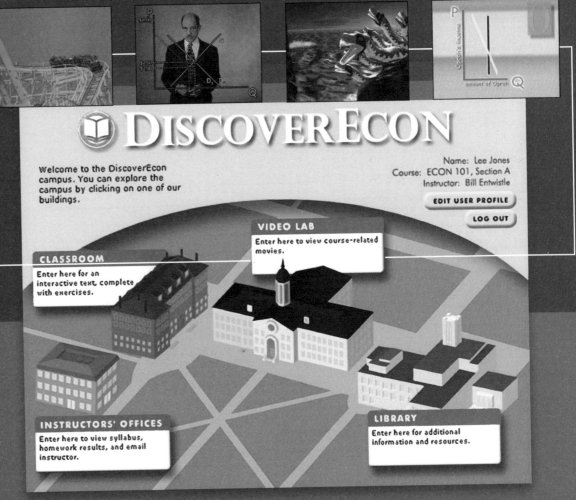

To use DiscoverEcon with Paul Solman Videos

1. Visit www.mhhe.com/economics/schiller10/discoverecon

2. Click Register to create a login username and password
   with this code:

   ## jkxhd-jpics-gewy9

   (Do only once)

PLEASE NOTE: This is a one time use only access code. This code
can only be used with new books.

3. Click the cover of the text you are using (The Economy Today,
   The Macro Economy Today, The Micro Economy Today)

4. Login with the username and password you created in Step 3.

5. Click the Classroom to use DiscoverEcon tutorials, exercises, and/or
   videos. Click the Video Lab for immediate access to the videos.

**If you're having problems accessing the software, please
visit our technical support website: www.mhhe.com/support
or call 800-331-5094.**

SYSTEM REQUIREMENTS

Multimedia PC with Pentium® 200 MHz or higher processor / Microsoft®
Windows 98™, Windows 2000 Professional™, Windows ME™ or Windows XP™
operating system / Internet Explorer 6.0™ with Java VM™ and valid Internet
Connection (JAVA™, Cookies and Active X™ enabled) / 32 MB of RAM for
Windows 98™; 64 MB for Windows 2000 Professional™ or Windows XP™ /
Microsoft ® Mouse, Microsoft ® IntelliMouse™, or compatible pointing device /
Super VGA, 16-bit or higher monitor supporting 800x600 screen resolution / Local
bus video with 1MB or more of video memory / 16-bit sound card with speakers or
headphones

**McGraw-Hill
Irwin**

ISBN: 0-07-304211-0

Don't throw this card out!

THE MACRO ECONOMY TODAY

Tenth Edition

BRADLEY R. SCHILLER

American University

Boston   Burr Ridge, IL   Dubuque, IA   Madison, WI   New York   San Francisco   St. Louis
Bangkok   Bogotá   Caracas   Kuala Lumpur   Lisbon   London   Madrid   Mexico City
Milan   Montreal   New Delhi   Santiago   Seoul   Singapore   Sydney   Taipei   Toronto

Mc Graw Hill | McGraw-Hill Irwin

THE MACRO ECONOMY TODAY

Published by McGraw-Hill/Irwin, a business unit of The McGraw-Hill Companies, Inc., 1221 Avenue of the Americas, New York, NY, 10020. Copyright © 2006, 2003, 2000, 1997, 1994, 1991, 1989, 1986, 1983, 1980 by The McGraw-Hill Companies, Inc. All rights reserved. No part of this publication may be reproduced or distributed in any form or by any means, or stored in a database or retrieval system, without the prior written consent of The McGraw-Hill Companies, Inc., including, but not limited to, in any network or other electronic storage or transmission, or broadcast for distance learning.

Some ancillaries, including electronic and print components, may not be available to customers outside the United States.

This book is printed on acid-free paper.

Printed in China

2 3 4 5 6 7 8 9 0 CTP/CTP 0 9 8 7 6 5

ISBN   0-07-297961-5

Publisher: *Gary Burke*
Executive sponsoring editor: *Paul Shensa*
Developmental editor: *Rebecca Hicks*
Editorial coordinator: *Heila Hubbard*
Senior marketing manager: *Martin D. Quinn*
Lead producer, Media technology: *Kai Chiang*
Project manager: *Harvey Yep*
Senior production supervisor: *Rose Hepburn*
Photo research coordinator: *Lori Kramer*
Lead media project manager: *Becky Szura*
Senior supplement producer: *Carol Loreth*
Developer, Media technology: *Brian Nacik*
Cover design: *Kami Carter*
Interior design: *Kami Carter*
Typeface: *10/12 Times New Roman*
Compositor: *GTS–York, PA Campus*
Printer: *CTPS*
Cover image: © David Parker/Photo Researchers, Inc./Description: Simulated detection of Higgs boson. Computer simulation of an event in which the decay of a Higgs boson particle produces four muons. Two of these muons are seen here (green tracks). The muons, along with countless other particles (red and blue tracks), are produced in a head-on collision between two protons. The Higgs boson is a localized clustering in the Higgs Field. This field permeates space, and local distortions of the Higgs Field are thought to be the way that particles gain mass. This image shows how the Higgs boson might be seen in the CMS detector on the Large Hadron Collider at CERN, the European particle physics laboratory.

Library of Congress Control Number: 2004116601

www.mhhe.com

Bradley R. Schiller has over three decades of experience teaching introductory economics at American University, the University of California (Berkeley and Santa Cruz), and the University of Maryland. He has given guest lectures at more than 300 colleges ranging from Fresno, California, to Istanbul, Turkey. Dr. Schiller's unique contribution to teaching is his ability to relate basic principles to current socioeconomic problems, institutions, and public policy decisions. This perspective is evident throughout *The Macro Economy Today.*

Dr. Schiller derives this policy focus from his extensive experience as a Washington consultant. He has been a consultant to most major federal agencies, many congressional committees, and political candidates. In addition, he has evaluated scores of government programs and helped design others. His studies of discrimination, training programs, tax reform, pensions, welfare, Social Security, and lifetime wage patterns have appeared in both professional journals and popular media. Dr. Schiller is also a frequent commentator on economic policy for television, radio, and newspapers.

Dr. Schiller received his Ph.D. from Harvard in 1969. He earned a B.A. degree, with great distinction, from the University of California (Berkeley) in 1965. He is now a professor of economics in the School of Public Affairs at American University in Washington, D.C.

THE 24/7 ECONOMY

24/7. That's the way the economy works. While you're sleeping, workers at the Texas Instrument plant in Kuala Lumpur are assembling the electronic circuits that will instruct your alarm clock to go off, relay the news via satellite TV or radio, enable video presentations in class or at remote locations, and help retrieve music files on the iPod you carry around. Venezuelan oil workers are pumping oil that will fuel your drive to class. Ethiopian farmers are harvesting the coffee beans that will help keep you alert. Traders in London, Hong Kong, and Tokyo are pushing the value of the dollar up or down, changing the cost of travel and trade. In an increasingly globalized economy, the economy truly never sleeps. It's in motion 24 hours a day, 7 days a week.

All of this perpetual motion makes teaching economics increasingly difficult. The parameters of the economy are constantly changing. Interest rates are up one day, down the next. The same with oil prices. Inflation looks worrisome one month and benign the next. Job growth looks great one month, then dismal the next. Even such famous prognosticators as Alan Greenspan have trouble keeping track of all these (changing) data, much less divining the implied direction of the economy.

At the micro level, incessant changes in the economy create similar problems. Market structures are continuously evolving. Products are always changing. With those changes, even market boundaries are on the move. Is your local cable franchise really a monopoly when satellite and Internet companies offer virtually identical products? Will Apple Computer, Inc., with a 70 percent market share in the portable MP3-player market, behave more like a monopolist or like a perfect competitor? With the Internet creating *global* shopping malls, how should industry concentration ratios be calculated? The Federal Trade Commission and the Antitrust Division of the U.S. Justice Department are vexed by ever-changing market boundaries and structures.

Coping with Change

So how do we cope with all this flux in the classroom? Or, for that matter, in a textbook that will be in print for three years? We could ignore the complexities of the real world and focus exclusively on abstract principles, perhaps "enlivening" the presentation with fables about the Acme Widget Company or the Jack and Jill Water Company. That approach not only bores students, but it also solidifies the misperception that economics is irrelevant to their daily life. Alternatively, we could spend countless hours reporting and discussing the economic news of the day. But that approach transforms the principles course into a current-events symposium.

The Macro Economy Today pursues a different strategy. I am convinced that economics is an exciting and very relevant field of study. I have felt this way since I attended my first undergraduate principles course. Despite an overbearing, boring textbook and a super-sized class (over 1,000 students!), I somehow discerned that economics could be an interesting topic. All it needed was a commitment to merging theoretical insights with the daily realities of shopping malls, stock markets, global integration, and policy development. Whew!

What Makes Economies Tick

How does this lofty ambition translate into the nuts and bolts of teaching? It starts by infusing the textbook and the course with a purposeful theme. Spotlighting scarcity and the necessity for choice is not enough; there's a much bigger picture. It's really about why some nations prosper while others languish. As we look around the world, how can we explain why millionaires abound in the United States, Hong Kong, the United Kingdom, and Australia, while 2.8 *billion* earthlings live on less than $2 a day? How is it that affluent consumers in developed nations carry around videophones while one-fourth of the world's population has never made a phone call? Surely, the way an economy is structured has something to do with this. At the micro level, Adam Smith taught us long ago that the degree of competition in product markets affects the quantity, quality, and price of consumer products.

Markets vs. Government

At the aggregate level, we've also seen that macro structure matters. Specifically, we recognize that the degree of government intervention in an economy is a critical determinant of its performance. The Chinese Communist Party once thought that central control of an economy would not only reduce inequalities but also accelerate growth. Since decentralizing parts of its economy, freeing up some markets, and even legalizing private property (see World View, p. 17), China has become the world's fastest-growing economy. India has heeded China's experience and is also pursuing a massive privatization and deregulation strategy (World View, p. 11).

This doesn't imply that *laissez faire* is the answer to all of our economic problems. What it does emphasize, however, is how important the choice between market reliance and government dependence can be.

We know that the three core questions in economics are WHAT, HOW, and FOR WHOM to produce. Instead of discussing them in a political and institutional void, we should energize these issues with more real-world context. We should also ask who should resolve these core questions, the governments or the marketplace? Where, when, and why do we expect market failure—suboptimal answers to the WHAT, HOW, and FOR WHOM questions. Where, when, and why can we expect government intervention to give us better answers—or to fail? This theme of market reliance versus government dependence runs through every chapter of *The Macro Economy Today.*

Real-World Concerns

Within the two-dimensional framework of three core questions and markets-versus-governments decision making, *The Macro Economy Today* pursues basic principles in an unwavering real-world context. The commitment to relevance is evident from the get-go. At the outset, the very serious trade-offs between arms spending and food production in North Korea (pp. 8–9) put the concept of opportunity costs into a meaningful context. Chapter 1 pursues the nature of opportunity cost into the future by examining the earthbound sacrifices we'll have to make for the proposed Lunar and Martian settlements (Chapter 1's "Economy Tomorrow" section, pp. 19–20). These kinds of concrete, page-one examples motivate students to learn *and retain* core economic principles.

Chapter 2 gives students a quick economic tour of the world. It shows how different nations have resolved the WHAT, HOW, and FOR WHOM questions. Students see how rich the USA is—and how poor other nations are (see World Views, pp. 28 and 29). They also see that inequality is not an ailment unique to "rich" nations (e.g., World View, p. 41). This chapter gives students an empirically based global perspective on economic outcomes that can spark a motivated search for explanations, that is, economic theory.

Macro Realities

In macro, we emphasize the cyclical problems of unemployment and inflation. But students don't get motivated to learn the origins or solutions for these problems just by citing the latest economics statistics (yawn). Most students don't have enough personal experience to know why 6 percent unemployment or 3.7 percent inflation are *serious* concerns. To fill that void, *The Macro Economy Today* takes students on a tour of unemployment and inflation. In Chapter 6, they see unemployment statistics translate into personal tragedies and social tensions. They see who loses their job when the unemployment rate rises (p. 118) and how devastating the experience can be (pp. 121–122). In Chapter 7, the devastation wrought by hyperinflation drives home the realization that price-level changes matter. These two chapters lay a global, historical, and personal foundation that gives purpose to the study of macro theory. Few other texts lay this foundation.

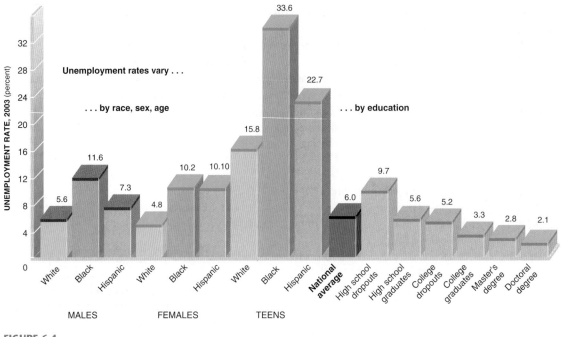

FIGURE 6.4
Unemployment Isn't Experienced Equally by Race, Sex, or Education

Minority groups, teenagers, and less-educated individuals experience higher rates of unemployment. Teenage unemployment rates are particularly high, especially for black and other minority youth. Source: U.S. Department of Labor (2003 data).

In the core macro chapters (8–18), *The Macro Economy Today* constantly reminds students of the real-world relevancy of core concepts. The potential instability of aggregate demand, for example, is illustrated with data on quarterly variance in consumption and investment (p. 192) as well as News accounts on investment decisions (p. 191) and consumer confidence (pp. 187, 219). The impacts of terrorism (News, p. 191) and "oil shocks" (News, p. 337) on both AD and AS get timely recognition, as do the successive tax cuts of 2001, 2002, 2003, and 2004. By tying core AS/AD concepts to real-world events, the textbook highlights the importance and relevance of macro theory.

When we peer into the long run, it's important to ask what makes economies grow and what institutions or policies can accelerate that growth. But students won't pay much attention until you demonstrate that economic growth is both *important* and *desirable.* Chapter 17 attempts this by reviewing the payoffs to growth and by directly confronting concerns about the limits to growth.

Nowhere is the commitment to a real-world context more evident than in Chapter 19. The very title of the chapter ("Theory vs. Reality") reveals its purpose. The chapter not only confronts but also *explains* the gap between the promise of macro theory and the reality of economic outcomes. The section entitled "Why Things Don't Always Work" (pp. 397–408) is a nice bridge between the blackboard and the boardroom for your students. Every macro course should include this chapter.

International Realities

International chapters (20 and 21) not only explain the core concepts of comparative advantage and exchange-rate determination but also assess the *resistance* to free trade and flexible exchange rates. By identifying the vested interests that resist trade, *The Macro Economy Today* bridges the gap between free-trade models and real-world trade disputes. Students see not only why trade is desirable but also how and why we pay for trade barriers. This is a lot more interesting than simply reciting the mathematics of comparative advantage in cloth and wine.

The bottom line here is simple and straight forward: ***by infusing the presentation of core concepts with a unifying theme and pervasive real-world application,*** *The Macro Economy Today offers an exciting and motivated introduction to economics.* As the accompanying News confirms, this is the kind of reality-based instruction today's students want.

IN THE NEWS

Real World 101

Colleges Scramble to Serve Students Looking for Classes That Elucidate Current Events

Who knew that the University of Nebraska houses American academia's only Afghanistan studies center? Or that a top-notch geography department would put Southwest Texas State University in San Marcos on the map for CIA recruiters? Before September 11, such specialties attracted scant attention and few students. But the speed with which colleges nationwide have raced to accommodate the stampede of under-graduates suddenly interested in war-related subject areas has stunned even seasoned educators (and turned scores into celebrity-experts).

—Mary Lord

Source: *U.S. News & World Report,* November 5, 2001. Reprinted with permission. www.usnews.com

Analysis: Real-world events and issues spark student interest in academic courses. No text brings the real world into the economics course as much as *The Macro Economy Today.*

EFFECTIVE PEDAGOGY

Despite the abundance of real-world applications, this is at heart a *principles* text, not a compendium of issues. Good theory and interesting applications are not mutually exclusive. This is a text that wants to *teach macroeconomics,* not just increase aware-ness of policy issues. To that end, *The Macro Economy Today* provides a logically organized and uncluttered theoretical structure for macro, and international theory. What distinguishes this text from others on the market is that it conveys theory in a lively, student-friendly manner.

Clean, Clear Theory

Student comprehension of core theory is facilitated with careful, consistent, and effec-tive pedagogy. This distinctive pedagogy includes the following features:

Concept Reinforcement

Graphs are *completely* labeled, colorful, and positioned on background grids. Because students often enter the principles course as graph-phobics, graphs are frequently accompanied by synchronized tabular data. Every table is also annotated. This shouldn't be a product-differentiating feature but, sadly, it is. Putting a table in a textbook without an annotation is akin to writing a cluster of numbers on the board, then leaving the classroom without any explanation.

Self-Explanatory Graphs and Tables

Key terms are defined in the margin when they first appear and, unlike in other texts, redefined as necessary in subsequent chapters. Web site references are directly

Reinforced Key Concepts

FIGURE 3.3
Shifts vs. Movements

A demand curve shows how a consumer responds to price changes. If the determinants of demand stay constant, the response is a *movement* along the curve to a new quantity demanded. In this case, the quantity demanded increases from 5 (point d_1), to 12 (point g_1), when price falls from $35 to $20 per hour.

If the determinants of demand change, the entire demand curve *shifts*. In this case, an increase in income increases demand. With more income, Tom is willing to buy 12 hours at the initial price of $35 (point d_2), not just the 5 hours he demanded before the lottery win.

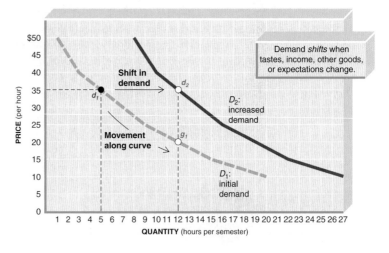

		Quantity Demanded (hours per semester)	
	Price (per hour)	Initial Demand	After Increase in Income
A	$50	1	8
B	45	2	9
C	40	3	10
D	35	5	12
E	30	7	14
F	25	9	16
G	20	12	19
H	15	15	22
I	10	20	27

tied to the book's content, not hung on like ornaments. End-of-chapter discussion questions use tables, graphs, and boxed news stories from the text, reinforcing key concepts.

Boxed and Annotated Applications

In addition to the real-world applications that run through the body of the text, *The Macro Economy Today* intersperses boxed domestic (In the News) and global (World View) case studies. Although nearly every text on the market now offers boxed applications, *The Macro Economy Today's* presentation is distinctive. First, the sheer number of In the News (65) and World View (55) boxes is unique. Second, and more important, *every* boxed application is referenced in the body of the text. Third, *every* News and World View comes with a brief, self-contained explanation. Fourth, the News and World View boxes are the subject of the end-of-chapter Discussion Questions and Student Problem Set exercises. In combination, these distinctive features assure that students will actually read the boxed applications and discern their economic content. The *Test Bank* and *DiscoverEcon with Paul Solman videos* also provide subsets of questions tied to the News and World View boxes so that instructors can confirm student use of this feature.

Photos and Cartoons

The text presentation is also enlivened with occasional photos and cartoons that reflect basic concepts. The photos on page 40 are much more vivid testimony to the extremes of inequality than the data in Figure 2.6 (p. 39). The cartoon on page x reminds students that not all economists are of the same mind. Every photo and cartoon is annotated and referenced in the body of the text. These visual features are an integral part of the presentation, not diversions.

© Alan Schein Photography/CORBIS

© Wolfgang Spunbarg/Photo Edit

Analysis: The market distributes income (and, in turn, goods and services) according to the resources an individual owns and how well they are used. If the resulting inequalities are too great, some redistribution via government intervention may be desired.

The one adjective invariably used to describe *The Macro Economy Today* is "readable." Professors often express a bit of shock when they realize that students actually enjoy reading the book. (Well, not as much as a Stephen King novel, but a whole lot better than most textbooks they've had to plow through.) The writing style is lively and issue-focused. Unlike any other textbook on the market, every boxed feature, every graph, every table, and every cartoon is explained and analyzed. Every feature is also referenced in the text, so students actually learn the material rather than skipping over it. Because readability is ultimately in the eye of the beholder, you might ask a couple of students to read and compare an analogous chapter in *The Macro Economy Today* and in another text. This is a test *The Macro Economy Today* usually wins.

I firmly believe that students must *work* with key concepts in order to really learn them. Weekly homework assignments are *de rigueur* in my own classes. To facilitate homework assignments, I have prepared the *Student Problem Set,* which includes built-in numerical and graphing problems that build on the tables, graphs, and boxed material in each chapter. Grids for drawing graphs are also provided. Each chapter's problem set is detachable and includes answer boxes that facilitate grading. (Answers are available in the *Instructor's Resource Manual,* in print, or in downloadable form on the book's Web site). The *Student Problem Set* is behind the tab at the end of this book.

All of these pedagogical features add up to an unusually supportive learning context for students. With this support, students will learn and retain more economic concepts—and maybe even enjoy the educational process.

DISTINCTIVE MACRO

The Macro Economy Today is well-known for its balanced presentation of different theoretical perspectives, its consistent use of the AS/AD framework, its global perspective, and its explicit juxtaposition of theory and reality.

This isn't a highly opinionated text. It doesn't assert that only long-run issues matter or that monetary policy is the only effective lever of short-run stabilization. Rather,

Readability

Student Problem Set

Balanced Macro Theory

Analysis: There are different theories about when and how the government should "fix" the economy. Policymakers must decide which advice to follow in specific situations.

The Macro Economy Today strives to offer students a *balanced* introduction to both short-and long-run macro concerns as well as an array of competing viewpoints. Keynes isn't dead, nor are supply-side policy options ignored. Instead, competing theories are presented in their best possible light, and then subjected to comparative scrutiny. This approach reflects my belief that students need to be exposed to a variety of perspectives if they're to understand the range and intensity of ongoing debates. Maybe we can't always answer the question posed in the accompanying cartoon with certainty. But our students should at least know the question is legitimate. That means we have to present alternative theories and opinions and help students sort them out. The benefits of such an eclectic and balanced approach were strikingly evident in the aftermath of the September 11, 2001, terrorist attacks. Not only did policy discussion shift abruptly from long-run issues (e.g., productivity growth and "saving Social Security") to short-run issues (stabilizing the economy), but even Milton Friedman and Alan Greenspan endorsed counter-cyclical fiscal policy! Shouldn't students have a broad foundation of principles that enables them to follow these developments? *The Macro Economy Today* offers such breadth of coverage.

Consistent AS/AD Framework

Too many textbooks still treat the aggregate supply/aggregate demand (AS/AD) framework as a separate theory. The AS/AD model is *not* a separate theory; it is just a convenient framework for illustrating macro theories in a world of changing prices. Keynes never said prices could not rise, so he would be surprised to see his macro theory of market instability confined to the "Keynesian cross" framework. The full measure of Keynesian theory can be better illustrated in the AS/AD framework, without any loss of content. Notice in Figures 10.6 (p. 215) and Figure 10.9 (p. 218) how the multiplier is illustrated by sequential AD shifts and measured along a horizontal plane (the prevailing price level, *not* an AS curve).

These AD multiplier effects are summarized again in Figure 11.4 (p. 229). This depiction of multiplier effects in the AS/AD framework spotlights the fact that AD shifts have both price and output effects (e.g., Figure 11.3, p. 227). Shouldn't students *start* their macro tour with this real-world perspective?

In view of this upfront AS/AD depiction of the multiplier, the core macro presentation is now exclusively rendered in the context of the AS/AD model. This greatly simplifies the presentation for students, who often got lost shuttling between two distinct models, sometimes in the same chapter. Since students have never encountered the Keynesian cross model, they won't miss it in *The Macro Economy Today*. For instructors who still want to use it, the Keynesian cross is now contained in the appendix to Chapter 9. As that appendix explains, the two models are simply different paths for reaching the same conclusions. The advantage of the AS/AD framework is that it generates more useful policy guidelines in a world of changing price levels. The single framework also facilitates contrasts of competing macro theories (see Figure 16.1, p. 332, for example) and time perspectives (long-run versus short-run).

Global Macro Constraints

The Macro Economy Today incorporates not only the reality of changing price levels but also the constraints of global linkages. The Fed's Board of Governors always looks over its collective shoulder at global markets when making decisions on domestic monetary policy. The impact of changing interest rates on the value of the dollar and global money flows is always discussed. Likewise, the effectiveness of fiscal-policy initiatives is always sensitive to potential export "leakage" and other trade effects. I have tried to convey a sense of how these global links constrain policy decisions and impacts in the "Global Macro" chapter. This unique chapter (18) is intended to introduce a dose of global reality into the macro course without delving into theories of trade or finance (Chapters 20 and 21). Chapter 18 is a stand-alone chapter in the macro section. It is designed for instructors who sense the need to offer more of a global perspective in the macro course, but don't have time to cover trade and finance theories.

Theory and Reality

The final chapter in the macro section serves two purposes. First, it brings together the various Keynesian, monetarist, supply-side, and growth theories into a convenient review format. No other text brings all the macro material into such a course-ending overview.

The second purpose of Chapter 19 is to examine why economic performance so often falls short of economic theory. This is a fun section, because it delves into the institutional and political constraints that shape and limit macro policy. Fiscal policy debates come alive when Republicans and Democrats start arguing over the size and content of antiterrorism stimulus policy (see News, p. 407). The chapter ends the macro course with the suggestion that the real world offers choices between *imperfect* markets and *imperfect* government intervention.

DISTINCTIVE INTERNATIONAL

The global economy runs through every chapter of *The Macro Economy Today.*

The most visible evidence of this globalism is in the 50 World View boxes that are distributed throughout the text. As noted earlier, these boxed illustrations offer specific global illustrations of basic principles. To facilitate their use, every World View has a brief caption that highlights the theoretical relevance of the example. The *Test Bank* and Student Problem Set also offer questions based on the World Views.

World Views

As noted earlier, Chapter 18 offers a unique global perspective on domestic macro policy. The global macro chapter is intended as a substitute for the traditional trade and finance chapters. It is designed for instructors who want to offer some international perspectives in the macro course but don't have time to cover trade and finance theory. In courses with more scope for international coverage, the global macro chapter can be used as a capstone to the more traditional chapters.

Global Macro

Consistent with the reality-based content of the entire text, the discussions of trade and finance theory go beyond basic principles to policy trade-offs and constraints. It's impossible to make sense of trade policy without recognizing the vested interests that battle trade principles. Chapters 20 and 21 emphasize that there are both winners and losers associated with every change in trade flows or exchange rates. Because vested interests are typically highly concentrated and well organized, they can often bend trade rules and flows to their advantage. Trade disputes over Mexican trucks, "dumped" steel, and sugar quotas help illustrate the realities of trade policy. The ongoing protest against the World Trade Organization is also assessed in terms of competing interests.

Vested Interests

DISTINCTIVE WEB SUPPORT

The tenth edition of *The Macro Economy Today* continues to set the pace for Web applications and support of the principles course.

A mini Web site directory is provided in each chapter's marginal WebNotes. These URLs aren't random picks; they were selected because they let students extend and update adjacent in-text discussions.

WebNotes

The Macro Economy Today's Web site now includes even more features that both instructors and students will find engaging and instructive. The Online Learning Center is user-friendly. Upon entering the site at **www.mhhe.com/economics/schiller10,** students and instructors will find three separate book covers: one for *The Economy Today,* one for *The Macroeconomy Today,* and one for *The Microeconomy Today.* By clicking on the appropriate cover, users will link to a specific site for the version of the book they are using.

www.mhhe.com/ economics/schiller10

Proceeding into the Student Center, students will find lots of brand-new interactive study material. Diane Keenan of Cerritos College has prepared 15 self-grading multiple-choice and five true-or-false questions per chapter, which are ideal for self-quizzing before a test. Solomon Namala, also of Cerritos College, has created a supplementary Student Problem Set for the site. Professors can assign the additional five problems per chapter as homework or students can access them for additional skills practice. Answers can be found on the password-protected Instructor's Edition of the Web site. Mark Maier of Glendale College has created two Web Activities per chapter and

15 Collaborative Activities, unique to the site. On top of all that, students have access to my periodic NewsFlashes, a User's Manual for the site, and links to Econ Graph Kit, *DiscoverEcon with Paul Solman* videos, Economics on the Web, and Career Opportunities. They will also have the option of purchasing PowerWeb access with their book, which supplies them with three to five news articles per week on the topics they are studying.

The password-protected Instructor Center includes some wonderful resources for instructors who want to include more interactive student activities in their courses. The downloadable *Instructor's Manual* and PowerPoints, auxiliary Student Problem Set and answers, and Instructor's Notes for the Collaborative Activities and Web Activities are available to provide guidance for instructors who collect these assignments and grade them. John Min of Northern Virginia Community College has created Online Lecture Launchers. These interactive PowerPoint presentations highlight current events relevant to key macro, micro, and international topics. They serve as excellent "jumping-off points" for in-class discussion and lectures and will be updated quarterly to provide the most current information.

DiscoverEcon with Paul Solman Videos

(www.mhhe.com/schiller10.com/discoverecon) A video and software program, this student online tutorial with accompanying videos is provided with every new copy of the tenth edition of *The Macro Economy Today.* It contains a fully updated and enhanced version of DiscoverEcon, developed by Gerald C. Nelson of the University of Illinois at Urbana-Champaign, featuring new learning opportunities for the students and easy integration into existing courses for the instructor. The software is like an interactive text: software chapters parallel text chapters and software pages include specific page references to the text. With Discover-Econ's e-submission, professors can manage the Discover-Econ exercise results of their students electronically. These results are available at anytime to the student and the instructor can easily set up a course management site to make this information available to them. The program provides links to related videos for key topics on the accompanying Web-streamed videos. Paul Solman, economics correspondent for the *Newsttour with Jim Lehrer* is the creator of the video component, which consists of over 250 minutes of video, broken down into segments ranging from 7 to 10 minutes in length. These video segments explain the key economic ideas such as economic growth, elasticity, and production possibilities in a memorable, accessible way.

Opportunities for active learning abound. All DiscoverEcon chapters contain a multiple-choice quiz, discussion questions with online links, and match-the-terms exercises. Interactive graphs, animated charts, and live tables let your students manipulate variables and study the outcomes. Links to the glossary and text references clarify key concepts, and Web-based exercises give students a direct link to the site in question. With the addition of a new syllabus development tool, instructors can create interactive syllabi by linking DiscoverEcon exercises, special Web sites, and Solman videos to their class syllabus. Access to DiscoverEcon is available online, via a password code card supplied with each new book. Link to *DiscoverEcon with Paul Solman* videos at **www.mhhe.com/schiller10/discoverecon.**

WHAT'S NEW IN THE TENTH

To previous users of *The Macro Economy Today,* all of its distinctive features have become familiar—and hopefully, welcome. For those instructors already familiar with *The Macro Economy Today,* the more urgent question is, What's new? The answer is *a lot.* By way of brief summary, you may want to note the following:

Focus on AS/AD Framework

As described above, the core macro section is now exclusively presented in the context of the AS/AD framework. Experience has shown that this streamlined presentation not only simplifies the macro discussion but also fully and faithfully conveys both Keynesian and competing theories. For instructors who still want to discuss the Keynesian aggregate-expenditure (Keynesian cross) model, the appendix to Chapter 9 has been expanded.

The chapter-ending "Economy Tomorrow" sections continue to challenge students with future-looking applications of core concepts. In Chapter 1, the "Journey to Mars" highlights opportunity costs. In Chapter 2, the new "A Better Tomorrow" ponders the prospects of fulfilling the World Bank's ambitious Millennium Declaration. In Chapter 6, the threat of "Outsourcing Jobs" is confronted. Chapter 12 peers into the looming financial crisis of the Social Security program ("Dipping into Social Security").

New "Economy Tomorrow"s

There are at least 21 all-new In the News applications in *The Macro Economy Today.* These range from consumer dissaving (pp. 181, 187) to the 2004 "oil shocks" (p. 337).

New In the News

World Views have also been updated throughout the test. The December 2003 legalization of private property in China (p. 17) is just one of the new World Views. They span a range from South Korean fiscal stimulus (p. 230) to Chinese monetary restraint (p. 296).

New World Views

The Macro Economy Today's set of arithmetic and graphing problems has proven to be an extremely valuable tool for homework and quizzes. In fact, it has become so widely used that it is now packaged in the text itself, at the back. As before, it offers quantitative and graphing problems (with grids!) explicitly tied to the text, including each chapter's figures, tables, In the News, and World Views. There are 50 new problems, as well as improvements to old ones. Answers are in the print *Instructor's Resource Manual,* also available on the password-protected instructor's section of the Web site.

Built-in Student Problem Set

There are at least 25 new end-of-chapter Questions for Discussion. As always these draw explicitly on the content of their respective chapters, including boxed applications and figures.

New Questions for Discussion

Previous WebNotes have been checked for currency and edited as needed, and a score of new WebNotes have been added as well. These are designed to enable students to update and extend in-text discussions.

New WebNotes

Besides all these salient updates, the entire text has been rendered up-to-date with the latest statistics and case studies. ***This unparalleled currency is a distinctive feature of* The Macro Economy Today.**

Thorough Updating

NEW AND IMPROVED SUPPLEMENTS

Test Bank. Linda Wilson and Jane Himarios of the University of Texas at Arlington have thoroughly revised the *Test Bank* for the tenth edition. This team assures a high level of quality and consistency of the test questions and the greatest possible correlation with the content of the text as well as the *Study Guide,* which was prepared by Linda Wilson with Mark Maier. All questions are coded according to level of difficulty and have a text-page reference where the student will find a discussion of the concept on which the question is based. The computerized *Test Bank* is available in Brownstone Diploma, a flexible and easy-to-use electronic testing program. Diploma systems can produce high-quality graphs from the test banks and feature the ability to generate multiple tests, with versions "scrambled" to be distinctive. This software will meet the various needs of the widest spectrum of computer users. Both the print and computerized test banks are offered in micro and macro versions, each of which contains nearly 4,000 questions including over 200 essay questions.

Instructor Aids

PowerPoint Presentations. Anthony Zambelli of Cuyamaca College created new presentation slides for the tenth edition. Developed using Microsoft PowerPoint software, these slides are a step-by-step review of the key points in each of the book's 36 chapters. They are equally useful to the student in the classroom as lecture aids or for personal review at home or the computer lab. The slides use animation to show students how graphs build and shift.

Overhead Transparencies. All of the text's tables and graphs have been reproduced as full-color overhead transparency acetates.

Instructor's Resource Manual. Mark Maier of Glendale College has prepared the *Instructor's Resource Manual* as well as much of the original content for the Web site. This has allowed him to integrate the two in a way that will make online Web resources easier than ever for instructors to use in class.

The *Instructor's Resource Manual* is available in book form or online, and it includes chapter summaries and outlines, "lecture launchers" to stimulate class discussion, and media exercises to extend the analysis. New features include a section that details common misconceptions regarding the material in a particular chapter; an annotated outline of the chapter; and answers to the Questions for Discussion and the Student Problem Sets. Rae Jean Goodman of the United States Naval Academy has worked with Mark to update the debate projects found in the *Instructor's Resource Manual*. In addition, there is a photocopy-ready Print Media Exercise for each chapter.

News Flashes. As up-to-date as *The Macro Economy Today* is, it can't foretell the future. As the future becomes the present, however, I write two-page News Flashes describing major economic events and relating them to specific text references. These News Flashes provide good lecture material and can be copied for student use. Adopters of *The Macro Economy Today* have the option of receiving News Flashes via fax or mail. They're also available on the Schiller Web site. Four to six News Flashes are sent to adopters each year. (Contact your local McGraw-Hill/Irwin sales representative to get on the mailing list.)

Student Aids

At the instructor's discretion, students have access to the News Flashes described above. In addition, the following supplements can facilitate learning.

Built-in Student Problem Set. The built-in *Student Problem Set* is found at the back of every copy of *The Macro Economy Today*. Each chapter has 8 to 10 numerical and graphing problems tied to the content of the text. Graphing grids are provided. The answer blanks are formatted to facilitate grading and all answers are contained in the *Instructor's Resource Manual*. For convenience, the *Student Problem Set* pages are also perforated.

Study Guide. The new *Study Guide* has been completely updated by Linda Wilson and Mark Maier. The *Study Guide* develops quantitative skills and the use of economic terminology, and enhances critical thinking capabilities. Each chapter includes a Quick Review which lists the key points in an easy-to-read bulleted format, Learning Objectives for the chapter, a crossword puzzle using key terms, 10 true-false questions with explanations, 20 multiple-choice questions, problems and applications that relate directly back to the text, and common student errors. Answers to all problems, exercises, and questions are provided at the end of each chapter.

A NOTE ABOUT THE COVER

The tenth edition cover image is a theoretical representation of the Higgs boson. Dubbed the "God Particle" by Nobel Prize-wining physicist Leon Lederman, the Higgs boson is an, as yet, undiscovered elementary particle. Scientists believe that Higgs particles generate a thick firmament through which other particles move, distorting the field and picking up drag that constitutes that particle's mass.

Scientists have spent years and millions of dollars in their quest to isolate the "God Particle". Perhaps the most ambitious of labs is the Centre Européen de Recherche Nucléaire (CERN), where they are constructing a $3 billion Large Hadron Collider (LHC). Two hundred feet under ground, the LHC sends particles zooming around its 17-mile circumference, smashing them into one another to create dozens of tinier particles whose data is calculated by the LHC's large computer grid system.

The LHC Computing Grid, created to process the 12-14 PetaBytes of data generated by the LHC each year (equivalent to 20 million CDs), incorporates over 200 scientists in 36 countries into a massive virtual computing organization. The Grid has the capacity to revolutionize the way we use the Internet, making it a more reliable way to quickly transmit large quantities of data. While the discovery of the Higgs boson could be years away, the LHC's computer grid has already provided real-world improvements for the economy today and a glimpse of the effects it could have on the economy tomorrow.

ACKNOWLEDGMENTS

This tenth edition is unquestionably the finest edition of *The Macro Economy Today,* and I am deeply grateful to all those people who helped develop it. Paul Shensa, my editor for the last thirty years, again picked a first-rate team and supported it well with budgets cajoled from Gary Burke, the economics publisher. The stand-out player was Becca Hicks, who as Development Editor not only kept the whole package together but also made many independent contributions to the text's content and style. Harvey Yep, the Project Manager, did an exceptional job in assuring that every page of the text was visually pleasing, properly formatted, error-free, and timely produced. The design team, led by Kami Carter, created a lively pallette of colors and features that enhanced *The Macro Economy Today's* readability. My thanks to all of them and their supporting staff. I also expect to be eternally grateful to Martin Quinn, who is in charge of marketing *The Macro Economy Today.* I trust he is already out knocking on office doors and setting new sales records.

I also want to express my heartfelt thanks to the professors who have shared their reactions (both good and bad) with me. Direct feedback from these users and reviewers has been a great source of continuing improvements in *The Macro Economy Today:*

User Survey Participants

James L. Allen, Jr.,
Wharton County Junior College

Louis Amato,
University of North Carolina—Charlotte

Janice C. Baldon,
University of Louisville

Nancy Brooks,
University of Vermont, Burlington

Bill Burrows,
Lane Community College

Mike Cohick,
Collin County Community College

Amy S. Cramer,
Pima Community College

Michael Ellis,
Texas Wesleyan College

Robert Eyler,
Sonoma State University

Kaya Ford,
Northern Virginia Community College

Alan Frishman,
Hobart and William Smith Colleges

Melissa A. Groves,
Towson University

Katherine M. Huger,
Charlestown Southern University

Marcha L. Hunley,
Cincinnati State University

Anisul M. Islam,
University of Houston—Downtown

Miren Ivankovic,
Southern Wesleyan University

James A. Janke,
Dakota State University

Paul E. Jorgensen,
Linn-Benton Community College

Emil Koren,
Hillsborough Community College

Ellen Lindeman,
Raritan Valley Community College

Cecil Mackey,
Michigan State University

Tom Masterson,
Westfield State College

Frederick W. May,
Trident Technical College

John Min,
North Virginia Community College

Stan Mitchell,
McLennan Community College

George L. Nagy,
Hudson Valley Community College

Michael L. Palmer,
Maplewood Community College

Norman Paul,
San Jacinto College

Peggy Pelt,
Gulf Coast Community College

Bob Potter,
University of Central Florida

Joe Prinzinger,
Lynchburg College
Taghi Ramin,
William Patterson University
John Romps,
St. Anselm College
Werner Sichel,
Western Michigan University
Noel S. Smith,
Palm Beach Community College
Carol O. Stivender,
University of North Carolina—Charlotte
Geetha Suresh,
Purdue University

Daniel A. Talley,
Dakota State University
Michael M. Tansey,
Rockhurst University
Deborah Thorsen,
Palm Beach Community College
Marjolein van der Veen,
Shoreline Community College
Richard D. Wolff,
University of Massachusetts
Virginia York,
Gulf Coast Community College
Andrea Zanter,
Hillsborough Community College

Reviewers

Gayla B. Ashford,
Calhoun Community College
Josiah Baker,
University of Central Florida
Millica Z. Bookman,
Saint Joseph's University
Wesley F. Booth,
San Antonio College
Nancy Brooks,
University of Vermont
Tim Burson,
Queens College (North Carolina)
James L. Butkiewitz,
University of Delaware
Suparna Chakraborty,
University of Minnesota
J. M. Cypher,
California State University—Fresno
Julie Edwards,
Blinn College
Harry Ellis, Jr.,
University of North Texas
Robert Eyler,
Sonoma State University
Indranil Ghosh,
Pennsylvania State University—Erie
Doug Greer,
San Jose State University
Rick Hirschi,
Brigham Young University (Idaho)
Jayvanath Ishwaran,
Stephen F. Austin State University
Kevin Klein,
Illinois College
Norman Knaub,
Pennsylvania State University—Altoona
Nazma Latif-Zaman,
Providence College

Tony Lima,
California State University—Hayward
Cathleen Leue,
University of Oregon
Jessica McCraw,
Texas Christian University
Carrie A. Meyer,
George Mason University
Francis D. Mummery,
Fullerton College
Judith E. Pasch,
University of Wisconsin
Sheila Amin Gutierrez de Piñeres,
University of Texas—Dallas
David R. Poma,
St. Francis College
Edward Price,
Oklahoma State University
Paddy Quick,
St. Francis College
George D. Santopietro,
Radford University
Reza Sepassi,
McLennan Community College
Mohamed Sharif,
University of Rhode Island
David J. St. Clair,
California State University
Carol O. Stivender,
University of North Carolina—Charlotte
Michael Stroup,
Stephen F. Austin State University
Geetha Suresh,
Purdue University
Kamal Upadhyaya,
University of New Haven

Finally, I'd like to thank all the professors and students who are going to use *The Macro Economy Today* as an introduction to economics principles. I welcome any responses (even the bad ones) you'd like to pass on for future editions.

—Bradley R. Schiller

CONTENTS IN BRIEF

CONTENTS

PART 1

The "God Particle"

The image on the cover is a theoretical depiction of a deteriorating "God Particle"—the most elusive speck of matter in the universe. Physicists believe that the God Particle, formally known as the Higgs boson, is the glue that holds the universe together. The God Particle is thought to emit a kind of soupy ether through which other particles move, picking up drag that turns matter into mass.

What does the God Particle have to do with economics? In their quest to isolate the God Particle, researchers are developing a supercomputing grid. The LHC Computing Grid will integrate computing resources from around the globe, creating a superpowerful *computation* network, similar in design to the Internet's global *communications* network. The LHC (for the Swiss-based $3-billion Large Hadron Collider) computer grid will allow individual users to tap into supercomputing power. The resultant computer power will vastly increase our technological abilities to process and interpret data. This will create new investment opportunities and enhance productivity in industries as diverse as film editing, drug design, and earthquake detection. In other words, pursuit of the God Particle, like the Internet, will expand the economy's production capacity and bring us still more goods and services in the economy tomorrow.

Economics: The Core Issues

I n February 2004, Intel Corporation announced a research breakthrough that stunned the high-tech industry. The company's engineers had created a new processor with 125 million transistors—the tiny parts that regulate the flow of electricity on a silicon chip. The new transistors are so small (90 nanometers, or less than one thousandth the width of a human hair) that 1 billion of them can be packed onto a single chip. That's a gargantuan leap from the 42-million-transistor Pentium 4 chip that now dominates the market and light-years away from the 2,300-transistor chip that powered IBM computers in 1972. What does all this have to do with you? For starters, it means that all electronic goods and services will be able to operate faster and with more options. In other words, the extraordinary array of goods we now confront in the marketplace will continue to expand and improve.

Maybe more isn't always better, but the history of humankind reveals a relentless quest for more and better output. To a large extent, the quest for more output has been driven by necessity. The world's population keeps growing, but the amount of land doesn't. That's why the English economist Thomas Malthus predicted in 1778 that the world would run out of food long before the nineteenth century ended. He didn't know that a few years later someone would invent the iron plow (1808), the reaper (1826), or the milking machine (1878). And Malthus had no conception of what biotechnology's "green revolution" might become and no clues at all about electronic circuits. So his prediction of global starvation turned out to be unduly pessimistic.

Although we've managed to increase global food output faster than the population has grown, we can't be complacent. The United Nations predicts that the world's population, now at 6.4 billion, will increase by another billion every 10 years. Even if we find ways for food output to keep pace, we can't be satisfied. Our future goals are much more ambitious. We want an ever higher standard of living, not just enough food on the table. No matter how fast our incomes grow, we always want more. The living standards earlier generations dreamed of we now take for granted. Today's luxuries—plasma TVs, camera phones, satellite radio—will most likely be viewed as necessities in a few years, but only if we keep squeezing more and more output out of available resources.

Ironically, some people fear we will do exactly that—and end up destroying the environment in the process. They foresee a Doomsday in which greenhouse gases generated by ever-rising production levels will overheat the earth, melt the solar icecaps, flood coastal areas, and destroy crops.

As the accompanying World View illustrates, no one really knows how the future will unfold. Even some of history's greatest minds have made predictions that turned out to be ludicrous. In gazing into the future, however, we can be certain of some fundamental principles. The first principle is that resources will always be scarce, relative to our desires. Second, how we use those scarce resources will shape our future. If we use resources today to miniaturize electronic circuits, we'll

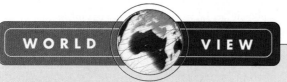

WORLD VIEW

Cloudy Days in Tomorrowland

We'd like to think all *our* predictions will prove right. But the highways of history are littered with wrong calls, false insights and bad guesses. Here's a sampler of twentieth-century futurology that flopped.

I confess that in 1901, I said to my brother Orville that man would not fly for 50 years . . . Ever since, I have distrusted myself and avoided all predictions.

—Wilbur Wright, *U.S. aviation pioneer, 1908*

I must confess that my imagination . . . refuses to see any sort of submarine doing anything but suffocating its crew and floundering at sea.

—H. G. Wells, *British novelist, 1901*

Airplanes are interesting toys but of no military value.

—Marshal Ferdinand Foch,
French military strategist and
future World War I commander, 1911

The horse is here to stay, but the automobile is only a novelty—a fad.

—A president of the Michigan Savings Bank advising Horace
Rackham *(Henry Ford's lawyer) not to invest in the Ford Motor
Co., 1903. Rackham ignored the advice, bought $5,000 worth
of stock and sold it several years later for $12.5 million.*

Radio has no future.

—Lord Kelvin, *Scottish mathematician and physicist, former
president of the Royal Society, 1897*

Everything that can be invented has been invented.

—Charles H. Duell, *U.S. commissioner of patents, 1899*

Who the hell wants to hear actors talk?

—Harry M. Warner, *Warner Brothers, 1927*

There is no reason for any individual to have a computer in their home.

—Kenneth Olsen, *president and founder of Digital Equipment
Corp., 1977*

[Man will never reach the moon] regardless of all future scientific advances.

—Dr. Lee De Forest, *inventor of the Audion tube and a father
of radio, February 25, 1967*

We don't like their sound. Groups of guitars are on the way out.

—Decca Records, *rejecting the Beatles, 1962*

What use could this company make of an electrical toy?

—*Western Union president* William Orton, *rejecting Alexander
Graham Bell's offer to sell his struggling telephone company to
Western Union for $100,000*

Computers in the future may . . . perhaps only weigh 1.5 tons.

—Popular Mechanics, *forecasting the development of
computer technology, 1949*

Stocks have reached what looks like a permanently high plateau.

—Irving Fisher, *professor of economics, Yale University,
October 17, 1929*

[Television] won't be able to hold on to any market it captures after the first six months. People will soon get tired of staring at a plywood box every night.

—Darryl F. Zanuck, *head of 20th Century-Fox, 1946*

Analysis: No one predicts the future well. But the economic choices we make today about the use of scarce resources will determine the kind of future we have.

Intel Corporation showcases its latest technology at www.intel.com/research/silicon.

economics: The study of how best to allocate scarce resources among competing uses.

be able to produce more and better products in the future. Likewise, if we build more factories and cyber networks today, we'll be able to produce more output tomorrow. If we install more pollution controls in cars, power plants, and factories today, we'll even have cleaner air tomorrow.

The science of economics helps us frame these choices. In a nutshell, **economics** is the study of how people use scarce resources. How do you decide how much time to spend studying? How does Amazon.com decide how many workers to hire? How does DaimlerChrysler decide whether to use its factories to produce sports utility vehicles or sedans? What share of a nation's resources should be devoted to space exploration, the delivery of health care services, or pollution control? In every instance, alternative ways of using scarce labor, land, and building resources are available, and we have to choose one use over another.

In this first chapter we explore the nature of scarcity and the kinds of choices it forces us to make. As we'll see, ***three core issues must be resolved:***

- ***WHAT to produce with our limited resources.***
- ***HOW to produce the goods and services we select.***
- ***FOR WHOM goods and services are produced;*** that is, who should get them.

We also have to decide who should answer these questions. Should the marketplace decide what gets produced and how and for whom? Or should the government dictate output choices, regulate production processes, and redistribute incomes? Should Microsoft decide what features get included in a computer's operating system, or should the government make that decision? Should private companies provide airport security or should the government assume that responsibility? Should interest rates be set by private banks alone, or should the government try to control interest rates? The battle over *who* should answer the core questions is often as contentious as the questions themselves.

THE ECONOMY IS US

To learn how the economy works, let's start with a simple truth: *The economy is us.* "The economy" is simply an abstraction referring to the grand sum of all our production and consumption activities. What we collectively produce is what the economy produces; what we collectively consume is what the economy consumes. In this sense, the concept of "the economy" is no more difficult than the concept of "the family." If someone tells you that the Jones family has an annual income of $42,000, you know that the reference is to the collective earnings of all the Joneses. Likewise, when someone reports that the nation's income is $11 trillion per year—as it now is—we should recognize that the reference is to the grand total of everyone's income. If we work fewer hours or get paid less, both family income *and* national income decline. The "meaningless statistics" (see accompanying cartoon) often cited in the news are just a summary of our collective market behavior.

The same relationship between individual behavior and aggregate behavior applies to specific outputs. If we as individuals insist on driving cars rather than taking public transportation, the economy will produce millions of cars each year and consume vast quantities of oil. In a slightly different way, the economy produces billions of dollars

"Meaningless statistics were up one-point-five per cent this month over last month."

Analysis: Many people think of economics as dull statistics. But economics is really about human behavior—how people decide to use scarce resources and how those decisions affect market outcomes.

of military hardware to satisfy our desire for national defense. In each case, the output of the economy reflects the collective behavior of the 300 million individuals who participate in the economy.

We may not always be happy with the output of the economy. But we can't ignore the link between individual action and collective outcomes. If the highways are clogged and the air is polluted, we can't blame someone else for the transportation choices we made. If we're disturbed by the size of our military arsenal, we must still accept responsibility for our choices (or nonchoices, if we failed to vote). In either case, we continue to have the option of reallocating our resources. We can create a different outcome the next day, month, or year.

SCARCITY: THE CORE PROBLEM

Although we can change economic outcomes, we can't have everything we want. If you go to the mall with $20 in your pocket, you can only buy so much. The money in your pocket sets a *limit* to your spending.

The output of the entire economy is also limited. The limits in this case are set not by money but by the resources available for producing goods and services. Everyone wants more housing, new schools, better transit systems, and a new car. But even a country as rich as the United States can't produce everything people want. So, like every other nation, we have to grapple with the core problem of **scarcity**—the fact that there aren't enough resources available to satisfy all our desires.

scarcity: Lack of enough resources to satisfy all desired uses of those resources.

The resources used to produce goods and services are called **factors of production.** *The four basic factors of production are*

Factors of Production

factors of production: Resource inputs used to produce goods and services, such as land, labor, capital, and entrepreneurship.

- *Land*
- *Labor*
- *Capital*
- *Entrepreneurship*

These are the *inputs* needed to produce desired *outputs*. To produce this textbook, for example, we needed paper, printing presses, a building, and lots of labor. We also needed people with good ideas who could put it together. To produce the education you're getting in this class, we need not only a textbook but a classroom, a teacher, and a blackboard as well. Without factors of production, we simply can't produce anything.

Land. The first factor of production, land, refers not just to the ground but to all natural resources. Crude oil, water, air, and minerals are all included in our concept of "land."

Labor. Labor too has several dimensions. It's not simply a question of how many bodies there are. When we speak of labor as a factor of production, we refer to the skills and abilities to produce goods and services. Hence, both the quantity and the quality of human resources are included in the "labor" factor.

capital: Final goods produced for use in the production of other goods, e.g., equipment, structures.

Capital. The third factor of production is capital. In economics the term **capital** refers to final goods produced for use in further production. The residents of fishing villages in southern Thailand, for example, braid huge fishing nets. The sole purpose of these nets is to catch more fish. The nets themselves become a factor of production in obtaining the final goods (fish) that people desire. Thus, they're regarded as *capital.* Blast furnaces used to make steel and desks used to equip offices are also capital inputs.

Entrepreneurship. The more land, labor, and capital available, the greater the amount of potential output. A farmer with 10,000 acres, 12 employees, and six tractors can grow more crops than a farmer with half those resources. But there's no guarantee that he will. The farmer with fewer resources may have better ideas about what to plant, when to irrigate, or how to harvest the crops. ***It's not just a matter of what resources you have but also of how well you use them.*** This is where the fourth factor of production—**entrepreneurship**—comes in. The entrepreneur is the person who sees the opportunity for new or better products and brings together the resources needed for producing them. If it weren't for entrepreneurs, Thai fishermen would still be using sticks to catch fish. Without entrepreneurship, farmers would still be milking their cows by hand. If someone hadn't thought of a way to miniaturize electronic circuits, you wouldn't have a cell phone.

The role of entrepreneurs in economic progress is a key issue in the market versus government debate. The Austrian economist Joseph Schumpeter argued that free markets unleash the "animal spirits" of entrepreneurs, propelling innovation, technology, and growth. Critics of government regulation argue that government interference in the marketplace, however well intentioned, tends to stifle those very same animal spirits.

> **entrepreneurship:** The assembling of resources to produce new or improved products and technologies.

Limits to Output

No matter how an economy is organized, there's a limit to how fast it can grow. The most evident limit is the amount of resources available for producing goods and services. These resource limits imply that we can't produce everything we want. When President Bush announced an ambitious plan to colonize the Moon and explore Mars, people were excited. But then people wondered how we'd pay for a trillion-dollar Mars expedition. In *dollar* terms, the money would have to come from other programs. In *economic* terms, the resources used for space exploration would be unavailable for producing more earthly goods like education, health care, and highways.

Opportunity Costs

The earthly sacrifices implied by an expedition to Mars go to the heart of the scarcity problem. ***Every time we use scarce resources in one way, we give up the opportunity to use them in other ways.*** If we use more resources to explore space, we have fewer resources available for producing earthly goods. The forgone earthly goods represent the **opportunity costs** of a Mars expedition. ***Opportunity cost is what is given up to get something else.*** Even a so-called free lunch has an opportunity cost (see cartoon). The resources used to produce the lunch could have been used to produce something else. A trip to Mars has a much higher opportunity cost.

Your economics class also has an opportunity cost. The building space used for your economics class can't be used to show movies at the same time. Your professor can't lecture (produce education) and repair motorcycles simultaneously. The decision to use these scarce resources (capital, labor) for an economics class implies producing less of other goods.

> **opportunity cost:** The most desired goods or services that are forgone to obtain something else.

"There's no such thing as a free lunch."

Analysis: All goods and services have an opportunity cost. Even the resources used to produce a "free lunch" could have been used to produce something else.

Even reading this book is costly. That cost is not measured in dollars and cents. The true (economic) cost is, instead, measured in terms of some alternative activity. What would you like to be doing right now? The more time you spend reading this book, the less time you have available for that alternative use of your time. The opportunity cost of reading this text is the best alternative use of your scarce time. If you are missing your favorite TV show, we'd say that show is the opportunity cost of reading this book. It is what you gave up to do this assignment. Hopefully, the benefits you get from studying will outweigh that cost. Otherwise this wouldn't be the best way to use your scarce time.

Guns vs. Butter

To see how the share of output allocated to national defense has changed in recent decades, visit the Congressional Budget Office web site at www.cbo.gov and search for "discretionary outlays."

One of the persistent national choices about resource use entails defense spending. After the September 11, 2001, terrorist attacks on the World Trade Center and Pentagon, American citizens overwhelmingly favored an increase in military spending. But where were the extra resources going to come from? Any resources employed in national defense must be taken from other industries. The 1.4 million men and women already serving in the armed forces aren't available to build schools, program computers, or teach economics. Similarly, the land, labor, capital, and entrepreneurship devoted to producing military hardware aren't available for producing civilian goods. An *increase* in national defense would imply still more sacrifices of civilian goods and services. This is the "guns versus butter" dilemma that all nations confront.

After the end of the Cold War in 1989, the United States had chosen to produce far fewer "guns." The defense budget declined from a high of 6.3 percent of total output in 1986 to only 3 percent in 2001. In the process, the armed forces had been cut by 500,000 men and women. These defense cutbacks freed up scarce resources that produced more civilian goods ("butter"). This is referred to as the "peace dividend" from military downsizing. The post-terrorist military buildup and the war in Iraq reversed part of that dividend.

PRODUCTION POSSIBILITIES

The opportunity costs implied by our every choice can be illustrated easily. Suppose a nation can produce only two goods, trucks and tanks. To keep things simple, assume that labor (workers) is the only factor of production needed to produce either good. Although other factors of production (land, machinery) are also needed in actual production, ignoring them for the moment does no harm. Let us assume further that we have a total of only 10 workers available per day to produce either trucks or tanks. Our initial problem is to determine the *limits* of output. How many trucks or tanks *can* be produced in a day with available resources?

Before going any further, notice how opportunity costs will affect the answer. If we use all 10 workers to produce trucks, no labor will be available to assemble tanks. In this case, forgone tanks would become the *opportunity cost* of a decision to employ all our resources in truck production.

We still don't know how many trucks could be produced with 10 workers or exactly how many tanks would be forgone by such a decision. To get these answers, we need more details about the production processes involved—specifically, how many workers are required to manufacture trucks or tanks.

The Production Possibilities Curve

production possibilities: The alternative combinations of final goods and services that could be produced in a given time period with all available resources and technology.

Table 1.1 summarizes the hypothetical choices, or **production possibilities,** that we confront in this case. Row *A* of the table shows the consequences of a decision to produce trucks only. With 10 workers available and a labor requirement of 2 workers per truck, we can manufacture a maximum of five trucks per day. By so doing, however, we use all available workers, leaving none for tank assembly. If we want tanks, we have to cut back on truck production; this is the essential choice we must make.

The remainder of Table 1.1 describes the full range of production choices. By cutting back truck production from five to four trucks per day (row *B*), we reduce labor use from 10 workers to 8. That leaves 2 workers available for other uses.

TABLE 1.1
Production Possibilities Schedule

As long as resources are limited, their use entails an opportunity cost. In this case, resources (labor) used to produce trucks can't be used for tank assembly at the same time. Hence, the forgone

tanks are the opportunity cost of additional trucks. If all our resources were used to produce trucks (row A), no tanks could be assembled.

	Total Available Labor	Truck Production				Tank Production		
		Output of Trucks per Day	× Labor Needed per Truck	=	Total Labor Required for Trucks	Labor Not Used for Trucks	Potential Output of Tanks per Day	Increase in Tank Output
A	10	5	2		10	0	0	
B	10	4	2		8	2	2.0	> 2.0
C	10	3	2		6	4	3.0	> 1.0
D	10	2	2		4	6	3.8	> 0.8
E	10	1	2		2	8	4.5	> 0.7
F	10	0	2		0	10	5.0	> 0.5

If we employ these remaining 2 workers to assemble tanks, we can build two tanks a day. We would then end up with four trucks and two tanks per day. What's the opportunity cost of these two tanks? It's the one additional truck (the fifth truck) that we could have produced but didn't.

As we proceed down the rows of Table 1.1, the nature of opportunity costs becomes apparent. Each additional tank built implies the loss (opportunity cost) of truck output. Likewise, every truck produced implies the loss of some tank output.

These trade-offs between truck and tank production are illustrated in the production possibilities curve of Figure 1.1. ***Each point on the production possibilities curve depicts an alternative mix of output*** that could be produced. In this case, each point represents a different combination of trucks and tanks that we could produce in a single day using all available resources (labor in this case).

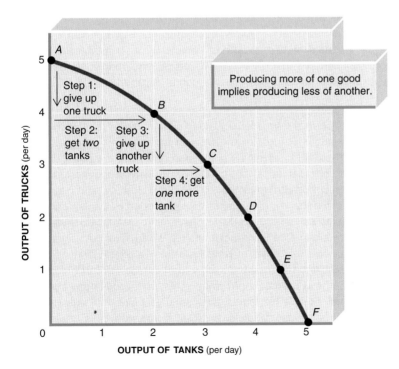

FIGURE 1.1
A Production Possibilities Curve

A production possibilities curve describes the various output combinations that could be produced in a given time period with available resources and technology. It represents a menu of output choices an economy confronts. Point B indicates that we could produce a combination of four trucks and two tanks per day. By producing one less truck, we could assemble a third tank, and thus move to point C. Points A, D, E, and F, illustrate still other output combinations that could be produced. This curve is a graphic illustration of the production possibilities schedule in Table 1.1.

Notice in particular how points *A* through *F* in Figure 1.1 represent the choices described in each row of Table 1.1. At point *A*, we're producing five trucks per day and no tanks. As we move down the curve from point *A* to point *B*, truck production drops from five to four vehicles per day while tank assembly increases from zero to two. In other words, we're giving up one truck to get two tanks assembled. The opportunity cost of those tanks is one truck that is given up. A production possibilities curve, then, is simply a graphic summary of production possibilities, as described in Table 1.1. It illustrates the alternative goods and services we could produce and the implied opportunity costs of each choice. In other words, ***the production possibilities curve illustrates two essential principles:***

- ***Scarce resources.*** There's a limit to the amount we can produce in a given time period with available resources and technology.
- ***Opportunity costs.*** We can obtain additional quantities of any desired good only by reducing the potential production of another good.

Increasing Opportunity Costs

The shape of the production possibilities curve reflects another limitation on our choices. Notice how opportunity costs increase as we move along the production possibilities curve. When we cut truck output from five to four (step 1, Figure 1.1), we get two tanks (step 2). When we cut truck production further, however (step 3), we get only one tank per truck given up (step 4). The opportunity cost of tank production is increasing. This process of increasing opportunity cost continues. By the time we give up the last truck (row *F*), tank output increases by only 0.5: We get only half a tank for the last truck given up. These increases in opportunity cost are reflected in the outward bend of the production possibilities curve.

Why do opportunity costs increase? Mostly because it's difficult to move resources from one industry to another. It's easy to transform trucks to tanks on a blackboard. In the real world, however, resources don't adapt so easily. Workers who assemble trucks may not have the same skills for tank assembly. As we continue to transfer labor from one industry to the other, we start getting fewer tanks for every truck we give up.

The difficulties entailed in transferring labor skills, capital, and entrepreneurship from one industry to another are so universal that we often speak of the *law of increasing opportunity cost*. This law says that we must give up ever-increasing quantities of other goods and services in order to get more of a particular good. The law isn't based solely on the limited versatility of individual workers. The *mix* of factor inputs makes a difference as well. Truck assembly requires less capital than tank assembly. In a pinch, wheels can be mounted on a truck almost completely by hand, whereas tank treads require more sophisticated machinery. As we move labor from truck assembly to tank assembly, available capital may restrict our output capabilities.

The Cost of North Korea's Military

The International Institute for Strategic Studies compiles data on national military forces (www.iiss.org). To determine what percentage of a nation's population is in the armed forces, try the Central Intelligence Agency (www.odci.gov/cia/publications/factbook).

The kind of opportunity costs that arise in truck production or tank assembly takes on even greater significance in the broader decisions nations make about WHAT to produce. Consider, for example, North Korea's decision to maintain a large military. North Korea is a relatively small country: Its population of 24 million ranks fortieth in the world. Yet North Korea maintains the fourth-largest army in the world. To do so, it must allocate 16 percent of all its resources to feeding, clothing, and equipping its military forces. As a consequence, there aren't enough resources available to produce food. Without adequate machinery, seeds, fertilizer, or irrigation, Korea's farmers can't produce enough food to feed the population (see World View). As Figure 1.2 illustrates, the opportunity cost of "guns" in Korea is a lot of needed "butter."

During World War II, the United States confronted a similar trade-off. In 1944, nearly 40 percent of all U.S. output was devoted to the military. Civilian goods were so scarce that they had to be rationed. Staples like butter, sugar, and gasoline were doled out in small quantities. Even golf balls were rationed. In North Korea, golf balls would be a luxury even without a military buildup. As the share of North Korea's output devoted to the military increased, even basic food production became more difficult.

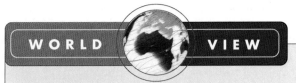

Food Shortages Plague N. Korea

BEIJING, Feb. 13—A severe food shortage has crippled the U.N. feeding program that sustains North Korea's most vulnerable and undernourished people, according to Masood Hyder, the U.N. humanitarian aid coordinator and World Food Program representative in Pyongyang.

He said his organization can now feed fewer than 100,000 of the 6.5 million people it normally does, many of them kindergarten-age children and pregnant women who cannot get what they need to stay healthy from the country's distribution system. . . .

Food shortages already produce stunted growth in four out of 10 North Korean students and allow pregnant women to gain only half of the 22 pounds they are expected to gain to give birth to healthy babies.

Some orphanages have started serving two meals a day instead of three because of the shortages, Masood said.

—Edward Cody

Source: *Washington Post,* February 14, 2004. © 2004 The Washington Post. Reprinted with permission. www.washingtonpost.com

North Korea Expanding Missile Programs

Despite international pressure to curtail its missile program, North Korea is building at least two new launch facilities for the medium-range Taepo Dong 1 and has stepped up production of short-range missiles, according to U.S. intelligence and diplomatic sources.

The projects, and a conclusion by U.S. intelligence agencies that North Korea intends to test-fire a second missile capable of striking Japan, are inflaming regional tensions, U.S. officials and Korea experts said.

—Dana Priest and Thomas W. Lippman

Source: *Washington Post,* November 20, 1998. © 1998 The Washington Post. Reprinted with permission. www.washingtonpost.com

Analysis: North Korea's inability to feed itself is partly due to maintaining its large army: Resources used for the military aren't available for producing food.

Russia confronted a similarly difficult trade-off. In September 2000, Russia decided it could no longer afford to devote such a large share of its resources to the military. It decided to shrink its armed forces by more than a fourth, releasing over 300,000 workers to produce civilian goods and services. As a result, Russia now has a smaller armed force than North Korea but also a lot more food. Figure 1.3 illustrates how other nations divide up available resources between military and civilian production. The $420 billion the United States now spends on national defense absorbs only 3.8 percent of total output. This made the opportunity costs of the war in Iraq and post-terrorist military buildup less painful.

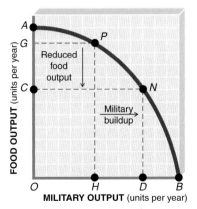

FIGURE 1.2
The Cost of War

North Korea devotes 16 percent of its output to the military. The opportunity cost of this decision is reduced output of food. As the military expands from *OH* to *OD,* food output drops from *OG* to *OC.*

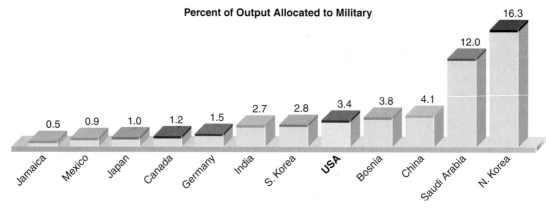

Percent of Output Allocated to Military

FIGURE 1.3
The Military Share of Output

The share of output allocated to the military is an indication of the opportunity cost of maintaining an army. North Korea has the highest cost, using 16 percent of its resources for military pur-

poses. Although China and the United States have much larger armies, their military *share* of output is much smaller.

Source: International Institute of Strategic Studies (2002 data).

Efficiency

Not all of the choices on the production possibilities curve are equally desirable. They are, however, all *efficient*. Efficiency means squeezing *maximum* output out of available resources. Every point of the production possibilities curve satisfies this condition. Although the *mix* of output changes as we move around the production possibilities curve (Figures 1.1 and 1.2), at every point we are getting as much *total* output as physically possible. Since **efficiency** in production means simply "getting the most from what you've got," every point on the production possibilities curve is efficient. At any point on the curve we are using all available resources in the best way we know how.

> **efficiency:** Maximum output of a good from the resources used in production.

Inefficiency

There's no guarantee, of course, that we'll always use resources so efficiently. *A production possibilities curve shows* **potential** *output, not necessarily* **actual** *output.* If we're inefficient, actual output will be less than that potential. This happens. In the real world, workers sometimes loaf on the job. Or they call in sick and go to a baseball game instead of working. Managers don't always give the clearest directions or stay in touch with advancing technology. Even students sometimes fail to put forth their best effort on homework assignments. This kind of slippage can prevent us from achieving maximum production. When that happens, we end up *inside* the production possibilities curve rather than *on* it.

Point *Y* in Figure 1.4 illustrates the consequences of inefficient production. At point *Y*, we're producing only three trucks and two tanks. This is less than our potential. We could assemble a third tank without cutting back truck production (point *C*). Or

FIGURE 1.4
Points Inside and Outside the Curve

Points outside the production possibilities curve (point *X*) are unattainable with available resources and technology. Points inside the curve (point *Y*) represent the incomplete use of available resources. Only points on the production possibilities curve (*A, B, C*) represent maximum use of our production capabilities.

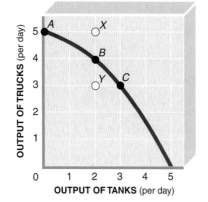

India's Economy Gets a New Jolt From Mr. Shourie

NEW DELHI—In March 2001, strikers opposed to the Indian government's sale of an aluminum company threatened to fast until they died, an act of civil disobedience made famous by the nation's founding father, Mahatma Gandhi. India's privatization czar, Arun Shourie, was unmoved. "I said you can do what you want," recalls Mr. Shourie, photos of Mr. Gandhi hanging on the office wall in front of him. "But we're still not going to talk to you." The strike folded weeks later.

The sale of Bharat Aluminum Co. was a big test of Mr. Shourie's three-year campaign to sell off the almost 250 companies owned by India's central government. . . .

Since becoming minister of disinvestment in 2000, Mr. Shourie has taken state-owned companies once thought sacrosanct, such as India's long-distance telephone company and its biggest auto maker, and placed them in private hands. . . .

In India, state-owned companies provide a vast patronage system to ministers, party officials, and even petty bureaucrats.

For that system's beneficiaries, privatization represents a "loss of control, prestige, and money," says a banker who has advised the government on privatizations. . . .

What Mr. Shourie learned about the condition of many state-owned companies shocked him. On one fact-finding trip, he toured a state-owned airport hotel in New Delhi that had only a 3% occupancy rate and inoperable toilets. A state-owned tourist hotel in the south of the country had a crematorium and two burial grounds on its land. And a fertilizer company in West Bengal hadn't produced an ounce of product in 14 years. "The employees just sat around all day playing carrom," says Mr. Shourie, referring to an Indian board game.

—Jay Solomon and Joanna Slater

Analysis: When resources are used inefficiently, a nation's output lies *inside* its production possibilities. By privatizing inefficient state enterprises, India hopes to increase total output and reach its production possibilities.

we could get an extra truck without sacrificing any tank output (point *B*). Instead, we're producing *inside* the production possibilities curve at point *Y.* Such inefficiencies plagued centrally planned economies. Government-run factories guaranteed everyone a job regardless of how much output he or she produced. They became bloated bureaucracies; as much as 40 percent of the workers were superfluous. When communism collapsed, many of these factories were "privatized," that is, sold to private investors. The privatized companies were able to fire thousands of workers and *increase* output. Governments in Europe and Latin America have also sold off many of their state-owned enterprises in the hopes of increasing efficiency and reaching the production possibilities curve. India's "Minister of Disinvestment" has been pursuing the same strategy, as the World View attests.

Unemployment

Countries may also end up inside their production possibilities curve if all available resources aren't used. In 2003, for example, as many as 8 million Americans were looking for work each week, but no one hired them. As a result, we were stuck *inside* the production possibilities curve, producing less output than we could have. A basic challenge for policymakers is to eliminate unemployment and keep the economy on its production possibilities curve. In 2004, the United States was closer to this goal.

Economic Growth

Figure 1.4 also illustrates an output mix that everyone would welcome. Point *X* lies *outside* the production possibilities curve. It suggests that we could get *more* goods than we're capable of producing! Unfortunately, point *X* is only a mirage: All output combinations that lie outside the production possibilities curve are unattainable with available resources and technology.

Things change, however. Every year, population growth and immigration increase our supply of labor. As we continue building factories and machinery, the stock of available capital also increases. The *quality* of labor and capital also increase when we train workers and pursue new technologies. Entrepreneurs may discover new products or better ways of producing old ones (e.g., Intel's latest chips). All these changes

FIGURE 1.5
Growth: Increasing Production Possibilities

A production possibilities curve is based on *available* resources and technology. If more resources or better technology becomes available, production possibilities will increase. This economic growth is illustrated by the *shift* from PP_1 to PP_2.

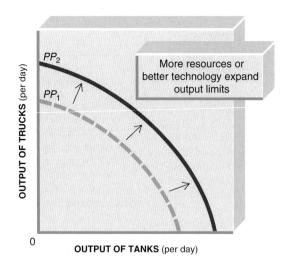

economic growth: An increase in output (real GDP); an expansion of production possibilities.

increase potential output. This is illustrated in Figure 1.5 by the outward *shift* of the production possibilities curve. Before the appearance of new resources or better technology, our production possibilities were limited by the curve PP_1. **With more resources or better technology, our production possibilities increase.** This greater capacity to produce is represented by curve PP_2. This outward shift of the production possibilities curve is the essence of **economic growth.** With economic growth, countries can have more guns *and* more butter. Without economic growth, living standards decline as the population grows. This is the problem that plagues some of the world's poorest nations, where population increases every year but output often doesn't.

BASIC DECISIONS

Production possibilities define the output choices that a nation confronts. From these choices every nation must make some basic decisions. As we noted at the beginning of this chapter, the three core economic questions are

- *WHAT to produce*
- *HOW to produce*
- *FOR WHOM to produce*

WHAT

There are millions of points along a production possibilities curve, and each one represents a different mix of output. We can choose only *one* of these points at any time. The point we choose determines what mix of output gets produced. That choice determines how many guns are produced, and how much butter.

The production possibilities curve doesn't tell us which mix of output is best; it just lays out a menu of available choices. It's up to us to pick out the one and only mix of output that will be produced at a given time. This WHAT decision is a basic decision every nation must make.

HOW

Decisions must also be made about HOW to produce. Should we generate electricity by burning coal, smashing atoms, or transforming solar power? Should we harvest ancient forests even if that destroys endangered owls or other animal species? Should we dump municipal and industrial waste into nearby rivers, or should we dispose of it in some other way? There are lots of different ways of producing goods and services, and someone has to make a decision about which production methods to use. The HOW decision is a question not just of efficiency but of social values as well.

FOR WHOM

After we've decided what to produce and how, we must address a third basic question: FOR WHOM? Who is going to get the output produced? Should everyone get an equal share? Should everyone wear the same clothes and drive identical cars? Should some people get to enjoy seven-course banquets while others forage in garbage cans for food scraps? How should the goods and services an economy produces be distributed? Are we satisfied with the way output is now distributed?

THE MECHANISMS OF CHOICE

Answers to the questions of WHAT, HOW, and FOR WHOM largely define an economy. But who formulates the answers? Who actually decides which goods are produced, what technologies are used, or how incomes are distributed?

The Invisible Hand of a Market Economy

Adam Smith had an answer back in 1776. In his classic work *The Wealth of Nations*, Smith said the "invisible hand" determines what gets produced, how, and for whom. The invisible hand he referred to wasn't a creature from a science fiction movie but, instead, a characterization of the way markets work.

Consider the decision about how many cars to produce in the United States. Who decides to produce over 16 million cars and trucks, a year? There's no "auto czar" who dictates production. Not even General Motors can make such a decision. Instead, the *market* decides how many cars to produce. Millions of consumers signal their desire to have a car by browsing the Internet, visiting showrooms, and buying cars. Their purchases flash a green light to producers, who see the potential to earn more profits. To do so, they'll increase auto output. If consumers stop buying cars, profits will disappear. Producers will respond by reducing output, laying off workers, and even closing factories. These interactions between consumers and producers determine how many cars are produced.

Notice how the invisible hand moves us along the production possibilities curve. If consumers demand more cars, the mix of output will include more cars and less of other goods. If auto production is scaled back, the displaced autoworkers will end up producing other goods and services, which will change the mix of output in the opposite direction.

Adam Smith's invisible hand is now called the **market mechanism.** Notice that it doesn't require any direct contact between consumers and producers. Communication is indirect, transmitted by market prices and sales. Indeed, *the essential feature of the market mechanism is the price signal.* If you want something and have sufficient income, you can buy it. If enough people do the same thing, the total sales of that product will rise, and perhaps its price will as well. Producers, seeing sales and prices rise, will want to exploit this profit potential. To do so, they'll attempt to acquire a larger share of available resources and use it to produce the goods we desire. That's how the "invisible hand" works.

market mechanism: The use of market prices and sales to signal desired outputs (or resource allocations).

The market mechanism can also answer the HOW question. To maximize their profits, producers will seek to use the lowest-cost method of producing a good. By observing prices in the marketplace, they can identify the cheapest method and adopt it.

The market mechanism can also resolve the FOR WHOM question. A market distributes goods to the highest bidder. Individuals who are willing and able to pay the most for a good tend to get it in a pure market economy.

Adam Smith was so impressed with the ability of the market mechanism to answer the basic WHAT, HOW, and FOR WHOM questions that he urged government to "leave it alone" (**laissez faire**). In his view, the price signals and responses of the marketplace were likely to do a better job of allocating resources than any government could.

laissez faire: The doctrine of "leave it alone," of nonintervention by government in the market mechanism.

Government Intervention and Command Economies

The laissez-faire policy Adam Smith favored has always had its share of critics. Karl Marx emphasized how free markets tend to concentrate wealth and power in the hands of the few, at the expense of the many. As he saw it, unfettered markets permit the capitalists (those who own the machinery and factories) to enrich themselves while the proletariat (the workers) toil long hours for subsistence wages. Marx argued that the government not only had to intervene but had to *own* all the means of production—the factories, the machinery, the land—in order to avoid savage inequalities. In *Das Kapital* (1867) and the *Communist Manifesto* (1848), he laid the foundation for a communist state in which the government would be the master of economic outcomes.

The British economist John Maynard Keynes seemed to offer a less drastic solution. The market, he conceded, was pretty efficient in organizing production and building better mousetraps. However, individual producers and workers had no control over the broader economy. The cumulative actions of so many economic agents could easily tip the economy in the wrong direction. A completely unregulated market might veer off in one direction and then another as producers all rushed to increase output at the same time or throttled back production in a herdlike manner. The government, Keynes reasoned, could act like a pressure gauge, letting off excess steam or building it up as the economy needed. With the government maintaining overall balance in the economy, the market could live up to its performance expectations. While assuring a stable, full-employment environment, the government might also be able to redress excessive inequalities. In Keynes's view, government should play an active but not all-inclusive role in managing the economy.

For more information on Smith, Malthus, Keynes, and Marx, visit the Federal Reserve Bank of San Francisco at www.frbsf.org/econedu and click on "Great Economists and Their Times" under "Publications and Resources."

Continuing Debates

These historical views shed perspective on today's political debates. The core of most debates is some variation of the WHAT, HOW, or FOR WHOM questions. Much of the debate is how these questions should be answered. Conservatives favor Adam Smith's laissez-faire approach, while liberals tend to think government intervention is likely to improve the answers. Conservatives resist workplace regulation, affirmative action, and minimum wages because such interventions might impair market efficiency. Liberals argue that such interventions temper the excesses of the market and promote both equity and efficiency.

The debate over how best to manage the economy is not unique to the United States. Countries around the world confront the same choice, between reliance on the market and reliance on the government. Few countries have ever relied exclusively on either one or the other to manage their economy. Even the former Soviet Union, where the government owned all the means of production and central planners dictated how they were to be used, made limited use of free markets. In Cuba, the government still manages the economy's resources but encourages farmers' markets and some private trade and investment. As a previous World View indicated, India is now letting the market play a larger role in deciding what is produced, how it is produced, and who gets the resulting output.

The World View below categorizes nations by the extent of their market reliance. Hong Kong scores high on this "Index of Economic Freedom" because its tax rates are relatively low, the public sector is comparatively small, and there are few restrictions on private investment or trade. By contrast, North Korea scores extremely low because the government owns all property, directly allocates resources, sets wages, and limits trade.

The rankings shown in the World View are neither definitive nor stable. In 1989, Russia began a massive transformation from a state-controlled economy to a more market-oriented economy. Some of the former republics (e.g., Estonia) became relatively free, while others (e.g., Turkmenistan) still rely on extensive government control of the economy. China has greatly expanded the role of private markets and Cuba is moving in the same direction in fits and starts. Even Libya—the second "least-free" nation on the Heritage list—is just now experimenting with some market reforms.

In the United States, the changes have been less dramatic. The most notable shift was President Franklin Roosevelt's New Deal, which greatly expanded the government's role in the economy. In more recent times, the tug-of-war between laissez faire and government intervention has been much less decisive. Although President Reagan often said that "government *is* the problem," he hardly made a dent in government growth during the eight years of his presidency. Likewise, President Clinton's very different conviction that the government can *fix* problems, not cause them, had only

To learn how the Heritage Foundation defines economic freedom, visit its Web site at www.heritage.org.

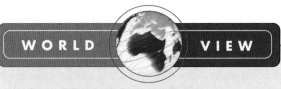

WORLD VIEW

Index of Economic Freedom

Hong Kong ranks number one among the world's nations in economic freedom. It achieves that status with low tax rates, free-trade policies, minimal government regulation, and secure property rights. These and other economic indicators place Hong Kong at the top of the Heritage Foundation's 2004 country rankings by the degree of "economic freedom." The "most free" and the "least free" (repressed) economies on the list of 155 countries are

Greatest Economic Freedom	Least Economic Freedom
Hong Kong	North Korea
Singapore	Libya
New Zealand	Zimbabwe
Luxembourg	Laos
Ireland	Burma
Estonia	Turkmenistan
United Kingdom	Uzbekistan
Denmark	Iran
Switzerland	Venezuela
United States	Tajikstan

Source: Heritage Foundation, *2004 Index of Economic Freedom,* Washington, DC, 2004.
www.heritage.org

Analysis: All nations must decide whether to rely on market signals or government directives to determine economic outcomes. Nations that rely the least on government intervention score highest on this Index of Economic Freedom.

minor effects on the size and scope of government activity. President George W. Bush has sought to not only lower taxes but also lessen government regulation of HOW goods are produced.

A Mixed Economy

Even if President Bush got all the tax cuts and deregulation he wanted, the government would still play a large role in the U.S. economy. No one wants to rely exclusively on Adam Smith's invisible hand. Nor is anyone willing to have the economy steered exclusively by the highly visible hand of the government. *The United States, like most nations, uses a combination of market signals and government directives to select economic outcomes.* The resulting compromises are called **mixed economies.**

The reluctance of countries around the world to rely exclusively on either market signals or government directives is due to the recognition that both mechanisms can and do fail on occasion. As we've seen, market signals are capable of answering the three core questions of WHAT, HOW, and FOR WHOM. But the answers may not be the best possible ones.

> **mixed economy:** An economy that uses both market signals and government directives to allocate goods and resources.

Market Failure

When market signals don't give the best possible answers to the WHAT, HOW, and FOR WHOM questions, we say that the market mechanism has *failed.* Specifically, **market failure** means that the invisible hand has failed to achieve the best possible outcomes. If the market fails, we end up with the wrong (*sub*optimal) mix of output, too much unemployment, polluted air, or an inequitable distribution of income.

In a market-driven economy, for example, producers will select production methods based on cost. Cost-driven production decisions, however, may lead a factory to spew pollution into the environment rather than to use cleaner but more expensive

> **market failure:** An imperfection in the market mechanism that prevents optimal outcomes.

methods of production. The resulting pollution may be so bad that society ends up worse off as a result of the extra production. In such a case we may need government intervention to force better answers to the WHAT and HOW questions.

We could also let the market decide who gets to consume cigarettes. Anyone who had enough money to buy a pack of cigarettes would then be entitled to smoke. What if, however, children aren't experienced enough to balance the risks of smoking against the pleasures? What if nonsmokers are harmed by secondhand smoke? In this case as well, the market's answer to the FOR WHOM question might not be optimal.

Government Failure

government failure: Government intervention that fails to improve economic outcomes.

Government intervention may move us closer to our economic goals. If so, the resulting mix of market signals and government directives would be an improvement over a purely market-driven economy. But government intervention may fail as well. **Government failure** occurs when government intervention fails to improve market outcomes or actually makes them worse.

The collapse of communism revealed how badly government directives can fail. But government failure also occurs in less spectacular ways. For example, the government may intervene to force an industry to clean up its pollution. The government's directives may impose such high costs that the industry closes factories and lays off workers. Some cutbacks in output might be appropriate, but they could also prove excessive. The government might also mandate pollution control technologies that are too expensive or even obsolete. None of this has to happen, but it might. If it does, government failure will have worsened economic outcomes.

The government might also fail if it interferes with the market's answer to the FOR WHOM question. For 50 years, communist China distributed goods by government directive, not market performance. Incomes were more equal, but uniformly low. To increase output and living standards, China has turned to market incentives (see World View on the next page). As entrepreneurs respond to these incentives, everyone may become better off—even while inequality increases.

Excessive taxes and transfer payments can also worsen economic outcomes. If the government raises taxes on the rich to pay welfare benefits for the poor, neither the rich nor the poor may see much purpose in working. In that case, the attempt to give everybody a "fair" share of the pie might end up shrinking the size of the pie. If that happened, society could end up worse off.

Seeking Balance

None of these failures has to occur, but each might. The challenge for society is to minimize failures by selecting the appropriate balance of market signals and government directives. This isn't an easy task. It requires that we know how markets work and why they sometimes fail. We also need to know what policy options the government has and how and when they might work.

WHAT ECONOMICS IS ALL ABOUT

Understanding how economies function is the basic purpose of studying economics. We seek to know how an economy is organized, how it behaves, and how successfully it achieves its basic objectives. Then, if we're lucky, we can discover better ways of attaining those same objectives.

End vs. Means

Economists don't formulate an economy's objectives. Instead, they focus on the *means* available for achieving given *goals*. In 1978, for example, the U.S. Congress identified "full employment" as a major economic goal. Congress then directed future presidents (and their economic advisers) to formulate policies that would enable us to achieve full employment. The economist's job is to help design policies that will best achieve this and other economic goals.

Macro vs. Micro

The study of economics is typically divided into two parts: macroeconomics and microeconomics. Macroeconomics focuses on the behavior of an entire economy—the "big picture." In macroeconomics we worry about such national goals as full employment, control of inflation, and economic growth, without worrying about the

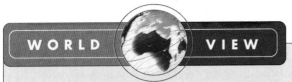

China's Leaders Back Private Property

SHANGHAI, Dec. 22—China's Communist Party leaders on Monday proposed amendments to the nation's constitution that would enshrine a legal right to private property while broadening the focus of the party to represent private businesses.

Virtually assured of adoption in the party-controlled National People's Congress, the amendments constitute a significant advance in China's ongoing transition from communism to capitalism. They amount to recognition that the economic future of the world's most populous country rests with private enterprise—a radical departure from the political roots of this land still known as the People's Republic of China.

Not since the Communist Party swept to power in 1949 in a revolution built on antipathy toward landowners and industrialists have Chinese been legally permitted to own property. Under the leadership of Chairman Mao, millions of people suffered persecution for being tainted with "bad" class backgrounds that linked them to landowning pasts.

But in present-day China the profit motive has come to pervade nearly every area of life. The site in Shanghai where the Communist Party was founded is now a shopping and entertainment complex anchored by a Starbucks coffee shop. From the poor villages in which most Chinese still live to the cities now dominated by high-rises, the market determines the price of most goods and decisions about what to produce. Business is widely viewed as a favored, even noble, undertaking.

The state-owned firms that once dominated China's economy have traditionally been sustained by credit from state banks, regardless of their balance sheets. Today, many are bankrupt, and banks are burdened by about $500 billion in bad loans, according to private economists. The government has cast privatization as the prescription for turning them around, creating management incentives to make them profitable.

—Peter S. Goodman

Source: *Washington Post*, December 23, 2003. © 2003 The Washington Post. Reprinted with permission. www.washingtonpost.com

Analysis: Government-directed production, prices, and incomes may increase equalities but blunt incentives. Private property and market-based incomes motivate higher productivity and growth.

well-being or behavior of specific individuals or groups. The essential concern of **macroeconomics** is to understand and improve the performance of the economy as a whole.

Microeconomics is concerned with the details of this big picture. In microeconomics we focus on the individuals, firms, and government agencies that actually compose the larger economy. Our interest here is in the behavior of individual economic actors. What are their goals? How can they best achieve these goals with their limited resources? How will they respond to various incentives and opportunities?

A primary concern of macroeconomics, for example, is to determine how much money, *in total,* consumers will spend on goods and services. In microeconomics, the focus is much narrower. In micro, attention is paid to purchases of *specific* goods and services rather than just aggregated totals. Macro likewise concerns itself with the level of *total* business investment, while micro examines how *individual* businesses make their investment decisions.

Although they operate at different levels of abstraction, macro and micro are intrinsically related. Macro (aggregate) outcomes depend on micro behavior, and micro (individual) behavior is affected by macro outcomes. One can't fully understand how an economy works until one understands how all the participants behave and why they behave as they do. But just as you can drive a car without knowing how its engine is constructed, you can observe how an economy runs without completely disassembling it. In macroeconomics we observe that the car goes faster when the accelerator is depressed and that it slows when the brake is applied. That's all we need to know in most situations. At times, however, the car breaks down. When it does, we have to know something more about how the pedals work. This leads us into micro studies. How does each part work? Which ones can or should be fixed?

Our interest in microeconomics is motivated by more than our need to understand how the larger economy works. The "parts" of the economic engine are people. To

macroeconomics: The study of aggregate economic behavior, of the economy as a whole.

microeconomics: The study of individual behavior in the economy, of the components of the larger economy.

the extent that we care about the welfare of individuals in society, we have a fundamental interest in microeconomic behavior and outcomes. In this regard, we examine how individual consumers and business firms seek to achieve specific goals in the marketplace. The goals aren't always related to output. Gary Becker won the 1992 Nobel Prize in economics for demonstrating how economic principles also affect decisions to marry, to have children, or to engage in criminal activities.

Theory vs. Reality

The distinction between macroeconomics and microeconomics is one of many simplifications we make in studying economic behavior. The economy is much too vast and complex to describe and explain in one course (or one lifetime). Accordingly, we focus on basic relationships, ignoring annoying detail. In so doing, we isolate basic principles of economic behavior and then use those principles to predict economic events and develop economic policies. This means that we formulate theories, or *models,* of economic behavior and then use those theories to evaluate and design economic policy.

Our model of consumer behavior assumes, for example, that people buy less of a good when its price rises. In reality, however, people *may* buy *more* of a good at increased prices, especially if those high prices create a certain snob appeal or if prices are expected to increase still further. In predicting consumer responses to price increases, we typically ignore such possibilities by *assuming* that the price of the good in question is the *only* thing that changes. This assumption of "other things remaining equal" (unchanged) (in Latin, **ceteris paribus**) allows us to make straightforward predictions. If instead we described consumer responses to increased prices in any and all circumstances (allowing everything to change at once), every prediction would be accompanied by a book full of exceptions and qualifications. We'd look more like lawyers than economists.

ceteris paribus: The assumption of nothing else changing.

Although the assumption of *ceteris paribus* makes it easier to formulate economic theory and policy, it also increases the risk of error. If other things do change in significant ways, our predictions (and policies) may fail. But, like weather forecasters, we continue to make predictions, knowing that occasional failure is inevitable. In so doing, we're motivated by the conviction that it's better to be approximately right than to be dead wrong.

Politics. Politicians can't afford to be quite so complacent about economic predictions. Policy decisions must be made every day. And a politician's continued survival may depend on being more than approximately right. George H. Bush's loss in the 1992 election resulted in part from his repeated predictions that the economy was "turning around." When this optimistic forecast proved wrong, voters lost faith in President Bush's ability to direct the economy. Ironically, his son gained a critical advantage in the superclose 2000 presidential election because of another economic slowdown and a slumping stock market. Once again, voters sought a new economic policy team.

After he took office, President George W. Bush immediately sought to change the mix of output. Even before the September 11, 2001, terrorist attacks, he wanted more "guns," as reflected in added defense spending. He also secured tax cuts to boost private consumption and investment. Were these the right choices? Economic theory can't completely answer that question. Choices about the mix of output are ultimately political—decisions that must take into account not only economic trade-offs (opportunity costs) but also social values. "Politics"—the balancing of competing interests—is an inevitable ingredient of economic policy.

Comparative data on the percentage of goods and services the various national governments provide is available from the Penn World Tables at www.pwt.econ.upenn.edu.

Imperfect Knowledge. One last word of warning before you read further. Economics claims to be a science, in pursuit of basic truths. We want to understand and explain how the economy works without getting tangled up in subjective value judgments. This may be an impossible task. First, it's not clear where the truth lies. For more than 200 years economists have been arguing about what makes the economy tick. None of the competing theories has performed spectacularly well. Indeed, few economists have successfully predicted major economic events with any consistency. Even annual forecasts of inflation, unemployment, and output are regularly in error. Worse still, never-ending arguments about what caused a major economic event continue long after it occurs. In fact, economists are still arguing over the primary causes of the Great Depression of the 1930s!

In part, this enduring controversy reflects diverse sociopolitical views on the appropriate role of government. Some people think a big public sector is undesirable, even if it improves economic performance. But the controversy has even deeper roots. Major gaps in our understanding of the economy persist. We know how much of the economy works, but not all of it. We're adept at identifying all the forces at work, but not always successful in gauging their relative importance. In point of fact, we may *never* find an absolute truth, because the inner workings of the economy change over time. When economic behavior changes, our theories must be adapted.

In view of all these debates and uncertainties, don't expect to learn everything there is to know about the economy today in this text or course. Our goals are more modest. We want to develop a reasonable perspective on economic behavior, an understanding of basic principles. With this foundation, you should acquire a better view of how the economy works. Daily news reports on economic events should make more sense. Congressional debates on tax and budget policies should take on more meaning. You may even develop some insights that you can apply toward running a business or planning a career, or—if the Nobel prize-winning economist Gary Becker is right—developing a lasting marriage.

THE ECONOMY TOMORROW

January 3, 2004, was a milestone in space exploration. That was the day the first robotic space vehicle—*Spirit*—landed on Mars. The pictures *Spirit* transmitted back to Earth unveiled a whole new boundary for human exploration. It created a challenge President Bush was quick to confront. Within days he announced an ambitious new agenda for America's space program:

The Journey to Mars

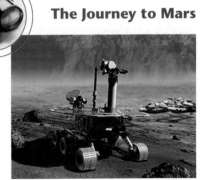

AFP/Getty Images

- By 2010 the United States is to complete the International Space Station.
- By 2008, a new Crew Exploration Vehicle, capable of ferrying astronauts and scientists to the Space Station, will be developed and ready for use.
- By 2015, the Crew Exploration Vehicle will begin extended human missions to the Moon.
- After 2015, human missions to Mars will begin.

Scientists and ordinary citizens around the world cheered both *Spirit's* accomplishments and President Bush's vision. People heard echoes of President Kennedy's May 1961 promise that mankind would soon set foot on the Moon—a promise that seemed equally implausible at the time, but ultimately proved to be attainable.

Opportunity Costs

The journey to Mars is not only a technological commitment but an economic commitment as well. The resources used to complete the Space Station, to colonize the Moon, and to journey onto Mars and worlds beyond all have alternative uses here on Earth. Some of the same scientists could be developing high-speed *rail* systems, safer domestic flights, or more eco-friendly technologies. The technological resources being poured into space exploration could be perfecting cell phone quality or simply accelerating online data transmissions. If we devoted as many resources to medical research as space research, we might find more ways to extend and improve life here on Earth. In other words, the journey to Mars will entail opportunity costs, that is, the sacrifice of earthly goods and services that could be produced with those same resources.

The journey to Mars won't be cheap. President Kennedy's *Apollo* program cost over $100 billion in today's dollars. Cost estimates for the journey to Mars run as high as $1 *trillion,* spread out over 20 years. That much money would fund a lot of earthly programs.

Earthly Benefits

NASA says the benefits of the Mars journey would outweigh those opportunity costs. Space exploration has already generated tangible benefits for us earthlings. NASA cites advances in weather forecasting, in communications technology, in robotics, in computing and electronics, and in search and rescue technology. The research behind the space program has also helped create the satellite telecommunications network and the Global Positioning System. Medical technologies such as the image processing used in CAT scanners and MRI machines also trace their origins to engineering work for space exploration. President Bush said we should expect still further benefits from the journey to Mars: not only tangible benefits like new resources and technological advance but also intangibles like the spiritual uplifting and heightened quest for knowledge that exploration promotes.

WEBNOTE

Review NASA's budget at www.whitehouse.gov or www.cbo.gov. For more information on the space program, visit www.nasa.gov.

Resource Allocations

As a society, we're going to have to make important choices about the economy tomorrow. Do we want to take the journey to Mars? If so, how fast do we want to get there? How many earthly goods and services do we want to give up to pay for the journey? Every year, the President and the U.S. Congress have to answer these questions. Their answers are reflected in the funds allocated to NASA (rather than other programs) in each year's federal budget. Would you allocate scarce resources for the economy tomorrow in the same way?

SUMMARY

- Scarcity is a basic fact of economic life. Factors of production (land, labor, capital, entrepreneurship) are scarce in relation to our desires for goods and services.
- All economic activity entails opportunity costs. Factors of production (resources) used to produce one output cannot simultaneously be used to produce something else. When we choose to produce one thing, we forsake the opportunity to produce some other good or service.
- A production possibilities curve illustrates the limits to production and the opportunity costs associated with different output combinations. It shows the alternative combinations of final goods and services that could be produced in a given period if all available resources and technology are used efficiently.
- The bent shape of the production possibilities curve reflects the law of increasing opportunity costs. This law states that increasing quantities of any good can be obtained only by sacrificing ever-increasing quantities of other goods.
- Inefficient or incomplete use of resources will fail to attain production possibilities. Additional resources or better

technologies will expand them. This is the essence of economic growth.
- Every country must decide WHAT to produce, HOW to produce, and FOR WHOM to produce with its limited resources.
- The choices of WHAT, HOW, and FOR WHOM can be made by the market mechanism or by government directives. Most nations are mixed economies, using a combination of these two choice mechanisms.
- Market failure exists when market signals generate suboptimal outcomes. Government failure occurs when government intervention worsens economic outcomes. The challenge for economic theory and policy is to find the mix of market signals and government directives that best fulfills our social and economic goals.
- The study of economics focuses on the broad question of resource allocation. Macroeconomics is concerned with allocating the resources of an entire economy to achieve aggregate economic goals (e.g., full employment). Microeconomics focuses on the behavior and goals of individual market participants.

Key Terms

economics
scarcity
factors of production
capital
entrepreneurship
opportunity cost

production possibilities
efficiency
economic growth
market mechanism
laissez faire
mixed economy

market failure
government failure
macroeconomics
microeconomics
ceteris paribus

Questions for Discussion

1. What opportunity costs did you incur in reading this chapter? If you read four more chapters of this book today, would your opportunity cost (per chapter) increase? Explain.
2. How much time could you spend on homework in a day? How much do you spend? How do you decide?
3. What's the real cost of the food in the free lunch cartoon?
4. What economic benefits might India get from privatizing state enterprises (World View, p. 11)?
5. How might a nation's production possibilities be affected by the following?
   a. A decrease in taxes.
   b. An increase in government regulation.
   c. An increase in military spending.
   d. An increase in college tuition.
   e. Faster, more powerful electronic chips.
6. Markets reward individuals according to their output; communism rewards people according to their needs. How might these different systems affect work effort?
7. How does government intervention affect college admissions? Who would go to college in a completely private (market) college system?
8. How will the Chinese economy benefit from private property? (See World View, page 17.) Is there any downside to greater entrepreneurial freedom?
9. How many resources should we allocate to space exploration? How will we make this decision?

 **PROBLEMS**   The Student Problem Set at the back of this book contains numerical and graphing problems for this chapter.

 **WEB ACTIVITIES**   to accompany this chapter can be found on the Online Learning Center: **http://www.mhhe.com/economics/schiller10**

APPENDIX

USING GRAPHS

Economists like to draw graphs. In fact, we didn't even make it through the first chapter without a few graphs. This appendix looks more closely at the way graphs are drawn and used. The basic purpose of a graph is to illustrate a relationship between two *variables*. Consider, for example, the relationship between grades and studying. In general, we expect that additional hours of study time will lead to higher grades. Hence, we should be able to see a distinct relationship between hours of study time and grade-point average.

Suppose that we actually surveyed all the students taking this course with regard to their study time and grade-point averages. The resulting information can be compiled in a table such as Table A.1.

TABLE A.1
Hypothetical Relationship of Grades to Study Time

Study Time (hours per week)	Grade-Point Average
16	4.0 (A)
14	3.5 (B+)
12	3.0 (B)
10	2.5 (C+)
8	2.0 (C)
6	1.5 (D+)
4	1.0 (D)
2	0.5 (F+)
0	0.0 (F)

According to the table, students who don't study at all can expect an F in this course. To get a C, the average student apparently spends 8 hours a week studying. All those who study 16 hours a week end up with an A in the course.

These relationships between grades and studying can also be illustrated on a graph. Indeed, the whole purpose of a graph is to summarize numerical relationships.

We begin to construct a graph by drawing horizontal and vertical boundaries, as in Figure A.1. These boundaries are called the *axes* of the graph. On the vertical axis (often called the *y*-axis) we measure one of the variables; the other variable is measured on the horizontal axis (the *x*-axis).

In this case, we shall measure the grade-point average on the vertical axis. We start at the *origin* (the intersection of the two axes) and count upward, letting the distance between horizontal lines represent half (0.5) a grade point. Each horizontal line is numbered, up to the maximum grade-point average of 4.0.

The number of hours each week spent doing homework is measured on the horizontal axis. We begin at the origin again, and count to the right. The *scale* (numbering) proceeds in increments of 1 hour, up to 20 hours per week.

FIGURE A.1

The Relationship of Grades to Study Time

The upward (positive) slope of the curve indicates that additional studying is associated with higher grades. The average student (2.0, or C grade) studies 8 hours per week. This is indicated by point *M* on the graph.

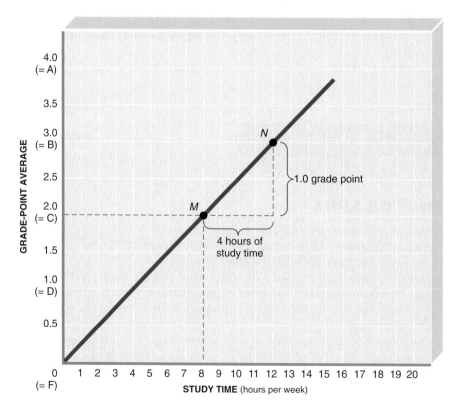

When both axes have been labeled and measured, we can begin illustrating the relationship between study time and grades. Consider the typical student who does 8 hours of homework per week and has a 2.0 (C) grade-point average. We illustrate this relationship by first locating 8 hours on the horizontal axis. We then move up from that point a distance of 2.0 grade points, to point *M*. Point *M* tells us that 8 hours of study time per week is typically associated with a 2.0 grade-point average.

The rest of the information in Table A.1 is drawn (or *plotted*) on the graph the same way. To illustrate the average grade for people who study 12 hours per week, we move upward from the number 12 on the horizontal axis until we reach the height of 3.0 on the vertical axis. At that intersection, we draw another point (point *N*).

Once we've plotted the various points describing the relationship of study time to grades, we may connect them with a line or curve. This line (curve) is our summary. In this case, the line slopes upward to the right—that is, it has a *positive* slope. This slope indicates that more hours of study time are associated with *higher* grades. Were higher grades associated with *less* study time, the curve in Figure A.1 would have a *negative* slope (downward from left to right).

Slopes

The upward slope of Figure A.1 tells us that higher grades are associated with increased amounts of study time. That same curve also tells us *by how much* grades tend to rise with study time. According to point *M* in Figure A.1, the average student studies 8 hours per week and earns a C (2.0 grade-point average). To earn a B (3.0 average), students apparently need to study an average of 12 hours per week (point *N*). Hence an increase of 4 hours of study time per week is associated with a 1-point increase in grade-point average. This relationship between *changes* in study time and *changes* in grade-point average is expressed by the steepness, or *slope,* of the graph.

The slope of any graph is calculated as

$$\text{Slope} = \frac{\text{vertical distance between two points}}{\text{horizontal distance between two points}}$$

In our example, the vertical distance between *M* and *N* represents a change in grade-point average. The horizontal distance between these two points represents the change in study time. Hence the slope of the graph between points *M* and *N* is equal to

$$\text{Slope} = \frac{3.0 \text{ grade} - 2.0 \text{ grade}}{12 \text{ hours} - 8 \text{ hours}} = \frac{1 \text{ grade point}}{4 \text{ hours}}$$

In other words, a 4-hour increase in study time (from 8 to 12 hours) is associated with a 1-point increase in grade-point average (see Figure A.1).

Shifts

The relationship between grades and studying illustrated in Figure A.1 isn't inevitable. It's simply a graphical illustration of student experiences, as revealed in our hypothetical survey. The relationship between study time and grades could be quite different.

Suppose that the university decided to raise grading standards, making it more difficult to achieve every grade other than an F. To achieve a C, a student now would need to study 12 hours per week, not just 8 (as in Figure A.1). Whereas students could previously expect to get a B by studying 12 hours per week, now they'd have to study 16 hours to get that grade.

Figure A.2 illustrates the new grading standards. Notice that the new curve lies to the right of the earlier curve. We say that the curve has *shifted* to reflect a change in the relationship between study time and grades. Point *R* indicates that 12 hours of study time now "produces" a C, not a B (point *N* on the old curve). Students who now study only 4 hours per week (point *S*) will fail. Under the old grading policy, they could have at least gotten a D. ***When a curve shifts, the underlying relationship between the two variables has changed.***

FIGURE A.2
A Shift

When a relationship between two variables changes, the entire curve *shifts*. In this case a tougher grading policy alters the relationship between study time and grades. To get a C, one must now study 12 hours per week (point *R*), not just 8 hours (point *M*).

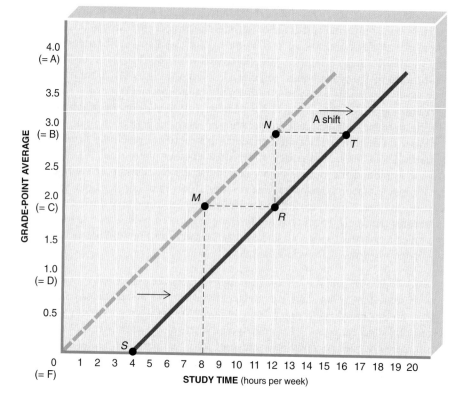

A shift may also change the slope of the curve. In Figure A.2, the new grading curve is parallel to the old one; it therefore has the same slope. Under either the new grading policy or the old one, a 4-hour increase in study time leads to a 1-point increase in grades. Therefore, the slope of both curves in Figure A.2 is

$$\text{Slope} = \frac{\text{vertical change}}{\text{horizontal change}} = \frac{1}{4}$$

This too may change, however. Figure A.3 illustrates such a possibility. In this case, zero study time still results in an F. But now the payoff for additional studying is reduced. Now it takes 6 hours of study time to get a D (1.0 grade point), not 4 hours as before. Likewise, another 4 hours of study time (to a total of 10) raises the grade by only two-thirds of a point. It takes 6 hours to raise the grade a full point. The slope of the new line is therefore

$$\text{Slope} = \frac{\text{vertical change}}{\text{horizontal change}} = \frac{1}{6}$$

The new curve in Figure A.3 has a smaller slope than the original curve and so lies below it. What all this means is that it now takes a greater effort to *improve* your grade.

Linear vs. Nonlinear Curves

In Figures A.1–A.3 the relationship between grades and studying is represented by a straight line—that is, a *linear curve*. A distinguishing feature of linear curves is that they have the same (constant) slope throughout. In Figure A.1, it appears that *every* 4-hour increase in study time is associated with a 1-point increase in average grades. In Figure A.3, it appears that every 6-hour increase in study time leads to a 1-point increase in grades. But the relationship between studying and grades may not be linear. Higher grades may be more difficult to attain. You may be able to raise a C to a B by studying 4 hours more per week. But it may be harder to raise a B to an A.

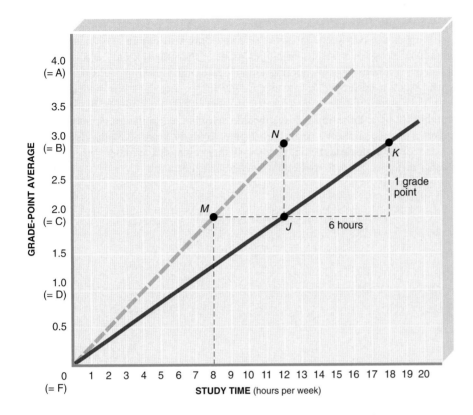

FIGURE A.3
A Change in Slope

When a curve shifts, it may change its slope as well. In this case, a new grading policy makes each higher grade more difficult to reach. To raise a C to a B, for example, one must study 6 additional hours (compare points *J* and *K*). Earlier it took only 4 hours to move the grade scale up a full point. The slope of the line has declined from $0.25 (= 1 \div 4)$ to $0.17 (= 1 \div 6)$.

According to Figure A.4, it takes an additional 8 hours of studying to raise a B to an A. Thus the relationship between study time and grades is *nonlinear* in Figure A.4; the slope of the curve changes as study time increases. In this case, the slope decreases as study time increases. Grades continue to improve, but not so fast, as more and more time is devoted to homework. You may know the feeling.

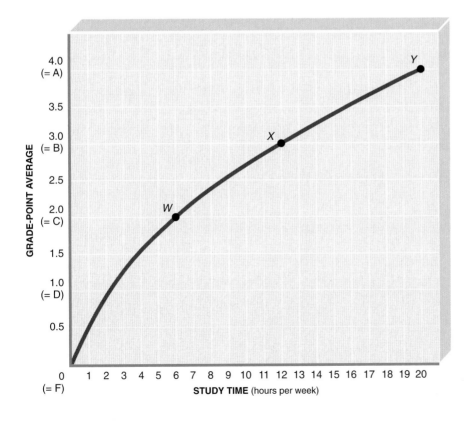

FIGURE A.4
A Nonlinear Relationship

Straight lines have a constant slope, implying a constant relationship between the two variables. But the relationship (and slope) may vary. In this case, it takes 6 extra hours of study to raise a C (point *W*) to a B (point *X*) but 8 extra hours to raise a B to an A (point *Y*). The slope decreases as we move up the curve.

Causation

For online practice with graphs, visit "Math Skills for Introductory Economics" at syllabus.syr.edu/cid/graph/book.html.

Figure A.4 doesn't by itself guarantee that your grade-point average will rise if you study 4 more hours per week. In fact, the graph drawn in Figure A.4 doesn't prove that additional study ever results in higher grades. The graph is only a summary of empirical observations. It says nothing about cause and effect. It could be that students who study a lot are smarter to begin with. If so, then less-able students might not get higher grades if they studied harder. In other words, the *cause* of higher grades is debatable. At best, the empirical relationship summarized in the graph may be used to support a particular theory (e.g., that it pays to study more). Graphs, like tables, charts, and other statistical media, rarely tell their own story; rather, they must be *interpreted* in terms of some underlying theory or expectation.

2 The U.S. Economy: A Global View

All nations must confront the central economic questions of WHAT to produce, HOW to produce, and FOR WHOM to produce it. However, the nations of the world approach these issues with vastly different production possibilities. China, Canada, the United States, and Brazil each has more than *3 million* acres of land. All that land gives them far greater production possibilities than Dominica, Tonga, Malta, or Lichtenstein, each of which has less than 500 acres of land. The population of China totals more than 1.3 billion people, five times that of the United States, and 25,000 times the population of Greenland. Obviously, these nations confront very different output choices.

In addition to vastly uneven production possibilities, the nations of the world use different mechanisms for deciding WHAT, HOW, and FOR WHOM to produce. Belarus, Romania, North Korea, and Cuba still rely heavily on central planning. By contrast, Singapore, New Zealand, Ireland, and the United States permit the market mechanism to play a dominant role in shaping economic outcomes.

With different production possibilities and mechanisms of choice, you'd expect economic outcomes to vary greatly across nations. And they do. This chapter assesses how the U.S. economy stacks up. Specifically,

- **WHAT goods and services does the United States produce?**
- **HOW is that output produced?**
- **FOR WHOM is the output produced?**

In each case, we want to see not only how the United States has answered these questions but also how America's answers compare with those of other nations.

WHAT AMERICA PRODUCES

The United States has less than 5 percent of the world's population and only 12 percent of the world's arable land, yet it produces more than 20 percent of the world's output.

GDP Comparisons

gross domestic product (GDP): The total market value of all final goods and services produced within a nation's borders in a given time period.

The World View shows how total U.S. production compares with other nations. These comparisons are based on the total market value of all the goods and services a nation produces—what we call **gross domestic product (GDP).**

In 2002, the U.S. economy produced about $10 trillion worth of output. The second-largest economy, China, produced only half that much. Japan came in third, with about a third of U.S. output. Cuba, by contrast, produced only $1.6 billion of output, less than the state of South Dakota. Russia, which was once regarded as a superpower, produced only $1.1 trillion, about as much as New York state. The entire 25-member European Union produces less than the United States.

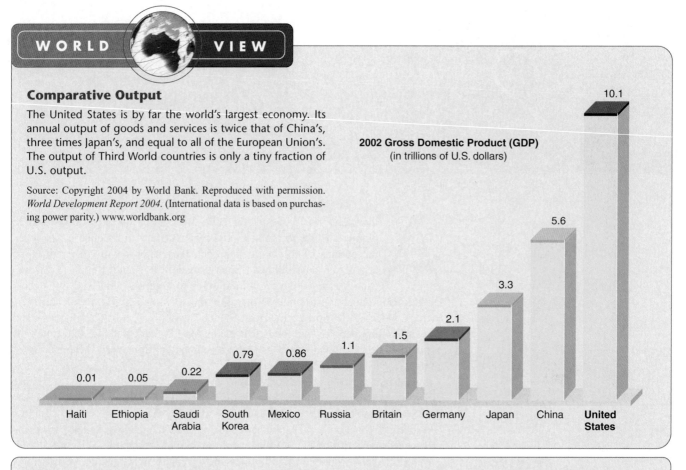

Comparative Output

The United States is by far the world's largest economy. Its annual output of goods and services is twice that of China's, three times Japan's, and equal to all of the European Union's. The output of Third World countries is only a tiny fraction of U.S. output.

Source: Copyright 2004 by World Bank. Reproduced with permission. *World Development Report 2004.* (International data is based on purchasing power parity.) www.worldbank.org

2002 Gross Domestic Product (GDP)
(in trillions of U.S. dollars)

Haiti	Ethiopia	Saudi Arabia	South Korea	Mexico	Russia	Britain	Germany	Japan	China	United States
0.01	0.05	0.22	0.79	0.86	1.1	1.5	2.1	3.3	5.6	10.1

Analysis: The market value of output (GDP) is a basic measure of an economy's size. The U.S. economy is far larger than any other and accounts for over one-fifth of the entire world's output.

per capita GDP: The dollar value of GDP divided by total population; average GDP.

Per Capita GDP. What makes the U.S. share of world output so noteworthy is that with only 5 percent of the world's population, the United States produces far more output *per person* than other countries do. This people-based measure of economic performance is called **per capita GDP.** Per capita GDP is simply total output divided by total population. Per capita GDP doesn't tell us how much any specific person gets. ***Per capita GDP is an indicator of how much output the average person would get if all output were divided up evenly among the population.***

In 2002, per capita GDP in the United States was more than $35,000—nearly five times as much as the average in the rest of the world. The following World View provides a global perspective on just how "rich" America is. Some of the country-specific comparisons are startling. China, which has the world's second-largest GDP, also contains one-fifth of the world's population. Hence, China has such a relatively low per capita income that most of its citizens would be considered "poor" by official American standards. Yet people in other nations (e.g., Haiti, Ethiopia) don't even come close to that low standard. According to the World Bank, nearly half of the people on Earth subsist on incomes of less than $2 a day. Seen in this context, it's

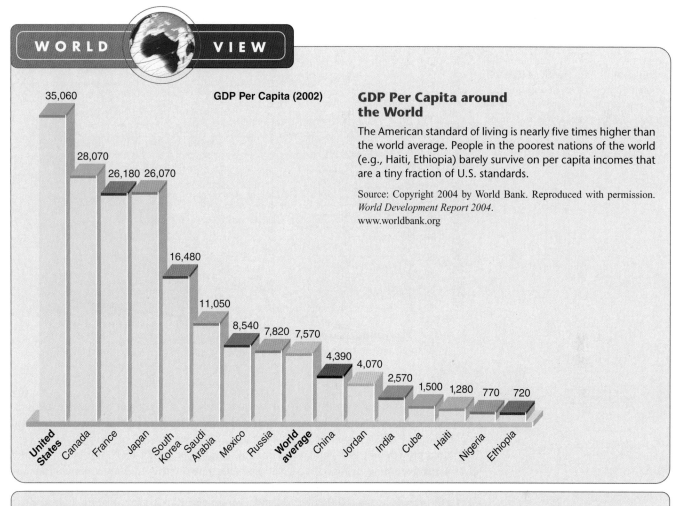

WORLD VIEW

GDP Per Capita around the World

The American standard of living is nearly five times higher than the world average. People in the poorest nations of the world (e.g., Haiti, Ethiopia) barely survive on per capita incomes that are a tiny fraction of U.S. standards.

Source: Copyright 2004 by World Bank. Reproduced with permission. *World Development Report 2004.* www.worldbank.org

GDP Per Capita (2002)

United States 35,060
Canada 28,070
France 26,180
Japan 26,070
South Korea 16,480
Saudi Arabia 11,050
Mexico 8,540
Russia 7,820
World average 7,570
China 4,390
Jordan 4,070
India 2,570
Cuba 1,500
Haiti 1,280
Nigeria 770
Ethiopia 720

Analysis: Per capita GDP is a measure of output that reflects average living standards. America's exceptionally high GDP per capita implies access to far more goods and services than people in other nations have.

easy to understand why the rest of the world envies (and sometimes resents) America's prosperity.

GDP Growth. What's even more startling about global comparisons is that the GDP gap between the United States and the world's poor nations keeps growing. The reason for that is **economic growth.** With few exceptions, U.S. output increases nearly every year. *On average, U.S. output has grown by roughly 3 percent a year, nearly three times faster than population growth (1 percent).* Hence, not only does *total* output keep rising, but *per capita* output keeps rising as well (see Figure 2.1).

Poor Nations. People in the world's poorest countries aren't so fortunate. China's economy has grown exceptionally fast in the last 20 years, propelling it to second place in the global GDP rankings. But in many other nations total output has actually *declined* year after year, further depressing living standards. Notice in Table 2.1, for example, what's been happening in Haiti. From 1990 to 2002, Haiti's output of

WEBNOTE

Data on the output of different nations are available from the Central Intelligence Agency at www.odci.gov/cia/publications/factbook.

economic growth: An increase in output (real GDP): an expansion of production possibilities.

FIGURE 2.1
**U.S. Output and Population
Growth Since 1900**

Over time, the growth of output in the United States has greatly exceeded population growth. As a consequence, GDP per capita has grown tremendously. GDP per capita was five times higher in 2000 than in 1900.

Source: U.S. Department of Labor.

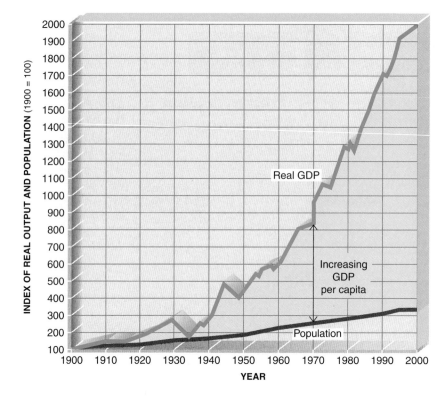

goods and services (GDP) declined by an average of 1.0 percent a year. As a result, total Haitian output in 2002 was 14 percent *smaller* than in 1990. During those same years, the Haitian population kept growing—by 2 percent a year. With *negative* economic growth and fast population growth, Haiti's per capita GDP fell below $1,300 a year. According to the United Nations, nearly two-thirds of Haiti's population was undernourished. As Table 2.1 shows, even some poor nations that had *positive* GDP growth in the 1990s (e.g., Kenya, Venezuela) didn't grow fast enough to raise

TABLE 2.1
Growth Rates in Selected Countries, 1990–2002

The relationship between GDP growth and population growth is very different in rich and poor countries. The populations of rich countries are growing very slowly, and gains in per capita GDP are easily achieved. In the poorest countries, population is still increasing rapidly, making it difficult to raise living standards. Notice how per capita incomes are *declining* in many poor countries (such as Kenya, Venezuela, Zimbabwe, and Haiti).

	Average Growth Rate (1990–2002) of		
	GDP	Population	Per Capita GDP
High-income countries			
United States	3.3	1.1	2.2
Canada	3.2	1.1	2.1
France	1.9	0.4	1.5
Japan	1.3	0.4	0.9
Low-income countries			
China	9.7	1.2	8.5
India	5.8	1.1	4.7
Ethiopia	4.6	2.6	2.0
Nigeria	2.4	2.8	−0.4
Kenya	1.9	2.9	−1.0
Venezuela	1.1	2.3	−1.2
Zimbabwe	1.1	2.7	−1.6
Haiti	−1.0	2.0	−3.0

Source: Copyright 2004 by World Bank. Reproduced with permission. *World Development Indicators, 2004.*

living standards. As a result, they fell even further behind America's (rising) level of prosperity.

Regardless of how much output a nation produces, the *mix* of output always includes both *goods* (such as cars, plasma TVs, potatoes) and *services* (like this economics course, visits to a doctor, or a professional baseball game). A century ago, about two-thirds of U.S. output consisted of farm goods (37 percent), manufactured goods (22 percent), and mining (9 percent). Since then, over 25 *million* people have left the farms and sought jobs in other sectors. As a result, today's mix of output is reversed: **Nearly 75 percent of U.S. output consists of services, not goods.** According to the U.S. Bureau of Labor Statistics, that trend is increasing. Over 98 percent of future job growth will be in service-producing industries such as health care, engineering, education, social services, and accounting. This trend will accelerate the change in the mix of output that has been underway for a long time (see Figure 2.2).

The *relative* decline in goods production (manufacturing, farming) doesn't mean that we're producing *fewer* goods today than in earlier decades. Quite the contrary. While some industries such as iron and steel have shrunk, others, such as chemicals, publishing, and telecommunications equipment, have grown tremendously. The result is that manufacturing output has increased fourfold since 1950. The same kind of thing has happened in the farm sector; where output keeps rising even though agriculture's *share* of total output has declined. It's just that output of *services* has increased so much faster.

Development Patterns. The transformation of the United States into a service economy is a reflection of our high incomes. In Ethiopia, where the most urgent concern is still to keep people from starving, over 50 percent of output comes from the farm sector. Poor people don't have enough income to buy dental services, vacations, or even an education, so the mix of output in poor countries is weighted toward goods, not services.

Services have become such a dominant share of the economy's output that we can say that **America is primarily a service economy and will become increasingly so in the future.** This generalization doesn't provide much detail, however, about exactly WHAT America produces. What kinds of services are being produced? Which goods?

We can develop a clearer picture of our answer to the WHAT question by examining the uses to which our output is put. **The four major uses of total output (GDP) are:**

* *Consumption*
* *Investment*
* *Government services*
* *Net exports*

The Mix of Output

Data on the mix of output in different nations are compiled in the World Bank's annual World Development Report, available at www.worldbank.org.

Today's Mix of Output

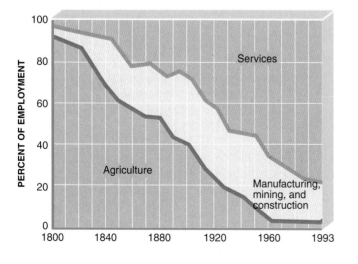

FIGURE 2.2
The Changing Mix of Output

Two hundred years ago, almost all U.S. output came from farms. Today, 75 percent of output consists of services, not farm or manufactured goods.

Source: US Department of Commerce.

FIGURE 2.3
WHAT America Produces

Two-thirds of America's output consists of consumer goods and services. Investment (such as plant, equipment, buildings) claims about 15 percent of total output. The public sector gets nearly 19 percent. Although we export more than 10 percent of domestic output, we import an even larger share of goods and services; *net* exports are negative.

Source: *Economic Report of the President, 2004.*

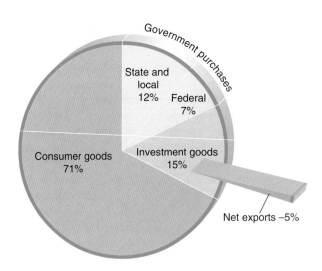

investment: Expenditures on (production of) new plant, equipment, and structures (capital) in a given time period, plus changes in business inventories.

income transfers: Payments to individuals for which no current goods or services are exchanged, e.g., Social Security, welfare, unemployment benefits.

Consumer Goods and Services. Most of America's output consists of consumer goods and services. This output includes everything from breakfast cereals (a good) to movie rentals (a service) and college education (another service)—anything and everything households buy for their own use. As Figure 2.3 illustrates, such consumption goods and services account for over two-thirds of all output.

Investment Goods and Services. Investment goods are a completely different type of output. **Investment** goods are the plant, machinery, equipment, and structures that are produced for the business sector. These investment goods are used to (1) replace worn-out equipment and factories, thus *maintaining* our production possibilities, and (2) increase and improve our stock of capital, thereby *expanding* our production possibilities.

Presently the United States devotes 15 percent of output to investment. The opportunity cost of building more plants and equipment is the extra consumer goods we could have produced instead. There's a payoff, however. New factories, buildings, and machinery allow us to produce *more* of all goods and services in the future.

Poor countries need capital investment desperately. Their incomes are so low, however, that they can't afford to cut back much on consumer goods. When Stalin wanted to make Russia an industrial power, he cut output of consumer goods and forced Russian households to scrape by with meager supplies of food, clothing, and even shelter for decades. Today, most poor nations have to depend on foreign aid and other capital inflows to finance needed investment. Without more investment, they run the risk of continuing stagnation or even a decline of living standards.

Government Services. The third type of output every nation produces is government services. Federal, state, and local governments purchase resources to police the streets, teach classes, write laws, and build highways. The resources the government sector uses for these purposes are unavailable for either consumption or investment. At present, the production of government services absorbs roughly one-fifth of total U.S. output (see Figure 2.3).

Notice the emphasis again on the production of real goods and services. The federal government now *spends* about $2.5 trillion a year. Much of that spending, however, consists of income transfers, not resource purchases. **Income transfers** are payments to individuals for which no direct service is provided. Social Security benefits, welfare checks, food stamps, and unemployment benefits are all transfer payments. This spending is *not* part of our output of goods and services. ***Only that part of federal spending used to acquire resources and produce services is counted in GDP.***

Federal purchases (production) of goods and services account for only 7 percent of total output.

State and local governments are large providers of public services. What state and local governments lack in size, they make up for in sheer numbers. In addition to the 50 state governments, there are 3000 counties, 18,000 cities, 17,000 townships, 21,000 school districts, and over 20,000 special districts. These are the government entities that build roads; provide schools, police, and firefighters; administer hospitals; and provide social services. The output of all these state and local governments accounts for roughly 12 percent of total GDP.

Net Exports. Finally, we should note that some of the goods and services we produce each year are used abroad rather than at home. In other words, we **export** some of our output to other countries.

International trade isn't a one-way street. While we export some of our own output, we also **import** goods and services from other countries. These imports may be used for consumption (sweaters from New Zealand, Japanese DVDs, travel), investment (German ball bearings, Lloyds of London insurance), or government (French radar screens). Theoretically, imports wouldn't affect the value of GDP since GDP includes only goods and services produced within a nation's borders. In practice, however, estimates of GDP are based on market *purchases,* not surveys of production. As a result, consumption, investment, and government purchases include imports as well as domestically produced goods. To get an accurate reading of *domestic* production, imports must be subtracted out.

Figure 2.4 summarizes America's trade. In 2003, we exported $726 billion worth of goods (e.g., airplanes, farm machinery, tobacco, food) and another $320 billion of services (e.g., movies, travel, engineering). These exports amounted to approximately 10 percent of total output. We imported even more goods and services, however, and so ended up with negative **net exports** (a trade deficit).

exports: Goods and services sold to foreign buyers.

imports: Goods and services purchased from foreign sources.

net exports: The value of exports minus the value of imports.

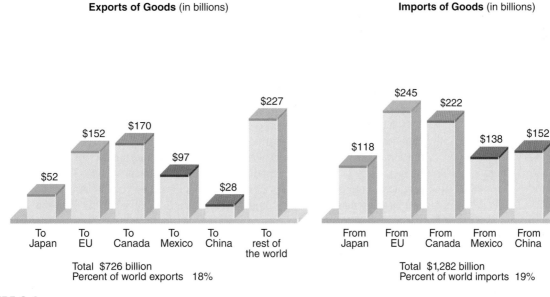

FIGURE 2.4
U.S. Exports and Imports

The United States is the world's largest exporter and importer. One-third of all U.S. trade is with Canada and Mexico. The European Union, Japan, and China account for another third. In 2003, U.S. merchandise (goods) imports exceeded exports by $556 billion. This merchandise trade gap was partially offset by net *service* exports, leaving $498 billion of *net imports* (of goods and services).

Comparative Advantage

comparative advantage: The ability of a country to produce a specific good at a lower opportunity cost than its trading partners.

The motivation for this international trade originates in our quest for more output. Most of the goods we import could be produced in the United States. In fact, most imported goods have domestically produced substitutes, for example, cars, computers, and tomatoes. Our decision to import them is not based on our inability to produce them but on the efficiency of importing them. International trade allows a nation to produce goods in which it has a cost advantage and then trade them for imported goods in which it has a cost disadvantage. This principle of **comparative advantage** entails exporting goods with low opportunity cost and importing goods with high opportunity cost. In other words, **international trade allows countries to produce and export what they do best and import goods they don't produce as efficiently.**

Although all nations gain from international trade, smaller countries are most in need of specialization. With few resources, a small economy can't produce the whole array of goods and services consumers want. So they need to *specialize*—producing goods they can sell (export) in world markets. Saudi Arabia, for example, exports 40 percent of its total output, mostly in the form of crude oil. It then uses its export earnings to buy desired cars, engineering services, and food that it can't produce efficiently itself.

HOW AMERICA PRODUCES

factors of production: Resource inputs used to produce goods and services, such as land, labor, capital, entrepreneurship.

All the goods and services included in gross domestic product are produced within the borders of the United States. The production process absorbs not only American-owned **factors of production** but also any foreign-owned land, labor, or capital used to produce goods or services in the United States. With the globalization of business ownership, it's often difficult to even identify who owns which factors of production. It's easy, however, to observe where the factors of production are. So GDP focuses on geographical boundaries. Japanese investors may *own* the Honda factory in Ohio, but the cars *produced* there are part of U.S. output. By contrast, all the shoes produced at Nike's Malaysian factories are counted as part of that nation's GDP.

Productivity

productivity: Output per unit of input, such as output per labor-hour.

A lot of people worry that the Nike factory in Malaysia is stealing U.S. jobs. Workers in Malaysia and other poor nations are willing to work for extremely low wages (recall that nearly half the world's population has incomes of less than $2 a day). But low foreign wages aren't as great a threat as they just appear. We also have to consider how much a worker *produces*. One reason wages are so low in the Third World is that workers produce so little. U.S. workers get paid an average of over $16 an hour because they *produce* so much.

If the sheer number of workers was the decisive factor for a nation's output, China would have the world's largest economy. In reality, **productivity**—the amount of output a worker produces—is at least as important as the number of available workers. In fact, high productivity explains how the United States, with 300 million people, produces more goods and services than the combined output of China, India, Indonesia, and Brazil—nations with a combined population 10 times larger than the U.S.'s!

Factors of Production

capital-intensive: Production processes that use a high ratio of capital to labor inputs.

Capital Stock. The exceptional productivity of U.S. workers is due in large part to an abundance of capital. America has accumulated a massive stock of capital—over $11 *trillion* worth of machinery, factories, and buildings. As a result of all this prior investment, U.S. production tends to be very **capital-intensive.** The contrast with *labor-intensive* production in poorer countries is striking. A Chinese farmer mostly works with his hands and crude implements, whereas a U.S. farmer works with computers, automated irrigation systems, and mechanized equipment (see photos on page 36). Russian business managers don't have the computer networks or telecommunications systems that make U.S. business so efficient. In Haiti and Ethiopia, even telephones, indoor plumbing, and dependable sources of power are scarce.

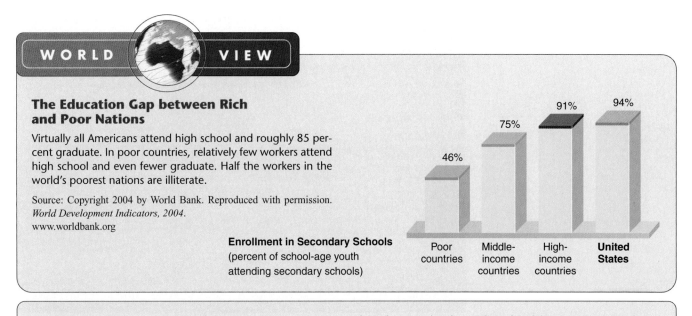

WORLD **VIEW**

The Education Gap between Rich and Poor Nations

Virtually all Americans attend high school and roughly 85 percent graduate. In poor countries, relatively few workers attend high school and even fewer graduate. Half the workers in the world's poorest nations are illiterate.

Source: Copyright 2004 by World Bank. Reproduced with permission. *World Development Indicators, 2004.*
www.worldbank.org

Enrollment in Secondary Schools
(percent of school-age youth attending secondary schools)

Poor countries	Middle-income countries	High-income countries	United States
46%	75%	91%	94%

Analysis: The high productivity of the American economy is explained in part by the quality of its labor resources. Workers in poorer, less developed countries get much less education or training.

Human Capital. Indoor plumbing and fiber-optic networks aren't the only kinds of capital a nation can accumulate. **Human capital**—the knowledge and skills workers possess—can also be accumulated. In the Stone Age, one's productive capacity was largely determined by physical strength and endurance. In today's economy, human capital is largely a product of education, training, and experience. Hence, a country can acquire more human capital even without more bodies.

> **human capital:** The knowledge and skills possessed by the workforce.

Over time, the United States has invested heavily in human capital. In 1940, only 1 out of 20 young Americans graduated from college; today, over 30 percent of young people are college graduates. High school graduation rates have jumped from 38 percent to over 85 percent in the same time period. In the less developed countries, only 1 out of 2 youth ever *attend* high school, much less graduate (see World View). As a consequence, the United Nations estimates that 1.2 billion people—a fifth of humanity—are unable to read a book or even write their own names. Without even functional literacy, such workers are doomed to low-productivity jobs. Despite low wages, they are not likely to "steal" many jobs from America's highly educated and trained workforce.

The huge output of the United States is thus explained not only by a wealth of resources but by their quality as well. ***The high productivity of the U.S. economy results from using highly educated workers in capital-intensive production processes.***

Factor Mobility. Our continuing ability to produce the goods and services that consumers demand also depends on our agility in *reallocating* resources from one industry to another. Every year, some industries expand and others contract. Thousands of new firms start up each year and almost as many others disappear. In the process, land, labor, capital, and entrepreneurship move from one industry to another in response to changing demands and technology. In 1975, Federal Express, Compaq Computer, Staples, Oracle, and Amgen didn't even exist. Today these companies employ 200,000 people. These workers came from other firms and industries that weren't growing as fast.

Technological Advance. One of the forces that keeps shifting resources from one industry to another is continuing advances in technology. On the first page of this text we noted Intel's breakthrough in nanoelectronics. The discovery of new technology for microscopic miniaturization of electronic circuits expanded our production possibilities.

© Richard Hamilton Smith/CORBIS

© Philippe Giraud/CORBIS SYGMA

Analysis: An abundance of capital equipment and advanced technology make American farmers and workers far more productive than workers in poor nations.

In the process, the productivity of workers in the electronics industry will rise, as will per capita GDP. A similar phenomenon happened when the fax machine was invented. That discovery not only made communication a lot faster and easier but it also released thousands of workers from the courier (bike messenger) business. Those workers moved to new industries where their productivity was higher. As e-mail replaces faxes, a similar transformation occurs. ***Whenever technology advances, an economy can produce more output with existing resources.***

Outsourcing and Trade. The same technological advances that fuel economic growth also facilitate *global* resource use. Telecommunications has become so sophisticated and inexpensive that phone workers in India or Grenada can answer calls directed to

U.S. companies. Likewise, programmers in India can work online to write computer code, develop software, or perform accounting chores for U.S. corporations. Although such "outsourcing" is often viewed as a threat to U.S. jobs, it is really another source of increased U.S. output. By outsourcing routine tasks to foreign workers, U.S. workers are able to focus on higher-value jobs. U.S. computer engineers do less routine programming and more systems design. U.S. accountants do less cost tabulation and more cost analysis. By utilizing foreign resources in the production process, U.S. workers are able to pursue their *comparative advantage* in high-skill, capital-intensive jobs. In this way, both productivity and total output increase. Although some U.S. workers suffer temporary job losses in this process, the economy overall gains.

Role of Government

In assessing HOW goods are produced and economies grow, we must also take heed of the role the government plays. As we noted in Chapter 1, the amount of economic freedom varies greatly among the 200-plus nations of the world. Moreover, the Heritage Foundation has documented a positive relationship between the degree of economic freedom and economic growth (see Figure 2.5). Quite simply, when entrepreneurs are unfettered by regulation or high taxes, they are more likely to design and produce better mousetraps. When the government owns the factors of production, imposes high taxes, or tightly regulates output, there is little opportunity or incentive to design better products or pursue new technology.

Recognizing the productive value of economic freedom isn't tantamount to rejecting all government intervention. No one really advocates the complete abolition of government. On the contrary, the government plays a critical role in establishing a framework in which private businesses can operate.

- *Providing a legal framework.* One of the most basic functions of government is to establish and enforce the rules of the game. In some bygone era maybe a person's word was sufficient to guarantee delivery or payment. Businesses today, however, rely more on written contracts. The government gives legitimacy to contracts by establishing the rules for such pacts and by enforcing their provisions. In the absence of contractual rights, few companies would be willing to ship goods without prepayment (in cash). Even the incentive to write textbooks would disappear if government copyright laws didn't forbid unauthorized photocopying.

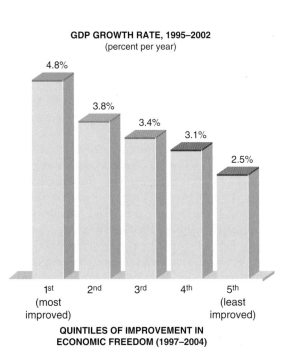

GDP GROWTH RATE, 1995–2002
(percent per year)

4.8% 3.8% 3.4% 3.1% 2.5%

| 1st (most improved) | 2nd | 3rd | 4th | 5th (least improved) |

QUINTILES OF IMPROVEMENT IN
ECONOMIC FREEDOM (1997–2004)

FIGURE 2.5
Economic Freedom and Growth

The extent of economic freedom (market reliance) affects a nation's ability to grow. The Heritage Foundation shows that as nations become "freer" (rely more on markets and less on government), output (real GDP) grows more quickly.

Source: Heritage Foundation, *2004 Index of Economic Freedom* (Washington, DC: 2004).

By establishing ownership rights, contract rights, and other rules of the game, the government lays the foundation for market transactions.

- *Protecting the environment.* The government also intervenes in the market to protect the environment. The legal contract system is designed to protect the interests of a buyer and a seller who wish to do business. What if, however, the business they contract for harms third parties? How are the interests of persons who *aren't* party to the contract to be protected?

  Numerous examples abound of how unregulated production may harm third parties. Earlier in the century, the steel mills around Pittsburgh blocked out the sun with clouds of sulfurous gases that spewed out of their furnaces. Local residents were harmed every time they inhaled. In the absence of government intervention, such side effects would be common. Decisions on how to produce would be based on costs alone, not on how the environment is affected. However, such **externalities**—spillover costs imposed on the broader community—affect our collective well-being. To reduce the external costs of production, the government limits air, water, and noise pollution and regulates environmental use.

  In poor countries, environmental protection often gets much less priority. In Haiti, residents keep cutting down newly planted saplings, destroying any hope of reforestation. They need the firewood *now* and can't afford to take the long-run view of economic growth. The Brazilian rain forests that are critical to the earth's ecosystem suffer the same fate. In the Caspian Sea, people poach so many sturgeon that the entire caviar industry is on the verge of destruction. In all these cases, the unbridled pursuit of individual gain has damaged broader economic welfare. More government regulation might both protect the environment and promote long-run growth.

- *Protecting consumers.* The government also uses its power to protect the interests of consumers. One way to do this is to prevent individual business firms from becoming too powerful. In the extreme case, a single firm might have a **monopoly** on the production of a specific good. As the sole producer of that good, a monopolist could dictate the price, the quality, and the quantity of the product. In such a situation, consumers would likely end up with the short end of the stick—paying too much for too little.

  To protect consumers from monopoly exploitation, the government tries to prevent individual firms from dominating specific markets. Antitrust laws prohibit mergers or acquisitions that would threaten competition. The U.S. Department of Justice and the Federal Trade Commission also regulate pricing practices, advertising claims, and other behavior that might put consumers at an unfair disadvantage in product markets.

  Government regulates the safety of many products. Consumers don't have enough expertise to assess the safety of various medicines, for example. If they rely on trial and error to determine drug safety, they might not get a second chance. To avoid this calamity, the government requires rigorous testing of new drugs, food additives, and other products.

- *Protecting labor.* The government also regulates how labor resources are used in the production process. In most poor nations, children are forced to start working at very early ages, often for minuscule wages. They often don't get the chance to go to school or to stay healthy. In Africa, 40 percent of children under age 14 work to survive or to help support their families. In the United States, child labor laws and compulsory schooling prevent minor children from being exploited. Government regulations also set standards for workplace safety, minimum wages, fringe benefits, and overtime provisions. After decades of bloody confrontations, the government also established the right of workers to organize and set rules for union-management relations. The introduction of unemployment insurance, Social Security, and disability insurance, and guarantees for private pension benefits also protect workers from the vagaries of the marketplace. These social benefits have profoundly affected how much people work, when they retire, and even how long they live.

externalities: Costs (or benefits) of a market activity borne by a third party.

monopoly: A firm that produces the entire market supply of a particular good or service.

All these government interventions are designed to change the way resources are used. Such interventions reflect the conviction that the market alone might not select the best possible way of producing goods and services. There's no guarantee, however, that government regulation of HOW goods are produced always makes us better off. Excessive regulation may inhibit production, raise product prices, and limit consumer choices. As noted in Chapter 1, *government* failure might replace *market* failure, leaving us no better off—possibly even worse off. This possibility underscores the importance of striking the right balance between market reliance and government regulation. The balance attained in the United States is surely not perfect, but it appears to be much more effective than the balances of regulation and free enterprise in most poor countries.

Striking a Balance

FOR WHOM AMERICA PRODUCES

As we've seen, America produces a huge quantity of output, using high-quality labor and capital resources. That leaves one basic question unanswered: FOR WHOM is all this output produced?

How many goods and services one gets largely depends on how much income one has to spend. The U.S. economy uses the market mechanism to distribute most goods and services. Those who receive the most income get the most goods. This goes a long way toward explaining why millionaires live in mansions and homeless people seek shelter in abandoned cars. This is the kind of stark inequality that fueled Karl Marx's denunciation of capitalism. Even today, people wonder how some Americans can be so rich while others are so poor.

Figure 2.6 illustrates the actual distribution of income in the United States. For this illustration the entire population is sorted into five groups of equal size, ranked by income. In this depiction, all the rich people are in the top **income quintile;** the

U.S. Income Distribution

income quintile: One-fifth of the population, rank-ordered by income (e.g., top fifth).

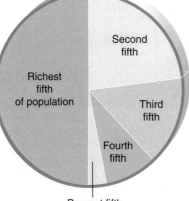

Income Quintile	2002 Income	Average Income	Share of Total Income (%)
Highest fifth	above $87,000	$147,000	49.8
Second fifth	$54,000–87,000	$ 69,000	23.4
Third fifth	$34,000–54,000	$ 44,000	14.8
Fourth fifth	$18,000–34,000	$ 26,000	8.7
Lowest fifth	$0–18,000	$ 10,000	3.4

Source: U.S. Department of Commerce, Bureau of the Census (averages rounded to thousands of dollars; 2002 data).

FIGURE 2.6
The U.S. Distribution of Income

The richest fifth of U.S. households gets nearly half of all the income—a huge slice of the income pie. By contrast, the poorest fifth gets only a sliver.

The most current data on the U.S. income distribution are available from the U.S. Bureau of the Census at www.census.gov/hhes/www/income.html.

poor are in the lowest quintile. To be in the top quintile in 2003, a household needed at least $87,000 of income. All the households in the lowest quintile had incomes under $18,000.

The most striking feature of Figure 2.6 is how large a slice of the income pie rich people get: ***The top 20 percent (quintile) of U.S. households gets nearly half of all U.S. income.*** By contrast, the poorest 20 percent (quintile) of U.S. households gets only a sliver of the income pie—less than 4 percent. Those grossly unequal slices explain why nearly half of all Americans believe the nation is divided into "haves" and "have nots."

Global Inequality

As unequal as U.S. incomes are, income disparities are actually greater in many other countries. Ironically, income inequalities are often greatest in the poorest countries. In Brazil, Guatamala, Zimbabwe, and South Africa, the richest *tenth* of the population has a far larger share of income than the richest 10 percent of Americans have. These and other comparisons of the FOR WHOM resolution are illustrated in the World View on the next page.

Comparisons across countries would manifest even greater inequality. As we saw earlier, Third World GDP per capita is far below U.S. levels. As a consequence, even **poor people in the United States receive far more goods and services than the average household in most low-income countries.**

© Alan Schein Photography/CORBIS

© Wolfgang Spunbarg/Photo Edit

Analysis: The market distributes income (and, in turn, goods and services) according to the resources an individual owns and how well they are used. If the resulting inequalities are too great, some redistribution via government intervention may be desired.

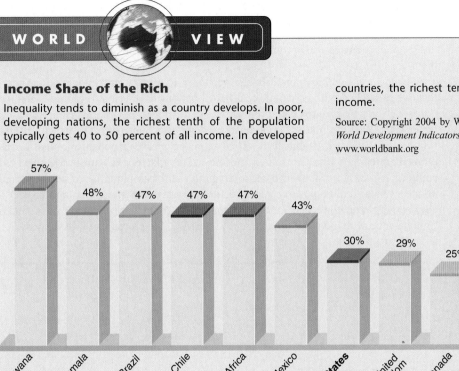

WORLD VIEW

Income Share of the Rich

Inequality tends to diminish as a country develops. In poor, developing nations, the richest tenth of the population typically gets 40 to 50 percent of all income. In developed countries, the richest tenth gets 20 to 30 percent of total income.

Source: Copyright 2004 by World Bank. Reproduced with permission. *World Development Indicators, 2004.* www.worldbank.org

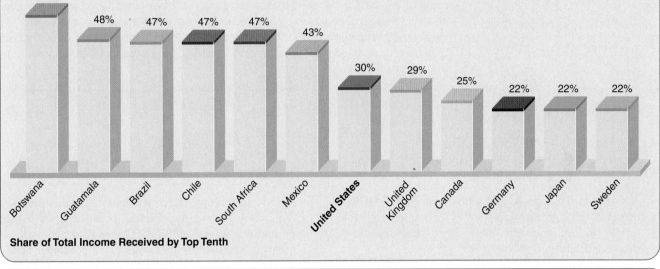

Share of Total Income Received by Top Tenth

Botswana	Guatemala	Brazil	Chile	South Africa	Mexico	United States	United Kingdom	Canada	Germany	Japan	Sweden
57%	48%	47%	47%	47%	43%	30%	29%	25%	22%	22%	22%

Analysis: The FOR WHOM question is reflected in the distribution of income. Although the U.S. distribution is very unequal, inequalities loom even larger in most Third World countries.

THE ECONOMY TOMORROW

A Better Tomorrow?

Global answers to the basic questions of WHAT, HOW, and FOR WHOM have been shaped by market forces and government intervention. Obviously, the answers aren't yet fully satisfactory. Over 3 billion people around the world live in abject poverty—with incomes of less than $2 a day. Over a fourth of the world's population is illiterate, nearly half have no access to sanitation facilities, and a fifth are chronically malnourished. In view of these problems, the World Bank has set ambitious goals for the economy tomorrow. In the Millennium Declaration of October 2000, the 180 nation-members of the World Bank set specific goals for world development. By 2015, they agreed to

- Reduce extreme poverty and hunger by at least half.
- Achieve universal primary education.
- Reduce child and maternal mortality by two-thirds.
- Reduce by half the number of people without access to potable water.

Achieving these goals would obviously help billions of people. But how will we fulfill them?

People in rich nations also aspire to higher living standards in the economy tomorrow. They already enjoy more comforts than people in poor nations even dream of. But that doesn't stop us from wanting more consumer goods, better schools, improved health care, a cleaner environment, and greater economic security. How will we get them?

A magic wand could transform the economy tomorrow into utopia. But short of that, we're saddled with economic reality. All nations have limited resources and technology. To get to a better place tomorrow, we've got to put those resources to even better uses. Will the market alone head us down the right path? As we've observed, (Figure 2.5), economies that have relied more on market mechanisms than on government directives have prospered the most. But that doesn't mean we must fully embrace laissez faire. Government intervention still has potential to accelerate economic growth, reduce poverty, raise health and education standards, and protect the environment. The challenge for the economy both today and tomorrow is to find the right balance of market and government forces. We'll explore this quest in more detail as the text proceeds.

SUMMARY

- Answers to the core WHAT, HOW, and FOR WHOM questions vary greatly across nations. These differences reflect varying production possibilities, choice mechanisms, and values.
- Gross domestic product (GDP) is the basic measure of how much an economy produces. The United States produces over $11 trillion of output per year, more than one-fifth of the world's total. The U.S. GDP per capita is five times the world average.
- The high level of U.S. per capita GDP reflects the high productivity of U.S. workers. Abundant capital, education, technology, training, and management all contribute to high productivity. The relatively high degree of U.S. economic freedom (market reliance) is also an important cause of superior economic growth.
- Over 75 percent of U.S. output consists of services, including government services. This is a reversal of historical ratios and reflects the relatively high incomes in the United States. Poor nations produce much higher proportions of food and manufactured goods.
- Most of America's output consists of consumer goods and services. Investment goods account for only 15 percent of total output, and government purchases almost 20 percent.
- Incomes are distributed very unequally among households, with households in the highest income class (quintile) receiving over 10 times more income than low-income households. Incomes are even less equally distributed in many poor nations.
- The mix of output, production methods, and the income distribution continue to change. The WHAT, HOW, and FOR WHOM answers in tomorrow's economy will depend on the continuing interplay of (changing) market signals and (changing) government policy.

Key Terms

gross domestic product (GDP)
per capita GDP
economic growth
investment
income transfers
exports

imports
net exports
comparative advantage
factors of production
productivity
capital-intensive

human capital
externalities
monopoly
income quintile

Questions for Discussion

1. Americans already enjoy living standards that far exceed world averages. Do we have enough? Should we even try to produce more?
2. Why is per capita GDP so much higher in the United States than in Mexico?
3. Why do people suggest that the United States needs to devote more output to investment goods? Why not produce just consumption goods?
4. The U.S. farm population has shrunk by over 25 million people since 1900. Where did all the people go? Why did they move?
5. How might the following government interventions affect a nation's economic growth?
   a. Mandatory school attendance.
   b. High income taxes.
   c. Copyright and patent protection.
   d. Political corruption.
6. How many people are employed by your local or state government? What do they produce? What is the opportunity cost of that output?
7. Why should the government regulate how goods are produced? Can regulation ever be excessive?
8. Should the government try to equalize incomes more by raising taxes on the rich and giving more money to the poor? How might such redistribution affect total output and growth?
9. Do we need more or less government intervention to achieve the World Bank's Millennium goals? Provide specific examples.

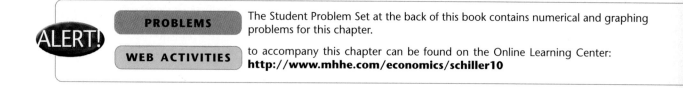

ALERT!

PROBLEMS   The Student Problem Set at the back of this book contains numerical and graphing problems for this chapter.

WEB ACTIVITIES   to accompany this chapter can be found on the Online Learning Center:
http://www.mhhe.com/economics/schiller10

Supply and Demand

The lights went out in California in January 2001. With only minutes of warning, sections of high-tech Silicon Valley, San Francisco, the state capital of Sacramento, and a host of smaller cities went dark. Schools closed early, traffic signals malfunctioned, ATM machines shut down, and elevators abruptly stopped. "It's like we're living in Bosnia," said Michael Mischer, an Oakland, California baker. "How could this happen?"[1]

California's governor, Gray Davis, had a ready answer. He said out-of-state power company "pirates" were gouging California residents with exorbitant prices they could not pay. As he saw it, the electricity crisis was just an example of market-driven greed. To resolve the crisis, the governor proposed stiff price controls, the state purchase of transmission lines, and state-ordered customer refunds from "profiteering" power companies. As he saw it, only the state government could keep the lights on.

Critics said the governor's explanation made for good politics but bad economics. Government intervention, not the market, was the cause of the electricity crisis, they said. Supply and demand were out of balance in California and only *higher* prices and *less* government intervention could keep the lights on. U.S. Treasury Secretary Paul O'Neill criticized the governor for trying "to defeat economics. . . I mean, you don't have to have an economics degree to understand that this is an unworkable situation." One of UC–Berkeley's Nobel-winning economists, Daniel McFadden, echoed that sentiment, blaming the state's "rigid regulation" for its energy woes. President Bush was equally adamant that "price controls will not solve the problem" and urged the state to rely more on the market than on state legislators to avoid future blackouts.

California's 2001 energy crisis is a classic illustration of why the choice between market reliance and government intervention is so critical and often so controversial. The goal of this chapter is to put that choice into a coherent framework. To do so, we'll focus on how unregulated markets work. How does the market mechanism decide WHAT to produce, HOW to produce, and FOR WHOM to produce? Specifically,

- **What determines the price of a good or service?**
- **How does the price of a product affect its production and consumption?**
- **Why do prices and production levels often change?**

Once we've seen how unregulated markets work, we'll observe how government intervention may alter market outcomes—for better or worse. Hopefully, the lights won't go off before we finish.

---

[1]Rene Sanchez and William Booth, "California Forced to Turn the Lights Off," *Washington Post,* January 18, 2001, p. 1.

MARKET PARTICIPANTS

A good way to start figuring out how markets work is to see who participates in them. The answer is simple: just about every person and institution on the planet. Domestically, over 300 million consumers, about 20 million business firms, and tens of thousands of government agencies participate directly in the U.S. economy. Millions of international buyers and sellers also participate in U.S. markets.

All these market participants come into the marketplace to satisfy specific goals. Consumers, for example, come with a limited amount of income to spend. Their objective is to buy the most desirable goods and services that their limited budgets will permit. We can't afford *everything* we want, so we must make *choices* about how to spend our scarce dollars. Our goal is to *maximize* the utility (satisfaction) we get from our available incomes.

Maximizing Behavior

Businesses also try to maximize in the marketplace. In their case, the quest is for maximum *profits.* Business profits are the difference between sales receipts and total costs. To maximize profits, business firms try to use resources efficiently in producing products that consumers desire.

The public sector also has maximizing goals. The economic purpose of government is to use available resources to serve public needs. The resources available for this purpose are limited too. Hence, local, state, and federal governments must use scarce resources carefully, striving to maximize the general welfare of society. International consumers and producers pursue these same goals when participating in our markets.

Market participants sometimes lose sight of their respective goals. Consumers sometimes buy impulsively and later wish they'd used their income more wisely. Likewise, a producer may take a two-hour lunch, even at the sacrifice of maximum profits. And elected officials sometimes put their personal interests ahead of the public's interest. In all sectors of the economy, however, ***the basic goals of utility maximization, profit maximization, and welfare maximization explain most market activity.***

The notion that buying and selling goods and services in the market might maximize our well-being originates in two simple observations. First, most of us are incapable of producing everything we desire to consume. Second, even if we *could* produce all our own goods and services, it would still make sense to specialize, producing only one product and trading it for other desired goods and services.

Specialization and Exchange

Suppose you were capable of growing your own food, stitching your own clothes, building your own shelter, and even writing your own economics text. Even in this little utopia, it would still make sense to decide how *best* to expend your limited time and energy and to rely on others to fill in the gaps. If you were *most* proficient at growing food, you would be best off spending your time farming. You could then exchange some of your food output for the clothes, shelter, and books you wanted. In the end, you'd be able to consume *more* goods than if you'd tried to make everything yourself.

Our economic interactions with others are thus necessitated by two constraints:

1. Our absolute inability as individuals to produce all the things we need or desire.
2. The limited amount of time, energy, and resources we have for producing those things we could make for ourselves.

Together, these constraints lead us to specialize and interact. Most of the interactions that result take place in the market.

THE CIRCULAR FLOW

Figure 3.1 summarizes the kinds of interactions that occur among market participants. Note first that the figure identifies four separate groups of participants. Domestically, the rectangle labeled "Consumers" includes all 300 million consumers in the United

The Circular Flow

Business firms supply goods and services to product markets (point *A*) and purchase factors of production in factor markets (*B*). Individual consumers supply factors of production such as their own labor (*C*) and purchase final goods and services (*D*). Federal, state, and local governments acquire resources in factor markets (*E*) and provide services to both consumers and business (*F*). International participants also take part by supplying imports, purchasing exports (*G*), and buying and selling factors of production (*H*).

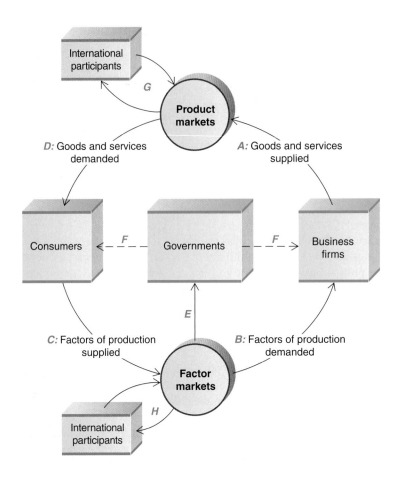

States. In the "Business firms" box are grouped all the domestic business enterprises that buy and sell goods and services. The third participant, "Governments," includes the many separate agencies of the federal government, as well as state and local governments. Figure 3.1 also illustrates the role of global actors.

The Two Markets

factor market: Any place where factors of production (e.g., land, labor, capital) are bought and sold.

product market: Any place where finished goods and services (products) are bought and sold.

The easiest way to keep track of all this market activity is to distinguish two basic markets. Figure 3.1 makes this distinction by portraying separate circles for product markets and factor markets. In **factor markets,** factors of production are exchanged. Market participants buy or sell land, labor, or capital that can be used in the production process. When you go looking for work, for example, you're making a factor of production—your labor—available to producers. The producers will hire you—purchase your services in the factor market—if you're offering the skills they need at a price they're willing to pay. The same kind of interaction occurs in factor markets when the government enlists workers into the armed services or when the Japanese buy farmland in Montana.

Interactions within factor markets are only half the story. At the end of a hard day's work, consumers go to the grocery store (or to a virtual store online) to buy desired goods and services—that is, to buy *products.* In this context, consumers again interact with business firms, this time purchasing goods and services those firms have produced. These interactions occur in **product markets.** Foreigners also participate in the product market by supplying goods and services (imports) to the United States and buying some of our output (exports).

The government sector also supplies services. (e.g., education, national defense, highways.) In California, Governor Davis even wanted the state to supply electricity to households and businesses. Most government services aren't explicitly sold in product markets, however. Typically, they're delivered "free," without an explicit price (e.g., public elementary schools, highways). This doesn't mean government services are truly free, though. There's still an opportunity cost associated with every service the government provides. Consumers and businesses pay that cost indirectly through taxes rather than directly through market prices.

In Figure 3.1, the arrow connecting product markets to consumers (point *D*) emphasizes the fact that consumers, by definition, don't supply products. When individuals produce goods and services, they do so within the government or business sector. For instance, a doctor, a dentist, or an economic consultant functions in two sectors. When selling services in the market, this person is regarded as a "business"; when away from the office, he or she is regarded as a "consumer." This distinction is helpful in emphasizing that *the consumer is the final recipient of all goods and services produced.*

Locating Markets. Although we refer repeatedly to two kinds of markets in this book, it would be a little foolish to go off in search of the product and factor markets. Neither market is a single, identifiable structure. The term *market* simply refers to a place or situation where an economic exchange occurs—where a buyer and seller interact. The exchange may take place on the street, in a taxicab, over the phone, by mail, or in cyberspace. In some cases, the market used may in fact be quite distinguishable, as in the case of a retail store, the Chicago Commodity Exchange, or a state employment office. But whatever it looks like, *a market exists wherever and whenever an exchange takes place.*

Dollars and Exchange

Figure 3.1 provides a useful summary of market activities, but it neglects one critical element of market interactions: dollars. Each arrow in the figure actually has two dimensions. Consider again the arrow linking consumers to product markets: It's drawn in only one direction because consumers, by definition, don't provide goods and services directly to product markets. But they do provide something: dollars. If you want to obtain something from a product market, you must offer to pay for it (typically, with cash, check, or credit card). Consumers exchange dollars for goods and services in product markets.

The same kinds of exchange occur in factor markets. When you go to work, you exchange a factor of production (your labor) for income, typically a paycheck. Here again, the path connecting consumers to factor markets really goes in two directions: one of real resources, the other of dollars. Consumers receive wages, rent, and interest for the labor, land, and capital they bring to the factor markets. Indeed, nearly *every market transaction involves an exchange of dollars for goods (in product markets) or resources (in factor markets).* Money is thus critical in facilitating market exchanges and the specialization the exchanges permit.

Supply and Demand

supply: The ability and willingness to sell (produce) specific quantities of a good at alternative prices in a given time period, *ceteris paribus.*

demand: The ability and willingness to buy specific quantities of a good at alternative prices in a given time period, *ceteris paribus.*

In every market transaction there must be a buyer and a seller. The seller is on the **supply** side of the market; the buyer is on the **demand** side. As noted earlier, we *supply* resources to the market when we look for a job—that is, when we offer our labor in exchange for income. We *demand* goods when we shop in a supermarket—that is, when we're prepared to offer dollars in exchange for something to eat. Business firms may *supply* goods and services in product markets at the same time they're *demanding* factors of production in factor markets. Whether one is on the supply side or the demand side of any particular market transaction depends on the nature of the exchange, not on the people or institutions involved.

DEMAND

To get a sense of how the demand side of market transactions work, we'll focus first on a single consumer. Then we'll aggregate to illustrate *market* demand.

Individual Demand

We can begin to understand how market forces work by looking more closely at the behavior of a single market participant. Let us start with Tom, a senior at Clearview

College. Tom has majored in everything from art history to government in his three years at Clearview. He didn't connect to any of those fields and is on the brink of academic dismissal. To make matters worse, his parents have threatened to cut him off financially unless he gets serious about his course work. By that, they mean he should enroll in courses that will lead to a job after graduation. Tom thinks he has found the perfect solution: Web design. Everything associated with the Internet pays big bucks. Plus, the girls seem to think Webbies are "cool." Or at least so Tom thinks. And his parents would definitely approve. So Tom has enrolled in Web-design courses.

Unfortunately for Tom, he never developed computer skills. Until he got to Clearview College, he thought mastering Sony's latest alien-attack video game was the pinnacle of electronic wizardry. His parents gave him a Wi-Fi laptop, but he used it only for surfing hot video sites. The concept of using his computer for course work, much less developing some Web content, was completely foreign to him. To compound his problems, Tom didn't have a clue about "streaming," "interfacing," "animation," or the other concepts the Web-design instructor outlined in the first lecture.

Given his circumstances, Tom was desperate to find someone who could tutor him in Web design. But desperation is not enough to secure the services of a Web architect. In a market-based economy, you must also be willing to *pay* for the things you want. Specifically, ***a demand exists only if someone is willing and able to pay for the good***—that is, exchange dollars for a good or service in the marketplace. Is Tom willing and able to *pay* for the Web-design tutoring he so obviously needs?

Let us assume that Tom has some income and is willing to spend some of it to get a tutor. Under these assumptions, we can claim that Tom is a participant in the *market* for Web-design services.

But how much is Tom willing to pay? Surely, Tom is not prepared to exchange *all* his income for help in mastering Web design. After all, Tom could use his income to buy more desirable goods and services. If he spent all his income on a Web tutor, that help would have an extremely high **opportunity cost.** He would be giving up the opportunity to spend that income on other goods and services. He'd pass his Web-design class but have little else. It doesn't sound like a good idea to Tom. Even though Tom says he would be willing to pay *anything* to pass the Web-design course, he probably has lower prices in mind. Indeed, it would be more reasonable to assume that there are *limits* to the amount Tom is willing to pay for any given quantity of Web-design tutoring. These limits will be determined by how much income Tom has to spend and how many other goods and services he must forsake in order to pay for a tutor.

Tom also knows that his grade in Web design will depend in part on how much tutoring service he buys. He can pass the course with only a few hours of design help. If he wants a better grade, however, the cost is going to escalate quickly.

Naturally, Tom wants it all: an A in Web design and a ticket to higher-paying jobs. But here again the distinction between *desire* and *demand* is relevant. He may *desire* to master Web design, but his actual proficiency will depend on how many hours of tutoring he is willing to *pay* for.

We assume, then, that when Tom starts looking for a Web-design tutor he has in mind some sort of **demand schedule,** like that described in Figure 3.2. According to row *A* of this schedule, Tom is willing and able to buy only 1 hour of tutoring service per semester if he must pay $50 an hour. At such an outrageous price he will learn minimal skills and pass the course. Just the bare minimum is all Tom is willing to buy at that price.

At lower prices, Tom would behave differently. According to Figure 3.2, Tom would purchase more tutoring services if the price per hour were less. At lower prices, he would not have to give up so many other goods and services for each hour of technical help. The reduced opportunity costs implied by lower service prices increase the attractiveness of professional help. Indeed, we see from row *I* of the demand schedule that Tom is willing to purchase 20 hours per semester—the whole bag of design tricks—if the price of tutoring is as low as $10 per hour.

opportunity cost: The most desired goods or services that are forgone in order to obtain something else.

demand schedule: A table showing the quantities of a good a consumer is willing and able to buy at alternative prices in a given time period, *ceteris paribus*.

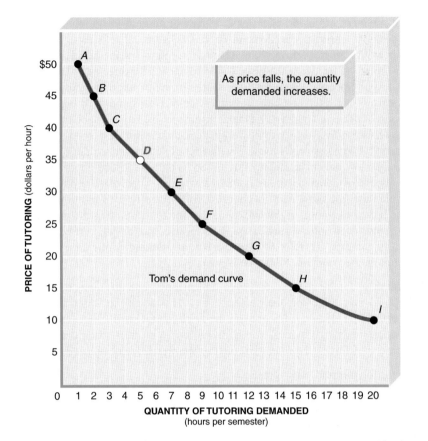

As price falls, the quantity demanded increases.

Tom's demand curve

PRICE OF TUTORING (dollars per hour)

QUANTITY OF TUTORING DEMANDED
(hours per semester)

FIGURE 3.2
A Demand Schedule and Curve

A demand schedule indicates the quantities of a good a consumer is able and willing to buy at alternative prices (*ceteris paribus*). The demand schedule below indicates that Tom would buy 5 hours of Web tutoring per semester if the price were $35 per hour (row *D*). If Web tutoring were less expensive (rows *E–I*), Tom would purchase a larger quantity.

A demand curve is a graphical illustration of a demand schedule. Each point on the curve refers to a specific quantity that will be demanded at a given price. If, for example, the price of Web tutoring were $35 per hour, this curve tells us the consumer would purchase 5 hours per semester (point *D*). If Web tutoring cost $30 per hour, 7 hours per semester would be demanded (point *E*). Each point on the curve corresponds to a row in the schedule.

	Tom's Demand Schedule	
	Price of Tutoring (per hour)	**Quantity of Tutoring Demanded (hours per semester)**
A	$50	1
B	45	2
C	40	3
D	35	5
E	30	7
F	25	9
G	20	12
H	15	15
I	10	20

Notice that the demand schedule doesn't tell us anything about *why* this consumer is willing to pay specific prices for various amounts of tutoring. Tom's expressed willingness to pay for Web-design tutoring may reflect a desperate need to finish a Web-design course, a lot of income to spend, or a relatively small desire for other goods and services. All the demand schedule tells us is what the consumer is *willing and able* to buy, for whatever reasons.

Also observe that the demand schedule doesn't tell us how many hours of design help the consumer will *actually* buy. Figure 3.2 simply states that Tom is *willing and able* to pay for one hour of tutoring per semester at $50 per hour, for two hours at $45 each, and so on. How much tutoring he purchases will depend on the actual price of such services in the market. Until we know that price, we cannot tell how much service will be purchased. Hence ***"demand" is an expression of consumer buying intentions, of a willingness to buy, not a statement of actual purchases.***

A convenient summary of buying intentions is the **demand curve,** a graphical illustration of the demand schedule. The demand curve in Figure 3.2 tells us again that this consumer is willing to pay for only one hour of tutoring per semester if the price is $50 per hour (point *A*), for two if the price is $45 (point *B*), for three at $40 an hour (point *C*), and so on. Once we know what the market price of tutoring actually is, a glance at the demand curve tells us how much service this consumer will buy.

What the notion of *demand* emphasizes is that the amount we buy of a good depends on its price. We seldom if ever decide to buy only a certain quantity of a good at whatever price is charged. Instead, we enter markets with a set of desires and a limited amount of money to spend. How much we actually buy of any good will depend on its price.

A common feature of demand curves is their downward slope. As the price of a good falls, people purchase more of it. In Figure 3.2 the quantity of Web-tutorial services demanded increases (moves rightward along the horizontal axis) as the price per hour decreases (moves down the vertical axis). This inverse relationship between price and quantity is so common we refer to it as the **law of demand.** Compaq used this law to increase computer sales in 2000 (see News).

Determinants of Demand

The demand curve in Figure 3.2 has only two dimensions—quantity demanded (on the horizontal axis) and price (on the vertical axis). This seems to imply that the amount of tutoring demanded depends only on the price of that service. This is surely not the case. A consumer's willingness and ability to buy a product at various prices depend on a variety of forces. *The determinants of market demand include*

- *Tastes* (desire for this and other goods).
- *Income* (of the consumer).
- *Other goods* (their availability and price).
- *Expectations* (for income, prices, tastes).
- *Number of buyers.*

IN THE NEWS

PC Prices Fall with Demand

Retailers Try to Minimize Losses with Big Rebates

Compaq Computer became the latest casualty of the weakening personal computer market, warning Tuesday that its fourth-quarter sales and profit will fall short of Wall Street's expectations.

The world's biggest PC maker blamed softening consumer and small-business demand—heightening expectations that PC makers may have to resort to price cuts to move excess inventory.

"We're seeing some of the biggest rebates we've ever seen in the PC industry," says Kevin Knox, a Gartner analyst in Stamford, Conn.

- Consumers can get rebates of $100 to $400 on PCs by Compaq, Hewlett-Packard and eMachines at Circuit City, Best Buy and other retailers.

- If sales don't pick up, bigger rebates are likely in January, analysts say.
- In a typical holiday bargain at Circuit City, shoppers can snap up a Compaq Presario computer, originally priced at $1,099, for $649. . . .

Analysts say PC makers and retail chains have inventory backlogs of eight to 12 weeks. The industry likes to see a backlog of three to four weeks. . . .

Worldwide, fourth-quarter PC shipments will be up 20 percent over the same period a year ago, says market research firm IDC.

—Edward Iwata

Source: *USA Today,* December 13, 2000. USA TODAY. Copyright 2000. Reprinted with permission. www.usatoday.com

Analysis: The law of demand predicted that Compaq would sell more computers if it reduced their price. That is exactly what happened.

Tom's "taste" for tutoring has nothing to do with taste buds. *Taste* is just another word for desire. In this case Tom's taste for Web-design services is clearly acquired. If he didn't have to pass a Web-design course, he would have no desire for related services, and thus no demand. If he had no income, he couldn't *demand* any Web-design tutoring either, no matter how much he might *desire* it.

Other goods also affect the demand for tutoring services. Their effect depends on whether they're *substitute* goods or *complementary* goods. A **substitute good** is one that might be purchased instead of tutoring services. In Tom's simple world, pizza is a substitute for tutoring. If the price of pizza fell, Tom would use his limited income to buy more pizzas and cut back on his purchases of Web tutoring. When the price of a substitute good falls, the demand for tutoring services declines.

A **complementary good** is one that's typically consumed with, rather than instead of, tutoring. If textbook prices or tuition increases, Tom might take fewer classes and demand *less* Web-design assistance. In this case, a price increase for a complementary good causes the demand for tutoring to decline.

Expectations also play a role in consumer decisions. If Tom expected to flunk his Web-design course anyway, he probably wouldn't waste any money getting tutorial help; his demand for such services would disappear. On the other hand, if he expects a Web tutor to determine his college fate, he might be more willing to buy such services.

> **substitute goods:** Goods that substitute for each other; when the price of good *x* rises, the demand for good *y* increases, *ceteris paribus*.

> **complementary goods:** Goods frequently consumed in combination; when the price of good *x* rises, the demand for good *y* falls, *ceteris paribus*.

Ceteris Paribus

If demand is in fact such a multidimensional decision, how can we reduce it to only the two dimensions of price and quantity? In Chapter 1 we first encountered this *ceteris paribus* trick. To simplify their models of the world, economists focus on only one or two forces at a time and *assume* nothing else changes. We know a consumer's tastes, income, other goods, and expectations all affect the decision to hire a tutor. But we want to focus on the relationship between quantity demanded and price. That is, we want to know what *independent* influence price has on consumption decisions. To find out, we must isolate that one influence, price, and assume that the determinants of demand remain unchanged.

> **ceteris paribus:** The assumption of nothing else changing.

The *ceteris paribus* assumption is not as farfetched as it may seem. People's tastes, income, and expectations do not change quickly. Also, the prices and availability of other goods don't change all that fast. Hence, a change in the *price* of a product may be the only factor that prompts a change in quantity demanded.

The ability to predict consumer responses to a price change is important. What would happen, for example, to enrollment at your school if tuition doubled? Must we guess? Or can we use demand curves to predict how the quantity of applications will change as the price of college goes up? ***Demand curves show us how changes in market prices alter consumer behavior.*** We used the demand curve in Figure 3.2 to predict how Tom's Web-design ability would change at different tutorial prices.

Shifts in Demand

Although demand curves are useful in predicting consumer responses to market signals, they aren't infallible. The problem is that ***the determinants of demand can and do change.*** When they do, a specific demand curve may become obsolete. A ***demand curve (schedule) is valid only so long as the underlying determinants of demand remain constant.*** If the *ceteris paribus* assumption is violated—if tastes, income, other goods, or expectations change—the ability or willingness to buy will change. When this happens, the demand curve will **shift** to a new position.

Suppose, for example, that Tom won $1,000 in the state lottery. This increase in his income would greatly increase his ability to pay for tutoring services. Figure 3.3 shows the effect of this windfall on Tom's demand. The old demand curve, D_1, is no longer relevant. Tom's lottery winnings enable him to buy more tutoring at any price, as illustrated by the new demand curve, D_2. According to this new curve, lucky Tom is now willing and able to buy 12 hours per semester at the price of $35 per hour

> **shift in demand:** A change in the quantity demanded at any (every) given price.

FIGURE 3.3
Shifts vs. Movements

A demand curve shows how a consumer responds to price changes. If the determinants of demand stay constant, the response is a *movement* along the curve to a new quantity demanded. In this case, the quantity demanded increases from 5 (point d_1), to 12 (point g_1), when price falls from $35 to $20 per hour.

If the determinants of demand change, the entire demand curve *shifts*. In this case, an increase in income increases demand. With more income, Tom is willing to buy 12 hours at the initial price of $35 (point d_2), not just the 5 hours he demanded before the lottery win.

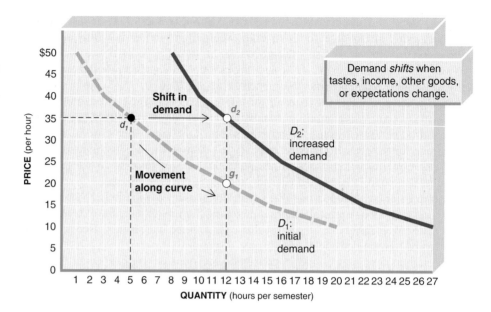

		Quantity Demanded (hours per semester)	
	Price (per hour)	Initial Demand	After Increase in Income
A	$50	1	8
B	45	2	9
C	40	3	10
D	35	5	12
E	30	7	14
F	25	9	16
G	20	12	19
H	15	15	22
I	10	20	27

(point d_2). This is a large increase in demand; previously (before winning the lottery) he demanded only 5 hours at that price (point d_1).

With his higher income, Tom can buy more tutoring services at every price. Thus, *the entire demand curve shifts to the right when income goes up.* Figure 3.3 illustrates both the old (prelottery) and the new (postlottery) demand curves.

Income is only one of the basic determinants of demand. Changes in any of the other determinants of demand would also cause the demand curve to shift. Tom's taste for Web tutoring might increase dramatically, for example, if his parents promised to buy him a new car for passing Web design. In that case, he might be willing to forgo other goods and spend more of his income on tutors. *An increase in taste (desire) also shifts the demand curve to the right.*

Pizza and Politics. A similar demand shift occurs at the White House when a political crisis erupts. On an average day, White House staffers order about $180 worth of pizza from the nearby Domino's. When a crisis hits, however, staffers work well into the night and their demand for pizza soars. On the days preceeding the March 2003 invasion of Iraq, White House staffers ordered more than $1,000 worth of pizza per day!

It's important to distinguish shifts of the demand curve from movements along the demand curve. ***Movements along a demand curve are a response to price changes for that good.*** Such movements assume that determinants of demand are unchanged. By contrast, ***shifts of the demand curve occur when the determinants of demand change.*** When tastes, income, other goods, or expectations are altered, the basic relationship between price and quantity demanded is changed (shifts).

For convenience, movements along a demand curve and shifts of the demand curve have their own labels. Specifically, take care to distinguish

- ***Changes in quantity demanded:*** movements along a given demand curve, in response to price changes of that good.
- ***Changes in demand:*** shifts of the demand curve due to changes in tastes, income, other goods, or expectations.

Tom's behavior in the Web-tutoring market will change if either the price of tutoring changes (a movement) or the underlying determinants of his demand are altered (a shift). Notice in Figure 3.3 that he ends up buying 12 hours of Web tutoring if either the price of tutoring falls or his income increases. Demand curves help us predict those market responses.

Whatever we say about demand for Web-design tutoring on the part of one wannabe Web master, we can also say about every student at Clearview College (or, for that matter, about all consumers). Some students have no interest in Web design and aren't willing to pay for related services: They don't participate in the Web-tutoring market. Other students want such services but don't have enough income to pay for them: They too are excluded from the Web-tutoring market. A large number of students, however, not only have a need (or desire) for Web tutoring but also are willing and able to purchase such services.

What we start with in product markets, then, is many individual demand curves. Fortunately, it's possible to combine all the individual demand curves into a single **market demand.** The aggregation process is no more difficult than simple arithmetic. Suppose you would be willing to buy one hour of tutoring per semester at a price of $80 per hour. George, who is also desperate to learn Web design, would buy two at that price; and I would buy none, since my publisher (McGraw-Hill) creates a Web page for me (try mhhe.com/economics/Schiller10). What would our combined (market) demand for hours of tutoring be at that price? Clearly, our individual inclinations indicate that we would be willing to buy a total of three hours of tutoring per semester if the price were $80 per hour. Our combined willingness to buy—our collective market demand—is nothing more than the sum of our individual demands. The same kind of aggregation can be performed for all consumers, leading to a summary of the total market demand for a specific good or service. This ***market demand is determined by the number of potential buyers and their respective tastes, incomes, other goods, and expectations.***

Figure 3.4 provides the basic market demand schedule for a situation in which only three consumers participate in the market. It illustrates the same market situation with demand curves. The three individuals who participate in the market demand for Web tutoring at Clearview College obviously differ greatly, as suggested by their respective demand schedules. Tom *has* to pass his Web-design classes or confront college and parental rejection. He also has a nice allowance (income), so can afford to buy a lot of tutorial help. His demand schedule is portrayed in the first column of the table (and is identical to the one we examined in Figure 3.2). George is also desperate to acquire some job skills and is willing to pay relatively high prices for Web-design tutoring. His demand is summarized in the second column under Quantity Demanded in the table.

The third consumer in this market is Lisa. Lisa already knows the nuts and bolts of Web design, so she isn't so desperate for tutorial services. She would like to upgrade

Movements vs. Shifts

Priceline.com is an online service for purchasing airline tickets, vacation packages, and car rentals. The site allows you to specify the *highest* price you're willing to pay for air travel between two cities. In effect, you reveal your demand curve to Priceline. If you use the price naming option and they find a ticket that costs no more than the price you're willing and able to pay, you must buy it. Priceline makes a profit by matching demand and supply. Try it at www.priceline.com.

Market Demand

market demand: The total quantities of a good or service people are willing and able to buy at alternative prices in a given time period; the sum of individual demands.

The Market Demand Curve

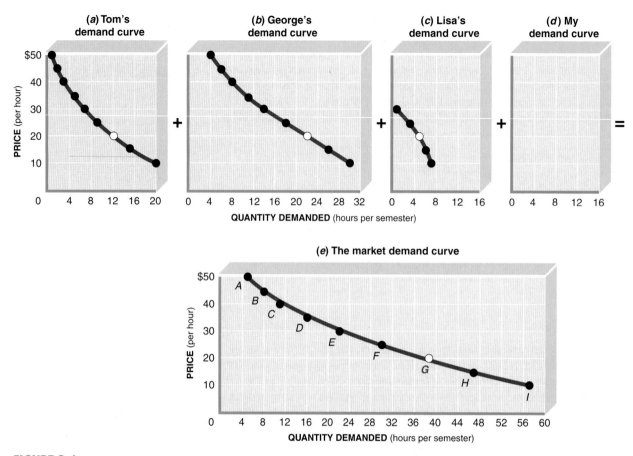

FIGURE 3.4
Construction of the Market Demand Curve

Market demand represents the combined demands of all market participants. To determine the total quantity of Web tutoring demanded at any given price, we add the separate demands of the individual consumers. Row *G* of this schedule indicates that a *total*

quantity of 39 hours per semester will be demanded at a price of $20 per hour. This same conclusion is reached by adding the individual demand curves, leading to point *G* on the market demand curve (see above).

	Price (per hour)	Tom	+	George	+	Lisa	+	Me	=	Market Demand
A	$50	1		4		0		0		5
B	45	2		6		0		0		8
C	40	3		8		0		0		11
D	35	5		11		0		0		16
E	30	7		14		1		0		22
F	25	9		18		3		0		30
G	20	12		22		5		0		39
H	15	15		26		6		0		47
I	10	20		30		7		0		57

her skills, however, especially in animation and e-commerce applications. But her limited budget precludes paying a lot for help. She will buy some technical support only if the price falls to $30 per hour. Should tutors cost less, she'd even buy quite a few hours of design services. Finally, there is my demand schedule (column 4 under Quantity Demanded), which confirms that I really don't participate in the Web-tutoring market.

The differing personalities and consumption habits of Tom, George, Lisa, and me are expressed in our individual demand schedules and associated curves in Figure 3.4. To determine the *market* demand for tutoring from this information, we simply add these four separate demands. The end result of this aggregation is, first, a *market* demand schedule and, second, the resultant *market* demand curve. These market summaries describe the various quantities of tutoring that Clearview College students are *willing and able* to purchase each semester at various prices.

How much Web tutoring will be purchased each semester? Knowing how much help Tom, George, Lisa, and I are willing to buy at various prices doesn't tell you how much we're actually going to purchase. To determine the actual consumption of Web tutoring, we have to know something about prices and supplies. Which of the many different prices illustrated in Figures 3.3 and 3.4 will actually prevail? How will that price be determined?

SUPPLY

To understand how the price of Web tutoring is established, we must also look at the other side of the market: the supply side. We need to know how many hours of tutoring services people are willing and able to *sell* at various prices, that is, the **market supply.** As on the demand side, the *market supply* depends on the behavior of all the individuals willing and able to supply Web tutoring at some price.

Let's return to the Clearview campus for a moment. What we need to know now is how much tutorial Web service people are willing and able to provide. Generally speaking, Web-page design can be fun, but it can also be drudge work, especially when you're doing it for someone else. Software programs like PhotoShop, Flash, and Fireworks have made Web-page design easier and more creative. And Wi-Fi laptops have made Web tutoring more convenient. But teaching someone else to design Web pages is still work. So few people offer to supply tutoring services just for the fun of it. Web designers do it for money. Specifically, they do it to earn income that they, in turn, can spend on goods and services they desire.

How much income must be offered to induce Web designers to do a job depends on a variety of things. The ***determinants of market supply include***

- *Technology*
- *Factor costs*
- *Other goods*
- *Taxes and subsidies*
- *Expectations*
- *Number of sellers*

The technology of Web design, for example, is always getting easier and more creative. With a program like PageOut, for example, it's very easy to create a bread-and-butter Web page. A continuous stream of new software programs (e.g., Fireworks, DreamWeaver) keeps stretching the possibilities for graphics, animation, interactivity, and content. These technological advances mean that Web-design services can be supplied more quickly and cheaply. They also make *teaching* Web design easier. As a result, they induce people to supply more tutoring services at every price.

How much Web-design service is offered at any given price also depends on the cost of factors of production. If the software programs needed to create Web pages are cheap (or, better yet, free), Web designers can afford to charge lower prices. If the required software inputs are expensive, however, they will have to charge more money per hour for their services.

market supply: The total quantities of a good that sellers are willing and able to sell at alternative prices in a given time period, *ceteris paribus.*

Determinants of Supply

law of supply: The quantity of a good supplied in a given time period increases as its price increases, *ceteris paribus*.

Other goods can also affect the willingness to supply Web-design services. If you can make more income waiting tables than you can tutoring lazy students, why would you even boot up the computer? As the prices paid for other goods and services change, they will influence people's decision about whether to offer Web services.

In the real world, the decision to supply goods and services is also influenced by the long arm of Uncle Sam. Federal, state, and local governments impose taxes on income earned in the marketplace. When tax rates are high, people get to keep less of the income they earn. Once taxes start biting into paychecks, some people may conclude that tutoring is no longer worth the hassle and withdraw from the market.

Expectations are also important on the supply side of the market. If Web designers expect higher prices, lower costs, or reduced taxes, they may be more willing to learn new software programs. On the other hand, if they have poor expectations about the future, they may just sell their computers and find something else to do.

Finally, we note that the number of available tutors will affect the quantity of service offered for sale at various prices. If there are lots of willing tutors on campus, a large quantity of tutorial service will be available.

All these considerations—factor costs, technology, expectations—affect the decision to offer Web services and at what price. In general, we assume that Web architects will be willing to provide more tutoring if the per-hour price is high and less if the price is low. In other words, there is a **law of supply** that parallels the law of demand. On the supply side the law says that *larger quantities will be offered for sale at higher prices.* Here again, the laws rest on the *ceteris paribus* assumption: The quantity supplied increases at higher prices *if* the determinants of supply are constant. *Supply curves are upward-sloping to the right,* as in Figure 3.5. Note how the *quantity supplied* jumps from 39 hours (point *d*) to 130 hours (point *h*) when the price of Web service doubles (from $20 to $40 per hour).

Market Supply

Figure 3.5 also illustrates how market supply is constructed from the supply decisions of individual sellers. In this case, only three Web masters are available. Ann is willing to provide a lot of tutoring at low prices, whereas Bob requires at least $20 an hour. Cory won't talk to students for less than $40 an hour.

By adding the quantity each Webhead is willing to offer at every price, we can construct the market supply curve. Notice in Figure 3.5, for example, how the quantity supplied to the market at $45 (point *i*) comes from the individual efforts of Ann (93 hours), Bob (33 hours), and Cory (14 hours). *The market supply curve is just a summary of the supply intentions of all producers.*

None of the points on the market supply curve (Figure 3.5) tells us how much Web tutoring is actually being sold on the Clearview campus. *Market supply is an expression of sellers' intentions—an offer to sell—not a statement of actual sales.* My next door neighbor may be willing to sell his 1994 Honda Civic for $8,000, but most likely he'll never find a buyer at that price. Nevertheless, his *willingness* to sell his car at that price is part of the *market supply* of used cars.

Shifts of Supply

As with demand, there's nothing sacred about any given set of supply intentions. Supply curves *shift* when the underlying determinants of supply change. Thus, we again distinguish

- *Changes in quantity supplied:* movements along a given supply curve.
- *Changes in supply:* shifts of the supply curve.

Our Latin friend *ceteris paribus* is once again the decisive factor. If the price of a product is the only variable changing, then we can *track changes in quantity supplied along the supply curve.* But if *ceteris paribus* is violated—if technology,

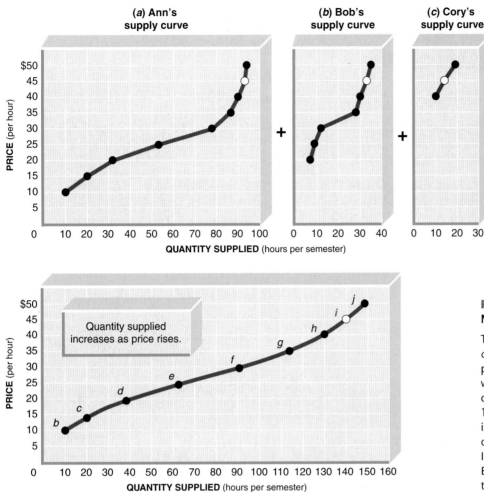

(a) Ann's supply curve

(b) Bob's supply curve

(c) Cory's supply curve

Quantity supplied increases as price rises.

FIGURE 3.5
Market Supply

The market supply curve indicates the *combined* sales intentions of all market participants. If the price of tutoring were $45 per hour (point *i*), the *total* quantity of services supplied would be 140 hours per semester. This quantity is determined by adding the supply decisions of all individual producers. In this case, Ann supplies 93 hours, Bob supplies 33, and Cory supplies the rest.

	Price (per hour)	Ann	+	Bob	+	Cory	=	Market
j	$50	94		35		19		148
i	45	93		33		14		140
h	40	90		30		10		130
g	35	86		28		0		114
f	30	78		12		0		90
e	25	53		9		0		62
d	20	32		7		0		39
c	15	20		0		0		20
b	10	10		0		0		10

Column header (spanning): **Quantity of Tutoring Supplied by**

factor costs, the profitability of producing other goods, tax rates, expectations, or the number of sellers change—then ***changes in supply are illustrated by shifts of the supply curve.***

The News on the next page illustrates how a supply shift sent lettuce prices soaring in 2002. When a burst of cold weather reduced harvests, the lettuce supply curve shifted leftward and price doubled.

Prices Soar As Cold Snap Shreds Iceberg Lettuce Supply

In a classic collision of supply and demand, a cold snap in Arizona and California has chopped the iceberg lettuce harvest just as Americans are eating more of the salad and sandwich staple.

Grocery prices have soared to $3 a head, school cafeterias have pulled lettuce out of ham sandwiches, restaurants have substituted cheaper baby spinach in salads and consumers are suffering sticker shock.

Farm prices for lettuce doubled in March to a record $86.50 per hundred pounds, up 477% from March 2001, according to the Department of Agriculture. Much of that increase was in the iceberg category, the most popular lettuce in the USA.

Reasons for the increase in lettuce prices:

- **Higher demand.** Farmers say demand has surged over the past five years because of the rising popularity of prepackaged "bag lettuce."
- **Bad weather.** It was unusually cold in Yuma, Ariz, and in the Imperial Valley in California, the nation's "salad bowl" during winter. That led to a delayed harvest and smaller yields.

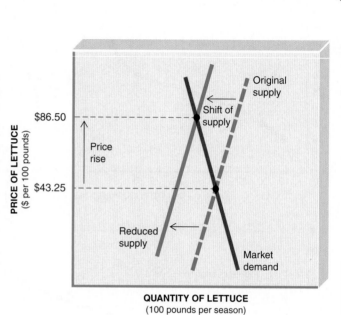

The weather isn't just making an impact on iceberg lettuce. Farm prices for cauliflower shot up 60% in March, while tomato prices rose 39%.

—Barbara Hagenbaugh

Source: *USA Today,* April 1, 2002. USA TODAY. Copyright 2002. Reprinted with permission.

Analysis: When factor costs or availability worsen, the supply curve shifts to the left. Such leftward supply-curve shifts push prices up the market demand curve.

EQUILIBRIUM

The abrupt spike in California lettuce prices offers some clues as to how the forces of supply and demand set, and change, market prices. To get a more detailed sense of how those forces work, we'll return to the mythical Clearview College Web tutoring market for a moment. How did supply and demand resolve the WHAT, HOW, and FOR WHOM questions in that market?

Figure 3.6 helps answer that question by bringing together the market supply and demand curves we've already examined (Figures 3.4 and 3.5). When we put the two curves together, we see that *only one price and quantity are compatible with the existing intentions of both buyers and sellers.* This equilibrium occurs at the intersection of the two curves in Figure 3.6. Once it's established, Web tutoring will cost $20 per hour. At that **equilibrium price,** campus Webheads will sell a total of 39 hours of tutoring per semester—the same amount that students wish to buy at that price. Those 39 hours of tutoring service will be part of WHAT is produced.

equilibrium price: The price at which the quantity of a good demanded in a given time period equals the quantity supplied.

Market Clearing

An equilibrium doesn't imply that everyone is happy with the prevailing price or quantity. Notice in Figure 3.6, for example, that some students who want to buy Web-design assistance services don't get any. These would-be buyers are arrayed along the demand curve *below* the equilibrium. Because the price they're *willing*

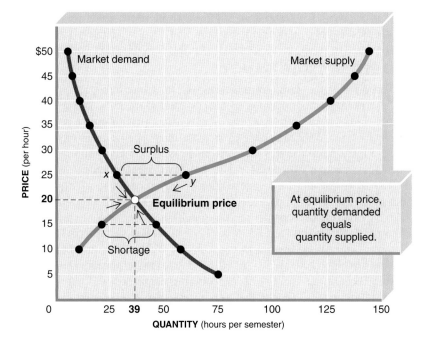

FIGURE 3.6
Equilibrium Price

Only at equilibrium is the quantity demanded equal to the quantity supplied. In this case, the equilibrium price is $20 per hour, and 39 hours is the equilibrium quantity. At higher prices, a market surplus exists—the quantity supplied exceeds the quantity demanded. At prices below equilibrium, a market shortage exists.

The intersection of the demand and supply curves in the graph represents equilibrium price and output in this market.

Price (per hour)	Quantity Supplied (hours per semester)		Quantity Demanded (hours per semester)
$50	148		5
45	140		8
40	130	market	11
35	114	surplus	16
30	90		22
25	62		30
20	39	equilibrium	39
15	20	market	47
10	10	shortage	57

to pay is less than the equilibrium price, they don't get any Web-design help. The market's FOR WHOM answer includes only those students willing and able to pay the equilibrium price.

Likewise, some would-be sellers in the market don't sell as much service as they might like. These people are arrayed along the supply curve *above* the equilibrium. Because they insist on being paid a price higher than the equilibrium price, they don't actually sell anything.

Although not everyone gets full satisfaction from the market equilibrium, that unique outcome is efficient. The equilibrium price and quantity reflect a compromise between buyers and sellers. No other compromise yields a quantity demanded that's exactly equal to the quantity supplied.

The Invisible Hand. The equilibrium price isn't determined by any single individual. Rather, it's determined by the collective behavior of many buyers and sellers, each acting out his or her own demand or supply schedule. It's this kind of impersonal price determination that gave rise to Adam Smith's characterization of the market mechanism as "the invisible hand." In attempting to explain how the **market mechanism** works, the famed eighteenth-century economist noted a certain feature of market

market mechanism: The use of market prices and sales to signal desired outputs (or resource allocations).

prices. The market behaves as if some unseen force (the invisible hand) were examining each individual's supply or demand schedule and then selecting a price that assured an equilibrium. In practice, the process of price determination isn't so mysterious: It's a simple process of trial and error.

Surplus and Shortage

price floor: Lower limit set for the price of a good.

market surplus: The amount by which the quantity supplied exceeds the quantity demanded at a given price; excess supply.

To appreciate the power of the market mechanism, consider interference in its operation. Suppose, for example, that campus Webheads banded together and agreed to charge a minimum price of $25 per hour. By establishing a **price floor,** a minimum price for their services, the Webheads hope to increase their incomes. But they won't be fully satisfied. Figure 3.6 illustrates the consequences of this *dis*equilibrium pricing. At $25 per hour, campus Webheads would be offering more tutoring services (point *y*) than Tom, George, and Lisa were willing to buy (point *x*) at that price. A **market surplus** of Web services would exist in the sense that more tutoring was being offered for sale (supplied) than students cared to purchase at the available price.

As Figure 3.6 indicates, at a price of $25 per hour, a market surplus of 32 hours per semester exists. Under these circumstances, campus Webheads would be spending many idle hours at their keyboards waiting for customers to appear. Their waiting will be in vain because the quantity of Web tutoring demanded will not increase until the price of tutoring falls. That is the clear message of the demand curve. As would-be tutors get this message, they'll reduce their prices. This is the response the market mechanism signals.

As sellers' asking prices decline, the quantity demanded will increase. This concept is illustrated in Figure 3.6 by the movement along the demand curve from point *x* to lower prices and greater quantity demanded. As we move down the market demand curve, the *desire* for Web-design help doesn't change, but the quantity people are *able and willing to buy* increases. When the price falls to $20 per hour, the quantity demanded will finally equal the quantity supplied. This is the *equilibrium* illustrated in Figure 3.6.

market shortage: The amount by which the quantity demanded exceeds the quantity supplied at a given price; excess demand.

An Initial Shortage. A very different sequence of events would occur if a market shortage existed. Suppose someone were to spread the word that Web-tutoring services were available at only $15 per hour. Tom, George, and Lisa would be standing in line to get tutorial help, but campus Web designers wouldn't be willing to supply the quantity desired at that price. As Figure 3.6 confirms, at $15 per hour, the quantity demanded (47 hours per semester) would greatly exceed the quantity supplied (20 hours per semester). In this situation, we may speak of a **market shortage,** that is, an excess of quantity demanded over quantity supplied. At a price of $15 an hour, the shortage amounts to 27 hours of tutoring services.

When a market shortage exists, not all consumer demands can be satisfied. Some people who are *willing* to buy Web help at the going price ($15) won't be able to do so. To assure themselves of sufficient help, Tom, George, Lisa, or some other consumer may offer to pay a *higher* price, thus initiating a move up the demand curve in Figure 3.6. The higher prices offered will in turn induce other enterprising Webheads to tutor more, thus ensuring an upward movement along the market supply curve. Thus, a higher price tends to evoke a greater quantity supplied, as reflected in the upward-sloping supply curve. Notice, again, that the *desire* to tutor Web design hasn't changed; only the quantity supplied has responded to a change in price.

Self-Adjusting Prices. What we observe, then, is that *whenever the market price is set above or below the equilibrium price, either a market surplus or a market shortage will emerge.* To overcome a surplus or shortage, buyers and sellers will change their behavior. Webheads will have to compete for customers by reducing prices when a market surplus exists. If a shortage exists, buyers will compete for service by offering to pay higher prices. Only at the *equilibrium* price will no further adjustments be required.

IN THE NEWS

For Fans, What's 4 Nights for U2?

After an 80-hour ordeal—four nights stuffed in a car, three days breathing bus exhaust, scarfing Cokes and franks, running blocks for pit stops—the three University of Maryland seniors who camped out at RFK Stadium prevailed. They beat the scalpers to U2 concert tickets.

At 8 A.M. today they would be, if all went as planned, first in line at the RFK box office. By 9 A.M. the 52,000-seat stadium will sell out, predicted a Ticketmaster official.

"It's what you got to do to get good seats," said Crawford Conniff, 22, stretched out near the stadium among traffic island dandelions.

"We have unlimited time," said Mike Collins, 22. "If we had a job making 50 grand, we could pay $150 to scalpers."

Actually, $150 sounds cheap for the $28.50 face-value tickets. Today's ticket sale for the Aug. 15 concert, one of the summer's hottest, is likely to ignite an orgy of profiteering.

When the band played Los Angeles, scalpers scored up to $1,200 a ticket for prime seats. In Washington, as early as Tuesday, ticket brokers had stationed students, unemployed and even homeless people at ticket outlets to snap up hundreds of choice seats.

—Laura Blumenfeld

Source: *Washington Post*, April 25, 1992. © 1992 The Washington Post. Reprinted with permission. www.washingtonpost.com

Analysis: In equilibrium, everyone who is willing and able to pay the equilibrium price gets to see the show. If price is below equilibrium, the quantity demanded exceeds the quantity supplied, so only people willing and able to stand in line for tickets will get them initially.

Sometimes the market price is slow to adjust, and a disequilibrium persists. This is often the case with tickets to rock concerts, football games, and other one-time events. People initially adjust their behavior by standing in ticket lines for hours, hoping to buy a ticket at the below-equilibrium price (see News). The tickets are typically resold ("scalped"), however, at prices closer to equilibrium.

Business firms can discover equilibrium prices by trial and error. If they find that consumer purchases aren't keeping up with production, they may conclude that their price is above the equilibrium price. They'll have to get rid of their accumulated inventory. To do so they'll have to lower their price (by a Grand End-of-Year Sale, perhaps). In the happy situation where consumer purchases are outpacing production, a firm might conclude that its price was a trifle too low and give it a nudge upward. In any case, the equilibrium price can be established after a few trials in the marketplace.

No equilibrium price is permanent. The equilibrium price established in the Clearview College tutoring market, for example, was the unique outcome of specific demand and supply schedules. Those schedules themselves were based on our assumption of *ceteris paribus.* We assumed that the "taste" (desire) for Web-design assistance was given, as were consumers' incomes, the price and availability of other goods, and expectations. Any of these determinants of demand could change. When one does, the demand curve has to be redrawn. Such a shift of the demand curve will lead to a new equilibrium price and quantity. Indeed, ***the equilibrium price will change whenever the supply or demand curve shifts.***

A Demand Shift. We can illustrate how equilibrium prices change by taking one last look at the Clearview College tutoring market. Our original supply and demand curves, together with the resulting equilibrium (point E_1), are depicted in Figure 3.7. Now suppose that all the professors at Clearview begin requiring class-specific Web pages from each student. The increased need (desire) for Web-design ability will affect market demand. Tom, George, and Lisa are suddenly willing to buy more Web tutoring

Changes in Equilibrium

FIGURE 3.7
Changes in Equilibrium

If demand or supply change (shift), market equilibrium will change as well.

Demand shift. In (a), the rightward shift of the demand curve illustrates an increase in demand. When demand increases, the equilibrium price rises (from E_1 to E_2).

Supply shift. In (b), the leftward shift of the supply curve illustrates a decrease in supply. This raises the equilibrium price to E_3.

Demand and supply curves shift only when their underlying determinants change, that is, when *ceteris paribus* is violated.

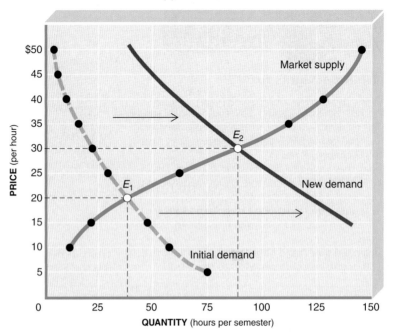

(a) A demand shift

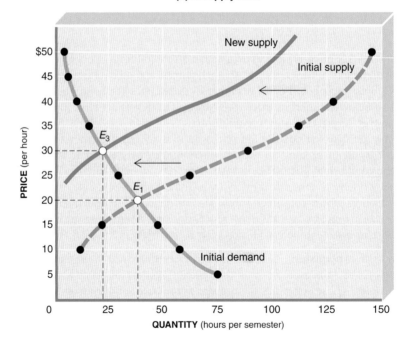

(b) A supply shift

at every price than they were before. That is, the *demand* for Web services has increased. We can represent this increased demand by a rightward *shift* of the market demand curve, as illustrated in Figure 3.7a.

Note that the new demand curve intersects the (unchanged) market supply curve at a new price (point E_2), the equilibrium price is now $30 per hour. This new equilibrium price will persist until either the demand curve or the supply curve shifts again.

A Supply Shift. Figure 3.7b illustrates a *supply* shift. The decrease (leftward shift) in supply might occur if some on-campus Webheads got sick. Or approaching exams might convince would-be tutors that they have no time to spare. ***Whenever supply decreases (shifts left), price tends to rise,*** as in Figure 3.7*b*.

The rock band U2 learned about changing equilibriums the hard way. As the NEWS on page 61 reported, ticket prices for the band's 1992 tour were below equilibrium, creating a *market shortage*. So U2 raised prices to as much as $52.50 a ticket for their 1997 tour—nearly double the 1992 price. By then, however, demand had shifted to the left, due to a lack of U2 hits and an increased number of competing concerts. By the time they got to their second city they were playing in stadiums with lots of empty seats. The apparent *market surplus* led critics to label the 1997 "Pop Mart" tour a disaster. For their 2001 "Elevation Tour," U2 offered "festival seating" for only $35.

Market outcomes shifted even more dramatically after the anthrax attacks on the U.S. mail in October 2001. Only one drug, Cipro, is approved to fight the deadly anthrax bacteria. When several people died from exposure to anthrax-laden mail, demand for Cipro soared (see NEWS below). This demand shift created an immediate market shortage.

The World View on the next page shows how rapid price adjustments can alleviate market shortages and surpluses. In this unusual case, a restaurant continuously adjusts its prices to ensure that everything on the menu is ordered.

MARKET OUTCOMES

Notice how the market mechanism resolves the basic economic questions of WHAT, HOW, and FOR WHOM.

The WHAT question refers to the amount of Web tutorial services to include in society's mix of output. The answer at Clearview College was 39 hours of tutoring per semester. This decision wasn't reached in a referendum, but instead in the market equilibrium (Figure 3.6). In the same way but on a larger scale, millions of consumers

WHAT

IN THE   NEWS

Demand for Cipro Rising

NYC Sees 62% Increase in Anti-Anthrax Prescriptions

Despite public health officials' admonitions against stockpiling drugs to protect against bioterrorism, new prescriptions for Cipro, the only drug approved to fight anthrax, in New York City have soared.

For the week ending Oct. 5, New York pharmacists filled 18,348 new prescriptions for the antibiotic, compared with just 11,313 for the same week in 2000, an increase of 62%, according to NDCHealth, a health-care information services company based in Atlanta.

Cipro, as well as a variety of other antibiotics, can prevent illness from anthrax exposure if taken before symptoms appear. Exposed individuals must take the drug for 60 days.

Still, Tommy Thompson, secretary of Health and Human Services, and other public health officials have urged Americans not to panic and hoard Cipro or other antibiotics. "You don't have to hoard antibiotics," Thompson said Friday at a briefing in which he announced a $643 million proposal to boost government stocks of antibiotics. "We're purchasing more."

Bayer, maker of Cipro, has said that it plans to reopen a German plant to meet increased demand for the drug.

—Rita Rubin

Source: *USA Today,* October 16, 2001. USA TODAY. Copyright 2001. Reprinted with permission.

Analysis: When a determinant of demand (e.g., tastes, expectations) changes, the demand curve shifts. When this happens, the equilibrium price will change.

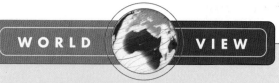

Dining on the Downtick

Americans aren't the only consumers who fall for packaging. Since late January, Parisians (not to mention TV crews from around the world) have been drawn to 6 rue Feydeau to try La Connivence, a restaurant with a new gimmick. The name means "collusion," and yes, of course, La Connivence is a block away from the Bourse, the French stock exchange.

What's the gimmick? Just that the restaurant's prices fluctuate according to supply and demand. The more a dish is ordered, the higher its price. A dish that's ignored gets cheaper.

Customers tune in to the day's menu (couched in trading terms) on computer screens. Among a typical day's options: *forte baisse du haddock* ("precipitous drop in haddock"), *vif recul de la côte de boeuf* ("rapid decline in beef ribs"), *la brochette de lotte au plus bas* ("fish kabob hits bottom"). Then comes the major decision—whether to opt for the price that's

listed when you order or to gamble that the price will have gone down by the time you finish your meal.

So far, only main dishes are open to speculation, but co-owners Pierre Guette, an ex-professor at a top French business school, and Jean-Paul Trastour, an ex-journalist at *Le Nouvel Observateur*, are adding wine to the risk list.

La Connivence is open for dinner, but the midday "session" (as the owners call it) is the one to catch. That's when the traders of Paris leave the floor to push their luck *à table*. But here, at least, the return on their $15 investment (the average price of a meal) is immediate—and usually good.

—Christina de Liagre

Source: *New York*, April 7, 1986. © 1986 K-III Magazine Corporation. All rights reserved. Reprinted with the permission of *New York* magazine. www.newyorkmag.com

Analysis: A market surplus signals that price is too high; a market shortage suggests that price is too low. This restaurant adjusts price until the quantity supplied equals the quantity demanded.

and a handful of auto producers decide to include 16 million or so cars and trucks in each year's mix of output. Auto prices and quantities adjust until consumers buy the same quantity that auto manufacturers produce.

HOW

The market mechanism also determines HOW goods are produced. Profit-seeking producers will strive to produce Web designs and automobiles in the most efficient way. They'll use market prices to decide not only WHAT to produce but also what resources to use in the production process. If new software simplifies Web design—and is priced low enough—Webheads will use it. Likewise, auto manufacturers will use robots rather than humans on the assembly line if robots reduce costs and increase profits.

FOR WHOM

Finally, the invisible hand of the market will determine who gets the goods produced. At Clearview College, who got Web tutoring? Only those students who were willing and able to pay $20 per hour for that service. FOR WHOM are all those automobiles produced each year? The answer is the same: those consumers who are willing and able to pay the market price for a new car.

Optimal, Not Perfect

Not everyone is happy with these answers, of course. Tom would like to pay only $10 an hour for a tutor. And some of the Clearview students don't have enough income to buy any tutoring. They think it's unfair that they have to design their own Web pages while richer students can have someone else do their design work for them. Students who can't afford cars are even less happy with the market's answer to the FOR WHOM question.

Although the outcomes of the marketplace aren't perfect, they're often optimal. Optimal outcomes are the best possible *given* our incomes and scarce resources. In other words, we expect the choices made in the marketplace to be the best possible choices for each participant. Why do we draw such a conclusion? Because Tom and George and everybody in our little Clearview College drama had (and continue to have) absolute freedom to make their own purchase and consumption decisions. And also because we assume that sooner or later they'll make the choices they find most satisfying. The results are *optimal* in the sense that everyone has done as well as she or he could, given their income and talents.

THE ECONOMY TOMORROW

Electric Shock: Energy-Price Spikes

The notion that markets generate optimal outcomes sounded absurd to Californians in 2000–01. As we noted earlier, wholesale energy prices jumped by over 1,000 percent in a single year. As Californians saw it, the only thing that protected them from these skyrocketing prices was government regulation. In 1996, the California legislature had set a ceiling on the *retail* price of electricity. The prices paid by consumers could *not* rise until at least 2002, no matter what happened to wholesale prices. As far as California's consumers were concerned, government intervention was their bulwark against the "price-gouging profiteers" that ruled the marketplace. Most of the state's residents welcomed Governor Gray Davis's January 2001 promises to keep cheap electricity flowing to the state's homes and businesses.

Equilibrium Pricing

As we've seen in this chapter, market prices aren't set by price-gouging profiteers. Sure, huge corporations, especially monopolies, can have a big influence on the market price of a good. But the equilibrium price must still reflect *both* sides of the market, that is, supply *and* demand. Furthermore, ***an increase in the equilibrium price can result from an increase (rightward shift) in demand or a decrease (leftward shift) of supply.*** Both shifts occurred in California.

Increased Demand

California's demand for electricity increases as its population grows and its economy expands. Abnormally cold winters or hot summers also increase the demand for electricity-driven heat and air conditioning. Between 1996 and 2001, the California economy grew by 29 percent. The winter of 2001 was colder than normal and the summer was a bit hotter than average. All these factors combined to shift the state's demand for electricity rightward as in Figure 3.8.

Decreased Supply

No new power plants or hydroelectric plants were built in California during the 1990s. The state managed to keep up with increased energy demand only by importing electricity from other states. With high-speed transmission lines, electricity can be shipped to California residents from power plants in Oregon, Idaho, and elsewhere. In 2001, however, several determinants of supply changed in adverse ways. Higher natural gas prices increased the cost of producing electricity in all states. Maintenance problems caused recurring shutdowns of California power plants. Low snowpacks reduced the power capacity of hydroelectric dams throughout the West. Market supply shifted to the left.

Disequilibrium Pricing

The consequences of a leftward supply shift and a rightward demand shift are evident in Figure 3.8; the equilibrium price of electricity skyrocketed. Residents of California didn't have to pay this higher price, however. Remember that the California legislature had put a **price ceiling** on retail electricity prices. By law, the retail price of electricity was stuck at 10 cents per kilowatt-hour, far below the new equilibrium price.

price ceiling: Upper limit imposed on the price of a good.

At first, Californians rejoiced at the low, government-set price. Then they learned the consequences of *dis*equilibrium pricing. At the ceiling price of 10 cents per kilowatt-hour, the quantity of electricity demanded (q_d in Figure 3.8) exceeded that quantity supplied (q_s). It was a classic case of *market shortage.* Because of the shortage, not everyone who was willing and able to pay the ceiling price (10 cents) could actually get the electricity they demanded. That's when the state had to resort to rolling blackouts. The blackouts left everyone with less electricity than they demanded. That experience helped convince Californians that price ceilings weren't as good as they appeared.

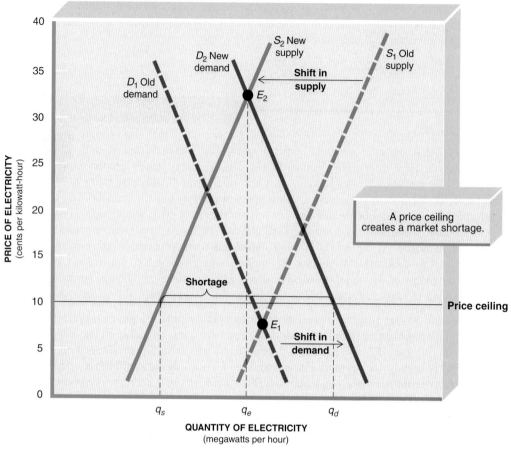

FIGURE 3.8
Price Ceilings Create Shortages

In 1996, the state of California set a price ceiling of 10 cents per kilowatt-hour. Initially, this price was above the market equilibrium (E_1) and had no impact. By 2001, however, demand had increased (to D_2) and supply had decreased (to S_2). At the ceiling price the quantity demanded (q_d) exceeded the quantity supplied (q_s), causing a market shortage and rolling blackouts. At the higher equilibrium (E_2) price there are no blackouts. Consumers reduce their energy consumption (to q_e from q_d) and power companies increase electricity deliveries (to q_e from q_s).

In fact, *price ceilings have three predictable effects; they*

- *Increase the quantity demanded.*
- *Decrease the quantity supplied.*
- *Create a market shortage.*

Given the choice between no electricity and high-priced electricity, state residents changed their view of market pricing. They didn't welcome higher prices but recognized that *higher prices*

- *Reduce quantity demanded.*
- *Increase quantity supplied.*
- *Alleviate market shortages.*

At the low, state-set price, consumers had no incentive to set air-conditioner thermostats higher, to set heater thermostats lower, or even turn off the lights and computer when they went out. At higher market prices, they'd think about those energy savings more often and reduce the quantity demanded. At the equilibrium price of E_2 in Figure 3.8, consumers are demanding (and using) less electricity than at q_d. On

IN THE NEWS

Federal Price Limits Backfire

Some Generators Withhold Power Rather Than Abide by Rate Caps

Officials in California and Nevada, after months of lobbying for federal regulators to cap Western power prices, warned yesterday that the newly imposed limits have had the unintended consequence of increasing a threat of blackouts in the two states.

The warnings were issued as California came within minutes of rolling blackouts yesterday afternoon, and one day after the first-ever rolling blackouts in Las Vegas forced energy-hungry casinos to shut off fountains and reduce air conditioning. . . .

The crux of the problem is that price limits kick in during shortages, yet power companies say these caps force them to sell power at below-market rates during periods of high demand.

Some companies have responded by holding back power rather than face the expense of shipping electricity from state to state. Each mile that electricity must be transmitted adds to the overall cost.

"No one's going to pay for transmission if the cost is near the caps," said Gary Ackerman, executive director of the Western Power Trading Forum, an energy-industry association in Menlo Park.

Ackerman said several companies in his organization decided that there was no economic advantage to offering power in regional markets when price controls are in effect.

"This means individual regions like California or Las Vegas could end up not having enough," Ackerman said. "It increases the threat of blackouts."

—David Lazarus

Source: *San Francisco Chronicle,* July 4, 2001. Copyright 2001 by the San Francisco Chronicle. Reprinted with permission. www.sfgate.com/news

Analysis: Price ceilings diminish the profitability of producing a good and so reduce the quantity supplied to the market. This may worsen market shortages.

the supply side, higher market prices encourage both in-state and out-of-state power providers to increase power-generating capacity and even sell it to California utilities. Once California residents recognized the virtue of equilibrium pricing, they saw that government intervention (price ceilings) might have been as much to blame as "power-producing profiteers" for the state's blackouts. In April 2001, the 1996 price ceiling was raised closer to equilibrium pricing with a 26 percent increase in retail electricity prices.

Other states have been affected by California's electricity crisis. The continuing demand of California residents for out-of-state power (a substitute good) has increased demand and raised electricity prices in Oregon, Nevada, Idaho, and other states in the interconnected Western power grid. As their own electricity prices rise, consumers in those states asked the government to intervene. In 2001, they convinced the federal government (the Federal Energy Regulatory Commission) to impose price ceilings across the Western grid. As the accompanying News reports, however, those price ceilings backfired. Power providers decided it made less sense to supply electricity to the price-controlled states, much less to add to power capacity; the quantity of electricity supplied declined. Blackouts soon hit other Western states.

As battles over access to energy sources continue, the patience of the public will be tested. Consumers want cheap electricity and expect elected officials to supply it. But politicians don't produce energy; private companies do. Cheap prices imposed by government not only encourage more consumption but discourage production. Moreover, power plants can't be built overnight, and new energy sources won't appear instantly. It takes *time* for market supply and demand to adjust. The greatest risk for the economy tomorrow is that political impatience today may slow the market adjustments needed to bring energy markets into equilibrium.

Looming Battles of the Power Grid

WEBNOTE

For another view of energy policy visit Public Citizen at www.citizen.org.

SUMMARY

- Individual consumers, business firms, government agencies, and foreigners participate in the marketplace by offering to buy or sell goods and services, or factors of production. Participation is motivated by the desire to maximize utility (consumers), profits (business firms), or the general welfare (government agencies) from the limited resources each participant has.
- All market transactions involve the exchange of either factors of production or finished products. Although the actual exchanges can occur anywhere, they take place in product markets or factor markets, depending on what is being exchanged.
- People willing and able to buy a particular good at some price are part of the market demand for that product. All those willing and able to sell that good at some price are part of the market supply. Total market demand or supply is the sum of individual demands or supplies.
- Supply and demand curves illustrate how the quantity demanded or supplied changes in response to a change in the price of that good, if nothing else changes (*ceteris paribus*). Demand curves slope downward; supply curves slope upward.
- Determinants of market demand include the number of potential buyers and their respective tastes (desires), incomes, other goods, and expectations. If any of these determinants change, the demand curve shifts. Movements along a demand curve are induced only by a change in the price of that good.
- Determinants of market supply include factor costs, technology, profitability of other goods, expectations, tax rates, and number of sellers. Supply shifts when these underlying determinants change.
- The quantity of goods or resources actually exchanged in each market depends on the behavior of all buyers and sellers, as summarized in market supply and demand curves. At the point where the two curves intersect, an equilibrium price—the price at which the quantity demanded equals the quantity supplied—is established.
- A distinctive feature of the equilibrium price and quantity is that it's the only price-quantity combination acceptable to buyers and sellers alike. At higher prices, sellers supply more than buyers are willing to purchase (a market surplus); at lower prices, the amount demanded exceeds the quantity supplied (a market shortage). Only the equilibrium price clears the market.
- Price ceilings are disequilibrium prices imposed on the marketplace. Such price controls create an imbalance between quantities demanded and supplied, resulting in market shortages.

Key Terms

factor market	law of demand	law of supply
product market	substitute goods	equilibrium price
supply	complementary goods	market mechanism
demand	*ceteris paribus*	price floor
opportunity cost	shift in demand	market surplus
demand schedule	market demand	market shortage
demand curve	market supply	price ceiling

Questions for Discussion

1. In our story of Tom, the student confronted with a Web-design assignment, we emphasized the great urgency of his desire for Web tutoring. Many people would say that Tom had an "absolute need" for Web help and therefore was ready to "pay anything" to get it. If this were true, what shape would his demand curve have? Why isn't this realistic?

2. With respect to the demand for college enrollment, which of the following would cause (1) a movement along the demand curve or (2) a shift of the demand curve?
   a. An increase in incomes.
   b. Lower tuition.
   c. More student loans.
   d. An increase in textbook prices.

3. Illustrate the market situation for the U2 concert (see page 61). Why didn't the concert promoters set an equilibrium price?

4. Which determinants of pizza demand change when the White House is in crisis (page 52)?

5. Can you explain the practice of scalping tickets for major sporting events in terms of market shortages? How else might tickets be distributed?

6. How else besides higher prices could the 2001 market shortage in California's electricity market have been alleviated? Consider both demand- and supply-side options.

7. What would happen in the apple market if the government set a *minimum* price of $2.00 per apple? What might motivate such a policy?

8. The World View on page 64 describes the use of prices to achieve an equilibrium in the kitchen. What happens to the food at more traditional restaurants?

9. Is there a shortage of on-campus parking at your school? How might the shortage be resolved?

10. Do Internet price information services tend to raise or lower the price consumers pay for a product?

ALERT!

PROBLEMS The Student Problem Set at the back of this book contains numerical and graphing problems for this chapter.

WEB ACTIVITIES to accompany this chapter can be found on the Online Learning Center: **http://www.mhhe.com/economics/schiller10**

The Public Sector

The market has a keen ear for private wants, but a deaf ear for public needs.
—Robert Heilbroner

Markets do work: The interaction of supply and demand in product markets *does* generate goods and services. Likewise, the interaction of supply and demand in labor markets *does* yield jobs, wages, and a distribution of income. As we've observed, the market is capable of determining WHAT goods to produce, HOW, and FOR WHOM.
But are the market's answers good enough? Is the mix of output produced by unregulated markets the best possible mix? Will producers choose the production process that strikes a desirable balance between production and the environment? Will the market-generated distribution of income be fair enough? Will there be enough jobs for everyone who wants one?

In reality, markets don't always give us the best-possible outcomes. Markets dominated by a few powerful corporations may charge excessive prices, limit output, provide poor service, or even retard technological advance. In the quest for profits, producers may sacrifice the environment for cost savings. In unfettered markets, some people may not get life-saving health care, basic education, or even adequate nutrition. When markets generate such outcomes, government intervention may be needed to ensure better answers to the WHAT, HOW, and FOR WHOM questions.

This chapter identifies the circumstances under which government intervention is desirable. To this end, we answer the following questions:

- **Under what circumstances do markets fail?**
- **How can government intervention help?**
- **How much government intervention is desirable?**

As we'll see, there's substantial agreement about how and when markets fail to give us the best WHAT, HOW, and FOR WHOM answers. But there's much less agreement about whether government intervention improves the situation. Indeed, an overwhelming majority of Americans are ambivalent about government intervention. They want the government to "fix" the mix of output, protect the environment, and ensure an adequate level of income for everyone. But voters are equally quick to blame government meddling for many of our economic woes.

MARKET FAILURE

We can visualize the potential for government intervention by focusing on the WHAT question. Our goal here is to produce the best-possible mix of output with existing resources. We illustrated this goal earlier with production possibilities curves. Figure 4.1 assumes that of all the possible combinations of output we

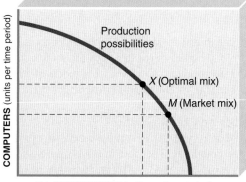

ALL OTHER GOODS (units per time period)

FIGURE 4.1
Market Failure

We can produce any mix of output on the production possibilities curve. Our goal is to produce the optimal (best-possible) mix of output, as represented by point X. Market forces, however, might produce another combination, like point M. In that case, the market fails—it produces a suboptimal mix of output.

could produce, the unique combination at point X represents the most desirable one. In other words, it's the **optimal mix of output,** the one that maximizes our collective social utility. We haven't yet figured out how to pinpoint that optimal mix; we're simply using the arbitrary point X in Figure 4.1 to represent that best-possible outcome.

Ideally, the **market mechanism** would lead us to point X. Price signals in the marketplace are supposed to move factors of production from one industry to another in response to consumer demands. If we demand more computers—offer to buy more at a given price—more resources (labor) will be allocated to computer manufacturing. Similarly, a fall in demand will encourage producers to stop making computers and offer their services in another industry. *Changes in market prices direct resources from one industry to another,* moving us along the perimeter of the production possibilities curve.

Where will the market mechanism take us? Will it move resources around until we end up at the optimal point X? Or will it leave us at another point on the production possibilities curve, with a *sub*optimal mix of output? (If point X is the *optimal,* or best-possible, mix, all other output mixes must be *sub*optimal.)

We use the term **market failure** to refer to situations where the market generates less than perfect (suboptimal) outcomes. If the invisible hand of the marketplace produces a mix of output that's different from the one society most desires, then it has failed. *Market failure implies that the forces of supply and demand haven't led us to the best point on the production possibilities curve.* Such a failure is illustrated by point M in Figure 4.1. Point M is assumed to be the mix of output generated by market forces. Notice that the market mix (M) doesn't represent the optimal mix, which is assumed to be at point X. The market in this case *fails;* we get the wrong answer to the WHAT question.

Market failure opens the door for government intervention. If the market can't do the job, we need some form of *nonmarket* force to get the right answers. In terms of Figure 4.1, we need something to change the mix of output—to move us from point M (the market mix of output) to point X (the optimal mix of output). Accordingly, *market failure establishes a basis for government intervention.* We look to the government to push market outcomes closer to the ideal.

Causes of Market Failure. Because market failure is the justification for government intervention, we need to know how and when market failure occurs. *The four specific sources of market failure are*

- *Public goods*
- *Externalities*
- *Market power*
- *Equity*

optimal mix of output: The most desirable combination of output attainable with existing resources, technology, and social values.

market mechanism: The use of market prices and sales to signal desired outputs (or resource allocations).

market failure: An imperfection in the market mechanism that prevents optimal outcomes.

We will first examine the nature of these problems, then see why government intervention is called for in each case.

Public Goods

The market mechanism has the unique capability to signal consumer demands for various goods and services. By offering to pay higher or lower prices for some goods, we express our preferences about WHAT to produce. However, this mode of communication works efficiently only if the benefits of consuming a particular good are available only to the individuals who purchase that product.

Consider doughnuts, for example. When you eat a doughnut, you alone get the satisfaction from its sweet, greasy taste—that is, you derive a private benefit. No one else benefits from your consumption of a doughnut: The doughnut you purchase in the market is yours alone to consume; it's a **private good.** Accordingly, your decision to purchase the doughnut will be determined only by your anticipated satisfaction, your income, and your opportunity costs.

> **private good:** A good or service whose consumption by one person excludes consumption by others.

No Exclusion. Most of the goods and services produced in the public sector are different from doughnuts—and not just because doughnuts look, taste, and smell different from "star wars" missile shields. When you buy a doughnut, you exclude others from consumption of that product. If Dunkin' Donuts sells you a particular pastry, it can't supply the same pastry to someone else. If you devour it, no one else can. In this sense, the transaction and product are completely private.

The same exclusiveness is not characteristic of national defense. If you buy a missile defense system to thwart enemy attacks, there's no way you can exclude your neighbors from the protection your system provides. Either the missile shield deters would-be attackers or it doesn't. In the former case, both you and your neighbors survive happily ever after; in the latter case, we're all blown away together. In that sense, you and your neighbors consume the benefits of a missile shield *jointly.* National defense isn't a divisible service. There's no such thing as exclusive consumption here. The consumption of nuclear defenses is a communal feat, no matter who pays for them. Accordingly, national defense is regarded as a **public good** in the sense that *consumption of a public good by one person doesn't preclude consumption of the same good by another person.* By contrast, a doughnut is a private good because if I eat it, no one else can consume it.

> **public good:** A good or service whose consumption by one person does not exclude consumption by others.

The Free-Rider Dilemma. The communal nature of public goods creates a dilemma. If you and I will *both* benefit from nuclear defenses, which one of us should buy the missile shield? I'd prefer that *you* buy it, thereby giving me protection at no direct cost. Hence, I may profess no desire for a missile shield, secretly hoping to take a **free ride** on your market purchase. Unfortunately, you too have an incentive to conceal your desire for national defenses. As a consequence, neither one of us may step forward to demand a missile shield in the marketplace. We'll both end up defenseless.

> **free rider:** An individual who reaps direct benefits from someone else's purchase (consumption) of a public good.

Flood control is also a public good. No one in the valley wants to be flooded out. But each landowner knows that a flood-control dam will protect *all* the landowners, regardless of who pays. Either the entire valley is protected or no one is. Accordingly, individual farmers and landowners may say they don't *want* a dam and aren't willing to *pay* for it. Everyone is waiting and hoping that someone else will pay for flood control. In other words, everyone wants a *free ride.* Thus, if we leave it to market forces, no one will *demand* flood control and all the property in the valley will be washed away.

The difference between public goods and private goods rests on *technical considerations* not political philosophy. The central question is whether we have the technical capability to exclude nonpayers. In the case of national defense or flood control, we simply don't have that capability. Even city streets have the characteristics of public goods. Although theoretically we could restrict the use of streets to those who paid to use them, a tollgate on every corner would be exceedingly expensive and impractical. Here again, joint or public consumption appears to be the only feasible alternative.

Napster Gets Napped

Shawn Fanning had a brilliant idea for getting more music: download it from friends' computers to the Internet. So he wrote software in 1999 that enabled online file-sharing of audio files. This peer-to-peer (P2P) online distribution system became an overnight sensation: in 2000–01 nearly 60 million consumers were using Napster's software to acquire recorded music.

At first blush, Napster's service looked like a classic "public good." The service was free, and one person's consumption did not impede another person from consuming the same service. Moreover, the distribution system was configured in such a way that nonpayers could not be excluded from the service.

The definition of "*public good*" relies, however, on whether nonpayers *can* be excluded, not whether they *are* excluded.

In other words, technology is critical in classifying goods as "public" or "private." In Napster's case, encryption technology that could exclude nonpayers was available, but the company had *chosen* not to use it. After being sued by major recording companies for copyright infringement, Napster changed its tune. In July 2001, it shut down its free download service. Two years later it re-opened with a *fee-based* service that could exclude nonpayers. Although free downloads are still available from offshore companies (e.g., Kazaa), fee-based services have sprung up all over (e.g., Apple's iTunes Music Store, Wal-Mart). For most consumers, music downloads are now a private good.

Source: "Napster is Back!" *NewsFlash*, October 2003.

Analysis: A product is a "public good" only if nonpayers *cannot* be excluded from its consumption. Napster had the technical ability to exclude nonpayers but initially chose not to do so. Fee-based music downloads are a private good.

As the accompanying News on Napster emphasizes, the technical capability to exclude nonpayers is the key factor in identifying "public goods."

To the list of public goods we could add snow removal, the administration of justice (including prisons), the regulation of commerce, the conduct of foreign relations, airport security, and even Fourth of July fireworks. These services—which cost tens of *billions* of dollars and employ thousands of workers—provide benefits to everyone, no matter who pays for them. In each instance it's technically impossible or prohibitively expensive to exclude nonpayers from the services provided.

Underproduction of Public Goods. The free riders associated with public goods upset the customary practice of paying for what you get. If I can get all the national defense, flood control, and laws I want without paying for them, I'm not about to complain. I'm perfectly happy to let you pay for the services while we all consume them. Of course, you may feel the same way. Why should you pay for these services if you can consume just as much of them when your neighbors foot the whole bill? It might seem selfish not to pay your share of the cost of providing public goods. But you'd be better off in a material sense if you spent your income on doughnuts, letting others pick up the tab for public services.

Because the familiar link between paying and consuming is broken, public goods can't be peddled in the supermarket. People are reluctant to buy what they can get free, a perfectly rational response for consumers who have limited incomes to spend. Hence, *if public goods were marketed like private goods, everyone would wait for someone else to pay.* The end result might be a total lack of public services. This is the kind of dilemma Robert Heilbroner had in mind when he spoke of the market's "deaf ear" (see quote at the beginning of this chapter).

The production possibilities curve in Figure 4.2 illustrates the dilemma created by public goods. Suppose that point *A* represents the optimal mix of private and public goods. It's the mix of goods and services we'd select if everyone's preferences were known and reflected in production decisions. The market mechanism won't lead us to point *A*, however, because the *demand* for public goods will be hidden. If we rely on

FIGURE 4.2
Underproduction of Public Goods

Suppose point *A* represents the optimal mix of output, that is, the mix of private and public goods that maximizes society's welfare. Because consumers won't demand purely public goods in the marketplace, the price mechanism won't allocate so many resources to their production. Instead, the market will tend to produce a mix of output like point *B*, which includes fewer public goods (*OR*) than is optimal (*OS*).

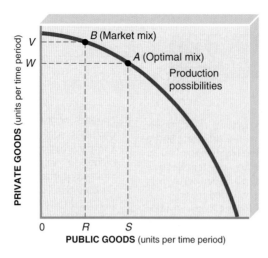

the market, nearly everyone will withhold demand for public goods, waiting for a free ride to point *A*. As a result, we'll get a smaller quantity of public goods than we really want. The market mechanism will leave us at a mix of output like that at point *B*, with few, if any, public goods. Since point *A* is assumed to be optimal, point *B* must be *suboptimal* (inferior to point *A*). The market fails: We can't rely on the market mechanism to allocate enough resources to the production of public goods, no matter how much they might be desired.

Note that we're using the term "public good" in a way different from how most people use it. To most people, "public good" refers to any good or service the government produces. In economics, however, the meaning is much more restrictive. The term "public good" refers only to those nonexcludable goods and services that must be consumed jointly, both by those who pay for them and by those who don't. Public goods can be produced by either the government or the private sector. Private goods can be produced in either sector as well. The problem is that ***the market tends to underproduce public goods and overproduce private goods.*** If we want more public goods, we need a *nonmarket* force—government intervention—to get them. The government will have to force people to pay taxes, then use the tax revenues to pay for the production of national defense, flood control, snow removal, and other public goods.

Externalities

The free-rider problem associated with public goods is one justification for government intervention. It's not the only justification, however. Further grounds for intervention arise from the tendency of costs or benefits of some market activities to "spill over" onto third parties.

Your demand for a good reflects the amount of satisfaction you expect from its consumption. The price you're willing to pay acts as a market signal to producers of your preferences. Often, however, your consumption may affect others. The purchase of cigarettes, for example, expresses a smoker's demand for that good. But others may suffer from that consumption. In this case, smoke literally spills over onto other consumers, causing them discomfort and possibly even ill health (see News on the next page). Yet their loss isn't reflected in the market: The harm caused to nonsmokers is *external* to the market price of cigarettes.

externalities: Costs (or benefits) of a market activity borne by a third party; the difference between the social and private costs (benefits) of a market activity.

The term **externalities** refers to all costs or benefits of a market activity borne by a third party, that is, by someone other than the immediate producer or consumer. ***Whenever externalities are present, market prices aren't a valid measure of a good's value to society.*** As a consequence, the market will fail to produce the right mix of output. Specifically, ***the market will underproduce goods that yield external benefits and overproduce those which generate external costs.***

Secondhand Smoke Poses Heart Attack Risk, CDC Warns

For the first time, the Centers for Disease Control and Prevention is warning people at risk of heart disease to avoid all buildings and gathering places that allow indoor smoking.

The CDC disclosed its new advisory in a commentary to a study published in the British Medical Journal yesterday, saying doctors need to warn people with heart problems that secondhand smoke can significantly increase their risk of a heart attack. The agency said that as little as 30 minutes' exposure can have a serious and even lethal effect.

The commentary accompanied a study showing that the number of heart attacks in Helena, Mont, decreased substantially after the city banned indoor smoking, then rose quickly to its former level after the law was struck down in court. . . .

Pechacek said the new study strengthens the growing body of research pointing to potentially fast and acute reactions to secondhand smoke, in addition to the long-term damage done to nonsmokers who live with smokers. The CDC has estimated that secondhand smoke causes 35,000 heart disease deaths a year in the United States, but Pechacek said that estimate is likely to be revised upward.

—Marc Kaufman

Source: *Washington Post*, April 23, 2004. © 2004 The Washington Post. Reprinted with permission.

Analysis: The health risks imposed on nonsmokers via "passive smoke" represent external costs. The market price of cigarettes doesn't reflect these costs borne by third parties.

External Costs. Figure 4.3 shows how external costs cause the market to overproduce cigarettes. The market demand curve includes only the wishes of smokers, that is, people who are willing and able to purchase cigarettes. The forces of market demand and supply result in a market equilibrium at E_M in which q_M cigarettes are produced and consumed. The market price P_M reflects the value of cigarettes to smokers.

The well-being of *non*smokers isn't reflected in the market equilibrium at E_M. To take the *non*smoker's interests into account, we must subtract the external costs

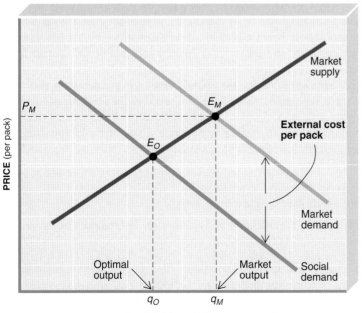

FIGURE 4.3
Externalities

The market responds to consumer demands, not externalities. Smokers demand q_M cigarettes. But external costs on nonsmokers imply that the *social* demand for cigarettes is less than (below) *market* demand. The socially optimal level of output is q_O, less than the market output q_M.

imposed on *them* from the value that *smokers* put on cigarettes. In general,

Social demand = market demand + externalities

In this case, the externality is a *cost,* so we must *subtract* the external cost from market demand to get a full accounting of social demand. The "social demand" curve in Figure 4.3 reflects this computation. To find this curve, we subtract the amount of external cost from every price on the market demand curve. What the *social* demand curve tells us is how much society would be willing and able to pay for cigarettes if the preferences of both smokers and nonsmokers were taken into account.

The social demand curve in Figure 4.3 creates a new equilibrium at q_O. This is the *optimal* quantity of cigarettes to produce (and consume). Yet the market alone would produce more than that (q_M). Government intervention may be needed to move the mix of output closer to society's optimal point.

The externalities associated with cigarette consumption have prompted many forms of government intervention, including mandatory health warnings on cigarette packaging, bans on advertising, and restrictions on locales where people may smoke. Courts have even determined that child custody decisions may be influenced by the smoking habits of the divorcing parents. All these interventions restrict the ability of individuals to maximize their personal utility in the marketplace. They're motivated by the recognition that the market mechanism responds only to the market demands of smokers and is unable to respond to nonmarketed externalities.

Externalities also exist in production. A power plant that burns high-sulfur coal damages the surrounding environment. Yet the damage inflicted on neighboring people, vegetation, and buildings is external to the cost calculations of the firm. Because the cost of such pollution is not reflected in the price of electricity, the firm will tend to produce more electricity (and pollution) than is socially desirable. To reduce this imbalance, the government has to step in and change market outcomes.

WEBNOTE

Check out the pollution problems in your neighborhood at www.epa.gov/epahome/commsearch.htm.

External Benefits. Externalities can also be beneficial. A product may generate external *benefits* rather than external *costs.* Your college is an example. The students who attend your school benefit directly from the education they receive. That's why they (and you) are willing to *pay* for tuition, books, and other services. The students in attendance aren't the only beneficiaries of this educational service, however. The research that a university conducts may yield benefits for a much broader community. The values and knowledge students acquire may also be shared with family, friends, and co-workers. These benefits would all be *external* to the market transaction between a paying student and the school. Positive externalities also arise from immunizations against infectious diseases.

If a product yields external benefits, the social demand is greater than the market demand. In this case, the social value of the good *exceeds* the market price (by the amount of external benefit). Accordingly, society wants *more* of the product than the market mechanism alone will produce at any given price. To get that additional output, the government may have to intervene with subsidies or other policies. We conclude then that *the market fails by*

- *Overproducing goods that have external costs.*
- *Underproducing goods that have external benefits.*

If externalities are present, the market won't produce the optimal mix of output. To get that optimal mix, we need government intervention.

Market Power

In the case of both public goods and externalities, the market fails to achieve the optimal mix of output because the price signal is flawed. The price consumers are willing and able to pay for a specific good doesn't reflect all the benefits or cost of producing that good.

The market may fail, however, even when the price signals are accurate. The *response* to price signals, rather than the signals themselves, may be flawed.

Restricted Supply. Market power is often the cause of a flawed response. Suppose there were only one airline company in the world. This single seller of airline travel would be a **monopoly**—that is, the only producer in that industry. As a monopolist, the airline could charge extremely high prices without worrying that travelers would flock to a competing airline. At the same time, the high prices paid by consumers would express the importance of that service to society. Ideally, such prices would act as a signal to producers to build and fly more planes—to change the mix of output. But a monopolist doesn't have to cater to every consumer's whim. It can limit airline travel and obstruct our efforts to achieve an optimal mix of output.

> **monopoly:** A firm that produces the entire market supply of a particular good or service.

Monopoly is the most severe form of **market power.** More generally, market power refers to any situation in which a single producer or consumer has the ability to alter the market price of a specific product. If the publisher (McGraw-Hill) charges a high price for this book, you'll have to pay the tab. McGraw-Hill has market power because there are relatively few economics textbooks and your professor has required you to use this one. You don't have power in the textbook market because your decision to buy or not won't alter the market price of this text. You're only one of the million students who are taking an introductory economics course this year.

> **market power:** The ability to alter the market price of a good or a service.

The market power McGraw-Hill possesses is derived from the copyright on this text. No matter how profitable textbook sales might be, no one else is permitted to produce or sell this particular book. Patents are another common source of market power because they also preclude others from making or selling a specific product. Market power may also result from control of resources, restrictive production agreements, or efficiencies of large-scale production.

Whatever the source of market power, the direct consequence is that one or more producers attain discretionary power over the market's response to price signals. They may use that discretion to enrich themselves rather than to move the economy toward the optimal mix of output. In this case, the market will again fail to deliver the most desired goods and services.

The mandate for government intervention in this case is to prevent or dismantle concentrations of market power. That's the basic purpose of **antitrust** policy. Another option is to *regulate* market behavior. This was one of the goals of the antitrust case against Microsoft. The government was less interested in breaking Microsoft's near monopoly on operating systems than in changing the way Microsoft behaved.

> **antitrust:** Government intervention to alter market structure or prevent abuse of market power.

In some cases, it may be economically efficient to have one large firm supply an entire market. Such a situation arises in **natural monopoly,** where a single firm can achieve economies of scale over the entire range of market output. Utility companies, local telephone service, subway systems, and cable all exhibit such scale (size) efficiencies. In these cases, a monopoly *structure* may be economically desirable. The government may have to regulate the *behavior* of a natural monopoly, however, to ensure that consumers get the benefits of that greater efficiency.

> **natural monopoly:** An industry in which one firm can achieve economies of scale over the entire range of market supply.

Public goods, externalities, and market power all cause resource misallocations. Where these phenomena exist, the market mechanism will fail to produce the optimal mix of output in the best-possible way.

Inequity

Beyond the questions of WHAT and HOW to produce, we're also concerned about FOR WHOM output is produced. The market answers this question by distributing a larger share of total output to those with the most income. Although this result may be efficient, it's not necessarily equitable. As we saw in Chapter 2, the market mechanism may enrich some people while leaving others to seek shelter in abandoned cars. If such outcomes violate our vision of equity, we may want the government to change the market-generated distribution of income.

Taxes and Transfers. The tax-and-transfer system is the principal mechanism for redistributing incomes. The idea here is to take some of the income away from those who have "too much" and give it to those whom the market has left with "too little." Taxes are levied to take back some of the income received from the market. Those tax revenues are then redistributed via transfer payments to those deemed needy, such as the poor, the aged, the unemployed. **Transfer payments** are income payments for which no goods or services are exchanged. They're used to bolster the incomes of those for whom the market itself provides too little.

> **transfer payments:** Payments to individuals for which no current goods or services are exchanged, like Social Security, welfare, and unemployment benefits.

Merit Goods. Often, our vision of what is "too little" is defined in terms of specific goods and services. There is a widespread consensus in the United States that everyone is entitled to some minimum levels of shelter, food, and health care. These are regarded as **merit goods,** in the same sense that everyone merits at least some minimum provision of such goods. When the market does not distribute that minimum provision, the government is called on to fill in the gaps. In this case, the income transfers take the form of *in-kind* transfers (e.g., Food Stamps, housing vouchers, Medicaid) rather than *cash* transfers (e.g., welfare checks, Social Security benefits).

> **merit good:** A food or service society deems everyone is entitled to some minimal quantity of.

Some people argue that we don't need the government to help the poor—that private charity alone will suffice. Unfortunately, private charity alone has never been adequate. One reason private charity doesn't suffice is the "free-rider" problem. If I contribute heavily to the poor, you benefit from safer streets (fewer muggers), a better environment (fewer slums and homeless people), and a clearer conscience (knowing fewer people are starving). In this sense, the relief of misery is a *public* good. Were I the only taxpayer to benefit substantially from the reduction of poverty, then charity would be a private affair. As long as income support substantially benefits the public at large, then income redistribution is a *public* good, for which public funding is appropriate. This is the *economic* rationale for public income-redistribution activities. To this rationale one can add such moral arguments as seem appropriate.

Macro Instability

The micro failures of the marketplace imply that we're at the wrong point on the production possibilities curve or inequitably distributing the output produced. There's another basic question we've swept under the rug, however. How do we get to the production possibilities curve in the first place? To reach the curve, we must utilize all available resources and technology. Can we be confident that the invisible hand of the marketplace will use all available resources? Or will some people face **unemployment**—that is, be willing to work but unable to find a job?

> **unemployment:** The inability of labor-force participants to find jobs.

And what about prices? Price signals are a critical feature of the market mechanism. But the validity of those signals depends on some stable measure of value. What good is a doubling of salary when the price of everything you buy doubles as well? Generally, rising prices will enrich people who own property and impoverish people who rent. That's why we strive to avoid **inflation**—a situation in which the *average* price level is increasing.

> **inflation:** An increase in the average level of prices of goods and services.

Historically, the marketplace has been wracked with bouts of both unemployment and inflation. These experiences have prompted calls for government intervention at the macro level. *The goal of macro intervention is to foster economic growth—to get us on the production possibilities curve (full employment), maintain a stable price level (price stability), and increase our capacity to produce (growth).*

GROWTH OF GOVERNMENT

The potential micro and macro failures of the marketplace provide specific justifications for government intervention. The question then turns to how well the activities of the public sector correspond to these implied mandates.

Until the 1930s the federal government's role was largely limited to national defense (a public good), enforcement of a common legal system (also a public good), and provision of postal service (equity). The Great Depression of the 1930s spawned a new range of government activities, including welfare and Social Security programs (equity), minimum wage laws and workplace standards (regulation), and massive public works (public goods and externalities). In the 1950s the federal government also assumed a greater role in maintaining macroeconomic stability (macro failure), protecting the environment (externalities), and safeguarding the public's health (externalities and equity).

These increasing responsibilities have greatly increased the size of the public sector. In 1902 the federal government employed fewer than 350,000 people and spent a mere $650 *million*. Today the federal government employs nearly 4 million people and spends roughly $2.5 *trillion* a year.

Direct Expenditure. Figure 4.4 summarizes the growth of the public sector since 1930. World War II caused a massive increase in the size of the federal government. Federal purchases of goods and services for the war accounted for over 40 percent of total output during the 1943–44 period. The federal share of total U.S. output fell abruptly after World War II, rose again during the Korean War (1950–53) and has declined slightly since then.

The decline in the federal share of total output is somewhat at odds with most people's perception of government growth. This discrepancy is explained by two phenomena. First, people see the *absolute* size of the government growing every year. But we're focusing here on the *relative* size of the public sector. Since the 1950s the public sector has grown a bit more slowly than the private sector, slightly reducing

FIGURE 4.4
Government Growth

During World War II the public sector purchased nearly half of total U.S. output. Since the early 1950s the public-sector share of total output has been closer to 20 percent. Within the public sector, however, there's been a major shift: State and local claims on resources have grown, while the federal share has declined significantly.

Source: *Economic Report of the President, 2004.*

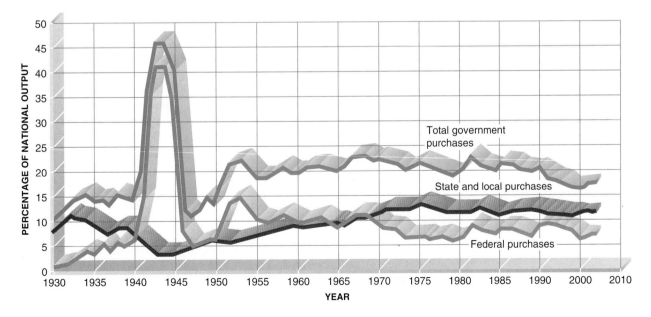

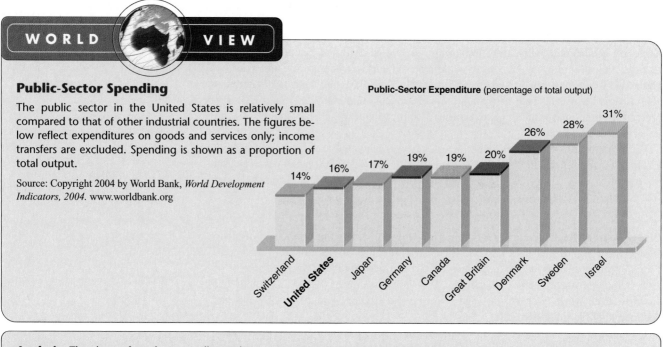

WORLD VIEW

Public-Sector Spending

The public sector in the United States is relatively small compared to that of other industrial countries. The figures below reflect expenditures on goods and services only; income transfers are excluded. Spending is shown as a proportion of total output.

Source: Copyright 2004 by World Bank, *World Development Indicators, 2004.* www.worldbank.org

Public-Sector Expenditure (percentage of total output)

- Switzerland 14%
- United States 16%
- Japan 17%
- Germany 19%
- Canada 19%
- Great Britain 20%
- Denmark 26%
- Sweden 28%
- Israel 31%

Analysis: The share of total output allocated to government services varies widely across nations. In the United States, the government share of output is relatively low.

its relative size. As the accompanying World View shows, other industrialized countries have significantly larger public sectors.

Income Transfers. Figure 4.4 depicts only government spending on goods and services, not *all* public spending. Not included in our depiction of government growth is spending on income transfers. Direct expenditure on goods and services absorbs real resources, but income transfers don't. Hence, income transfers don't directly alter the mix of output. Their effect is primarily *distributional* (the FOR WHOM question), not *allocative* (the WHAT question). Were income transfers included, the relative size and growth of the federal government would be larger than Figure 4.4 depicts. This is because **most of the growth in federal spending has come from increased income transfers, not purchases of goods and services.**

State and Local Growth

State and local spending on goods and services has followed a very different path from federal expenditure. Prior to World War II, state and local governments dominated public-sector spending. During the war, however, the share of total output going to state and local governments fell, hitting a low of 3 percent in that period (Figure 4.4).

State and local spending caught up with federal spending in the mid-1960s and has exceeded it ever since. Today more than 80,000 state and local government entities buy much more output than Uncle Sam and employ five times as many people.

Figure 4.5 is an overview of state and local budgets. Education is a huge expenditure at both levels of government. Most direct state spending is on colleges; most local spending is for elementary and secondary education. The fastest-growing areas for state expenditure are prisons (public safety) and welfare. At the local level, sewage and trash services are claiming an increasing share of budgets.

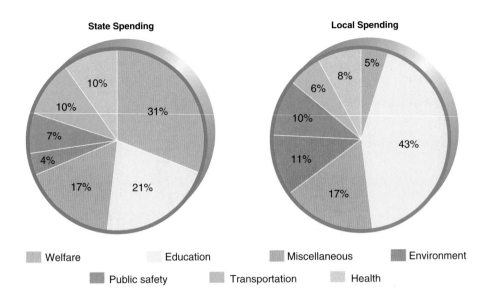

FIGURE 4.5
State and Local Spending

Spending on education and welfare accounts for half of all state and local expenditure. There are important differences, however, in the content of spending at each level of government.

Source: U.S. Bureau of the Census.

TAXATION

Whatever we may think of any specific government expenditure, we must recognize one basic fact of life: We pay for government spending. We pay not just in terms of tax *dollars* but in the more fundamental form of a changed mix of output. Government expenditures on goods and services absorb factors of production that could be used to produce consumer goods. The mix of output changes toward *more* public services and *less* private goods and services. Resources used to produce missile shields or elementary schools aren't available to produce cars, houses, or restaurant meals. In real terms, **the cost of government spending is measured by the private-sector output sacrificed when the government employs scarce factors of production.**

The **opportunity costs** of public spending aren't always apparent. We don't directly hand over factors of production to the government. Instead, we give the government part of our income in the form of taxes. Those dollars are then used to buy factors of production or goods and services in the marketplace. Thus, *the primary function of taxes is to transfer command over resources (purchasing power) from the private sector to the public sector.* Although the government sometimes also borrows dollars to finance its purchases, taxes are the primary source of government revenues.

As recently as 1902, much of the revenue the federal government collected came from taxes imposed on alcoholic beverages. The federal government didn't have authority to collect income taxes. As a consequence, *total* federal revenue in 1902 was only $653 million.

Income Taxes. All that has changed. The Sixteenth Amendment to the U.S. Constitution, enacted in 1915, granted the federal government authority to collect income taxes. The government now collects nearly $1 *trillion* in that form alone. Although the federal government still collects taxes on alcoholic beverages, the individual income tax has become the largest single source of government revenue (see Figure 4.6).

In theory, the federal income tax is designed to be **progressive**—that is, to take a larger *fraction* of high incomes than of low incomes. In 2004, for example, a single person with less than $7,800 of income paid no federal income tax. The next $7,000 of income was taxed at 10 percent, however. People with incomes of $50,000–$70,000 confronted a 25 percent tax rate on their additional income. The marginal tax rate got as high as 35 percent for people earning more than $300,000 in income. Thus people with high incomes not only pay more taxes but also pay a larger *fraction* of their income in taxes.

opportunity costs: The most desired goods or services that are forgone in order to obtain something else.

Federal Taxes

progressive tax: A tax system in which tax rates rise as incomes rise.

FIGURE 4.6
Federal Taxes

Taxes transfer purchasing power from the private sector to the public sector. The largest federal tax is the individual income tax. The second-largest source of federal revenue is the Social Security payroll tax.

Source: Office of Management and Budget, FY2005 data.

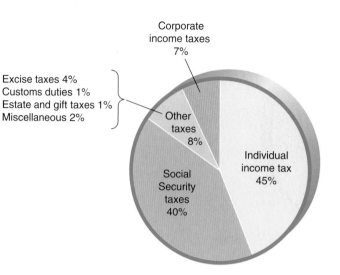

Corporate income taxes 7%

Excise taxes 4%
Customs duties 1%
Estate and gift taxes 1%
Miscellaneous 2%

Other taxes 8%

Social Security taxes 40%

Individual income tax 45%

proportional tax: A tax that levies the same rate on every dollar of income.

regressive tax: A tax system in which tax rates fall as incomes rise.

WEBNOTE

The Office of Management and Budget's "A Citizen's Guide to the Federal Budget" provides convenient charts and data on federal revenues. See www.whitehouse.gov/omb/budget or www.access.gpo.gov.su_docs/budgetguide.html.

Social Security Taxes. The second major source of federal revenue is the Social Security payroll tax. People working now transfer part of their earnings to retired workers by making "contributions" to Social Security. There's nothing voluntary about these "contributions"; they take the form of mandatory payroll deductions. In 2004, each worker paid 7.65 percent of his or her wages to Social Security and employers contributed an equal amount. As a consequence, the government collected nearly $750 billion.

At first glance, the Social Security payroll tax looks like a **proportional tax,** that is, a tax that takes the *same* fraction of every taxpayer's income. But this isn't the case. The Social Security (FICA) tax isn't levied on every payroll dollar. Incomes above a certain ceiling (roughly $90,000 per year) aren't taxed. As a result, workers with really high salaries turn over a smaller fraction of their incomes to Social Security than do low-wage workers. This makes the Social Security payroll tax a **regressive tax.**

Corporate Taxes. The federal government taxes the profits of corporations as well as the incomes of consumers. But there are far fewer corporations (less than 4 million) than consumers (300 million), and their profits are small in comparison to total consumer income. In 2004, the federal government collected only $150 billion in corporate income taxes, despite the fact that it imposed a top tax rate of 38 percent on corporate profits.

"I can't find anything wrong here, Mr. Truffle . . . you just seem to have too much left after taxes."

Analysis: Taxes are a financing mechanism that enable the government to purchase scarce resources. Higher taxes imply less private-sector purchases.

Excise Taxes. The last major source of federal revenue is excise taxes. Like the early taxes on whiskey, excise taxes are sales taxes imposed on specific goods and services. The federal government taxes not only liquor ($13.50 per gallon) but also gasoline (18.4 cents per gallon), cigarettes (39 cents per pack), telephone service (3 percent), air fares, and a variety of other goods and services. Such taxes not only discourage production and consumption of these goods—by raising their price and thereby reducing the quantity demanded—they also raise a substantial amount of revenue.

Taxes. State and local governments also levy taxes on consumers and businesses. In general, cities depend heavily on property taxes, and state governments rely heavily on sales taxes (see Figure 4.7). Although nearly all states and many cities also impose income taxes, effective tax rates are so low (averaging less than 2 percent of personal income) that income tax revenues are much less than sales and property tax revenues.

Like the Social Security payroll tax, state and local taxes tend to be *regressive*—that is, they take a larger share of income from the poor than from the rich. Consider a 4 percent sales tax, for example. It might appear that a uniform tax rate like this would affect all consumers equally. But people with lower incomes tend to spend most of their income on goods and services. Thus, most of their income is subject to sales taxes. By contrast, a person with a high income can afford to save part of his or her income and thereby shelter it from sales taxes. A family that earns $40,000 and spends $30,000 of it on taxable goods and services, for example, pays $1,200 in sales taxes when the tax rate is 4 percent. In effect, then, they are handing over 3 percent of their *income* ($1,200 ÷ $40,000) to the state. By contrast, the family that makes only $12,000 and spends $11,500 of it for food, clothing, and shelter pays $460 in sales taxes in the same state. Their total tax is smaller, but it represents a much larger *share* (3.8 versus 3.0 percent) of their income.

Local property taxes are also regressive because poor people devote a larger portion of their incomes to housing costs. Hence, a larger share of a poor family's income is subject to property taxes. According to the Advisory Council on Intergovernmental Relations, a family earning $50,000 a year devotes only 2.5 percent of its income to property taxes, whereas a family earning $10,000 pays out 4.5 percent of its income in property taxes. State lotteries are also regressive, for the same reason (see News). Low-income players spend 1.4 percent of their incomes on lottery tickets while upper-income players devote only 0.1 percent of their income to lottery purchases.

Current excise tax rates are available from the U.S. Bureau of Alcohol, Tobacco, and Firearms. See www.atf.treas.gov.

State and Local Revenues

The U.S. Census Bureau compiles the most comprehensive data on state and local government finances. For details visit www.census.gov/ftp/pub.

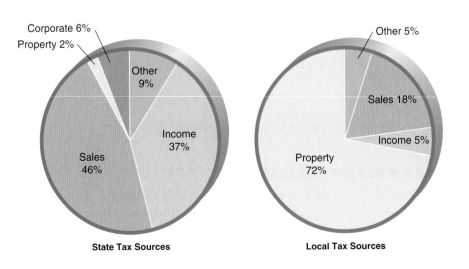

State Tax Sources

- Corporate 6%
- Property 2%
- Other 9%
- Income 37%
- Sales 46%

Local Tax Sources

- Other 5%
- Sales 18%
- Income 5%
- Property 72%

FIGURE 4.7
State and Local Tax Sources

State governments get half their tax revenue from sales taxes. By contrast, local governments depend heavily on property taxes.

Source: U.S. Department of Commerce (2000–01 data).

Soaking the Poor:

The Incidence of State-Sponsored Gambling

With many states suffering tax shortfalls and budget deficits, state-sponsored gambling again is offering a temptingly easy source of new revenue. Some argue that state-sponsored lotteries, slot machines, and other gambling opportunities simply give the local government the gambling profits that otherwise would have gone elsewhere, to other states or to the illegal gambling industry. Opponents of state-sponsored gambling respond that revenues derived from gambling take money that families otherwise would have spent on other kinds of consumption and that it affects the poor more than the rich;

these "voluntary taxes" are highly regressive, amounting to little more than the state picking the pocket of the poor and the ignorant.

A new study sheds light on this debate. Professor Melissa Kearney of Wellesley College reports that . . . the poor spend about the same number of dollars on lottery tickets (about $165 per adult per year) as those who are better off, so they spend a much larger share of their income on state lotteries.

—Bernard Wasow

Source: The Century Foundation, November 2002.

Analysis: Poor people spend a larger percentage of their income on lottery tickets than do rich people. This makes lotteries a regressive source of government revenue.

---

categorical grants: Federal grants to state and local governments for specific expenditure purposes.

Federal Aid. Up until 1986, the federal government gave state and local governments some of its revenues for whatever purposes those entities desired. But such general *revenue sharing* was always small. Most federal aid to state and local governments is in the form of **categorical grants,** that is, grants that can be used only for specific activities. For example, the federal government spent $30 billion on natural resources and environment in 2004. But one-fifth of this amount was simply given to local communities for the construction of sewage treatment plants. The local governments actually purchased or built these plants; the federal government only provided the necessary revenue. Accordingly, the federal government maintained control over WHAT to produce, but local governments exercised some judgment on HOW to produce it.

In 2004, the federal government gave over $400 billion to state and local governments in the form of categorical grants (including those for employment programs, Medicaid, schools, and highways). These federal grants accounted for about one-fifth of all state and local revenues.

user charge: Fee paid for the use of a public-sector good or service.

User Charges. The third major source of state and local revenues consists of **user charges.** The tuition that college students (or their parents) pay for attending a state university or community college is an all-too-familiar user charge. But tuition fees never cover the full costs of maintaining public colleges. Part of the costs of providing higher education are borne by all state taxpayers, whether or not they attend college. Public hospitals and highways are financed the same way, with users paying part of the costs directly and all taxpayers paying the remaining costs through state and local taxes. Hence, user charges aren't identical to market prices because they're not intended to cover the full costs of supplying a particular good.

GOVERNMENT FAILURE

Some government intervention in the marketplace is clearly desirable. The market mechanism can fail for a variety of reasons, leaving a laissez-faire economy short of its economic goals. But how much government intervention is desirable? Communist nations once thought that complete government control of production, consumption,

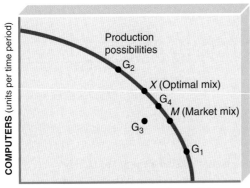

FIGURE 4.8
Government Failure

When the market produces a subop-timal mix of output (point *M*), the goal of government is to move output to the social optimum (point *X*). A move to G_4 would be an improvement in the mix of output. But government inter-vention *may* move the economy to points G_1, G_2, or G_3—all reflecting government failure.

and distribution decisions was the surest path to utopia. They learned the hard way that not only markets but governments as well can fail.

In this context, **government failure** means that government intervention fails to move us closer to our economic goals.

In Figure 4.8, the goal of government intervention is to move the mix of output from point *M* (failed market outcome) to point *X* (the social optimum). But gov-ernment intervention might unwittingly move us to point G_1, making matters worse. Or the government might overreact, sending us to point G_2. Red tape and onerous regulation might even force us to point G_3, *inside* the production possibilities curve (with less total output than at point *M*). All those possibilities (G_1, G_2, G_3) repre-sent government failure. Government intervention is desirable only to the extent that it *improves* market outcomes (e.g., G_4). Government intervention in the FOR WHOM question is desirable only if the distribution of income gets better, not worse, as a result of taxes and transfers. Even when outcomes improve, government failure may occur if the costs of government intervention exceeded the benefits of an improved output mix, cleaner production methods, or a fairer distribution of income.

> **government failure:** Government intervention that fails to improve economic outcomes.

Taxpayers seem to have strong opinions about government failure. When asked whether the government "wastes" their tax dollars or uses them well, the majority see waste in government (see News on "Persistent Doubts"). The average taxpayer now believes that state governments waste 29 cents out of each dollar, while the federal government wastes 42 cents out of each tax dollar!

Government "waste" implies that the public sector isn't producing as many serv-ices as it could with the sources at its disposal. Such inefficiency implies that we're producing somewhere *inside* our production possibilities curve rather than on it (e.g., point G_3 in Figure 4.8). If the government is wasting resources this way, we can't possibly be producing the optimal mix of output.

Perceptions of Waste

Even if the government weren't wasting resources, it might still be guilty of govern-ment failure. As important as efficiency in government may be, it begs the larger question of how many government services we really want. In reality, *the issue of government waste encompasses two distinct questions:*

Opportunity Cost

- *Efficiency:* Are we getting as much service as we could from the resources we allocate to government?
- *Opportunity cost:* Are we giving up too many private-sector goods in order to get those services?

If the government is producing goods inefficiently, we end up *inside* the produc-tion possibilities curve, with less output than attainable. Even if the government is efficient, however, the *mix* of output may not be optimal, as points G_1 and G_2 in

IN THE NEWS

Persistent Doubts about Government Waste

Question: Do you think that people in government waste a lot of the money we pay in taxes, waste some of it, or don't waste very much of it?

Source: University of Michigan. www.umich.edu

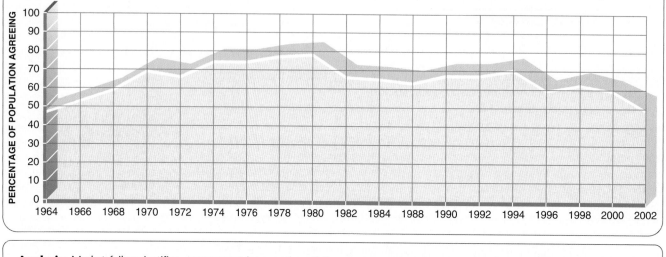

"The Government Wastes a Lot of Tax Money"

Analysis: Market failure justifies government intervention. If the government wastes resources, however, it too may fail to satisfy our economic goals.

WEBNOTE

For more public opinion on the role of government, visit the University of Michigan's National Election Studies site at www.umich.edu/~nes/nesguide/gd-index.htm.

Figure 4.8 illustrate. ***Everything the government does entails an opportunity cost.*** The more police officers or schoolteachers employed by the public sector, the fewer workers available to private producers and consumers. Similarly, the more computers, pencils, and paper consumed by government agencies, the fewer accessible to individuals and private companies.

When assessing government's role in the economy, ***we must consider not only what governments do but also what we give up to allow them to do it.*** The theory of public goods tells us only what activities are appropriate for government, not the proper *level* of such activity. National defense is clearly a proper function of the public sector. Not so clear, however, is how much the government should spend on tanks, aircraft carriers, and missile shields. The same is true of environmental protection or law enforcement.

The concept of opportunity costs puts a new perspective on the whole question of government size. Before we can decide how big is "too big," we must decide what we're willing to give up to support the public sector. A military force of 1.4 million men and women is "too big" from an economic perspective only if we value the forgone private production and consumption more highly than we value the added strength of our defenses. The government has gone "too far" if the highway it builds is less desired than the park and homes it implicitly replaced. In these and all cases, the assessment of bigness must come back to a comparison of what is given up with what is received. The assessment of government failure thus comes back to points on the production possibilities curve. Has the government moved us closer to the optimal mix of output (e.g., point G_4 in Figure 4.8) or not?

This is a tough question to answer in the abstract. We can, however, use the concept of opportunity cost to assess the effectiveness of specific government interventions. From this perspective, *additional public-sector activity is desirable only if the benefits from that activity exceed its opportunity costs.* In other words, we compare the benefits of a public project to the value of the private goods given up to produce it. By performing this calculation repeatedly along the perimeter of the production possibilities curve, we could locate the optimal mix of output—the point at which no further increase in public-sector spending activity is desirable.

This same principle can be used to decide *which* goods to produce within the public sector. A public project is desirable only to the extent that it promises to yield some benefits (or utility). But all public projects involve opportunity costs. Hence, a project should be pursued only if its anticipated benefits exceeded the value of alternative resource uses. In this sense, the public sector confronts the same kind of dilemma we consumers have. There are hundreds of goods and services we'd *like* to have, but scarce resources require us to select only the best possible ones. That implies getting the highest possible ratio of benefits to costs.

Valuation Problems. Although the principles of cost-benefit analysis are simple enough, they're deceptive. How are we to measure the potential benefits of improved police services, for example? Should we estimate the number of robberies and murders prevented, calculate the worth of each, and add up the benefits? And how are we supposed to calculate the worth of a saved life? By a person's earnings? value of assets? number of friends? And what about the increased sense of security people have when they know the police are patrolling in their neighborhood? Should this be included in the benefit calculation? Some people will attach great value to this service; others will attach little. Whose values should be the standard?

When we're dealing with (private) market goods and services, we can gauge the benefits of a product by the amount of money consumers are willing to pay for it. This price signal isn't available for most public services, however, because of externalities and the nonexclusive nature of pure public goods (the free-rider problem). Hence, *the value (benefits) of public services must be estimated because they don't have (reliable) market prices.* This opens the door to endless political squabbles about how beneficial any particular government activity is.

The same problems arise in evaluating the government's efforts to redistribute incomes. Government transfer payments now go to retired workers, disabled people, veterans, farmers, sick people, students, pregnant women, unemployed people, poor people, and a long list of other recipients. To pay for all these transfers, the government must raise tax revenues. With so many people paying taxes and receiving transfer payments, the net effects on the distribution of income aren't easy to figure out. Yet we can't determine whether this government intervention is worth it until we know how the FOR WHOM answer was changed and what the tax-and-transfer effort cost us. Here again, there's at least a possibility of government failure.

In practice, we rely on political mechanisms, not cost-benefit calculations, to decide what to produce in the public sector and how to redistribute incomes. *Voting mechanisms substitute for the market mechanism in allocating resources to the public sector and deciding how to use them.* Some people have even suggested that the variety and volume of public goods are determined by the most votes, just as the variety and volume of private goods are determined by the most dollars. Thus, governments choose that level and mix of output (and related taxation) that seem to command the most votes.

Sometimes the link between the ballot box and output decisions is very clear and direct. State and local governments, for example, are often compelled to get voter approval before building another highway, school, housing project, or sewage plant. *Bond referenda* are direct requests by a government unit for the authority and

Cost-Benefit Analysis

Ballot Box Economics

The National Conference of State Legislatures tracks bond referenda and other ballot issues. Visit them at www.ncsl.org to review recent ballots.

purchasing power to expand the production of particular public goods. In 2002, for example, governments sought voter approval for $22 billion of new borrowing to finance public expenditure; over 60 percent of those requests were approved.

Although the direct link between bond referenda and spending decisions is important, it's more the exception than the rule. Bond referenda account for less than 1 percent of state and local expenditures (and none of federal expenditures). As a consequence, voter control of public spending is much less direct. Although federal agencies must receive authorization from Congress for all expenditures, consumers get a chance to elect new representatives only every two years. Much the same is true at state and local levels. Voters may be in a position to dictate the general level and pattern of public expenditures but have little direct influence on everyday output decisions. In this sense, the ballot box is a poor substitute for the market mechanism.

Even if the link between the ballot box and allocation decisions were stronger, the resulting mix of output might not be optimal. A democratic vote, for example, might yield a 51 percent majority for approval of new local highways. Should the highways then be built? The answer isn't obvious. After all, a large minority (49 percent) of the voters have stated that they don't want resources used this way. If we proceed to build the highways, we'll make those people worse off. Even the voters who voted for the highways may end up worse off, depending on how the benefits and costs of the highway are distributed and what other opportunities exist. The basic dilemma is really twofold. *We don't know what the real demand for public services is, and votes alone don't reflect the intensity of individual demands.* Moreover, real-world decision making involves so many choices that a stable consensus is impossible.

Public-Choice Theory

In the midst of all this complexity and uncertainty, another factor may be decisive—namely, self-interest. In principle, government officials are supposed to serve the people. It doesn't take long, however, before officials realize that the public is indecisive about what it wants and takes very little interest in government's day-to-day activities. With such latitude, government officials can set their own agendas. Those agendas may give higher priority to personal advancement than to the needs of the public. Agency directors may foster new programs that enlarge their mandate, enhance their visibility, and increase their prestige or income. Members of Congress may likewise pursue legislative favors like tax breaks for supporters more diligently than they pursue the general public interest. In such cases, the probability of attaining the optimal mix of output declines.

public choice: Theory of public-sector behavior emphasizing rational self-interest of decision makers and voters.

The theory of **public choice** emphasizes the role of self-interest in public decision making. Public-choice theory essentially extends the analysis of market behavior to political behavior. Public officials are assumed to have specific personal goals (for example, power, recognition, wealth) that they'll pursue in office. *A central tenet of public-choice theory is that bureaucrats are just as selfish (utility maximizing) as everyone else.*

Public-choice theory provides a neat and simple explanation for public-sector decision making. But critics argue that the theory provides a woefully narrow view of public servants. Some people do selflessly pursue larger, public goals, such critics argue, and ideas can overwhelm self-interest. Steven Kelman of Harvard, for example, argues that narrow self-interest can't explain the War on Poverty of the 1960s, the tax revolt of the 1970s, or the deregulation movement of the 1980s. These tidal changes in public policy reflect the power of ideas, not simple self-interest.

Although self-interest can't provide a complete explanation of public decision making, it adds important perspectives on the policy process. James Buchanan of George Mason University (Virginia) won the 1986 Nobel Prize in economics for helping develop this public-choice perspective. It adds a personal dimension to the faceless mechanics of ballot box economics, cost-benefit analysis, and other "objective" mechanisms of public-sector decision making.

Downsizing Government

The Great Depression of the 1930s devastated the world economy. For many people, it was compelling evidence that the market alone couldn't be trusted to answer the WHAT, HOW, and FOR WHOM questions. With unemployment, hunger, and homelessness at record levels, people everywhere turned to government for help. In the United States, Franklin Roosevelt's New Deal envisioned a more activist government, restoring full employment and assuring everyone some minimal level of economic security. In Eastern Europe, the Communist Party advanced the notion that outright government *control* of the economy was the only sure way to attain economic justice for all.

Confidence in the ability of government to resolve core economic issues continued to increase in the post–World War II era. Securing national defenses during the Cold War (1948–89) justified the maintenance of a large military establishment, both in the United States and elsewhere. The War on Poverty that began in the mid-1960s brought about a huge increase in government social programs and income transfers. As the U.S. population has aged, the government's health care and retirement programs (e.g., Social Security, military and civilian government pensions) have grown rapidly. In each case, there was a political consensus that expanded public services would enhance society's welfare. That consensus helped grow *total* federal spending (including purchases and income transfers) from 17 percent of GDP in 1965 to over 23 percent in 1982.

Deficit Financing. President Reagan railed against the relentless growth of the federal government. To reverse that growth, he pushed a massive tax cut through Congress, hoping thereby to cut off the major source of government finances. But he couldn't convince Congress to reduce social-program spending, and he wanted more military spending. So the federal government kept growing, using *borrowed* money to replace the lost tax revenue.

Military Cutbacks. The end of the Cold War sparked a significant cutback in military outlays. Between 1991 and 1998, annual military spending declined by $35 *billion* a year. The size of the armed forces shrank by nearly 500,000 personnel. All these "guns" weren't converted to civilian "butter," however. As military spending declined in the 1990s, federal social spending continued to increase. As a result, the federal share of total output declined very slowly.

Nonmilitary Downsizing. Public opinion has not kept pace with the continued growth of federal programs. As we noted earlier, most taxpayers think the government wastes a lot of money. More to the point, a 2003 CBS news survey revealed that Americans are highly skeptical about the federal government's ability to fix things. As the News on the next page shows, only 4 percent of the population "always" trusts the government to do what is right. A lot of people now suspect government intervention *creates* more problems than it solves.

The increasing skepticism about government intervention has prompted a worldwide downsizing of the public sector. The downsizing has been most dramatic in the former communist nations, like the Soviet Union, where the mechanisms of central planning have been removed. In Europe, Latin America, and Asia, the downsizing of government has taken the form of privatization of government-owned industries such as railroads, airlines, and telephone service. In the United States, every president since Reagan has made the downsizing of government a policy priority. To achieve that goal, however, requires chipping away at specific programs. That's always the hard part. The war against terrorism that began in September 2001 abruptly reversed the downtrend in defense spending, leaving social spending the only target for budget cuts. With baby boomers rapidly approaching retirement, spending on Social Security, Medicare, and

IN THE NEWS

Little Confidence in Government

Public-opinion polls reveal that Americans have little confidence in government, as the following responses illustrate.

Question: How much of the time do you think you can trust the government in Washington to do what is right—just about always, most of the time, or only some of the time?

Source: Conducted by CBS News/New York Times, July 13–July 27, 2003.

Answers

Just about always	4%
Most of the time	32%
Some of the time	60%
Never (vol.)	3%
Don't know/No answer	1%

Analysis: In principle, governments intervene to remedy market failure. But the public has little confidence in government performance.

Medicaid is also sure to rise substantially, however. That leaves little room for serious cutbacks in government spending. And even desirable cutbacks in other areas are sure to encounter stiff resistance from beneficiaries and bureaucrats. As a result, few seasoned observers expect the government sector to shrink any further in the economy tomorrow.

SUMMARY

- Government intervention in the marketplace is justified by market failure, that is, suboptimal market outcomes.
- The micro failures of the market originate in public goods, externalities, market power, and an inequitable distribution of income. These flaws deter the market from achieving the optimal mix of output or distribution of income.
- Public goods are those that can't be consumed exclusively; they're jointly consumed regardless of who pays. Because everyone seeks a free ride, no one demands public goods in the marketplace. Hence, the market underproduces public goods.
- Externalities are costs (or benefits) of a market transaction borne by a third party. Externalities create a divergence between social and private costs or benefits, causing suboptimal market outcomes. The market overproduces goods with external costs and underproduces goods with external benefits.
- Market power enables a producer to thwart market signals and maintain a suboptimal mix of output. Antitrust policy seeks to prevent or restrict market power. The government may also regulate the behavior of powerful firms.
- The market-generated distribution of income may be unfair. This inequity may prompt the government to intervene with taxes and transfer payments that redistribute incomes.

- The macro failures of the marketplace are reflected in unemployment and inflation. Government intervention is intended to achieve full employment and price stability.
- The federal government expanded greatly after 1930. More recent growth, however, has been in transfer payments, which now account for over half of federal expenditure.
- State and local governments purchase more output (12 percent of GDP) than the federal government (7 percent) and employ five times as many workers.
- Income and payroll taxes provide most federal revenues. States get most revenue from sales taxes; local governments rely on property taxes.
- Government failure occurs when intervention moves us away from rather than toward the optimal mix of output (or income). Failure may result from outright waste (operational inefficiency) or from a misallocation of resources.
- All government activity must be evaluated in terms of its opportunity cost, that is, the *private* goods and services forgone to make resources available to the public sector.
- Allocation decisions within the public sector may be based on cost-benefit analysis or votes. The self-interests of government agents may also affect decisions of when and how to intervene.

Key Terms

optimal mix of output	market power	progressive tax
market mechanism	antitrust	proportional tax
market failure	natural monopoly	regressive tax
private good	transfer payments	categorical grants
public good	merit good	user charge
free rider	unemployment	government failure
externalities	inflation	public choice
monopoly	opportunity cost	

Questions for Discussion

1. Why should taxpayers subsidize public colleges and universities? What external benefits are generated by higher education?
2. If everyone seeks a free ride, what mix of output will be produced in Figure 4.2? Why would anyone voluntarily contribute to the purchase of public goods like flood control or snow removal?
3. Could local fire departments be privately operated, with their services sold directly to customers? What problems would be involved in such a system?
4. Why might Fourth of July fireworks be considered a public good? Who should pay for them? What about airport security?
5. What is the specific market-failure justification for government spending on (*a*) public universities,
(*b*) health care, (*c*) trash pickup, (*d*) highways, (*e*) police? Would a purely private economy produce any of these services?
6. Why should the well-being of nonsmokers affect the price and quantity of cigarettes produced?
7. The government now spends over $400 billion a year on Social Security benefits. Why don't we leave it to individuals to save for their own retirement?
8. What government actions might cause failures like points G_1, G_2, and G_3 in Figure 4.8? Can you give examples?
9. Are subway fares progressive or regressive? How about highway tolls?
10. Should the government be downsized? Which functions should be cut back?

PROBLEMS	The Student Problem Set at the back of this book contains numerical and graphing problems for this chapter.
WEB ACTIVITIES	to accompany this chapter can be found on the Online Learning Center: **http://www.mhhe.com/economics/schiller10**

PART 2

Measuring Macro Outcomes

Macroeconomics focuses on the performance of the entire economy rather than on the behavior of individual participants (a micro concern). The central concerns of macroeconomics are (1) the short-term business cycle and (2) long-term economic growth. In the long run, the focus is on expanding the economy's capacity to produce goods and services, thereby raising future living standards. In the short run, the emphasis is on fully using available capacity, thereby maximizing output and minimizing unemployment. Chapters 5 through 7 focus on the measurement tools used to gauge the nation's macroeconomic performance (both short-run and long-run). Also examined are the social and economic damage caused by the problems of unemployment and inflation.

National-Income Accounting

A favorite cliché of policymakers in Washington is that government likes to tackle only those problems it can measure. Politicians need visible results. They want to be able to brag to their constituents about the miles of new highways built, the number of students who graduated, the number of families that left welfare, and the number of unemployed workers who found jobs. To do this, they must be able to measure economic outcomes.

The Great Depression of the 1930s was an abject lesson in the need for better measures of economic performance. There were plenty of anecdotes about factories closing, farms failing, and people selling apples on the streets. But nobody knew the dimensions of the nation's economic meltdown until millions of workers had lost their jobs. The need for more timely information about the health of the national economy was evident. From that experience a commitment to **national-income accounting**—the measurement of aggregate economic activity—emerged. During the 1930s the economist Simon Kuznets (who later received a Nobel Prize for his work) and the U.S. Department of Commerce developed an accounting system that gauges the economy's health. That national-accounting system now churns out reams of data that are essential to tracking the economy's performance. They answer such questions as

- **How much output is being produced? What is it being used for?**
- **How much income is being generated in the marketplace?**
- **What's happening to prices and wages?**

It's tempting, of course, to ignore all these measurement questions, especially since they tend to be rather dull. But if we avoid measurement problems, we severely limit our ability to understand how the economy works or how well (or poorly) it's performing. We also limit our ability to design policies for improving economic performance.

National-income accounting also provides a useful perspective on the way the economy works. It shows how factor markets relate to product markets, how output relates to income, and how consumer spending and business investment relate to production. It also shows how the flow of taxes and government spending may alter economic outcomes.

national-income accounting: The measurement of aggregate economic activity, particularly national income and its components.

MEASURES OF OUTPUT

The array of goods and services we produce is truly massive, including everything from professional baseball to guided-missile systems. All these things are part of our total output; the problem is to find a summary measure.

Itemizing the amount of each good or service produced each year won't solve our measurement problems. The resulting list would be so long that it would be both unwieldy and meaningless. We couldn't even add it up, since it would contain diverse goods measured in a variety of units (e.g., miles, packages, pounds, quarts). Nor could we compare one year's output to another's. Suppose that last year we produced 2 billion oranges, 2 million bicycles, and 700 rock concerts, whereas this year we produced 3 billion oranges, 4 million bicycles, and 600 rock concerts. Which year's output was larger? With more of some goods, but less of others, the answer isn't obvious.

Gross Domestic Product

To facilitate our accounting chores, we need some mechanism for organizing annual output data into a more manageable summary. The mechanism we use is price. *Each good and service produced and brought to market has a price. That price serves as a measure of value for calculating total output.* Consider again the problem of determining how much output was produced this year and last. There's no obvious way to answer this question in physical terms alone. But once we know the price of each good, we can calculate the *value* of output produced. The total dollar value of final output produced each year is called the **gross domestic product (GDP).** GDP is simply the sum of all final goods and services produced for the market in a given time period, with each good or service valued at its market price.

> **gross domestic product (GDP):** The total market value of all final goods and services produced within a nation's borders in a given time period.

Table 5.1 illustrates the use of prices to value total output in two hypothetical years. If oranges were 20 cents each last year and 2 billion oranges were produced, then the *value* of orange production last year was $400 million ($0.20 × 2 billion). In the same manner, we can determine that the value of bicycle production was $100 million and the value of rock concerts was $700 million. By adding these figures, we can say that the value of last year's production—last year's GDP—was $1,200 million (Table 5.1*a*).

Now we're in a position to compare one year's output to another's. Table 5.1*b* shows that the use of prices enables us to say that the *value* of this year's output is $1,400 million. Hence, *total output* has increased from one year to the next. *The use of prices to value market output allows us to summarize output activity and to compare the output of one period with that of another.*

Output	Amount
a. Last Year's Output	
In physical terms:	
Oranges	2 billion
Bicycles	2 million
Rock concerts	700
Total	?
In monetary terms:	
2 billion oranges @ $0.20 each	$ 400 million
2 million bicycles @ $50 each	100 million
700 rock concerts @ $1 million each	700 million
Total	$1200 million
b. This Year's Output	
In physical terms:	
Oranges	3 billion
Bicycles	4 million
Rock concerts	600
Total	?
In monetary terms:	
3 billion oranges @ $0.20 each	$ 600 million
4 million bicycles @ $50 each	200 million
600 rock concerts @ $1 million each	600 million
Total	$1400 million

TABLE 5.1
The Measurement of Output

It's impossible to add up all output when output is counted in *physical* terms. Accordingly, total output is measured in *monetary* terms, with each good or service valued at its market price. GDP refers to the total market value of all goods and services produced in a given time period. According to the numbers in this table, the total *value* of the oranges, bicycles, and rock concerts produced "last" year was $1.2 billion and $1.4 billion "this" year.

GDP vs. GNP. The concept of GDP is of relatively recent use in U.S. national-income accounts. Prior to 1992, most U.S. statistics focused on gross *national* product or G*N*P. Gross *national* product refers to the output produced by American-owned factors of production regardless of where they're located. Gross *domestic* product refers to output produced within America's borders. Thus, GNP would include some output from an Apple computer factory in Singapore but exclude some of the output produced by a Honda factory in Ohio. In an increasingly global economy, where factors of production and ownership move easily across international borders, the calculations of GNP became ever more complex. It also became a less dependable measure of the nation's economic health. ***GDP is geographically focused, including all output produced within a nation's borders regardless of whose factors of production are used to produce it.*** Apple's output in Singapore ends up in Singapore's GDP; the cars produced at Honda's Ohio plant are counted in America's GDP.

International Comparisons. The geographic focus of GDP facilitates international comparisons of economic activity. Is Japan's output as large as that of the United States? How could you tell? Japan produces a mix of output different from ours, making *quantity*-based comparisons difficult. We can compare the *value* of output produced in each country, however. The World View, "Comparative Output" in Chapter 2, shows that the value of America's GDP is three times larger than Japan's.

GDP per Capita. International comparisons of total output are even more vivid in *per capita terms.* **GDP per capita** relates the total value of annual output to the number of people who share that output; it refers to the average GDP per person. In 2004, America's total GDP of $11 trillion was shared by 290 million citizens. Hence, our average, or *per capita,* GDP was nearly $38,000. By contrast, the average GDP for the entire world's inhabitants was only $8,000. In these terms, America's position as the richest country in the world clearly stands out.

> **GDP per capita:** Total GDP divided by total population; average GDP.

Statistical comparisons of GDP across nations are abstract and lifeless. They do, however, convey very real differences in the way people live. The accompanying World View examines some everyday realities of living in a poor nation, compared with a rich nation. Disparities in per capita GDP mean that people in low-income countries have little access to telephones, televisions, paved roads, or schools. They also die a lot younger than do people in rich countries.

But even the World View fails to fully convey how tough life is for people at the *bottom* of the income distribution in both poor and rich nations. Per capita GDP isn't a measure of what every citizen is getting. In the United States, millions of individuals have access to far more goods and services than our average per capita GDP, while millions of others must get by with much less. Although per capita GDP in Kuwait is three times larger than that of Brazil's, we can't conclude that the typical citizen of Kuwait is three times as well off as the typical Brazilian. The only thing these figures tell us is that the average Kuwaiti *could have* almost three times as many goods and services each year as the average Brazilian *if* GDP were distributed in the same way in both countries. ***Measures of per capita GDP tell us nothing about the way GDP is actually distributed or used: they're only a statistical average.*** When countries are quite similar in structure, institutions, and income distribution, however—or when historical comparisons are made within a country—per capita GDP can be viewed as a rough-and-ready measure of relative standards of living.

Global data on per capita incomes and other social indicators are available from the United Nations at www.un.org/depts/unsd/social/inc-eco.htm.

Measurement Problems

Nonmarket Activities. Although the methods for calculating GDP and per capita GDP are straightforward, they do create a few problems. For one thing, GDP measures exclude most goods and services that are *produced* but not *sold* in the market. This may appear to be a trivial point, but it isn't. Vast quantities of output never reach the market. For example, the homemaker who cleans, washes, gardens, shops, and cooks definitely contributes to the output of goods and services. Because she's not

WORLD VIEW

Global Inequalities

The 2.5 billion residents of the world's low-income nations have comparatively few goods and services. Their average income (per capita GDP) is only $2,100 a year, a *fourteenth* of the average income in high-income nations such as the United States, Japan, and Germany. It's not just a colossal *income* disparity; it's also a disparity in the quality and even the duration of life. Some examples:

Total population
2.5 billion
1.0 billion

Per capita income
$2,100
$28,480

Life expectancy (years)
59
78

Child mortality (per 1,000)
121
7

Access to sanitation
43%
93%

Paved roads (% of total)
19%
94%

Electricity use per capita (kilowatt-hours per year)
317
8,421

Cars (per 1,000 people)
8
436

Televisions (per 1,000 people)
91
735

Telephones (per 1,000 people)
28
585

Personal computers (per 1,000 people)
7.5
467

Public health spending (% of GDP)
1.1
6.0

◼ Low-income nations
◻ High-income nations

Source: Copyright 2004 by World Bank, *World Development Report, 2004* and *World Development Indicators, 2004.* Reproduced with permission. www.worldbank.org

Analysis: Hidden behind dry statistical comparisons of per capita GDP lie very tangible and dramatic differences in the way people live. Low GDP per capita reflects a lot of deprivation.

paid a market wage for these services, however, her efforts are excluded from the calculation of GDP. At the same time, we do count the efforts of those workers who sell identical homemaking services in the marketplace. This seeming contradiction is explained by the fact that a homemaker's services aren't sold in the market and therefore carry no explicit, market-determined value.

The exclusion of homemakers' services from the GDP accounts is particularly troublesome when we want to compare living standards over time or between countries. In the United States, for example, most women now work outside the home. As a result households make greater use of *paid* domestic help (e.g., child care, house cleaning). Accordingly, a lot of housework and child care that were previously excluded from GDP statistics (because they were unpaid family help) are now included (because they're done by paid help). In this respect, our historical GDP figures may exaggerate improvements in our standard of living.

Homemaking services aren't the only output excluded. If a friend helps you with your homework, the services never get into the GDP accounts. But if you hire a tutor or engage the services of a term paper-writing agency, the transaction becomes part of GDP. Here again, the problem is simply that we have no way to determine how much output was produced until it enters the market and is purchased.[1]

Unreported Income. The GDP statistics also fail to capture market activities that aren't reported to tax or census authorities. Many people work "off the books," getting paid in unreported cash. This so-called underground economy is motivated by tax avoidance and the need to conceal illegal activities. Although illegal activities capture most of the headlines, tax evasion on income earned in otherwise legal pursuits accounts for most of the underground economy. The Internal Revenue Service estimates that over two-thirds of underground income comes from legitimate wages, salaries, profits, interest, and pensions that simply aren't reported. As the accompanying News indicates, unreported income is particularly common in the service sector.

IN THE NEWS

A Lot Going On under the Table

- Percentage of households making untaxed or unmeasured "underground" purchases: 83
- Estimated unreported income per person in 2000, excluding illegal activities: $4,300
- Percentage of unreported income from wages and salaries: 18
- Percentage of unreported income from capital gains: 13
- Unreported income as a percentage of GDP: 12
- Taxes lost from unreported income in 2000: $195 billion

The underground economy—transactions that are untaxed or unaccounted for in GDP—involves a lot more than nannies and drug deals.

	Estimated Percentage of Services Supplied by the Underground Economy
Lawn maintenance	90
Domestic help	83
Child care	49
Home repair/improvements	34
Laundry/sewing services	25
Appliance repair	17
Car repairs	13
Haircuts/beauty service	8
Catering	8

Data from University of Michigan Institute for Social Research, U.S. Department of Labor.

Source: U.S. Internal Revenue Service. www.irs.gov

Analysis: GDP statistics include only the value of reported market transactions. Unreported transactions in the underground economy can't be counted and may therefore distort perceptions of economic activity.

---

[1]The U.S. Commerce Department does, however, *estimate* the value of some nonmarket activities (e.g., food grown by farmers for their own consumption, the rental value of homeownership) and includes such estimates in GDP calculations.

Stages of Production	Value of Transaction	Value Added
1. Farmer grows wheat, sells it to miller	$0.12	$0.12
2. Miller converts wheat to flour, sells it to baker	0.28	0.16
3. Baker bakes bagel, sells it to bagel store	0.60	0.32
4. Bagel store sells bagel to consumer	0.75	0.15
Total	$1.75	$0.75

TABLE 5.2
Value Added in Various Stages of Production

The value added at each stage of production represents a contribution to total output. Value added equals the market value of a product minus the cost of intermediate goods.

People who mow lawns, clean houses, paint walls, or provide child care services are apt to get paid in cash that isn't reported. The volume of such mundane transactions greatly exceeds the underground income generated by drug dealers, prostitutes, or gambling.

Value Added

Not every reported market transaction gets included at full value in GDP statistics. If it did, the same output would get counted over and over. The problem here is that the production of goods and services typically involves a series of distinct stages. Consider the production of a bagel, for example. For a bagel to reach Einstein's or some other bagel store, the farmer must grow some wheat, the miller must convert it to flour, and the baker must make bagels with it. Table 5.2 illustrates this chain of production.

Notice that each of the four stages of production depicted in Table 5.2 involves a separate market transaction. The farmer sells to the miller (stage 1), the miller to the baker (stage 2), the baker to the bagel store (stage 3), and finally, the store to the consumer. If we added up the separate value of each market transaction, we'd come to the conclusion that $1.75 of output had been produced. In fact, though, only one bagel has been produced, and it's worth only 75 cents. Hence, we should increase GDP—the value of output—only by 75 cents.

To get an accurate measure of GDP we must distinguish between *intermediate* goods and *final* goods. **Intermediate goods** are goods purchased for use as input in further stages of production. Final goods are the goods produced at the end of the production sequence, for use by consumers (or other market participants).

intermediate goods: Goods or services purchased for use as input in the production of final goods or in services.

We can compute the value of *final* output in one of two ways. The easiest way would be to count only market transactions entailing final sales (stage 4 in Table 5.2). To do this, however, we'd have to know who purchased each good or service in order to know when we had reached the end of the process. Such a calculation would also exclude any output produced in stages 1, 2, and 3 in Table 5.2 but not yet reflected in stage 4.

Another way to calculate GDP is to count only the **value added** at each stage of production. Consider the miller, for example. He doesn't really contribute $0.28 worth of production to total output, but only $0.16. The other $0.12 reflected in the price of his flour represents the contribution of the farmer who grew the wheat. By the same token, the baker *adds* only $0.32 to the value of output, as part of his output was purchased from the miller. By considering only the value *added* at each stage of production, we eliminate double counting. We don't count twice the *intermediate* goods and services that producers buy from other producers, which are then used as inputs. As Table 5.2 confirms, we can determine that value of final output by summing up the value added at each stage of production. (Note that $0.75 is also the price of a bagel.)

value added: The increase in the market value of a product that takes place at each stage of the production process.

Although prices are a convenient measure of market value, they can also distort perceptions of real output. Imagine what would happen to our calculations of GDP if

Real vs. Nominal GDP

all prices were to double from one year to the next. Suppose, for example, that the price of oranges, as shown in Table 5.1, rose from $0.20 to $0.40, the price of bicycles to $100, and the price of rock concerts to $2 million each. How would such price changes alter measured GDP? Obviously, the price increases would double the *value* of final output. Measured GDP would rise from $1,400 million to $2,800 million.

Such a rise in GDP doesn't reflect an increase in the *quantity* of goods and services available to us. We're still producing the same quantities shown in Table 5.1; only the prices of those goods have changed. Hence, ***changes in GDP brought about by changes in the price level can give us a distorted view of economic activity.*** Surely we wouldn't want to assert that our standard of living had improved just because price increases raised measured GDP from $1,400 million to $2,800 million.

To distinguish increases in the quantity of goods and services from increases in their prices, we must construct a measure of GDP that takes into account price-level changes. We do so by distinguishing between *real* GDP and *nominal* GDP. **Nominal GDP** is the value of final output measured in *current* prices, whereas **real GDP** is the value of output measured in *constant* prices. ***To calculate real GDP, we adjust the market value of goods and services for changing prices.***

Note, for example, that in Table 5.1 prices were unchanged from one year to the next. When prices in the marketplace are constant, interyear comparisons of output are simple. But if all prices double, the comparison becomes more complicated. If all prices doubled from last year to this year, this year's nominal GDP would rise to $2,800 million. But these price increases wouldn't alter the quantity of goods produced. In other words, *real* GDP, valued at constant prices, would remain at $1,400 million. Thus, ***the distinction between nominal and real GDP is important whenever the price level changes.***

Because the price level does change every year, both real and nominal GDP are regularly reported. Nominal GDP is computed simply by adding the current dollar value of production. Real GDP is computed by making an adjustment for changes in prices from year to year.

Consider the GDP statistics for 2001 and 2002, as displayed in Table 5.3. The first row shows nominal GDP in each year: nominal GDP increased by $380 billion between 2001 and 2002 (row 2). This 3.8 percent increase looks impressive. However, some of that gain was fueled by higher prices, not increased output. Row 3 indicates that the price level rose by 1.5 percent during that same period.

Row 4 in Table 5.3 adjusts the GDP comparison for the change in prices. We deflate the 2002 nominal GDP by factoring out the 1.5 percent price increase. Simple division is all we need to compute *real* GDP in 2002 as being $10,326 billion. Hence, *real* GDP increased by only $225 billion in 2002 (row 5), not by the larger inflation-exaggerated amount in row 2.

Notice in Table 5.3 that in 2001 real and nominal GDP are identical because we're using that year as the basis of comparison. We're comparing performance in 2002 to that of the 2001 **base period.** Real GDP can be expressed in the prices of a particular

nominal GDP: The value of final output produced in a given period, measured in the prices of that period (current prices).

real GDP: The value of final output produced in a given period, adjusted for changing prices.

base period: The time period used for comparative analysis; the basis for indexing, for example, of price changes.

TABLE 5.3
Computing Real GDP

Real GDP is the inflation-adjusted value of nominal GDP. Between 2001 and 2002, nominal GDP increased by $380 billion (row 2). Some of this gain was due to rising prices (row 3). After adjusting for inflation, real GDP increased only by $225 billion (row 5).

		2001	2002
1.	Nominal GDP (in billions)	$10,101	$10,481
2.	Change in nominal GDP		+$380
3.	Change in price level, 2001 to 2002		1.5%
4.	Real GDP in 2001 dollars	$10,101	$10,326 $\left(=\dfrac{\$10,481}{\dfrac{101.5}{100.0}}\right)$
5.	Change in real GDP		+$225

year; that year serves as the base for computing price-level and output changes. The general formula for computing real GDP is

$$\text{Real GDP in year } t = \frac{\text{nominal GDP in year } t}{\text{price index}}$$

The price index shows how average prices have changed between the base year and year *t*. Between 2001 and 2002, average prices rose 1.5 percent. This price-level change is indexed as 101.5. Thus, real GDP in 2002 is calculated as

$$\begin{array}{l}\text{Real GDP in 2002}\\ \text{(2001 prices)}\end{array} = \frac{\$10,481 \text{ billion}}{\dfrac{101.5}{100.0}} = \$10,326 \text{ billion}$$

This is the figure shown in row 4, Table 5.3.

The distinction between nominal and real GDP becomes critical when more distant years are compared. Between 1933 and 2003, for example, prices rose by 1,300 percent. Table 5.4 shows how such price-level changes can distort our views of how living

Find out how much real GDP fell per year during the Great Depression (1929–40) at www.bea.doc.gov/bea/dn/0898nip3/table1.htm.

Suppose we want to determine how much better off the average American was in 2003, as measured in terms of new goods and services, than people were during the Great Depression. To do this, we'd compare GDP per capita in 2003 with GDP per capita in 1933. The following data make that comparison.

	GDP	Population	Per Capita GDP
1933	$ 56 billion	126 million	$ 444
2003	10,988 billion	291 million	37,760

In 1933, the nation's GDP of $56 billion was shared by 126 million Americans, yielding a *per capita* GDP of $444. By contrast, GDP in 2003 was almost 200 times larger, at $10,988 billion. This vastly larger GDP was shared by 291 million people, giving us a per capita GDP of $37,760. Hence, it would appear that our standard of living in 2003 was 85 times higher than the standard of 1933.

But this increase in *nominal* GDP vastly exaggerates our material well-being. The average price of goods and services—the *price level*—increased by 1,300 percent between 1933 and 2003. The goods and services you might have bought for $1 in 1933 cost $14 in 2003. In other words, we needed a lot more dollars in 2003 to buy any given combination of real goods and services.

To compare our *real* GDP in 2003 with the real GDP of 1933, we have to adjust for this tremendous jump in prices (inflation). We do so by measuring both years' output in terms of *constant* prices. Since prices went up, on average, fourteenfold between 1933 and 2003, we simply divide the 2003 *nominal* output by 14. The calculation is

$$\begin{array}{l}\text{Real GDP}\\ \text{in 2003} \\ \text{(1933 prices)}\end{array} = \text{nominal 2003 GDP} \times \frac{\text{1933 price level}}{\text{2003 price level}}$$

By arbitrarily setting the level of prices in 1933 at 100 and noting that prices have increased fourteenfold since then, we can calculate

$$\begin{array}{l}\text{Real GDP}\\ \text{in 2003} \\ \text{(1933 prices)}\end{array} = \$10,988 \text{ billion} \times \frac{100}{1,400}$$

$$= \$785 \text{ billion}$$

With a population of 291 million, this left us with real GDP per capita of $2,698 in 2003—as measured in 1933 dollars. This was more than six times the *real* per capita GDP of the depression ($444), but not nearly so great an increase as comparisons of *nominal* GDP suggest.

TABLE 5.4
Real vs. Nominal GDP: A Historical View

standards have changed since the Great Depression: In *nominal* terms, our per capita income has risen a whopping 85 times over; in *real* terms, however, the income gain is a much less spectacular six times over.

Figure 5.1 shows how nominal and real GDP have changed since 1990. Real GDP is calculated here on the basis of the level of prices prevailing in 2000. (Note that real and nominal GDP are identical in that base year.) The dollar value of output produced each year has risen considerably faster than the quantity of output, reflecting persistent increases in the price level—that is, **inflation.**

Notice in particular that continuing inflation tends to obscure the actual *declines* in real output. Real GDP actually declined in 1991, though nominal GDP kept rising. Although the *value* of final output continued to rise in that year, the actual production of goods and services was falling; nominal and real GDP moved in opposite directions.

Chain-Weighted Price Adjustments. Although the distinction between real and nominal GDP is critical in measuring the nation's economic health, the procedure for making inflation adjustments isn't perfect. When we use the prices of a specific year as the base for computing real GDP, we're implicitly freezing *relative* prices as well as *average* prices. Over time, however, relative prices change markedly. Computer prices, for example, have fallen sharply in recent years in both absolute and relative terms.

> **inflation:** An increase in the average level of prices of goods and services.

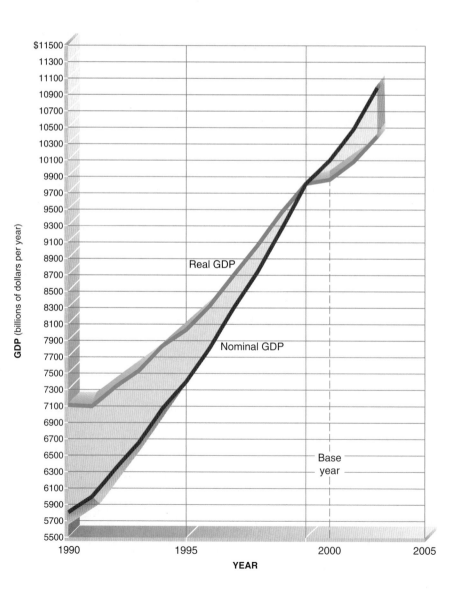

FIGURE 5.1

Changes in GDP: Nominal vs. Real

Increases in *nominal* GDP reflect higher prices as well as more output. Increases in *real* GDP reflect more output only. To measure these real changes, we must value each year's output in terms of common base prices. In this figure the reference year is 2000. Notice that *real* GDP declined in 1991, although *nominal* GDP continued to rise. Nominal GDP rises faster than real GDP as a result of inflation.

Source: *Economic Report of the President, 2004.*

During the same period, unit sales of computers have increased by 20 to 25 percent a year. If we used the higher computer prices of 5 years ago to compute that sales growth, we'd greatly exaggerate the *value* of today's computer output. If we use today's prices, however, we'll underestimate the value of output produced in the past. To resolve this problem, the U.S. Department of Commerce uses a *chain-weighted* price index to compute real GDP. Instead of using the prices of a *single* base year to compute real GDP, **chain-weighted indexes use a moving average** *of price levels in consecutive years as an inflation adjustment.* When chain-weighted price adjustments are made, real GDP still refers to the inflation-adjusted value of GDP but isn't expressed in terms of the prices prevailing in any specific base year. All official estimates of real GDP are now based on chain-weighted price indexes.

Changes in real GDP from one year to the next tell us how much the economy's output is growing. Some of that growth, however, may come at the expense of future output. Recall that our **production possibilities** determine how much output we can produce. Those limits are, in turn, established by the availability of factors of production and technology. If we use up some of these resources to produce this year's output, future production possibilities may shrink. *Next year we won't be able to produce as much output unless we replace factors of production we use this year.*

We routinely use up plant and equipment (capital) in the production process. To maintain our production possibilities, therefore, we have to at least replace what we've used. The value of capital used up in producing goods and services is commonly called **depreciation.**[2] In principle, it's the amount of capital worn out by use in a year or made obsolete by advancing technology. In practice, the amount of capital depreciation is estimated by the U.S. Department of Commerce.

By subtracting depreciation from GDP we get **net domestic product (NDP).** This is the amount of output we could consume without reducing our stock of capital and therewith next year's production possibilities.

The distinction between GDP and NDP is mirrored in a distinction between *gross* investment and *net* **investment. Gross investment** is positive as long as some new plant and equipment are being produced. But *the stock of capital—the total collection of plant and equipment—won't grow unless gross investment exceeds depreciation.* That is, the *flow* of new capital must exceed depreciation, or our *stock* of capital will decline. Whenever the rate of gross investment exceeds depreciation, **net investment** is positive.

Notice that net investment can be negative as well; in such situations we're wearing out plant and equipment faster than we're replacing it. When net investment is negative, our capital stock is shrinking. This was the situation during the Great Depression. Gross investment fell so sharply in 1932–34 (see front endpaper of book) that it wasn't even replacing used-up machinery and structures. As a result, the economy's ability to produce goods and services declined.

THE USES OF OUTPUT

The role of investment in maintaining or expanding our production possibilities helps focus attention on the uses to which GDP is put. It's not just the total value of annual output that matters, its also the use that we make of that output. *The GDP accounts also tell us what mix of output we've selected, that is, society's answer to the core issue of WHAT to produce.*

The major uses of total output conform to the four sets of market participants we encountered in Chapter 2, namely, consumers, business firms, government, and foreigners. Those goods and services used by households are called *consumption goods* and range all the

WEBNOTE

If you want to see some great charts on GDP and other economic statistics, visit Dr. Ed Yardeni's Web site at www.prudential.com/yardeni.

Net Domestic Product

production possibilities: The alternative combinations of final goods and services that could be produced in a given time period with all available resources and technology.

depreciation: The consumption of capital in the production process; the wearing out of plant and equipment.

net domestic product (NDP): GDP less depreciation.

investment: Expenditures on (production of) new plant, equipment, and structures (capital) in a given time period, plus changes in business inventories.

gross investment: Total investment expenditure in a given time period.

net investment: Gross investment less depreciation.

Consumption

---

[2]The terms *depreciation* and *capital consumption allowance* are used interchangeably. The depreciation charges firms commonly make, however, are determined in part by income tax regulations and thus may not accurately reflect the amount of capital consumed.

way from doughnuts to online computer services. Included in this category are all goods and services households purchase in product markets. As we observed in Chapter 2, all this consumer spending claims two-thirds of our annual output (see Figure 2.3).

Investment

Investment goods represent another use of GDP. Investment goods are the plant, machinery, and equipment we produce. Net changes in business inventories and expenditures for residential construction are also counted as investment. To produce any of these investment goods, we must use scarce resources that could be used to produce something else. Investment spending claims about one-sixth of our total output.

Government Spending

The third major use of GDP is the *public sector*. Federal, state, and local governments purchase resources to police the streets, teach classes, write laws, and build highways. The resources purchased by the government sector are unavailable for either consumption or investment purposes. At present, government spending on goods and services (*not* income transfers) claims roughly one-fifth of total output.

Net Exports

exports: Goods and services sold to international buyers.

imports: Goods and services purchased from international sources.

net exports: The value of exports minus the value of imports.

Finally, remember that some of the goods and services we produce each year are used abroad rather than at home. That is, we **export** some of our output to other countries, for whatever use they care to make of it. Thus, GDP—the value of output produced—will be larger than the sum of our own consumption, investment, and government purchases to the extent that we succeed in exporting goods and services.

We **import** goods and services as well. A flight to London on British Air is an imported service; a Jaguar is an imported good. These goods and services aren't part of America's GDP since they weren't produced within our borders (even though Jaguar is owned by Ford, the cars are produced in England). In principle, these imports never enter the GDP accounts. In practice, however, it's difficult to distinguish imports from domestic-made products, especially when goods include value added from both foreign and domestic producers. Even "American-made" cars typically incorporate parts manufactured in Japan, Mexico, Thailand, Britain, Spain, or Germany, with final assembly here in the United States. Should that car be counted as an "American" product or as an import? Rather than try to sort out all these products and parts, the U.S. Commerce Department simply subtracts the value of all imports from the value of total spending. Thus, exports are *added* to GDP and *imports* are subtracted. The difference between the two expenditure flows is called **net exports.**

GDP Components

Once we recognize the components of output, we discover a simple method for computing GDP. ***The value of GDP can be computed by adding up the expenditures of market participants.*** Specifically, we note that

$$GDP = C + I + G + (X - M)$$

where C = consumption expenditure
I = investment expenditure
G = government expenditure
X = exports
M = imports

This approach to GDP accounting emphasizes the fact that all the output produced in the economy must be claimed by someone. If we know who's buying our output, we know how much was produced and what uses were made of it.

MEASURES OF INCOME

There's another way of looking at GDP. Instead of looking at who's *buying* our output, we can look at who's *being paid* to produce it. Like markets themselves. ***GDP accounts have two sides: One side focuses on expenditure (the demand side), the other side focuses on income (the supply side).***

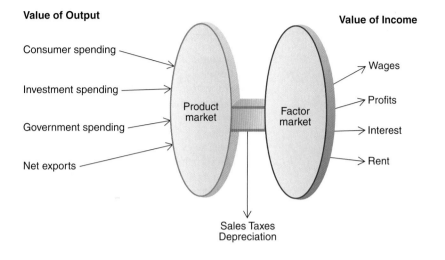

Value of Output

Consumer spending

Investment spending

Government spending

Net exports

Product market

Factor market

Wages

Profits

Interest

Rent

Value of Income

Sales Taxes
Depreciation

FIGURE 5.2
Output = Income

All the spending that establishes the value of output also determines the value of incomes. With minor exceptions, the market value of incomes must equal the market value of output.

We've already observed (see Figure 3.1) that every market transaction involves an *exchange* of dollars for a good or resource. Moreover, the *value* of each good or resource is measured by the amount of money exchanged for it (its market price). Hence, ***the total value of market incomes must equal the total value of final output, or GDP.*** In other words, one person's expenditure always represents another person's income.

Figure 5.2 illustrates the link between spending on output and incomes. This is a modified version of the circular flow we saw in Chapter 3. The spending that flows into the product market gets funneled into the factor market when resources are employed to produce the goods people want. The expenditure then flows into the hands of business owners, workers, landlords, and other resource owners. With the exception of sales taxes and depreciation, all spending on output becomes income to factors of production.

The equivalence of output and income isn't dependent on any magical qualities possessed by money. Were we to produce only one product—say, wheat—and pay everyone in bushels and pecks, total income would still equal total output. People couldn't receive in income more wheat than we produced. On the other hand, all the wheat produced would go to *someone*. Hence, one could say that the production possibilities of the economy define the limits to real income. The amount of income actually generated in any year depends on the production and expenditure decisions of consumers, firms, and government agencies.

Table 5.5 shows the actual flow of output and income in the U.S. economy during 2003. Total output is made up of the familiar components of GDP: consumption, investment, government goods and services, and net exports. The figures on the left side of Table 5.5 indicate that consumers spent $7,757 billion, businesses spent $1,671 billion on plant and equipment, governments spent $2,055 billion, and net imports were $465 billion. Our total output value (GDP) was thus nearly $11 trillion in 2003.

The right-hand side of Table 5.5 indicates who received the income generated from these markets transactions. Every dollar spent on goods and services provides income to someone. It may go to a worker (as wage or salary) or to a business firm (as profit and depreciation allowance). It may go to a landlord (as rent), to a lender (as interest), or to government (as sales or property tax). None of the dollars spent on goods and services disappears into thin air.

Although it may be exciting to know that we collectively received nearly $11 trillion of income in 2003, it might be of more interest to know who actually got all that income. After all, in addition to the 290 million pairs of outstretched palms among

National Income

TABLE 5.5
The Equivalence of Expenditure and Income (in billions of dollars)

The value of total expenditure must equal the value of total income. Why? Because every dollar spent on output becomes a dollar of income for someone.

Expenditure		Income	
Consumer goods and services	$ 7,757	Wages and salaries	$ 6,203
		Corporate profits	1,070
Investment in plant,		Proprietors' income	827
equipment, and		Farm income	20
inventory	1,671	Rents	164
Government goods		Interest	583
and services	2,055	Sales taxes	740
Exports	1,049	Depreciation	1,311
Imports	(1,544)	Statistical discrepancy	70
Total value of output	$10,988 =	Total value of income	$10,988

Source: U.S. Department of Commerce (2003 data).

us, millions of businesses and government agencies were also competing for those dollars and the goods and services they represent. By charting the flow of income through the economy, we can see FOR WHOM our output was produced.

Depreciation. The annual income flow originates in product-market sales. Purchases of final goods and services create a flow of income to producers and, through them, to factors of production. But a major diversion of sales revenues occurs immediately, as a result of depreciation charges made by businesses. As we noted earlier, some of our capital resources are used up in the process of production. For the most part, these resources are owned by business firms that expect to be compensated for such investments. Accordingly, they regard some of the sales revenue generated in product markets as reimbursement for wear and tear on capital plant and equipment. They therefore subtract *depreciation charges* from gross revenues in calculating their incomes. Depreciation charges reduce GDP to the level of *net* domestic product (NDP) before any income is available to current factors of production. As we saw earlier,

$$NDP = GDP - depreciation$$

Net Foreign Factor Income. Remember that some of the income generated in U.S. product markets belongs to foreigners. Wages, interest, and profits paid to foreigners are not part of U.S. income. So we need to subtract that outflow.

Recall also that U.S. citizens own factors of production employed in other nations (e.g., a Ford plant in Mexico; a McDonald's outlet in Singapore). This creates an *in*flow of income to U.S. households. To connect the value of U.S. output to U.S. incomes, we must add back in the net inflow of foreign factor income.

Once depreciation charges are subtracted from GDP and net foreign factor income added, we're left with **national income (NI),** which is the total income earned by U.S. factors of production. Thus,

national income (NI): Total income earned by current factors of production: GDP less depreciation and indirect business taxes, plus net foreign factor income.

$$NI = NDP + net\ foreign\ factor\ income$$

As Table 5.6 illustrates, our national income in 2003 was $9,680 billion, roughly $1.3 trillion less than GDP.

Personal Income

We're not quite through counting the gaps between the total sales revenue that gets registered in product markets and the amount of income actually received by households.

Income Flow	Amount (in billions)
Gross domestic product (GDP)	$11,004
Less depreciation	(1,354)
Net domestic product (NDP)	9,650
Plus net foreign factor income	54
Less statistical discrepancy	(24)
National income (NI)	9,680
Less indirect business taxes	(751)
Less corporate taxes	(235)
Less retained earnings*	(391)
Less Social Security taxes	(1,150)
Plus transfer payments	1,335
Plus net interest	674
Personal income (PI)	9,162
Less personal taxes	(1,002)
Disposable income (DI)	8,160

*Retained earnings are net of inventory valuation changes and depreciation.
Source: U.S. Department of Commerce.

TABLE 5.6
The Flow of Income, 2003

The revenue generated from market transactions passes through many hands. Households end up with disposable income equal to about 70 percent of GDP, after depreciation and taxes are taken out and net interest and transfer payments are added back in. Disposable income is either spent (consumption) or saved by households.

Indirect Business Taxes. Another major diversion of the income flow occurs at its point of origin. When goods are sold in the marketplace, their purchase price is typically encumbered with some sort of sales tax. Thus, some of the revenue generated in product markets disappears before any factor of production gets a chance to claim it. These *indirect business taxes,* as they're called, must be deducted from national income because they don't represent payment to factors of production.

Corporate Taxes and Retained Earnings. Theoretically, all the income corporations receive represents income for their owners—the households who hold stock in the corporations. But the flow of income through corporations to stockholders is far from complete. First, corporations may pay taxes on their profits. Accordingly, some of the income received on behalf of a corporation's stockholders goes into the public treasury rather than into private bank accounts. Second, corporate managers typically find some urgent need for cash. As a result, part of the profits is retained by the corporation rather than passed on to the stockholders in the form of dividends. Accordingly, both *corporate taxes* and *retained earnings* must be subtracted from national income before we can determine how much income flows into the hands of consumers.

Still another deduction must be made for *Social Security taxes*. Nearly all people who earn a wage or salary are required by law to pay Social Security "contributions." In 2004, the Social Security tax rate for workers was 7.65 percent of the first $87,900 of earnings received in the year. Workers never see this income because it is withheld by employers and sent directly to the U.S. Treasury. Thus, the flow of national income is reduced considerably before it becomes **personal income (PI),** the amount of income received by households before payment of personal taxes.

Not all of our adjustments to national income are negative. Households receive income in the form of transfer payments from the public treasury. More than 47 million people receive monthly Social Security checks, for example, and another 20 million receive some form of public welfare. These income transfers represent income for the people who receive them. People also receive interest payments in excess of those they pay (largely because of interest payments on the government

personal income (PI): Income received by households before payment of personal taxes.

debt). This *net* interest is another source of personal income. Accordingly, our calculation of personal income is as follows:

- *National income* (= income earned by factors of production)
  less indirect business taxes
  corporate taxes
  retained earnings
  Social Security taxes
  plus transfer payments
  net interest
- *Equals **personal income*** (= income received by households)

The total flow of income generated in production is significantly reduced before it gets into the hands of individual households. But we haven't yet reached the end of the reduction process. We have to set something aside for personal income taxes. To be sure we don't forget about our obligations, Uncle Sam and his state and local affiliates usually arrange to have their share taken off the top. Personal income taxes are withheld by the employer, who thus acts as a tax collector. Accordingly, to calculate **disposable income (DI),** which is the amount of income consumers may themselves spend (dispose of), we reduce personal income by the amount of personal taxes:

$$\text{Disposable income} = \text{personal income} - \text{personal taxes}$$

> **disposable income (DI):** After-tax income of households; personal income less personal taxes.

Disposable income is the end of the accounting line. As Table 5.6 shows, households end up with roughly 70 percent of the revenues generated from final market sales (GDP). Once consumers get this disposable income in their hands, they face two choices. They may choose to *spend* their disposable income on consumer goods and services. Or they may choose to *save* it. These are the only two choices in GDP accounting. **Saving,** in this context, simply refers to disposable income that isn't spent on consumption. In the analysis of income and saving flows, we don't care whether savings are hidden under a mattress, deposited in the bank, or otherwise secured. All we want to know is whether disposable income is spent. Thus, ***all disposable income is, by definition, either consumed or saved; that is,***

> **saving:** That part of disposable income not spent on current consumption; disposable income less consumption.

$$\text{Disposable income} = \text{consumption} + \text{saving}$$

THE FLOW OF INCOME

For the latest data on GDP and its components visit the Bureau of Economic Analysis at www.bea.doc.gov.

Figure 5.3 summarizes the relationship between expenditure and income. The essential point again is that every dollar spent on goods and services flows into somebody's hands. Thus, ***the dollar value of output will always equal the dollar value of income.*** Specifically, total income (GDP) ends up distributed in the following way:

- To *households,* in the form of disposable income.
- To *business,* in the form of retained earnings and depreciation allowances.
- To *government,* in the form of taxes.

Income and Expenditure

The annual flow of income to households, businesses, and government is part of a continuing process. Households rarely stash their disposable income under the mattress; they spend most of it on consumption. This spending adds to GDP in the next round of activity, thereby helping to keep the flow of income moving.

Business firms also have a lot of purchasing power tied up in retained earnings and depreciation charges. This income, too, may be recycled—returned to the circular flow—in the form of business investment.

Even the income that flows into public treasuries finds its way back into the marketplace, as government agencies hire police officers, soldiers, and clerks, or they buy goods and services. Thus, ***the flow of income that starts with GDP ultimately returns to the market in the form of new consumption (C), investment (I), and government purchases (G).*** A new GDP arises, and the flow starts all over. In later chapters we examine in detail these *expenditure* flows, with particular emphasis on their ability to keep the economy producing at its full potential.

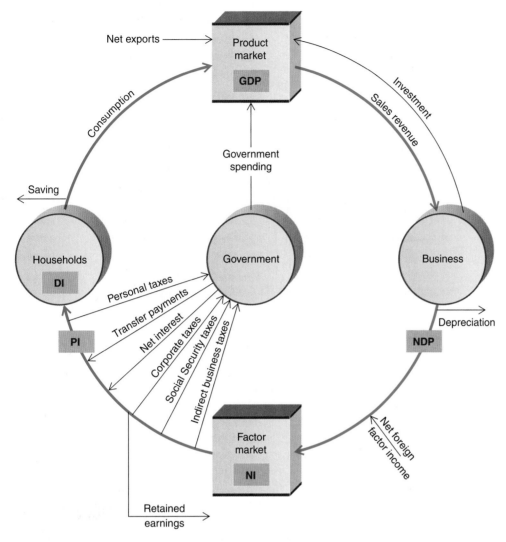

FIGURE 5.3
The Circular Flow of Spending and Income

GDP represents the dollar value of final output sold in the product market. The revenue stream flowing from GDP works its way through NDP, NI, and PI before reaching households in the form of smaller DI. DI is in turn either spent or saved by consumers. This consumption, plus investment, government spending, and net exports, continues the circular flow.

THE ECONOMY TOMORROW

Money, money, money—it seems that's all we talk about. Why don't we talk about important things like beauty, virtue, or the quality of life? Will the economy of tomorrow be filled with a glut of products but devoid of real meaning? Do the GDP accounts—either the expenditure side or the income side—tell us anything we really want to know about the quality of life? If not, why should we bother to examine them?

The Quality of Life

All the economic measures discussed in this chapter are important indexes of individual and collective welfare; they tell us something about how well people are living. They don't, however, capture the completeness of the way in which we view the world or the totality of what makes our lives satisfying. A clear day, a sense of accomplishment, even a smile can do more for a person's sense of well-being than

Intangibles

© 1996 Harley Schwadron.

Analysis: GDP includes *everything* produced and sold in the product market, no matter how much each good or service contributes to our social well-being.

can favorable movements in the GDP accounts. Or, as John Kenneth Galbraith put it, "In a rational lifestyle, some people could find contentment working moderately and then sitting by the street—and talking, thinking, drawing, painting, scribbling, or making love in a suitably discreet way. None of these requires an expanding economy."[3]

The emphasis on economic outcomes arises not from ignorance of life's other meanings but from the visibility of the economic outcomes. We all realize that well-being arises from both material and intangible pleasures, but the intangibles tend to be elusive. It's not easy to gauge individual happiness, much less to ascertain the status of our collective satisfaction. We have to rely on measures we can see, touch, and count. As long as the material components of our environment bear some positive relation to our well-being, they at least serve a useful purpose.

In some situations, however, more physical output may actually worsen our collective welfare. If increased automobile production raises congestion and pollution levels, the rise in GDP occasioned by those additional cars is a misleading index of society's welfare. In such a case, the rise in GDP might actually mask a *decrease* in the well-being of the population. We might also wonder whether more casinos, more prisons, more telemarketing, more divorce litigation, and more Prozac—all of which contribute to GDP growth—are really valid measures of our well-being (see cartoon). Exclusive emphasis on measurable output would clearly be a mistake in many cases.

What is true of automobile production might also be true of other outputs. Increased development of urban areas may cause a loss of social welfare if that development occurs at the expense of space, trees, and tranquillity. Increased mechanization on the farm may raise agricultural output but isolate and uproot farmers. So, too, increased productivity in factories and offices might contribute to a sense of alienation. These ill effects of increased output needn't occur; but if they do, indexes of output tell us less about social or individual well-being.

Index of Well-Being

Researchers at Fordham University devised an alternative index of well-being. Their Index of Social Health includes a few economic parameters (such as unemployment and weekly earnings) but puts more emphasis on sociological behavior (such as

[3]Cited in Leonard Silk, *Nixonomics,* 2nd ed. (New York: Praeger, 1973), p. 163.

IN THE NEWS

America's Declining Social Health

National-income accounts are regularly reported and widely quoted. They do not, however, adequately reflect the nation's *social* performance. To measure more accurately the country's social health, a Fordham University team of social scientists has devised an Index of Social Health with 16 indicators, including infant mortality, drug abuse, health-insurance coverage, and

poverty among the aged. According to this index, America's social health deteriorated sharply in the mid-1970s. The index of social health stayed flat in the 1980s, despite a sustained rise in the nation's economy. It rose with GDP after 1993 but peaked again in 1999 at a level far below that of 1973.

Source: Fordham Institute, *2003 Index of Social Health*, Tarrytown, NY.

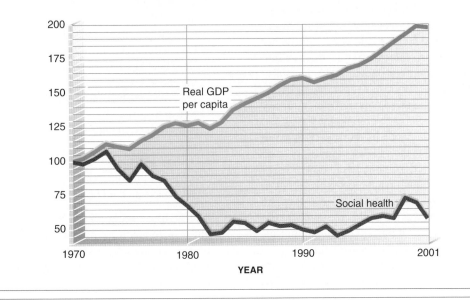

Analysis: The national-income accounts emphasize material well-being. They are an important, but not complete, gauge of our societal welfare.

child abuse and teen suicides). They claim that this broader view points to stagnation in societal well-being over the past two decades, even though GDP was rising (see News.)

Even if the Index of Social Health is a valid gauge of our collective well-being, we shouldn't conclude that the national-income accounts are useless or irrelevant. These points help underscore the fact that *social welfare* and *economic welfare* aren't synonymous. The GDP accounts tell us whether our economic welfare has increased, as measured by the value of goods and services produced. They don't tell us how highly we value additional goods and services relative to nonmarket phenomena. Nor do they even tell us whether important social costs were incurred in the process of production. These judgments must be made outside the market; they're social decisions.

Finally, note that any given level of GDP can encompass many combinations of output. Choosing WHAT to produce is still a critical question, even after the goal of *maximum* production has been established. The quality of life in the economy tomorrow will depend on what specific mix of goods and services we include in GDP.

WEBNOTE

The United Nations has constructed a Human Development Index that offers a broader view of social well-being than GDP alone. For details and country rankings, visit www.undp.org. Also check the Genuine Progress Indicator at www.rprogress.org.

SUMMARY

- National-income accounting measures annual output and income flows. The national-income accounts provide a basis for assessing our economic performance, designing public policy, and understanding how all the parts of the economy interact.
- The most comprehensive measure of output is gross domestic product (GDP), the total market value of all final goods and services produced within a nation's borders during a given time period.
- In calculating GDP, we include only the value added at each stage of production. This procedure eliminates the possibility of the double counting that would result because business firms buy intermediate goods from other firms and include the associated costs in their selling price. For the most part, only marketed goods and services are included in GDP.
- To distinguish physical changes in output from monetary changes in its value, we compute both nominal and real GDP. Nominal GDP is the value of output expressed in *current* prices. Real GDP is the value of output expressed in *constant* prices (the prices of some *base* year).
- Each year some of our capital equipment is worn out in the process of production. Hence, GDP is larger than the amount of goods and services we could consume without reducing our production possibilities. The amount of capital used up each year is referred to as *depreciation*.
- By subtracting depreciation from GDP we derive net domestic product (NDP). The difference between NDP and GDP is also equal to the difference between *gross* investment—the sum of all our current plant and equipment expenditures—and *net* investment—the amount of investment over and above that required to replace wornout capital.
- All the income generated in market sales (GDP) is received by someone. The sequence of flows involved in this process is

  GDP
  less depreciation
  equals NDP
  plus net foreign factor income
  equals national income (NI)
  less indirect business taxes,
       corporate taxes,
       retained earnings, and
       Social Security taxes
  plus transfer payments and
       net interest
  equals personal income (PI)
  less personal income taxes
  equals disposable income (DI)

- The incomes received by households, business firms, and governments provide the purchasing power required to buy the nation's output. As that purchasing power is spent, further GDP is created and the circular flow continues.

Key Terms

national-income accounting	inflation	exports
gross domestic product (GDP)	production possibilities	imports
GDP per capita	depreciation	net exports
intermediate goods	net domestic product (NDP)	national income (NI)
value added	investment	personal income (PI)
nominal GDP	gross investment	disposable income (DI)
real GDP	net investment	saving
base period		

Questions for Discussion

1. The manuscript for this book was typed by a friend. Had I hired a secretary to do the same job, GDP would have been higher, even though the amount of output would have been identical. Why is this? Does this make sense?
2. GDP in 1981 was $2.96 trillion. It grew to $3.07 trillion in 1982, yet the quantity of output actually decreased. How is this possible?
3. If gross investment is not large enough to replace the capital that depreciates in a particular year, is net investment greater or less than zero? What happens to our production possibilities?
4. Can we increase consumption in a given year without cutting back on either investment or government services? Under what conditions?

5. Why is it important to know how much output is being produced? Who uses such information?
6. What jobs are likely part of the underground economy?
7. How might the quality of life be adversely affected by an increase in GDP?

8. Is the Fordham Index of Social Health, discussed in the NEWS on p. 111, a better barometer of well-being than GDP? What are its relative advantages or disadvantages?

ALERT!

PROBLEMS   The Student Problem Set at the back of this book contains numerical and graphing problems for this chapter.

WEB ACTIVITIES   to accompany this chapter can be found on the Online Learning Center:
http://www.mhhe.com/economics/schiller10

Unemployment

George H. had worked at the textile mill in Kannapolis, North Carolina for 18 years. Now he was 46 years old, with a wife and three children. With his base salary of $38,200 and the performance bonus he received nearly every year, he was doing pretty well. He had his own home, two cars, company-paid health insurance for the family, and a growing nest egg in the company's pension plan. The H. family wasn't rich, but they were comfortable and secure.

Or so they thought. Overnight the H. family's comfort was shattered. With little warning, the mill was closed in July 2003. George H., along with 4,800 fellow workers, was permanently laid off. The weekly paychecks and the company-paid health insurance stopped immediately; the pension nest egg was in doubt. Within a few weeks, George H. was on the street looking for a new job—an experience he hadn't had since high school. The unemployment benefits the state provided didn't come close to paying the mortgage payment, groceries, insurance, and other necessities. And even those benefits soon ran out. The H. family quickly used up its savings, including the $5,000 they'd set aside for the children's college education.

George H. stayed unemployed for nearly two years. His wife found a part-time waitressing job, and his oldest son went to work rather than college. George himself ultimately found a warehousing job that paid only half as much as his previous job.

In the recession of 2001 and its aftermath nearly 2 *million* workers lost their jobs as companies "downsized," "restructured," or simply closed. Not all these displaced workers fared as badly as George H. and his family. But the job loss was a painful experience for every one of those displaced workers. That's the human side of an economic downturn.

The pain of joblessness is not confined to those who lose their jobs. In recessions, students discover that jobs are hard to find in the summer. In the recession of 2001, college graduates found out that jobs weren't waiting for them. No matter how good their grades were or how nice their résumés looked, some graduates just didn't get any job offers. Those who did get job offers were dismayed when start dates were postponed—or the offer was rescinded. Even people with jobs felt some economic pain: Their paychecks shrank when hours or wages were scaled back.

In this chapter we take a closer look at the problem of unemployment, focusing on the following questions:

- **When is a person "unemployed"?**
- **What are the costs of unemployment?**
- **What's an appropriate policy goal for "full employment"?**

As we answer these questions, we'll develop a sense of why full employment is a major goal of macro policy and begin to see some of the obstacles we face in achieving it.

THE LABOR FORCE

To assess the dimensions of our unemployment problems, we first need to decide who wants a job. Millions of people are jobless, yet they're not part of our unemployment problem. Full-time students, young children playing with their toys, and older people living in retirement are all jobless. We don't expect them to be working, so we don't regard them as part of the unemployment problem. We're not concerned that *everybody* be put to work, only with ensuring jobs for all those persons who are ready and willing to work.

To distinguish between those people who want a job from those who don't, we separate the entire population into two distinct groups. One group consists of *labor-force participants;* the other group encompasses all *nonparticipants.*

The **labor force** includes everyone age 16 and older who is actually working plus all those who aren't working but are actively seeking employment. Individuals are also counted as employed in a particular week if their failure to work is due to vacation, illness, labor dispute (strike), or bad weather. All such persons are regarded as "with a job but not at work." Also, unpaid family members working in a family enterprise (farming, for example) are counted as employed. ***People who are neither employed nor actively seeking work aren't counted as part of the labor force;*** they're referred to as *nonparticipants.* As Figure 6.1 shows, only half the U.S. population participates in the labor force.

Note that our definition of labor-force participation excludes most household and volunteer activities. A person who chooses to devote their energies to household responsibilities or to unpaid charity work isn't counted as part of the labor force, no matter how hard he or she works. Because they are neither in paid employment nor seeking such employment in the marketplace, they are regarded as outside the labor market (a nonparticipant). But if he or she decides to seek a paid job outside the home, we'd say that they are "entering the labor force." Students too are typically out of the labor force until they leave school. They *"enter"* the labor force when they go looking for a job, either during the summer or after graduation. People *"exit"* the labor force when they go back to school, return to household activities, go to prison, or retire. These entrants and exits keep changing the size and composition of the labor force.

> **labor force:** All persons over age 16 who are either working for pay or actively seeking paid employment.

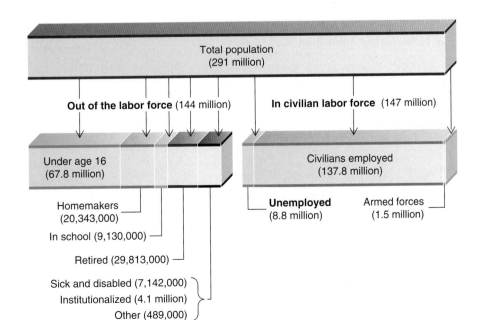

FIGURE 6.1

The Labor Force, 2003

Only half the total U.S. population participates in the civilian labor force. The rest of the population is too young, in school, at home, retired, or otherwise unavailable.

Unemployment statistics count only those participants who aren't currently working but are actively seeking paid employment. Nonparticipants are neither employed nor actively seeking employment.

Source: U.S. Bureau of Labor Statistics.

FIGURE 6.2
A Growing Labor Force

The labor force expands as the birth rate and immigration increase. A big increase in the participation rate of women has also added to labor-force growth.

Source: *Economic Report of the President, 2004.*

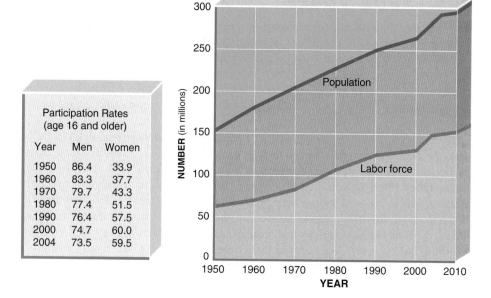

Participation Rates (age 16 and older)		
Year	Men	Women
1950	86.4	33.9
1960	83.3	37.7
1970	79.7	43.3
1980	77.4	51.5
1990	76.4	57.5
2000	74.7	60.0
2004	73.5	59.5

Since 1960, the U.S. labor force has more than doubled in size. As Figure 6.2 indicates, this labor-force growth has come from two distinct sources: population growth and a rising **labor-force participation rate.** The U.S. population has increased by only 50 percent since 1960, just half as fast as the labor force. The difference is explained by the rapid increase in the labor-force participation of women. Notice in Figure 6.2 that only one out of three women participated in the labor force in 1950–60, whereas 6 out of 10 now do so. The labor-force participation of men actually declined during the same period, even though it remains higher than that of women.

labor-force participation rate: The percentage of the working-age population working or seeking employment.

Future growth of the U.S. labor force will come primarily from population growth and immigration. These two sources add more than 1.5 million persons to the labor force each year. This labor-force growth is an important source of the nation's economic growth. As we first saw in Chapter 1, the quantity of goods and services an economy can produce in any time period is limited by two factors:

- *Availability of factors of production.*
- *Our technological know-how.*

Growth of Production Possibilities

As the available labor force has grown, the nation's **production possibilities** curve has shifted outward, as in Figure 6.3. With those shifts has come an increased capacity for producing goods and services, the essence of long-run **economic growth.**

production possibilities: The alternative combinations of final goods and services that could be produced in a given time period with all available resources and technology.

FIGURE 6.3
Labor-Force Growth

The amount of labor available for work—the *labor force*—is a prime determinant of a nation's production possibilities. As the labor force grows, so does the capacity to produce. To produce at capacity, however, the labor force must be fully employed. At point *F*, resources are unemployed.

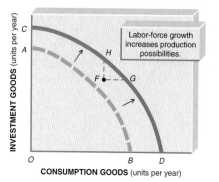

Institutional Constraints. We could grow the economy even faster if we used more labor and natural resources. But we've chosen to impose institutional constraints on resource exploitation. Child labor laws, for example, prohibit small children from working, no matter how much they or their parents yearn to contribute to total output. Yet we could produce more output this year if we put all those little bodies to work. In fact, we could produce a little more output this year if you were to put down this book and get a job. To the extent that small children, students, and others are precluded from working, both the size of our labor force (our *available* labor) and our potential output shrink.

Constraints are also imposed on the use of material resources and technology. We won't cut down all the forests this year and build everybody a wooden palace. We've collectively decided to preserve some natural habitat for owls and other endangered species. Therefore, the federal government limits each year's tree harvest on public lands. The federal government also restricts the use of nuclear technology. In both cases, the need for environmental protection constrains the use of resources or technology and limits annual output. These are *institutional* constraints on our productive capacity. Without such constraints, we could produce more output. Our production possibilities in any year therefore depend not only on what resources and technology are available but also on how we choose to restrict their use.

An expanding labor force not only increases our capacity to produce but also implies the need to keep creating new jobs. Even in the short run (with given resources and technology), we have to confront the issue of job availability.

We can't reach points beyond the production possibilities curve, but we can easily end up somewhere inside that curve, as at point *F* in Figure 6.3. When that happens, we're not producing at (short-run) capacity, and some available resources remain underused. ***To make full use of available production capacity, the labor force must be fully employed.*** If we fail to provide jobs for all labor-force participants, we end up with less than capacity output and the related problem of **unemployment.** With the labor force growing by 1.5 million people a year, the challenge of keeping all labor-force participants employed never disappears.

Okun's Law. Arthur Okun quantified the relationship between the production possibilities curve and unemployment. According to the original formulation of **Okun's Law,** each additional 1 percent of unemployment translated into a loss of 3 percent in real output. More recent estimates of Okun's Law put the ratio at about 1 to 2, largely due to the changing composition of both the labor force (more women and teenagers) and output (more services). Using that 2-to-1 ratio allows us to put a dollar value on the aggregate cost of unemployment. In 2003, high unemployment left us $450 billion short of our production possibilities. That output shortfall implied a loss of $1,500 of goods and services for every American.

MEASURING UNEMPLOYMENT

To determine how many people are actually unemployed, the U.S. Census Bureau surveys about 60,000 households each month. The Census interviewers first determine whether a person is employed—that is, worked for pay in the previous week (or didn't work due to illness, vacation, bad weather, or a labor strike). If the person isn't employed, he or she is either unemployed or out of the labor force. To make that distinction, the Census interviewers ask whether the person actively looked for work in the preceding four weeks. ***If a person is not employed and actively seeking a job, he or she is counted as unemployed.*** Individuals neither employed nor actively seeking a job are counted as outside the labor force (nonparticipants). The responses to this survey provide the basis for estimating the total number of people who are unemployed across the country.

---

economic growth: An increase in output (real GDP); an expansion of production possibilities.

Unemployment

unemployment: The inability of labor-force participants to find jobs.

Okun's Law: 1 percent more unemployment is estimated to equal 2 percent less output.

The Unemployment Rate

unemployment rate: The proportion of the labor force that is unemployed.

WEBNOTE

Data on unemployment by race and gender from 1948 to the present are available from the Bureau of Labor Statistics at www.bls.gov.

In 2003, an average of 8.8 million persons were counted as unemployed in any month. As Figure 6.1 shows, these unemployed individuals accounted for 6.0 percent of our total labor force. Accordingly, the average **unemployment rate** in 2003 was 6 percent.

$$\text{Unemployment rate} = \frac{\text{number of unemployed people}}{\text{labor force}}$$

The monthly unemployment figures indicate not only the total amount of unemployment in the economy but also which groups are suffering the greatest unemployment. Typically, teenagers just entering the labor market have the greatest difficulty finding (or keeping) jobs. They have no job experience and relatively few marketable skills. Employers are reluctant to hire them, especially if they must pay the federal minimum wage. As a consequence, teenage unemployment rates are typically three times higher than adult unemployment rates (see Figure 6.4).

Minority workers also experience above-average unemployment. Notice in Figure 6.4 that black and hispanic unemployment rates are much higher than white worker's unemployment rates.

Education also affects the chances of being unemployed. If you graduate from college, your chances of being unemployed drop sharply, regardless of gender or race (Figure 6.4). Advancing technology and a shift to services from manufacturing have put a premium on better-educated workers. Very few people with master's or doctoral degrees stand in unemployment lines.

FIGURE 6.4

Unemployment Isn't Experienced Equally by Race, Sex, or Education

Minority groups, teenagers, and less-educated individuals experience higher rates of unemployment. Teenage unemployment rates are particularly high, especially for black and other minority youth.
Source: U.S. Department of Labor (2003 data).

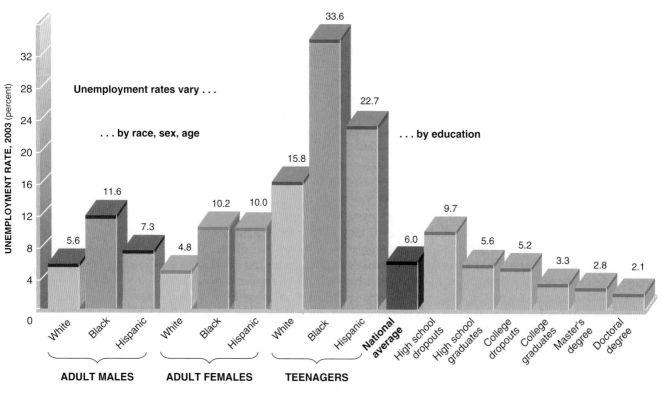

Duration	Percent of Unemployed
Less than 5 weeks	31.7%
5 to 14 weeks	29.8
15 to 26 weeks	16.4
27 weeks or more	22.1

Source: U.S. Bureau of Labor Statistics (2003 data).

TABLE 6.1
Duration of Unemployment

The severity of unemployment depends on how long the spell of joblessness lasts. About one-third of unemployed workers return to work quickly, but many others remain unemployed for six months or longer.

Although high school dropouts are more likely to be unemployed than college graduates, they don't *stay* unemployed. In fact, most people who become unemployed remain jobless for a relatively brief period of time. As Table 6.1 indicates, the median spell of unemployment in 2003 was 10 weeks. Less than one out of four unemployed individuals had been jobless for as long as six months (27 weeks or longer). People who lose their jobs do find new ones. **When the economy is growing, both unemployment rates and the average duration of unemployment decline.** Recessions have the opposite effect—raising the costs of unemployment significantly.

The reason a person becomes unemployed also affects the length of time the person stays jobless. A person just entering the labor market might need more time to identify job openings and develop job contacts. By contrast, an autoworker laid off for a temporary plant closing can expect to return to work quickly. Figure 6.5 depicts these and other reasons for unemployment. In 2003, half the unemployed were job losers (laid off or fired), and 1 in 11 were job leavers (quit). The rest were new entrants (primarily teenagers) or reentrants (primarily mothers returning to the workforce). Like the duration of unemployment, the reasons for joblessness are very sensitive to economic conditions. In really bad years, most of the unemployed are job losers, and they remain out of work a long time.

Unemployment statistics don't tell the complete story about the human costs of a sluggish economy. When unemployment persists, job seekers become increasingly frustrated. After repeated rejections, job seekers often get so discouraged that they give up the search and turn to their families, friends, or public welfare for income support. When the Census Bureau interviewer asks whether they're actively seeking employment, such **discouraged workers** are apt to reply no. Yet they'd like to be working, and they'd probably be out looking for work if jobs prospects were better.

The Duration of Unemployment

Reasons for Unemployment

Discouraged Workers

discouraged worker: An individual who isn't actively seeking employment but would look for or accept a job if one were available.

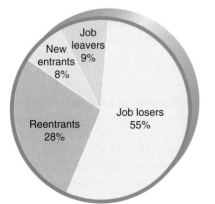

FIGURE 6.5
Reasons for Unemployment

People become unemployed for various reasons. Roughly half of the unemployed were job losers in 2003. About a third of the unemployed were entering or reentering the labor market in search of a job. In recessions, the proportion of job losers shoots up.

"*I've stopped looking for work, which, I believe, helps the economic numbers.*"

Analysis: People who stop searching for a job aren't officially counted as "unemployed." They are called "discouraged workers."

Discouraged workers aren't counted as part of our unemployment problem because they're technically out of the labor force (see cartoon). The Labor Department estimates that over 400,000 individuals fell into this uncounted class of discouraged workers in 2003. In years of higher unemployment, this number jumps sharply.

Underemployment

underemployment: People seeking full-time paid employment who work only part-time or are employed at jobs below their capability.

Some people can't afford to be discouraged. Many people who become jobless have family responsibilities and bills to pay: They simply can't afford to drop out of the labor force. Instead, they're compelled to take some job—any job—just to keep body and soul together. The resultant job may be part-time or full-time and may pay very little. Nevertheless, any paid employment is sufficient to exclude the person from the count of the unemployed, though not from a condition of **underemployment.**

Underemployed workers represent labor resources that aren't being fully utilized. They're part of our unemployment problem, even if they're not officially counted as *unemployed.* In 2003, nearly 4 million workers were underemployed in the U.S. economy.

The Phantom Unemployed

For the most recent data on unemployment in the United States, visit the U.S. Bureau of Labor Statistics at www.bls.gov.

Although discouraged and underemployed workers aren't counted in official unemployment statistics, some of the people who *are* counted probably shouldn't be. Many people report that they're actively seeking a job even when they have little interest in finding employment. To some extent, public policy actually encourages such behavior. For example, welfare recipients are often required to look for a job, even though some welfare mothers would prefer to spend all their time raising their children. Their resultant job search is likely to be perfunctory at best, including perhaps only one trip to the state employment office. Similarly, most states require people receiving unemployment benefits to provide evidence that they're looking for a job, even though some recipients may prefer a brief period of joblessness. Here again, reported unemployment may conceal labor-force nonparticipation. More generous benefits in European nations are thought to create similar problems (see the following World View).

WORLD VIEW

Europe's Unemployment Woes

Years of sluggish economic growth (low demand) raised unemployment rates in Europe to levels rarely seen in the United States. Generous unemployment benefits cushion the personal losses from joblessness, but they also discourage European workers from accepting new jobs (less supply).

Source: U.S. Department of Labor (2003 data). http://stats.bls.gov/fls

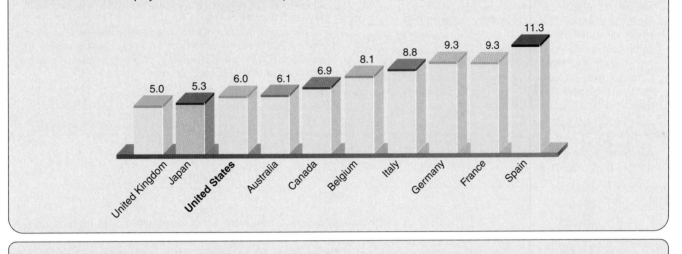

Analysis: Unemployment rates are typically significantly higher in Europe than in the United States. Analysts blame both sluggish economic growth and high unemployment benefits.

THE HUMAN COSTS

Although our measures of unemployment aren't perfect, they're a reliable index to a serious macro problem. Unemployment statistics tell us that millions of people are jobless. That may be all right for a day or even a week, but if you need income to keep body and soul together, prolonged unemployment can hurt.

The most visible impact of unemployment on individuals is the loss of income. For workers who've been unemployed for long periods of time, such losses can spell financial disaster. Typically, an unemployed person must rely on a combination of savings, income from other family members, and government unemployment benefits for financial support. After these sources of support are exhausted (see News on next page), public welfare is often the only legal support left.

Not all unemployed people experience such a financial disaster, of course. College students who fail to find summer employment are unlikely to end up on welfare the following semester. Similarly, teenagers and others looking for part-time employment won't suffer great economic losses from unemployment. Nevertheless, the experience of unemployment—of not being able to find a job when you want one—can still be painful. This sensation isn't easily forgotten, even after one has finally found employment.

It is difficult to measure all the intangible effects of unemployment on individual workers. Studies have shown, however, that joblessness causes more crime, more health problems, more divorces, and other problems (see News on page 123). Such findings underscore the notion that prolonged unemployment poses a real danger. Like George H., the worker discussed at the beginning of this chapter, many unemployed workers simply can't cope with the resulting stress. Thomas Cottle, a lecturer at Harvard Medical School, stated the case more bluntly: "I'm now convinced that unemployment is *the* killer disease in this country—responsible for wife beating, infertility, and even tooth decay."

WEBNOTE

Compare unemployment rates of different countries at <u>stats.bls.gov/fls/home.htm</u>.

Unemployment Benefits Not for Everyone

In 2003, nearly 10 million people collected unemployment benefits averaging $262 per week. But don't rush to the state unemployment office yet—not all unemployed people are eligible. To qualify for weekly unemployment benefits you must have worked a substantial length of time and earned some minimum amount of wages, both determined by your state. Furthermore, you must have a "good" reason for having lost your last job. Most states will not provide benefits to students (or their professors!) during summer vacations, to professional athletes in the off-season, or to individuals who quit their last jobs.

If you qualify for benefits, the amount of benefits you receive each week will depend on your previous wages. In most states the benefits are equal to about one-half of the previous weekly wage, up to a state-determined maximum. The maximum benefit in 2004 ranged from $205 in Arizona to a high of $508 in Massachusetts.

Unemployment benefits are financed by a tax on employers and can continue for as long as 26 weeks. During periods of high unemployment, the duration of benefit eligibility may be extended another 13 weeks or more.

Source: U.S. Employment and Training Administration. www.workforcesecurity.doleta.gov

Analysis: Some of the income lost due to unemployment is replaced by unemployment insurance benefits. Not all unemployed persons are eligible, however, and the duration of benefits is limited.

German psychiatrists have also observed that unemployment can be hazardous to your health. They estimate that the anxieties and other nervous disorders that accompany one year of unemployment can reduce life expectancy by as much as five years. In Japan, the suicide rate jumped by more than 50 percent in 1999 when the economy plunged into recession. In New Zealand, suicide rates are twice as high for unemployed workers than for employed ones.

There's an upside to these relationships as well. When the U.S. unemployment rate fell steadily in the late 1990s, so did crime rates, premarital births, divorce rates, and child abuse. Declining unemployment rates weren't the only cause of these trends, but they certainly helped.

DEFINING FULL EMPLOYMENT

In view of the economic and social losses associated with unemployment, it's not surprising that *full employment* is one of our basic macroeconomic goals. You may be surprised to learn, however, that *"full"* employment isn't the same thing as *"zero"* unemployment. There are in fact several reasons for regarding some degree of unemployment as inevitable and even desirable.

Seasonal Unemployment

seasonal unemployment: Unemployment due to seasonal changes in employment or labor supply.

Some joblessness is virtually inevitable as long as we continue to grow crops, build houses, or go skiing at certain seasons of the year. At the end of each such season, thousands of workers must go searching for new jobs, experiencing some **seasonal unemployment** in the process.

Seasonal fluctuations also arise on the supply side of the labor market. Teenage unemployment rates, for example, rise sharply in the summer as students look for temporary jobs. To avoid such unemployment completely, we'd either have to keep everyone in school or ensure that all students went immediately from the classroom to the workroom. Neither alternative is likely, much less desirable.[1]

[1]Seasonal variations in employment and labor supply not only create some unemployment in the annual averages but also distort monthly comparisons. Unemployment rates are always higher in February (when farming and housing construction come to a virtual standstill) and June (when a mass of students go looking for summer jobs). The Labor Department adjusts monthly unemployment rates according to this seasonal pattern and reports "seasonally adjusted" unemployment rates for each month. Seasonal adjustments don't alter *annual* averages, however.

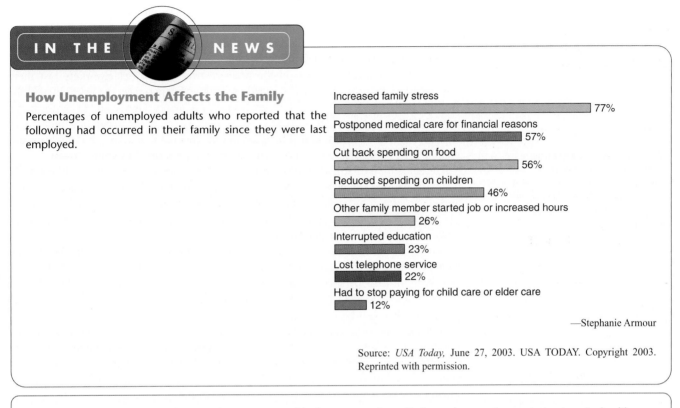

IN THE NEWS

How Unemployment Affects the Family

Percentages of unemployed adults who reported that the following had occurred in their family since they were last employed.

Increased family stress	77%
Postponed medical care for financial reasons	57%
Cut back spending on food	56%
Reduced spending on children	46%
Other family member started job or increased hours	26%
Interrupted education	23%
Lost telephone service	22%
Had to stop paying for child care or elder care	12%

—Stephanie Armour

Source: *USA Today,* June 27, 2003. USA TODAY. Copyright 2003. Reprinted with permission.

Analysis: The cost of unemployment is not measured in lost wages alone. Prolonged unemployment also impairs health, social relationships, and productivity.

There are other reasons for expecting a certain amount of unemployment. Many workers have sound financial or personal reasons for leaving one job to look for another. In the process of moving from one job to another, a person may well miss a few days or even weeks of work without any serious personal or social consequences. On the contrary, people who spend more time looking for work may find *better* jobs.

The same is true of students first entering the labor market. It's not likely that you'll find a job the moment you leave school. Nor should you necessarily take the first job offered. If you spend some time looking for work, you're more likely to find a job you like. The job-search period gives you an opportunity to find out what kinds of jobs are available, what skills they require, and what they pay. Accordingly, a brief period of job search may benefit labor market entrants and the larger economy. The unemployment associated with these kinds of job searches is referred to as **frictional unemployment.**

Three factors distinguish frictional unemployment from other kinds of unemployment. First, enough jobs exist for those who are frictionally unemployed—that is, there's adequate *demand* for labor. Second, those individuals who are frictionally unemployed have the skills required for available jobs. Third, the period of job search will be relatively short. Under these conditions, frictional unemployment resembles an unconventional game of musical chairs. There are enough chairs of the right size for everyone, and people dance around them for only a brief period of time.

No one knows for sure just how much of our unemployment problem is frictional. Most economists agree, however, that friction alone is responsible for an unemployment rate of 2 to 3 percent. Accordingly, our definition of *"full employment"* should allow for at least this much unemployment.

Frictional Unemployment

frictional unemployment: Brief periods of unemployment experienced by people moving between jobs or into the labor market.

Structural Unemployment

structural unemployment:
Unemployment caused by a mismatch between the skills (or location) of job seekers and the requirements (or location) of available jobs.

For many job seekers, the period between jobs may drag on for months or even years because they don't have the skills that employers require. Imagine, for example, the predicament of steelworkers. During the 1980s, the steel industry contracted as consumers demanded fewer and lighter-weight cars and as construction of highways, bridges, and buildings slowed. In the process, over 300,000 steelworkers lost their jobs. Most of these workers had a decade or more of experience and substantial skill. But the skills they'd perfected were no longer in demand. They couldn't perform the jobs available in computer software, biotechnology, or other expanding industries. Although there were enough job vacancies in the labor market, the steelworkers couldn't fill them: These workers were victims of **structural unemployment.**

The same kind of structural displacement hit the defense industry in the 1990s. Cutbacks in national defense spending forced weapons manufactures, aerospace firms, and electronics companies to reduce output and lay off thousands of workers. The displaced workers soon discovered that their highly developed skills weren't immediately applicable in nondefense industries.

Teenagers from urban slums also suffer from structural unemployment. Most poor teenagers have an inadequate education, few job-related skills, and little work experience. From their perspective, almost all decent jobs are "out of reach." As a consequence, these teenagers, many of whom are from minority groups, remain unemployed far longer than can be explained by frictional forces.

Structural unemployment violates the second condition for frictional unemployment: that the job seekers can perform the available jobs. Structural unemployment is analogous to a musical chairs game in which there are enough chairs for everyone, but some of them are too small to sit on. It's a more serious concern than frictional unemployment and incompatible with any notion of full employment.

Cyclical Unemployment

cyclical unemployment:
Unemployment attributable to a lack of job vacancies, that is, to an inadequate level of aggregate demand.

The fourth type of unemployment is **cyclical unemployment**—joblessness that occurs when there aren't simply enough jobs to go around. Cyclical unemployment exists when the number of workers demanded falls short of the number of persons supplied (in the labor force). This isn't a case of mobility between jobs (frictional unemployment) or even of job seekers' skills (structural unemployment). Rather, it's simply an inadequate level of demand for goods and services and thus for labor. Cyclical unemployment resembles the most familiar form of musical chairs, in which the number of chairs is always less than the number of players.

The Great Depression is the most striking example of cyclical unemployment. The dramatic increase in unemployment rates that began in 1930 (see Figure 6.6) wasn't due to any increase in friction or sudden decline in workers' skills. Instead, the high rates of unemployment that persisted for a *decade* were caused by a sudden decline in the market demand for goods and services. How do we know? Just notice what happened to our unemployment rate when the demand for military goods and services increased in 1941!

Slow Growth. Cyclical unemployment can emerge even when the economy is expanding. Keep in mind that the labor force is always growing, due to population growth and continuing immigration. If these additional labor-force participants are to find jobs, the economy must grow. Specifically, *the economy must grow at least as fast as the labor force to avoid cyclical unemployment.* When economic growth slows below this threshold, unemployment rates start to rise.

The Full-Employment Goal

In later chapters we examine the causes of cyclical unemployment and explore some potential policy responses. At this point, however, we're just establishing some perspective on the goal of full employment. In the Employment Act of 1946, Congress committed the federal government to pursue a goal of "maximum" employment but didn't specify exactly what that rate was. Presumably, this meant avoiding as much cyclical and structural unemployment as possible while keeping frictional unemployment within reasonable bounds. As guidelines for public policy, these perspectives are admittedly vague.

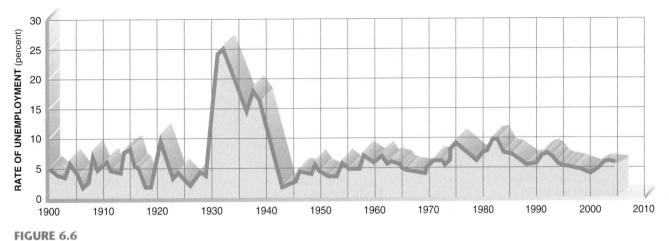

FIGURE 6.6
The Unemployment Record

Unemployment rates reached record heights (25 percent) during the Great Depression. In more recent decades, the unemployment rate has varied from 4 percent in full-employment years to over 10 percent in recession years. Keeping the labor force fully employed is a primary macro policy goal.

Source: U.S. Department of Labor.

Inflationary Pressures. The first attempt to define *full employment* more precisely was undertaken in the early 1960s. At that time the Council of Economic Advisers (itself created by the Employment Act of 1946) decided that our proximity to full employment could be gauged by watching *prices.* As the economy approached its production possibilities, labor and other resources would become increasingly scarce. As market participants bid for these remaining resources, wages and prices would start to rise. Hence, **rising prices are a signal that employment is nearing capacity.**

After examining the relationship between unemployment and inflation, the Council of Economic Advisers decided to peg full employment at 4 percent unemployment. The unemployment rate could fall below 4 percent. If it did, however, price levels would begin to rise. Thus, 4 percent unemployment was regarded as an acceptable compromise of our employment and price goals.

Changes in Structural Unemployment. During the 1970s and early 1980s, this view of our full-employment potential was considered overly optimistic. Unemployment rates stayed far above 4 percent, even when the economy expanded. Moreover, inflation began to accelerate at higher levels of unemployment. Critics suggested that structural barriers to full employment had intensified, necessitating a redefinition of our full-employment goal. These structural barriers included the following:

- *More youth and women.* Between 1956 and 1979, the proportion of teenagers in the labor force increased from 6 percent to 9 percent. During the same period, the proportion of adult women in the labor force grew tremendously (see Figure 6.2). Many of these women were entering the labor force for the first time—or reentering it after long periods of homemaking. These trends increased frictional and structural unemployment.
- *Liberal transfer payments.* Higher benefits and easier rules for unemployment insurance, food stamps, welfare, and Social Security made unemployment less painful. As a result, critics suggested, more people were willing to stay unemployed rather than work.
- *Structural changes in demand.* Changes in consumer demand, technology, and trade shrank the markets in steel, textiles, autos, and other industries. The workers dislocated from these industries couldn't be absorbed fast enough in new high-tech and other service industries.

In view of these factors, the Council of Economic Advisers later raised the level of unemployment thought to be compatible with price stability. In 1983, the Reagan administration concluded that the "inflation-threshold" unemployment rate was between 6 and 7 percent (see cartoon).

Declining Structural Pressures. The structural barriers that intensified inflationary pressures in the 1970s and early 1980s receded in the 1990s. The number of teenagers declined by 3 million between 1981 and 1993. The upsurge in women's participation in the labor force also leveled off. High school and college attendance and graduation rates increased. All these structural changes made it easier to reduce unemployment rates without increasing inflation. In 1991, the first Bush administration concluded that **full employment** was equivalent to 5.5 percent unemployment. In 1999, the Clinton administration suggested the full-employment threshold might have dropped even further, to 5.3 percent. In reality, the national unemployment rate stayed below even that benchmark for four years (Figure 6.6) without any upsurge in inflation. In 2004 the Bush administration set the full-employment threshold at 5.1 percent.

full employment: The lowest rate of unemployment compatible with price stability; variously estimated at between 4 percent and 6 percent unemployment.

The "Natural" Rate of Unemployment

natural rate of unemployment: Long-term rate of unemployment determined by structural forces in labor and product markets.

The ambiguity about which rate of unemployment might trigger an upsurge in inflation has convinced some analysts to abandon the inflation-based concept of full employment. They prefer to specify a "natural" rate of unemployment that doesn't depend on inflation trends. In this view, the natural rate of unemployment consists of frictional and structural components only. It's the rate of unemployment that will prevail in the long run. In the short run, both the unemployment rate and the inflation rate may go up and down. However, the economy will tend to gravitate toward the long-run **natural rate of unemployment.**

Although the natural rate concept avoids specifying a short-term inflation trigger, it too is subject to debate. As we've seen, the *structural* determinants of

"I don't like six-per-cent unemployment, either. But I can live with it."

Analysis: So-called full employment entails a compromise between employment and inflation goals. That compromise doesn't affect everyone equally.

unemployment (e.g., age and composition of the labor force) change over time. When structural forces change, the level of natural unemployment presumably changes as well.

Although most economists agree that an unemployment rate of 4 to 6 percent is consistent with either natural or full employment, Congress has set tougher goals for macro policy. According to the Full Employment and Balanced Growth Act of 1978 (commonly called the Humphrey-Hawkins Act), our national goal is to attain a 4 percent rate of unemployment. The act also requires a goal of 3 percent inflation. There was an escape clause, however. In the event that both goals couldn't be met, the president could set higher, provisional definitions of full employment.

Congressional Targets

To see the Fed's annual Humphrey-Hawkins report to Congress, go to www.federalreserve.gov/boarddocs/hh.

THE HISTORICAL RECORD

Although there's some ambiguity about the specific definition of full employment, the historical record is littered with evident failures. Our greatest failure occurred during the Great Depression, when as much as one-fourth of the labor force was unemployed. As Figure 6.6 shows, unemployment rates were extraordinarily high throughout the 1930s.

Unemployment rates fell dramatically during World War II. In 1944, virtually anyone who was ready and willing to work quickly found a job: The civilian unemployment rate hit a rock-bottom 1.2 percent.

Since 1950, the unemployment rate has fluctuated from a low of 2.8 percent during the Korean War (1953) to a high of 10.8 percent during the 1981–82 recession. From 1982 to 1989 the unemployment rate receded, but it shot up again in the 1990–91 recession. As many as 10 million workers were unemployed at one time during that recession. Millions more experienced joblessness during the course of that economic downturn. During the last half of the 1990s the unemployment rate fell steadily and hit the low end of the full-employment range in 2000. Slow GDP growth in 2000–01 and the economic stall caused by the September 11, 2001, terrorist attacks, pushed the unemployment rate sharply higher in late 2001 (see News).

To get a more vivid image of the Great Depression than unemployment statistics provide, see the photo collection of the Farm Security Administration at memory.loc.gov/ammem/fsowhome.html.

IN THE NEWS

Unemployment Soars by 700,000

The U.S. jobless rate surged to 5.4 percent last month, the highest level in almost five years, as companies laid off hundreds of thousands of workers in the wake of the Sept. 11 terrorist attacks, the Labor Department reported yesterday.

The rate jumped from 4.9 percent in September, for the biggest monthly increase since the recession of 1980.

As the economy deteriorated, jobless rates rose significantly for every major demographic group—adult men and women, teens, whites, blacks and persons of Hispanic origin—as the ranks of the unemployed soared to 7.7 million from 7 million.

The number of people working part time, either because their workweeks were cut back or because they could not find full-time jobs, is also growing. Over the past two months, this group has increased by 1.1 million, to 4.5 million.

—John M. Berry

Source: *Washington Post*, November 3, 2001, p. 1. © 2001 The Washington Post. Reprinted with permission. www.washingtonpost.com

Analysis: A slowdown in economic growth causes the unemployment rate to rise—sometimes sharply.

THE ECONOMY TOMORROW

Outsourcing Jobs

outsourcing: The relocation of production to foreign countries

To keep unemployment rates low in the economy tomorrow, job growth in U.S. product markets must exceed labor-force growth. As we've observed, this will require at least 1.5 million *new* jobs every year. To make matters worse, a lot of U.S. firms are shutting down U.S. operations and relocating production to Mexico, China, and other foreign nations. Other firms are **outsourcing** a lot of their U.S. production to workers in India, Poland, Malaysia, and elsewhere.

Cheap Labor

Low wages are the primary motivation for all this outsourcing. As the accompanying World View documents, telephone operators and clerks in India are paid a tenth of their U.S. counterparts. Indian accountants and paralegals get paid less than half their U.S. counterparts. Polish workers are even cheaper. With cheap, high-speed telecommunications, that offshore labor is an attractive substitute for U.S. workers. Over the next 10 years, over 3 million U.S. jobs are expected to move offshore in response to such wage differentials.

Small Numbers

In the short run, outsourcing clearly worsens the U.S. employment outlook. But there's a lot more to the story. To begin with, the total number of outsourced jobs averages less than 300,000 per year. That amounts to only .002 of all U.S. jobs, and only 3–5 percent of total U.S. *un*employment. So even in the worst case, outsourcing can't be a major explanation for U.S. unemployment.

WORLD VIEW

Salary Gap

Programmers' Pay

A Hungarian computer programmer starts at a salary of $4,800 per year; an American programmer begins at $60,000.

Average Salaries of Computer Programmers

Country	Salary Range
Poland and Hungary	$4,800–8,000
India	$5,880–11,000
Philippines	$6,564
Malaysia	$7,200
Russian Federation	$5,000–7,500
China	$8,952
Canada	$28,174
Ireland	$23,000–34,000
Israel	$15,000–38,000
United States	$60,000–80,000

Wages, India Versus U.S.

Wages in the United States in some occupations are twice as high as in India, and in others 12 times as high.

Hourly Wages for Selected Occupations, U.S. and India, 2002–2003

Occupation	U.S.	India
Telephone Operator	$12.57	Under $1.00
Health Record Technologist/ Medical Transcriptionist	$13.17	$1.50–2.00
Payroll Clerk	$15.17	$1.50–2.00
Legal Assistant/Paralegal	$17.86	$6.00–8.00
Accountant	$23.35	$6.00–15.00
Financial Researcher/Analyst	$33.00–35.00	$6.00–15.00

Source: Ashok Deo Bardhan and Cynthia Kroll, "The New Wave of Outsourcing" (November 2, 2003). *Fisher Center for Real Estate and Urban Economics. Fisher Center Reports*: Report # 1103. http://repositories. cdlib.org/iber/fcrene/reports/1103.

Analysis: Cheap foreign labor is a substitute for U.S. labor. These and similar salary gaps encourage U.S. firms to relocate production offshore.

We also have to recognize that outsourcing of U.S. jobs has a counterpart in the "insourcing" of foreign production. The German BMW company builds cars in Alabama to reduce production and distribution costs, so German autoworkers lose some job opportunities to U.S. autoworkers. Other foreign companies invest billions of dollars every year in U.S. production facilities. In addition to this direct investment, foreign nations and firms hire U.S. workers to design, build, and deliver a wide variety of products. In other words, ***trade in both products and labor resources is a two-way street.*** Looking at the flow of jobs in only one direction distorts the jobs picture.

Insourcing

Even the gross flow of outsourced jobs is not all bad. The cost savings realized by U.S. firms due to outsourcing increases U.S. profits. Those profits may finance new investment or consumption in U.S. product markets, thereby creating new jobs. The accompanying News suggests more jobs are gained than lost as a result. Outsourcing

Productivity and Growth

IN THE NEWS

Outsourcing May Create U.S. Jobs

Higher Productivity Allows For Investment in Staffing, Expansion, a Study Finds

WASHINGTON—U.S. companies sending computer-systems work abroad yielded higher productivity that actually boosted domestic employment by 90,000 across the economy last year, according to an industry-sponsored study.

The analysis, one of the few that attaches detailed dollar values to offshore outsourcing's costs and benefits, was conducted for

More Jobs
Estimated new U.S. jobs created from outsourcing abroad, according to an industry study

	2003	2008
Natural Resources & Mining	1,046	1,182
Construction	19,815	75,757
Manufacturing	3,078	25,010
Wholesale Trade	20,456	43,359
Retail Trade	12,552	30,931
Transportation & Utilities	18,895	63,513
Publishing, Software & Communications	−24,860	−50,043
Financial Services	5,604	32,066
Professional & Business Services	14,667	31,623
Education & Health Services	18,015	47,260
Leisure, Hospitality & Other Services	4,389	12,506
Government	−3,393	4,203
Total Employment	**90,264**	**317,367**

Source: Global Insight and North American Industry Classification System.

a coalition of business groups working to combat a growing backlash on Capitol Hill and in statehouses against the loss of U.S. jobs.

Expected to be released today, the study's premise is that U.S. companies' use of foreign workers lowers costs, increases labor productivity and produces income that companies can use to expand both in the U.S. and abroad. . . .

The study claims that twice the number of U.S. jobs are created than displaced, producing wage increases in various sectors. The report takes a rather narrow focus, tracking the outsourcing of computer-services jobs, but not other work increasingly being done abroad such as manufacturing, call centers or medical X-ray reading.

Among the study's conclusions, spending for global outsourcing of computer software and services is expected to grow at a compound annual rate of almost 26%, increasing to $31 billion in 2008—or 6.2% of all information-technology spending by U.S. companies—from about $10 billion in 2003.

During the same period, total savings from lower wages, among other things, are estimated to grow to $20.9 billion from $6.7 billion. The savings are expected to translate into the creation of 317,000 U.S. jobs by 2008, including in construction, education, health care and financial services. Since the beginning of 2003, 104,000 jobs were displaced because of outsourcing, the study concludes.

Demand for U.S. exports is expected to increase due to the relatively lower prices of U.S.-produced goods and services and higher incomes in foreign countries where U.S. work is done. Exports increased by $2.3 billion in 2003 because of the practice, and are expected to expand $9 billion by 2008, the study said.

—Michael Schroeder

Analysis: Outsourcing increases U.S. productivity and profits while reducing U.S. production costs and prices. These outcomes may increase demand for U.S. jobs by more than the immediate job loss.

routine tasks to foreign workers also raises the productivity of U.S. workers by allowing U.S. workers to focus on more complex and high-value tasks. In other words, outsourcing promotes specialization and higher productivity both here and abroad. ***Production possibilities expand, not contract, with outsourcing.***

Creating Jobs   Greater efficiency and expanded production possibilities don't guarantee jobs in the economy tomorrow. The challenge is still to *use* that expanded capacity to the fullest. To do so, we have to use macroeconomic tools to keep output growing faster than the labor force. Stopping the outsourcing of jobs won't achieve that goal—and may even worsen income and job prospects in the economy tomorrow.

SUMMARY

- To understand unemployment, we must distinguish the labor force from the larger population. Only people who are working (employed) or spend some time looking for a job (unemployed) are participants in the labor force. People neither working nor looking for work are outside the labor force.
- The size of the labor force affects production possibilities. As the labor force grows, so does the capacity to produce goods and services.
- Unemployment implies that we're producing inside the production possibilities curve rather than on it.
- The macroeconomic loss imposed by unemployment is reduced output of goods and services. Okun's Law suggests that 1 percentage point in unemployment is equivalent to a 2 percentage point decline in output.
- The human cost of unemployment includes not only financial losses but social, physical, and psychological costs as well.
- Unemployment is distributed unevenly; minorities, teenagers, and the less educated have much higher rates of unemployment. Also hurt are discouraged workers—those who've stopped looking for work at part-time or menial

jobs because they can't find full-time jobs equal to their training or potential.
- There are four types of unemployment: seasonal, frictional, structural, and cyclical. Because some seasonal and frictional unemployment is inevitable and even desirable, full employment is not defined as zero unemployment. These considerations, plus fear of inflationary consequences, result in full employment being defined as an unemployment rate of 4 to 6 percent.
- The economy (output) must grow at least as fast as the labor force to keep the unemployment rate from rising.
- The natural rate of unemployment is based on frictional and structural forces, without reference to short-term price (inflation) pressures.
- Unemployment rates got as high as 25 percent in the 1930s. Since 1960, the unemployment rate has ranged from 3.4 to 10.8 percent.
- Outsourcing of U.S. production directly reduces domestic employment. But the indirect effects of higher U.S. productivity, profits, and global competitiveness may create even more jobs.

Key Terms

labor force
labor-force participation rate
production possibilities
economic growth
unemployment
Okun's Law

unemployment rate
discouraged worker
underemployment
seasonal unemployment
frictional unemployment

structural unemployment
cyclical unemployment
full employment
natural rate of unemployment
outsourcing

Questions for Discussion

1. Is it possible for unemployment rates to increase at the same time that the number of employed persons is increasing? How?

2. If more teenagers stay in school longer, what happens to (*a*) production possibilities? (*b*) unemployment rates?

3. What factors might explain (*a*) the rising labor-force participation rate of women and (*b*) the declining participation of men? (See Figure 6.2 for trends.)

4. Why might job (re)entrants have a harder time finding a job than job losers?

5. If the government guaranteed some income to all unemployed persons, how might the unemployment rate be affected? Who should get unemployment benefits? (See News, page 122.)

6. Can you identify three institutional constraints on the use of resources (factors of production)? What has motivated these constraints?

7. Why is frictional unemployment deemed desirable?

8. Why do people expect inflation to heat up when the unemployment rate approaches 4 percent?

9. Identify (*a*) two jobs at your school that could be outsourced and (*b*) two jobs that would be hard to outsource.

10. How can the outsourcing of U.S. computer jobs generate new U.S. jobs in construction or retail trade? (See News, p. 129.)

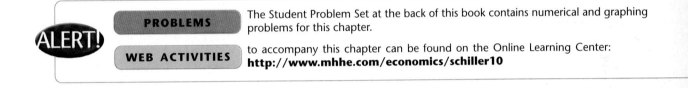

ALERT!

PROBLEMS The Student Problem Set at the back of this book contains numerical and graphing problems for this chapter.

WEB ACTIVITIES to accompany this chapter can be found on the Online Learning Center: **http://www.mhhe.com/economics/schiller10**

Inflation

Germany set a record in 1923 that no other nation wants to beat. In that year, prices in Germany rose a *trillion* times over. Prices rose so fast that workers took "shopping breaks" to spend their twice-a-day paychecks before they became worthless. Menu prices in restaurants rose while people were still eating! Accumulated savings became worthless, as did outstanding loans. People needed sacks of currency to buy bread, butter, and other staples. With prices more than doubling every *day,* no one could afford to save, invest, lend money, or make long-term plans. In the frenzy of escalating prices, production of goods and services came to a halt, unemployment rose tenfold, and the German economy all but collapsed.

Hungary had a similar episode of runaway inflation in 1946, as did Japan. More recently, Russia, Bulgaria, Brazil, Zaire, Yugoslavia, Argentina, and Uruguay have all witnessed at least a tenfold jump in prices in a single year.

The United States has never experienced such a price frenzy. During the Revolutionary War, prices did double in one year, but that was a singular event. In the last decade, U.S. prices have risen just 1 to 4 percent a year. Despite this enviable record, Americans still *worry* a lot about inflation. In response to this anxiety, every president since Franklin Roosevelt has expressed a determination to keep prices from rising. In 1971, the Nixon administration took drastic action to stop inflation. With prices rising an average of only 3 percent, President Nixon imposed price controls on U.S. producers to keep prices from rising any faster. For 90 days all wages and prices were frozen by law—price increases were prohibited. For three more years, wage and price increases were limited by legal rules.

In 1990, U.S. prices were rising at a 6 percent clip—twice the pace that triggered the 1971–74 wage and price controls. Calling such price increases "unacceptable," Federal Reserve Chairman Alan Greenspan set a goal of *zero* percent inflation. In pursuit of that goal, the Fed slowed economic growth so much that the economy fell into a recession. The Fed did the same thing again in early 2000. With even less evidence of inflation, the Fed slowed the economy to the brink of another recession.

In later chapters we'll examine how the Fed and other policymakers slow the economy down or speed it up. Before looking at the levers of macro policy, however, we need to examine our policy goals. Why is inflation so feared? How much inflation is unacceptable? To get a handle on this basic issue, we'll ask and answer the following questions:

- **What kind of price increases are referred to as *inflation?***
- **Who is hurt (or helped) by inflation?**
- **What is an appropriate goal for *price stability?***

As we'll discover, inflation is a serious problem, but not for the reasons most people cite. We'll also see why deflation—falling prices—isn't so welcome either.

WHAT IS INFLATION?

Most people associate **inflation** with price increases on specific goods and services. The economy isn't necessarily experiencing an inflation, however, every time the price of a cup of coffee goes up. We must be careful to distinguish the phenomenon of inflation from price increases for specific goods. *Inflation is an increase in the average level of prices, not a change in any specific price.*

> **inflation:** An increase in the average level of prices of goods and services.

The Average Price

Suppose you wanted to know the average price of fruit in the supermarket. Surely you wouldn't have much success in seeking out an average fruit—nobody would be quite sure what you had in mind. You might have some success, however, if you sought out the prices of apples, oranges, cherries, and peaches. Knowing the price of each kind of fruit, you could then compute the average price of fruit. The resultant figure wouldn't refer to any particular product but would convey a sense of how much a typical basket of fruit might cost. By repeating these calculations every day, you could then determine whether fruit prices, *on average,* were changing. On occasion, you might even notice that apple prices rose while orange prices fell, leaving the *average* price of fruit unchanged.

The same kinds of calculations are made to measure inflation in the entire economy. We first determine the average price of all output—the average price level—then look for changes in that average. A rise in the average price level is referred to as inflation.

The average price level may fall as well as rise. A decline in average prices—a **deflation**—occurs when price decreases on some goods and services outweigh price increases on all others. This happened in Japan in 1995, and again in 2003 (see World View "Worldwide Inflation," p. 146). Such deflations are rare, however: The United States has not experienced any general deflation since 1940.

> **deflation:** A decrease in the average level of prices of goods and services.

Relative Prices vs. the Price Level

Because inflation and deflation are measured in terms of average price levels, it's possible for individual prices to rise or fall continuously without changing the average price level. We already noted, for example, that the price of apples can rise without increasing the average price of fruit, so long as the price of some other fruit, such as oranges, falls. In such circumstances, **relative prices** are changing, but not average prices. An increase in the *relative* price of apples simply means that apples have become more expensive in comparison with other fruits (or any other goods or services).

> **relative price:** The price of one good in comparison with the price of other goods.

Changes in relative prices may occur in a period of stable average prices, or in periods of inflation or deflation. In fact, in an economy as vast as ours—in which literally millions of goods and services are exchanged in the factor and product markets—relative prices are always changing. Indeed, relative price changes are an essential ingredient of the market mechanism. Recall from Chapter 3 what happens when the market price of Web-design services rises relative to other goods and services. This (relative) price rise alerts Web architects (producers) to increase their output, cutting back on other production or leisure activities.

A general inflation—an increase in the average price level—doesn't perform this same market function. If all prices rise at the same rate, price increases for specific goods are of little value as market signals. In less extreme cases, when most but not all prices are rising, changes in relative prices do occur but aren't so immediately apparent. Table 7.1 reminds us that some prices do fall even during periods of general inflation.

REDISTRIBUTIVE EFFECTS OF INFLATION

The distinction between relative and average prices helps us determine who's hurt by inflation—and who's helped. Popular opinion notwithstanding, it's simply not true that everyone is worse off when prices rise. *Although inflation makes some people worse off, it makes other people better off.* Some people even get rich when prices rise! The micro consequences of inflation are reflected in redistributions of income and wealth, not general declines in either measure of our economic welfare. These redistributions

TABLE 7.1
Prices That Have Fallen

Inflation refers to an increase in the *average* price level. It doesn't mean that *all* prices are rising. In fact, many prices fall, even during periods of general inflation.

Item	Early Price	2004 Price
Long-distance telephone call (per minute)	$ 6.90 (1915)	$ 0.05
Pocket electronic calculator	200.00 (1972)	2.99
Digital watch	2,000.00 (1972)	1.99
Polaroid camera (color)	150.00 (1963)	29.95
Pantyhose	2.16 (1967)	1.29
Ballpoint pen	0.89 (1965)	0.29
Transistor radio	55.00 (1967)	5.99
Videocassette recorder	1,500.00 (1977)	69.00
DVD player	800.00 (1997)	79.00
Laptop computer	3,500.00 (1986)	900.00
Airfare (New York–Paris)	490.00 (1958)	328.00
Microwave oven	400.00 (1972)	79.00
Contact lenses	275.00 (1972)	39.00
Television (19-inch, color)	469.00 (1980)	169.00
Compact disk player	1,000.00 (1985)	29.00
Digital camera	748.00 (1994)	140.00
Digital music player	399.00 (2001)	149.00

occur because people buy different combinations of goods and services, own different assets, and sell distinct goods or services (including labor). The impact of inflation on individuals therefore depends on how prices change for the goods and services each person actually buys or sells.

Price Effects

Price changes are the most visible consequence of inflation. If you've been paying tuition, you know how painful a price hike can be. Ten years ago, the average in-state tuition at public colleges and universities was $500 per year. Today the average in-state tuition exceeds $3,800. At private universities, tuition has increased eightfold in the past 10 years, to over $17,000. Even community colleges are getting expensive (see News). You don't need a whole course in economics to figure out the implications

IN THE NEWS

Tuition Is Up 11.5% at Community Colleges, Survey Finds; State Budget Cuts Are Blamed

Tuition for the current academic year jumped by 11.5 percent at community colleges, largely because of state budget cuts, according to a survey released last week by the American Association of Community Colleges.

In more than half of the states, community-college tuition rose by more than 10 percent. California and Virginia colleges had the highest percentage increases, at 60 percent and 42 percent, respectively. Maine and West Virginia did not raise tuition at all, although some two-year colleges in those states increased fees slightly.

The association conducted the survey because of concerns that "the tremendous cuts in state revenues were big enough

that they are beginning to affect our core values, namely access," said George R. Boggs, the group's president.

Still, the survey found, average tuition at public two-year colleges—$1,560 annually for full-time students—remains the lowest in higher education. The 11.5-percent increase amounts to a rise of roughly $80 per semester.

The survey also found that community colleges received 61.3 percent of their revenue last year from state and local governments. That's up from 56 percent in the 1998–99 academic year, according to a 2001 survey by the association.

—Jamilah Evelyn

Source: *Chronicle of Higher Education,* September 26, 2003. Copyright 2003, the Chronicle of Higher Education. Reprinted with permission.

Analysis: Tuition increases reduce the real income of students. How much you suffer from inflation depends on what happens to the prices of the products you purchase.

of these tuition hikes. To stay in college, you (or your parents) must forgo increasing amounts of other goods and services. You end up being worse off since you can't buy as many goods and services as you could before tuition went up.

The effect of tuition increases on your economic welfare is reflected in the distinction between nominal income and real income. **Nominal income** is the amount of money you receive in a particular time period; it's measured in current dollars. **Real income,** by contrast, is the purchasing power of that money, as measured by the quantity of goods and services your dollars will buy. If the number of dollars you receive every year is always the same, your *nominal income* doesn't change—but your *real income* will rise or fall with price changes.

Suppose your parents agree to give you $6,000 a year while you're in school. Out of that $6,000 you must pay for your tuition, room and board, books, and everything else. The budget for your first year at school might look like this:

nominal income: The amount of money income received in a given time period, measured in current dollars.

real income: Income in constant dollars; nominal income adjusted for inflation.

FIRST YEAR'S BUDGET

Nominal income	$6,000
Consumption	
Tuition	$3,000
Room and board	2,000
Books	300
Everything else	700
Total	$6,000

After paying for all your essential expenses, you have $700 to spend on clothes, entertainment, or anything else you want. That's not exactly living high, but it's not poverty.

Now suppose tuition increases to $3,500 in your second year, while all other prices remain the same. What will happen to your nominal income? Nothing. Unless your parents take pity on you, you'll still be getting $6,000 a year. Your nominal income is unchanged. Your *real* income, however, will suffer. This is evident in the second year's budget:

SECOND YEAR'S BUDGET

Nominal income	$6,000
Consumption	
Tuition	$3,500
Room and board	2,000
Books	300
Everything else	200
Total	$6,000

You now have to use more of your income to pay tuition. This means you have less income to spend on other things. Since room and board and books still cost $2,300 per year, there's only one place to cut: the category of "everything else." After tuition increases, you can spend only $200 per year on movies, clothes, pizzas, and dates—not $700, as in the "good old days." This $500 reduction in purchasing power represents a *real* income loss. Even though your *nominal* income is still $6,000, you have $500 less of "everything else" in your second year than you had in the first.

Although tuition hikes reduce the real income of students, nonstudents aren't hurt by such price increases. In fact, if tuition *doubled,* nonstudents really wouldn't care. They could continue to buy the same bundle of goods and services they'd been buying all along. Tuition increases reduce the real incomes only of people who go to college.

Two basic lessons about inflation are to be learned from this sad story:

- *Not all prices rise at the same rate during an inflation.* In our example, tuition increased substantially while other prices remained steady. Hence, the "average" price increase wasn't representative of any particular good or service. Typically, some prices rise rapidly, others only modestly, and some actually fall.

The average rate of inflation conceals substantial differences in the price changes of specific goods and services. The impact of inflation on individuals depends in part on which goods and services are consumed. People who buy goods whose prices are rising fastest lose more real income. In 2003, drivers and college students were particularly hard-hit by inflation.

Prices That Rose (%)		Prices That Fell (%)	
Gasoline	+16.5%	Airfares	−0.1%
Eggs	+13.8	Video rentals	−5.4
College tuition	+8.4	Butter	−7.1
Textbooks	+6.5	Televisions	−13.0
Coffee	+1.6	Computers	−20.7
Average inflation rate: +2.3%			

Source: U.S. Bureau of Labor Statistics.

- *Not everyone suffers equally from inflation.* This follows from our first observation. Those people who consume the goods and services that are rising faster in price bear a greater burden of inflation; their real incomes fall further. Other consumers bear a lesser burden, or even none at all, depending on how fast the prices rise for the goods they enjoy.

Table 7.2 illustrates some of the price changes that occurred in 2003. The average rate of inflation was only 2.3 percent. This was little solace to college students, however, who confronted tuition increases of 8.4 percent, and 6.5 percent price hikes on textbooks (sorry!). On the other hand, price reductions on video rentals and computers spared consumers of these products from the pain of the *average* inflation rate.

Income Effects

Even if all prices rose at the *same* rate, inflation would still redistribute income. The redistributive effects of inflation originate not only in *expenditure* patterns but also *income* patterns. Some people have fixed incomes that *don't* go up with inflation. Fixed-income groups include those retired people who depend primarily on private pensions and workers with multiyear contracts that fix wage rates at preinflation levels. Lenders (like banks) that have lent funds at fixed interest rates also suffer real income losses when price levels rise. They continue to receive interest payments fixed in *nominal* dollars that have increasingly less *real* value. All these market participants experience a declining share of real income (and output) in inflationary periods.

Not all market participants suffer a real income decline when prices rise. Some people's nominal income rises *faster* than average prices, thereby boosting their *real* incomes. Keep in mind that there are two sides to every market transaction. **What looks like a price to a buyer looks like an income to a seller.** If students all pay higher tuition, the university will take in more income. When the nominal incomes colleges receive increase faster than average prices, they actually *benefit* from inflation. They end up being able to buy *more* goods and services (including faculty, buildings, and library books) after a period of inflation than they could before. Their real income rises. When the price of this textbook goes up, my *nominal* income goes up. If the text prices rises faster than other prices, my *real* income increases as well. In either case, you lose (sorry!).

Once we recognize that nominal incomes and prices don't all increase at the same rate, it makes no sense to say that "inflation hurts everybody." **If prices are rising, incomes must be rising too.** In fact, on *average,* incomes rise just as fast as prices (see Figure 7.1). That fact is of little comfort, however, to those who end up losing real income in the inflation game.

Wealth Effects

Still more winners and losers of the inflation game are selected on the basis of the assets they hold. Suppose you deposit $100 in a savings account on January 1, where it earns 5 percent interest. At the end of the year you'll have more nominal wealth ($105) than you started with ($100). But what if all prices have doubled in the meantime? In that case, your $105 will buy you no more at the end of the year than $52.50

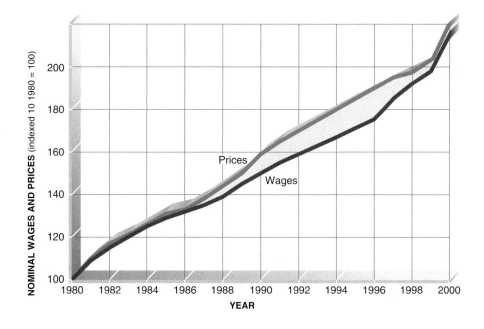

FIGURE 7.1
Nominal Wages and Prices

Inflation implies not only higher prices but higher incomes as well. Hence, inflation can't make *everyone* worse off. In fact, average wages increase along with average prices. They rise faster than prices when productivity increases. Wages rise slower than prices when fringe benefits or payroll taxes are increasing.

Source: *Economic Report of the President, 2004.*

would have bought you at the beginning. Inflation in this case reduces the *real* value of your savings, and you end up worse off than those individuals who spent all their income earlier in the year!

Table 7.3 shows how the value of various assets has changed. Between 1991 and 2001, the average price level increased 32 percent. The average value of stocks, diamonds, and homes rose much faster than the price level, increasing the *real* value of those assets. Farmland prices rose too, but just a bit more than average prices. People who owned bonds, silver, and gold weren't so lucky; their *real* wealth declined.

By altering relative prices, incomes, and the real value of wealth, inflation turns out to be a mechanism for redistributing incomes and wealth. ***The redistributive mechanics of inflation include:***

Redistributions

- *Price effects.* People who prefer goods and services that are increasing in price the fastest end up with fewer goods and services.
- *Income effects.* People whose nominal incomes rise more slowly than the rate of inflation end up with fewer goods and services.
- *Wealth effects.* People who own assets that are declining in real value end up with less real wealth.

Asset	Change in Value (%), 1991–2001
Stocks	+250%
Diamonds	+71
Oil	+66
Housing	+56
U.S. farmland	+49
Average price level	+32
Silver	+22
Bonds	+20
Stamps	−9
Gold	−29

TABLE 7.3
The Real Story of Wealth

Households hold their wealth in many different forms. As the value of various assets changes, so does a person's wealth. Between 1991 and 2001, inflation was very good to people who held stocks. By contrast, the real value of bonds, gold, and silver fell.

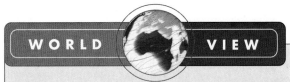

On the other hand, people whose nominal incomes increase faster than inflation end up with larger shares of total output. The same thing is true of those who enjoy goods that are rising slowest in price or who hold assets whose real value is increasing. In this sense, *inflation acts just like a tax, taking income or wealth from one group and giving it to another.* But we have no assurance that this particular tax will behave like Robin Hood, taking from the rich and giving to the poor. In reality, inflation often redistributes income in the opposite direction.

Social Tensions

Because of its redistributive effects, inflation also increases social and economic tensions. Tensions—between labor and management, between government and the people, and among consumers—may overwhelm a society and its institutions. As Gardner Ackley of the University of Michigan observed, "A significant real cost of inflation is what it does to morale, to social coherence, and to people's attitudes toward each other." "This society," added Arthur Okun, "is built on implicit and explicit contracts. . . . They are linked to the idea that the dollar means something. If you cannot depend on the value of the dollar, this system is undermined. People will constantly feel they've been fooled and cheated."[1] This is how the middle class felt in Germany in 1923 and in China in 1948, when the value of their savings was wiped out by sudden and unanticipated inflation. A surge in prices also stirred social and political tensions in Russia as it moved from a price-controlled economy to a market-driven economy in the 1990s. A similar political backlash occurred in Mexico in 1999 when tortilla prices jumped (see World View). On a more personal level, psychotherapists report that "inflation stress" leads to more frequent marital spats, pessimism, diminished self-confidence, and even sexual insecurity. Some people turn to crime as a way of solving the problem.

Money Illusion

money illusion: The use of nominal dollars rather than real dollars to gauge changes in one's income or wealth.

Even those people whose nominal incomes keep up with inflation often feel oppressed by rising prices. People feel that they *deserve* any increases in wages they receive. When they later discover that their higher (nominal) wages don't buy any additional goods, they feel cheated. They feel worse off, even though they haven't suffered any actual loss of real income. This phenomenon is called **money illusion.** People suffering from money illusion are forever reminding us that they used to pay only $5 to see a movie or $20 for a textbook. What they forget is that nominal incomes were also a lot lower in the "good old days" than they are today.

[1]Quoted in *BusinessWeek*, May 22, 1978, p. 118.

MACRO CONSEQUENCES

Although redistributions of income and wealth are the primary consequences of inflation, inflation has *macroeconomic* effects as well. Inflation can alter the rate and mix of output by changing consumption, work, saving, investment, and trade behavior.

One of the most immediate consequences of inflation is uncertainty. When the average price level is changing significantly in either direction, economic decisions become more difficult. As the accompanying cartoon suggests, even something as simple as ordering a restaurant meal is more difficult if menu prices are changing (as they did during Germany's 1923 runaway inflation). Longer-term decisions are even more difficult. Should you commit yourself to four years of college, for example, if you aren't certain that you or your parents will be able to afford the full costs? In a period of stable prices you can be fairly certain of what a college education will cost. But if prices are rising, you can no longer be sure how large the bill will be. Under such circumstances, some individuals may decide not to enter college rather than risk the possibility of being driven out later by rising costs.

Price uncertainties affect production decisions as well. Imagine a firm that wants to build a new factory. Typically, the construction of a factory takes two years or more, including planning, site selection, and actual construction. If construction costs change rapidly, the firm may find that it's unable to complete the factory or to operate it profitably. Confronted with this added uncertainty, the firm may decide not to build a new plant. This deprives the economy of new investment and expanded production possibilities.

Inflation threatens not only to reduce the level of economic activity but to change its very nature. If you really expect prices to rise, it makes sense to buy goods and resources now for resale later. If prices rise fast enough, you can make a handsome profit. These are the kinds of thoughts that motivate people to buy houses, precious metals, commodities, and other assets. But such speculation, if carried too far, can detract from the production process. If speculative profits become too easy, few people will engage in production; instead, everyone will be buying and selling existing goods. People may even be encouraged to withhold resources from the production process, hoping to sell them later at higher prices. Such speculation may fuel **hyperinflation,** as spending accelerates and production declines. This happened in Germany in the 1920s, China in 1948–49, and in Russia in the early 1990s. Russian prices rose by 200 percent in 1991 and by another 1,000 percent in 1992. These price increases

Uncertainty

To see how much the cost of college or any product will change at different inflation rates, use the CPI inflator provided by the Federal Reserve Bank of Minneapolis at woodrow.mpls.frb.us/ research/data/us/calc.

Speculation

Want a "down-under" view of inflation? The Reserve Bank of New Zealand offers insights into the problems of inflation at www.rbnz.govt.nz/statistics/ 0135595.html.

hyperinflation: Inflation rate in excess of 200 percent, lasting at least one year.

" DO I HAVE YOUR ASSURANCE THAT PRICES WILL NOT BE INCREASED BEFORE WE ARE SERVED ? "

From *The Wall Street Journal*. Permission, Cartoon Features Syndicate.

Analysis: The uncertainty caused by rising prices causes stress and may alter consumption and investment decisions.

rendered the Russian ruble nearly worthless. No one wanted to hold rubles or trade for them. Farmers preferred to hold potatoes rather than sell them. Producers of shoes and clothes likewise decided to hold rather than sell their products. The resulting contraction in supply caused a severe decline in Russian output.

Bracket Creep

> **bracket creep:** The movement of taxpayers into higher tax brackets (rates) as nominal incomes grow.

Another reason that savings, investment, and work effort decline when prices rise is that taxes go up, too. Federal income tax rates are *progressive;* that is, tax rates are higher for larger incomes. The intent of these progressive rates is to redistribute income from rich to poor. However, inflation tends to increase *everyone's* income. In the process, people are pushed into higher tax brackets and confront higher tax rates. The process is referred to as **bracket creep.** In recent years, bracket creep has been limited by the inflation indexing of personal income tax rates and a reduction in the number of tax brackets. However, Social Security payroll taxes and most state and local taxes aren't indexed.

Although the public sector still reaps some gain from inflation, inflation stress tends to create a political backlash. Voters are quick to blame the government for inflation. If the administration doesn't put a stop to inflation, the voters will turn to someone who promises to do so.

Deflation Dangers

Ironically, a *falling* price level—a deflation—might not make people happy either. In fact, a falling price level can do the same kind of harm as a rising price level. When prices are falling, people on fixed incomes and long-term contracts gain more *real* income. Lenders win and creditors lose. People who hold cash or bonds win: Homeowners and stamp collectors lose. A deflation simply reverses the kinds of redistributions caused by inflation.

A falling price level also has similar macro consequences. Time horizons get shorter. Businesses are more reluctant to borrow money or to invest. People lose confidence in themselves and public institutions when declining price levels deflate their incomes and assets.

MEASURING INFLATION

In view of the macro and micro consequences of price-level changes, the measurement of inflation serves two purposes: to gauge the average rate of inflation and to identify its principal victims.

Consumer Price Index

> **Consumer Price Index (CPI):** A measure (index) of changes in the average price of consumer goods and services.

> **inflation rate:** The annual percentage rate of increase in the average price level.

The most common measure of inflation is the **Consumer Price Index (CPI).** As its name suggests, the CPI is a mechanism for measuring changes in the average price of consumer goods and services. It's analogous to the fruit price index we discussed earlier. The CPI doesn't refer to the price of any particular good but to the average price of all consumer goods.

By itself, the "average price" of consumer goods isn't a very useful number. But once we know the average price of consumer goods, we can observe whether that average rises—that is, whether inflation is occurring. By observing the extent to which prices increase, we can calculate the **inflation rate.**

We can get a better sense of how inflation is measured by observing how the CPI is constructed. The process begins by identifying a market basket of goods and services the typical consumer buys. For this purpose, the Bureau of Labor Statistics surveys a large sample of families every year to determine what goods and services consumers actually buy. Figure 7.2 summarizes the results of the 2002 survey, which reveal that 32.7 cents out of every consumer dollar is spent on housing (shelter, furnishings, and utilities), 13.2 cents on food, and another 19 cents on transportation. Only 5 cents of every consumer dollar is spent on entertainment.

Within these broad categories of expenditure, the Bureau of Labor Statistics itemizes specific goods and services. The details of the expenditure survey show, for example, that private expenditures for reading and education account for only 2 percent of

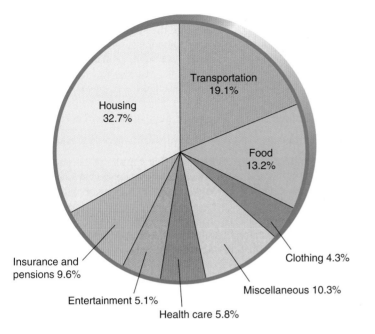

FIGURE 7.2
The Market Basket

To measure changes in average prices, we must first know what goods and services consumers buy. This diagram, based on consumer surveys, shows how the typical urban consumer spends each dollar. Housing, transportation, and food account for over two-thirds of consumer spending.

Source: U.S. Bureau of Labor Statistics (2002 data).

the typical consumer's budget, less than is spent on alcoholic beverages and tobacco. It also shows that we spend 7 cents out of every dollar on fuel, to drive our cars (3.2 cents) and to heat and cool our houses (3.8 cents).

Once we know what the typical consumer buys, it's relatively easy to calculate the average price of a market basket. The Bureau of Labor Statistics actually goes shopping in 85 cities across the country, recording the prices of the 184 items that make up the typical market basket. Approximately 19,000 stores are visited, and 60,000 landlords, renters, and homeowners are surveyed—every month!

As a result of these massive, ongoing surveys, the Bureau of Labor Statistics can tell us what's happening to consumer prices. Suppose, for example, that the market basket cost $100 last year and that the same basket of goods and services cost $110 this year. On the basis of those two shopping trips, we could conclude that consumer prices had risen by 10 percent in one year.

In practice, the CPI is usually expressed in terms of what the market basket cost in a specific **base period.** The price level in the base period is arbitrarily designated as 100. In the case of the CPI, the average price level for the period 1982–84 is usually used as the base for computing price changes. Hence, the price index for that base period is set at 100. In July 2004, the CPI registered 184. In other words, it cost $184 in 2004 to buy the same market baskets that cost only $100 in the base period. Prices had increased by an average of 84 percent over that period. Each month the Bureau of Labor Statistics updates the CPI, telling us how the current cost of that same basket compares to its cost between 1982 and 1984.[2]

Table 7.4 illustrates how changes in the official CPI are computed. Notice that all price changes don't have the same impact on the inflation rate. Rather, *the effect of a specific price change on the inflation rate depends on the product's relative importance in consumer budgets.*

The relative importance of a product in consumer budgets is reflected in its **item weight,** which refers to the percentage of a typical consumer budget spent on the item.

At the U.S. Bureau of Labor Statistics, www.bls.gov, you can find the CPI for the most recent month and the same month last year.

base period: The time period used for comparative analysis: the basis for indexing, for example, of price changes.

item weight: The percentage of total expenditure spent on a specific product; used to compute inflation indexes.

---

[2]Since January 1978, the Bureau of Labor Statistics has actually been computing two CPIs, one for urban wage earners and clerical workers and the second and larger one for all urban consumers (about 80 percent of the population). A third index, which uses rent rather than ownership costs of shelter, was introduced in 1983. The "urban/rental" index is most commonly cited.

TABLE 7.4
Computing Changes in the CPI

The impact of any price change on the average price level depends on the importance of an item in the typical consumer budget.

The Consumer Expenditure Survey of 2002 revealed that the average household spends 0.85 cent of every consumer dollar on college tuition. Households without college students don't pay any tuition, of course. And your family probably devotes *more* than 0.85 cent of each consumer dollar to tuition. On *average,* however, 0.85 cent is the proportion of each dollar spent on tuition. This figure is the *item weight* of tuition in computing the CPI.

The impact on the CPI of a price change for a specific good is calculated as follows:

Item weight × percentage change in price of item = percentage change in CPI

Suppose that tuition prices suddenly go up 20 percent. What impact will this single price increase have on the CPI? In this case, where tuition is the only price that increases, the impact on the CPI will be only 0.17 percent (0.0085 × 20) as illustrated below. Thus, a very large increase in the price of tuition (20 percent) has a tiny impact (0.17 percent) on the *average* price level.

Housing, on the other hand, accounts for 32.7 percent of consumer expenditure. Thus if housing prices increase 20 percent, and housing is the only price that increases, the impact on the CPI will be 6.54 percent, as shown below.

The relative importance of an item in consumer budgets—its item weight—is a key determinant of its inflationary impact.

Item	Item Weight	×	Price Increase for the Item	=	Impact on the CPI
College tuition	0.0085		20%		0.17%
Housing	0.327		20		6.54

WEBNOTE

The U.S. Bureau of Labor Statistics updates the CPI and PPI every month. For the latest inflation data visit the bureau at stats.bls.gov/cpi. Visit stats.bls.gov/ppi for an explanation of how the PPI and CPI differ.

Table 7.4 shows the item weights for college tuition and housing. College tuition may loom very large in your personal budget, but less than 1 percent of *all* consumer expenditure is spent on college tuition. Hence, the item weight for college tuition in the *average* consumer budget is only 0.0085.

Housing costs absorb a far larger share of the typical consumer budget. As Table 7.4 shows, the item weight for housing is 0.327. Accordingly, rent increases have a much larger impact on the CPI than do tuition hikes.

WEBNOTE

The importance of housing prices is emphasized in Steven Cecchetti's 'Inflation Updates' at http://people.brandeis.edu/~cecchett.

Producer Price Indexes

In addition to the familiar Consumer Price Index, there are three Producer Price Indexes (PPIs). The PPIs keep track of average prices received by *producers.* One index includes crude materials, another covers intermediate goods, and the last covers finished goods. The three PPIs don't include all producer prices but primarily those in mining, manufacturing, and agriculture. Like the CPI, changes in the PPIs are identified in monthly surveys.

Over long periods of time, the PPIs and the CPI generally reflect the same rate of inflation. In the short run, however, the PPIs usually increase before the CPI, because it takes time for producers' price increases to be reflected in the prices that consumers pay. For this reason, the PPIs are watched closely as a clue to potential changes in consumer prices.

The GDP Deflator

GDP deflator: A price index that refers to all goods and services included in GDP.

The broadest price index is the GDP deflator. The GDP deflator covers all output, including consumer goods, investment goods, and government services. Unlike the CPI and PPIs, the **GDP deflator** isn't based on a fixed "basket" of goods or services. Rather, it allows the contents of the basket to change with people's consumption and investment patterns. The GDP deflator therefore isn't a pure measure of price change. Its value reflects both price changes and market responses to those price changes, as reflected in new expenditure patterns. Hence, the GDP deflator typically registers a lower inflation rate than the CPI.

Real vs. Nominal GDP. The GDP deflator is used to adjust nominal output values for changing price levels. Recall that **nominal GDP** refers to the *current*-dollar value of output, whereas **real GDP** denotes the *inflation-adjusted* value of output. These two measures of output are connected by the GDP deflator:

$$\text{Real GDP} = \frac{\text{nominal GDP}}{\text{GDP deflator}} \times 100$$

The nominal values of GDP were \$10 trillion in 2000 and \$5.7 trillion in 1990. At first blush, this would suggest that output had increased by 75 percent. However, the price level rose by 24 percent between those years. Hence, *real* GDP in 2000 in the base-period prices of 1990 was

$$\frac{\text{2000 real GDP}}{\text{(in 1990 prices)}} = \frac{\text{nominal GDP}}{\text{price deflator}} = \frac{\$10 \text{ trillion}}{\dfrac{124}{100}} = \frac{\$10 \text{ trillion}}{1.24} = \$8.06 \text{ trillion}$$

In reality, then, output increased by only 41 percent in the 1990s. Changes in real GDP are a good measure of how output and living standards are changing. Nominal GDP statistics, by contrast, mix up output and price changes.

THE GOAL: PRICE STABILITY

In view of the inequities, anxieties, and real losses caused by inflation, it's not surprising that price stability is a major goal of economic policy. As we observed at the beginning of this chapter, every U.S. president since Franklin Roosevelt has decreed price stability to be a foremost policy goal. Unfortunately, few presidents (or their advisers) have stated exactly what they mean by "price stability." Do they mean *no* change in the average price level? Or is some upward creep in the price index acceptable?

An explicit numerical goal for **price stability** was established for the first time in the Full Employment and Balanced Growth Act of 1978. According to that act, the goal of economic policy is to hold the rate of inflation under 3 percent.

Why did Congress choose 3 percent inflation rather than zero inflation as the benchmark for price stability? One reason was concern about unemployment. To keep prices from rising, the government might have to restrain spending in the economy. Such restraint could lead to cutbacks in production and an increase in joblessness. In other words, there might be a trade-off between declining inflation and rising unemployment. From this perspective, a little bit of inflation might be the "price" the economy has to pay to keep unemployment rates from rising.

Recall how the same kind of logic was used to define the goal of full employment. The fear there was that price pressures would increase as the economy approached its production possibilities. This suggested that some unemployment might be the "price" the economy has to pay for price stability. Accordingly, the goal of "full employment" was defined as the lowest rate of unemployment *consistent with stable prices.* The same kind of thinking is apparent here. The amount of inflation regarded as tolerable depends in part on the effect of anti-inflation strategies on unemployment rates. After reviewing our experiences with both unemployment and inflation, Congress concluded that 3 percent inflation was a safe target.

The second argument for setting our price-stability goal above zero inflation relates to our measurement capabilities. The Consumer Price Index isn't a perfect measure of inflation. In essence, the CPI simply monitors the price of specific goods over time. Over time, however, the goods themselves change, too. Old products become better as a result of *quality improvements.* A plasma TV set costs more today than a TV did

---

nominal GDP: The value of final output produced in a given period, measured in the prices of that period (current prices).

real GDP: The value of final output produced in a given period, adjusted for changing prices.

A Numerical Goal

Unemployment Concerns

price stability: The absence of significant changes in the average price level; officially defined as a rate of inflation of less than 3 percent.

Quality Changes

IN THE NEWS

Ignoring Cell Phones Biases CPI Upward

Cellular telephones have been in commercial operation in the United States for 13 years. Beginning in Chicago in late 1983, and then at the Los Angeles Olympic Games in 1984, cellular telephone usage spread first to the top 30 Metropolitan Statistical Areas (MSAs), then to the other 300 or so MSAs, and finally to rural areas. At year-end 1996, there were over 40 million cellular subscribers in the United States. . . .

Yet the cellular telephone will not be included in the calculation of the Consumer Price Index (CPI) until 1998 or 1999. "This neglect of new goods leads to an upward bias in the CPI," NBER Research Associate Jerry Hausman concludes.

The CPI estimates that since 1988, telecommunications prices have increased by 8.5 percent, or 1.02 percent per year. A corrected index that includes cellular service decreased 1.28 percent per year since 1988, Hausman figures. "Thus, the bias in the BLS [Bureau of Labor Statistics] telecommunications services CPI equals approximately 2.3 percentage points per year."

Source: National Bureau of Economic Research, *NBER Digest*, June 1997. www.nber.org/digest

Analysis: Since the CPI tracks prices for a fixed basket of goods, it misses the effects of falling prices on new goods that appear between survey periods.

in 1955, but today's television also delivers a bigger, clearer picture, in digital sound and color, and with a host of on-screen programming options. Hence, increases in the price of TV sets tend to exaggerate the true rate of inflation: Most of the higher price represents more product.

The same is true of automobiles. The best-selling car in 1958 (a Chevrolet Bel Air) had a list price of only $2,618. That makes a 2004 Ford Taurus look awfully expensive at $20,605. The quality of today's cars is much better, however. Improvements since 1958 include seat belts, air bags, variable-speed windshield wipers, electronic ignitions, rear-window defrosters, radial tires, antilock brakes, emergency flashers, remote-control mirrors, crash-resistant bodies, a doubling of fuel mileage, and a 100-fold decrease in exhaust pollutants. As a result, today's higher car prices also buy cars that are safer, cleaner, and more comfortable.

The U.S. Bureau of Labor Statistics does adjust the CPI for quality changes. Such adjustments inevitably entail subjective judgments, however. Critics are quick to complain that the CPI overstates inflation because quality improvements are undervalued.

New Products   The problem of measuring quality improvements is even more difficult in the case of new products. The computers and word processors used today didn't exist when the Census Bureau conducted its 1972–73 survey of consumer expenditure. The 1982–84 expenditure survey included those products but not still newer ones such as the cellular phone. As the News above explains, the omission of cellular phones caused the CPI to overstate the rate of inflation. The consumer expenditure survey of 1993–95 included cell phones but not digital cameras, HDTVs, or DVD players—all of which have had declining prices. As a result, there's a significant (though unmeasured) element of error in the CPI insofar as it's intended to gauge changes in the average prices paid by consumers. The goal of 3 percent inflation allows for such errors.

THE HISTORICAL RECORD

In the long view of history, the United States has done a good job of maintaining price stability. On closer inspection, however, our inflation performance is very uneven. Table 7.5 summarizes the long view, with data going back to 1800. The base

Year	CPI	Year	CPI	Year	CPI	Year	CPI
1800	17.0	1900	8.3	1940	14.0	1980	82.4
1825	11.3	1915	10.1	1950	24.1	1982–84	100.0
1850	8.3	1920	20.0	1960	29.6	1990	130.5
1875	11.0	1930	16.7	1970	38.8	2000	172.8

Note: Data from 1915 forward reflect the official all-items Consumer Price Index, which used the pre-1983 measure of shelter costs. Estimated indexes for 1800 through 1900 are drawn from several sources.

Source: U.S. Bureau of Labor Statistics.

TABLE 7.5
Two Centuries of Price Changes

Before World War II, the average level of prices rose in some years and fell in others. Since 1945, prices have risen continuously. The Consumer Price Index has more than doubled since 1980.

period for pricing the market basket of goods is again 1982–84. Notice that the same market basket cost only $17 in 1800. Consumer prices increased 500 percent in 183 years. But also observe how frequently the price level *fell* in the 1800s and again in the 1930s. These recurrent deflations held down the long-run inflation rate. Because of these periodic deflations, average prices in 1945 were at the same level as in 1800!

Figure 7.3 provides a closer view of our more recent experience with inflation. In this figure we transform annual changes in the CPI into percentage rates of inflation. The CPI increased from 72.6 to 82.4 during 1980. This 9.8-point jump in the CPI translates into a 13.5 percent rate of inflation (9.8 ÷ 72.6 = 0.135). This inflation rate, represented by point *A* in Figure 7.3, was the highest in a generation. Since then, prices have continued to increase, but at much slower rates.

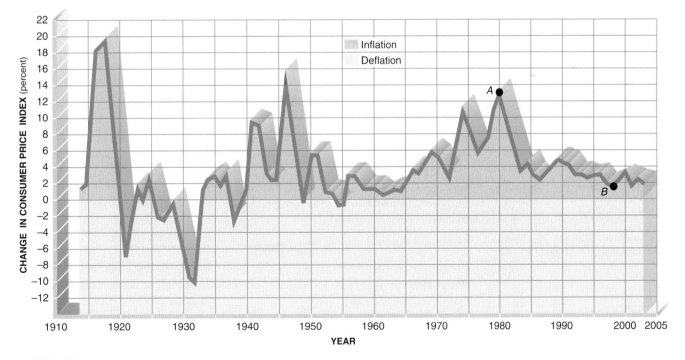

FIGURE 7.3
Annual Inflation Rates

During the 1920s and 1930s, consumer prices fell significantly, causing a general deflation. Since the Great Depression, however, average prices have risen almost every year. But even during this inflationary period, the annual rate of price increase has varied widely. In 1980, the rate of inflation was 13.5 percent (point *A*); in 1998, average prices rose only 1.6 percent (point *B*).

Source: U.S. Bureau of Labor Statistics.

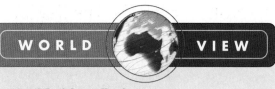

Worldwide Inflation

In many countries prices rise at rates much higher than those in the United States. In 2003, the inflation rate in Zimbabwe was so high that prices rise 15 percent every *month*.

In the United States the inflation rate for the entire *year* was only 2.4 percent. In Japan, the price level actually *fell* by 0.2 percent. What are the implications of such wildly different inflation rates?

Country	Inflation Rate	Country	Inflation Rate
Zimbabwe	432	Canada	2.7
Angola	98	**United States**	2.4
Haiti	33	Germany	1.1
Venezuela	31	Japan	−0.2
Belarus	28		
Turkey	25		

Source: International Monetary Fund, *World Economic Outlook*, 2004. www.imf.org

Analysis: Although inflation is regarded as a major macro problem in the United States, American inflation rates are comparatively low. Many developing countries have extraordinarily fast price increases.

As the accompanying World View documents, the low rates of inflation the United States has experienced are far below the pace in other nations. In 2003, for example, the inflation rate in the United States was lower than in Europe and incomprehensibly low for Zimbabweans, who saw their prices rise 15 percent per *month*.

CAUSES OF INFLATION

The evident variation in year-to-year inflation rates requires explanation. So do the horrifying bouts of hyperinflation that have erupted in other nations at various times. What causes price levels to rise or fall?

In the most general terms, this is an easy question to answer. Recall that all market transactions entail two converging forces, namely, *demand* and *supply*. Accordingly, any explanation of changing price levels must be rooted in one of these two market forces.

Demand-Pull Inflation

Excessive pressure on the demand side of the economy is often the cause of inflation. Suppose the economy was already producing at capacity but that consumers were willing and able to buy even more goods. With accumulated savings or easy access to credit, consumers could end up trying to buy more output than the economy was producing. This would be a classic case of "too much money chasing too few goods." As consumers sought to acquire more goods, store shelves (inventory) would begin to empty. Seeing this, producers would begin raising prices. The end result would be a demand-driven rise in average prices, or demand-pull inflation.

Cost-Push Inflation

The pressure on prices could also originate on the supply side. When the Organization of Petroleum Exporting Countries (OPEC) abruptly increased oil prices in 2000–01, production costs increased in a broad array of industries. To cover these higher costs, producers raised output prices. When Hurricane Mitch devastated

Honduras in 1998, it destroyed a huge portion of that country's production capacity, including its farm output. As market participants scurried for the remaining output, prices rose across the board.

Inflationary pressures could also originate in higher wages. If labor unions were able to abruptly push up wage rates, the costs of production would increase, putting pressure on product prices.

PROTECTIVE MECHANISMS

Whatever the *causes* of inflation, market participants don't want to suffer the consequences. Even at a relatively low rate of inflation, the real value of money declines over time. If prices rise by an average of just 4 percent a year, the real value of $1,000 drops to $822 in 5 years and to only $676 in 10 years (see Table 7.6). *Low rates of inflation don't have the drama of hyperinflation, but they still redistribute real wealth and income.*

Market participants can protect themselves from inflation by *indexing* their nominal incomes, as is done with Social Security benefits, for example. In any year that the rate of inflation exceeds 3 percent, Social Security benefits go up *automatically* by the same percentage as the inflation rate. This **cost-of-living adjustment (COLA)** ensures that nominal benefits keep pace with the rising prices. Because of the COLA, much of the real income of retirees is protected (private pensions typically don't include COLAs).

Landlords often protect their real incomes with COLAs as well, by including in their leases provisions that automatically increase rents by the rate of inflation. COLAs are also common in labor union agreements, government transfer programs (like food stamps), and many other contracts. In every such case, *a COLA protects real income from inflation.*

Cost-of-living adjustments have also become more common in loan agreements. As we observed earlier, debtors win and creditors lose when the price level rises. Suppose a loan requires interest payments equal to 5 percent of the amount (principal) borrowed. If the rate of inflation jumps to 7 percent, prices will be rising faster than interest is accumulating. Hence, the **real interest rate**—the inflation-adjusted rate of interest—will actually be negative. The interest payments made in future years will buy fewer goods than can be bought today.

WEBNOTE

For current news stories on inflation, check out the Excite server money.excite.com/ht/nw/tbeconomy.html. Search for "inflation."

COLAs

cost-of-living adjustment (COLA): Automatic adjustments of nominal income to the rate of inflation.

ARMs

real interest rate: The nominal interest rate minus the anticipated inflation rate.

TABLE 7.6
Inflation's Impact, 2005–2015

In the past 20 years, the U.S. rate of inflation ranged from a low of 1 percent to a high of 13 percent. Does a range of 12 percentage points really make much difference? One way to find out is to see how a specific sum of money will shrink in real value in a decade.

Here's what would happen to the real value of $1,000 from January 1, 2005, to January 1, 2015, at different inflation rates. At 2 percent inflation, $1,000 held for 10 years would be worth $820. At 10 percent inflation that same $1,000 would buy only $386 worth of goods in the year 2015.

	Annual Inflation Rate				
Year	2%	4%	6%	8%	10%
2005	$1,000	$1,000	$1,000	$1,000	$1,000
2006	980	962	943	926	909
2007	961	925	890	857	826
2008	942	889	840	794	751
2009	924	855	792	735	683
2010	906	822	747	681	621
2011	888	790	705	630	564
2012	871	760	665	584	513
2013	853	731	627	540	467
2014	837	703	592	500	424
2015	820	676	558	463	386

Sky-High Interest Rates in Africa

Fed up with those measly interest payments the bank pays on your hard-earned savings? Why not move your savings account to Zimbabwe, where banks were paying interest rates of 400 percent or more on savings accounts in 2003? That's right, 400 percent!

These sky-high interest rates look tempting, but there's a catch. The inflation rate in Zimbabwe in 2003 was close to 430 percent (see World View; p. 146.). So those high interest payments didn't keep up with rising prices. After inflation, savers had less buying power than when they first put money in the bank. The *real* interest rate—the nominal interest rate minus inflation was actually *negative*. That hardly justifies a trip to Africa.

Source: International Monetary Fund
www.imf.org

Analysis: The appropriate measure of a return on savings is the *real* interest rate. The real rate equals the *nominal* rate minus anticipated inflation.

The real rate of interest is calculated as

$$\text{Real interest rate} = \text{nominal interest rate} - \text{anticipated rate of inflation}$$

In this case, the nominal interest rate is 5 percent and inflation is 7 percent. Hence, the *real* rate of interest is *minus* 2 percent. The World View above illustrates how inflation can make even sky-high (nominal) interest rates look pretty mundane.

The distinction between real and nominal interest rates isn't too important if you're lending or borrowing money for just a couple of days. But the distinction is critical for long-term loans like home mortgages. Mortgage loans typically span a period of 25 to 30 years. If the inflation rate stays higher than the nominal interest rate during this period, the lender will end up with less *real* wealth than was initially lent.

To protect against such losses, the banking industry offers home loans with adjustable interest rates. An **adjustable-rate mortgage (ARM)** stipulates an interest

adjustable-rate mortgage (ARM): A mortgage (home loan) that adjusts the nominal interest rate to changing rates of inflation.

CPI Overstates Inflation, Senate Panel Says

The government's most widely used inflation gauge, the consumer price index, will overstate future inflation by about one percentage point every year, according to a panel of five experts appointed by the Senate Finance Committee. . . .

The Congressional Budget Office has calculated that by shaving one percentage point off the cost-of-living increases in entitlement programs, the government would save the government about $140 billion a year by 2005. That would cut the projected budget deficit that year by about a third. . . .

In its interim report, the advisory committee estimated that the CPI now overstates the rise in living costs for the average household by somewhere from 0.7 percent to 2.0 percent each year, and has been doing so for at least the past 20 years.

—Steven Pearlstein

Source: *Washington Post*, September 15, 1995. © 1995 The Washington Post. Reprinted with permission. www.washingtonpost.com

Analysis: Changes in product quality and expenditure patterns may cause inflation to be overestimated. Any overstatement will increase federal outlays and reduce tax revenues because of inflation indexing.

rate that changes during the term of the loan. A mortgage paying 5 percent interest in a stable (3 percent inflation) price environment may later require 9 percent interest if the inflation rate jumps to 7 percent. Such an adjustment would keep the real rate of interest at 2 percent.

The proliferation of COLAs and ARMs has made the CPI a critical statistic in today's economy. The problem is simple: If the CPI goes up, so do government transfer payments, union wages, and nominal interest rates. Critics charge that the Bureau of Labor Statistics has persistently exaggerated the inflation rate by undervaluing quality improvements, new products, and changes in expenditure patterns. If the CPI overstates inflation by just one percentage point, the federal government loses $140 billion per year in increased outlays and reduced tax revenues (see News). In 1998, the CPI's market basket of goods and services was overhauled. The new index, based on 1993–95 expenditure patterns, includes more new products such as cell phones and new adjustments for quality improvements. As products continue to emerge and change, however, the CPI will remain an imperfect but highly useful measure of inflation.

The Cost of Mismeasurement

THE ECONOMY TOMORROW

The End of Inflation?

The earth spins, the sun shines, prices rise: two generations have grown up believing that inflation is an unalterable fact of life. No wonder. A dollar today is worth only 13 cents in 1945 money; a pound is worth only 6p. Much of the damage was done in the 1970s and early 1980s, and much has improved since then. In the OECD countries inflation is now hovering around its 1960s level of 3–4 percent. That gives governments the best chance they have had for decades to kill it off and achieve price stability. Sadly, they may fluff it.

Historical Stability

Price stability is not as extraordinary as it sounds. It does not mean that all prices stay the same: some will fall, others rise, but the average price level remains constant. Anyway, inflation, in the sense of continuously rising prices, is historically the exception, not the rule. On the eve of the first world war, prices in Britain were on average no higher than at the time of the fire of London in 1666. . . . During those 250 years, the longest unbroken run of rising prices was six years. Since 1946, by contrast, prices in Britain have risen every year, and the same is true of virtually every other OECD country.

It is easy to say that double-digit inflation is bad, but harder to agree on the ideal rate. Should governments aim for 5 percent, 3 percent, or 0 percent? Some claim that the extra benefits of zero inflation are tiny and would be outweighed by the short-term cost—lost output, lost jobs—of pushing inflation lower. A little bit of inflation, they say, acts like a lubricant, helping relative prices and wages to adjust more efficiently, since all wages and most prices are hard to cut in absolute terms. But a little inflation sounds like "a little drink" for an alcoholic. It can too easily accelerate. That is the lesson of the past 40 years—that and the fact that the economies with the lowest inflation have tended to be the ones with the least unemployment. Beyond the short term governments cannot choose to have a bit faster growth in exchange for a bit more inflation. The choice does not exist.

The Virtue of Zero

The rewards of reducing inflation from 5 percent to 0 percent may be smaller than those from crunching inflation from 5,000 percent to 5 percent, but they are still highly desirable. The best inflation rate is one that least affects the behaviour of companies, investors, shoppers and workers. That means zero, because anything higher interferes with the most fundamental function of prices—their ability to provide information about relative scarcities. If prices in general are rising by 5 percent a year, the fact that the price of one particular product rises by 8 percent goes largely unnoticed. Yet that product's relative 3 percent increase ought to attract the attention of potential new producers, and to encourage buyers to look elsewhere—in short, to set in train the changes that maximize economic efficiency. It would do that if the 3 percent rise was like a hillock in an otherwise flat landscape; but, in the mountains of generalized inflation, nobody notices a crag. Even with an annual inflation rate of 5 percent, the general price level doubles every 14 years, obscuring changes in relative prices.

Now imagine a world without inflation. Once it was believable, it would transform the way people behave. Companies would be confident about borrowing long-term money, and lenders confident about providing it. Real interest rates would fall. Firms would invest more because the probable pay-out would be clearer; the same would be true of individuals investing time and money on their education. Governments could budget for infrastructural projects, knowing that their plans would not be derailed by unexpected surges in prices. In general, everyone would think more about the long term because the long term would be easier to see.

Source: *The Economist,* January 22, 1992. © 1992 The Economist Newspaper Ltd. All Rights Reserved. Reprinted with permission. Further reproduction prohibited. www.economist.com.

SUMMARY

- Inflation is an increase in the average price level. Typically it's measured by changes in a price index such as the Consumer Price Index (CPI).
- At the micro level, inflation redistributes income by altering relative prices, income, and wealth. Because not all prices rise at the same rate and because not all people buy (and sell) the same goods or hold the same assets, inflation doesn't affect everyone equally. Some individuals actually gain from inflation, whereas others suffer a loss of real income or wealth.
- At the macro level, inflation threatens to reduce total output because it increases uncertainties about the future and thereby inhibits consumption and production decisions. Fear of rising prices can also stimulate spending, forcing the government to take restraining action that threatens full employment. Rising prices also encourage speculation and hoarding, which detract from productive activity.
- Fully anticipated inflation reduces the anxieties and real losses associated with rising prices. However, few people can foresee actual price patterns or make all the necessary adjustments in their market activity.

- The U.S. goal of price stability is defined as an inflation rate of less than 3 percent per year. This goal recognizes potential conflicts between zero inflation and full employment as well as the difficulties of measuring quality improvements and new products.
- From 1800 to 1945, prices both rose and fell, leaving the average price level unchanged. Since then, prices have risen nearly every year but at widely different rates.
- Inflation is caused by either excessive demand (demand-pull inflation) or structural changes in supply (cost-push inflation).
- Cost-of-living adjustments (COLAs) and adjustable-rate mortgages (ARMs) help protect real incomes from inflation. Universal indexing, however, wouldn't eliminate inflationary redistributions of income and wealth.
- Worldwide inflation rates have diminished in recent years. Experience with inflation and changing patterns of asset ownership are creating political pressure for greater price stability.

Key Terms

inflation	bracket creep	nominal GDP
deflation	Consumer Price Index (CPI)	real GDP
relative price	inflation rate	price stability
nominal income	base period	cost-of-living adjustment (COLA)
real income	item weight	real interest rate
money illusion	GDP deflator	adjustable-rate mortgage (ARM)
hyperinflation		

Questions for Discussion

1. Why would farmers rather store their output than sell it during periods of hyperinflation? How does this behavior affect prices?
2. How might rapid inflation affect college enrollments?
3. Who gains and who loses from rising house prices?
4. Whose real wealth (see Table 7.3) declined in the 1990s? Who else might have lost real income or wealth? Who gained as a result of inflation?
5. If *all* prices increased at the same rate (i.e., no *relative* price changes), would inflation have any redistributive effects?
6. Would it be advantageous to borrow money if you expected prices to rise? Would you want a fixed-rate loan or one with an adjustable interest rate?
7. Are people worse off when the price level rises as fast as their income? Why do people often feel worse off in such circumstances?
8. Identify two groups that benefit from deflation and two that lose.
9. Could demand-pull inflation occur before an economy was producing at capacity? How?
10. Why would anyone borrow money at 400 percent interest, as was the case in Zimbabwe in 2003? (See World View, "Sky-High Interest Rates" (p. 148). Why would a bank lend money in that situation?

ALERT!

PROBLEMS   The Student Problem Set at the back of this book contains numerical and graphing problems for this chapter.

WEB ACTIVITIES   to accompany this chapter can be found on the Online Learning Center:
http://www.mhhe.com/economics/schiller10

PART 3

Cyclical Instability

One of the central concerns of macroeconomics is the short-run business cycle—recurrent bouts of expansion and contraction of the nation's output. These cycles affect jobs, prices, economic growth, and international trade and financial balances. Chapters 8 through 10 focus on the nature of the business cycle and the market forces that might affect it.

The Business Cycle

n 1929 it looked as though the sun would never set on the U.S. economy. For eight years in a row, the U.S. economy had been expanding rapidly. During the Roaring Twenties, the typical American family drove its first car, bought its first radio, and went to the movies for the first time. With factories running at capacity, virtually anyone who wanted to work found a job readily.

Everyone was optimistic. In his Acceptance Address in November 1928, President-elect Herbert Hoover echoed this optimism by declaring: "We in America today are nearer to the final triumph over poverty than ever before in the history of any land. . . . We shall soon with the help of God be in sight of the day when poverty will be banished from this nation."

The booming stock market seemed to confirm this optimistic outlook. Between 1921 and 1927 the stock market's value more than doubled, adding billions of dollars to the wealth of U.S. households and businesses. The stock market boom accelerated in 1927, causing stock prices to double again in less than two years. The roaring stock market made it look easy to get rich in America.

The party ended abruptly on October 24, 1929. On what came to be known as Black Thursday, the stock market crashed. In a few short hours, the market value of U.S. corporations tumbled, in the most frenzied selloff ever seen (see News). The next day President Hoover tried to assure America's stockholders that the economy was "on a sound and prosperous basis." But despite his assurances and the efforts of leading bankers to stem the decline, the stock market continued to plummet. The following Tuesday (October 29) the pace of selling quickened. By the end of the year, more than $40 billion of wealth had vanished in the Great Crash. Rich men became paupers overnight; ordinary families lost their savings, their homes, and even their lives.

The devastation was not confined to Wall Street. The financial flames engulfed the farms, the banks, and industry. Between 1930 and 1935, millions of rural families lost their farms. Automobile production fell from 4.5 million cars in 1929 to only 1.1 million in 1932. So many banks were forced to close that newly elected President Roosevelt had to declare a "bank holiday" in March 1933 to stem the outflow of cash to anxious depositors.

Throughout these years, the ranks of the unemployed continued to swell. In October 1929, only 3 percent of the workforce was unemployed. A year later the total was over 9 percent, and millions of additional workers were getting by on lower wages and shorter hours. But things got worse. By 1933, over one-fourth of the labor force was unable to find work. People slept in the streets, scavenged for food, and sold apples on Wall Street.

The Great Depression seemed to last forever. In 1933, President Roosevelt lamented that one-third of the nation was ill-clothed, ill-housed, and ill-fed. Thousands of unemployed workers marched to the Capitol to demand jobs and aid. In 1938, nine years after Black Thursday, nearly 20 percent of the workforce was still idle.

IN THE NEWS

Market in Panic As Stocks Are Dumped in 12,894,600 Share Day; Bankers Halt It

Effect Is Felt on the Curb and throughout Nation—Financial District Goes Wild

The stock markets of the country tottered on the brink of panic yesterday as a prosperous people, gone suddenly hysterical with fear, attempted simultaneously to sell a record-breaking volume of securities for whatever they would bring.

The result was a financial nightmare, comparable to nothing ever before experienced in Wall Street. It rocked the financial district to its foundations, hopelessly overwhelmed its mechanical facilities, chilled its blood with terror.

In a society built largely on confidence, with real wealth expressed more or less inaccurately by pieces of paper, the entire fabric of economic stability threatened to come toppling down.

Into the frantic hands of a thousand brokers on the floor of the New York Stock Exchange poured the selling orders of the world. It was sell, sell, sell—hour after desperate hour until 1:30 P.M.

—Laurence Stern

Source: *The World*, October 25, 1929.

Analysis: Stock markets are a barometer of confidence in the economy. If people have doubts about the economy, they're less willing to hold stocks. The crash of 1929 mirrored and worsened consumer confidence.

The Great Depression shook not only the foundations of the world economy but also the self-confidence of the economics profession. No one had predicted the depression, and few could explain it. The ensuing search for explanations focused on three central questions:

- **How stable is a market-driven economy?**
- **What forces cause instability?**
- **What, if anything, can the government do to promote steady economic growth?**

The basic purpose of **macroeconomics** is to answer these questions—to *explain* how and why economies grow and what causes the recurrent ups and downs of the economy that characterize the **business cycle.** In this chapter we introduce the theoretical model economists use to describe and explain the short-run business cycle. We'll also preview some of the policy options the government might use to dampen those cycles.

macroeconomics: The study of aggregate economic behavior, of the economy as a whole.

business cycle: Alternating periods of economic growth and contraction.

STABLE OR UNSTABLE?

Prior to the 1930s, macro economists thought there could never be a Great Depression. The economic thinkers of the time asserted that a market-driven economy was inherently stable. There was no need for government intervention.

This **laissez-faire** view of macroeconomics seemed reasonable at the time. During the nineteenth century and the first 30 years of the twentieth, the U.S. economy experienced some bad years in which the nation's output declined and unemployment increased. But most of these episodes were relatively short-lived. The dominant feature of the Industrial Era was growth: an expanding economy, with more output, more jobs, and higher incomes nearly every year.

A Self-Regulating Economy. In this environment, classical economists, as they later became known, propounded an optimistic view of the macro economy. *According to the classical view, the economy "self-adjusts" to deviations from its long-term growth trend.* Producers might occasionally reduce their output and

Classical Theory

laissez faire: The doctrine of "leave it alone," of nonintervention by government in the market mechanism.

throw people out of work, but these dislocations would cause little damage. If output declined and people lost their jobs, the internal forces of the marketplace would quickly restore prosperity. Economic downturns were viewed as temporary setbacks, not permanent problems.

The cornerstones of classical optimism were flexible prices and flexible wages. If producers couldn't sell all their output at current prices, they had two choices. They could reduce the rate of output and throw some people out of work, or they could reduce the price of their output, thereby stimulating an increase in the quantity demanded. According to the **law of demand,** price reductions cause an increase in unit sales. If prices fall far enough, all the output produced can be sold. Thus, flexible prices—prices that would drop when consumer demand slowed—virtually guaranteed that all output could be sold. No one would have to lose a job because of weak consumer demand.

Flexible prices had their counterpart in factor markets. If some workers were temporarily out of work, they'd compete for jobs by offering their services at lower wages. As wage rates declined, producers would find it profitable to hire more workers. Ultimately, flexible wages would ensure that everyone who wanted a job would have a job.

These optimistic views of the macro economy were summarized in Say's Law. **Say's Law**—named after the nineteenth-century economist Jean-Baptiste Say—decreed that "supply creates its own demand." Whatever was produced would be sold. All workers who sought employment would be hired. *Unsold goods and unemployed labor could emerge in this classical system, but both would disappear as soon as people had time to adjust prices and wages.* There could be no Great Depression—no protracted macro failure—in this classical view of the world.

Macro Failure. The Great Depression was a stunning blow to classical economists. At the onset of the depression, classical economists assured everyone that the setbacks in production and employment were temporary and would soon vanish. Andrew Mellon, Secretary of the U.S. Treasury, expressed this optimistic view in January 1930, just a few months after the stock market crash. Assessing the prospects for the year ahead, he said: "I see nothing . . . in the present situation that is either menacing or warrants pessimism. . . . I have every confidence that there will be a revival of activity in the spring and that during the coming year the country will make steady progress."[1] Merrill Lynch, one of the nation's largest brokerage houses, was urging that people should buy stocks. But the depression deepened. Indeed, unemployment grew and persisted *despite* falling prices and wages (see Figure 8.1). The classical self-adjustment mechanism simply didn't work.

The Keynesian Revolution

The Great Depression effectively destroyed the credibility of classical economic theory. As the British economist John Maynard Keynes pointed out in 1935, classical economists

> were apparently unmoved by the lack of correspondence between the results of their theory and the facts of observation:—a discrepancy which the ordinary man has not failed to observe. . . .
>
> The celebrated optimism of [classical] economic theory . . . is . . . to be traced, I think, to their having neglected to take account of the drag on prosperity which can be exercised by an insufficiency of effective demand. For there would obviously be a natural tendency towards the optimum employment of resources in a Society which was functioning after the manner of the classical postulates. It may well be that the classical theory represents the way in which we should like our Economy to behave. But to assume that it actually does so is to assume our difficulties away.[2]

Glossary definitions

law of demand: The quantity of a good demanded in a given time period increases as its price falls, *ceteris paribus.*

Say's Law: Supply creates its own demand.

---

[1]David A. Shannon, *The Great Depression* (Englewood Cliffs, NJ: Prentice Hall, 1960), p. 4.
[2]John Maynard Keynes, *The General Theory of Employment, Interest and Money* (London: Macmillan, 1936), pp. 33–34.

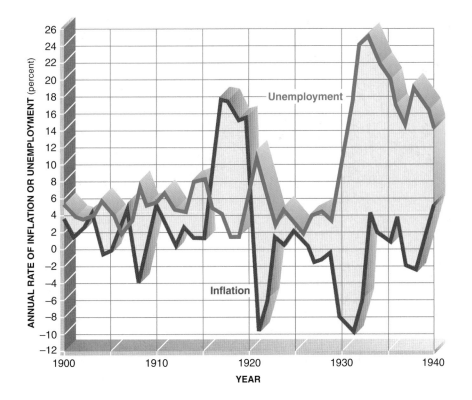

FIGURE 8.1
Inflation and Unemployment, 1900–1940

In the early 1900s, falling price levels (deflation) appeared to limit increases in unemployment. Periods of high unemployment also tended to be brief. These experiences bolstered the confidence of classical economists in the stability of the macro economy. Say's Law seemed to work.

In the 1930s, unemployment rates rose to unprecedented heights and stayed high for a decade. Falling wages and prices did not restore full employment. This macro failure prompted calls for new theories and policies to control the business cycle.

Source: U.S. Bureau of the Census, *The Statistics of the United States,* 1957.

Inherent Instability. Keynes went on to develop an alternative view of the macro economy. Whereas the classical economists viewed the economy as inherently stable, *Keynes asserted that a market-driven economy is inherently unstable.* Small disturbances in output, prices, or unemployment were likely to be magnified, not muted, by the invisible hand of the marketplace. The Great Depression was not a unique event, Keynes argued, but a calamity that would recur if we relied on the market mechanism to self-adjust.

Government Intervention. In Keynes's view, the inherent instability of the marketplace required government intervention. When the economy falters, we can't afford to wait for some assumed self-adjustment mechanism but must instead intervene to protect jobs and income. The government can do this by "priming the pump": buying more output, employing more people, providing more income transfers, and making more money available. When the economy overheats, the government must cool it down with higher taxes, spending reductions, and less money.

Keynes's denunciation of classical theory didn't end the macroeconomic debate. On the contrary, economists continue to wage fierce debates about the stability of the economy. Those debates fill the pages of the next few chapters. But before examining them, let's first take a quick look at the economy's actual performance.

HISTORICAL CYCLES

The upswings and downturns of the business cycle are gauged in terms of changes in total output. An economic upswing, or expansion, refers to an increase in the volume of goods and services produced. An economic downturn, or contraction, occurs when the total volume of production declines. Changes in employment typically mirror these changes in production.

Figure 8.2 depicts the stylized features of a business cycle. Over the long run, the output of the economy grows at roughly 3 percent per year. There's a lot of year-to-year

FIGURE 8.2
The Business Cycle

The model business cycle resembles a roller coaster. Output first climbs to a peak, then decreases. After hitting a trough, the economy recovers, with real GDP again increasing.

A central concern of macroeconomic theory is to determine whether a recurring business cycle exists, and if so, what forces cause it.

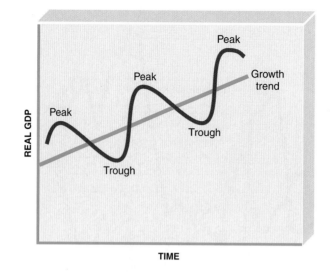

real GDP: The value of final output produced in a given period, adjusted for changing prices.

variation around this growth trend, however. The short-run cycle looks like a roller coaster, climbing steeply, then dropping from its peak. Once the trough is reached, the upswing starts again.

In reality, business cycles aren't as regular or as predictable as Figure 8.2 suggests. The U.S. economy has experienced recurrent upswings and downswings, but of widely varying length, intensity, and frequency.

Figure 8.3 illustrates the actual performance of the U.S. economy since 1929. Changes in total output are measured by changes in **real GDP,** the inflation-adjusted value of all goods and services produced. From a long-run view, the growth of real

FIGURE 8.3
The Business Cycle in U.S. History

From 1929 to 2004, real GDP increased at an average rate of 3 percent a year. But annual growth rates have departed widely from that average. Years of above-average growth seem to alternate with years of sluggish growth (*growth recessions*) and actual decreases in total output (*recessions*).

Source: U.S. Department of Commerce (2004).

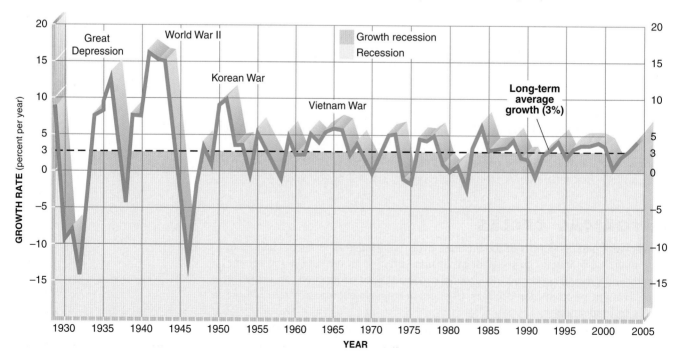

GDP has been impressive: Real GDP today is eight times larger than it was in 1929. Americans now consume a greater variety of goods and services, and in greater quantities, than earlier generations ever dreamed possible.

Our long-term success in raising living standards is clouded, however, by a spate of short-term macro setbacks. On closer inspection, *the growth path of the U.S. economy isn't a smooth, rising trend but a series of steps, stumbles, and setbacks.* This short-run instability is evident in Figure 8.3. The dashed line represents the long-term *average* growth rate of the U.S. economy. From 1929 through 2004, the U.S. economy expanded at an average rate of 3 percent per year. But Figure 8.3 clearly shows that we didn't grow so nicely every year. There were lots of years when real GDP grew by less than 3 percent. Worse still, there were many years of *negative* growth, with real GDP *declining* from one year to the next. These successive short-run contractions and expansions are the essence of the business cycle.

The most prolonged departure from our long-term growth path occurred during the Great Depression. Between 1929 and 1933, total U.S. output steadily declined. Notice in Figure 8.3 how the growth rate is negative in each of these years. During these four years of negative growth, real GDP contracted a total of nearly 30 percent. Investments in new plant and equipment virtually ceased. Economies around the world came to a grinding halt (see World View).

The U.S. economy rebounded in April 1933 and continued to expand for 3 years (see positive growth rates in Figure 8.3). By 1937, however, the rate of output was still below that of 1929. Then things got worse again. During 1938 and 1939 output again contracted and more people lost their jobs. At the end of the decade GDP per capita was lower than it had been in 1929.

World War II greatly increased the demand for goods and services and ended the Great Depression. During the war years, real GDP grew at unprecedented rates—almost 19 percent in a single year (1942). Virtually everyone was employed, either in the armed forces or in the factories. Throughout the war, America's productive capacity was strained to the limit.

The Great Depression

The National Archives provides a wealth of information on the Great Depression in the Hoover Presidential Library. Visit www.hoover.nara.gov. and click on "Research Our Collection" and "research/historical materials."

World War II

Global Depression

The Great Depression wasn't confined to the U.S. economy. Most other countries suffered substantial losses of output and employment over a period of many years. Between 1929 and 1932, industrial production around the world fell 37 percent. The United States and Germany suffered the largest losses, while Spain and the Scandinavian countries lost only modest amounts of output.

Some countries escaped the ravages of the Great Depression altogether. The Soviet Union, largely insulated from Western economic structures, was in the midst of Stalin's forced industrialization drive during the 1930s. China and Japan were also relatively isolated from world trade and finance and so suffered less damage from the depression.

Country	Decline in Industrial Output
Chile	−22%
France	−31
Germany	−47
Great Britain	−17
Japan	−2
Norway	−7
Spain	−12
United States	−46

Analysis: International trade and financial flows tie nations together. When the U.S. economy tumbled in the 1930s, other nations lost export sales. Such interactions made the Great Depression a worldwide calamity.

TABLE 8.1
Business Slumps

The U.S. economy has experienced 13 business slumps since 1929. In the post–World War II period, these downturns have been much less severe. The typical recession lasts around 10 months. When will the next recession occur, and how long will it last?

Dates	Duration (months)	Percentage Decline in Real GDP	Peak Unemployment Rate
Aug. '29–Mar. '33	43	53.4%	24.9%
May '37–June '38	13	32.4	20.0
Feb. '45–Oct. '45	8	38.3	4.3
Nov. '48–Oct. '49	11	9.9	7.9
July '53–May '54	10	10.0	6.1
Aug. '57–Apr. '58	8	14.3	7.5
Apr. '60–Feb. '61	10	7.2	7.1
Dec. '69–Nov. '70	11	8.1	6.1
Nov. '73–Mar. '75	16	14.7	9.0
Jan. '80–July '80	6	8.7	7.6
July '81–Nov. '82	16	12.3	10.8
July '90–Feb. '91	8	2.2	6.5
Mar. '01–Nov. '01	8	0.6	5.6

The Postwar Years

recession: A decline in total output (real GDP) for two or more consecutive quarters.

After World War II, the U.S. economy resumed a pattern of alternating growth and contraction. The contracting periods are called *recessions*. Specifically, we use the term **recession** to mean a decline in real GDP that continues for at least two successive quarters. As Table 8.1 indicates, there have been 11 recessions since 1944. The most severe postwar recession occurred immediately after World War II ended. Sudden cutbacks in defense production caused GDP to decline sharply in 1945. That postwar recession was relatively brief, however. Pent-up demand for consumer goods and a surge in investment spending helped restore full employment. The Korean War (1950–53) further increased the demand for goods, accelerating economic growth.

The 1980s

The 1980s started with two recessions, the second lasting 16 months (July 1981–November 1982). Despite the onset of a second recession at midyear, the economy's total output actually increased in 1981. But the growth rate was so slow (1.9 percent) that few people noticed any improvement in their standard of living. Indeed, because output was growing more slowly than the labor force, the number of unemployed workers actually increased in 1981. These kinds of experiences are called **growth recessions**—the economy grows, but at a slower rate than the long-run (3 percent) average: Thus, *a growth recession occurs when the economy expands too slowly. A recession occurs when real GDP actually contracts.* A depression is an extremely deep and long recession—or when you don't even get socks for Christmas (see cartoon).

growth recession: A period during which real GDP grows, but at a rate below the long-term trend of 3 percent.

In November 1982, the U.S. economy began an economic expansion that lasted over seven years. During that period, real GDP increased by over $1 trillion and nearly 20 million new jobs were created. It was the second-longest peacetime expansion in American history. As the expansion continued, however, the *rate* of economic growth diminished. By the end of the decade, economic growth had slowed to a crawl and another growth recession occurred.

The 1990s and 2000–

The 1990s started poorly as a result. The growth recession of 1989 became a full-blown recession in 1990. Beginning in July 1990, real GDP started declining. Although the recession officially ended eight months later (February 1991), subsequent growth was so slow that unemployment kept increasing. By the end of 1991, the recession had destroyed 2 million jobs and reduced total output by nearly 2 percent.

In 1992, the economy started to grow a bit faster, but unemployment rates stayed high for the entire year. The increase in output was so small that unemployment kept rising to a peak of 7.7 percent in June of that year. Economic growth accelerated in the late 1990s, again creating millions of new jobs. In the fall of 2000,

Analysis: Recessions occur when total output in the economy declines. In recessions, household income and spending fall.

the national unemployment rate fell to 3.9 percent, the lowest in over three decades, and the economic expansion set a longevity record. Shortly thereafter, however, GDP growth slowed so much that the United States experienced another brief recession in 2001.

A MODEL OF THE MACRO ECONOMY

The bumpy growth record of the U.S. economy lends some validity to the notion of a recurring business cycle. Every decade seems to contain at least one boom or bust cycle. But the historical record doesn't really answer our key questions. Are business cycles *inevitable?* Can we do anything to control them? *Keynes and the classical economists weren't debating whether business cycles occur but whether they're an appropriate target for government intervention.* That debate continues.

To determine whether and how the government should try to control the business cycle, we first need to understand its origins. What causes the economy to expand or contract? What marketplace forces dampen (self-adjust) or magnify economic swings?

Figure 8.4 sets the stage for answering these questions. This diagram provides a bird's-eye view of how the macro economy works. This basic macro model emphasizes that the performance of the economy depends on a surprisingly small set of determinants.

On the right side of Figure 8.4 the primary measures of macroeconomic performance are arrayed. These basic *macro outcomes include*

- *Output:* total value of goods and services produced (real GDP).
- *Jobs:* levels of employment and unemployment.
- *Prices:* average price of goods and services.
- *Growth:* year-to-year expansion in production capacity.
- *International balances:* international value of the dollar; trade and payment balances with other countries.

These macro outcomes define our economic welfare; we measure our economic well-being in terms of the value of output produced, the number of jobs created, price stability, and rate of economic expansion. We also seek to maintain a certain balance in our international trade and financial relations. The economy's performance is rated by the "scores" on these five macro outcomes.

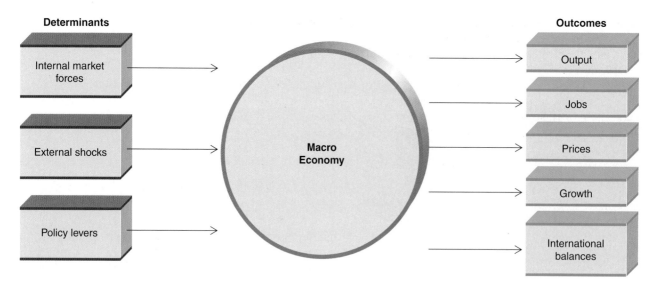

FIGURE 8.4
The Macro Economy

The primary outcomes of the macro economy are output of goods and services, jobs, prices, economic growth, and international balances (trade, currency). These outcomes result from the interplay of internal market forces such as population growth, innovation, and spending patterns; external shocks such as wars, weather, and trade disruptions; and policy levers such as tax, budget, and regulatory decisions.

On the left side of Figure 8.4 three very broad forces that shape macro outcomes are depicted. These **determinants of macro performance are**

- **Internal market forces:** population growth, spending behavior, invention and innovation, and the like.
- **External shocks:** wars, natural disasters, terrorist attacks, trade disruptions, and so on.
- **Policy levers:** tax policy, government spending, changes in the availability of money, and regulation, for example.

In the absence of external shocks or government policy, an economy would still function: It would still produce output, create jobs, develop prices, and maybe even grow. The U.S. economy operated with minimal government intervention for much of its history. Even today, many less developed countries operate in relative isolation from government or international events. In these situations, macro outcomes depend exclusively on internal market forces.

The crucial macro controversy is whether such pure, market-driven economies are inherently stable or unstable. Classical economists viewed internal market forces as self-stabilizing and saw no need for the box in Figure 8.4 labeled "Policy levers." Keynes argued that policy levers were both effective and necessary. Without such intervention, Keynes believed, the economy was doomed to bouts of repeated macro failure.

Modern economists hesitate to give policy intervention that great a role. Nearly all economists recognize that policy intervention affects macro outcomes. But there are great arguments about just how effective any policy lever is. Some economists even echo the classical notion that policy intervention may be either ineffective or, worse still, inherently destabilizing.

AGGREGATE DEMAND AND SUPPLY

To determine which views of economic performance are valid, we need to examine the inner workings of the macro economy. All Figure 8.4 tells us is that macro outcomes depend on certain identifiable forces. But the figure doesn't reveal *how* the determinants and outcomes are connected. What's in the mysterious circle labeled "Macro Economy" at the center of Figure 8.4?

When economists peer into the mechanics of the macro economy they see the forces of supply and demand at work. All the macro outcomes depicted in Figure 8.4 are the result of market transactions—an interaction between supply and demand. Hence, ***any influence on macro outcomes must be transmitted through supply or demand.***

By conceptualizing the inner workings of the macro economy in supply and demand terms, economists have developed a remarkably simple model of how the economy works. To operationalize that model, however, we need to know more about the macroeconomic dimensions of supply and demand.

Economists use the term *aggregate demand* to refer to the collective behavior of all buyers in the marketplace. Specifically, **aggregate demand** refers to the various quantities of output (real GDP) that all people, taken together, are willing and able to buy at alternative price levels in a given period. Our view here encompasses the collective demand for *all* goods and services rather than the demand for any single good.

To understand the concept of aggregate demand better, imagine that everyone is paid on the same day. With their incomes in hand, people then enter the product market. The question becomes: How much output will people buy?

To answer this question, we have to know something about prices. If goods and services are cheap, people will be able to buy more with their available income. On the other hand, high prices will limit both the ability and willingness to purchase goods and services. Note that we're talking here about the *average* price level, not the price of any single good.

Figure 8.5 illustrates this simple relationship between average prices and real spending. The horizontal axis depicts the various quantities of (real) output that might be purchased. The vertical axis shows various price levels that might exist.

The aggregate demand curve illustrates how the real value of purchases varies with the average level of prices. The downward slope of the aggregate demand curve suggests that with a given (constant) level of income, people will buy more goods and services at lower price levels. Why would this be the case? ***Three separate reasons explain the downward slope of the aggregate demand curve:***

- ***The real-balances effect.***
- ***The foreign-trade effect.***
- ***The interest-rate effect.***

Aggregate Demand

aggregate demand: The total quantity of output (real GDP) demanded at alternative price levels in a given time period, *ceteris paribus.*

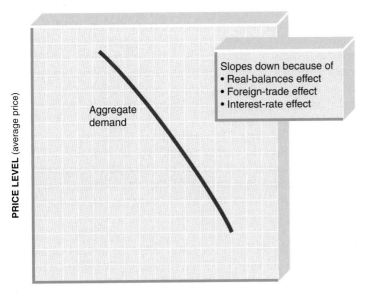

PRICE LEVEL (average price)

Aggregate demand

Slopes down because of
• Real-balances effect
• Foreign-trade effect
• Interest-rate effect

REAL OUTPUT (quantity per year)

FIGURE 8.5
Aggregate Demand

Aggregate demand refers to the total output (real GDP) demanded at alternative price levels, *ceteris paribus.* The vertical axis measures the average level of all prices rather than the price of a single good. Likewise, the horizontal axis refers to the real value of all goods and services, not the quantity of only one product.

The downward slope of the aggregate demand curve is due to the real-balances, foreign-trade, and interest-rate effects.

Real-Balances Effect. The most obvious explanation for the downward slope of the aggregate demand curve is that cheaper prices make dollars more valuable. Suppose you had $1,000 in your savings account. How much output could you buy with that savings balance? That depends on the price level. At current prices, you could buy $1,000 worth of output. But what if the price level rose? Then your $1,000 wouldn't stretch as far. *The real value of money is measured by how many goods and services each dollar will buy.* When the *real* value of your savings declines, your ability to purchase goods and services declines as well.

Suppose inflation pushes the price level up by 25 percent in a year. What will happen to the real value of your savings balance? At the end of the year, you'll have

$$\text{Real value of savings at year-end} = \frac{\text{savings balance}}{\frac{\text{price level at year-end}}{\text{price level at year-start}}}$$

$$= \frac{\$1,000}{\frac{125}{100}} = \frac{\$1,000}{1.25}$$

$$= \$800$$

In effect, inflation has wiped out a chunk of your purchasing power. At year's end, you can't buy as many goods and services as you could have at the beginning of the year. The quantity of output you demand will decrease. In Figure 8.5 this would be illustrated by a movement up the aggregate demand curve.

A declining price level (deflation) has the opposite effect. Specifically, lower price levels make you "richer": *The cash balances you hold in your pocket, in your bank account, or under your pillow are worth more when the price level falls.* As a result, you can buy *more* goods, even though your *nominal income* hasn't changed.

Lower price levels increase the purchasing power of other dollar-denominated assets as well. Bonds, for example, tend to rise in value when the price level falls. This may tempt consumers to use some of their bonds to buy goods and services. With greater real wealth, consumers might also decide to save less and spend more of their current income. In either case, the quantity of goods and services demanded at any given income level will increase. These real-balances effects create an inverse relationship between the price level and the real value of output demanded—that is, a downward-sloping aggregate demand curve.

Foreign-Trade Effect. The downward slope of the aggregate demand curve is reinforced by changes in imports and exports. Consumers have the option of buying either domestic or foreign goods. A decisive factor in choosing between them is their relative price. If the average price of U.S.-produced goods is rising, Americans may buy more imported goods and fewer domestically produced products. Conversely, falling price levels in the United States may convince consumers to buy more "Made in the USA" output and fewer imports.

International consumers are also swayed by relative price levels. When our price levels decline, overseas tourists flock to Disney World. Global consumers also buy more U.S. wheat, airplanes, and computers when our price levels decline. Conversely, the quantity of U.S. output demanded by international consumers declines when our price level rises. These changes in imports and exports contribute to the downward slope of the aggregate demand curve.

Interest-Rate Effect. Changes in the price level also affect the amount of money people need to borrow and so tend to affect interest rates. At lower price levels, consumer borrowing needs are smaller. As the demand for loans diminishes, interest rates tend to decline as well. This "cheaper" money stimulates more borrowing and loan-financed purchases. These interest-rate effects reinforce the downward slope of the aggregate demand curve, as illustrated in Figure 8.5.

Although lower price levels tend to increase the volume of output demanded, they have the opposite effect on the aggregate quantity *supplied*. As we observed, our production possibilities are defined by available resources and technology. Within those limits, however, producers must decide how much output they're *willing* to supply. Their supply decisions are influenced by changes in the price level.

Profit Effect. The primary motivation for supplying goods and services is the chance to earn a profit. Producers can earn a profit so long as the prices they receive for their output exceed the costs they pay in production. Hence, ***changing price levels will affect the profitability of supplying goods.***

If the price level declines, profits tend to drop. In the short run, producers are saddled with some relatively constant costs like rent, interest payments, negotiated wages, and inputs already contracted for. If output prices fall, producers will be hard-pressed to pay these costs, much less earn a profit. Their response will be to reduce the rate of output.

Higher output prices have the opposite effect. Because many costs are relatively constant in the short run, higher prices for goods and services tend to widen profit margins. As profit margins widen, producers will want to produce and sell more goods. Thus, ***we expect the rate of output to increase when the price level rises.*** This expectation is reflected in the upward slope of the aggregate supply curve in Figure 8.6. **Aggregate supply** reflects the various quantities of real output that firms are willing and able to produce at alternative price levels, in a given time period.

Cost Effect. The upward slope of the aggregate supply curve is also explained by rising costs. The profit effect depends on some costs remaining constant when the average price level rises. Not all costs will remain constant, however. Producers may have to pay overtime wages, for example, to increase output, even if *base* wages are constant. Tight supplies of other inputs may also unleash cost increases. Such cost pressures tend to multiply as the rate of output increases. As time passes, even costs that initially stayed constant may start creeping upward.

All these cost pressures will make producing output more expensive. Producers will be willing to supply additional output only if prices rise at least as fast as costs.

Aggregate Supply

aggregate supply: The total quantity of output (real GDP) producers are willing and able to supply at alternative price levels in a given time period, *ceteris paribus*.

The slope of the aggregate supply curve depends in part on what producers pay for their inputs. Find out about producer prices at www.bls.gov/ppi.

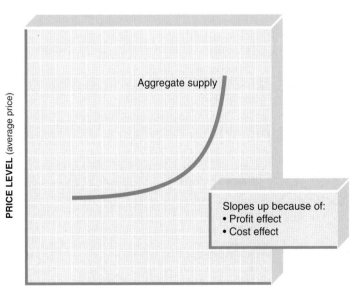

REAL OUTPUT (quantity per year)

FIGURE 8.6
Aggregate Supply

Aggregate supply is the real value of output (real GDP) producers are willing and able to bring to the market at alternative price levels, *ceteris paribus*. The upward slope of the aggregate supply curve reflects both profit effects (the lure of widening profit margins) and cost effects (increasing cost pressures).

The upward slope of the aggregate supply curve in Figure 8.6 illustrates this cost effect. Notice how the aggregate supply curve is practically horizontal at low rates of aggregate output and then gets increasingly steeper. At high output levels the aggregate supply curve almost turns straight up. This changing slope reflects the fact that *cost pressures are minimal at low rates of output but intense as the economy approaches capacity.*

Macro Equilibrium

When all is said and done, what we end up with here is two rather conventional looking supply and demand curves. But these particular curves have special significance. Instead of describing the behavior of buyers and sellers in a single product market, *aggregate supply and demand curves summarize the market activity of the whole (macro) economy.* These curves tell us what *total* amount of goods and services will be supplied or demanded at various price levels.

These graphic summaries of buyer and seller behavior provide some important clues about the economy's performance. The most important clue is point E in Figure 8.7, where the aggregate demand and supply curves intersect. This is the only point at which the behavior of buyers and sellers is compatible. We know from the aggregate demand curve that people are willing and able to buy the quantity Q_E when the price level is at P_E. From the aggregate supply curve we know that businesses are prepared to sell quantity Q_E at the price level P_E. Hence, buyers and sellers are willing to trade exactly the same quantity (Q_E) at that price level. We call this situation **macro equilibrium**—the unique combination of prices and output compatible with both buyers and sellers' intentions.

To appreciate the significance of macro equilibrium, suppose that another price or output level existed. Imagine, for example, that prices were higher, at the level P_1 in Figure 8.7. How much output would people want to buy at that price level? How much would business want to produce and sell?

The aggregate demand curve tells us that people would want to buy only the quantity D_1 at the higher price level P_1. In contrast, business firms would want to sell a larger quantity, S_1. This is a *dis*equilibrium situation in which the intentions of buyers and sellers are incompatible. The aggregate *quantity supplied* (S_1) exceeds the aggregate *quantity demanded* (D_1). Accordingly, a lot of goods will remain unsold at price level P_1.

To sell these goods, producers will have to reduce their prices. As prices drop, producers will decrease the volume of goods sent to market. At the same time, the quantities that consumers seek to purchase will increase. This adjustment process will

equilibrium (macro): The combination of price level and real output that is compatible with both aggregate demand and aggregate supply.

FIGURE 8.7
Macro Equilibrium

The aggregate demand and supply curves intersect at only one point (E). At that point, the price level (P_E) and output (Q_E) combination is compatible with both buyers' and sellers' intentions. The economy will gravitate to those equilibrium price (P_E) and output (Q_E) levels. At any other price level (e.g., P_1), the behavior of buyers and sellers is incompatible.

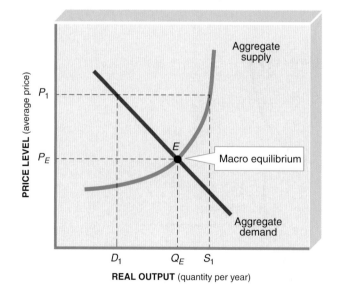

continue until point E is reached and the quantities demanded and supplied are equal. At that point, the lower price level P_E will prevail.

The same kind of adjustment process would occur if a lower price level first existed. At lower prices, the aggregate quantity demanded would exceed the aggregate quantity supplied. The resulting shortages would permit sellers to raise their prices. As they did so, the aggregate quantity demanded would decrease, and the aggregate quantity supplied would increase. Eventually, we would return to point E, where the aggregate quantities demanded and supplied are equal.

Equilibrium is unique; it's the only price-output combination that is mutually compatible with aggregate supply and demand. In terms of graphs, it's the only place the aggregate supply and demand curves intersect. At point E there's no reason for the level of output or prices to change. The behavior of buyers and sellers is compatible. By contrast, any other level of output or prices creates a *dis*equilibrium that requires market adjustments. All other price and output combinations, therefore, are unstable. They won't last. Eventually, the economy will return to point E.

There are two potential problems with the macro equilibrium depicted in Figure 8.7. The *two potential problems with macro equilibrium are*

- *Undesirability:* The price-output relationship at equilibrium may not satisfy our macroeconomic goals.
- *Instability:* Even if the designated macro equilibrium is optimal, it may be displaced by macro disturbances.

Undesirability. The macro equilibrium depicted in Figure 8.7 is simply the intersection of two curves. All we know for sure is that people want to buy the same quantity of output that businesses want to sell at the price level P_E. This quantity (Q_E) may be more or less than our full-employment capacity. This contingency is illustrated in Figure 8.8. The output level Q_F represents our **full-employment GDP** potential. In this case, the equilibrium rate of output (Q_E) falls far short of capacity production. We've failed to achieve our goal of full employment.

Similar problems may arise from the equilibrium price level. Suppose that P^* represents the most desired price level. In Figure 8.8, we see that the equilibrium price level P_E exceeds P^*. If market behavior determines prices, the price level will rise

Macro Failures

full-employment GDP: The total market value of final goods and services that could be produced in a given time period at full employment; potential GDP.

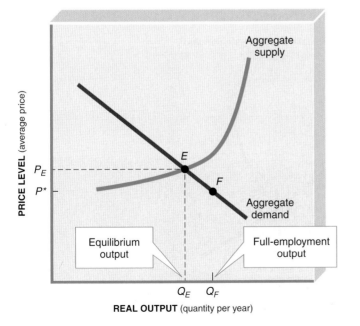

FIGURE 8.8
An Undesired Equilibrium

Equilibrium establishes only the level of prices and output that are compatible with both buyers' and sellers' intentions. These outcomes may not satisfy our policy goals. In this case, the equilibrium price level is too high (above P^*) and the equilibrium output rate falls short of full employment (Q_F).

inflation: An increase in the average level of prices of goods and services.

above the desired level. The resulting increase in the average level of prices is what we call **inflation.**

It could be argued, of course, that our apparent macro failures are simply an artifact. We could have drawn the aggregate supply and demand curves to intersect at point *F* in Figure 8.8. At that intersection we'd be assured of both price stability and full employment. Why didn't we draw them there, instead of intersecting at point *E*?

On the graph we can draw curves anywhere we want. In the real world, however, *only one set of aggregate supply and demand curves will correctly express buyers' and sellers' behavior.* We must emphasize here that these "correct" curves may *not* intersect at point *F*, thus denying us price stability or full employment, or both. That is the kind of economic outcome illustrated in Figure 8.8.

Instability. Figure 8.8 is only the beginning of our macro worries. Suppose, just suppose, that the aggregate supply and demand curves actually intersected in the perfect spot. That is, imagine that macro equilibrium yielded the optimal levels of both employment and prices. If this happened, could we settle back and stop fretting about the state of the economy?

Unhappily, even a "perfect" macro equilibrium doesn't ensure a happy ending. The aggregate supply and demand curves aren't permanently locked into their respective positions. They can *shift*—and they will, whenever the behavior of buyers and sellers changes.

AS Shifts. Suppose the Organization of Petroleum Exporting Countries (OPEC) increased the price of oil, as it did in early 2004. These oil price hikes directly increased the cost of production in a wide range of U.S. industries, making producers less willing and able to supply goods at prevailing prices. Thus, the aggregate supply curve *shifted to the left,* as in Figure 8.9*a.*

FIGURE 8.9
Macro Disturbances

(a) **Aggregate supply shifts** A decrease (leftward shift) of the aggregate-supply curve tends to reduce real GDP and raise average prices. When supply shifts from AS_0 to AS_1, the equilibrium moves from *F* to *G*. At *G*, output is lower and prices are higher than at *F*. Such a supply shift may result from higher import prices, changes in tax policy, or other events.

(b) **Aggregate demand shifts** A decrease (leftward shift) in aggregate demand tends to reduce output and price levels. When demand shifts from AD_0 to AD_1, both real output and the price level decline. A fall in demand may be caused by decreased export demand, changes in expectations, taxes, or other events.

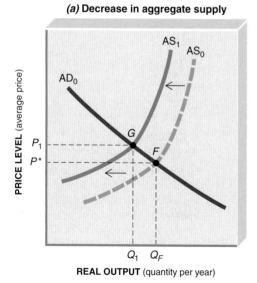

(a) Decrease in aggregate supply

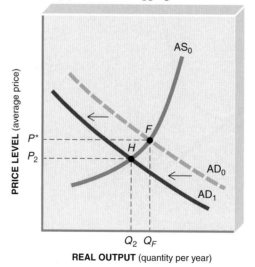

(b) Decrease in aggregate demand

The September 11, 2001, terrorist strikes against the World Trade Center and Pentagon also caused a leftward shift of aggregate supply. Physical destruction and fear of further terrorism kept some producers out of the market. Intensified security of transportation systems and buildings also increased the costs of supplying goods and services to the market.

The impact of a leftward supply shift on the economy is evident in Figure 8.9. Whereas macro equilibrium was originally located at the optimal point *F*, the new equilibrium is located at point *G*. At point *G*, less output is produced and prices are higher. Full employment and price stability have vanished before our eyes.

AD Shifts. A shift of the aggregate demand curve could do similar damage. In the wake of the September 11, 2001, terrorist attacks, Americans were worried about their physical and economic security. Consumers were afraid to go shopping at the mall, and even more afraid to board airplanes. Businesses were also fearful of starting new projects. As a result, the AD curve shifted left, as illustrated in Figure 8.9*b*. As the accompanying News relates, the slow recovery of confidence kept the AD curve from shifting back to the right in a timely manner.

Multiple Shifts. The situation gets even crazier when the aggregate supply and demand curves shift repeatedly in different directions. A leftward shift of the aggregate demand curve can cause a recession, as the rate of output falls. A later rightward shift of the aggregate demand curve can cause a recovery, with real GDP (and employment) again increasing. Shifts of the aggregate supply curve can cause similar upswings and downswings. Thus, *business cycles are likely to result from recurrent shifts of the aggregate supply and demand curves.*

IN THE NEWS

Slack Demand Hinders Economy

Businesses Have Few Incentives to Expand or Hire, Economists Say

To understand why the U.S. economy can't seem to muster a stronger recovery, it helps to look for clues in Victorville, Calif., where 500 unused and unwanted passenger jets—some of them brand new—sit wingtip to wingtip in the desert.

Or in Detroit, where the Big Three continue to churn out large numbers of passenger cars that they sell at little or no profit, just to keep their factories busy.

Or in nearly every major metropolitan area, where office vacancy rates are still rising after 18 months, and have reached 25 percent in Dallas, 24 percent in Raleigh-Durham, N.C., and 18 percent in San Francisco.

But perhaps the best explanation can be found in those falling prices shoppers find for clothing, televisions, hotel rooms and cellular phone service. While the bargains are great for American consumers, they are being paid in the form of continued corporate layoffs, lackluster stock prices and a sky-high trade deficit—in short, an economy that's having trouble building up a head of steam.

Economists refer to this phenomenon as overcapacity, which is really nothing more than too much supply chasing too little demand. . . .

To be sure, overcapacity is a feature of every recession. A slowdown in consumer spending and a decline in business investment suddenly leave too many companies with too many workers, underutilized plants and underperforming stores. In most cases, it is only after most of that excess is cut back, and supply and demand get back into some rough balance, that businesses begin hiring and investing again, laying the foundation for another period of economic expansion.

This time, however, that process is turning out to be longer and more drawn out than in the past, making for a slower and weaker recovery than forecasters, executives and policymakers had expected.

—Steven Pearlstein

Source: *Washington Post*, August 25, 2002. © 2002 The Washington Post. Reprinted with permission.

Analysis: When AD shifts left, goods remain unsold, workers are laid off, and prices fall. The longer full-employment supply exceeds aggregate demand, the greater the economic pain.

COMPETING THEORIES OF SHORT-RUN INSTABILITY

Figures 8.8 and 8.9 hardly inspire optimism about the macro economy. Figure 8.8 suggests that the odds of the market generating an equilibrium at full employment and price stability are about the same as finding a needle in a haystack. Figure 8.9 suggests that if we're lucky enough to find the needle, we'll probably drop it again. From this perspective, it appears that our worries about the business cycle are well founded.

The classical economists had no such worries. As we saw earlier, they believed that the economy would gravitate toward full employment. Keynes, on the other hand, worried that the macro equilibrium might start out badly and get worse in the absence of government intervention.

The AS/AD model doesn't really settle this controversy. It does, however, provide a convenient framework for comparing these and other theories about how the economy works. Essentially, *macro controversies focus on the shape of aggregate supply and demand curves and the potential to shift them.* With the right shape—or the correct shift—any desired equilibrium could be attained. As we'll see, there are differing views as to whether and how this happy outcome might come about. These differing views can be classified as demand-side explanations, supply-side explanations, or some combination of the two.

Demand-Side Theories

Keynesian Theory. Keynesian theory is the most prominent of the demand-side theories. Keynes argued that a deficiency of spending would tend to depress an economy. This deficiency might originate in consumer saving, inadequate business investment, or insufficient government spending. Whatever its origins, the lack of spending would leave goods unsold and production capacity unused. This contingency is illustrated by point E_1 in Figure 8.10a. Notice that the equilibrium at E_1 leaves the economy at Q_1, below its full-employment potential (Q_F). Thus, *Keynes concluded that inadequate aggregate demand would cause persistently high unemployment.*

Keynes developed his theory during the Great Depression, when the economy seemed to be stuck at a very low level of equilibrium output, far below full-employment GDP. The only way to end the depression, he argued, was for someone to start demanding more goods. He advocated a big hike in government spending to start the economy

FIGURE 8.10

Demand-Side Theories

Inadequate demand may cause unemployment. In part (*a*), the demand AD_1 creates an equilibrium at E_1. The resulting output Q_1 falls short of full employment Q_F.

In part (*b*), excessive aggregate demand causes inflation. The price level rises from P_0 to P_2 when aggregate demand expands to AD_2 Demand-side theories emphasize how inadequate or excessive AD can cause macro failures.

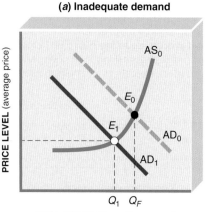

(*a*) Inadequate demand

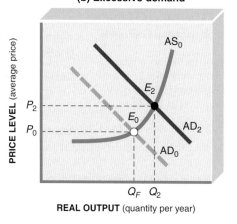

(*b*) Excessive demand

WORLD VIEW

Economy Expands, Barely

The U.S. economy skirted the edge of a recession this spring as increases in consumer and government purchases narrowly offset the biggest drop in business spending in almost 20 years, the Commerce Department reported yesterday.

The economy grew in the second quarter at only a 0.7 percent annual rate, the smallest quarterly gain in eight years. After expanding more than 4 percent a year for several years, growth slowed abruptly in mid-2000 and over the past 12 months has averaged only a 1.3 percent annual rate.

— John M. Berry

Source: *Washington Post*, July 28, 2001. © 2001 The Washington Post. Reprinted with permission. www.washingtonpost.com

Japan Sees Slight Drop in Its GDP

TOKYO—Japan's economy contracted slightly in the first three months of this year, government data showed Monday, raising fears that the world's second-biggest economy is sinking into another recession.

Gross domestic product fell 0.2 percent in the three months ended March 31 from the previous quarter, seasonally adjusted, the government said today. Economists had expected the economy to expand 0.1 percent after growing 0.7 percent in the fourth quarter.

Business investment, the main source of economic growth the last two years, gave way in the first quarter, falling 1 percent from the fourth quarter, when it increased 6.7 percent. That was the first decline in three quarters.

— Ann Saphir and Neha Ku

Source: Bloomberg News, *Los Angeles Times*, June 11, 2001. Reprinted with permission. www.latimes.com

China Reports 7.9% Growth

SHANGHAI, July 17—China said today that its economy expanded 7.9 percent in the first six months of this year, exceeding the forecasts of many private experts and defying the global slowdown.

The State Statistical Bureau, which announced the increase, predicted that, in the absence of further deterioration in the economic outlook for the rest of the world, China's growth for the full year could top the government's target of 7 percent.

Analysts attribute the vigorous performance of China's economy to the strength of the nation's domestic market, with 1.3 billion consumers clamoring for new goods and services and the government providing an extra boost to demand by spending heavily on infrastructure and public works.

—Clay Chandler

Source: *Washington Post*, July 18, 2001. © 2001 The Washington Post. Reprinted with permission. www.washingtonpost.com

Analysis: Why do short-term growth rates vary across countries? In these stories, shifts of aggregate demand are emphasized, as in Figure 8.10.

moving toward full employment. At the time his advice was largely ignored. When the United States mobilized for World War II, however, the sudden surge in government spending shifted the aggregate demand curve sharply to the right, restoring full employment (e.g., a reverse shift from AD_1 to AD_0 in Figure 8.10a). In times of peace, Keynes also advocated changing government taxes and spending to shift the aggregate demand curve in whatever direction is desired.

The accompanying World View contrasts GDP growth in the United States, Japan, and China in early 2001. Notice the role that aggregate demand plays in the stories. A decline in business spending is blamed for the U.S. slowdown and the Japanese recession. In China, an increase in consumer and government spending is credited for the spurt in real GDP. This is entirely consistent with Keynesian theory, which will be examined more closely in Chapters 9 through 11.

Monetary Theories. Another demand-side theory emphasizes the role of money in financing aggregate demand. Money and credit affect the ability and willingness of people to buy goods and services. If credit isn't available or is too expensive, consumers won't be able to buy as many cars, homes, or other expensive products. "Tight" money might also curtail business investment. In these circumstances, aggregate demand might prove to be inadequate, as illustrated in Figure 8.10a. In this case, an increase in the money supply may be required to shift the aggregate demand curve into the desired position.

Both the Keynesian and monetarist theories also regard aggregate demand as a prime suspect for inflationary problems. In Figure 8.10b, the curve AD$_2$ leads to an equilibrium at E_2. At first blush, that equilibrium looks desirable, as it offers more output (Q_2) than the full-employment threshold (Q_F). Notice, however, what's happening to prices: The price level rises from P_0 to P_2. Hence, ***excessive aggregate demand may cause inflation.***

The more extreme monetary theories attribute all our macro successes and failures to management of the money supply. According to these *monetarist* theories, the economy will tend to stabilize at something like full-employment GDP. Thus, only the price level will be affected by changes in the money supply and resulting shifts of aggregate demand. We'll examine the basis for this view in a moment. At this juncture we simply note that ***both Keynesian and monetarist theories emphasize the potential of aggregate-demand shifts to alter some macro outcomes.***

Supply-Side Theories

Figure 8.11 illustrates an entirely different explanation of the business cycle. Notice that the aggregate *supply* curve is on the move in Figure 8.11. The initial equilibrium is again at point E_0. This time, however, aggregate demand remains stationary, while aggregate supply shifts. The resulting decline of aggregate supply causes output and employment to decline (to Q_3 from Q_F).

Figure 8.11 tells us that aggregate supply may be responsible for downturns as well. Our failure to achieve full employment may result from the unwillingness of producers to provide more goods at existing prices. That unwillingness may originate in simple greed, in rising costs, in resource shortages, or in government taxes and regulation. Inadequate investment in infrastructure (e.g., roads, sewer systems) or skill training may also limit supply potential. Whatever the cause, if the aggregate supply curve is AS$_1$ rather than AS$_0$, full employment will not be achieved with the demand AD$_0$.

The inadequate supply illustrated in Figure 8.11 causes not only unemployment but inflation as well. At the equilibrium E_3, the price level has risen from P_0 to P_3. Hence, a decrease in aggregate supply can cause multiple macro problems. On the other hand, an increase—a rightward shift—in aggregate supply can move us closer to both our price-stability and full-employment goals. Chapter 16 examines the many ways of inducing such a shift.

Eclectic Explanations

Not everyone blames either the demand side or the supply side exclusively. The various macro theories tell us that both supply and demand can cause us to achieve or miss our policy goals. These theories also demonstrate how various shifts of the aggregate supply and demand curves can achieve any specific output or price level. One could also shift *both* the AS and AD curves to explain unemployment, inflation, or recurring business cycles. Such eclectic explanations of macro failure draw from both sides of the market.

WEBNOTE

The U.S. Bureau of Economic Analysis compiles data on gross domestic product. Using data from its Web site at www.bea.doc.gov, determine the GDP growth rate for each of the last six quarters. What supply or demand shifts might explain recent quarterly fluctuations in real GDP?

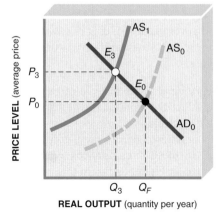

FIGURE 8.11
Supply-Side Theories

Inadequate supply can keep the economy below its full-employment potential and cause prices to rise as well. AS$_1$ leads to output Q_3 and increases the price level from P_0 to P_3. Supply-side theories emphasize how AS shifts can worsen or improve macro outcomes.

LONG-RUN SELF-ADJUSTMENT

Some economists argue that these various theories of short-run instability aren't only confusing but also pointless. As they see it, what really matters is the *long*-run trend of the economy, not *short*-run fluctuations around those trends. In their view, month-to-month or quarter-to-quarter fluctuations in real output or prices are just statistical noise. The *long*-term path of output and prices is determined by more fundamental factors.

This emphasis on long-term outcomes is reminiscent of the classical theory: the view that the economy will self-adjust. A decrease in aggregate demand is only a *temporary* problem. Once producers and workers make the required price and wage adjustments, the economy will return to its long-run equilibrium growth path.

The monetarist theory we encountered a moment ago has a similar view of long-run stability. According to the monetarist theory, the supply of goods and services is determined by institutional factors such as the size of the labor force and technology. These factors determine a natural rate of output that's relatively immune to short-run fluctuations in aggregate demand. If this argument is valid, the long-run aggregate supply curve is vertical, not sloped.

Figure 8.12 illustrates the classical/monetarist view of long-run stability. The vertical long-run AS curve is anchored at the natural rate of output Q_N. The natural rate Q_N is itself determined by demographics, technology, market structure, and the institutional infrastructure of the economy.

If the long-run AS curve is really vertical, as the classical and monetarist theories assert, some startling conclusions follow. The most startling implication is that ***aggregate demand shifts affect prices but not output in the long run.*** Notice in Figure 8.12 how the shift from AD_1 to AD_2 raises the price level but leaves output anchored at Q_N.

What has happened here? Didn't we suggest earlier that an increase in aggregate demand would spur producers to increase output? And aren't rising prices an extra incentive for doing so?

Monetarists concede that *short-run* price increases tend to widen profit margins. This profit effect is an incentive to increase the rate of output. In the *long run,* however, costs are likely to catch up with rising prices. Workers will demand higher

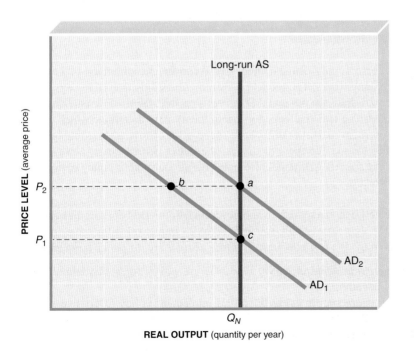

FIGURE 8.12
The "Natural" Rate of Output

Monetarists and neoclassical theorists assert that the level of output is fixed at the natural rate Q_N by the size of the labor force, technology, and other institutional factors. As a result, fluctuations in aggregate demand affect the price level but not real output.

wages, landlords will increase rents, and banks will charge higher interest rates as the price level rises. Hence, a rising price level has only a *temporary* profit effect on supply behavior. In the *long run,* cost effects will dominate. In the *long run,* a rising price level will be accompanied by rising costs, giving producers no special incentive to supply more output. Accordingly, output will revert to its natural rate Q_N.

Classical economists use the vertical AS curve to explain also how the economy self-adjusts to temporary setbacks. If AD declines from AD_2 to AD_1 in Figure 8.12, the economy may move from point *a* to point *b*, leaving a lot of unsold output. As producers respond with price cuts, however, the volume of output demanded increases as the economy moves from point *b* to point *c*. At point *c*, full employment is restored. Thus flexible prices (and wages) enable the economy to maintain the natural rate of output Q_N.

Short- vs. Long-Run Perspectives

All this may well be true. But as Keynes pointed out, it's also true that "in the long run we are all dead." How long are we willing to wait for the promised "self-adjustment"? In the Great Depression, people waited for 10 years—and still saw no self-adjustment.

Whatever the long run may hold, it's in the short run that we must consume, invest, and find a job. However stable and predictable the long run might be, short-run variations in macro outcomes will determine how well we fare in any year. Moreover, *the short-run aggregate supply curve is likely to be upward-sloping,* as shown in our earlier graphs. This implies that both aggregate supply and aggregate demand influence short-run macro outcomes.

By distinguishing between short-run and long-run aggregate supply curves, competing economic theories achieve a standoff. Theories that highlight the necessity of policy intervention emphasize the importance of short-run macro outcomes. On the other hand, theories that emphasize the "natural" stability of the market point to the predictability of long-run outcomes. Even this fragile truce, however, is easily broken when the questions turn to the duration of the "short" run or the effectiveness of any particular policy option.

THE ECONOMY TOMORROW

Macro Policy Options

The aggregate supply-demand model is a convenient summary of how the macro economy works. The model raises more questions than it answers, however. We could draw the AS and AD curves—or shift them—to create any outcome we wanted. The real challenge for macro theory is to determine which curves (or shifts) best represent market reality. We'll spend a lot of time sifting through evidence and looking for the "correct" theory. At the outset of that quest, however, we might consider how the AS/AD model also helps define our macro policy options for the economy tomorrow.

Basic Policy Strategies

The basic choice between market-driven and government-directed behavior underlies all policy options. The aggregate supply-demand (AS/AD) framework adds a new dimension to this dichotomy. We can now identify ***three distinct macro policy strategies:***

- ***Shift the aggregate demand curve.*** Find and use policy tools that stimulate or restrain total spending.
- ***Shift the aggregate supply curve.*** Find and implement policy levers that reduce the cost of production or otherwise stimulate more output at every price level.
- ***Laissez faire.*** Don't interfere with the market; let markets self-adjust.

These very different policy strategies generate a variety of specific policy options, including the following:

Classical Approaches. The classical approach to economic policy embraced the laissez-faire perspective. Prior to the Great Depression, most economists were convinced that the economy would self-adjust to full employment. If the initial equilibrium rate of output were too low, the resulting imbalances would alter prices and wages, inducing changes in market behavior. The aggregate supply and demand curves would "naturally" shift, until they reached the intersection where full employment (Q_F) prevails.

Recent versions of the classical theory—dubbed the "new classical economics"—stress not only the market's "natural" ability to self-adjust to *long-run* equilibrium but also the inability of the government to improve *short-run* market outcomes. New classical economists point to the increasing ability of market participants to anticipate government policies and to take defensive actions that thwart them.

Fiscal Policy. The Great Depression cast serious doubt on the classical self-adjustment concept. According to Keynes's view, the economy would *not* self-adjust. Rather, it might stagnate until aggregate demand was forcibly shifted. An increase in government spending on goods and services might provide the necessary shift. Or a cut in taxes might be used to stimulate greater consumer and investor spending. These budgetary tools are the hallmark of fiscal policy. Specifically, **fiscal policy** is the use of government tax and spending powers to alter economic outcomes.

fiscal policy: The use of government taxes and spending to alter macroeconomic outcomes.

Fiscal policy is an integral feature of modern economic policy. Every year the president and Congress debate the budget. They argue about whether the economy needs to be stimulated or restrained. They then argue about the level of spending or taxes required to ensure the desired outcome. This is the heart of fiscal policy.

Monetary Policy. The government budget doesn't get all the action. As suggested earlier, the amount of money in circulation may also affect macro equilibrium. If so, then the policy arsenal must include some levers to control the money supply. These are the province of monetary policy. **Monetary policy** refers to the use of money and credit controls to alter economic outcomes.

monetary policy: The use of money and credit controls to influence macroeconomic outcomes.

The Federal Reserve (the "Fed") has direct control over monetary policy. The Fed is an independent regulatory body, charged with maintaining an "appropriate" supply of money. In practice, the Fed increases or decreases the money supply in accordance with its views of macro equilibrium.

Supply-Side Policy. Fiscal and monetary policies focus on the demand side of the market. Both are motivated by the conviction that appropriate shifts of the aggregate demand curve can bring about desired changes in output or price levels. **Supply-side policies** offer an alternative; they seek to shift the aggregate supply curve.

supply-side policy: The use of tax incentives, (de)regulation, and other mechanisms to increase the ability and willingness to produce goods and services.

There are scores of supply-side levers. The most familiar are the tax cuts implemented by the Reagan administration in 1981. These tax cuts were designed to increase *supply,* not just demand (as does traditional fiscal policy). By reducing tax rates on wages and profits, the Reagan tax cuts sought to increase the willingness to supply goods at any given price level. The promise of greater after-tax income was the key incentive for the supply shift. President George W. Bush pushed Congress to reduce taxes on both personal income and business income for the same reasons.

Trade Policy. International trade and money flows offer yet another option for shifting aggregate supply and demand. A reduction in trade barriers makes imports cheaper and more available. This shifts the aggregate supply to the right, reducing price pressures at every output level. Changing the international value (exchange rate) of the dollar alters the relative price of U.S.-made goods, thereby shifting both aggregate demand and supply. Hence, trade policy is another tool in the macroeconomic toolbox.

Eclecticism. Few presidents commit themselves entirely to one macroeconomic strategy. Herbert Hoover, for example, was a fervent proponent of laissez faire. But even he was prepared to accelerate public works spending and income transfers to stop the Great Depression. Ironically, Franklin Roosevelt campaigned against these fiscal policies, arguing that such demand-side levers would unbalance the federal deficit. He later became a fervent believer in Keynesian-style fiscal policy.

Ronald Reagan was a champion of supply-side economics. But he also "primed the pump" with a huge increase in defense expenditures, a demand-side policy option. George H. Bush repeatedly expressed his confidence in the market's ability to self-adjust. But when the recession of 1990–91 began to cloud his reelection prospects, President Bush pushed for supply-side tax incentives and accelerated government spending. President Clinton emphasized the need for supply-side investments in human and physical capital to promote his "New Direction." He also relied on tax hikes and spending cuts (fiscal policy), however, to achieve his macroeconomic goals. For his part, President George W. Bush emphasized the importance of long-run strategies but pushed hard for short-run personal tax cuts when economic growth stalled and for business tax breaks and more government spending in the aftermath of the September 11, 2001, terrorist attacks.

In part, the eclectic use of policy options reflects a "do-whatever-it-takes-to-win" attitude on the part of politicians. But "politics" isn't the only explanation for the lack of clear-cut policy strategies. No economic theory has proved infallible. As we'll see, different theories provide important insights into how the economy works, but each falls short in explaining one or more of our economic problems. In these circumstances, policymakers are reluctant to put all their economic eggs in one basket. They prefer more "flexible" strategies. So we're likely to witness an eclectic mix of classical, fiscal, monetary, and supply-side policies in the economy tomorrow rather than single-minded adherence to any one theory.

SUMMARY

- The long-term growth rate of the U.S. economy is approximately 3 percent a year. But output doesn't increase 3 percent every year. In some years, real GDP grows much faster than that; in other years growth is slower. Sometimes total output actually declines.

- These short-run variations in GDP growth are a central focus of macroeconomics. Macro theory tries to explain the alternating periods of growth and contraction that characterize the business cycle; macro policy attempts to control the cycle.

- The primary outcomes of the macro economy are output, prices, jobs, and international balances. The outcomes result from the interplay of internal market forces, external shocks, and policy levers.

- All the influences on macro outcomes are transmitted through aggregate supply or aggregate demand. Aggregate supply and demand determine the equilibrium rate of output and prices. The economy will gravitate to that unique combination of output and price levels.

- Macro equilibrium may not be consistent with our nation's employment or price goals. Macro failure occurs when the economy's equilibrium isn't optimal.

- Macro equilibrium may be disturbed by changes in aggregate supply (AS) or aggregate demand (AD). Such changes are illustrated by shifts of the AS and AD curves, and they lead to a new equilibrium.

- Competing economic theories try to explain the shape and shifts of the aggregate supply and demand curves, thereby explaining the business cycle. Specific theories tend to emphasize demand or supply influences.

- In the long run the AS curve tends to be vertical, implying that changes in aggregate demand affect prices but not output. In the short run, however, the AS curve is sloped, making macro outcomes sensitive to both supply and demand.

- Macro policy options range from laissez faire (the classical approach) to various strategies for shifting either the aggregate demand curve or the aggregate supply curve.

Key Terms

macroeconomics
business cycle
laissez faire
law of demand
Say's Law
real GDP

recession
growth recession
aggregate demand
aggregate supply
equilibrium (macro)

full-employment GDP
inflation
fiscal policy
monetary policy
supply-side policy

Questions for Discussion

1. If business cycles were really inevitable, what purpose would macro policy serve?
2. What events might prompt consumers to demand fewer goods at current prices?
3. If equilibrium is compatible with both buyers' and sellers' intentions, how can it be undesirable?
4. The stock market plunge following the September 11, 2001, terrorist attacks greatly reduced the wealth of the average U.S. household. How might this have affected aggregate demand? Aggregate supply?
5. What exactly did Say mean when he said "supply creates its own demand"?
6. What's wrong with the Classical theory of self-adjustment? Why didn't sales and employment increase in 1929–33 in response to declining prices and wages (see Figure 8.1)?
7. What might have caused real GDP to decline so dramatically in (*a*) 1929 and (*b*) 1946 (see Figure 8.3)? What caused output to increase again in each case?
8. How would a sudden jump in U.S. prices affect (*a*) imports from Mexico, (*b*) exports to Mexico, and (*c*) U.S. aggregate demand?
9. Why might rising prices stimulate short-run production but have no effect on long-run production?
10. How might a tax cut affect both AD *and* AS?

PROBLEMS   The Student Problem Set at the back of this book contains numerical and graphing problems for this chapter.

WEB ACTIVITIES   to accompany this chapter can be found on the Online Learning Center: **http://www.mhhe.com/economics/schiller 10**

Aggregate Demand

The terrorist attacks of September 11, 2001, destroyed billions of dollars' worth of capital and killed nearly 3,000 people. As terrible as this devastation was, however, that physical damage made only a tiny dent in the $11 *trillion* production capacity of the U.S. economy. The *supply* of goods and services was relatively unscathed.

On the *demand* side of the economy the damage was much greater. The 9/11 terrorist strike instilled fear of further attacks. So much fear that Americans were hesitant to go shopping, much less travel. Businesses, too, were fearful of building new factories or equipment. As a result, aggregate demand shifted left, prolonging a recession.

Should the government have waited for the economy to self-adjust? Or should it have intervened to increase aggregate demand? We know how the British economist John Maynard Keynes would have answered this question. The Great Depression revealed the undependability of the classical self-adjustment process. Who knows how long another "self-adjustment" process might last. Rather than wait forever—until, as Keynes put it, we're all "dead"—the government should intervene to boost total spending and get the economy back on track.

In this and the next two chapters we focus on the demand side of the macro economy. We start with the same questions Keynes posed:

- **What are the components of aggregate demand?**
- **What determines the level of spending for each component?**
- **Will there be enough demand to maintain full employment?**

By working through the demand side of the macro economy, we'll get a better view of what might cause business cycles and what might cure them. Later on we'll examine the aggregate supply side more closely as well.

MACRO EQUILIBRIUM

In Chapter 8 we got a bird's-eye view of how macro equilibrium is established. Producers have some notion of how much output they're willing and able to produce at various price levels. Likewise, consumers, businesses, governments, and foreign buyers have some notion of how much output they're willing and able to buy at different price levels. These forces of **aggregate demand** and **aggregate supply** confront each other in the marketplace. Eventually, buyers and sellers discover that only one price level and output combination is acceptable to *both* sides. This is the price-output combination we designate as **(macro) equilibrium.** At equilibrium, the aggregate quantity of goods demanded exactly equals the aggregate quantity supplied. In the absence of macro disturbances, the economy will gravitate toward equilibrium.

aggregate demand: The total quantity of output demanded at alternative price levels in a given time period, *ceteris paribus.*

aggregate supply: The total quantity of output producers are willing and able to supply at alternative price levels in a given time period, *ceteris paribus.*

equilibrium (macro): The combination of price level and real output that is compatible with both aggregate demand and aggregate supply.

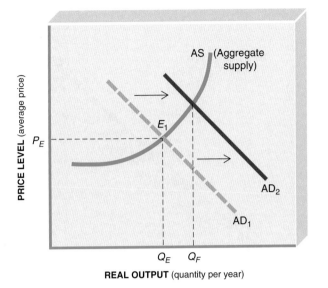

FIGURE 9.1
Escaping a Recession

Aggregate demand (AD) might be in-sufficient to ensure full employment (Q_F), as illustrated by the intersection of AD_1 and the aggregate supply curve. The question is whether and how AD will increase—that is, *shift* rightward—say to AD_2. To answer these questions, the components or demand must be examined.

The Desired Adjustment

Figure 9.1 illustrates again this general view of macro equilibrium. In the figure, aggregate supply (AS) and demand (AD_1) establish an equilibrium at E_1. At this particular equilibrium, the value of real output is Q_E, significantly short of the economy's full-employment potential at Q_F. Accordingly, the economy depicted in Figure 9.1 is saddled with excessive unemployment. This is the kind of situation the U.S. economy confronted in 2001.

All economists recognize that such a *short-run* macro failure is possible. We also realize that the unemployment problem depicted in Figure 9.1 would disappear if either the AD or AS curve shifted rightward. A central macro debate is over whether the curves *will* shift on their own (self-adjust). If not, the government might have to step in and do some heavy shifting.

Components of Aggregate Demand

To assess the possibilities for self-adjustment, we need to examine the nature of aggregate demand more closely. Who's buying the output of the economy? What factors influence their purchase decisions?

We can best understand the nature of aggregate demand by breaking it down into its various components. *The four components of aggregate demand are*

- *Consumption (C)*
- *Investment (I)*
- *Government spending (G)*
- *Net exports (X − M)*

Each of these components represents a stream of spending that contributes to aggregate demand. What we want to determine is how these various spending decisions are made. We also want to know what factors might *change* the level of spending, thereby *shifting* aggregate demand.

CONSUMPTION

Consider first the largest component of aggregate demand, namely, **consumption.** Consumption refers to expenditures by households (consumers) on final goods and services. As we observed in Chapter 2, *consumer expenditures account for two-thirds of total spending.* Hence, whatever factors alter consumer behavior are sure to have an impact on aggregate demand.

consumption: Expenditure by consumers on final goods and services.

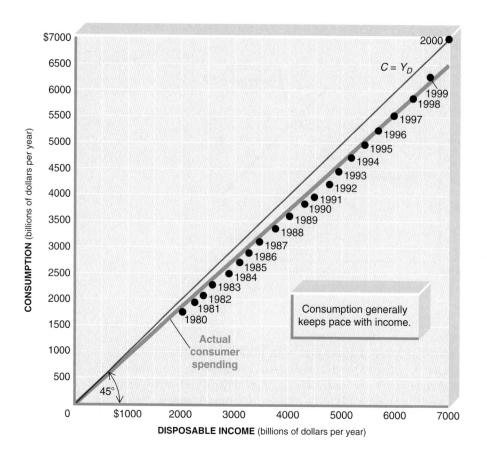

FIGURE 9.2

U.S. Consumption and Income

The points on the graph indicate the actual rates of U.S. disposable income and consumption for the years 1980–2000. By connecting these dots, we can approximate the long-term consumption function. Clearly, consumption rises with income. Indeed, consumers spend almost every extra dollar they receive.

Income and Consumption

The aggregate demand curve asserts that the *real* value of output demanded depends on the price level. Keynes, however, argued that consumers don't really think in such terms. The typical consumer simply decides how much he or she is going to *spend,* in dollars. The most decisive influence on that spending decision is available income: ***Most consumers simply spend most of whatever income they have.***

Figure 9.2 seems to confirm Keynes's view. Year after year, consumer spending has risen in tandem with income. Accordingly, if we know how much income consumers have, we should be able to predict roughly how much they'll spend on consumption.

Disposable income is the key concept here. As noted in Chapter 5, **disposable income** is the amount of income consumers actually take home after all taxes have been paid, transfers (e.g., Social Security benefits) have been received, and depreciation charges and retained earnings have been subtracted (see Table 5.6).

What will consumers do with their disposable income? There are only two choices: They can either spend their disposable income on consumption, or they can save (not spend) it. At this point we don't care what form household **saving** might take (e.g., cash under the mattress, bank deposits, stock purchases); all we want to do is distinguish that share of disposable income spent on consumer goods and services from the remainder that is *not* spent. By definition, then, ***all disposable income is either consumed (spent) or saved (not spent);*** that is,

> **disposable income:** After-tax income of consumers; personal income less personal taxes.

> **saving:** That part of disposable income not spent on current consumption; disposable income less consumption.

$$\text{Disposable income} = \text{consumption} + \text{saving}$$
$$(Y_D) \qquad\qquad (C) \qquad\quad (S)$$

Consumption vs. Saving

What intrigued Keynes about this formula was the recognition that consumers might *not* spend all their income. This could pose a problem for macro equilibrium. Specifically, too much saving might leave aggregate demand short of its full-employment potential. This possibility led Keynes to take a closer look at the relationship of consumer spending to disposable income.

Keynes discovered two different ways of describing the consumption-income relationship. The first way focuses on the ratio of *total* consumption to *total* disposable income. The second method focuses on the relationship of *changes* in consumption to *changes* in disposable income.

The proportion of *total* disposable income spent on consumer goods and services is referred to as the **average propensity to consume (APC).** To determine the APC, we simply observe how much consumers spend in a given time period out of that period's disposable income. In 2001, for example, the disposable income of U.S. households amounted to $7,469 billion. Out of this amount, consumers spent $7,342 billion and saved only $127 billion. Accordingly, we may calculate the *average* propensity to consume as

$$APC = \frac{\text{total consumption}}{\text{total disposable income}} = \frac{C}{Y_D}$$

For 2001 this works out to

$$APC = \frac{\$7{,}342 \text{ billion}}{\$7{,}469 \text{ billion}} = 0.98$$

In other words, U.S. consumers spent just about every penny they received in 2001. Specifically, consumers spent, on average, 98 cents out of every dollar of income. Only 2 cents out of every disposable dollar was saved.

The relatively high APC in the United States distinguishes our consumer-oriented economy. In recent years, the U.S. APC has even *exceeded* 1.0 on occasion, forcing U.S. households to finance some of their consumption with credit or past savings. Prior to 9/11, a lot of U.S. households were doing exactly that, as the accompanying News reports.

> **average propensity to consume (APC):** Total consumption in a given period divided by total disposable income.

The Marginal Propensity to Consume

If the APC can change from year to year, then consumers aren't always spending the same fraction of every dollar received (the APC is just an average). This led Keynes to develop a second measure of consumption behavior, called the *marginal* propensity

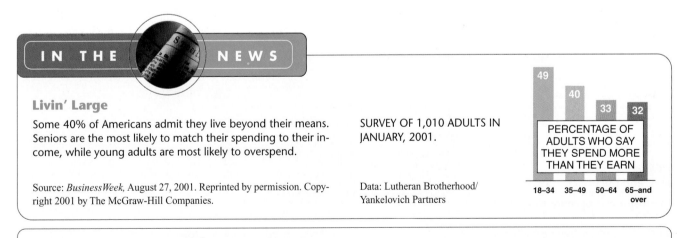

IN THE NEWS

Livin' Large

Some 40% of Americans admit they live beyond their means. Seniors are the most likely to match their spending to their income, while young adults are most likely to overspend.

Source: *BusinessWeek*, August 27, 2001. Reprinted by permission. Copyright 2001 by The McGraw-Hill Companies.

SURVEY OF 1,010 ADULTS IN JANUARY, 2001.

Data: Lutheran Brotherhood/Yankelovich Partners

PERCENTAGE OF ADULTS WHO SAY THEY SPEND MORE THAN THEY EARN

18–34	35–49	50–64	65–and over
49	40	33	32

Analysis: When consumer spending exceeds disposable income, consumer saving is negative; households are *dissaving*. Dissaving is financed with credit or prior savings.

marginal propensity to consume (MPC): The fraction of each additional (marginal) dollar of disposable income spent on consumption; the change in consumption divided by the change in disposable income.

to consume. The **marginal propensity to consume (MPC)** tells us how much consumer expenditure will *change* in response to *changes* in disposable income. With the delta symbol, Δ, representing "change in," MPC can be written as

$$MPC = \frac{\text{change in consumption}}{\text{change in disposable income}} = \frac{\Delta C}{\Delta Y_D}$$

To calculate the marginal propensity to consume, we could ask how consumer spending in 2001 was affected by the *last* dollar of disposable income. That is, how did consumer spending change when disposable income increased from \$7,468,999,999 to \$7,469,000,000? If consumer spending increased by 80 cents when this last \$1.00 was received, we'd calculate the *marginal* propensity to consume as

$$MPC = \frac{\Delta C}{\Delta Y_D} = \frac{\$0.80}{\$1.00} = 0.8$$

Notice that the MPC in this particular case (0.8) is lower than the APC (0.98). Suppose we had incorrectly assumed that consumers would always spend \$0.98 of every dollar's income. Then we'd have expected the rate of consumer spending to rise by 98 cents as the last dollar was received. In fact, however, the rate of spending increased by only 80 cents. In other words, consumers responded to an *increase* in their income differently than past averages implied.

No one would be upset if our failure to distinguish the APC from the MPC led to an error of only 18 cents in forecasts of consumer spending. After all, the rate of consumer spending in the U.S. economy now exceeds \$8 *trillion* per year! But those same trillion-dollar dimensions make the accuracy of the MPC that much more important. Annual *changes* in disposable income entail hundreds of billions of dollars. When we start playing with those sums—the actual focus of economic policymakers—the distinction between APC and MPC is significant.

The Marginal Propensity to Save

marginal propensity to save (MPS): The fraction of each additional (marginal) dollar of disposable income not spent on consumption; 1 − MPC.

Once we know how much of their income consumers will spend, we also know how much they'll save. Remember that all *disposable income is, by definition, either consumed (spent on consumption) or saved.* Saving is just whatever income is left over after consumption expenditures. Accordingly, if the MPC is 0.80, then 20 cents of each additional dollar is being saved and 80 cents is being spent (see Figure 9.3). The **marginal propensity to save (MPS)**—the fraction of each additional dollar saved (that is, *not* spent)—is simply

$$MPS = 1 - MPC$$

As Table 9.1 illustrates, if we know how much of their income consumers spend, we also know how much of it they save.

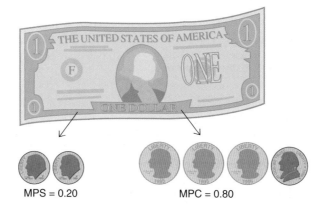

FIGURE 9.3
MPC and MPS

The marginal propensity to consume (MPC) tells us what portion of an extra dollar of income will be spent. The remaining portion will be saved. The MPC and MPS help us predict consumer behavior.

MPS = 0.20   MPC = 0.80

MPC. The marginal propensity to consume (MPC) is the *change* in consumption that accompanies a *change* in disposable income; that is,

$$MPC = \frac{\Delta C}{\Delta Y_D}$$

MPS. The marginal propensity to *save* (MPS) is the fraction of each additional (marginal) dollar of disposable income *not* spent—that is, saved. This is summarized as

$$MPS = \frac{\Delta S}{\Delta Y_D}$$

MPS equals 1 − MPC, since every additional dollar is either spent (consumed) or not spent (saved).

APC. We may also be interested in the proportion of *total* disposable income that's spent on consumption. This is referred to as the *average* propensity to consume and is computed:

$$APC = \frac{C}{Y_D}$$

APS. The average *propensity* to save is $\frac{S}{Y_D}$ and must equal 1 − APC.

TABLE 9.1
Average and Marginal Propensities

WEBNOTE

Go to the U.S. Bureau of Economic Activity (BEA) Web site at www.bea.doc.gov, and determine the rate of disposable income and consumer spending in the most recent two quarters. What was the APC in the most recent quarter? What was the MPC between the two quarters?

THE CONSUMPTION FUNCTION

The MPC, MPS, APC, and APS are simply statistical measures of observed consumer behavior. What we really want to know is what drives these measures. If we know, then we'll be in a position to *predict* rather than just *observe* consumer behavior. This ability would be of immense value in anticipating and controlling short-run business cycles.

Keynes had several ideas about the determinants of consumption. Although he observed that consumer spending and income were highly correlated (Figure 9.2), he knew consumption wasn't *completely* determined by current income. In extreme cases, this is evident. People who have no income in a given period continue to consume goods and services. They finance their purchases by dipping into their savings accounts (past income) or using credit (future income) instead of spending current income. We also observe that people's spending sometimes *changes* even when income doesn't, suggesting that income isn't the *only* determinant of consumption. Other, *non*income determinants of consumption include

- *Expectations:* People who anticipate a pay raise, a tax refund, or a birthday check often start spending more money even before the extra income is received. Conversely, workers who anticipate being laid off tend to save more and spend less. Hence, *expectations* may alter consumer spending before income itself changes.
- *Wealth:* The amount of wealth an individual owns also affects a person's ability and willingness to consume. A homeowner may take out a home equity loan to buy a plasma TV, a vacation, or a new car. In this case, consumer spending is being financed by wealth, not current income. *Changes* in wealth will also *change* consumer behavior. When the stock market rises, stockholders respond by saving less and spending more of their current income. This **wealth effect** was particularly evident in the late 1990s, when a persistent rise in the stock market helped fuel a consumption spree (and a negative savings rate). When the stock market reversed direction in 2000, consumers cut back their spending.

Autonomous Consumption

wealth effect: A change in consumer spending caused by a change in the value of owned assets.

- *Credit:* The availability of credit allows people to spend more than their current income. On the other hand, the need to repay past debts may limit current consumption. Here again, *changes* in credit availability or cost (interest rates) may alter consumer behavior.
- *Taxes:* Taxes are the link between total and disposable income. The tax cuts enacted in 2001–3 put more income into consumer hands immediately (via tax rebates) and left them with more income from future pay checks (via tax-rate cuts). These tax reductions stimulated more aggregate demand. Were income taxes to go up, disposable incomes and consumer spending would decline.
- *Price levels:* Rising price levels reduce the real value of money balances and may cause people to curtail spending. (This is the real-balances effect, which also helps explain aggregate demand.)

Income-Dependent Consumption

In recognition of these many determinants of consumption, Keynes distinguished between two kinds of consumer spending: (1) spending *not* influenced by current income and (2) spending that *is* determined by current income. This simple categorization is summarized as

$$\text{Total consumption} = \frac{\text{autonomous}}{\text{consumption}} + \text{income-dependent consumption}$$

where *autonomous* consumption refers to that consumption spending independent of current income. The level of autonomous spending depends instead on expectations, wealth, credit, taxes, price levels, and other nonincome influences.

These various determinants of consumption are summarized in an equation called the **consumption function,** which is written as

$$C = a + bY_D$$

consumption function: A mathematical relationship indicating the rate of desired consumer spending at various income levels.

where C = current consumption
a = autonomous consumption
b = marginal propensity to consume
Y_D = disposable income

At first blush, the consumption function is just a mathematical summary of consumer behavior. It has important *predictive* power, however: ***The consumption function provides a precise basis for predicting how changes in income (Y_D) will affect consumer spending (C).*** It also shows how changes in *non*income forces will affect consumer spending.

One Consumer's Behavior

To see how the consumption function works, consider the plight of Justin, a college freshman who has no income. How much will Justin spend? Obviously he must spend *something,* otherwise he'll starve to death. At a very low rate of income—in this case, zero—consumer spending depends less on current income than on basic survival needs, past savings, and credit. The *a* in the consumption function expresses this autonomous consumption: let's assume it's $50 per week. Thus, the weekly rate of consumption expenditure in this case is

$$C = \$50 + bY_D$$

Now suppose that Justin finds a job and begins earning $100 per week. Will his spending be affected? The $50 per week he'd been spending didn't buy much. Now that he's earning a little income, Justin will want to improve his lifestyle. That is, ***we expect consumption to rise with income.*** The marginal propensity to consume tells us how fast spending will rise.

Suppose Justin responds to the new-found income by increasing his consumption from $50 per week to $125. The *change* in his consumption is therefore $75. Dividing this *change* in his consumption ($75) by the *change* in income ($100) reveals that his marginal propensity to consume is 0.75.

Once we know the level of autonomous consumption ($50 per week) and the marginal propensity to consume (0.75), we can predict consumer behavior with uncanny accuracy. In this case, Justin's consumption function is

$$C = \$50 + 0.75Y_D$$

With these numerical values we can advance from simple *observation* (what he's spending now) to *prediction* (what he'll spend at different income levels). Figure 9.4 summarizes this predictive power.

We've already noted that Justin will spend $125 per week when his income is only $100. This observation is summarized in row *B* of the table in Figure 9.4 and by point *B* on the graph. Notice that his spending exceeds his income by $25 at this point. The other $25 is still being begged, borrowed, or withdrawn from savings. Without peering further into Justin's personal finances, we simply say that he's **dissaving** $25 per week. ***Dissaving occurs whenever current consumption exceeds current income.*** As the News on p. 181 revealed, dissaving is common in the United States, especially among younger people who are "livin' large."

dissaving: Consumption expenditure in excess of disposable income; a negative saving flow.

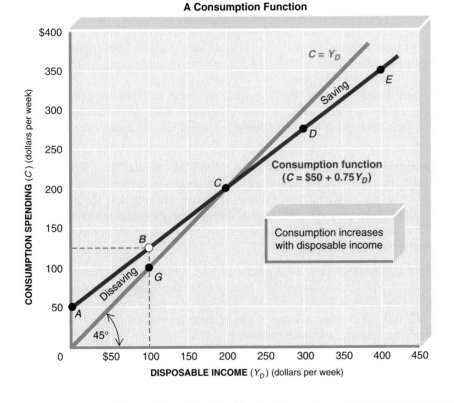

A Consumption Function

	Disposable Income (Y_D)	Consumption ($C = \$50 + 0.75\,Y_D$)				
		Autonomous Consumption	+	Income Dependent Consumption	=	Total Consumption
A	$ 0	$50		$ 0		$ 50
B	100	50		75		125
C	200	50		150		200
D	300	50		225		275
E	400	50		300		350
F	500	50		375		425

FIGURE 9.4
Justin's Consumption Function

The rate of consumer spending (*C*) depends on disposable income (Y_D). The marginal propensity to consume indicates how much consumption will increase with each added dollar of income. In this case, when disposable income rises from $100 to $200, consumption increases by $75 (from point *B* to point *C*). The MPC = 0.75.

The consumption function can be expressed in an equation, a table, or a graph. Point *B* on the graph, for example, corresponds to row *B* in the table. Both indicate that this consumer desires to spend $125 per week when his income is $100 per week. The difference between income and consumption equals (dis)saving.

If Justin's income continues to rise, he'll stop dissaving at some point. Perhaps he'll even start saving enough to pay back all the people who have sustained him through these difficult months. Figure 9.4 shows just how and when this will occur.

The 45-Degree Line. The green line in Figure 9.4, with a 45-degree angle, represents all points where consumption and income are exactly equal ($C = Y_D$). Recall that Justin currently has an income of $100 per week. By moving up from the horizontal axis at $Y_D = \$100$, we see all the consumption possibilities he confronts. Were he to spend exactly $100 on consumption, he'd end up on the 45-degree line at point *G*. But we already know he doesn't stop there. Instead, he proceeds further, to point *B*. At point *B* the consumption function lies above the 45-degree line, so consumption exceeds income; dissaving is occurring.

Observe, however, what happens when his disposable income rises to $200 per week (row *C* in the table in Figure 9.4). The upward slope of the consumption function (see graph) tells us that consumption spending continues to rise with income. In fact, *the slope of the consumption function equals the marginal propensity to consume.* In this case, we see that when income increases from $100 to $200, consumption rises from $125 (point *B*) to $200 (point *C*). Thus the *change* in consumption ($75) equals three-fourths of the *change* in income. The MPC is still 0.75.

Point *C* has further significance. At an income of $200 per week Justin is no longer dissaving but is now breaking even—that is, disposable income equals consumption, so saving equals zero. Notice that point *C* lies on the 45-degree line, where current consumption equals current income.

What would happen to spending if income increased still further? According to Figure 9.4, Justin will start *saving* once income exceeds $200 per week. To the right of point *C*, the consumption function always lies below the 45-degree line.

The Aggregate Consumption Function

Repeated studies of consumers suggest that there's nothing remarkable about Justin. The consumption function we've constructed for him can be used to depict all consumers simply by changing the numbers involved. Instead of dealing in hundreds of dollars per week, we now play with trillions of dollars per year. But the basic relationship is the same. This aggregate relationship between consumption spending and disposable income was already observed in Figure 9.2, and is confirmed again in the News at the top of the next page.

Shifts of the Consumption Function

Although the consumption function is a handy device for predicting consumer behavior, it's not infallible. People change their behavior. Neither autonomous consumption (the *a* in the consumption function) nor the marginal propensity to consume (the *b* in $C = a + bY_D$) is set in stone. Whenever one of these parameters changes, the entire consumption function *shifts* to a new position.

Consider first the value for *a*. We noted earlier that autonomous consumption depends on wealth, credit, expectations, taxes, and price levels. If any of these non-income determinants changes, the value of the *a* in the consumption function will change as well.

We noted earlier how the 9/11 terrorist attacks heightened fears for both physical and economic security. Market disruptions and job layoffs added to the sense of insecurity. All these pressures derailed consumer confidence. As the News at the bottom of the next page reports, the index of consumer confidence plunged in October 2001. As a result, the value of autonomous consumption declined from a_1 to a_2 and the consumption function *shifted* downward, as in Figure 9.5 on page 188.

Shifts of Aggregate Demand. Shifts of the consumption function are reflected in shifts of the aggregate demand curve. Consider again the October 2001 downward shift of the consumption function. A decrease in consumer spending at any given income level implies a decrease in aggregate demand as well. Recall that the aggregate demand curve depicts how much real output will be demanded at various price

Consumer Spending Increased, Personal Income Rose in March

WASHINGTON–U.S. consumer spending grew at a healthy pace in March, while another upbeat economic report showed personal income rising.

The U.S. Commerce Department said Friday that consumers boosted spending by 0.4% in March, matching a revised increase in February. In a separate Commerce report, personal income increased by 0.4% in March, after climbing a revised 0.5% in February.

—Jeff Bater

Personal Income

Here is the Commerce Department's latest report on personal income. The figures are at seasonally adjusted annual rates in trillions of dollars.

	March 2004	February 2004
Personal income	$9.524	$9.495
Wages and salaries	5.236	5.223
Factory payrolls	.682	.682
Transfer payments	1.427	1.426
Disposable personal income	8.541	8.507
Personal outlays	8.375	8.344
Consumption expenditures	8.088	8.055
Other outlays	4.968	4.960
Personal savings	.166	.163

Analysis: When household incomes increase, consumer spending increases as well. The marginal propensity to consume summarizes this relationship.

Consumer Confidence Drops to Seven-Year Low

Consumer confidence plunged this month to the lowest level in seven years, raising new concerns about whether consumers worried about their jobs and terrorist attacks may reduce their spending at a time when the U.S. economy is already faltering.

The Conference Board said yesterday that its confidence index fell to 85.5 this month, the lowest level since February 1994, from 97.0 in September. It was the fourth consecutive monthly decline.

"This is a very worrisome report, and what's worse is that by Friday morning it could be old news," said economist Oscar Gonzalez at John Hancock Financial Services in Boston, referring to the Friday release of the government's October unemployment report. If, as expected, the report shows a sharp rise in unemployment and decline in job growth, "it could be a crushing blow to confidence." "Having a job is probably the single biggest factor in consumers having confidence," Gonzalez said.

Analysts are keenly interested in consumers' attitudes because their spending accounts for two-thirds of the nation's economic output. Earlier this year, steady increases in consumer spending helped keep the economy growing despite big declines in business investment. Many economists now believe that the nation is slipping into recession and worry that a steep falloff in consumer spending could make it longer and more painful than otherwise.

—John M. Berry

Analysis: Expectations of *future* income affect consumer spending. When consumer confidence in the future declines, autonomous spending drops and the consumption function shifts downward (as in Figure 9.5).

FIGURE 9.5
A Shift in the Consumption Function

Consumers' willingness to spend current income is affected by their confidence in the future. If consumers become more worried or pessimistic, autonomous consumption may decrease from a_1 to a_2. This change will shift the entire consumption function downward.

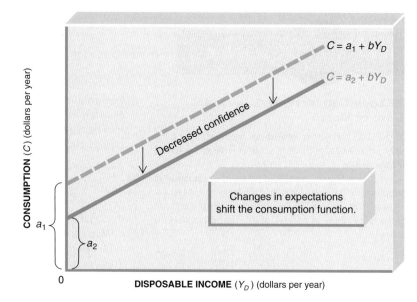

levels, *with income held constant.* When the consumption function shifts downward, households spend less of their income. Hence, less real output is demanded at any given price level. To summarize,

- *A downward shift of the consumption function implies a leftward shift of the aggregate demand curve.*
- *An upward shift of the consumption function implies an increase (a rightward shift) in aggregate demand.*

These relationships are illustrated in Figure 9.6.

FIGURE 9.6
AD Effects of Consumption Shifts

A downward shift of the consumption function implies that households want to spend less of their income. Here consumption at the income level Y_1 decreases from f_1 to f_2. This decreased expenditure is reflected in a leftward shift of the aggregate demand curve. At the initial price level P_1 consumers demanded Q_1 output. At that same price level, consumers now demand less output, $Q_2 [= Q_1 - (f_1 - f_2)]$. (*Note:* Both income and the price level are being held constant here.)

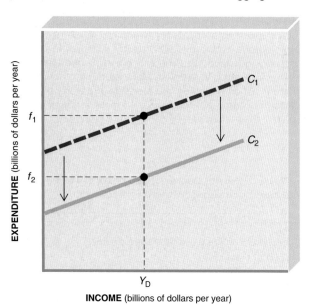

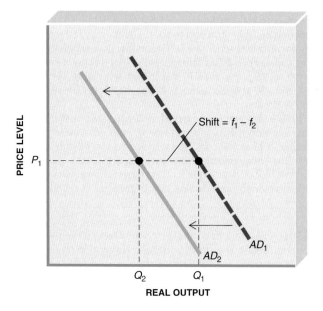

A change in consumer confidence is only one factor that might shift the aggregate demand curve. ***Shift factors include all nonincome (autonomous) determinants of consumption, including***

- ***Changes in consumer confidence (expectations).***
- ***Changes in wealth.***
- ***Changes in credit conditions.***
- ***Changes in tax policy.***

As we observed earlier, a change in the value of a household's assets (wealth) will alter autonomous consumption. The Council of Economic Advisers estimated that rising stock market prices added one percentage point to the average propensity to consume in 1997 and 1998.

The wealth effect turned negative, however, in 2000, when the stock market plunged (see News below). With consumers spending less at every income level, aggregate demand fell (shifted leftward) in 2000–2001 (Figure 9.6).

The same emphasis on *change* applies to other shift factors. A *change* in tax rates or interest rates (credit conditions) is what *shifts* the consumption function up or down. These same changes therefore shift the aggregate demand curve left or right (Figure 9.6). In short, ***shifts of the AD curve occur when nonincome determinants of consumption change.***

Shifts of aggregate demand can be a cause of macro instability. As we first observed in Chapter 8, recurrent shifts of aggregate demand may cause real output to alternately expand and contract, thereby giving rise to short-run business cycles. What we've observed here is that those aggregate demand shifts may originate in consumer

IN THE NEWS

Falling Stocks Smash Nest Eggs

"Wealth Effect" Has Gone Poof, and So Have Many Investors' Spending Plans

For a long time, the stock market was very good to Chuck Yanus—so good that he and his wife went out and bought themselves two Suzuki motorcycles for about $10,000 in cash.

The Yanus family felt so flush that when Honda introduced its new top-of-the-line Gold Wing touring bike (price tag: $17,000-plus) this year, the couple began making plans to give one to themselves for Christmas.

But then the markets plunged, vaporizing more than $2 trillion in stock value in the nine months since stocks peaked in March. The tech-heavy Nasdaq is down a stunning 36 percent this year and about 48 percent from its exhilarating high last spring. The Dow Jones industrial average, sober avatar of the Old Economy, is better, but not enough to avoid pain: It's down about 7 percent this year, after being up 25 percent last year.

Stock portfolios that gave investors thoughts of early retirement or made almost anything seem affordable were devastated.

"When you lop 25 percent off your bottom line, it makes you stop and think," says Yanus, 46, a district manager for Sun Microsystems in Syracuse, N.Y. Big-ticket items like the Gold Wing are out. "I said the hell with it, let's wait," Yanus says.

For many Americans like the Yanuses, the thrill is gone. The "wealth effect"—that giddy feeling of richness that consumers got as they watched the value of their portfolios and their homes soar—has been killed, or at least badly wounded, by the prolonged market decline.

Spending Spree May Be Over. Interviews with consumers around the country suggest that the market-driven shopping spree may be over. Many of the motorcycles, cars, houses, home renovations, big-screen TVs and other big-ticket purchases Americans would have made without hesitation a year or even six months ago are on hold.

—George Hager and Dina Temple-Raston

Source: *USA Today,* December 19, 2000. USA TODAY. Copyright 2001. Reprinted with permission. www.usatoday.com

Analysis: The stock market plunge of 2000–2001 reduced consumer wealth and autonomous consumption. This shifted the consumption function downward and the aggregate demand curve leftward.

behavior. Changes in consumer confidence, in wealth, or in credit conditions alter the rate of consumer spending. If consumer spending increases abruptly, demand-pull inflation may follow. If consumer spending slows abruptly, a recession may occur.

INVESTMENT

Although consumer spending can be unstable, the economy need not suffer every time the consumption function shifts. There are, after all, three other sources of aggregate demand: investment (I), government spending (G), and net exports ($X - M$). These components of aggregate demand could potentially offset any shortfalls or instability in consumer spending. To assess this possibility, we will first examine how the level of investment is determined and how stable it is.

Determinants of Investment

As we observed in Chapter 5, investment spending accounts for roughly 15 percent of total output. That spending includes not only expenditures on new plant, equipment, and business software (all referred to as *fixed investment*) but also spending on inventories (called *inventory investment*). Residential construction is also counted in investment statistics because houses and apartment buildings continue to produce housing services for decades. All these forms of **investment** represent a demand for output.

> **investment:** Expenditures on (production of) new plant, equipment, and structures (capital) in a given time period, plus changes in business inventories.

Expectations. Expectations play a critical role in investment decisions. No firm wants to purchase new plant and equipment unless it is convinced people will later buy the output produced by that plant and that equipment. Nor do producers want to accumulate inventories of goods unless they expected consumers to eventually buy them. Thus, *favorable expectations of future sales are a necessary condition for investment spending.*

Interest Rates. A second determinant of investment spending is the rate of interest. Business firms typically borrow money in order to purchase plant and equipment. The higher the rate of interest, the costlier it is to invest. Accordingly, we anticipate a lower rate of investment spending when interest rates are high, more investment at lower rates, *ceteris paribus.*

Technology and Innovation. A third determinant of investment is changes in technology and innovation. When scientists learned how to miniaturize electronic circuitry, an entire new industry of electronic calculators, watches, and other goods sprang to life. In this case, the demand for investment goods shifted to the right as a result of improved miniaturized circuits and imaginative innovation (the use of the new technology in pocket calculators). More recently, technological advances and cost reductions have stimulated an investment spree in digital music players, laptop computers, cellular phones, video conferencing, fiber-optic networks, and anything associated with the Internet.

The curve I_1, in Figure 9.7, depicts the general shape of the investment function. To find the rate of investment spending in this figure, we simply have to know the rate of interest. At an interest rate of 8 percent, for example, we expect to see $150 billion of investment (point A in Figure 9.7). At 6 percent interest, we'd expect $300 billion of investment (point B).

Shifts of Investment

These predictions about investment spending depend on a critical assumption; namely, that investor expectations are stable. In truth, that's a very tenuous assumption. While no one is entirely sure what shapes investors' expectations, experience shows that they are often quite volatile.

Altered Expectations. Business expectations are essentially a question of confidence in future sales. An upsurge in current consumer spending could raise investor expectations for future sales, shifting the investment function rightward (to I_2). New business software might induce a similar response. New business tax breaks might have

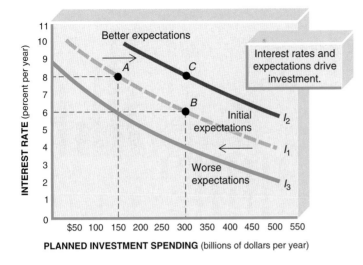

(The figure shows a graph with INTEREST RATE (percent per year) on the vertical axis from 0 to 11, and PLANNED INVESTMENT SPENDING (billions of dollars per year) on the horizontal axis from $50 to 550. It includes curves labeled I_1 (Initial expectations), I_2 (Better expectations), and I_3 (Worse expectations), with points A, B, and C marked. A box states "Interest rates and expectations drive investment.")

FIGURE 9.7
Investment Demand

The rate of desired investment depends on expectations, the rate of interest, and innovation. A *change* in expectations will *shift* the investment-demand curve. With given expectations, a change in the rate of interest will lead to *movements* along the existing investment-demand curve. In this case, an increase in investment beyond $150 billion per year (point *A*) may be caused by lower interest rates (point *B*) or improved expectations (point *C*). Keynes emphasized the role of investor expectations in maintaining full-employment spending.

the same effect. If any of these things happened, businesses would be more eager to invest. They'd borrow *more* money at any given interest rate (e.g., point *C* in Figure 9.7) and use it to buy more plant, equipment, and inventory.

Business expectations could worsen as well. The terrorist strikes of September 11, 2001, put a lot of investment plans on hold (see News). A transportation strike or spike in oil prices might worsen sales expectations as well. These kinds of events will shift the investment function leftward, as to I_3 in Figure 9.7. ***When investment spending declines, the aggregate demand curve shifts to the left.***

Empirical Instability. Figure 9.8 shows that unstable investment is more than just a theoretical threat to macro stability. What is depicted here are the quarter-to-quarter changes in both consumer spending and investor spending for the years 1999–2004. Quarterly changes in *consumer* spending never exceeded 7 percent and never became negative. By contrast, *investment* spending plummeted by 13.3 percent in the

---

IN THE NEWS

Small-Business Owners Pare Spending, Fearing Sales Will Dwindle After Attacks

Small-business owners expect the Sept. 11 terrorist attacks will sap fourth-quarter sales and have cut back fast on hiring and other spending plans. . . .

A survey by the National Federation of Independent Business, a small-business lobbying group in Washington, found during the days after the attacks on the World Trade Center and Pentagon a sharp downturn in expectations of sales growth for the next three months. . . .

The lower sales expectations led business owners to pare plans to hire workers, invest in capital equipment and in

inventory, the NFIB said. That collective hunkering down would, of course, contribute further to recessionary pressures. . . .

Capital-spending plans in the post-Sept. 11 period were at their lowest level in the survey's 15-year history, and hiring plans were at the lowest level since 1993.

—Jeff Bailey

Source: *The Wall Street Journal*, October 3, 2001. Reprinted by permission of *The Wall Street Journal.* © 2001 Dow Jones & Company, Inc. All Rights Reserved Worldwide. www.wsj.com

---

Analysis: Business investment is based more on expected future sales than on current sales and income. When expectations for future sales growth diminish, investment spending on plant, equipment, and inventory drops.

FIGURE 9.8
Volatile Investment Spending

Investment spending fluctuates more than consumption. Shown here are the quarter-to-quarter changes in the real rate of spending for fixed investment (excluding residential construction and inventory changes) and total consumption. Notice the sharp drops in investment spending just prior to the recession that began in March 2001 and again after the 9/11 attacks.

Source: *U.S. Bureau of Economic Analysis* (quarterly data seasonally adjusted).

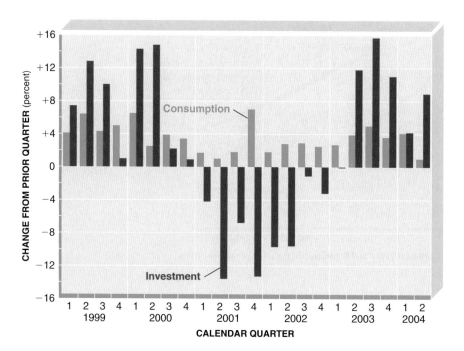

Check the U.S. Bureau of Economic Activity (BEA) Web site at www.stat-usa.gov to see how much seasonally adjusted investment has varied in percentage terms over the past six quarters.

post-9/11 quarter and jumped by over 14 percent in three other quarters. Those abrupt changes in investment were a major cause of the 2001 recession and also an important source of subsequent recovery.

GOVERNMENT AND NET EXPORT SPENDING

The apparent volatility of investment spending heightens rather than soothes anxiety about short-run macro instability. Together, consumption and investment account for roughly 80 percent of total output. As we have seen, the investment component of aggregate demand can be both uncertain and unstable. The consumption component of aggregate demand may shift abruptly as well. As we have seen, such shifts can sow the seeds of macro failure. Will the other components of aggregate demand improve the odds of macro success? What determines the level of government and net export spending? How stable are they?

Government Spending

At present, the government sector (federal, state, and local) spends over $2 trillion on goods and services, all of which is part of aggregate demand (unlike income transfers, which are not). As we observed in Chapter 2, about two-thirds of this spending occurs at the state and local levels. That nonfederal spending is limited by tax receipts, because state and local governments typically confront legal limitations on borrowing money. As a consequence, state and local spending has a mild pro-cyclical component, with expenditure rising slightly as the economy (and tax receipts) expands and declining somewhat when the economy (and tax receipts) slumps. This doesn't auger well for macro stability, much less "self-adjustment." *If consumption and investment spending decline, the subsequent decline in state-local government spending will aggravate rather than offset the leftward shift of the AD curve.*

Federal spending on goods and services isn't so constrained by tax receipts. Uncle Sam can *borrow* money, thereby allowing federal spending to exceed tax receipts. In fact, the federal government typically operates "in the red," with large annual budget deficits. This gives the federal government a unique *counter*-cyclical power. If private-sector spending and incomes decline, federal tax revenues will fall in response. Unlike state and local governments, however, the federal government can *increase* its spending despite declining tax revenues. In other words, Uncle Sam can help reverse AD

Canada Forecasts Slower 2001 Growth, Citing U.S. "Spillover"

OTTAWA—Citing the impact of the slowing U.S. economy, the Bank of Canada lowered its forecast of gross domestic product growth this year to about 3 percent from a previous range of 3 percent to 4 percent.

In a revision of its monetary-policy report of last November. Canada's central bank said "the slowdown of the U.S. economy has been more abrupt than anticipated," and has had a "spillover effect" on Canada. More than 85 percent of Canadian exports go to the U.S.

Bank of Canada governor David Dodge said yesterday the economy is now likely to grow at the low end of the bank's 3–4 percent forecast made in November. The bank said that it estimates the Canadian economy grew last year by 5 percent.

The bank also said it expects total consumer price inflation to ease to an annual pace of 2 percent by the end of this year, reflecting declines in oil prices.

—Joel Baglole

Source: *The Wall Street Journal*, February 7, 2001. Reprinted by permission of *The Wall Street Journal*. © 2001 Dow Dones & Company, Inc. All Rights Reserved Worldwide. www.wsj.com

Analysis: Most Canadian exports go to the United States. So when the U.S. economy slows, Canada experiences a decline in export demand—a leftward shift in that country's aggregate demand.

shifts by changing its own spending. This is exactly the kind of government action that Keynes advocated. We examine its potential more closely in Chapter 11.

The fourth and final source of aggregate demand is net exports. Our gross exports depend on the spending behavior of foreign consumers and businesses. If foreign consumers and investors behave like Americans, their demand for U.S. products will be subject to changes in *their* income, expectations, wealth, and other factors. In the Asian currency crisis of 1997–99, this was alarmingly evident: Once incomes in Asia began falling, U.S. exports to Asia of rice, corn, lumber, computers, and other goods and services fell sharply. So did the number of Asian students applying to U.S. colleges (a demand for U.S.-produced educational services). This decline in export spending represented a leftward shift of U.S. aggregate demand. The same kind of shift occurred in Canada's aggregate demand when the U.S. economy slowed in early 2001 (see World View).

Imports, too, can be unstable, and for the same reasons. Most U.S. imports are consumer goods and services. Imports, therefore, just get caught up in the ebb and flow of consumer spending. When consumer confidence slips or the stock market dips, import spending declines along with the rest of consumption (and investment). As a consequence, *net* exports can be both uncertain and unstable, creating further shifts of aggregate demand.

Net Exports

MACRO FAILURE

Once the potential instability of aggregate demand is recognized, the anxiety about macro instability begins to make sense. There is only one macro equilibrium at any one time—an equilibrium located at the intersection of the aggregate supply and demand curves. *Keynes had two chief concerns about macro equilibrium, namely,*

1. *The market's macro equilibrium might not give us full employment or price stability.*
2. *Even if the market's macro equilibrium were perfectly positioned (i.e., with full employment and price stability), it might not last.*

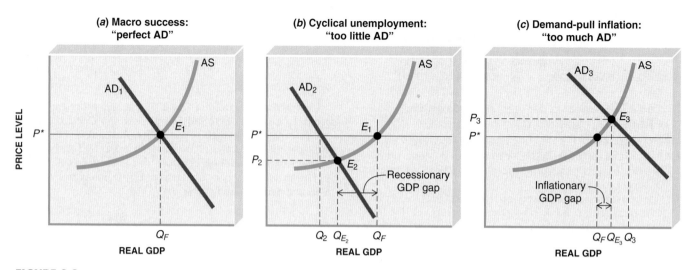

FIGURE 9.9
Macro Failures

Keynesian theory emphasizes that the combined spending decisions of consumers, investors, governments, and net exporters may not be compatible with the desired full employment (Q_F)–price stability (P^*) equilibrium (as they are in Figure a).

Aggregate demand may be too small (Figure b) or too great (Figure c) causing cyclical unemployment (b) or demand-pull inflation (c). Worse yet, even a desirable macro equilibrium (a) may be upset by abrupt *shifts* of aggregate demand.

Undesired Equilibrium

Figure 9.9a depicts the perfect macro equilibrium that everyone hopes for. Aggregate demand and aggregate supply intersect at E_1. At that macro equilibrium we get both full employment (Q_F) and price stability (P^*)—an ideal situation.

Keynes didn't think such a perfect outcome was likely. Why should aggregate demand intersect with aggregate supply exactly at point E_1? As we've observed, consumers, investors, government, and foreigners make independent spending decisions, based on many influences. Why should all these decisions add up to just the right amount of aggregate demand? Keynes didn't think they would. ***Because market participants make independent spending decisions, there's no reason to expect that the sum of their expenditures will generate exactly the right amount of aggregate demand.*** Instead, there's a high likelihood that we'll confront an imbalance between desired spending and full-employment output levels—that is, too much or too little aggregate demand.

full-employment GDP: The value of total output (real GDP) produced at full employment.

Recessionary GDP Gap. Figure 9.9b illustrates one of the undesired equilibriums that Keynes worried about. **Full-employment GDP** is still at Q_F and stable prices are at the level P^*. In this case, however, the rate of output demanded at price level P^* is only Q_2, far short of full-employment GDP (Q_F). How could this happen? Quite simple: The spending plans of consumers, investors, government, and export buyers don't generate enough aggregate demand at current (P^*) prices.

equilibrium GDP: The value of total output (real GDP) produced at macro equilibrium (AS = AD).

The economy depicted in Figure 9.9b is in trouble. At full employment, a lot more output would be produced than market participants would be willing to buy. As unsold inventories rose, production would get cut back, workers would get laid off, and prices would decline. Eventually, the economy would settle at E_2, where AD_2 and AS intersect. **Equilibrium GDP** would be equal to Q_{E2} and the equilibrium price level would be at P_2.

recessionary GDP gap: The amount by which equilibrium GDP falls short of full-employment GDP.

E_2 is clearly not a happy equilibrium. What particularly concerned Keynes was the **recessionary GDP gap,** the amount by which equilibrium GDP falls short of full-employment GDP. In Figure 9.9b, the recessionary GDP gap equals Q_F minus Q_{E2}. This gap represents unused productive capacity: lost GDP and unemployed workers. It is the breeding ground of **cyclical unemployment.**

cyclical unemployment: Unemployment attributable to a lack of job vacancies; that is, to inadequate aggregate demand.

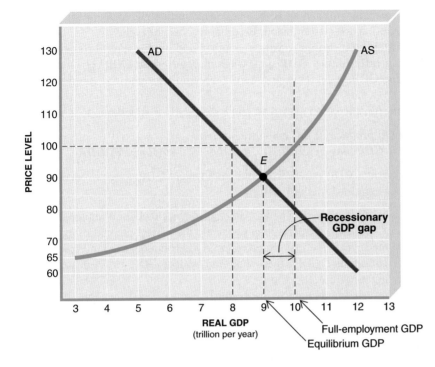

FIGURE 9.10
A Recessionary GDP Gap

The level of aggregate demand de-pends on the spending behavior of market participants. In this case, the level of GDP demanded at current prices (*P* = 100) ($8 trillion) is less than full-employment GDP ($10 trillion). This results in a lower equilibrium GDP ($9 trillion) and a recessionary GDP gap ($1 trillion). The price level also declines from 100 to 90.

Real GDP Demanded (in $ trillions) by:						
Price Level	Consumers +	Investors +	Government +	Net Exports =	Aggregate Demand	Aggregate Supply
130	3.0	0.25	1.5	0.25	5.0	12.0
120	3.5	0.50	1.5	0.50	6.0	11.5
110	4.0	0.75	1.5	0.75	7.0	11.0
100	4.5	1.00	1.5	1.0	8.0	10.0
90	5.0	1.25	1.5	1.25	9.0	9.0
80	5.5	1.50	1.5	1.50	10.0	7.0
70	6.0	1.75	1.5	1.75	11.0	5.0
60	6.5	2.0	1.5	2.0	12.0	3.0

Figure 9.10 illustrates this dilemma with more details on aggregate demand. The table depicts the demand for GDP at different price levels by consumers, investors, government, and net export buyers. Full-employment GDP is set at $10 trillion and the price level at 100. As is evident, however, the quantity of output demanded at that price level is only $8 trillion. This shortfall of aggregate demand will lead to output and price reductions, pushing the economy downward to equilibrium GDP, at point *E*. At that AS = AD intersection, the *equilibrium* GDP is at $9 trillion, with a price level of 90. The recessionary GDP gap is therefore $1 trillion ($Q_F - Q_E$).

Inflationary GDP Gap. Aggregate demand won't always fall short of potential out-put. But Keynes saw it as a distinct possibility. He also realized that aggregate demand might even *exceed* the economy's full-employment/price stability capacity. This con-tingency is illustrated in Figure 9.9*c*.

In Figure 9.9*c*, the AD_3 curve represents the combined spending plans of all mar-ket participants. According to this aggregate demand curve, market participants demand more output (Q_3) at current prices than the economy can produce (Q_F). To meet this excessive demand, producers will use overtime shifts and strain capacity. This will push

inflationary GDP gap: The amount by which equilibrium GDP exceeds full-employment GDP.

demand-pull inflation: An increase in the price level initiated by excessive aggregate demand.

Unstable Equilibrium

business cycle: Alternating periods of economic growth and contraction.

Macro Failures

Self-Adjustment?

prices up. The economy will end up at the macro equilibrium E_3. At E_3 the price level is higher (inflation) and short-run output exceeds sustainable levels.

What we end up with in Figure 9.9c is another undesirable equilibrium. In this case we have an **inflationary GDP gap,** wherein equilibrium GDP (Q_{E3}) exceeds full-employment GDP (Q_F). This is a fertile breeding ground for **demand-pull inflation.**

The GDP gaps illustrated in Figure 9.9b and c are clearly troublesome. In a nutshell,

- *The goal is to produce at full employment, but*
- *Equilibrium GDP may be greater or less than full-employment GDP.*

Whenever equilibrium GDP differs from full-employment GDP, we confront a macro failure (unemployment or inflation).

Things need not always work out so badly. Although Keynes thought it improbable, the spending plans of market participants *might* generate the perfect amount of aggregate demand, leaving the economy at the desired macro equilibrium depicted in Figure 9.9a. In Figure 9.9a, equilibrium GDP equals full-employment GDP. Unfortunately, that happy outcome might not last.

As we've observed, market participants may change their spending behavior abruptly. The stock market may boom or bust, shifting the consumption component of aggregate demand. Changed sales forecasts (expectations) may alter investment plans. Crises in foreign economies may disrupt export sales. A terrorist attack or outbreak of war may rock everybody's boat. Any of these events will cause the aggregate demand curve to shift. When this happens, the AD curve will get knocked out of its "perfect" position in Figure 9.9a, sending us to undesirable outcomes like 9.9b and 9.9c. Recurrent shifts of aggregate demand could even cause a **business cycle.**

Economies can get into macro trouble from the supply side of the market place as well, as we'll see later (Chapter 16). Keynes's emphasis on demand-side inadequacies serves as an early warning of potential macro failure, however. *If aggregate demand is too little, too great, or too unstable, the economy will not reach and maintain the goals of full employment and price stability.*

As we noted earlier, not everyone is as pessimistic as Keynes was about the prospects for macro bliss. The critical question is not whether undesirable outcomes might *occur* but whether they'll *persist.* In other words, the seriousness of any short-run macro failure depends on how markets *respond* to GDP gaps. If markets self-adjust, as classical economists asserted, then macro failures would be temporary.

How might markets self-adjust? If investors stepped up *their* spending whenever consumer spending faltered, the right amount of aggregate demand could be maintained. Such self-adjustment requires that some components of aggregate demand shift in the right direction at just the right time. In other words, self-adjustment requires that any shortfalls in one component of aggregate demand be offset by spending in another component. If such offsetting shifts occurred, then the desired macro equilibrium in Figure 9.9a could be maintained. Keynes didn't think that likely, however, for reasons we'll explore in the next chapter.

THE ECONOMY TOMORROW

Looking for AD Shifts

The Index of Leading Indicators

Keynes's theory of macro failure gave economic policymakers a lot to worry about. If Keynes was right, abrupt changes in aggregate demand could ruin even the best of economic times. Even if he was wrong about the ability of the economy to self-adjust, sudden shifts of aggregate demand could cause a lot of temporary pain. To minimize such pain, policymakers need some way of peering into

Indicator	Expected Impact
1. Average workweek	Hours worked per week typically increase when greater output and sales are expected.
2. Unemployment claims	Initial claims for unemployment benefits reflect changes in industry layoffs.
3. Delivery times	The longer it takes to deliver ordered goods, the greater the ratio of demand to supply.
4. Credit	Changes in business and consumer borrowing indicate potential purchasing power.
5. Materials prices	When producers step up production they buy more raw materials, pushing their prices higher.
6. Equipment orders	Orders for new equipment imply increased production capacity and higher anticipated sales.
7. Stock prices	Higher stock prices reflect expectations of greater sales and profits.
8. Money supply	Faster growth of the money supply implies a pickup in aggregate demand.
9. New orders	New orders for consumer goods trigger increases in production and employment.
10. Building permits	A permit represents the first step in housing construction.
11. Inventories	Companies build up inventory when they anticipate higher sales.

TABLE 9.2
The Leading Economic Indicators

Everyone wants a crystal ball to foresee future economic events. In reality, forecasters must reckon with very crude predictors of the future. One of the most widely used predictors is the Index of Leading Economic Indicators, which includes 11 factors believed to predict economic activity three to six months in advance. Changes in the leading indicators are used to forecast changes in GDP.

The leading indicators rarely move in the same direction at the same time. They're weighted together to create the index. Up-and-down movements of the index are reported each month by the nonprofit Conference Board.

the future—to foresee coming shifts of aggregate demand. With such a crystal ball, they might be able to take defensive actions and keep the economy on track.

Market participants have developed all kinds of crystal balls for anticipating AD shifts. The Foundation for the Study of Cycles has identified 4,000 different crystal balls people use to foretell changes in spending. They include the ratio of used-car to new-car sales (it rises in economic downturns); the number of divorce petitions (it rises in bad times); animal population cycles (they peak just before economic downturns); and even the optimism/pessimism content of popular music (a reflection of consumer confidence).

One of the most widely used crystal balls is the Index of Leading Indicators. What's appealing about that index is the plausible connection between its components and future spending. Equipment orders, for example, is one of the leading indicators (number 6 in Table 9.2). This seems eminently reasonable, since businesses don't order equipment unless they later plan to buy it. The same is true of building permits (indicator 10); people obtain permits only if they plan to build something. Hence, both indicators appear to be dependable signs of future investment.

Unfortunately, the Leading Indicators aren't a perfect crystal ball. Equipment orders are often canceled. Building plans get delayed or abandoned. Hence, shifts of aggregate demand still occur without warning. No crystal ball could predict a terrorist strike or the timing and magnitude of a natural disaster. Compared to other crystal balls, however, the Index of Leading Indicators has a pretty good track record—and a very big audience. It helps investors and policymakers foresee what the economy tomorrow might look like.

SUMMARY

- Macro failure occurs when the economy fails to achieve full employment and price stability.
- Too much or too little aggregate demand, relative to full employment, can cause macro failure. Too little aggregate demand causes cyclical unemployment; too much aggregate demand causes demand-pull inflation.
- Aggregate demand reflects the spending plans of consumers (C), investors (I), government (G), and foreign buyers (net exports $= X - M$).
- Consumer spending is affected by nonincome (autonomous) factors and current income, as summarized in the consumption function: $C = a + bY_D$.
- Autonomous consumption (a) depends on wealth, expectations, taxes, credit, and price levels. Income-dependent consumption depends on the marginal propensity to consume (MPC), the b in the consumption function.

- Consumer saving is the difference between disposable income and consumption (that is, $S = Y_D - C$). All disposable income is either spent (C) or saved (S).
- The consumption function shifts up or down when autonomous influences such as wealth and expectations change. Shifts of the consumption function at a constant price level are reflected in shifts of the aggregate demand curve.
- Investment spending depends on interest rates, expectations for future sales, and innovation. Changes in expectations may abruptly alter investment spending.
- Government spending and net exports are influenced by a variety of cyclical and noncyclical factors and may also change abruptly.
- Even a "perfect" macro equilibrium may be upset by abrupt shifts of spending behavior. Recurrent shifts may cause a business cycle.

Key Terms

aggregate demand	marginal propensity to consume (MPC)	equilibrium GDP
aggregate supply	marginal propensity to save (MPS)	recessionary GDP gap
equilibrium (macro)	wealth effect	cyclical unemployment
consumption	consumption function	inflationary GDP gap
disposable income	dissaving	demand-pull inflation
saving	investment	business cycle
average propensity to consume (APC)	full-employment GDP	

Questions for Discussion

1. What percentage of last month's income did you spend? How much more would you spend if you won a $1,000 lottery prize? Why might your average and marginal propensities to consume differ?
2. Why do rich people have a higher marginal propensity to save than poor people?
3. How do households dissave? Where do they get the money to finance their extra consumption? Can everyone dissave at the same time?
4. What events might change consumer confidence? (See News, page 187).
5. According to the News on p. 191, why did businesses cut investment spending in October 2001? Was this a rational response?

6. If state governments can't borrow money for noncapital expenditures, how will their level of spending be affected by (a) a recession, (b) an economic boom?
7. What factors influence the level of (a) U.S. exports to Mexico, (b) U.S. imports from Mexico?
8. Why wouldn't market participants always want to buy all the output produced?
9. If an inflationary GDP gap exists, what will happen to business inventories. How will producers respond?
10. How might a "perfect" macro equilibrium (Figure 9.9a) be affected by (a) a stock market crash, (b) the death of a president, (c) a recession in Canada, (d) a spike in oil prices?

PROBLEMS The Student Problem Set at the back of this book contains numerical and graphing problems for this chapter.

WEB ACTIVITIES to accompany this chapter can be found on the Online Learning Center: **http://www.mhhe.com/economics/schiller10**

THE KEYNESIAN CROSS

The Keynesian view of the macro economy emphasizes the potential instability of the private sector and the undependability of a market-driven self-adjustment. We have illustrated this theory with shifts of the AD curve and resulting real GDP gaps. The advantage of the AS/AD model is that it illustrates how both real output and the price level are simultaneously affected by AD shifts. At the time Keynes developed his theory of instability, however, inflation was not a threat. In the Great Depression prices were *falling*. With unemployment rates reaching as high as 25 percent, no one worried that increased aggregate demand would push price levels up. The only concern was to get back to full employment.

Because inflation was not seen as an adequate threat, early depictions of Keynesian theory didn't use the AS/AD model. Instead, they used a different basic graph, called the "Keynesian cross." The Keynesian cross focuses on the relationship of total spending to the value of total output, without an explicit distinction between price levels and real output. As we'll see, the Keynesian cross doesn't change any conclusions we've come to about macro instability. It simply offers an alternative, and historically important, framework for explaining macro outcomes.

Keynes said that in a really depressed economy we could focus exclusively on the rate of *spending* in the economy, without distinguishing between real output and price levels. All he worried about was whether **aggregate expenditure**—the sum of consumer, investor, government, and net export buyers' spending plans—would be compatible with the dollar value of full-employment output.

For Keynes, the critical question was how much each group of market participants would spend at different levels of nominal *income*. As we saw earlier, Keynes showed that consumer spending directly varies with the level of income. That's why the consumption function in Figure 9.4 had *spending* on the vertical axis and nominal *income* on the horizontal axis.

Figure 9A.1 puts the consumption function into the larger context of the macro economy. In this figure, the focus is exclusively on *nominal* incomes and spending. Y_F indicates the dollar value of full-employment output at current prices. In this figure, $3,000 billion is assumed to be the value of Y_F. The 45-degree line shows all points where total spending equals total income.

The consumption function in Figure 9A.1 is the same one we used before, namely

$$C = \$100 + 0.75(Y_D)$$

Notice again that consumers *dissave* at lower income levels but *save* at higher income levels.

What particularly worried Keynes was the level of intended consumption at full employment. At full employment, $3 trillion of income (output) is generated. But

Focus on Aggregate Expenditure

> **aggregate expenditure:** The rate of total expenditure desired at alternative levels of income, *ceteris paribus.*

The Consumption Shortfall

FIGURE 9A.1

The Consumption Shortfall

To determine how much output consumers will demand at full-employment output (Y_F), we refer to the consumption function. First locate full-employment output on the horizontal axis (at Y_F). Then move up until you reach the consumption function. In this case, the amount C_F (equal to $2,350 billion per year) will be demanded at full-employment output ($3,000 billion per year). This leaves $650 billion of output not purchased by consumers.

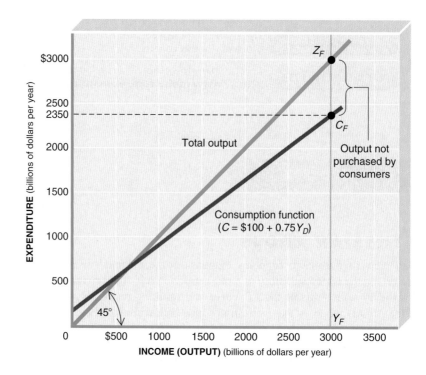

consumers plan to spend only

$$C = \$100 + 0.75(\$3,000\ \text{billion}) = \$2,350\ \text{billion}$$

and save the rest ($650 billion).[1] Were product-market sales totally dependent on consumers, this economy would be in trouble: Consumer spending falls short of full-employment output. In Figure 9A.1, this consumption shortfall is the vertical difference between points Z_F and C_F.

Nonconsumer Spending

The evident shortfall in consumer spending need not doom the economy to macro failure. There are other market participants, and their spending will add to aggregate expenditure. Keynes, however, emphasized that the spending decisions of investors, governments, and net export buyers are made independently. They *might* add up to just the right amount—or they might *not*.

To determine how much other market participants might spend, we'd have to examine their behavior. Suppose we did so and ended up with the information in Figure 9A.2. The data in that figure reveal how many dollars will be spent at various income levels. By vertically stacking these expenditure components, we can draw on *aggregate* (total) expenditure curve as in Figure 9A.2. The aggregate expenditure curve shows how *total* spending varies with income.

A Recessionary Gap

Keynes used the aggregate expenditure curve to assess the potential for macro failure. He was particularly interested in determining how much market participants would spend if the economy were producing at full-employment capacity.

---

[1]In principle, we first have to determine how much *disposable* income is generated by any given level of *total* income, then use the consumption function to determine how much consumption occurs. If Y_D is a constant percentage of Y, this two-step computation boils down to

$$Y_D = dY$$

where d = the share of total income received as disposable income, and

$$C = a + b(dY)$$
$$= a + (b \times d)Y$$

The term $(h \times d)$ is the marginal propensity to consume out of *total* income.

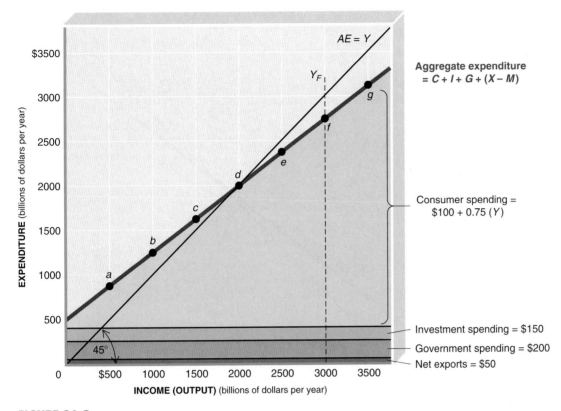

FIGURE 9A.2
Aggregate Expenditure

The aggregate expenditure curve depicts the desired spending of market participants at various income (output) levels. In this case, I, G, and $(X - M)$ don't vary with income, but C does. Adding these four components gives us total desired spending. If total income were $1,000 billion, desired spending would total $1,250 billion, as shown in row b in the table and by point b in the graph.

	At Income (output) of	Consumers Desire to Spend	+	Investors Desire to Spend	+	Governments Desire to Spend	+	Net Export Spending	=	Aggregate Expenditure
a	$ 500	$ 475		$150		$200		$50		$ 875
b	1,000	850		150		200		50		1,250
c	1,500	1,225		150		200		50		1,625
d	2,000	1,600		150		200		50		2,000
e	2,500	1,975		150		200		50		2,375
f	3,000	2,350		150		200		50		2,750
g	3,500	2,725		150		200		50		3,125

With the information in Figure 9A.2, it is easy to answer that question. At full employment (Y_F), total income is $3,000 billion. From the table, we see that total spending at that income level is:

$$\text{Consumer spending at} \quad Y_F = \$100 + 0.75(\$3,000) = \$2,350$$
$$\text{Investment spending at} \quad Y_F \qquad\qquad\qquad = \quad 150$$
$$\text{Government spending at} \quad Y_F \qquad\qquad\qquad = \quad 200$$
$$\text{Net export spending at} \quad Y_F \qquad\qquad\qquad = \quad\underline{50}$$
$$\text{Aggregate spending at} \quad Y_F \qquad\qquad\qquad = \$2,750$$

FIGURE 9A.3

Expenditure Equilibrium

There's only one rate of output at which desired expenditure equals the value of output. This expenditure equilibrium occurs at point E, where the aggregate expenditure and 45-degree lines intersect. At this equilibrium, $2,000 billion of output is produced and willingly purchased.

At full-employment output ($Y_F = $3,000$), aggregate expenditure is only $2,750 billion. This spending shortfall leaves $250 billion of output unsold. The difference between full-employment output (point h) and desired spending at full employment (point f) is called the recessionary gap.

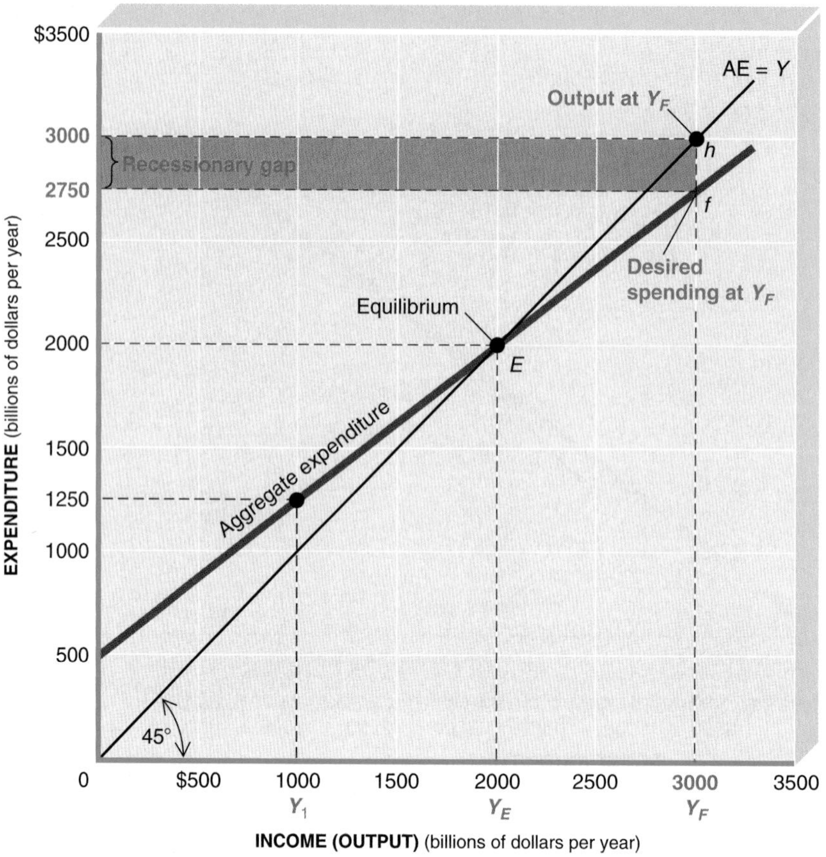

recessionary gap: The amount by which aggregate spending at full employment falls short of full-employment output.

expenditure equilibrium: The rate of output at which desired spending equals the value of output.

In this case, we end up with less aggregate expenditure in product markets ($2,750 billion) than the value of full-employment output ($3,000 billion). This is illustrated by point f in Figure 9A.3.

The economy illustrated in Figure 9A.3 is in trouble. If full employment were achieved, it wouldn't last. At full employment, $3,000 billion of output would be produced. But only $2,750 of output would be sold. There isn't enough aggregate expenditure at current price levels to sustain full employment. As a result, $250 billion of unsold output piles up in warehouses and on store shelves. That unwanted inventory pileup is a harbinger of trouble.

The difference between full-employment output and desired spending at full employment is called a **recessionary gap.** Not enough output is willingly purchased at full employment to sustain the economy. Producers may react to the spending shortfall by cutting back on production and laying off workers.

A Single Equilibrium. You might wonder whether the planned spending of market participants would ever be exactly equal to the value of output. It will, but not necessarily at the rate of output we seek.

Figure 9A.3 illustrates where this **expenditure equilibrium** exists. Recall the significance of the 45-degree line in that figure. The 45-degree line represents all points where expenditure *equals* income. At any point on this line there would be no difference between total spending and the value of output.

The juxtaposition of the aggregate expenditure function with the 45-degree line is called the Keynesian cross. *The Keynesian cross relates aggregate expenditure to total income (output),* without explicit consideration of (changing) price levels. As is evident in Figure 9A.3, the aggregate expenditure curve crosses the 45-degree line only once, at point *E*. At that point, therefore, desired spending is *exactly* equal to the value of output. In Figure 9A.3 this equilibrium occurs at an output rate of $2,000 billion. Notice in the accompanying table how much market participants desire to spend at that rate of output. We have

Consumer spending at	$Y_E = \$100 + 0.75(\$2,000) =$	$1,600
Investment spending at	Y_E =	150
Government spending at	Y_E =	200
Net export spending at	Y_E =	50
Aggregate spending at	Y_E =	$2,000

At Y_E we have spending behavior that's completely compatible with the rate of production. At this equilibrium rate of output, no goods remain unsold. At that one rate of output where desired spending and the value of output are exactly equal, an expenditure equilibrium exists. ***At macro equilibrium producers have no incentive to change the rate of output because they're selling everything they produce.***

Unfortunately, the equilibrium depicted in Figure 9A.3 isn't the one we hoped to achieve. At Y_E the economy is well short of its full-employment goal (Y_F).

The expenditure equilibrium won't always fall short of the economy's productive capacity. Indeed, market participants' spending desires could also *exceed* the economy's full-employment potential. This might happen if investors, the government, or foreigners wanted to buy more output or if the consumption function shifted upward. In such circumstances an **inflationary gap** would exist. An inflationary gap arises when market participants want to *spend more* income than can be produced at full employment. The resulting scramble for goods may start a bidding war that pushes price levels even higher. This would be another symptom of macro failure.

The Keynesian analysis of aggregate *expenditure* looks remarkably similar to the Keynesian analysis of aggregate *demand*. In fact, it is: Both approaches lead to the same conclusions about macro instability. The key difference between the "old" (expenditure) analysis and the "new" (AD) analysis is the level of detail about macro outcomes. In the old aggregate-expenditure analysis, the focus was simply on total spending, the product of output and prices. In the newer AD analysis, the separate effects of macro instability on prices and real output are distinguished.[2] In a world where changes in both real output and price levels are important, the AD/AS framework is more useful.

Macro Failure

inflationary gap: The amount by which aggregate spending at full employment exceeds full-employment output.

Two Paths to the Same Conclusion

[2]This distinction is reflected in the differing definitions for the traditional *recessionary gap* (the *spending* shortfall at full-employment income) and the newer *recessionary GDP gap* (real output gap between full-employment GDP and equilibrium GDP).

Self-Adjustment or Instability?

John Maynard Keynes took a dim view of a market-driven macro economy. He emphasized that (1) macro failure is likely to occur in such an economy, and worse yet, (2) macro failure isn't likely to go away. As noted earlier, the first prediction wasn't all that controversial. The classical economists had conceded the possibility of occasional recession or inflation. In their view, however, the economy would quickly self-adjust, restoring full employment and price stability. Keynes's second proposition challenged this view. The most distinctive, and frightening, proposition of Keynes's theory was that there'd be no automatic self-adjustment; the economy could stagnate in *persistent* unemployment or be subjected to *continuing* inflation.

President Herbert Hoover was a believer in the market's ability to self-adjust. So was President George H. Bush. As Hoover and Bush Sr. waited for the economy to self-adjust, however, they both lost their reelection bids. President George W. Bush wasn't willing to take that chance. As soon as he was elected, he pushed tax cuts through Congress that boosted consumer disposable incomes and helped bolster a sagging economy. After the terrorist attacks of September 11, 2001, he called for even greater government intervention.

These different presidential experiences don't resolve the self-adjustment debate; rather, they emphasize how important the debate is. In this chapter we'll focus on the *adjustment process,* that is, how markets *respond* to an undesirable equilibrium. We're especially concerned with the following questions:

- **Why does anyone think the market might self-adjust (returning to a desired equilibrium)?**
- **Why might markets *not* self-adjust?**
- **Could market responses actually *worsen* macro outcomes?**

LEAKAGES AND INJECTIONS

Chapter 9 demonstrated how the economy could end up at the wrong macro equilibrium—with too much or too little aggregate demand. Such an undesirable outcome might result from an initial imbalance between **aggregate demand** at the current price level and full-employment GDP. Or the economy could fall into trouble from a shift in aggregate demand that pushes the economy out of a desirable full-employment–price-stability equilibrium. Whatever the sequence of events might be, the bottom line is the same: Total spending doesn't match total output at the desired full-employment–price-stability level.

aggregate demand (AD): The total quantity of output demanded at alternative price levels in a given time period, *ceteris paribus.*

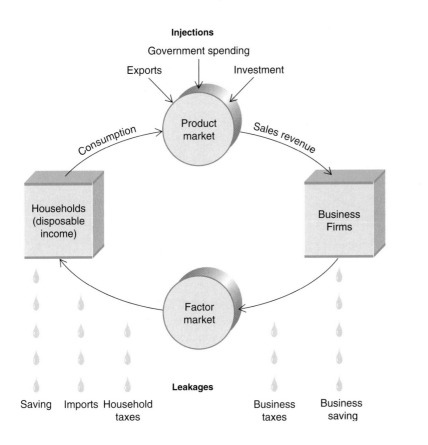

Injections

Government spending

Exports   Investment

Consumption   Product market   Sales revenue

Households (disposable income)   Business Firms

Factor market

Leakages

Saving   Imports   Household taxes   Business taxes   Business saving

FIGURE 10.1
Leakages and Injections

The income generated in production doesn't return completely to product markets in the form of consumer spending. Consumer saving, imports, taxes, and business saving all leak from the circular flow, reducing aggregate demand. If this leakage isn't offset, some of the output produced will remain unsold.

Business investment, government purchases of goods and services, and exports inject spending into the circular flow, adding to aggregate demand. The focus of macro concern is whether desired injections will offset desired leakage at full employment.

The Circular Flow. The circular flow of income illustrates both how such an undesirable outcome comes about and how it might be resolved. Recall that all income originates in product markets, where goods and services are sold. If the economy were producing at **full-employment GDP,** then enough income would be available to buy everything a fully employed economy produces. As we've seen, however, aggregate demand isn't so certain. It could happen that market participants opt *not* to spend all their income, leaving some goods unsold. Alternatively, they might try to buy *more* than full-employment output, pushing prices up.

To see how such imbalances might arise, Keynes distinguished *leakages* from the circular flow and *injections* into that flow, as illustrated in Figure 10.1.

As we observed in Chapter 9, consumers typically don't spend *all* the income they earn in product markets; they *save* some fraction of it. This is the first leak in the circular flow. Some income earned in product markets isn't being instantly converted into spending. This circular flow **leakage** creates the potential for a spending shortfall.

Suppose the economy were producing at full employment, with $3,000 billion of output at the current price level, indexed at $P = 100$. This initial output rate is marked by point F in Figure 10.2. Suppose further that *all* of the income generated in product markets went to consumers. In that case, would consumers *spend* enough to *maintain* full employment? We already observed in Chapter 9 that such an outcome is unlikely. Typically, consumers *save* a small fraction of their incomes.

If the consumption function were $C_F = \$100$ billion $+ 0.75Y$, consumers will spend only

$$C_F = \$100 \text{ billion} + 0.75(\$3{,}000 \text{ billion})$$

$$= \$2{,}350 \text{ billion}$$

at the current price level. This consumption behavior is illustrated in Figure 10.2 by the point C_F. Consumers would demand more real output with their current income

full-employment GDP: The value of total output (real GDP) produced at full employment.

Consumer Saving

leakage: Income not spent directly on domestic output but instead diverted from the circular flow, for example, saving, imports, taxes.

FIGURE 10.2
Leakage and AD

The disposable income consumers receive is only about 70 percent of total income (GDP), due to taxes and income held by businesses. Consumers also tend to save some of their disposable income and buy imported products. As a result of these leakages, consumers will demand less output at the current price level ($P = 100$) than the economy produces at full-employment GDP (Q_F). In this case, consumers demand only \$2,350 billion of output at the price level $P = 100$ (point C_F) when \$3,000 billion of output (income) is produced (point F).

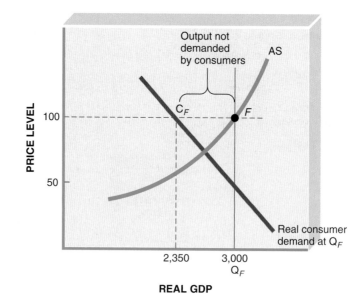

if prices were to fall. Hence, the consumption component of aggregate demand slopes downward from point C_F. Our immediate concern, however, focuses on how much (real) output consumers will purchase at the current price level. At the price level $P = 100$ consumers choose to save \$650 billion, leaving consumption (\$2,350 billion) far short of full employment GDP (\$3,000 billion).

The decision to save some fraction of household income isn't necessarily bad, but it does present a potential problem. Unless other market participants, such as business, government, and foreigners, buy this unsold output, goods will pile up on producers' shelves. As undesired inventory accumulates, producers will reduce the rate of output and unemployment will rise.

Imports and Taxes

Saving isn't the only source of leakage. ***Imports also represent leakage from the circular flow.*** When consumers buy imported goods, their spending leaves (that is, leaks out of) the domestic circular flow and goes to foreign producers. As a consequence, income spent on imported goods and services is not part of the aggregate demand for domestic output.

In the real world, ***taxes are a form of leakage as well.*** A lot of revenue generated in market sales gets diverted into federal, state, and local government coffers. Sales taxes are taken out of the circular flow in product markets. Then payroll taxes and income taxes are taken out of wages. Households never get the chance to spend any of that income. They start with disposable income, which is much less than the total income generated in product markets. In 2004, disposable income was only \$8 trillion while total income (GDP) was \$11 trillion. Hence, consumers couldn't buy everything produced with their current incomes even if they saved nothing.

Business Saving

The business sector also keeps part of the income generated in product markets. Some revenue is set aside to cover the costs of maintaining, repairing, and replacing plant and equipment. The revenue held aside for these purposes is called a depreciation allowance. In addition, corporations keep some part of total profit (retained earnings) for other business uses rather than turn all profits over to the business owners in the form of stockholder dividends. The total value of depreciation allowances and retained earnings is called **gross business saving.** Whatever businesses save in these forms represents further leakage from the circular flow—income that doesn't automatically flow directly back into product markets.

gross business saving: Depreciation allowances and retained earnings.

Although leakage from the circular flow is a potential source of unemployment problems, we shouldn't conclude that the economy will sink as soon as consumers start saving some of their income, buy a few imports, or pay their taxes. Consumers aren't the only ones who buy goods and services in product markets; business firms and government agencies also contribute to total spending. So do international consumers who buy our exports. So before we run out into the streets screaming "The circular flow is leaking!" we need to look at what other market participants are doing.

The top half of Figure 10.1 completes the picture of the circular flow by depicting **injections** of new spending. When businesses buy plant and equipment, they add to the dollar value of product market sales. Government purchases and exports also inject spending into the product market. These *injections of investment, government, and export spending help offset leakage from saving, imports, and taxes.* As a result, there may be enough aggregate demand to maintain full employment at the current price level, even if consumers aren't spending every dollar of income.

The critical issue for macro stability is whether spending injections will actually equal spending leakage at full employment. If so, the economy will stabilize at full employment and we can stop worrying about macro problems. If not, we've still got some work to do.

As we noted earlier, classical economists had no worries. They assumed that spending injections would always equal spending leakage. That was the foundation of their belief in the market's self-adjustment. The mechanism assuring the equality of leakages and injections was the interest rate.

Flexible Interest Rates. Ignore all other injections and leakages for the moment and focus on just consumer saving and business investment (Figure 10.3). If consumer saving exceeds business investment, unspent income must be piling up somewhere (in bank accounts, for example). These unspent funds will be a tempting lure for business investors. In the classical view, businesses are always looking for funds to finance expansion or modernization. So they aren't likely to leave a pile of consumer savings sitting idle. Moreover, the banks and other institutions that are holding consumer savings will be eager to lend more funds as consumer savings piles up. To make more loans, they can lower the interest rate. As we observed in Chapter 9 (Figure 9.7), lower interest rates prompt businesses to borrow and invest more. Hence, *classical economists concluded that if interest rates fell far enough, business investment (injections) would equal consumer saving (leakage).* From this perspective, any spending shortfall would soon be closed by this self-adjustment of leakage and injection flows. Aggregate demand would be maintained at full-employment GDP, because investment spending would soak up all consumer saving.

Changing Expectations. Keynes argued that classical economists ignored the role of expectations in business investments. As Figure 9.7 illustrated, the level of investment *is* sensitive to interest rates. But the whole investment function *shifts* when business expectations change. Keynes thought it preposterous that investment spending would *increase* in response to *declining* sales. A decline in investment is more likely, Keynes argued.

Injections into the Circular Flow

injection: An addition of spending to the circular flow of income.

Self-Adjustment?

Check the U.S. Bureau of Economic Analysis (BEA) Web site at www.bea.doc.gov to see how much investment varied in the last year. Click on "Gross Domestic Product," then "Selected NIPA Tables."

Leakages	Injections
Consumer saving	Investment
Business saving	Government spending
Taxes	Exports
Imports	

FIGURE 10.3
Leakages and Injections

Macro stability depends on the balance between injections and leakages. Of these, consumer saving and business investment are the primary sources of (im)balance in a wholly private and closed economy. Hence the relationship between saving and investment reveals whether a market-driven economy will self-adjust to full employment and price stability.

The Bogeyman of Deflation

WELL, WE FACE A NEW DANGER: DEFLATION. So says the FOMC, the Federal Reserve's main policymaking body. It's astonishing what a few words can do, and these words riveted attention on something that, until recently, seemed a historic curiosity. Deflation signifies a general decline of prices; it hasn't happened in the United States since the Great Depression. . . .

Deflation would arise from too much supply (of everything from computer chips to airplane seats) chasing too little demand. Prices would drop as companies competed for buyers. . . . Why would that be bad? Lower prices would allow people to buy more with their wages: the economy could benefit.

But what's also true is that deflation poses dangers: (1) lower prices could squeeze corporate profits, hurt the stock market and pressure companies to fire workers and cut wages;

(2) falling prices could lower overnight interest rates to near zero, making it harder for the Fed to stimulate the economy; (3) companies and farmers may default on loans, which are fixed while the prices they receive fall, and (4) consumers might delay purchases, believing future prices will be lower.

In the Depression, the dangers materialized. From 1929 to 1933, retail prices dropped 24 percent. Thousands of businesses and farmers went bankrupt. About 40 percent of banks failed. By 1933, unemployment was 25 percent. Although the Fed cut interest rates, the economy didn't respond. (In the summer of 1931, the Fed's discount rate was 1.5 percent; but prices were down 9 percent, making the price-adjusted interest rate almost 11 percent.)

—Robert J. Samuelson

Source: Washington Post Writers Group, May 19, 2003. © 2003 The Washington Post. Reprinted with permission.

Analysis: Deflation does make products cheaper for consumers. But declining prices also reduce business revenues, profits, and sales expectations.

Flexible Prices. There is another way the economy could self-adjust. Look at Figure 10.2 again. It says consumers will demand only $2,350 billion of output *at the current price level.* But what if prices *fell?* Then consumers would buy more output. In fact, if prices fell far enough, consumers might buy *all* the output produced at full employment. In Figure 10.2, the price level $P = 50$ elicits such a response.

Expectations (again). Keynes again chided the classical economists for their naiveté. Sure, a nationwide sale might prompt consumers to buy more goods and services. But how would businesses react? They had planned on selling Q_F amount of output at the price level $P = 100$. If prices must be cut in half to move their merchandise, businesses are likely to rethink their production and investment plans. Keynes argued that declining (retail) prices were likely to prompt investment cutbacks, as the accompanying News also suggests.

THE MULTIPLIER PROCESS

Keynes not only rejected the classical notion of self-adjustment, he also argued that things were likely to get *worse*, not better, once a spending shortfall emerged.

To understand Keynes's fears, imagine that the economy is initially at the desired full-employment GDP equilibrium, as represented again by point F in Figure 10.4. Included in that full-employment equilibrium GDP is

Consumption	=	$2,350 billion
Investment	=	400 billion
Government	=	150 billion
Net exports	=	100 billion
Aggregate demand at current price level	=	$3,000 billion

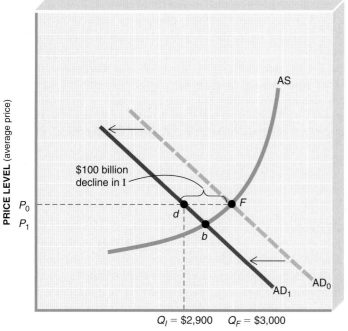

FIGURE 10.4
AD Shift

When investment spending drops, aggregate demand shifts to the left. In the short run, this causes output and the price level to fall. The initial equilibrium at *F* is pushed to a new equilibrium at point *b*.

Everything looks good in this macro economy. This is pretty much how the U.S. economy looked from 1993 until early 2001.

Now suppose that business expectations for future sales worsen. In early 2001, business forecasts of consumer spending were already declining. After the terrorist attacks of September 11, expectations fell even further. As expectations worsened, businesses cut back on investment spending (see News).

A Decline in Investment

Undesired Inventory. When business investment was cut back, unsold capital goods started piling up. Unsold trucks, office equipment, machinery, and airplanes quickly reached worrisome levels.

At the Economics Briefing Room of the White House at www.whitehouse.gov/fsbr/output.html, find current data on output.

IN THE NEWS

Small Businesses Hold Off on Big Purchases

Capital Spending Helps Drive Economy, So Drop-off May Hurt

SAN FRANCISCO—Small companies are buying fewer trucks, computers and other big-ticket items—the capital purchases that could lift the U.S. economy.

About 28% of small firms plan big purchases, a major survey out Monday said. That's down from about 32% before the terrorist attacks.

Capital spending by small firms is critical. It helps them be more productive and boosts sales at big companies like Ford Motor and Dell Computer. . . .

— Jim Hopkins

Source: *USA Today,* October 16, 2001. USA TODAY. Copyright 2001. Reprinted with permission. www.usatoday.com

Analysis: Worsened sales expectations may cause a decline in investment spending that shifts the AD curve to the left, leading to pileups of unwanted inventory.

Ironically, this additional inventory is counted as part of investment spending. (Recall that our definition of investment spending includes changes in business inventories.) This additional inventory is clearly undesired, however, as producers had planned on selling these goods.

To keep track of these unwanted changes in investment, we *distinguish* **desired (or planned) investment from actual investment.** *Desired* investment represents purchases of new plant and equipment plus any *desired* changes in business inventories. By contrast, *actual* investment represents purchases of new plant and equipment plus *actual* changes in business inventories, desired or otherwise. In other words,

$$\frac{\text{Actual}}{\text{investment}} = \frac{\text{desired}}{\text{investment}} + \frac{\text{undesired}}{\text{investment}}$$

Falling Output and Prices. How are business firms likely to react when they see undesired inventory piling up on car lots and store shelves? They could regard the inventory pileup as a brief aberration and continue producing at full-employment levels. But the inventory pileup might also set off sales alarms, causing businesses to alter their pricing, production, and investment plans. If that happens, they're likely to start cutting prices in an attempt to increase the rate of sales. Producers are also likely to reduce the rate of new output. Figure 10.4 illustrates these two responses. Assume that investment spending declines by $100 billion at the existing price level P_0. This shifts the aggregate demand curve leftward from AD_0 to AD_1 and immediately moves the economy from point F to point d. If no other changes were to occur, the economy would gravitate toward a new **equilibrium GDP** at point b. At point b, the rate of output (Q_1) is less than the full-employment level (Q_F) and the price level has fallen from P_0 to P_1.

> **equilibrium GDP:** The value of total output (real GDP) produced at macro equilibrium (AS = AD).

Household Incomes

The decline in GDP depicted in Figure 10.4 isn't pretty. But Keynes warned that the picture would get uglier when *consumers* start feeling the impact of the production cutbacks.

So far we've treated the production cutbacks that accompany a GDP gap as a rather abstract problem. But the reality is that when production is cut back, people suffer. When producers decrease the rate of output, workers lose their jobs or face pay cuts, or both. Cutbacks in investment spending on September 2001 (prior News) led to layoffs at Honeywell, Advanced Micro Devices, and other capital-equipment manufacturers (see News on next page). An abrupt decline in travel caused even larger layoffs at airlines and aircraft manufacturers. As workers get laid off or have their wages cut, household incomes decline. Thus, *a reduction in investment spending implies a reduction in household incomes.*

Income-Dependent Consumption

We saw in Chapter 9 the kind of threat a reduction in household income poses. Those consumers who end up with less income won't be able to purchase as many goods and services as they did before. As a consequence, aggregate demand will fall further, leading to still larger stocks of unsold goods, more job layoffs, and further reductions in income. It's this sequence of events—called the *multiplier process*—that makes a sudden decline in aggregate demand so frightening. What starts off as a relatively small spending shortfall quickly snowballs into a much larger problem.

We can see the multiplier process at work by watching what happens to the $100 billion decline in investment spending as it makes its way around the circular flow (Figure 10.5 on page 212). At first (step 1), the only thing that happens is that unsold goods appear (in the form of undesired inventories). Producers adjust to this problem by cutting back on production and laying off workers or reducing wages and prices (step 2). In either case, consumer income falls $100 billion per year shortly after the investment cutbacks occur (step 3).

Terror's Aftermath: Layoffs

Who knows how many of these might have come anyway? But since Sept. 11, companies have cut more than 160,000 jobs.

Airlines were the hardest hit, but other industries were also affected. Here are some of the biggest.

Company	Cuts	Industry
Boeing	30,000	Aerospace
American Airlines	20,000	Airline
United	20,000	Airline
Delta	13,000	Airline
Continental	12,000	Airline
Starwood Hotels & Resorts	12,000	Hotel
US Airways	11,000	Airline
Northwest	10,000	Airline
British Airways	7,000	Airline
Air Canada	5,000	Airline
Honeywell International	3,800	Aerospace/Diversified materials
Swissair	3,000	Airline
Alitalia	2,500	Airline
Textron	2,500	Aircraft manufacturing
EMC	2,400	Data storage
Advanced Micro Devices	2,300	Microprocessors
America West	2,000	Airline
Applied Materials	2,000	Semiconductors

Source: *BusinessWeek*, October 8, 2001. Reprinted with permission. Copyright 2001 by The McGraw-Hill Companies. www.businessweek.com

Analysis: Cutbacks in production cause employee layoffs. The newly unemployed workers curtail *their* spending, causing sequential layoffs in other industries. These "snowball" effects give rise to the multiplier.

How will consumers respond to this drop in disposable income? *If disposable income falls, we expect consumer spending to drop as well.* In fact, the consumption function tells us just how much spending will drop. The **marginal propensity to consume (MPC)** is the critical variable in this process. Since we've specified that $C = \$100$ billion $+ 0.75Y$, we anticipate that consumers will reduce their spending by $0.75 for every $1.00 of lost income. In the present example, the loss of $100 billion of annual income will induce consumers to reduce their rate of spending by $75 billion per year (0.75 × $100 billion). This drop in spending is illustrated by step 4 in Figure 10.5.

The multiplier process doesn't stop here. A reduction in consumer spending quickly translates into more unsold output (step 5). As additional goods pile up on producers' shelves, we anticipate further cutbacks in production, employment, and disposable income (step 6).

As disposable incomes are further reduced by job layoffs and wage cuts (step 7), more reductions in consumer spending are sure to follow (step 8). Again the marginal propensity to consume (MPC) tells us how large such reductions will be. With an MPC of 0.75, we may expect spending to fall by another $56.25 billion per year (0.75 × $75 billion) in step 8.

> **marginal propensity to consume (MPC):** The fraction of each additional (marginal) dollar of disposable income spent on consumption; the change in consumption divided by the change in disposable income.

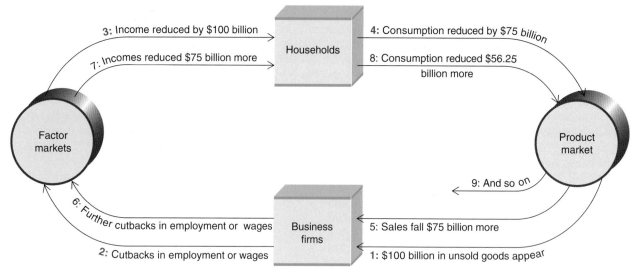

FIGURE 10.5
The Multiplier Process

A decline in investment (step 1) may lead to a cutback in production and income (step 2). A reduction in total income (step 3) will in turn lead to a reduction in consumer spending (step 4). These additional cuts in spending cause a further decrease in income, leading to additional spending reductions, and so on. This sequence of adjustments is referred to as the *multiplier process.*

The Multiplier

The multiplier process continues to work until the reductions in income and sales become so small that no one's market behavior is significantly affected. We don't have to examine each step along the way. As you may have noticed, all the steps begin to look alike once we've gone around the circular flow a few times. Instead of examining each step, we can look ahead to see where they are taking us. Each time the multiplier process works its way around the circular flow, the reduction in spending equals the previous drop in income multiplied by the MPC. Accordingly, by pressing a few keys on a calculator, we can produce a sequence of events like that depicted in Table 10.1 on the next page.

The impact of the multiplier is devastating. The ultimate reduction in real spending resulting from the initial drop in investment isn't $100 billion per year but $400 billion! Even if one is accustomed to thinking in terms of billions and trillions, this is a huge drop in demand. What the multiplier process demonstrates is that the dimensions of an initial spending gap greatly understate the severity of the economic dislocations that will follow in its wake. ***The eventual decline in spending will be much larger than the initial (autonomous) decrease in aggregate demand.*** This was evident in the recession of 2001, when layoffs snowballed from industry to industry (see News), ultimately leaving millions of people unemployed.

The ultimate impact of an AD shift on total spending can be determined by computing the change in income and consumption at each cycle of the circular flow, for an infinite number of cycles. This is the approach summarized in Table 10.1, with each row representing a spending cycle. The entire computation can be simplified considerably by using a single figure, the multiplier. The **multiplier** tells us the extent to which the rate of total spending will change in response to an initial change in the flow of expenditure. The multiplier summarizes the sequence of steps described in Table 10.1.[1] In its simplest form, the multiplier can be computed as:

$$\text{Multiplier} = \frac{1}{1 - \text{MPC}}$$

Do sports teams create multiplier effects for cities? Read about this at www.brookings.edu/dybdocroot/press/books/sports.htm.

multiplier: The multiple by which an initial change in spending will alter total expenditure after an infinite number of spending cycles; 1/(1 − MPC).

[1]The multiplier summarizes the geometric progression $1 + \text{MPC} + \text{MPC}^2 + \text{MPC}^3 + \cdots + \text{MPC}^n$, which equals $1/(1 - \text{MPC})$ when n becomes infinite.

Spending Cycles	Change in This Cycle's Spending and Income (billions per year)	Cumulative Decrease in Spending and Income (billions per year)
First cycle: recessionary gap emerges	$100.00	$100.00 } Δ*I*
Second cycle: consumption drops by MPC × $100	75.00	175.00
Third cycle: consumption drops by MPC × $75	56.25	231.25
Fourth cycle: consumption drops by MPC × $56.25	42.19	273.44
Fifth cycle: consumption drops by MPC × $42.19	31.64	305.08 } Δ**C**
Sixth cycle: consumption drops by MPC × $31.64	23.73	328.81
Seventh cycle: consumption drops by MPC × $23.73	17.80	346.61
Eighth cycle: consumption drops by MPC × $17.80	13.35	359.95
⋮	⋮	⋮
*n*th cycle and beyond		400.00

TABLE 10.1
The Multiplier Cycles

The circular flow of income implies that an initial change in income will lead to cumulative changes in consumer spending and income. Here, an initial income loss of $100 billion (first cycle) causes a cutback in consumer spending in the amount of $75 billion (second cycle). At each subsequent cycle, consumer spending drops by the amount MPC × prior change in income. Ultimately, total spending (and income) falls by $400 billion, or $1/(1 - MPC) \times$ initial change in spending.

IN THE NEWS

Companies Begin Another Round of Job Cuts

Even More Layoffs Could Threaten if Recession Closes In

When it comes to layoffs, employers are finding once is not enough.

The ongoing economic downturn means companies that have already laid off workers are cutting again. For example:

- Compaq Computer last week reported that it was laying off about 4,000 additional workers. That's in addition to about 4,500 cuts earlier this year. . . .
- Even though 8,500 workers at Lucent Technologies have accepted an early retirement offer, CEO Henry Schacht said last week that the beleaguered company plans its third round of job cuts since January. . . . The Murray Hill, N.J.–based company announced in January that it would eliminate 10,000 jobs and sell facilities employing an additional 6,000 workers as part of a restructuring and cost-cutting program.

- Santa Clara, Calif.–based Exodus Communications in June announced an unspecified number of layoffs. That follows the announcement in May that the web-hosting company would shed 675 positions, or about 15 percent of its workforce.
- Santa Clara–based equipment maker 3Com in May announced it was laying off 3,000 employees. That follows job cuts of about 1,200 in March.

This may just be the beginning of what's to come if the economy slides closer to a recession, some experts say.

—Stephanie Armour

Source: *USA Today*, July 17, 2001. USA TODAY. Copyright 2001. Reprinted with permission. www.usatoday.com

Analysis: Few industries escape damage from a recession. Spending slowdowns spread from industry to industry in a multiplier-like way. Job layoffs reduce disposable income and consumption.

In our example, the initial change in spending occurs when investment drops by $100 billion per year at full-employment output ($3,000 billion per year). Table 10.1 indicates that this gap will lead to a $400 billion reduction in the rate of total spending at the current price level. Using the multiplier, we arrive at the same conclusion by observing that

$$\text{Total change in spending} = \text{multiplier} \times \text{initial change in aggregate spending}$$

$$= \frac{1}{1 - \text{MPC}} \times \$100 \text{ billion per year}$$

$$= \frac{1}{1 - 0.75} \times \$100 \text{ billion per year}$$

$$= 4 \quad\quad \times \$100 \text{ billion per year}$$

$$= \$400 \text{ billion per year}$$

In other words, *the cumulative decrease in total spending ($400 billion per year) resulting from a shortfall in aggregate demand at full employment is equal to the initial shortfall ($100 billion per year) multiplied by the multiplier (4).* More generally, we may observe that the larger the fraction (MPC) of income respent in each round of the circular flow, the greater the impact of any autonomous change in spending on cumulative aggregate demand. The cumulative process of spending adjustments can also have worldwide effects. As the World View illustrates, Asia's economic growth slowed when the U.S. economy slumped in 2001.

WORLD VIEW

U.S. Slowdown Helps Derail Asia
High-Tech Firms Suffer Vicious Circle

SAN FRANCISCO—Waves from the U.S. high-tech and economic slump continue to crash onto Asian shores: Analysts fear the onset of a global recession and Japanese tech giant Fujitsu said Monday that it will cut 16,400 workers.

"The U.S. economy—especially the technology sector—was the primary locomotive for the export economies of Japan, Korea, Taiwan and Malaysia," says Sung Won Sohn, chief economist at Wells Fargo Bank. "Now that the bubble has burst here, it's having a devastating effect on Asia."

Among the dire signs:

- Fujitsu, the No. 2 maker of personal computers in Japan and a leading maker of flash-memory chips, will lay off 10 percent of its workers, including 5,000 employees in Japan and 11,400 employees at plants in Thailand, Vietnam and the Philippines. . . .
- The economy of Taiwan, a leading manufacturer and exporter of high-tech parts and goods, officially has entered a recession. In the first year-to-year drop in 26 years, Taiwan's gross domestic product plunged 2 percent in the second quarter from the same time last year, Taiwan's government said Friday. . . .
- When the U.S. economy started limping last year, Asia's economies were still dashing ahead at double-digit growth rates. Now, export-oriented Asia is expected to grow only 2 percent this year, with Japan's economy flat-lining. China predicts its huge economy will rise 8 percent this year. But analysts long skeptical of China's economic data say 4 percent to 6 percent is a more realistic figure. . . .

Like a boomerang, the economic chill in Asia is circling back and hurting the USA. Economists call it the "international-multiplier effect."

Cash-poor Asian nations can no longer buy high-tech goods and other products from U.S. companies, which also rely heavily on overseas trade.

—Edward Iwata

Analysis: Multiplier effects can spill over national borders. The 2001 economic slump in the United States reduced U.S. demand for Asian exports, setting off a sequence of spending cuts in Japan, Taiwan, and other Asian nations.

MACRO EQUILIBRIUM REVISITED

The key features of the Keynesian adjustment process are

- *Producers cut output and employment when output exceeds aggregate demand at the current price level (leakage exceeds injections).*
- *The resulting loss of income causes a decline in consumer spending.*
- *Declines in consumer spending lead to further production cutbacks, more lost income, and still less consumption.*

Figure 10.6 illustrates the ultimate impact of the multiplier process. Notice that the AD curve shifts *twice*. The first shift—from AD_0 to AD_1—represents the $100 billion drop in investment spending. As we saw earlier in Figure 10.4, this initial shift of aggregate demand will start the economy moving toward a new equilibrium at point *b*.

Along the way, however, the multiplier kicks in and things get worse. *The decline in household income caused by investment cutbacks sets off the multiplier process, causing a secondary shift of the AD curve.* We measure these multiplier effects at the initial price level of P_0. With a marginal propensity to consume of 0.75, we've seen that induced consumption declines by $300 billion when autonomous investment declines by $100 billion. In Figure 10.6 this is illustrated by the *second* shift of the aggregate demand curve, from AD_1 to AD_2. Notice that the horizontal distance between AD_1 and AD_2 is $300 billion.

Although aggregate demand has fallen (shifted) by $400 billion, real output doesn't necessarily drop that much. *The impact of a shift in aggregate demand is reflected in both output and price changes.* This is evident in Figure 10.7, which is a close-up view of Figure 10.6. When AD shifts from AD_0 to AD_2 the macro equilibrium moved down the sloped AS curve to point *c*. At point *c* the new equilibrium output is Q_E and the new price level is P_E.

Recessionary GDP Gap. As long as the aggregate supply curve is upward-sloping, the shock of any AD shift will be spread across output and prices. In Figure 10.7, the

Sequential AD Shifts

Price and Output Effects

> **recessionary GDP gap:** The amount by which equilibrium GDP falls short of full-employment GDP.

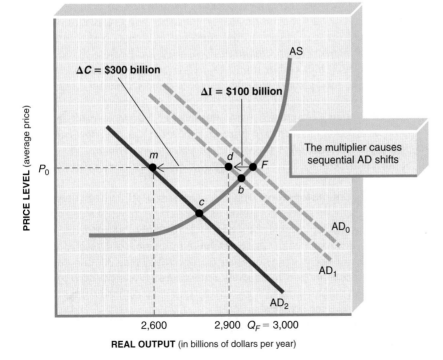

FIGURE 10.6
Multiplier Effects

A decline in investment spending reduces household income, setting off negative multiplier effects. Hence, the *initial* shift of AD_0 to AD_1 is followed by a *second* shift from of AD_1 to AD_2. The second shift represents reduced consumption.

FIGURE 10.7
Recessionary GDP Gap

The real GDP gap is the difference between equilibrium GDP (Q_E) and full-employment GDP (Q_F). It represents the lost output due to a recession.

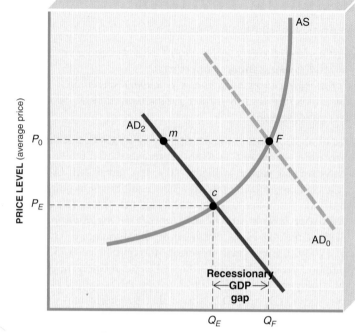

REAL OUTPUT (in billions of dollars per year)

cyclical unemployment: Unemployment attributable to a lack of job vacancies, that is, to an inadequate level of aggregate demand.

Short-Run Inflation-Unemployment Trade-Offs

full employment: The lowest rate of unemployment compatible with price stability; variously estimated at between 4 and 6 percent unemployment.

net effect on real output is shown as the real GDP gap. *The recessionary GDP gap equals the difference between equilibrium real GDP (Q_E) and full-employment real GDP (Q_F).* It represents the amount by which the economy is underproducing during a recession. As we noted in Chapter 9, this is a classic case of **cyclical unemployment.**

Figure 10.7 not only illustrates how much output declines when AD falls but also provides an important clue about the difficulty of restoring full employment. Suppose the recessionary GDP gap were $200 billion, as illustrated in Figure 10.8. How much more AD would we need to get back to full employment?

Upward-Sloping AS. Suppose aggregate demand at the equilibrium price level (P_E) were to increase by exactly $200 billion (including multiplier effects), as illustrated by the shift to AD_3. Would that get us back to full-employment output? Not according to Figure 10.8. *When AD increases, both output and prices go up.* Because the AS curve is upward-sloping, the $200 billion shift from AD_2 to AD_3 moves the new macro equilibrium to point *g* rather than point *f*. We'd like to get to point *f* with full employment and price stability. But as demand picks up, producers are likely to raise prices. This leads us up the AS curve to point *g*. At point *g*, we're still short of full employment and have experienced a bit of inflation (an increased price level). *So long as the short-run AS is upward-sloping, there's a trade-off between unemployment and inflation.* We can get lower rates of unemployment (more real output) only if we accept some inflation.

"Full" vs. "Natural" Unemployment. The short-term trade-off between unemployment and inflation is the basis for the definition of "full" employment. We don't define full employment as *zero* unemployment; we define it as the rate of unemployment *consistent with price stability.* As noted in Chapter 6, **full employment** is typically defined as a 4 to 6 percent rate of unemployment. What the upward-sloping AS curve tells us is that *the closer the economy gets to capacity output, the greater the risk of inflation.* To get back to full employment in Figure 10.8, aggregate demand would have to increase to AD_4, with the price level rising to P_4.

Not everyone accepts this notion of full employment. As we saw in Chapter 8, neoclassical and monetarist economists prefer to focus on *long*-run outcomes. In their view, the long-run AS curve is vertical (see Figure 8.12). In that long-run context,

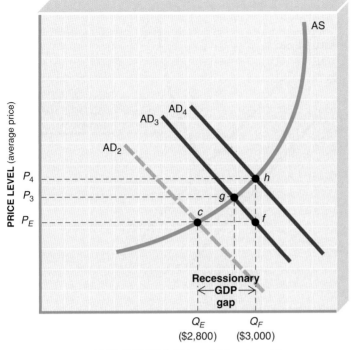

FIGURE 10.8
The Unemployment-Inflation Trade-Off

If the short-run AS curve is upward-sloping, an AD increase will raise output *and* prices. If AD increases by the amount of the recessionary GDP gap only (AD_2 to AD_3), full employment (Q_F) won't be reached. Macro equilibrium moves to point *g*, not point *f*.

there's no unemployment-inflation trade-off: An AD shift doesn't change the "natural" (institutional) rate of unemployment but does alter the price level. We'll examine this argument in Chapters 16 and 17.

ADJUSTMENT TO AN INFLATIONARY GDP GAP

As we've observed, a sudden shift in aggregate demand can have a cumulative effect on macro outcomes that's larger than the initial imbalance. This multiplier process works both ways: Just as a *decrease* in investment (or any other injection) can send the economy into a recessionary tailspin, an *increase* in investment might initiate an inflationary spiral.

Figure 10.9 illustrates the consequences of a sudden jump in investment spending. We start out again in the happy equilibrium (point *F*), where full employment (Q_F) and price stability (P_0) prevail. Initial spending consists of

$$C = \$2,350 \text{ billion} \qquad G = \$150 \text{ billion}$$
$$I = \$400 \text{ billion} \qquad X - M = \$100 \text{ billion}$$

Then investors suddenly decide to step up the rate of investment. Perhaps their expectations for future sales have risen. Maybe new technology has become available that compels firms to modernize their facilities. Whatever the reason, investors decide to raise the level of investment from $400 billion to $500 billion at the current price level (P_0). This change in investment spending shifts the aggregate demand curve from AD_0 to AD_5 (a horizontal shift of $100 billion).

Increased Investment

Inventory Depletion. One of the first things you'll notice when AD shifts like this is that available inventories shrink. Investors can step up their *spending* more quickly than firms can increase their *production*. A lot of the increased investment demand will have to be satisfied from existing inventory. When this happens, *desired* investment (including desired inventory) will fall below actual investment. The decline in inventory is a signal to producers that it might be a good time to raise prices a bit. Thus, ***inventory depletion is a warning sign of impending inflation.*** As the economy moves up from point *F* to point *r* in Figure 10.9, that inflation starts to become visible.

FIGURE 10.9
Demand-Pull Inflation

An increase in investment or other autonomous spending sets off multiplier effects shifting AD to the right. AD shifts to the right *twice,* first (AD$_0$ to AD$_5$) because of increased investment, then (AD$_5$ to AD$_6$) because of increased consumption. The increased AD moves the economy up the short-run AS curve, causing some inflation. How much inflation results depends on the slope of the AS curve.

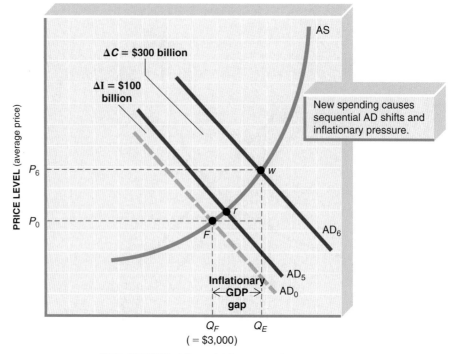

REAL OUTPUT (in billions of dollars per year)

Household Incomes

Whether or not prices start rising quickly, household incomes will get a boost from the increased investment. Producers will step up the rate of output to rebuild inventories and supply more investment goods (equipment and structures). To do so, they'll hire more workers or extend working hours. The end result for workers will be fatter paychecks.

Induced Consumption

What will households do with these heftier paychecks? By now, you know what the consumer response will be. The marginal propensity to consume prompts an increase in consumer spending. Eventually, consumer spending increases by a *multiple* of the income change. In this case, the consumption increase is $300 billion (see Table 10.1).

Figure 10.9 illustrates the secondary shift of AD caused by multiplier-induced consumption. Notice how the AD curve shifts a second time, from AD$_5$ to AD$_6$.

A New Equilibrium

> **demand-pull inflation:** An increase in the price level initiated by excessive aggregate demand.

The ultimate impact of the investment surge is reflected in the new equilibrium at point *w.* As before, the shift of AD has affected both real output and prices. Real output does increase beyond the full-employment level, but it does so only at the expense of accelerating inflation. This is a classic case of **demand-pull inflation.** The initial increase in investment was enough to kindle a little inflation. The multiplier effect worsened the problem by forcing the economy further along the ever-steeper AS curve. The **inflationary GDP gap** ends up as $Q_E - Q_F$.

Booms and Busts

> **inflationary GDP gap:** The amount by which equilibrium GDP exceeds full-employment GDP.

The Keynesian analysis of leakages, injections, and the multiplier paints a fairly grim picture of the prospects for macro stability. *The basic conclusion of the Keynesian analysis is that the economy is vulnerable to abrupt changes in spending behavior and won't self-adjust to a desired macro equilibrium.* A shift in aggregate demand can come from almost anywhere. The September 2001 terrorist attack on the World Trade Center shook both consumer and investor confidence. Businesses starting cutting back production even *before* inventories started piling up. Worsened *expectations* rather than rising inventories caused investment demand to shift, setting off the multiplier process.

When the aggregate demand curve shifts, macro equilibrium will be upset. Moreover, the responses of market participants to an abrupt AD shift are likely to worsen rather than improve market outcomes. As a result, the economy may gravitate toward an equilibrium of stagnant recession (point *c* in Figure 10.6) or persistent inflation (point *w* in Figure 10.9).

As Keynes saw it, the combination of alternating AD shifts and multiplier effects also causes recurring business cycles. A drop in consumer or business spending can set off a recessionary spiral of declining GDP and prices. A later increase in either consumer or business spending can set the ball rolling in the other direction. This may result in a series of economic booms and busts.

THE ECONOMY TOMORROW

Maintaining Consumer Confidence

This chapter emphasized how a sudden change in investment might set off the multiplier process. Investors aren't the only potential culprits, however. A sudden change in government spending or exports could just as easily start the multiplier ball rolling. In fact, the whole process could originate with a change in *consumer* spending.

Consumer Confidence

Recall the two components of consumption: *autonomous* consumption and *induced* consumption. These two components may be expressed as

$$C = a + bY$$

We've seen that autonomous consumption is influenced by *non*income factors, including consumer confidence. What's more, consumer confidence can change abruptly, as Figure 10.10 confirms. When it does, the value of *a* in the consumption

FIGURE 10.10
Consumer Confidence

Consumer confidence is affected by various financial, political, and international events. Changes in consumer confidence affect consumer behavior and thereby shift the AD curve.

Source: University of Michigan

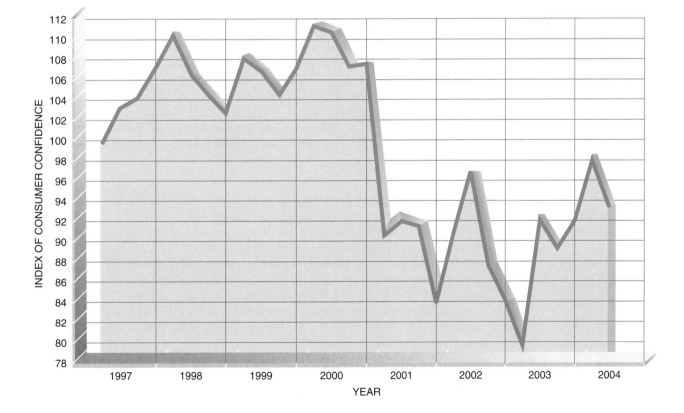

Thrift Shift—The More the Japanese Save for a Rainy Day, the Gloomier It Gets

Stuffing Yen into the Drawer

A decade ago, when Japan was considered economically mighty and the U.S. was struggling, many economists agreed that a big reason for the disparity was savings: The thrifty Japanese had plenty to invest in their future, the wanton Americans too little.

Today, the average Japanese family puts away more than 13 percent of its income, the average American family 4 percent. Yet Japan is in the tank while the U.S. prospers.

Is saving no longer an economic virtue and profligacy no longer a vice? Did Benjamin Franklin get it all wrong? Maybe not—but it isn't as simple as Franklin's Poor Richard's Almanac made it seem:

An economy can save too much.

Japan is the first major developed country since World War II to confront the "paradox of thrift," the condition John Maynard Keynes worried about, where bad times lead individuals to save more, suppressing overall demand and making a country even worse off.

But these days, the pressing savings crisis is in Tokyo. Interest rates on bank deposits run below 1 percent, and still "households are saving too much," says Kengo Inoue, a Bank of Japan economist. "That's depressing demand and, over time, corporate investment." That, in turn, has become a drag on all of Asia.

So the Japanese government nudges its citizens to live it up. The Finance Ministry, concerned that families would simply tuck away a recent $500-a-household income-tax cut, launched a media blitz to advise people on how to spend the money.

—Jacob M. Schlesinger and David P. Hamilton

Source: *The Wall Street Journal*, July 2, 1998. Reprinted by permission of *The Wall Street Journal*. © 1998 Dow Jones & Company, Inc. All Rights Reserved Worldwide. www.wsj.com

Analysis: When Japanese consumers became more pessimistic about their economy, they started saving more and spending less. This shifted AD leftward and deepened the recession. Government officials urged them to spend more.

For data on consumer confidence visit the University of Michigan at www.sca.isr.umich.edu

function will change and the consumption function itself will shift. A change in consumer confidence might also change the marginal propensity to consume, the b in the equation. According to a recent World Bank study, every 1 percent change in consumer confidence alters autonomous consumer spending by $1.1 billion.

The reverberation of a change in consumer confidence will cause *two* shifts of the AD curve. The first shift will be due to the effect of changed consumer confidence on *autonomous* consumption. The second shift will result from the multiplier effects on *induced* consumption. This is exactly the kind of dilemma that prolonged the Japanese recession (see World View). As the outlook got gloomier, Japanese households decided to decrease autonomous consumption and reduce the marginal propensity to consume. Unfortunately, their attempt to save more and spend less worsened Japan's recession.

The Official View: Always a Rosy Outlook

Because consumer spending vastly outweighs any other component of aggregate demand, the threat of abrupt changes in consumer behavior is serious. Although U.S. consumers have an optimistic bent (see News), an abrupt decline in consumer confidence is always a possibility. Recognizing this, public officials strive to maintain consumer confidence in the economy tomorrow, even when such confidence might not be warranted. That's what Japanese officials were doing in 1998, described in the World View. That's also why President Hoover, bank officials, and major brokerage houses tried to assure the public in 1929 that the outlook was still rosy. (Look back at the first few pages of Chapter 8.) The "rosy outlook" is still the official perspective on the economy tomorrow. The White House is always upbeat about prospects for the economy. If it weren't—if it were even to hint at the possibility of a recession—consumer and investor confidence might wilt. Then the economy might quickly turn ugly.

Harris Poll: Wiser but Unbowed

How has the boom/bust economy of recent years affected Americans' perennial optimism? A *BusinessWeek*/Harris Poll of 1,022 adults, conducted July 20–25, found that most Americans believe the good times will return soon. Still, this outlook is tempered by a sense that the Brave New World of technology may not be quite the panacea it was once thought to be. Highlights of the poll:

Now, for the Turnaround

How optimistic or pessimistic are you that the U.S. can avoid a lengthy downturn marked by more large-scale job layoffs, further weakness in the stock market, and a decline in Americans' living standards?

Very optimistic   13%
Somewhat optimistic   50

Somewhat pessimistic 23%
Very pessimistic   8
Not sure/refused   7

The Future Is Ours

How confident are you that after the economic downturn ends, America can return to rapid economic growth, rising incomes, and good job opportunities?

Very confident   21%
Somewhat confident   55
Not very confident   17
Not at all confident   5
Not sure/refused   2

Analysis: The willingness of consumers to keep spending depends on their outlook for the economy. U.S. consumers are relatively optimistic about future growth, even during recessions.

SUMMARY

- The circular flow of income has offsetting leakages (consumer saving, taxes, business saving, imports) and injections (autonomous consumption, investment, government spending, exports).
- When desired injections equal leakage, the economy is in equilibrium.
- An imbalance of injections and leakages will cause the economy to expand or contract. An imbalance at full-employment GDP will cause cyclical unemployment or demand-pull inflation. How serious these problems become depends on how the market responds to the initial imbalance.
- Classical economists believed (changing) interest rates and price levels would equalize injections and leakages (especially consumer saving and investment), restoring full-employment equilibrium.

- Keynes showed that spending imbalances might actually *worsen* if consumer and investor expectations changed.
- An abrupt change in autonomous spending (injections) shifts the AD curve, setting off a sequential multiplier process that magnifies changes in equilibrium GDP.
- The multiplier itself is equal to $1/(1 - MPC)$. It indicates the cumulative change in demand that follows an initial (autonomous) disruption of spending flows.
- As long as the short-run aggregate supply curve slopes upward, AD shifts will affect both real output and prices.
- The recessionary GDP gap measures the amount by which equilibrium GDP falls short of full-employment GDP.
- Sudden changes in consumer confidence would destabilize the economy. To avoid this, policymakers always maintain a rosy outlook.

Key Terms

aggregate demand
full-employment GDP
leakage
gross business saving
injection

equilibrium GDP
marginal propensity to consume (MPC)
multiplier
recessionary GDP gap

cyclical unemployment
full employment
demand-pull inflation
inflationary GDP gap

Questions for Discussion

1. How might declining prices affect a firm's decision to borrow and invest?
2. Why wouldn't investment and saving flows at full employment always be equal?
3. When unwanted inventories pile up in retail stores, how is production affected? What are the steps in this process?
4. How can equilibrium output exceed full-employment output (as in Figure 10.9)?
5. How might the airline industry job losses described in the News feature on page 211 affect incomes in the clothing and travel industries?
6. Why would Asian economies stall when the U.S. economy slumps (World View, page 214)? How could the Asian economies self-adjust? Is that likely?
7. What forces might turn an economic bust into an economic boom? What forces might put an end to the boom?
8. What might trigger an abrupt decline in consumer spending?
9. What might get the international multiplier effect (World View, page 214) moving in the right direction?
10. Will the price level always rise when AD increases? Why or why not?

ALERT!

PROBLEMS The Student Problem Set at the back of this book contains numerical and graphing problems for this chapter.

WEB ACTIVITIES to accompany this chapter can be found on the Online Learning Center: **http://www.mhhe.com/economics/schiller10**

PART 4

Fiscal Policy Levers

The government's tax and spending activities influence economic outcomes. Keynesian theory emphasizes the market's lack of self-adjustment, particularly in recessions. If the market doesn't self-adjust, then the government may have to intervene. Specifically, the government may have to use its tax and spending power (fiscal policy) to stabilize the macro economy. Chapters 11 and 12 look closely at these policy options.

Fiscal Policy

The Keynesian theory of macro instability is practically a mandate for government intervention. From a Keynesian perspective, too little aggregate demand causes unemployment; too much aggregate demand causes inflation. Since the market itself won't correct these imbalances, the federal government must. Keynes concluded that the government must intervene to manage the level of aggregate demand. This implies increasing aggregate demand when it's deficient and decreasing aggregate demand when it's excessive.

This chapter examines some tools the federal government can use to alter macroeconomic outcomes. The questions we confront are

- **Can government spending and tax policies help ensure full employment?**
- **What policy actions will help fight inflation?**
- **What are the risks of government intervention?**

As we'll see, the government's tax and spending activities affect not only the *level* of output and prices but the *mix* of output as well.

TAXES AND SPENDING

Article I of the U.S. Constitution empowers Congress "to lay and collect taxes, duties, imposts and excises, to pay the debts and provide for the common defense and general welfare of the United States." Up until 1915, however, the federal government collected few taxes and spent little. In 1902, the federal government employed fewer than 350,000 people and spent a mere $650 million. Today, the federal government employs over 4 million people and spends more than $2 trillion a year.

Government Revenue

The tremendous expansion of the federal government started with the Sixteenth Amendment to the U.S. Constitution (1913); it extended the government's taxing power to *incomes*. Prior to that, most government revenue came from taxes on imports, whiskey, and tobacco. Once the federal government got the power to tax incomes, it had the revenue base to finance increased expenditure.

Today, the federal government collects over $2 trillion a year in tax revenues. Nearly half of that revenue comes from individual income taxes (see Figure 4.6). Social Security payroll taxes are the second-largest revenue source, followed at a distance by corporate income taxes. The customs, whiskey, and tobacco taxes on which the federal government depended in 1902 now count for very little.

Government Expenditure

In 1902, federal government expenditures mirrored tax revenues: Both were very small. Today, things are very different. The federal government now spends all of its much larger tax revenues—and more. Uncle Sam even borrows additional funds to pay for federal spending. In Chapter 12 we look at the implications of the budget deficits that help finance federal spending. In this chapter we focus on how government spending *directly* affects **aggregate demand.**

Purchases vs. Transfers. To understand how government spending affects aggregate demand, we must again distinguish between government *purchases* and *income transfers*. Government spending on defense, highways, and health care entail the purchase of goods and services in product markets; they're part of aggregate demand. By contrast, the government doesn't buy anything when it mails out Social Security checks. Those checks simply transfer income from taxpayers to retired workers. **Income transfers** don't become part of aggregate demand until the transfer recipients decide to spend that income.

As we observed in Chapter 4, less than half of all federal government spending entails the purchase of goods and services. The rest of federal spending is either an income transfer or an interest payment on the national debt.

The federal government's tax and spending powers give it a great deal of influence over aggregate demand. ***The government can alter aggregate demand by***

Fiscal Policy

- *Purchasing more or fewer goods and services.*
- *Raising or lowering taxes.*
- *Changing the level of income transfers.*

Fiscal policy entails the use of these various budget levers to influence macroeconomic outcomes. ***From a macro perspective, the federal budget is a tool that can change aggregate demand and macroeconomic outcomes.*** Figure 11.1 puts this tool into the framework of the basic AS/AD model.

Although fiscal policy can be used to pursue any of our economic goals, we begin our study by exploring its potential to ensure full employment. We then look at its impact on inflation. Along the way we also observe the potential of fiscal policy to alter the mix of output and the distribution of income.

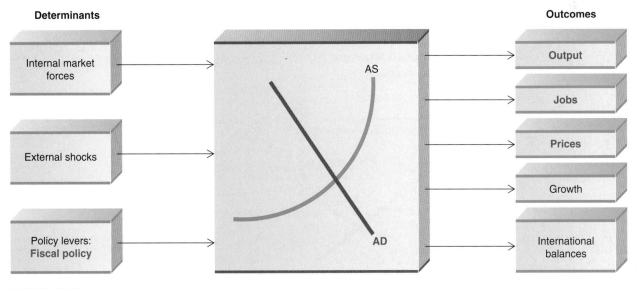

FIGURE 11.1
Fiscal Policy

Fiscal policy refers to the use of the government tax and spending powers to alter macro outcomes. Fiscal policy works principally through shifts of the aggregate demand curve.

equilibrium (macro): The combination of price level and real output that is compatible with both aggregate demand and aggregate supply.

Keynesian Strategy

recessionary GDP gap: The amount by which equilibrium GDP falls short of full-employment GDP.

fiscal stimulus: Tax cuts or spending hikes intended to increase (shift) aggregate demand.

The Fiscal Target

aggregate supply: The total quantity of output producers are willing and able to supply at alternative price levels in a given time period, *ceteris paribus*.

FISCAL STIMULUS

The basic premise of fiscal policy is that the market's short-run macro equilibrium may not be a desirable one. This is clearly the case in Figure 11.2. **Macro equilibrium** occurs at Q_E, where $5.6 trillion of output is being produced. Full-employment GDP occurs at Q_F, where the real value of output is $6 trillion. Accordingly, the economy depicted in Figure 11.2 confronts a **recessionary GDP gap** of $400 billion.

The Keynesian model of the adjustment process helps us not only understand how an economy can get into such trouble but also see how it might get out. Keynes emphasized how the aggregate demand curve *shifts* with changes in spending behavior. He also emphasized how new injections of spending into the circular flow multiply into much larger changes in total spending. From a Keynesian perspective, then, the way out of recession is obvious: Get someone to spend more on goods and services. Should desired spending increase, the aggregate demand curve would *shift* to the right, leading the economy out of recession. That additional spending impetus could come from increased government purchases or from tax cuts that induce increased consumption or investment. Such a **fiscal stimulus** might propel the economy out of recession.

Although the general strategy for Keynesian fiscal policy is clear, the scope of desired intervention isn't so evident. Two strategic policy questions must be addressed:

- By how much do we want to shift the AD curve to the right?
- How can we induce the desired shift?

At first glance, the size of the desired AD shift might seem obvious. If the GDP gap is $400 billion, why not just increase aggregate demand by that amount?

The Naive Keynesian Model. Keynes thought that policy might just work. The intent of the expansionary fiscal policy is to achieve full employment. In Figure 11.3, this goal would be attained at point *b*. When the AD curve shifts rightward by $400 billion, the new AD₂ curve in fact passes through point *b*, creating the possibility of achieving our full-employment goal.

Will the economy move so easily from point *a* to point *b*? Only under very special conditions. The economy would move from point *a* to point *b* in Figure 11.3 only if the **aggregate supply** curve were horizontal. In other words, we'd achieve full employment at the current price level (P_E) with the shift to AD₂ only if prices didn't rise when the economy expanded. This is the expectation of the naive Keynesian model. In fairness to Keynes, we must recall that he developed this approach during the Great Depression, when prices were *falling*. No one was worried that prices would rise if demand increased.

FIGURE 11.2
The Policy Goal

If the economy is in a recessionary equilibrium like point *a*, the policy goal is to increase output to full employment (Q_F). Keynes urged the government to use its tax and spending powers to shift the AD curve rightward.

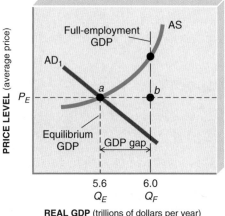

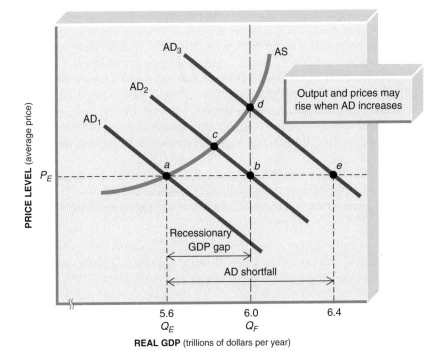

FIGURE 11.3
The AD Shortfall

If aggregate demand increased by the amount of the recessionary GDP gap, which is the shift from AD_1 to AD_2, equilibrium would occur at point c, leaving the economy short of full employment (Q_F). (Some of the increased demand pushes up prices instead of output.) To reach full-employment equilibrium (point d), the AD curve must shift to AD_3, thereby eliminating the entire AD shortfall. The AD shortfall—the horizontal distance between point a and point e—is the fiscal policy target for achieving full employment.

Price-Level Changes. Even in today's economy, prices may not rise every time aggregate demand increases. Over some ranges of real output, the AS curve may actually be horizontal. Eventually, however, we expect the AS curve to slope upward. When it does, any increase in aggregate demand affects both real output *and* prices. In those circumstances, an increase in aggregate demand doesn't translate dollar-for-dollar into increased real GDP. Instead, *when the AD curve shifts to the right, the economy moves up the aggregate supply (AS) curve, not horizontally to the right. As a result both real output and the price level change.*

Figure 11.3 illustrates the consequences of the upward-sloping aggregate supply curve. Suppose we actually increased aggregate demand by $400 billion, an amount equal to the initial GDP gap. When the aggregate demand curve shifts from AD_1 to AD_2, the economy moves to the macro equilibrium at point c, not to point b. As demand picks up, we expect cost pressures to increase, pushing the price level up the upward-sloping AS curve. At point c, the AS and AD_2 curves intersect, establishing a new equilibrium. At that equilibrium, the price level is higher than it was initially (P_E). Real output is higher as well but still short of the full-employment target (Q_F). Hence, the naive Keynesian policy fails to achieve full employment. To do better, we must recognize that *shifting (increasing) aggregate demand by the amount of the GDP gap will achieve full employment only if the price level doesn't rise.*

The AD Shortfall. Although the naive Keynesian approach doesn't work, we needn't forsake fiscal policy. Figure 11.3 simply tells us that the naive Keynesian policy prescription (increasing AD by the amount of the GDP gap) probably won't cure all our unemployment ills. It also suggests, however, that a *larger* dose of fiscal stimulus might just work. *So long as the AS curve slopes upward, we must increase aggregate demand by more than the size of the recessionary GDP gap in order to achieve full employment.*

Figure 11.3 illustrates this new policy target. The **AD shortfall** is the amount of additional aggregate demand needed to achieve full employment *after allowing for*

AD shortfall: The amount of additional aggregate demand needed to achieve full employment after allowing for price-level changes.

price-level changes. Notice in Figure 11.3 that full employment (Q_F) is achieved only when the AD curve intersects the AS curve at point *d*. To get there, the aggregate demand curve must shift from AD_1 all the way to AD_3. That third aggregate demand curve passes through point *e* as well. Hence, aggregate demand must increase until it passes through point *e*. This **horizontal distance between point a and point e in Figure 11.3 measures the AD shortfall.** Aggregate demand must increase (shift) by the amount of the AD shortfall in order to achieve full employment. Thus, **the AD shortfall is the fiscal target.** In Figure 11.3, the AD shortfall amounts to $800 billion ($0.8 trillion). That's how much *additional* aggregate demand is required to reach full employment (Q_F).

Were we to increase AD by enough to attain full employment, it's apparent in Figure 11.3 that prices would increase as well. We'll examine this dilemma later; for the time being we focus on the policy options for increasing aggregate demand by the desired amount.

More Government Spending

The simplest way to shift aggregate demand is to increase government spending. If the government were to step up its purchases of tanks, highways, schools, and other goods, the increased spending would add directly to aggregate demand. This would shift the aggregate demand curve rightward, moving us closer to full employment. Hence, **increased government spending is a form of fiscal stimulus.**

Multiplier Effects. It isn't necessary for the government to make up the entire shortfall in aggregate demand. Suppose that the fiscal target was to increase aggregate demand by $800 billion, the AD shortfall illustrated in Figure 11.3. Were government spending to increase by that amount, the AD curve would actually shift *beyond* point *e* in Figure 11.3. In that case we'd quickly move from a situation of *inadequate* aggregate demand (point *a*) to a situation of *excessive* aggregate demand.

The origins of this apparent riddle lie in the circular flow of income. When the government buys more goods and services, it creates additional income for market participants. The recipients of this income will in turn spend it. Hence, each dollar gets spent and respent many times. This is the multiplier adjustment process we encountered in Chapter 10. As a result of this process, **every dollar of new government spending has a multiplied impact on aggregate demand.**

How much "bang" the economy gets for each government "buck" depends on the value of the **multiplier.** Specifically,

> **multiplier:** The multiple by which an initial change in aggregate spending will alter total expenditure after an infinite number of spending cycles; $1/(1 - MPC)$.

$$\frac{\text{Total change}}{\text{in spending}} = \text{multiplier} \times \text{new spending injection}$$

The multiplier adds a lot of punch to fiscal policy. Suppose that households have a **marginal propensity to consume** equal to 0.75. In this case, the multiplier would have a value of 4 and each dollar of new government expenditure would increase total expenditure by $4.

> **marginal propensity to consume (MPC):** The fraction of each additional (marginal) dollar of disposable income spent on consumption; the change in consumption divided by the change in disposable income.

Figure 11.4 illustrates that leveraged impact of government spending. Aggregate demand shifts from AD_1 to AD_2 when the government buys an additional $200 billion of output. Multiplier effects then increase consumption spending by $600 billion. This additional consumption shifts aggregate demand further, to AD_3. Thus, **the impact of fiscal stimulus on aggregate demand includes both the new government spending and all subsequent increases in consumer spending triggered by the additional government outlays.** In Figure 11.4, the shift from AD_1 to AD_3 includes

AD_1 to AD_2: Shift due to $200 billion injection of new government spending.
AD_2 to AD_3: Shift due to multiplier-induced increase in consumption ($600 billion).

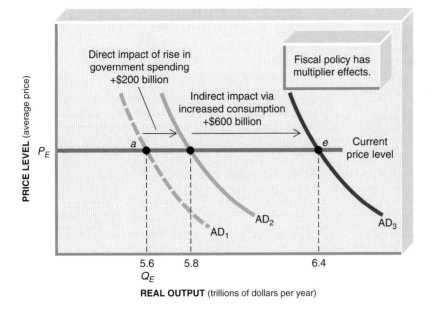

FIGURE 11.4
Multiplier Effects

Fiscal stimulus will set off the multiplier process. As a result of this, aggregate demand will increase (shift) in two distinct steps: (1) the initial fiscal stimulus (AD_1 to AD_2) and (2) induced changes in consumption (AD_2 to AD_3). In this case, a $200 billion increase in government spending causes an $800 billion increase in aggregate demand at the *existing* price level.

As a result of these initial and multiplier-induced shifts, aggregate demand at the current price level (P_E) increases by $800 billion. Thus,

$$\text{Cumulative increase (horizontal shift) in AD} = \text{new spending injection (fiscal stimulus)} + \text{induced increase in consumption}$$

$$= \text{multiplier} \times \text{fiscal stimulus (new spending injection)}$$

The second equation is identical to the first but expressed in the terminology of fiscal policy. The "fiscal stimulus" is the "new spending injection" that sets the multiplier process in motion.

The Desired Stimulus. Multiplier effects make changes in government spending a powerful policy lever. The multiplier also increases the risk of error, however. Whereas too little fiscal stimulus may leave the economy in a recession, too much can rapidly lead to excessive spending and inflation. This was the dilemma President George W. Bush confronted in his first year. He wanted a $1.6 trillion tax cut spread out over several years. Critics worried, however, that too much fiscal stimulus might accelerate inflation. A compromise of $1.35 trillion was struck in early 2001.

After the terrorist attacks of September 11, 2001, too *little,* not too much fiscal stimulus, was a greater risk. The attacks put an immediate damper on consumer and investor spending, widening the recessionary GDP gap. President Bush quickly asked Congress to approve more government spending and additional tax cuts to keep the economy growing.

Policy decisions would be a lot easier if we could anticipate such events. If we knew the exact dimensions of aggregate demand, as in Figure 11.3, we could easily calculate the required increase in the rate of government spending. The general formula for computing the *desired* stimulus is a simple rearrangement of the earlier formula:

$$\text{Desired fiscal stimulus} = \frac{\text{AD shortfall}}{\text{the multiplier}}$$

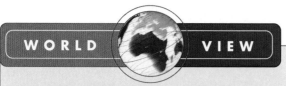

Seoul Plans Spending to Boost Economy

South Korea's finance minister, Jin Nyum, said the government, state-run companies and funds would increase third-quarter spending on infrastructure and other projects by 4.3 trillion won ($3.35 billion) to a total 30.3 trillion won, in a move to bolster an economy that has been hurt by declining exports. He spoke after President Kim Dae Jung met with economic

ministers. Among planned steps to boost the economy are a cut in interest rates on loans to companies that participate in state projects and increased financial support to exporters. The government is also considering a tax cut, Mr. Jin said.

Source: *The Wall Street Journal*, August 8, 2001. Reprinted by permission of The Wall Street Journal. © 2001 Dow Jones Company, Inc. All rights reserved worldwide. www.wsj.com

Analysis: Fear of a pending decline in aggregate demand prompted South Korea's government to increase government spending on roads, bridges, and telecom networks. The government hoped such a fiscal stimulus would offset a decline in export sales and avert recession.

In the economy in Figure 11.3, we assumed the policy goal was to increase aggregate demand by the amount of the AD shortfall ($800 billion). Accordingly, we conclude that

$$\text{Desired fiscal stimulus} = \frac{\$800 \text{ billion}}{4}$$

$$= \$200 \text{ billion}$$

In other words, a $200 billion increase in government spending at the current price level would be enough fiscal stimulus to close the $800 billion AD shortfall and achieve full employment.

In practice, we rarely know the exact size of the shortfall in aggregate demand. The multiplier is also harder to calculate when taxes and imports enter the picture. Nevertheless, the foregoing formula does provide a useful rule of thumb for determining how much fiscal stimulus is needed to achieve any desired increase in aggregate demand. Such calculations helped the South Korean government decide how much fiscal stimulus was needed in 2001 to keep its economy out of recession (see World View).

WEBNOTE

To see what happened to real GDP in South Korea after the 2001 fiscal stimulus, check out GDP data at koreaeconomy.org.

Tax Cuts

Although injections of government spending can close a GDP gap, increased government purchases aren't the only way to get there. The increased demand required to raise output and employment levels from Q_E to Q_F could emerge from increases in autonomous consumption or investment as well as from increased government spending. It could also come from abroad, in the form of increased demand for our exports. In other words, any "Big Spender" would help, whether from the public sector or the private sector. Of course, the reason we're initially at Q_E instead of Q_F in Figure 11.3 is that consumers, investors, and export buyers have chosen *not* to spend as much as required for full employment.

Consumer and investor decisions are subject to change. Moreover, fiscal policy can encourage such changes. Congress not only buys goods and services but also levies taxes. By lowering taxes, the government increases the **disposable income** of the private sector. This was the objective of the early Bush tax cuts, which gave all tax payers a rebate of $300–600 in the summer of 2001. By putting $38 billion more after-tax income into the hands of consumers, Congress hoped to stimulate (shift) the consumption component of aggregate demand.

disposable income: After-tax income of consumers; personal income less personal taxes.

Taxes and Consumption. A tax cut directly increases the disposable income of consumers. The question here, however, is how a tax cut affects *spending*. By how much will consumption increase for every dollar of tax cuts?

Spending Propels Growth

Fueled by a surge in consumer spending, the U.S. economy took off in the July–September period, with growth running perhaps as high as a 7 percent annual rate, a number of economists said yesterday.

Such predictions got a boost from a Commerce Department report yesterday that retail sales grew at a 12.2 percent annual rate in the third quarter, despite a 0.2 percent decline last month.

Some analysts said the federal personal income tax cut that took effect July 1 was partially responsible for the jump in spending.

"You give consumers a tax cut and they'll spend it," said Ken Mayland of ClearView Economics in Cleveland. "That's the way America works."

—John M. Berry

Source: *The Washington Post,* October 16, 2003. © 2003 The Washington Post. Reprinted with permission.

Analysis: Tax cuts increase disposable incomes. Typically, consumers use most of this increased income to buy more products, thereby shifting AD rightward.

The answer lies in the marginal propensity to consume. Consumers won't spend every dollar of tax cuts; they'll *save* some of the cut and spend the rest. The MPC tells us how the tax-cut dollar will be split between saving and spending. If the MPC is 0.75, consumers will spend $0.75 out of every tax-cut $1.00. In other words,

$$\text{Initial increase in consumption} = \text{MPC} \times \text{tax cut}$$

If taxes were cut by $200 billion, the resulting spree would amount to

$$\text{Initial increase in consumption} = 0.75 \times \$200 \text{ billion}$$

$$= \$150 \text{ billion}$$

Hence, *the effect of a tax cut that increases disposable incomes is to stimulate consumer spending.* A tax cut therefore shifts the aggregate demand curve to the right. This chain of events is what the accompanying News calls "the way America works."

The initial consumption spree induced by a tax cut starts the multiplier process in motion. The new consumer spending creates additional income for producers and workers, who will then use the additional income to increase their own consumption. This will propel us along the multiplier path already depicted in Figure 11.4. The cumulative change in total spending will be

$$\begin{array}{c}\text{Cumulative change} \\ \text{in spending}\end{array} = \text{multiplier} \times \begin{array}{c}\text{initial change} \\ \text{in consumption}\end{array}$$

In this case, the cumulative change is

$$\begin{array}{c}\text{Cumulative change} \\ \text{in spending}\end{array} = \frac{1}{1 - \text{MPC}} \times \$150 \text{ billion}$$

$$= 4 \times \$150 \text{ billion}$$

$$= \$600 \text{ billion}$$

Here again we see that the multiplier increases the impact on aggregate demand of a fiscal policy stimulus. There's an important difference here, though. When we increased government spending by $200 billion, aggregate demand increased by $800 billion. When we cut taxes by $200 billion, however, aggregate demand increases by only $600 billion. Hence, *a tax cut contains less fiscal stimulus than an increase in government spending of the same size.*

FIGURE 11.5
The Tax Cut Multiplier

Only part of a tax cut is used to increase consumption; the remainder is saved. Accordingly, the initial spending injection is less than the tax cut. This makes tax cuts less stimulative than government purchases of the same size. The multiplier still goes to work on that new consumer spending, however.

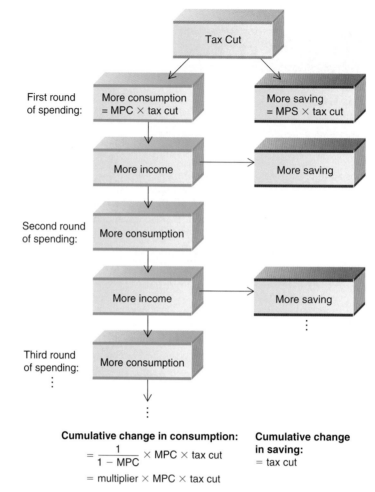

The lesser stimulative power of tax cuts is explained by consumer saving. Only part of a tax cut gets spent. Consumers save the rest. This is evident in Figure 11.5 which illustrates the successive rounds of the multiplier process. Notice that the tax cut is used to increase both consumption and saving, according to the MPC. Only that part of the tax cut that's used for consumption enters the circular flow as a spending injection. Hence, *the initial spending injection is less than the size of the tax cuts.* By contrast, every dollar of government purchases goes directly into the circular flow. Accordingly, tax cuts are less powerful than government purchases because the initial *spending* injection is smaller.

This doesn't mean we can't close the AD shortfall with a tax cut. It simply means that the desired tax cut must be larger than the required stimulus. It remains true that

$$\text{Desired fiscal stimulus} = \frac{\text{AD shortfall}}{\text{the multiplier}}$$

But now we're using a consumption shift as the fiscal stimulus rather than increased government spending. Hence, we have to allow for the fact that the initial surge in consumption (the fiscal stimulus) will be *less* than the tax cut. Specifically,

$$\text{Initial consumption injection} = \text{MPC} \times \text{tax cut}$$

Hence, if we want to use a consumer tax cut to close a GDP gap, we have

$$\text{Desired tax cut} = \frac{\text{desired fiscal stimulus}}{\text{MPC}}$$

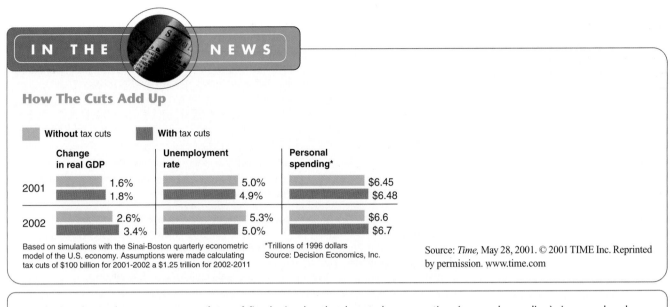

How The Cuts Add Up

■ **Without** tax cuts   ■ **With** tax cuts

	Change in real GDP	Unemployment rate	Personal spending*
2001	1.6% / 1.8%	5.0% / 4.9%	$6.45 / $6.48
2002	2.6% / 3.4%	5.3% / 5.0%	$6.6 / $6.7

Based on simulations with the Sinai-Boston quarterly econometric model of the U.S. economy. Assumptions were made calculating tax cuts of $100 billion for 2001-2002 a $1.25 trillion for 2002-2011

*Trillions of 1996 dollars
Source: Decision Economics, Inc.

Source: *Time*, May 28, 2001. © 2001 TIME Inc. Reprinted by permission. www.time.com

Analysis: The Bush tax cuts were a form of fiscal stimulus that boosted consumption (personal spending), increased real GDP growth, and reduced unemployment.

In the economy in Figure 11.3, we assumed that the desired stimulus is $200 billion and the MPC equals 0.75. Hence, the desired tax cut is

$$\text{Desired tax cut} = \frac{\$200 \text{ billion}}{0.75} = \$267 \text{ billion}$$

By cutting taxes $267 billion, we directly increase disposable income by the same amount. Consumers then increase their rate of spending $200 billion (0.75 × $267 billion); they save the remaining $67 billion. As the added spending enters the circular flow, it starts the multiplier process, ultimately increasing aggregate demand by $800 billion per year.

This comparison of government purchases and tax cuts clearly reveals their respective power. What we've demonstrated is that *a dollar of tax cuts is less stimulative than a dollar of government purchases.* This doesn't mean that tax cuts are undesirable, just that they need to be larger than the desired injection of spending. The nearby News shows that the 2001 tax cut boosted both consumer spending and, as a result, real GDP growth.

The different effects of tax cuts and increased government spending have an important implication for government budgets. Because some of the power of a tax cut "leaks" into saving, tax increases don't "offset" government spending of equal value. This unexpected result is described in Table 11.1.

Taxes and Investment. A tax cut may also be an effective mechanism for increasing *investment* spending. As we observed in Chapter 9, investment decisions are guided by expectations of future profit. If a cut in corporate taxes raises potential after-tax profits, it should encourage additional investment. Once an increase in the rate of investment spending enters the circular flow, it has a multiplier effect on total spending like that which follows an initial change in consumer spending.

Tax cuts designed to stimulate consumption (*C*) and investment (*I*) have been used frequently. In 1963, President John F. Kennedy announced his intention to reduce taxes in order to stimulate the economy, citing that the marginal propensity to consume for the average U.S. family at that time appeared to be exceptionally high. His successor, Lyndon Johnson, concurred with Kennedy's reasoning. Johnson agreed to "shift emphasis sharply from expanding federal expenditure to boosting private consumer

Different views of how the Bush tax cuts might affect spending, employment, and real GDP are available from the Heritage Foundation at www.heritage.org/research/taxes/issues2004.cfm and the Brookings Institution at www.brookings.edu/comm/policybriefs/pb101.htm.

TABLE 11.1
The Balanced Budget Multiplier

An increase in government spending paid for by a tax cut of equal size shifts aggregate demand. This box explains why.

Many taxpayers and politicians demand that any new government spending be balanced with new taxes. Such balancing at the margin, it's asserted, will keep the budget deficit from rising, while avoiding further economic stimulus.

However, changes in government spending (*G*) are more powerful than changes in taxes (*T*) or transfers. This implies that an increase in *G* apparently offset with an equal rise in *T* will actually increase aggregate demand.

To see how this curious result comes about, suppose that the government decided to spend $50 billion per year on a new fleet of space shuttles and to pay for them by raising income taxes by the same amount. Thus

$$\text{Change in } G = +\$50 \text{ billion per year}$$
$$\text{Change in } T = +\$50 \text{ billion per year}$$
$$\text{Change in budget balance} = 0$$

How will this pay-as-you-go (balanced) budget initiative affect total spending?

The increase in the rate of government spending represents a new injection of $50 billion. But the higher taxes don't increase leakage by the same amount. Households will pay taxes by reducing *both* consumption and saving. The initial reduction in annual consumer spending equals only MPC × $50 billion.

The reduction in consumption is therefore less than the increase in government spending, implying a net increase in *aggregate* spending. The *initial* change in aggregate demand brought about by this balanced budget expenditure is

$$\text{Initial increase in government spending} = \$50 \text{ billion}$$
$$\underline{\text{less Initial reduction in consumer spending} = \text{MPC} \times \$50 \text{ billion}}$$
$$\text{Net initial change in total spending} = (1 - \text{MPC})\$50 \text{ billion}$$

Like any other changes in the rate of spending, this initial increase in aggregate spending will start a multiplier process in motion. The *cumulative* change in expenditure will be much larger, as indicated by the multiplier. In this case, the cumulative (ultimate) change in total spending is

$$\frac{\text{The}}{\text{multiplier}} \times \frac{\text{initial change}}{\text{in spending per year}} = \frac{\text{cumulative change}}{\text{in total spending}}$$

$$\frac{1}{1 - \text{MPC}} \times (1 - \text{MPC})\$50 \text{ billion} = \$50 \text{ billion}$$

Thus, the balanced budget multiplier is equal to 1. In this case, a $50 billion increase in annual government expenditure combined with an equivalent increase in taxes increases aggregate demand by $50 billion per year.

WEBNOTE

To follow the ups and downs of Federal income tax as a percentage of GDP, go to the Congressional Budget Office at www.cbo.gov and choose "Historical Budget Data."

demand and business investment." He proceeded to cut personal and corporate taxes $11 billion. President Johnson proclaimed that "the $11 billion tax cut will challenge American businessmen, investors, and consumers to put their enlarged incomes to work in the private economy to expand output, investment, and jobs." He added, "I am confident that our private decision makers will rise to this challenge." They apparently did, because *C* + *I* increased $33 billion in 1963 and another $46 billion in 1965 (in part as a result of multiplier effects, of course).

The second-largest tax cut in history was initiated by President Ronald Reagan. In 1981, Congress cut personal taxes $250 billion over a three-year period and cut business taxes another $70 billion. The resulting increase in disposable income stimulated consumer spending and helped push the economy out of the 1981–82 recession. When the economy slowed down at the end of the 1980s, President George H. Bush proposed to cut the capital gains tax, hoping to stimulate investment. President Clinton also embraced the notion of tax incentives for investment. He favored a tax credit for new investments in plant and equipment to increase the level of investment and set off multiplier effects for many years.

President George W. Bush pulled out all the tax-cut stops. Immediately upon taking office in 2001, he convinced Congress to pass a $1.35 trillion tax cut for consumers, spread over several years. He followed that up with business tax cuts in 2002 and 2003. The cumulative impact of these tax cuts shifted AD significantly to the right and accelerated recovery from the 2001 recession.

Increased Transfers

A third fiscal policy option for stimulating the economy is to increase transfer payments. If Social Security recipients, welfare recipients, unemployment insurance beneficiaries, and veterans get larger benefit checks, they'll have more disposable income to spend. The resulting increase in consumption will boost aggregate demand.

Increased transfer payments don't, however, increase injections dollar-for-dollar. Here again, we have to recognize that consumers will save some of their additional transfer payments; only part (MPC) of the additional income will be injected into the spending stream. Hence, *the initial fiscal stimulus (AD shift) of increased transfer payments is*

Initial fiscal stimulus (injection) = MPC × increase in transfer payments.

This initial stimulus sets the multiplier in motion, shifting the aggregate demand curve further to the right.

FISCAL RESTRAINT

The objective of fiscal policy isn't always to increase aggregate demand. At times the economy is already expanding too fast and **fiscal restraint** is more appropriate. In these circumstances, policymakers are likely to be focused on inflation, not unemployment. Their objective will be to *reduce* aggregate demand, not to stimulate it.

> **fiscal restraint:** Tax hikes or spending cuts intended to reduce (shift) aggregate demand.

The means available to the federal government for restraining aggregate demand emerge again from both sides of the budget. The difference here is that we use the budget tools in reverse. We now want to reduce government spending, increase taxes, or decrease transfer payments.

The Fiscal Target

As before, our first task is to determine how much we want aggregate demand to fall. To determine this, we must consult Figure 11.6. The initial equilibrium in this case occurs at point E_1, where the AS and AD_1 curves intersect. At that equilibrium the

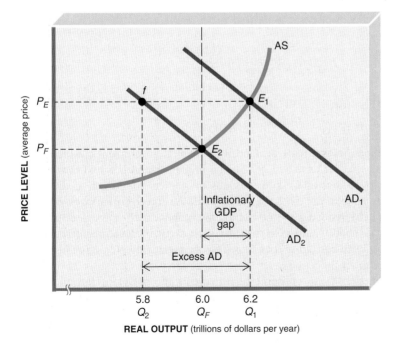

FIGURE 11.6
Excess Aggregate Demand

Too much aggregate demand (AD_1) causes the price level to rise (P_E) above its desired level (P_F). To restore price stability, the AD curve must shift leftward by the entire amount of the excess AD (here shown as $Q_1 - Q_2$). In this case, the excess AD amounts to $400 billion. If AD shifts by that much (from AD_1 to AD_2), the excess AD is eliminated and equilibrium moves from E_1 to E_2.

unemployment rate falls below the rate consistent with full employment (Q_F) and we produce the output Q_1. The resulting strains on production push the price level to P_E, higher than we're willing to accept. Our goal is to maintain the price level at P_F, which is consistent with our notion of full employment *and* price stability.

In this case, we have an **inflationary GDP gap**—that is, equilibrium GDP exceeds full-employment GDP by the amount $Q_1 - Q_F$, or \$200 billion. If we want to restore price stability (P_F), however, we need to reduce aggregate demand by *more* than this GDP gap. The **AD excess** takes into account potential changes in the price level. Observe that *the AD excess exceeds the inflationary GDP gap.* In Figure 11.6, the AD excess equals the horizontal distance from E_1 to point f, which amounts to \$400 billion. This excess aggregate demand is our fiscal policy target. To restore price stability, we must shift the AD curve leftward until it passes through point f. The AD_2 curve does this. The shift to AD_2 moves the economy to a new equilibrium at E_2. At E_2 we have less output but also a lower price level (less inflation).

Knowing the dimensions of excess aggregate demand, we can compute the desired fiscal restraint as

$$\frac{\text{Desired}}{\text{fiscal restraint}} = \frac{\text{excess AD}}{\text{the multiplier}}$$

In other words, first we determine how far we want to shift the AD curve. Generally, the desired AD reduction will equal the excess AD. Then we compute how much government spending or taxes must be changed to achieve the desired shift, taking into account multiplier effects.

Budget Cuts

The first option to consider is budget cuts. By how much should we reduce government expenditure on goods and services? The answer is simple in this case: We first calculate the desired fiscal restraint, as computed above. Then we cut government expenditure by that amount.

The GDP gap in Figure 11.6 amounts to \$200 billion ($Q_1 - Q_F$). If aggregate demand is reduced by that amount, however, some of the restraint will be dissipated in price-level reductions. To bring *equilibrium* GDP down to the full-employment (Q_F) level, even more of a spending reduction is needed. In this case, the excess AD amounts to \$400 billion.

Budgets cuts of less than \$400 billion will achieve the desired reduction in aggregate demand. If we assume a marginal propensity to consume of 0.75, the multiplier equals 4. In these circumstances, the desired fiscal restraint is

$$\frac{\text{Desired}}{\text{fiscal restraint}} = \frac{\text{excess AD}}{\text{the multiplier}}$$
$$= \frac{\$400 \text{ billion}}{4}$$
$$= \$100 \text{ billion}$$

What would happen to aggregate demand if the federal government cut that much spending out of, say, the defense budget? Such a military cutback would throw a lot of aerospace employees out of work. Thousands of workers would get smaller paychecks, or perhaps none at all. These workers would be forced to cut back on their own spending, thereby reducing the consumption component of aggregate demand. Hence, aggregate demand would take two hits: first a cut in government spending, then induced cutbacks in consumer spending. The accompanying News highlights the impact of this multiplier process.

The marginal propensity to consume again reveals the power of the multiplier process. If the MPC is 0.75, the consumption of aerospace workers will drop by \$75 billion when the government cutbacks reduce their income by \$100 billion. (The rest of the income loss will be covered by a reduction in saving.)

Economy Is Already Feeling the Impact of Federal Government's Spending Cuts

WASHINGTON—Skeptical about the federal government's pledge to tighten its belt? Consider this: It already has, and that's one reason the economy is so sluggish.

Federal purchases of goods and services dropped 3.3 percent in 1992, the first decline in three years and the largest in almost 20. Behind the decline were huge defense cutbacks: These purchases tumbled more than 6.0 percent during the year.

But nondefense purchases are showing signs of shrinking, too. For two years in a row their rate of increase has slowed, and in the second quarter of this year they actually fell 1.8 percent. . . .

The economy has felt the pinch. Kurl Karl of the WEFA Group, economic consultants based in suburban Philadelphia,

estimates that cuts in purchases by the federal government knocked as much as 0.5 percentage point off the gross domestic product last year, costing roughly 400,000 jobs, and will probably do the same in 1993.

"Government cuts in defense spending have definitely been a drag" on the economy, says Jim O'Sullivan, economist with Morgan Guaranty in New York.

—Lucinda Harper

Analysis: Reductions in governmental spending on goods and services directly decrease aggregate demand. Multiplier effects induce additional cutbacks in consumption, further reducing aggregate demand.

From this point on the story should sound familiar. The $100 billion government cutback will ultimately reduce consumer spending by $300 billion. The total drop in spending is thus $400 billion. Like their mirror image, *budget cuts have a multiplied effect on aggregate demand.* The total impact is equal to

$$\text{Cumulative reduction in spending} = \text{multiplier} \times \text{initial budget cut (fiscal restraint)}$$

This cumulative reduction in spending would eliminate excess aggregate demand. We conclude, then, that *the budget cuts should equal the size of the desired fiscal restraint.*

Tax increases can also be used to shift the aggregate demand curve to the left. The direct effect of a tax increase is a reduction in disposable income. People will pay the higher taxes by reducing their consumption *and* saving less. Only the reduced consumption results in less aggregate demand. As consumers tighten their belts, they set off the multiplier process, leading again to a much larger, cumulative shift of aggregate demand.

Because people pay higher tax bills by reducing both consumption and saving (by MPC and MPS, respectively), *taxes must be increased more than a dollar to get a dollar of fiscal restraint.* This leads us to the following guideline:

$$\text{Desired increase in taxes} = \frac{\text{desired fiscal restraint}}{\text{MPC}}$$

In other words, changes in taxes must always be larger than the desired change in leakages or injections. How much larger depends on the marginal propensity to consume. In this case

$$\begin{aligned}\text{Desired fiscal restraint} &= \frac{\text{excess AD}}{\text{the multiplier}} \\[6pt] &= \frac{\$400 \text{ billion}}{4} \\[6pt] &= \$100 \text{ billion}\end{aligned}$$

Tax Hikes

Therefore, the appropriate tax increase is

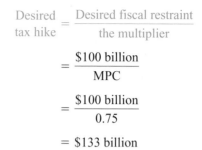

$$\frac{\text{Desired}}{\text{tax hike}} = \frac{\text{Desired fiscal restraint}}{\text{the multiplier}}$$

$$= \frac{\$100 \text{ billion}}{\text{MPC}}$$

$$= \frac{\$100 \text{ billion}}{0.75}$$

$$= \$133 \text{ billion}$$

Were taxes increased by this amount, consumers would reduce their consumption by $100 billion (= 0.75 × $133 billion). This cutback in consumption would set off the multiplier, leading to a cumulative reduction in spending of $400 billion. In Figure 11.6, aggregate demand would shift from AD_1 to AD_3.

Tax increases have been used to "cool" the economy on several occasions. In 1968, for example, the economy was rapidly approaching full employment and Vietnam War expenditures were helping to drive up prices. Congress responded by imposing a 10 percent surtax (temporary additional tax) on income, which took more than $10 billion in purchasing power away from consumers. Resultant multiplier effects reduced spending in 1969 over $20 billion and thus helped restrain price pressures.

In 1982 there was great concern that the 1981 tax cuts had been excessive and that inflation was emerging. To reduce that inflationary pressure, Congress withdrew some of its earlier tax cuts, especially those designed to increase investment spending. The net effect of the Tax Equity and Fiscal Responsibility Act of 1982 was to increase taxes roughly $90 billion for the years 1983 to 1985. This shifted aggregate demand leftward, thus reducing price-level pressures.

Reduced Transfers

The third option for fiscal restraint is to reduce transfer payments. *A cut in transfer payments works like a tax hike, reducing the disposable income of transfer recipients.* With less income, consumers spend less, as reflected in the MPC. The appropriate size of the transfer cut can be computed exactly as the desired tax increase in the preceding formula.

Although transfer cuts have the same fiscal impact as a tax hike, they're seldom used. An outright cut in transfer payments has a direct and very visible impact on recipients, including the aged, the poor, the unemployed, and the disabled. Hence, this policy option smacks of "balancing the budget on the backs of the poor." In practice, *absolute* cuts in transfer payments are rarely proposed. Instead, this lever is sometimes used to reduce the rate of increase in transfer benefits. Then only *future* benefits are reduced, and not so visibly.

FISCAL GUIDELINES

A Primer: Simple Rules

The essence of fiscal policy entails deliberate shifting of the aggregate demand curve. The steps required to formulate fiscal policy are straightforward:

- *Specify the amount of the desired AD shift* (excess AD or AD shortfall).
- *Select the policy tools needed to induce the desired shift.*

As we've seen, the fiscal policy toolbox contains a variety of tools for managing aggregate demand. When the economy is in a slump, the government can stimulate the economy with more government purchases, tax cuts, or an increase in transfer payments. When the economy is overheated, the government can reduce inflationary pressures by reducing government purchases, raising taxes, and cutting transfer payments. Table 11.2 summarizes the policy options and the desired use of each. As confusing as this list of options might at first appear, the guidelines are pretty simple.

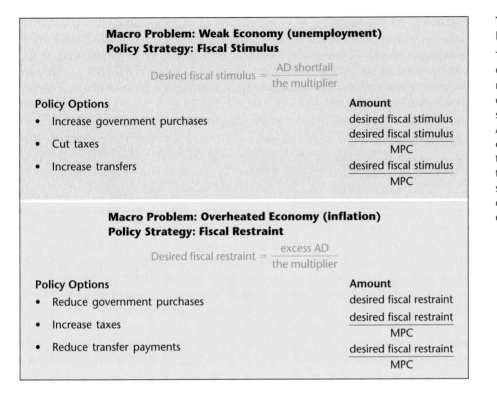

Macro Problem: Weak Economy (unemployment)
Policy Strategy: Fiscal Stimulus

$$\text{Desired fiscal stimulus} = \frac{\text{AD shortfall}}{\text{the multiplier}}$$

Policy Options	Amount
• Increase government purchases	desired fiscal stimulus
• Cut taxes	$\dfrac{\text{desired fiscal stimulus}}{\text{MPC}}$
• Increase transfers	$\dfrac{\text{desired fiscal stimulus}}{\text{MPC}}$

Macro Problem: Overheated Economy (inflation)
Policy Strategy: Fiscal Restraint

$$\text{Desired fiscal restraint} = \frac{\text{excess AD}}{\text{the multiplier}}$$

Policy Options	Amount
• Reduce government purchases	desired fiscal restraint
• Increase taxes	$\dfrac{\text{desired fiscal restraint}}{\text{MPC}}$
• Reduce transfer payments	$\dfrac{\text{desired fiscal restraint}}{\text{MPC}}$

TABLE 11.2
Fiscal Policy Primer

The goal of fiscal policy is to eliminate GDP gaps by shifting the AD curve rightward (to reduce unemployment) or leftward (to curb inflation). The desired shifts may be measured by the AD shortfall or the AD excess. In either case the desired fiscal initiative is equal to the desired shift divided by the multiplier. Once the size of the desired stimulus or restraint is known, the size of the appropriate policy options is easily calculated.

To use them all one needs to know is the size of the AD shortfall or excess and the marginal prosperity to consume.

The fiscal policy guidelines in Table 11.2 are a useful guide. However, they neglect a critical dimension of fiscal policy. Notice that we haven't said anything about how the government is going to *finance* its expenditures. Suppose the government wanted to stimulate the economy with a $50 billion increase in federal purchases. How would it pay for those purchases? If the government raised taxes for this purpose, the fiscal stimulus would be largely offset by resultant declines in consumption and investment. If, instead, the government *borrows* the money from the private sector, less credit may be available to finance consumption and investment, again creating an offsetting reduction in private demand. In either case, government spending may "crowd out" some private expenditure. If this happens, some of the intended fiscal stimulus may be offset by the **crowding out** of private expenditure. We examine this possibility further in Chapter 12 when we look at the budget deficits that help finance fiscal policy.

A Warning: Crowding Out

crowding out: A reduction in private-sector borrowing (and spending) caused by increased government borrowing.

Time Lags

Another limitation on fiscal policy is *time*. In the real world it takes time to recognize that the economy is in trouble. A blip in the unemployment or inflation rate may not signal a trend. Before intervening, we may want to be more certain that a recessionary or inflationary GDP gap is emerging. Then it will take time to develop a policy strategy and to get Congress to pass it. Once implemented, we'll have to wait for the many steps in the multiplier process to unfold. In the best of circumstances, the fiscal policy rescue may not arrive for quite a while. In the meantime, the very nature of our macro problems could change if the economy is hit with other internal or external shocks.

Pork Barrel Politics

Before putting too much faith in fiscal policy, we should also remember who designs and implements tax and spending initiatives: the U.S. Congress. Once a tax or spending plan arrives at the Capitol, politics take over. However urgent fiscal

restraint might be, members of Congress are reluctant to sacrifice any spending projects in their own districts. And if taxes are to be cut, they want *their* constituents to get the biggest tax savings. And no one in Congress wants a tax hike or spending cut *before* the election. This kind of pork barrel politics can alter the content and timing of fiscal policy. We'll examine the *politics* of fiscal policy further in Chapters 12 and 19.

THE ECONOMY TOMORROW

The Concern for Content

The guidelines for fiscal policy don't say anything about how the government spends its revenue or whom it taxes. The important thing is that the right amount of spending take place at the right time. In other words, insofar as our stabilization objectives are concerned, the content of total spending is of secondary interest; the level of spending is the only thing that counts.

The "Second Crisis"

But it does matter, of course, whether federal expenditures are devoted to military hardware, urban transit systems, or tennis courts. Our economic goals include not only full employment and price stability but also a desirable mix of output, an equitable distribution of income, and adequate economic growth. These other goals are directly affected by the content of total spending. The relative emphasis on, and sometimes exclusive concern for, stabilization objectives—to the neglect of related GDP content—has been designated by Joan Robinson as the "second crisis of economic theory." She explains:

> The first crisis arose from the breakdown of a theory which could not account for the *level* of employment. The second crisis arises from a theory that cannot account for the *content* of employment.
>
> Keynes was arguing against the dominant orthodoxy which held that government expenditure could not increase employment. He had to prove, first of all, that it could. He had to show that an increase in investment will increase consumption—that more wages will be spent on more beer and boots whether the investment is useful or not. He had to show that the secondary increase in real income [the multiplier effect] is quite independent of the object of the primary outlay. Pay men to dig holes in the ground and fill them up again if you cannot do anything else.
>
> There was an enormous orthodox resistance to this idea. The whole weight of the argument had to be on this one obvious point.
>
> The war was a sharp lesson in Keynesism. Orthodoxy could not stand up any longer. Government accepted the responsibility to maintain a high and stable level of employment. Then economists took over Keynes and erected the new orthodoxy. Once the point had been established the question should have changed. Now that we all agree that government expenditure can maintain employment, we should argue about what the expenditure should be for. Keynes did not *want* anyone to dig holes and fill them.[1]

The alternatives to paying people for digging and filling holes in the ground are virtually endless. With $2 trillion to spend each year, the federal government has great influence not only on short-run prices and employment but also on the mix of output, the distribution of income, and the prospects for long-run growth. In other words, fiscal policy helps shape the dimensions of the economy tomorrow.

---

[1]From "The Second Crisis of Economic Theory," by Joan Robinson, *American Economic Review,* May 1972, p. 6. Used by permission of American Economic Association.

One of the most debated issues in fiscal policy is the balance between the public and private sectors. Critics of Keynesian theory object to its apparent endorsement of government growth. They fear that depending on government spending to stabilize the economy will lead to an ever-larger public sector. They attribute the growth of the government's GDP share (from 10 percent in 1930 to 19 percent today) to the big-government bias of Keynesian fiscal policy.

In principle, this big-government bias doesn't exist. Keynes never said government spending was the only lever of fiscal policy. Even in 1934 he advised President Roosevelt to pursue only *temporary* increases in government spending. As we've seen, tax policy can be used to alter consumer and investor spending as well. Hence, fiscal policy can just as easily focus on changing the level of *private*-sector spending as on changing *public*-sector spending. In 1934, however, business confidence was so low that tax-induced increases in investment seemed unlikely. In less desperate times, the choice of which fiscal tool to use is a political decision, not a Keynesian mandate. President Clinton favored increased government spending to stimulate the economy, whereas President George W. Bush has favored tax cuts that bolster private spending.

In addition to choosing whether to increase public or private spending, fiscal policy must also consider the specific content of spending within each sector. Suppose we determine that stimulation of the private sector is preferable to additional government spending as a means of promoting full employment. We still have many choices. We could, for example, cut corporate taxes, cut individual taxes, reduce excise taxes, or increase Social Security benefits. Each alternative implies a different mix of consumption and investment and a different distribution of income. Congressional Democrats, for example, characterized President George W. Bush's original 2001 tax-cut plan as a "fat cat's tax break." They objected that too much of the tax cuts went to high-income taxpayers. They wanted a smaller tax cut for the rich, more tax relief for the poor, and more government spending on social programs. After months of negotiation, they got a compromise that altered both the mix of output and the distribution of income a bit more to their liking. The same kind of differences about the content of fiscal stimulus slowed the policy response to the September 11, 2001, terrorist attacks (see News).

Public vs. Private Spending

Output Mixes within Each Sector

IN THE NEWS

Bush Seeks More Tax Cuts, Democrats Higher Spending

Economic Stimulus Package Sparks Debate over Size of Unemployment Help

WASHINGTON—President Bush and Democrats played tug-of-war over an economic stimulus package, as the administration insisted on more tax cuts and Democrats appealed for more direct spending.

Administration officials told congressional leaders that Mr. Bush wants the bulk of his proposed $60 billion to $75 billion package to go toward tax cuts. The rest would go to spending—much of it earmarked for a package of unemployment and health-care benefits for jobless workers.

Democratic leaders generally are comfortable with the size of the White House proposal but want to spend much more of it on worker benefits. Many Democrats also favor massive spending on bridges, road and other infrastructure to stimulate the economy rather than tax cuts, which they argue would go mostly to businesses and wealthy individuals.

—John D. McKinnon

Source: *The Wall Street Journal,* October 5, 2001. Reprinted by permission of The Wall Street Journal. © 2001 Dow Jones and Company, Inc. All rights reserved worldwide. www.wsj.com

Analysis: Even when the need for fiscal stimulus is accepted, tough decisions still have to be made about whose taxes to cut, whose benefits to increase, or which programs to spend more on.

SUMMARY

- The economy's short-run macro equilibrium may not co-incide with full employment and price stability. Keynes advocated government intervention to shift the AD curve to a more desirable equilibrium.
- Fiscal policy refers to the use of the government's tax and spending powers to achieve desired macro outcomes. Options for fiscal stimulus include increasing government purchases, reducing taxes, and raising income transfers.
- Fiscal restraint may originate in reductions in government purchases, increases in taxes, or cuts in income transfers.
- Government purchases add directly to aggregate demand; taxes and transfers have an indirect effect by inducing changes in consumption and investment. This makes changes in government spending more powerful per dollar than changes in taxes or transfers.
- Fiscal policy initiatives have a multiplied impact on total spending and output. An increase in government spending,

for example, will result in more disposable income, which will be used to finance further consumer spending.
- The objective of fiscal policy is to close GDP gaps. To do this, the aggregate demand curve must shift by more than the size of the GDP gap to compensate for changing price levels. The desired shift is equal to the aggregate demand shortfall (or excess).
- Because of multiplier effects, the desired fiscal stimulus or restraint is always less than the size of the AD shortfall or excess.
- Changes in government spending and taxes alter the content of GDP and thus influence what to produce. Fiscal policy affects the relative size of the public and private sectors as well as the mix of output in each sector.

Key Terms

aggregate demand
income transfers
fiscal policy
equilibrium (macro)
recessionary GDP gap

fiscal stimulus
aggregate supply
AD shortfall
multiplier
marginal propensity to consume (MPC)

disposable income
fiscal restraint
inflationary GDP gap
AD excess
crowding out

Questions for Discussion

1. How can you tell if the economy is in equilibrium? How could you estimate the GDP gap?
2. Will an extra $20 billion per year spent on housing have the same impact on the economy as an extra $20 billion spent on interstate highways? Explain.
3. What happens to aggregate demand when transfer payments and the taxes to pay them both rise?
4. Why are the AD shortfall and AD excess larger than their respective GDP gaps? Are they ever the same size?
5. Will consumers always spend the same percentage of any tax cut? Why might they spend more or less than usual?
6. How does the slope of the AS curve affect the size of the AD shortfall? If the AS curve were horizontal, how large would the AD shortfall be in Figure 11.3?
7. According to the World View on page 230, what prompted South Korea's fiscal stimulus in 2001? Had the government not intervened, what might have happened?
8. How quickly should Congress act to remedy an AD excess or shortfall? What are the risks of quick fiscal policy responses?
9. Why do critics charge that fiscal policy has a "big-government bias"?
10. In the 2004 presidential election compaign, John Kerry proposed more government spending paid for with higher taxes on "the rich." What impact would those options have on macro equilibrium?

ALERT!

PROBLEMS The Student Problem Set at the back of this book contains numerical and graphing problems for this chapter.

WEB ACTIVITIES to accompany this chapter can be found on the Online Learning Center: **http://www.mhhe.com/economics/schiller10**

Deficits, Surpluses, and Debt

resident George W. Bush's string of massive tax cuts (2001–3) were the centerpiece of his fiscal policy. As we observed in the previous chapter, those cuts provided timely fiscal stimulus to the U.S. economy. They weren't an unmixed macro blessing, however. First of all, critics charged that the tax *cuts* were excessively skewed toward the rich. Second, Senator John Kerry and other leading Democrats pointed out that increased government spending on infrastructure and social programs would have provided even more fiscal stimulus and maybe a more desirable mix of output. Finally, a slew of Democrats and Republicans alike expressed alarm about the huge budget deficits that accompanied the tax cuts. Professor Laura Tyson, president Clinton's former economic adviser, went so far as to proclaim that those tax-cut deficits were "sapping America's strength" (see News on next page). As she saw it, the Bush tax cuts would ultimately hurt, not help, the U.S. economy.

How can this be?! Didn't we just show how tax cuts shift aggregate demand rightward, propelling the economy toward full employment? Why would anyone have misgivings about such beneficial intervention?

The core critique of fiscal stimulus focuses on the *budget* consequences of government pump-priming. Fiscal stimulus entails either tax cuts or increased government spending. Either option increases the size of the government's budget deficit. Hence, we have to ask more questions about how fiscal stimulus is *financed* and how the economy is affected by that financing. We start with these questions:

- **How do deficits arise?**
- **What harm, if any, do deficits cause?**
- **Who will pay off the accumulated national debt?**

As we'll see, the answers to these questions add another dimension to fiscal policy debates.

BUDGET EFFECTS OF FISCAL POLICY

Keynesian theory highlights the potential of **fiscal policy** to solve our macro problems. The guidelines are simple. Use fiscal stimulus—stepped-up government spending, tax cuts, increased transfers—to eliminate unemployment. Use fiscal restraint—less spending, tax hikes, reduced transfers—to keep inflation under control. From this perspective, the federal budget is a key policy lever for controlling the economy.

Use of the budget to stabilize the economy implies that federal expenditures and receipts won't always be equal. In a recession, for example, the government has sound reasons both to cut taxes and to increase its own spending. By reducing tax revenues and increasing expenditures simultaneously, however, the federal government will throw its budget out of balance. This practice is called **deficit spending,** a situation in which the government borrows funds to pay for spending that exceeds

fiscal policy: The use of government taxes and spending to alter macroeconomic outcomes.

Budget Surpluses and Deficits

The Bush Tax Cuts are Sapping America's Strength

When George W. Bush became President, the federal government enjoyed a projected 10-year budget surplus of $5.6 trillion. Today, less than three years later. Washington confronts sizable annual budget deficits regardless of the cyclical ups and downs of the economy. A growing number of private forecasters now predict a 10-year deficit of around $4 trillion—$6.7 trillion excluding the Social Security surplus. Government debt and interest payments are slated to double as a share of the economy over the next decade, crowding out private investment and government spending on anything else.

President Bush claims that the economic slowdown and the war on terrorism have triggered the nation's fiscal woes. But they are only part of the story. According to the Congressional Budget Office, over the next two years, the Bush tax cuts enacted since 2001 will cost nearly three times as much as the fighting and occupation in Afghanistan and Iraq, reconstruction and relief after September 11, and homeland security combined. What's more, these tax cuts are scheduled to explode, totaling $2 trillion over the decade. And that's assuming the sunset provisions phasing them out are enacted. If, as

seems likely, they are not, the 10-year budgetary costs of the tax cuts will rise by another $2 trillion.

The Administration argues that its tax cuts are necessary to stimulate growth in a sluggish economy. But this argument is specious. The economy may have needed a temporary infusion of additional demand during the past three years. But . . . even the Republican-controlled Joint Committee on Taxation, using a variety of dynamic scoring assumptions, was forced to admit that these cuts are likely to reduce the economy's long-term growth. Why? Any positive business-investment incentives from lower taxes will be out weighed by the curtailing of national saving and investment caused by mammoth budget deficits. To the extent that larger deficits diminish domestic saving, they eat into productive investment. To the extent that larger deficits are funded by borrowing from the rest of the world, they raise the nation's foreign debt and drive future income into servicing this debt. Contrary to the claims of Administration ideologues, larger deficits mean lower future living standards.

—Laura D'Andrea Tyson

Source: *BusinessWeek*, August 11, 2003. Reprinted by permission. Copyright 2003 by The McGraw-Hill Companies.

Analysis: Tax cuts reduce tax revenues and thereby enlarge the government's budget deficit. Larger deficits, in turn, may create new macro problems.

---

deficit spending: The use of borrowed funds to finance government expenditures that exceed tax revenues.

budget deficit: Amount by which government spending exceeds government revenue in a given time period.

budget surplus: An excess of government revenues over government expenditures in a given time period.

tax revenues. The size of the resulting **budget deficit** is equal to the difference between expenditures and receipts:

$$\text{Budget deficit} = \text{government spending} - \text{tax revenues} > 0$$

As Table 12.1 shows, the federal government had a huge budget deficit in 2004. In that year the government spent $2.3 trillion but had revenues of just less than $1.9 trillion, leaving a budget deficit of over $400 billion.

As Figure 12.1 illustrates, the 2004 deficit was the largest one in over 30 years—by a long shot. The figure also reveals, however, that budget deficits have been common. In fact, the few years (1969, 1998–2001) in which the government ran a **budget surplus** were clearly a rare departure from the historical pattern.

Keynesian View. What made the budget deficits of 2003–5 so remarkable was not only their absolute size but also their sudden emergence after a brief string of budget

TABLE 12.1
Budget Deficits and Surpluses

Budget deficits arise when government outlays (spending) exceed revenues (receipts). When revenues exceed outlays, a budget surplus exists.

Budget Totals (in billions of dollars)	2000	2001	2002	2003	2004
Revenues	2,025	1,991	1,853	1,782	1,871
Outlays	−1,789	−1,864	−2,011	−2,157	−2,293
Surplus (deficit)	236	127	(158)	(375)	(422)
Source: Congressional Budget Office.					

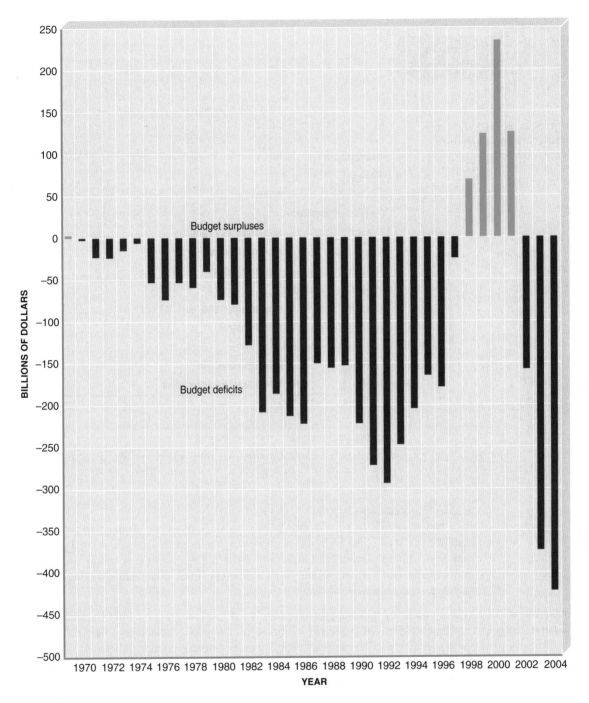

FIGURE 12.1
A String of Deficits

Budget deficits are overwhelmingly the rule, not the exception. A budget surplus was achieved in only four years (1998–2001) since 1970. These deficits result from both cyclical slowdowns and discretionary policies.

Source: Congressional Budget Office.

surpluses (1998–2001). Keynes wouldn't have been too surprised by such a turnaround however. As far as he was concerned, budget deficits and surpluses are just a routine byproduct of countercyclical fiscal policy. Deficits can easily arise when the government uses fiscal stimulus to increase aggregate demand, just as fiscal restraint (tax hikes; spending cuts) may cause a budget surplus. As Keynes saw it, ***the goal of macro policy is not to balance the budget but to balance the economy (at full employment).***

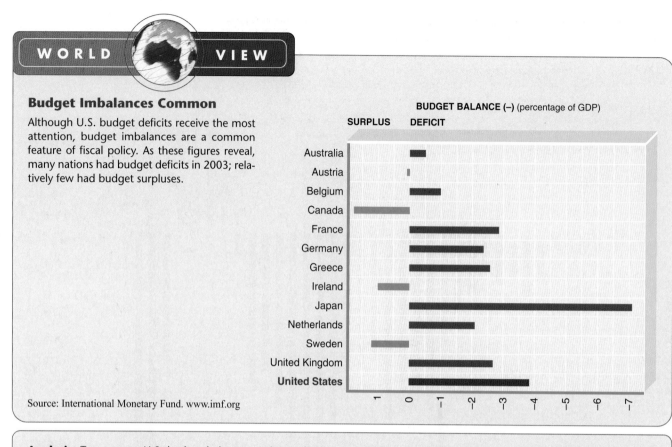

WORLD VIEW

Budget Imbalances Common

Although U.S. budget deficits receive the most attention, budget imbalances are a common feature of fiscal policy. As these figures reveal, many nations had budget deficits in 2003; relatively few had budget surpluses.

BUDGET BALANCE (−) (percentage of GDP)

SURPLUS   DEFICIT

Australia
Austria
Belgium
Canada
France
Germany
Greece
Ireland
Japan
Netherlands
Sweden
United Kingdom
United States

Source: International Monetary Fund. www.imf.org

Analysis: To compare U.S. budget balances to those of other industrialized countries, we must adjust for differences in size by forming the *ratio* of deficits or surpluses to GDP. By this measure, U.S. budget imbalances haven't been that large.

If a budget deficit or surplus was needed to shift aggregate demand to the desired equilibrium, then so be it. In Keynes's view, a balanced budget would be appropriate only if all other injections and leakages were in balance and the economy was in full-employment equilibrium. As the World View confirms, other nations evidently subscribe to that conclusion as well.

Discretionary vs. Automatic Spending

Theory aside, budget analysts have concluded that Congress couldn't balance the federal budget every year even if it wanted to. Congress doesn't have as much control over spending and revenues as people assume. Hence, neither deficits nor surpluses are necessarily the result of fiscal policy decisions. To understand the limits of budget management, we have to take a closer look at how budget outlays and receipts are actually determined.

At the beginning of each year, the president and Congress put together a budget blueprint for the next **fiscal year (FY).** They don't start from scratch, however. Most budget line items reflect commitments made in earlier years. In FY 2004, for example, the federal budget included $493 billion in Social Security benefits. The FY 2004 budget also provided for $34 billion in veterans benefits, $156 billion for interest payments on the national debt, and many billions more for completion of projects begun in previous years. Short of repudiating all prior commitments, there's little that Congress or the president can do to alter these expenditures in any given year. *To a large extent, current revenues and expenditures are the result of decisions made in prior years.* In this sense, much of each year's budget is considered "*uncontrollable.*"

At present, uncontrollables account for roughly 80 percent of the federal budget. This leaves only 20 percent for **discretionary fiscal spending**—that is, spending decisions

fiscal year (FY): The 12-month period used for accounting purposes; begins October 1 for the federal government.

discretionary fiscal spending: Those elements of the federal budget not determined by past legislative or executive commitments.

not "locked in" by prior legislative commitments. In recent years, rising interest payments and increasing entitlements (Social Security, Medicare, civil service pensions, etc.) have reduced the discretionary share of the budget even further. This doesn't mean that discretionary fiscal policy is no longer important; it simply means that the potential for *changing* budget outlays in any year is much smaller than it might first appear. Yet, the ability to *change* tax or spending levels is the force behind Keynesian fiscal policy. Recall that deliberate changes in government spending or taxes are the essence of **fiscal restraint** and **fiscal stimulus.** If most of the budget is uncontrollable, those policy levers are less effective.

Automatic Stabilizers. Most of the uncontrollable line items in the federal budget have another characteristic that directly affects budget deficits: their value *changes* with economic conditions. Consider unemployment insurance benefits. The unemployment insurance program, established in 1935, provides that persons who lose their jobs will receive some income (an average of $270 per week) from the government. The law establishes the *entitlement* to unemployment benefits but not the amount to be spent in any year. Each year's expenditure depends on how many workers lose their jobs and qualify for benefits. In 2002, for example, outlays for unemployment benefits increased by $17 billion. That increase in federal spending wasn't the result of any new policy decisions. Spending went up simply because more workers lost their jobs in the 2001 recession. The spending increase was *automatic,* not *discretionary.*

Welfare benefits also increased by $5 billion in 2002. This increase in spending also occurred automatically in response to changing economic conditions. As more people lost jobs and used up their savings, they turned to welfare for help. They were *entitled* to welfare benefits according to eligibility rules already written; no new congressional or executive action was required to approve this increase in government spending.

Notice that ***outlays for unemployment compensation and welfare benefits increase when the economy goes into recession.*** This is exactly the kind of fiscal policy that Keynes advocated. The increase in **income transfers** helps offset the income losses due to recession. These increased transfers therefore act as **automatic stabilizers**— injecting new spending into the circular flow during economic contractions. Conversely, transfer payments decline when the economy is expanding and fewer people qualify for unemployment or welfare benefits. Hence, no one has to pull the fiscal policy lever to inject more or less entitlement spending into the circular flow; much of it happens automatically.

Automatic stabilizers also exist on the revenue side of the federal budget. Income taxes are an important stabilizer because they move up and down with the value of spending and output. As we've observed, if household incomes increase, a jump in consumer spending is likely to follow. The resultant multiplier effects might create some demand-pull inflation. The tax code lessens this inflationary pressure. When you get more income, you have to pay more taxes. Hence, income taxes siphon off some of the increased purchasing power that might have found its way to product markets. Progressive income taxes are particularly effective stabilizers, as they siphon off increasing proportions of purchasing power when incomes are rising and decreasing proportions when aggregate demand and output are falling.

Automatic stabilizers imply that policymakers don't have total control of each year's budget. In reality, ***the size of the federal deficit or surplus is sensitive to expansion and contraction of the macro economy.***

Table 12.2 shows just how sensitive the budget is to cyclical forces. When the GDP growth rate falls by 1 percent, tax revenues decline by $28 billion. As the economy slows, people also turn to the government for additional income support: Unemployment benefits and other transfer payments increase by $2 billion. As a consequence, the budget deficit increases by $30 billion. This is exactly what happened in FY 2002: The recession that began in March 2001 shrank the budget surplus by roughly $30 billion.

fiscal restraint: Tax hikes or spending cuts intended to reduce (shift) aggregate demand.

fiscal stimulus: Tax cuts or spending hikes intended to increase (shift) aggregate demand.

income transfers: Payments to individuals for which no current goods or services are exchanged, such as Social Security, welfare, unemployment benefits.

automatic stabilizer: Federal expenditure or revenue item that automatically responds counter-cyclically to changes in national income, like unemployment benefits, income taxes.

Cyclical Deficits

TABLE 12.2

The Budget Impact of Cyclical Forces (in 2005 dollars)

Changes in economic conditions alter federal revenue and spending. When GDP growth slows, tax revenues decline and income transfers increase. This widens the budget deficit.

Higher rates of inflation increase both outlays and revenues but not equally.

The cyclical balance reflects these budget impacts.

- *Changes in Real GDP Growth*

When the GDP growth rate decreases by one percentage point:

1. Government spending (*G*) automatically increases for:
   - Unemployment insurance benefits
   - Food stamps
   - Welfare benefits
   - Social Security benefits
   - Medicaid

   Total increase in outlays: +$2 billion

2. Government tax revenues (*T*) automatically decline for:
   - Individual income taxes
   - Corporate income taxes
   - Social Security payroll taxes:

   Total decline in revenues: −$28 billion

3. **The deficit increases by $30 billion**

- *Changes in Inflation*

When the inflation rate increases by one percentage point:

1. Government spending (*G*) automatically increases for:
   - Indexed retirement and Social Security benefits
   - Higher interest payments

   Total increase in outlays: +$35 billion

2. Government tax revenues (*T*) automatically increase for:
   - Corporate income taxes
   - Social Security payroll taxes

   Total increase in revenues: +$42 billion

3. **The deficit shrinks by $7 billion**

Source: Congressional Budget Office (first year effects).

Inflation also affects the budget. Because Social Security benefits are automatically adjusted to inflation, federal outlays increase as the price level rises. This added expenditure is offset, however, by inflation-swollen tax receipts. Both Social Security payroll taxes and corporate profit taxes rise automatically with inflation. These offsetting expenditure and revenue effects almost cancel each other out: Table 12.2 shows that a one-point increase in the inflation rate *shrinks* the budget deficit by only $7 billion.

The most important implication of Table 12.2 is that neither the president nor the Congress has complete control of the federal deficit. ***Actual budget deficits and surpluses may arise from economic conditions as well as policy.*** Perhaps no one learned this better than President Reagan. In 1980 he campaigned on a promise to balance the budget. The 1981–82 recession, however, caused the actual deficit to soar. The president later had to admit that actual deficits aren't solely the product of big spenders in Washington.

President George H. Bush explained the persistence of huge deficits during his presidency on the same basis. During the recession of 1990–91, the nation's unemployment rate jumped by more than two percentage points. That setback alone added roughly $84 billion to the federal deficit.

President Clinton had more luck with the deficit. Although he increased discretionary spending in his first two years, the annual budget deficit *shrank* by over $90 billion between 1993 and 1995. Most of the deficit reduction was due to automatic stabilizers that kicked in as GDP growth accelerated and the unemployment rate fell. As the economy continued to grow sharply, the unemployment rate fell to 4 percent. That surge in the economy affected the budget by increasing tax revenues, reducing income transfers, and propelling the 1998 budget into surplus.

It was primarily the economy, not the president or the Congress, that produced the first budget surplus in a generation.

That part of the federal deficit attributable to cyclical disturbances (unemployment and inflation) is referred to as the **cyclical deficit.** As we've observed,

- *The cyclical deficit widens when GDP growth slows or inflation decreases.*
- *The cyclical deficit shrinks when GDP growth accelerates or inflation increases.*

If observed budget balances don't necessarily reflect fiscal policy decisions, how are we to know whether fiscal policy is stimulative or restrictive? Clearly, some other indicator is needed.

To isolate the effects of fiscal policy, economists break down the actual budget balance into *cyclical* and *structural* components:

$$\frac{\text{Total budget}}{\text{balance}} = \frac{\text{cyclical}}{\text{balance}} + \frac{\text{structural}}{\text{balance}}$$

The cyclical portion of the budget balance reflects the impact of the business cycle on federal tax revenues and spending. The **structural deficit** reflects fiscal policy decisions. Rather than comparing actual outlays to actual receipts, the structural deficit compares the outlays and receipts that would occur if the economy were at full employment.[1] This technique eliminates budget distortions caused by cyclical conditions. Any remaining changes in spending or outlays must be due to policy decisions. Hence, *part of the deficit arises from cyclical changes in the economy; the rest is the result of discretionary fiscal policy.*

Table 12.3 shows how the total, cyclical, and structural balances have behaved in recent years. Consider what happened to the federal budget in 2000–2001. In 2000 the federal surplus was $236 billion. In 2001 the surplus shrunk to $127 billion. The shrinking surplus suggests that the government was trying to stimulate economic activity with expansionary fiscal policies (tax cuts, spending hikes). But this wasn't the case. The primary reason for the smaller 2001 surplus was an abrupt halt in GDP growth. As the economy slipped into recession, the *cyclical* component shifted from a *surplus* of $128 billion in 2000 to only $21 billion in 2001. This $107 billion swing in the cyclical budget accounted for nearly all the increase in the total budget deficit. By contrast, the *structural* surplus decreased by only $2 billion, reflecting minimal *discretionary* fiscal stimulus.

By distinguishing between the structural budget and the actual budget, we can evaluate fiscal policy more accurately. Only changes in the structural deficit are relevant.

cyclical deficit: That portion of the budget balance attributable to short-run changes in economic conditions.

Structural Deficits

structural deficit: Federal revenues at full employment minus expenditures at full employment under prevailing fiscal policy.

For more historical data on cyclical and structural deficits, visit the U.S. Congressional Budget Office Web site at www.cbo.gov and look for "Historical Budget Data."

TABLE 12.3
Cyclical vs. Structural Budget Balances (in billions of dollars)

The budget balance includes both cyclical and structural components. Changes in the structural component result from policy changes; changes in the cyclical component result from changes in the economy. Between FY 2000 and FY 2001 the structural surplus shrank by only $2 billion, implying near-zero policy intervention. The cyclical surplus shrank by $107 billion, however, as the economy fell into a recession. As a result, the federal surplus was cut nearly in half.

Fiscal Year	Budget Balance	=	Cyclical Component	+	Structural Component
1995	−164		−17		−147
1996	−107		−11		−96
1997	−22		+61		−83
1998	+69		+91		−32
1999	+126		+114		+12
2000	+236		+128		+108
2001	+127		+21		+106
2002	−158		−12		−146
2003	−357		−44		−313

Source: Congressional Budget Office.

[1]The structural deficit is also referred to as the "full-employment," "high-employment," or "standardized" deficit.

Fiscal Policy in the Great Depression

In 1931 President Herbert Hoover observed, "Business depressions have been recurrent in the life of our country and are but transitory." Rather than proposing fiscal stimulus, Hoover complained that expansion of public-works programs had unbalanced the federal budget. In 1932 he proposed *cut-backs* in government spending and *higher* taxes. In his view, the "unquestioned balancing of the federal budget . . . is the first necessity of national stability and is the foundation of further recovery."

Franklin Roosevelt shared this view of fiscal policy. He criticized Hoover for not balancing the budget, and in 1933, warned Congress that "all public works must be considered from the point of view of the ability of the government treasury to pay for them."

As the accompanying figure shows, the budget deficit persisted throughout the Great Depression. But these deficits were the result of a declining economy, not stimulative fiscal policy. The structural deficit actually *decreased* from 1931 to 1933 (see figure), thereby restraining aggregate spending at a time when producers were desperate for increasing sales. Only when the structural deficit was expanded tremendously by spending during World War II did fiscal policy have a decidedly positive effect. Federal defense expenditures jumped from $2.2 billion in 1940 to $87.4 billion in 1944!

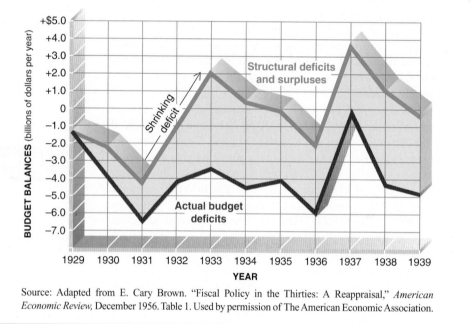

Source: Adapted from E. Cary Brown. "Fiscal Policy in the Thirties: A Reappraisal," *American Economic Review,* December 1956. Table 1. Used by permission of The American Economic Association.

Analysis: From 1931 to 1933, the structural deficit decreased from $4.5 billion to a $2 billion *surplus*. This fiscal restraint reduced aggregate demand and deepened the Great Depression.

In fact, ***only changes in the structural budget balance measure the thrust of fiscal policy.*** By this measure we categorize fiscal policy in the following ways:

- ***Fiscal stimulus is measured by the increase in the structural deficit*** (or shrinkage in the structural surplus).
- ***Fiscal restraint is gauged by the decrease in the structural deficit*** (or increase in the structural surplus).

According to this measure, fiscal policy was actually restrictive during the Great Depression, when fiscal stimulus was desperately needed (see News). Both Presidents Hoover and Roosevelt thought the government should rein in its spending when tax revenues declined, so as to keep the federal budget balanced. It took years of economic devastation before the fiscal policy lever was reversed. Also notice in Table 12.3 the abrupt shift from structural surplus (+$106) in 2001 to structural deficit (−$146) in 2002. This $252 billion swing in the structural balance reflects the fiscal stimulus at the Bush tax cuts and increased defense spending.

ECONOMIC EFFECTS OF DEFICITS

No matter what the origins of budget deficits, most people are alarmed by them. Should they be? What are the *consequences* of budget deficits?

We've already encountered one potential consequence of deficit financing: *If the government borrows funds to finance deficits, the availability of funds for private-sector spending may be reduced.* This is the **crowding-out** problem first noted in Chapter 11. If crowding out occurs, the increase in government expenditure will be at least partially offset by reductions in consumption and investment.

If the economy were operating at full employment, crowding out would be inevitable. At full employment, we'd be on the production possibilities curve, using all available resources. As Figure 12.2 reminds us, additional government purchases can occur only if private-sector purchases are reduced. In real terms, *crowding out implies less private-sector output.*

Crowding out is complete only if the economy is at full employment. If the economy is in recession. it's possible to get more public-sector output (like highways, schools, defense) without cutbacks in private-sector output. This possibility is illustrated by the move from point *c* to point *b* in Figure 12.2.

Tax cuts have crowding-out effects as well. The purpose of the 2001 tax cuts was to stimulate consumer spending. As the economy approaches full employment, however, how can more consumer output be produced? At the production possibilities limit, the added consumption will force cutbacks in either investment or government services. This was the outcome Professor Tyson feared would eventually "sap America's strength" (see News, p. 244).

What Figure 12.2 emphasizes is that *the risk of crowding out is greater the closer the economy is to full employment.* This implies that deficits are less appropriate at high levels of employment but more appropriate at low levels of employment.

Even if crowding out does occur, that doesn't mean that deficits are necessarily too big. Crowding out simply reminds us that there's an **opportunity cost** to government spending. We still have to decide whether the private-sector output crowded out by government expenditure is more or less desirable than the increased public-sector output.

Crowding Out

crowding out: A reduction in private-sector borrowing (and spending) caused by increased government borrowing.

Opportunity Cost

opportunity cost: The most desired goods or services that are forgone in order to obtain something else.

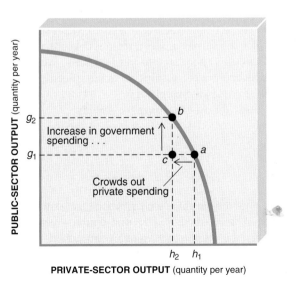

PUBLIC-SECTOR OUTPUT (quantity per year)

g_2 — Increase in government spending . . .

g_1 — Crowds out private spending

PRIVATE-SECTOR OUTPUT (quantity per year)

h_2 h_1

FIGURE 12.2
Crowding Out

If the economy is fully employed, an increase in public-sector expenditure (output) will reduce private-sector expenditure (output). In this case a deficit-financed increase in government expenditure moves the economy from point *a* to point *b*. In the process the quantity $h_1 − h_2$ of private-sector output is crowded out to make room for the increase in public-sector output (from g_1 to g_2). If the economy started at point *c*, however, with unemployed resources, crowding out need not occur.

The deficits of the 1980s financed a substantial military buildup. Private investment spending stagnated, however. Hence, the deficits were desirable only if the resulting change in the mix of output was itself desired.

President Clinton agreed that deficit reduction was desirable. He also, however, defended government expenditure on education, training, and infrastructure as public "investment." He believed that crowding out of private-sector expenditure wasn't necessarily an unwelcome outcome, especially if government investments were well targeted. Public investments in education, health care, and transportation systems might even accelerate long-term economic growth.

President George W. Bush saw things differently. He preferred a mix of output that included less public-sector output and more private-sector output. Accordingly, he doesn't really count any crowding out of government spending as a real loss. To minimize the crowding out of private-sector investment, he pushed *business* tax cuts in 2002 and 2003.

Interest-Rate Movements

Although the production possibilities curve illustrates the inevitability of crowding out at full employment, it doesn't explain *how* the crowding out occurs. Typically, the mechanism that enforces crowding out is the rate of interest. When the government borrows more funds to finance larger deficits, it puts pressure on financial markets. That added pressure may cause interest rates to rise. If they do, households will be less eager to borrow more money to buy cars, houses, and other debt-financed products. Businesses, too, will be more hesitant to borrow and invest. Hence, *rising interest rates are both a symptom and a cause of crowding out.*

Rising interests may also crowd out *government* spending in the wake of tax cuts. We know consumers will use their tax cuts to buy more goods and services. In the process, they'll undoubtedly borrow more money as well, to make larger purchases (plasma TVs, cars, etc.). This added borrowing will push interest rates up. As interest rates rise, government borrowing costs rise as well. According to the Congressional Budget Office, a one-point rise in interest rates increases Uncle Sam's debt expenses by over $100 billion over four years. These higher interest costs leave less room in government budgets for financing new projects.

How much interest rates rise again depends on how close the economy is to its productive capacity. If there is lots of excess capacity, interest-rate induced crowding out isn't very likely. As capacity is approached, however, interest rates and crowding out are both likely to increase.

ECONOMIC EFFECTS OF SURPLUSES

Although budget deficits are clearly the norm, we might at least ponder the economic effects of budget *surpluses*. Essentially, they are the mirror image of those for deficits.

Crowding In

When the government takes in more revenue than it spends, it adds to leakage in the circular flow. But Uncle Sam doesn't hide the surplus under a mattress. And the sums involved (such as $236 billion in FY 2000) are too large to put in a bank. Were the government to buy corporate stock with the budget surplus, it would effectively be nationalizing private enterprises. So where does the surplus go?

There are really only four potential uses for a budget surplus, namely,

- *Spend it on goods and services.*
- *Cut taxes.*
- *Increase income transfers.*
- *Pay off old debt ("save it").*

The first three options effectively wipe out the surplus by changing budget outlays or receipts. There are important differences here, though. The first option—increased government spending—not only reduces the surplus but enlarges the public sector. Cutting taxes or increasing income transfers, by contrast, puts the money into the hands of consumers and enlarges the private sector.

The fourth budget option is to use the surplus to pay off some of the debt accumulated from earlier deficits. This has a similar but less direct **crowding-in** effect. If Uncle Sam pays off some of his accumulated debt, households that were holding that debt (government bonds) will end up with more money. If they use that money to buy goods and services, then private-sector output will expand.

crowding in: An increase in private-sector borrowing (and spending) caused by decreased government borrowing.

Even people who haven't lent any money to Uncle Sam will benefit from the debt reduction. When the government reduces its level of borrowing, it takes pressure off market interest rates. As interest rates drop, consumers will be more willing and able to purchase big-ticket items such as cars, appliances, and houses, thus changing the mix of output in favor of private-sector production.

Cyclical Sensitivity

Like crowding out, the extent of crowding in depends on the state of the economy. In a recession, a surplus-induced decline in interest rates isn't likely to stimulate much spending. If consumer and investor confidence are low, even a surplus-financed tax cut might not lift private-sector spending much. This was clearly the case in 2001. Taxpayers were slow to spend their tax-rebate checks and businesses were initially unpersuaded by low interest rates to increase their investment spending.

THE ACCUMULATION OF DEBT

Because the U.S. government has had more years of budget deficits than budget surpluses, Uncle Sam has accumulated a large **national debt.** In fact, the United States started out in debt. The Continental Congress needed to borrow money in 1777 to continue fighting the Revolutionary War. The Congress tried to raise tax revenues and even printed new money (the Continental dollar) in order to buy needed food, tents, guns, and ammunition. But by the winter of 1777, these mechanisms for financing the war were failing. To acquire needed supplies, the Continental Congress plunged the new nation into debt.

national debt: Accumulated debt of the federal government.

Debt Creation

As with today's deficits, the Continental Congress acknowledged its loans by issuing bonds. Today the U.S. Treasury is the fiscal agent of the U.S. government. The Treasury collects tax revenues, signs checks for federal spending, and—when necessary—borrows funds to cover budget deficits. When the Treasury borrows funds, it issues **Treasury bonds;** these are IOUs of the federal government. People buy bonds—lend money to the U.S. Treasury—because bonds pay interest and are a very safe haven for idle funds.

Treasury bonds: Promissory notes (IOUs) issued by the U.S. Treasury.

The total stock of all outstanding bonds represents the national debt. It's equal to the sum total of our accumulated deficits, less net repayments in years when a budget surplus existed. In other words, *the national debt is a stock of IOUs created by annual deficit flows.* Whenever there's a budget deficit, the national debt increases. In years when a budget surplus exists, the national debt can be pared down.

Early History, 1776–1900

The United States began accumulating debt as soon as independence was declared. By 1783, the United States had borrowed over $8 million from France and $250,000 from Spain. Most of these funds were secretly obtained to help finance the Revolutionary War.

During the period 1790–1812, the United States often incurred debt but typically repaid it quickly. The War of 1812, however, caused a massive increase in the national debt. With neither a standing army nor an adequate source of tax revenues to acquire one, the U.S. government had to borrow money to repel the British. By 1816, the national debt was over $129 million. Although that figure seems tiny by today's standards, it amounted to 13 percent of national income in 1816.

1835–1836: Debt-Free! After the War of 1812, the U.S. government used recurrent budget surpluses to repay its debt. These surpluses were so frequent that the U.S. government was completely out of debt by 1835. In 1835 and again in 1836, the government had neither national debt nor a budget deficit. The dilemma in those years was how to use the budget *surplus!* Since there was no accumulated debt, the option of using the surplus to reduce the debt didn't exist. In the end, Congress decided simply to distribute the surplus funds to the states. That was the last time the U.S. government was completely out of debt.

The Mexican-American War (1846–48) necessitated a sudden increase in federal spending. The deficits incurred to fight that war caused a fourfold increase in the debt. That debt was pared down the following decade. Then the Civil War (1861–65) broke out, and both sides needed debt financing. By the end of the Civil War, the North owed over $2.6 billion, or approximately half its national income. The South depended more heavily on newly printed Confederate currency to finance its side of the Civil War, relying on bond issues for only one-third of its financial needs. When the South lost, however, neither Confederate currency nor Confederate bonds had any value.[2]

The Twentieth Century

The Spanish-American War (1898) also increased the national debt. But all prior debt was dwarfed by World War I, which increased the national debt from 3 percent of national income in 1917 to 41 percent at the war's end.

The national debt declined during the 1920s because the federal government was consistently spending less revenue than it took in. Budget surpluses disappeared quickly when the economy fell into the Great Depression, however, and the cyclical deficit widened (see News, page 250).

World War II. The most explosive jump in the national debt occurred during World War II, when the government had to mobilize all available resources. Rather than raise taxes to the fullest, the U.S. government restricted the availability of consumer goods. With consumer goods rationed, consumers had little choice but to increase their saving. Uncle Sam encouraged people to lend their idle funds to the U.S. Treasury by buying U.S. war bonds. The resulting bond purchases raised the national debt from 45 percent of GDP in 1940 to over 125 percent of GDP in 1946 (see Figure 12.3).

The 1980s. During the 1980s, the national debt jumped again—by nearly $2 *trillion*. This 10-year increase in the debt exceeded all the net debt accumulation since the country was founded. This time, however, the debt increase wasn't war-related. Instead, the debt explosion of the 1980s originated in recessions (1980–82 and 1990–91), massive tax cuts (1981–84), and increased defense spending. The recessions caused big jumps in the cyclical deficit while the Reagan tax cuts and military buildup caused the structural deficit to jump fourfold in only four years (1982–86).

The 1990s. The early 1990s continued the same trend. Discretionary federal spending increased sharply in the first two years of the George H. Bush administration. The federal government was also forced to bail out hundreds of failed savings and loan associations. Although taxes were raised a bit and military spending was cut back, the structural deficit was little changed. Then the recession of 1990–91 killed any chance of achieving smaller deficits. In only four years (1988–92) the national debt increased by another $1 trillion.

In 1993, the Clinton administration persuaded Congress to raise taxes, thereby reducing the structural deficit. Continuing recovery from the 1990–91 recession also reduced the cyclical deficit (see Table 12.3). Nevertheless, the budget deficits of 1993–96 pushed the national debt to over $5 trillion.

2000–. After a couple of years of budget surplus, the accumulated debt still exceeded $5.6 trillion in 2002. Then the Bush tax cuts and the defense buildup kicked in. As the structural deficit soared (Table 12.3) the national debt surged again. By 2005 the debt surpassed $8 trillion, which works out to nearly $27,000 of debt for every U.S. citizen.

WEBNOTE

The U.S. National Debt Clock tracks the debt. To see it, visit www.brillig.com/debt_clock or http://www.publicdebt.treas.gov/opd/opdpdodt.htm.

---

[2]In anticipation of this situation, European leaders had forced the South to guarantee most of its loans with cotton. When the South was unable to repay its debts, these creditors could sell the cotton they had held as collateral. But most holders of Confederate bonds or currency received nothing.

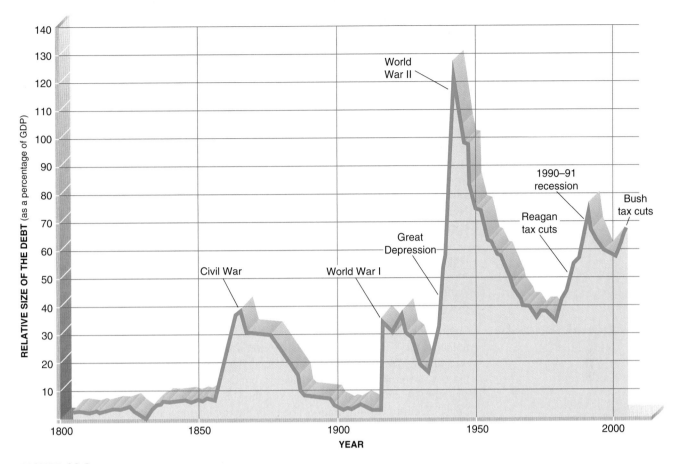

FIGURE 12.3
Historical View of the Debt/GDP Ratio

From 1790 to 1917, the national debt exceeded 10 percent of GDP only during the Civil War years. After 1917, however, the debt ratio grew sharply. World War I, the Great Depression, and World War II all caused major increases in the debt ratio. The tax cuts of 1981–84 and 2001–5 and the recessions of 1990–91 and 2001 caused further increases in the debt/GDP ratio.

Source: Office of Management and Budget.

Year	Total Debt Outstanding (millions of dollars)	Year	Total Debt Outstanding (millions of dollars)
1791	75	1920	24,299
1800	83	1930	16,185
1810	53	1940	42,967
1816	127	1945	258,682
1820	91	1960	286,331
1835	0	1970	370,919
1850	63	1980	914,300
1865	2,678	1985	1,827,500
1890	1,122	1990	3,163,000
1900	1,263	1995	5,076,000
1915	1,191	2000	5,629,000
		2005 (est)	8,133,000

Source: Office of Management and Budget.

TABLE 12.4
The National Debt

It took nearly a century for the national debt to reach $1 trillion. Then the debt tripled in a mere decade. The accumulated debt now exceeds $8 trillion.

WHO OWNS THE DEBT?

To the average citizen, the accumulated national debt is both incomprehensible and frightening. Who can understand debts that are measured in *trillions* of dollars? Who can ever be expected to pay them?

Liabilities = Assets

liability: An obligation to make future payment; debt.

asset: Anything having exchange value in the marketplace; wealth.

The first thing to note about the national debt is that it represents not only a liability but an asset as well. When the U.S. Treasury borrows money, it issues bonds. Those bonds are a **liability** for the federal government since it must later repay the borrowed funds. But those same bonds are an **asset** to the people who hold them. Bondholders have a claim to future repayment. They can even convert that claim into cash by selling their bonds in the bond market. Therefore, *national debt creates as much wealth (for bondholders) as liabilities (for the U.S. Treasury).* Neither money nor any other form of wealth disappears when the government borrows money.

The fact that total bond assets equal total bond liabilities is of little consolation to taxpayers confronted with $8 trillion of national debt and worry when, if ever, they'll be able to repay it. The fear that either the U.S. government or its taxpayers will be "bankrupted" by the national debt always lurks in the shadows. How legitimate is that fear?

Ownership of the Debt

Figure 12.4 shows who owns the bonds the U.S. Treasury has issued. The largest bondholder is the U.S. government itself: *Federal agencies hold roughly 50 percent of all outstanding Treasury bonds.* The Federal Reserve System, an independent agency of the U.S. government, acquires Treasury bonds in its conduct of monetary policy (see Chapters 14 and 15). Other agencies of the U.S. government also purchase bonds. The Social Security Administration, for example, maintains a trust fund balance to cover any shortfall between monthly payroll tax receipts and retirement benefits. Most of that balance is held in the form of interest-bearing Treasury bonds. Thus, one arm of the federal government (the U.S. Treasury) owes another arm (the U.S. Social Security Administration) a significant part of the national debt. Because Social Security has been accumulating huge annual reserves in recent years, it's now the largest single holder of the national debt.

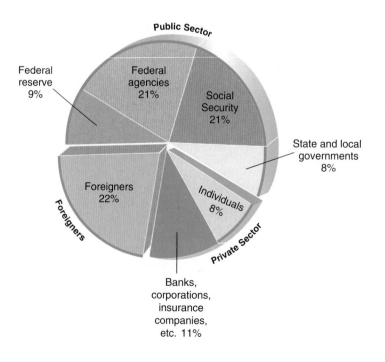

FIGURE 12.4
Debt Ownership

The bonds that create the national debt represent wealth that's owned by bondholders. Half of that wealth is held by the U.S. government itself. The private sector in the United States holds only 20 percent of the debt, and foreigners own about 22 percent.

Source: U.S. Treasury Department (2004 data).

State and local governments hold another 8 percent of the national debt. This debt, too, arises when state and local governments use their own budget surpluses to purchase interest-bearing Treasury bonds.

The general public owns *directly* only about 8 percent of the national debt. This private wealth is in the form of familiar U.S. savings bonds or other types of Treasury bonds. Even more private wealth is held *indirectly*. As Figure 12.4 shows, 11 percent of the national debt is held by banks, insurance companies, money-market funds, corporations, and other institutions. All this wealth is ultimately owned by the people who have deposits at the bank or in money market funds, who own stock in corporations, or who are insured by companies that hold Treasury bonds. Thus, *U.S. households hold nearly 20 percent of the national debt, either directly or indirectly.*

All the debt held by U.S. households, institutions, and government entities is referred to as **internal debt.** As Figure 12.4 illustrates, 80 percent of the national debt is internal. In other words, we owe most of the national debt to ourselves.

The remaining 22 percent of the national debt is held by foreign banks, corporations, households, and governments. U.S. Treasury bonds are attractive to global participants because of their relative security, the interest they pay, and the general acceptability of dollar-denominated assets in world trade. All the bonds held by foreign households and institutions is referred to as **external debt.**

internal debt: U.S. government debt (Treasury bonds) held by U.S. households and institutions.

external debt: U.S. government debt (Treasury bonds) held by foreign households and institutions.

refinancing: The issuance of new debt in payment of debt issued earlier.

BURDEN OF THE DEBT

It may be comforting to know that most of our national debt is owned internally, and much of it by the government itself. Figure 12.4 won't still the fears of most taxpayers, however, especially those who don't hold any Treasury bonds. From their perspective, the total debt still looks frightening.

How much of a "burden" the debt really represents isn't so evident. For nearly 30 years (1970–97), the federal government kept piling up more debt without apparent economic damage. As we saw earlier (Figure 12.3), deficits and debt stretched out over even longer periods in earlier decades.

How was the government able to pile debt upon debt? Quite simple: As debts have become due, the federal government has simply borrowed new funds to pay them off. New bonds have been issued to replace old bonds. This **refinancing** of the debt is a routine feature of the U.S. Treasury's debt management.

The ability of the U.S. Treasury to refinance its debt raises an intriguing question. What if the debt could be eternally refinanced? What if no one *ever* demanded to be paid off more than others were willing to lend Uncle Sam? Then the national debt would truly grow forever.

Two things are worrisome about this scenario. First, eternal refinancing seems like a chain letter that promises to make everyone rich. In this case, the chain requires that people hold ever-larger portions of their wealth in the form of Treasury bonds. People worry that the chain will be broken and that they'll be forced to repay all the outstanding debt. Parents worry that the scheme might break down in the next generation, unfairly burdening their own children or grandchildren (see cartoon).

Aside from its seeming implausibility, the notion of eternal refinancing seems to defy a basic maxim of economics, namely, that "there ain't no free lunch." Eternal refinancing makes it look as though government borrowing has no cost, as though federal spending financed by the national debt is really a free lunch.

There are two flaws in this way of thinking. The first relates to the interest charges that accompany debt. The second, and more important, oversight relates to the real economic costs of government activity.

Refinancing

"What's this I hear about you adults mortgaging my future?"

Analysis: The fear that present generations are passing the debt burden to future generations is exaggerated.

Debt Service

debt service: The interest required to be paid each year on outstanding debt.

Find out about the U.S. Treasury government bills, notes, and bonds at www.publicdebt.treas.gov/of/ofaucrt.htm.

With over $8 trillion in accumulated debt, the U.S. government must make enormous interest payments every year. **Debt service** refers to these annual interest payments. In FY 2005, the U.S. Treasury paid over $200 billion in interest charges. These interest payments force the government to reduce outlays for other purposes or to finance a larger budget each year. In this respect, *interest payments restrict the government's ability to balance the budget or fund other public-sector activities.*

Although the debt-servicing requirements may pinch Uncle Sam's spending purse, the real economic consequences of interest payments are less evident. Who gets the interest payments? What economic resources are absorbed by those payments?

As noted, most of the nation's outstanding debt is internal—that is, owned by domestic households and institutions. Therefore, most interest payments are made to people and institutions within the United States. *Most debt servicing is simply a redistribution of income from taxpayers to bondholders.* In many cases, the taxpayer and bondholder are the same person. In all cases, however, the income that leaks from the circular flow in the form of taxes to pay for debt servicing returns to the circular flow as interest payments. Total income is unchanged. Thus, debt servicing may not have any direct effect on the level of aggregate demand.

Debt servicing also has little impact on the real resources of the economy. The collection of additional taxes and the processing of interest payments require the use of some land, labor, and capital. But the value of the resources used for the processing of debt service is trivial—a tiny fraction of the interest payments themselves. This means that *interest payments themselves have virtually no direct opportunity cost.* The amount of goods and services available for other purposes is virtually unchanged as a result of debt servicing.

Opportunity Costs

If debt servicing absorbs few economic resources, can we conclude that the national debt really does represent a free lunch? Unfortunately not. But the concept of opportunity cost does provide a major clue about the true burden of the debt and who bears it.

Opportunity costs are incurred only when real resources (factors of production) are used. The amount of that cost is measured by the other goods and services that could have been produced with those resources, but weren't. As noted earlier, the *process* of debt servicing absorbs few resources and so has negligible opportunity cost. To understand the true burden of the national debt, we have to look at what that debt financed. *The true burden of the debt is the opportunity cost of the activities financed by the debt.* To assess that burden, we need to ask what the government did with the borrowed funds.

Government Purchases. Suppose Congress decides to upgrade our naval forces and borrows $10 billion for that purpose. What's the opportunity cost of that decision? The economic cost of the fleet upgrade is measured by the goods and services forgone in order to build more ships. The labor, land, and capital used to upgrade the fleet can't be used to produce something else. We give up the opportunity to produce another $10 billion worth of private goods and services when Congress upgrades the fleet.

The economic cost of the naval buildup is unaffected by the method of government finance. Whether the government borrows $10 billion or increases taxes by that amount, the forgone civilian output will still be $10 billion. *The opportunity cost of government purchases is the true burden of government activity, however financed.* The decision to finance such activity with debt rather than taxes doesn't materially alter that cost.

Transfer Payments. Suppose the government uses debt financing to pay for increased transfer payments rather than the purchase of real goods and services. What would be the burden of debt in this case?

Note first that transfer payments entail few real costs. Income transfers entail a redistribution of income from the taxpayer to the transfer recipient. The only direct costs of those transfer payments are the land, labor, and capital involved in the administrative process of making that transfer. Those direct costs are so trivial that they can be ignored. Whatever changes in output or prices occur because of transfer payments result from *indirect* behavioral responses. If taxpayers or transfer recipients respond to transfers by working, saving, or investing less, the economy may suffer. These important *indirect* effects must be distinguished from the *direct* cost of the transfers, which are minimal. As a result, the amount of income transferred isn't a meaningful measure of economic burden. Hence, the debt that originated in deficit-financed income transfers can't be viewed as a unique "burden" either.

The Real Trade-Offs

Although the national debt poses no special burden to the economy, the transactions it finances have a substantial impact on the basic questions of WHAT, HOW, and FOR WHOM to produce. The mix of output is influenced by how much deficit spending the government undertakes. The funds obtained by borrowing allow the federal government to bid for scarce resources. Private investors and consumers will have less access to loanable funds and be less able to acquire incomes or goods. The larger the deficit, the more the private sector gets squeezed. Hence, deficit financing allows the government to obtain more resources and change the mix of output. In general, *deficit financing tends to change the mix of output in the direction of more public-sector goods.*

As noted earlier, the deficits of the 1980s helped finance a substantial military buildup. The same result could have been financed with higher taxes. Taxes are more visible and always unpopular, however. By borrowing rather than taxing, the federal government's claim on scarce resources is less apparent. Either financing method allows the public sector to expand at the expense of the private sector. This resource reallocation reveals the true burden of the debt: *The burden of the debt is really the opportunity cost (crowding out) of deficit-financed government activity.* How large that burden is depends on how many unemployed resources are available and the behavioral responses of consumers and investors to increased government activity.

Notice also *when* that cost is incurred. If the military is upgraded this year, then the opportunity cost is incurred this year. It's only while resources are actually being used by the military that we give up the opportunity to use them elsewhere. Opportunity costs are incurred at the time a government activity takes place, not when the resultant debt is paid. In other words, *the primary burden of the debt is incurred when the debt-financed activity takes place.*

If the entire military buildup is completed this year, what costs are borne next year? None. The land, labor, and capital available next year can be used for whatever purposes are then desired. Once the military buildup is completed, no further resources are allocated to that purpose. The real costs of government projects can't be postponed until a later year. In other words, the real burden of the debt can't be passed on to future generations. On the contrary, future generations will benefit from the sacrifices made today to build ships, parks, highways, dams, and other public-sector projects. Future taxpayers will be able to *use* these projects without incurring the opportunity costs of their construction.

Economic Growth. Although future generations may benefit from current government spending, they may also be adversely affected by today's opportunity costs. Of particular concern is the possibility that government deficits might crowd out private investment. Investment is essential to enlarging our production possibilities and attaining higher living standards in the future. If federal deficits and debt-servicing requirements crowd our private investment, the rate of economic growth will slow, leaving future generations with less productive capacity than they would otherwise have. Thus, *if debt-financed government spending crowds out private investment, future generations will bear some of the debt burden.* Their burden will take the form of smaller-than-anticipated productive capacity. This is the kind of cost professor Tyson worried about (see News, p. 244).

There's no certainty that such crowding out will occur. Also, any reduction in private investment may be offset by public works (such as highways, schools, defense systems) that benefit future generations. So future generations may not suffer a net loss in welfare even if the national debt slows private investment and economic growth. From this perspective, *the whole debate about the burden of the debt is really an argument over the* **optimal mix of output.** If we permit more deficit spending, we're promoting more public-sector activity. On the other hand, limits on deficit financing curtail growth of the public sector. Battles over deficits and debts are a proxy for the more fundamental issue of private versus public spending.

Repayment. All this sounds a little too neat. Won't future generations have to pay interest on the debts we incur today? And might they even have to pay off some of the debt?

We've already observed that the collection of taxes and processing of interest payments absorb relatively few resources. Hence, the mechanisms of repayment entail little burden.

Notice also who *receives* future interest payments. When we die, we leave behind not only the national debt but also the bonds that represent ownership of that debt. Hence, future grandchildren will be both taxpayers *and* bondholders. If interest payments are made 30 years from today, only people who are alive and holding bonds at that time will receive interest payments. *Future interest payments entail a redistribution of income among taxpayers and bondholders living in the future.*

The same kind of redistribution occurs if and when our grandchildren decide to pay off the debt. Tax revenues will be used to pay off the debt. The debt payments will go to people then holding Treasury bonds. The entire redistribution will occur among people living in the future.

EXTERNAL DEBT

The nature of opportunity costs makes it difficult but not impossible to pass the debt burden on to future generations. The exception is the case of external debt.

No Crowding Out

When we borrow funds from abroad, we increase our ability to consume, invest, and finance government activity. In effect, other nations are lending us the income necessary to *import* more goods. If we can buy imports with borrowed funds (without offsetting exports), our real income will exceed our production possibilities. As Figure 12.5 illustrates, external borrowing allows us to enjoy a mix of output that lies *outside* our production possibilities curve. Specifically, *external financing allows us to get more public-sector goods without cutting back on private-sector production (or vice versa).* When we use external debt to finance government spending, we move

FIGURE 12.5
External Financing

A closed economy must forsake some private-sector output in order to increase public-sector output (see Figure 12.2). External financing temporarily eliminates that opportunity cost. Instead of having to move from *a* to *b*, external borrowing allows us to move from *a* to *d*. At point *d* we have more public output and no less private output.

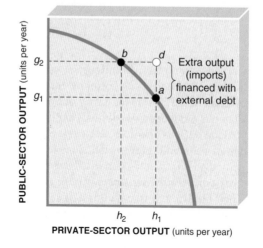

from point *a* to point *d* in Figure 12.5. Imported goods and services eliminate the need to cut back on private-sector activity, a cutback that would otherwise force us to point *b*. External financing eliminates this opportunity cost. The move from point *a* to point *d* reflects the additional imports financed by external debt.

The imports needn't be public-sector goods. A tax cut at point *b* might increase consumption and imports by $h_1 - h_2$, moving the economy to point *d*. At *d* we have *more* consumption and *no less* government activity.

External financing appears to offer the proverbial free lunch. It would be a free lunch if foreign lenders were willing to accumulate U.S. Treasury bonds forever. They would then own stacks of paper (Treasury bonds), and we'd consume some of their output (our imports) each year. ***As long as outsiders are willing to hold U.S. bonds, external financing imposes no real cost.*** No goods or services are given up to pay for the additional output received.

Repayment

Foreign investors may not be willing to hold U.S. bonds indefinitely. At some point they'll want to collect their bills. To do this, they'll cash in (sell) their bonds, then use the proceeds to buy U.S. goods and services. When this happens, the United States will be *exporting* goods and services to pay off its debts. Recall that the external debt was used to acquire imported goods and services. Hence, ***external debt must be repaid with exports of real goods and services.***

DEFICIT AND DEBT LIMITS

Although external and internal debts pose very different problems, most policy discussions overlook these distinctions. In policy debates, the aggregate size of the national debt is usually the only concern. The key policy questions are whether and how to limit or reduce the national debt.

The only way to stop the growth of the national debt is to eliminate the budget deficits that create debt. The first step in debt reduction, therefore, is a balanced annual budget. A balanced budget will at least stop the debt from growing further. **Deficit ceilings** are explicit limitations on the size of the annual budget deficit. A deficit ceiling of zero compels a balanced budget.

Deficit Ceilings

deficit ceiling: An explicit, legislated limitation on the size of the budget deficit.

The Balanced Budget and Emergency Deficit Control Act of 1985—popularly referred to as the Gramm-Rudman-Hollings Act—was the first explicit attempt to force the federal budget into balance. The essence of the Gramm-Rudman Act was simple:

- First, it set a lower ceiling on each year's deficit, until budget balance was achieved.
- Second, it called for automatic cutbacks in spending if Congress failed to keep the deficit below the ceiling.

The original Gramm-Rudman law required Congress to pare the deficit from over $200 billion in FY 1985 to zero (a balanced budget) by 1991. But Congress wasn't willing to cut spending and increase taxes enough to meet those targets. And the Supreme Court declared that the "automatic" mechanism for spending cuts was unconstitutional.

In 1990, President George H. Bush and the Congress developed a new set of rules for reducing the deficit. They first acknowledged that they lacked total control of the deficit. At best, Congress could close the *structural* deficit by limiting discretionary spending or raising taxes. The Budget Enforcement Act (BEA) of 1990 laid out a plan for doing exactly this. The BEA set separate limits on defense spending, discretionary domestic spending, and international spending. It also required that any new spending initiative be offset with increased taxes or cutbacks in other programs.

The Budget Enforcement Act was successful in reducing the structural deficit somewhat. But the political pain associated with spending cuts and higher taxes was too great for elected officials to bear. President George H. Bush's reelection bid was

For a discussion of deficits and deficit-reduction efforts, visit the U.S. Congressional Budget Office at www.cbo.gov.

damaged by his willingness to raise taxes. And Democrats took heat for reducing the growth of social programs.

Soon thereafter, legislated deficit ceilings proved to be more political ornaments than binding budget mandates. They didn't surface again until 2004.

Debt Ceilings

debt ceiling: An explicit, legislated limit on the amount of outstanding national debt.

Explicit **debt ceilings** are another mechanism for forcing Congress to adopt specific fiscal policies. A debt ceiling can be used either to stop the accumulation of debt or to force the federal government to start *reducing* the accumulated national debt. In effect, debt ceilings are a backdoor approach to deficit reduction. *Like deficit ceilings, debt ceilings are really just political mechanisms for forging compromises on how best to use budget surpluses or deficits.*

THE ECONOMY TOMORROW

Dipping into Social Security

The Social Security Trust Fund has been a major source of funding for the federal government for over 20 years. Since 1985, the Trust Fund has collected more payroll (FICA) taxes each year than it has paid out in retirement benefits. As we noted already, all of those surpluses have been "invested" in Treasury securities, making the Social Security Trust Fund the U.S. Treasury's largest creditor. The Trust Fund now holds more than $1.5 trillion of Treasury securities and is still accumulating more. Between 2005 and 2014, the Trust Fund will acquire another $2 trillion in Treasury securities.

Aging Baby Boomers

The persistent surpluses in the Social Security Trust Fund are largely the result of aging Baby Boomers. In the 15 years after World War II ended, birthrates soared. These Baby Boomers are now in their peak earning years (45–60) and paying lots of payroll taxes. This keeps the Social Security Trust Fund flush with cash.

As we peer into the economy tomorrow, however, the fiscal outlook is not so bright. The Baby Boomers are fast approaching retirement age. When they do retire, the Baby Boomers will throw the budget of the Social Security Trust Fund out of whack. Today, there are 3.2 active (tax-paying) workers for every retiree. By 2015, that worker-retiree ratio will slip to 2.7. By 2030, there'll be only 2 workers for every retiree (see Table 12.5). By then, the Trust Fund payroll-tax collections will be a lot smaller than the benefit promises made to retired Baby Boomers. When that happens, a primary source of government financing will disappear.

Social Security Deficits

In fact, the Trust Fund balance shifts from annual surpluses to annual deficits as soon as 2014. After that, Social Security will be able to pay promised benefits only if (1) the U.S. Treasury pays all interest due on bonds held by the Trust Fund and, ultimately, (2) the U.S. Treasury redeems the $3 trillion-plus of bonds the Trust Fund will then be holding. This is what scares aging Baby Boomers (and should worry you!).

TABLE 12.5
Changing Worker-Retiree Ratios

Fifty years ago there were over 16 tax-paying workers for every retiree. Today there are only 3.2, and the ratio slips below 3 when the Baby Boomers start retiring. This demographic change will convert Social Security surpluses into deficits, causing future budget problems.

Year	Workers per Beneficiary	Year	Workers per Beneficiary
1950	16.5	2000	3.4
1960	5.1	2015	2.7
1970	3.7	2030	2.0

Source: U.S. Social Security Administration.

The Baby Boomers wonder where the Treasury is going to get the funds needed to repay the Social Security Trust Fund. There really aren't many options. ***To pay back Social Security loans, the Congress will have to raise future taxes significantly, make substantial cuts in other (non–Social Security) programs or sharply increase budget deficits.*** None of these options is attractive. Worse yet, the budget squeeze created by the Social Security payback will severely limit the potential for discretionary fiscal policy.

When GDP growth slows in the economy tomorrow, it will be increasingly difficult to cut taxes or increase government spending while the U.S. Treasury is scurrying to repay Social Security Trust Fund loans. Aging Baby Boomers worry that Congress might instead cut their promised retirement benefits.

SUMMARY

- Budget imbalances result from both discretionary fiscal policy (structural deficits and surpluses) and cyclical changes in the economy (cyclical deficits and surpluses).
- Fiscal restraint is measured by the reduction in the structural deficit; fiscal stimulus occurs when the structural deficit increases.
- Automatic stabilizers increase federal spending and reduce tax revenues during recessions. When the economy expands, they have the reverse effect, thereby shrinking the cyclical deficit.
- Deficit financing of government expenditure may crowd out private investment and consumption. The risk of crowding out increases as the economy approaches full employment. If investment becomes the opportunity cost of increased government spending or consumer tax cuts, economic growth may slow.
- Crowding in refers to the increase in private-sector output made possible by a decline in government borrowing.
- Each year's deficit adds to the national debt. The national debt grew sporadically until World War II and then skyrocketed. Tax cuts, recessions, and increased government spending since 1980 have increased the national debt to over $8 trillion.

- Budget surpluses may be used to finance tax cuts or more government spending, or used to reduce accumulated national debt.
- Every dollar of national debt represents a dollar of assets to the people who hold U.S. Treasury bonds. Most U.S. bonds are held by government agencies, U.S. households, and U.S. banks, insurance companies, and other institutions.
- The real burden of the debt is the opportunity cost of the activities financed by the debt. That cost is borne at the time the deficit-financed activity takes place. The benefits of debt-financed activity may extend into the future.
- External debt permits the public sector to expand without reducing private-sector output. External debt also makes it possible to shift some of the real debt burden on to future generations.
- Deficit and debt ceilings are largely symbolic efforts to force consideration of real trade-offs, to restrain government spending, and to change the mix of output.
- The coming retirement of the Baby Boomers (born 1946–60) will transform Social Security surpluses into deficits, imposing severe constraints on future fiscal policy.

Key Terms

fiscal policy
deficit spending
budget deficit
budget surplus
fiscal year (FY)
discretionary fiscal spending
fiscal restraint
fiscal stimulus
income transfers

automatic stabilizer
cyclical deficit
structural deficit
crowding out
opportunity cost
crowding in
national debt
Treasury bonds
liability

asset
internal debt
external debt
refinancing
debt service
optimal mix of output
deficit ceiling
debt ceiling

Questions for Discussion

1. Who paid for the Revolutionary War? Did the deficit financing initiated by the Continental Congress pass the cost of the war on to future generations?

2. In what ways do future generations benefit from this generation's deficit spending? Cite three examples.

3. What's considered "too much" debt or "too large" a deficit? Are you able to provide any guidelines for deficit or debt ceilings?

4. If deficit spending "crowds out" some private investment, could future generations be worse off? If external financing eliminates crowding out, are future generations thereby protected?

5. If tax cuts crowd out government spending, is the economy worse off? (see News, p. 244.)

6. A constitutional amendment has been proposed that would require Congress to balance the budget each year. Is it possible to balance the budget each year? Is it desirable?

7. What should the government do with a budget surplus?

8. By how much did defense spending increase in 1940 to 1944? (See back endpapers of this book.) What was crowded out?

9. How long would it take to pay off the national debt? How would the economy be affected?

10. Which of the following options do you favor for resolving future Social Security deficits? What are the advantages and disadvantages of each option? (a) cutting Social Security benefits, (b) raising payroll taxes, (c) cutting non–Social Security programs, (d) raising income taxes.

ALERT!

PROBLEMS The Student Problem Set at the back of this book contains numerical and graphing problems for this chapter.

WEB ACTIVITIES to accompany this chapter can be found on the Online Learning Center: **http://www.mhhe.com/economics/schiller10**

PART 5

Monetary Policy Options

Monetary policy tries to alter macro outcomes by managing the amount of money available in the economy. By changing the money supply and/or interest rates, monetary policy seeks to shift aggregate demand in the desired direction. Chapters 13 through 15 illustrate how this policy lever works.

Money and Banks

Sophocles, the ancient Greek playwright, had very strong opinions about the role of money. As he saw it, "Of evils upon earth, the worst is money. It is money that sacks cities, and drives men forth from hearth and home; warps and seduces native intelligence, and breeds a habit of dishonesty."

In modern times, people may still be seduced by the lure of money and fashion their lives around its pursuit. Nevertheless, it's hard to imagine an economy functioning without money. Money affects not only morals and ideals but also the way an economy works.

This and the following two chapters examine the role of money in the economy today. We begin with a very simple question:

- **What is money?**

As we'll discover, money isn't exactly what you might think it is. There's a lot more money in the economy than there is cash. And there's a lot more income around than money. So money is something quite different from either cash or income. Once we've established the characteristics of money, we go on to ask:

- **How is money created?**
- **What role do banks play in the circular flow of income and spending?**

In Chapter 14 we look at how the Federal Reserve System controls the amount of money created. In Chapter 15 we look at the implications for monetary policy, another policy lever in our basic macro model.

WHAT IS "MONEY"?

To appreciate the significance of money for a modern economy, imagine for a moment that there were no such thing as money. How would you get something for breakfast? If you wanted eggs for breakfast, you'd have to tend your own chickens or go see Farmer Brown. But how would you pay Farmer Brown for his eggs? Without money, you'd have to offer him some goods or services that he could use. In other words, you'd have to engage in primitive **barter**—the direct exchange of one good for another—in order to get eggs for breakfast. You'd get those eggs only if Farmer Brown happened to want the particular goods or services you had to offer.

barter: The direct exchange of one good for another, without the use of money.

The use of money greatly simplifies market transactions. It's a lot easier to exchange money for eggs at the supermarket than to go into the country and barter with farmers every time you crave some eggs. Our ability to use money in market transactions, however, depends on the grocer's willingness to accept money as a *medium of exchange*. The grocer sells eggs for money only because he can use the same money to pay his help and buy the goods he himself desires. He too can exchange money for goods and services.

WORLD VIEW

The Cashless Society

Bartering Chokes Russian Economy

NARO-FOMINSK, RUSSIA—Natalya Karpova, a supervisor at a fabric factory here on the outskirts of Moscow, heard good news a couple of weeks ago. Three carloads of concrete utility poles had arrived at the train station.

This was a matter of utmost importance to Karpova, because her factory was a year behind on its electric bill and had no cash on hand. The electric company agreed to accept utility poles instead, but how to pay for utility poles with no rubles?

Simple. First, her factory shipped fabric 200 miles to a sewing factory in Nizhny Novgorod. In exchange for the fabric, that factory sewed shirts for the security guards who work at a nearby automobile manufacturer. In exchange for the shirts, the auto factory shipped a car and truck to a concrete plant. In exchange for the vehicles, the concrete plant delivered the poles to the electric company.

Thus did the Narfomsholk fabric factory pay for the power to run its dye machines.

But only for a while. "Now they want a steam shovel," said Karpova, with a little sigh.

This is how Karpova's factory and much of Russia's industry survives these days: barter. By some estimates, it accounts for almost three-fourths of all transactions.

Barter is poisoning the development of capitalism in Russia because it consumes huge amounts of time that would be better spent producing goods.

Many workers have no expectation of a real paycheck. Unpaid wages now amount to an estimated $11 billion. Instead of money, the workers are stuck with whatever the factory or farm is handing out, usually what it produces. The practice is so common now that only the more bizarre substitutes for wages draw notice, such as bras or coffins.

—Sharon LaFraniere

Source: *Washington Post*, September 3, 1998. © 1998, The Washington Post. Reprinted with permission. www.washingtonpost.com

Analysis: When the Russian ruble lost its value, people would no longer accept it in payment. Market transactions had to be bartered, a clumsy and inefficient process.

Without money, the process of acquiring goods and services would be much more difficult and time-consuming. This was evident when the value of the Russian ruble plummeted. Trading goods for Farmer Brown's eggs seems simple compared to the complicated barter deals Russian factories had to negotiate when paper money was no longer accepted (see World View). And Russian workers certainly would've preferred to be paid in cash rather than in bras and coffins.

THE MONEY SUPPLY

Many Types of Money

Although markets can't function well without money, they can get along without *dollars*. In the early days of colonial America, there were no U.S. dollars; a lot of business was conducted with Spanish and Portuguese gold coins. Later, people used Indian wampum, then tobacco, grain, fish, and furs as mediums of exchange. Throughout the colonies, gunpowder and bullets were frequently used for small change. These forms of money weren't as convenient as U.S. dollars, but they did the job.

This historical perspective on money highlights its essential characteristics. *Anything that serves all the following purposes can be thought of as money:*

- *Medium of exchange:* is accepted as payment for goods and services (and debts).
- *Store of value:* can be held for future purchases.
- *Standard of value:* serves as a yardstick for measuring the prices of goods and services.

All the items used during the colonial days satisfied these conditions and were thus properly regarded as money.

WEBNOTE

For a brief history of coins and to learn how coins are made, visit the U.S. mint at www.usmint.gov.

After the colonies became an independent nation, the U.S. Constitution prohibited the federal government from issuing paper money. Money was instead issued by state-chartered banks. Between 1789 and 1865, over 30,000 different paper bills were issued by 1,600 banks in 34 states. People often preferred to get paid in gold, silver, or other commodities rather than in one of these uncertain currencies.

The first paper money the federal government issued consisted of $10 million worth of "greenbacks," printed in 1861 to finance the Civil War. The National Banking Act of 1863 gave the federal government permanent authority to issue money.

Modern Concepts

The "greenbacks" we carry around today aren't the only form of "money" we use. Most people realize this when they offer to pay for goods with a check rather than cash. People do distinguish between "cash" and "money," and for good reason. The "money" you have in a checking account can be used to buy goods and services or to pay debts, or it can be retained for future use. In these respects, your checking account balance is as much a part of your "money" as are the coins and dollars in your pocket or purse. You can access your balance by writing a check or using an ATM or debit card. Checks are more convenient than cash because they eliminate trips to the bank. Checks are also safer: Lost or stolen cash is gone forever; checkbooks and credit cards are easily replaced at little or no cost. We might use checks even more frequently if everyone accepted them.

> **money:** Anything generally accepted as a medium of exchange.

There's nothing unique about cash, then, insofar as the market is concerned. *Checking accounts can and do perform the same market functions as cash.* Accordingly, we must include checking account balances in our concept of **money.** The essence of money isn't its taste, color, or feel but, rather, its ability to purchase goods and services.

Credit cards are another popular medium of exchange. People use credit cards for about one-third of all purchases over $100. This use is not sufficient, however, to qualify credit cards as a form of "money." Credit card balances must be paid by check or cash. The same holds true for balances in online electronic credit accounts ("e-cash"). Electronic purchases on the Internet or online services are ultimately paid by withdrawals from a bank account (by check or computer). Online payment mechanisms and credit cards are a payment *service,* not a final form of payment (credit card companies charge fees and interest for this service). The cards themselves are not a store of value, in contrast to cash or bank account balances.

The Diversity of Bank Accounts. To determine how much money is available to purchase goods and services, we need to count up all our coins and currency—as well as our bank account balances. This effort is complicated by the variety of bank accounts people have. In addition to simple no-interest checking accounts at full-service banks, people have bank accounts that pay interest, offer automatic transfers, require minimum holding periods, offer overdraft protection, or limit the number of checks that can be written. People also have "bank" accounts in credit unions, brokerage houses, and other nontraditional financial institutions.

Although all bank account balances can be spent, they're not all used the same way. People use regular checking accounts all the time to pay bills or make purchases. But consumers can't write checks on most savings accounts. And few people want to cash in a certificate of deposit just to go to the movies. Hence, *some bank accounts are better substitutes for cash than others.*

M1: Cash and Transactions Accounts

> **money supply:** (M1) Currency held by the public, plus balances in transactions accounts.

Several different measures of money have been developed to accommodate the diversity of bank accounts and other payment mechanisms. The narrowest definition of the **money supply** is designated **M1,** *which includes*

- *Currency in circulation*
- *Transactions account balances*
- *Traveler's checks*

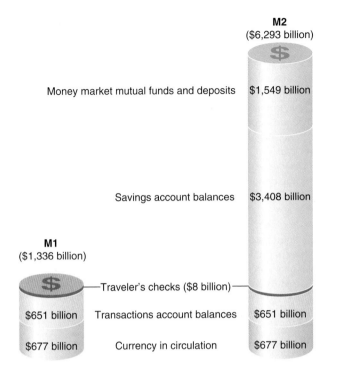

FIGURE 13.1
Composition of the Money Supply

Cash is only a part of the money supply. People also have easy access to transactions account balances and various savings account balances that are counted in measures of the money supply (M1 and M2). Because people hold so much money in money market mutual funds and savings (time-deposit) accounts, M2 is nearly five times larger than M1.

Source: Federal Reserve (June 2004 data).

As Figure 13.1 indicates, the second largest component of this basic money supply (M1) is **transactions account** balances, which are the balances in bank accounts that are readily accessed by check. Most people refer to these simply as "checking accounts." The term "transactions account" is broader, however, including NOW accounts, ATS accounts, credit union share drafts, and demand deposits at mutual savings banks. *The distinguishing feature of all transactions accounts is that they permit direct payment to a third party (by check or debit card),* without requiring a trip to the bank to make a special withdrawal. Because of this feature, transactions accounts are the readiest substitutes for cash in market transactions. Traveler's checks issued by nonbank firms such as American Express can also be used directly in market transactions, just like good old-fashioned cash.

Transactions accounts aren't the only substitute for cash. People can and do dip into savings accounts on occasion. People sometimes even cash in their certificates of deposit in order to buy something, despite the interest penalty associated with early withdrawal. And banks have made it easy to transfer funds from one type of account to another. Savings accounts can be transformed into transactions accounts with a phone call or computer instruction. As a result, *savings account balances are almost as good a substitute for cash as transactions account balances.*

Another popular way of holding money is to buy shares of money market mutual funds. Deposits into money market mutual funds are pooled and used to purchase interest-bearing securities such as Treasury bills. The interest rates paid on these funds are typically higher than those paid by banks. Moreover, the deposits made into the funds can often be withdrawn immediately, just like those in transactions accounts. When interest rates are high, deposits move out of regular transactions accounts into these money market mutual funds in order to earn a higher return.

Additional measures of the money supply have been constructed to account for the possibility of using savings account balances, money market mutual funds, and various other deposits to finance everyday spending. The most widely watched money measure is **M2,** which includes all of M1 *plus* balances in savings accounts, money market mutual funds, and some CDs ("time deposits"). As Figure 13.1 shows, M2 is

transactions account: A bank account that permits direct payment to a third party, for example, with a check.

M2: M1 + Savings Accounts, etc.

Everything you want to know about currency can be found at www.frbatlanta.org/publica/brochure/fundfac/money.htm.

M2 money supply: M1 plus balances in most savings accounts and money market mutual funds.

TABLE 13.1
Alternative Measures of the Money Supply

Measures of the money supply are intended to gauge the extent of purchasing power held by consumers. But the extent of purchasing power depends on how accessible assets are and how often people use them. The various money supply measures reflect variations in the liquidity and accessibility of assets.

Measure	Components
M1	Currency in circulation outside of bank vaults
	Demand deposits at commercial banks
	NOW and ATS accounts
	Credit union share drafts
	Demand deposits at mutual savings banks
	Traveler's checks (nonbank)
M2	M1 plus:
	Savings accounts
	Time deposits of less than $100,000
	Money market mutual funds
M3	M2 plus:
	Time deposits larger than $100,000
	Repurchase agreements
	Overnight Eurodollars
L	M3 plus other liquid assets, for example:
	Treasury bills
	U.S. savings bonds
	Bankers' acceptances
	Term Eurodollars
	Commercial paper

aggregate demand: The total quantity of output demanded at alternative price levels in a given time period, *ceteris paribus*.

nearly five times as large as M1. Table 13.1 summarizes the content of these and two other measures of money.

Our concern about the specific nature of money stems from our broader interest in **aggregate demand.** What we want to know is how much purchasing power consumers have, since this will affect their ability to purchase goods and services. What we've observed, however, is that money isn't so easily defined. How much spending power people have depends not only on the number of coins in their pockets but also on their willingness to write checks, make trips to the bank, or convert other assets into cash.

In an increasingly complex financial system, the core concept of "money" isn't easy to pin down. Nevertheless, the official measures of the money supply (particularly M1 and M2) are fairly reliable benchmarks for gauging how much purchasing power market participants have.

CREATION OF MONEY

Once we've decided what money is, we still have to explain where it comes from. Part of the explanation is simple. Currency must be printed. Some nations use private printers for this purpose, but all U.S. currency is printed by the Bureau of Engraving and Printing in Washington, D.C. Coins come from the U.S. mints located in Philadelphia and Denver. As we observed in Figure 13.1, however, currency is a small fraction of our total money supply. So we need to look elsewhere for the origins of most money. Specifically, where do all the transactions accounts come from? How do people acquire transactions deposits? How does the total amount of such deposits—and therefore the money supply of the economy—change?

Deposit Creation

Most people assume that all transactions account balances come from cash deposits. But this isn't the case. Direct deposits of paychecks, for example, are carried out by computer, not by the movement of cash (see cartoon). Moreover, the employer who issues the paycheck probably didn't make any cash deposits. It's more likely that she covered those paychecks with customers' checks that she deposited or with loans granted by the bank itself.

Analysis: People see very little of their money—most deposits and loans are computer entries in the banking system.

The ability of banks to lend money opens up a whole new set of possibilities for creating money. *When a bank lends someone money, it simply credits that individual's bank account.* The money appears in an account just as it would with a cash deposit. And the owner of the account is free to spend that money as with any positive balance. Hence, *in making a loan, a bank effectively creates money because transactions account balances are counted as part of the money supply.*

To understand the origins of our money supply then, we must recognize two basic principles:

- Transactions account balances are a large portion of the money supply.
- Banks can create transactions account balances by making loans.

The following two sections examine this process of **deposit creation** more closely. We determine how banks actually create deposits and what forces might limit the process of deposit creation.

deposit creation: The creation of transactions deposits by bank lending.

Bank Regulation. Banks' deposit-creation activities are regulated by the government. The most important agency in this regard is the Federal Reserve System. "The Fed" puts limits on the amount of bank lending, thereby controlling the basic money supply. We'll discuss the structure and functions of the Fed in the next chapter; here we focus on the process of deposit creation itself.

A Monopoly Bank

Table 13.2 documents that there are thousands of banks, of various sorts, in the United States. To understand how banks create money, however, we'll simplify reality greatly. We'll assume for the moment that there's only one bank in town, University Bank. Imagine also that you've been saving some of your income by putting loose change into a piggy bank. Now, after months of saving, you break the bank and discover that your thrift has yielded $100. You immediately deposit this money in a new checking account at University Bank. How will this deposit affect the money supply?

Your initial deposit will have no immediate effect on the money supply. The coins in your piggy bank were already counted as part of the money supply (M1 and M2) because they represented cash held by the public. *When you deposit cash or coins in a bank, you're only changing the composition of the money supply, not its size.* The public (you) now holds $100 less of coins but $100 more of transactions deposits. Accordingly, no money is created by the demise of your piggy bank (the initial deposit). This accounting outcome is reflected in the following "T account" of University Bank and the composition of the money supply:

University Bank		Money Supply	
Assets	Liabilities	Cash held by the public	−$100
+$100 in coins	+$100 in deposits	Transactions deposits at bank	+$100
		Change in M	0

TABLE 13.2
What Is a Bank?

The essential functions of a bank are to
- Accept deposits
- Offer drafts (check writing privileges)
- Make loans

In the United States, roughly 19,000 depository institutions fulfill these functions. These "banks" are typically classified into four general categories, even though most banks (and many other financial institutions) now offer similar services.

Type of Bank	Characteristics
Commercial banks	The nearly 8,000 commercial banks in the United States provide a full range of banking services, including savings ("time") and checking accounts and loans for all purposes. They hold nearly all demand deposits and nearly half of total savings deposits.
Savings and loan associations	Begun in 1831 as a mechanism for pooling the savings of a neighborhood in order to provide funds for home purchases, which is still the basic function of such banks. The nearly 500 S&Ls channel virtually all their savings deposits into home mortgages.
Mutual savings banks	Originally intended to serve very small savers (like the Boston Five Cents Savings Bank). They now use their deposits for a wider variety of purposes, including investment bonds and blue chip stocks. Almost all the 1,000 or so mutual savings banks are located in only five states: New York, Massachusetts, Connecticut, Pennsylvania, and New Jersey.
Credit unions	Cooperative societies formed by individuals bound together by some common tie, such as a common employer or labor union. Credit union members hold savings accounts and enjoy access to the pooled savings of all members. Most credit union loans are for consumer purchases. Although there are close to 10,000 credit unions in the United States, they hold less than 5 percent of total savings deposits.

The T account shows that your coins are now held by University Bank. In exchange, the bank has credited your checking account $100. This balance is a liability for the bank since it must allow you to withdraw the deposit on demand.

The total money supply is unaffected by your cash deposit because two components of the money supply change in opposite directions (i.e., less cash, more bank deposits). This initial deposit is just the beginning of the money creation process, however. Banks aren't in business for your convenience; they're in business to earn a profit. To earn a profit on your deposit, University Bank will have to put your money to work. This means using your deposit as the basis for making a loan to someone who's willing to pay the bank interest for use of money. If the function of banks was merely to store money, they wouldn't pay interest on their accounts or offer free checking services. Instead, you'd have to pay them for these services. Banks pay you interest and offer free (or inexpensive) checking because they can use your money to make loans that earn interest.

The Initial Loan. Typically, a bank doesn't have much difficulty finding someone who wants to borrow money. Someone is always eager to borrow money. The question is: How much money can a bank lend? Can it lend your entire deposit? Or must University Bank keep some of your coins in reserve, in case you want to withdraw them?

To answer this question, suppose that University Bank decided to lend the entire $100 to Campus Radio. Campus Radio wants to buy a new antenna but doesn't have any money in its own checking account. To acquire the antenna, Campus Radio must take out a loan.

When University Bank agrees to lend Campus Radio $100, it does so by crediting the account of Campus Radio. Instead of giving Campus Radio $100 cash, University

Bank simply adds $100 to Campus Radio's checking account balance. That is, the loan is made with a simple bookkeeping entry as follows:

University Bank		Money Supply	
Assets	Liabilities	Cash held by the public	no change
		Transactions deposits at bank	+$100
$100 in coins	$100 your account balance	Change in M	+$100
$100 in loans	$100 Campus Radio account		

This simple bookkeeping procedure is the key to creating money. When University Bank lends $100 to the Campus Radio account, it "creates" money. Keep in mind that transactions deposits are counted as part of the money supply. Once the $100 loan is credited to its account, Campus Radio can use this new money to purchase its desired antenna, without worrying that its check will bounce.

Or can it? Once University Bank grants a loan to Campus Radio, both you and Campus Radio have $100 in your checking accounts to spend. But the bank is holding only $100 of **reserves** (your coins). In other words, the increased account balance obtained by Campus Radio doesn't limit your ability to write checks. There's been a net *increase* in the value of transactions deposits but no increase in bank reserves.

> **bank reserves:** Assets held by a bank to fulfill its deposit obligations.

Secondary Deposits. What happens if Campus Radio actually spends the $100 on a new antenna? Won't this "use up all" the reserves held by the bank, endangering your check writing privileges? The answer is no.

Consider what happens when Atlas Antenna receives the check from Campus Radio. What will Atlas do with the check? Atlas could go to University Bank and exchange the check for $100 of cash (your coins). But Atlas may prefer to deposit the check in its own checking account at University Bank (still the only bank in town). This way, Atlas not only avoids the necessity of going to the bank (it can deposit the check by mail) but also keeps its money in a safe place. Should Atlas later want to spend the money, it can simply write a check. In the meantime, the bank continues to hold its entire reserves (your coins), and both you and Atlas have $100 to spend.

Fractional Reserves. Notice what's happened here. The money supply has increased by $100 as a result of deposit creation (the loan to Campus Radio). Moreover, the bank has been able to support $200 of transaction deposits (your account and either the Campus Radio or Atlas account) with only $100 of reserves (your coins). In other words, **bank reserves are only a fraction of total deposits.** In this case, University Bank's reserves (your $100 in coins) are only 50 percent of total deposits. Thus the bank's **reserve ratio** is 50 percent—that is,

> **reserve ratio:** The ratio of a bank's reserves to its total transactions deposits.

$$\text{Reserve ratio} = \frac{\text{bank reserves}}{\text{total deposits}}$$

The ability of University Bank to hold reserves that are only a fraction of total deposits results from two facts: (1) people use checks for most transactions, and (2) there's no other bank. Accordingly, reserves are rarely withdrawn from this monopoly bank. In fact, if people *never* withdrew their deposits and *all* transactions accounts were held at University Bank, University Bank wouldn't need *any* reserves. In this most unusual case, University Bank could make as many loans as it wanted. Every loan it made would increase the supply of money.

In reality, many banks are available, and people both withdraw cash from their accounts and write checks to people who have accounts in other banks. In addition, bank lending practices are regulated by the Federal Reserve System. *The Federal Reserve System requires banks to maintain some minimum reserve ratio.* This reserve requirement directly limits banks' ability to grant new loans.

Required Reserves. The potential impact of Federal Reserve requirements on bank lending can be readily seen. Suppose that the Federal Reserve imposed a minimum reserve requirement of 75 percent on University Bank. Such a requirement would prohibit University Bank from lending $100 to Campus Radio. That loan would result in $200 of deposits, supported by only $100 of reserves. The actual ratio of reserves to deposits would be 50 percent ($100 of reserves ÷ $200 of deposits), which would violate the Fed's assumed 75 percent reserve requirement. A 75 percent reserve requirement means that University Bank must hold **required reserves** equal to 75 percent of *total* deposits, including those created through loans.

The bank's dilemma is evident in the following equation:

$$\text{Required reserves} = \text{required reserve ratio} \times \text{total deposits}$$

To support $200 of total deposits, University Bank would need to satisfy this equation:

$$\text{Required reserves} = 0.75 \times \$200 = \$150$$

But the bank has only $100 of reserves (your coins) and so would violate the reserve requirement if it increased total deposits to $200 by lending $100 to Campus Radio.

University Bank can still issue a loan to Campus Radio. But the loan must be less than $100 in order to keep the bank within the limits of the required reserve formula. Thus, *a minimum reserve requirement directly limits deposit-creation possibilities.* It's still true, however, as we'll now illustrate, that the banking system, taken as a whole, can create multiple loans (money) from a single deposit.

A Multibank World

Table 13.3 illustrates the process of deposit creation in a multibank world with a required reserve ratio. In this case, we assume that legally required reserves must equal at least 20 percent of transactions deposits. Now when you deposit $100 in your checking account, University Bank must hold at least $20 as required reserves.[1]

Excess Reserves. The remaining $80 the bank obtains from your deposit is regarded as **excess reserves.** These reserves are "excess" in that your bank is *required* to hold in reserve only $20 (equal to 20 percent of your initial $100 deposit):

$$\text{Excess reserves} = \text{total reserves} - \text{required reserves}$$

The $80 of excess reserves isn't required and may be used to support additional loans. Hence, the bank can now lend $80. In view of the fact that banks earn profits (interest) by making loans, we assume that University Bank will try to use these excess reserves as soon as possible.

To keep track of the changes in reserves, deposit balances, and loans that occur in a multibank world we'll have to do some bookkeeping. For this purpose we'll again use the same balance sheet, or "T account," that banks themselves use. On the left side of the balance sheet, a bank lists all its assets. *Assets* are things the bank owns or are owed by others, including cash held in a bank's vaults, IOUs (loan obligations) from bank customers, reserve credits at the Federal Reserve (essentially the bank's own deposits at the central bank), and securities (bonds) the bank has purchased.

On the right side of the balance sheet a bank lists all its liabilities. *Liabilities* are things the bank owes to others. The largest liability is represented by the deposits of bank customers. The bank owes these deposits to its customers and must return them "on demand."

---

required reserves: The minimum amount of reserves a bank is required to hold; equal to required reserve ratio times transactions deposits.

excess reserves: Bank reserves in excess of required reserves.

WEBNOTE

Find the most recent data on total bank reserves, borrowed reserves, excess reserves, and required reserves at the U.S. Federal Reserve: www.Federalreserve.gov/releases. Click on "Aggregate Reserves of Depository Institutions."

---

[1]The reserves themselves may be held in the form of cash in the bank's vault but are usually held as credits with one of the regional Federal Reserve banks.

Step 1: You deposit cash at University Bank. The deposit creates $100 of reserves, $20 of which are designated as required reserves.

University Bank				Banking System	
Assets		Liabilities		Change in Transactions Deposits	Change in M
Required reserves	$ 20	Your deposit	$100	+$100	$0
Excess reserves	80				
Total	$100		100		

Step 2: The bank uses its excess reserves ($80) to make a loan to Campus Radio. Total deposits now equal $180. The money supply has increased.

University Bank				Banking System	
Assets		Liabilities		Δ Deposits	Δ M
Required reserves	$ 36	Your account	$100	+$80	+$80
Excess reserves	64	Campus Radio account	80		
Loans	80				
Total	$180	Total	$180		

Step 3: Campus Radio buys an antenna. This depletes Campus Radio's account but increases Atlas's balance. Eternal Savings gets $80 of reserves when the Campus Radio check clears.

University Bank				Eternal Savings				Banking System	
Assets		Liabilities		Assets		Liabilities		Δ Deposits	Δ M
Required reserves	$ 20	Your account	$100	Required reserves	$16	Atlas Antenna account	$80	$0	$0
Excess reserves	0	Campus Radio account	0	Excess reserves	64				
Loan	80								
Total	$100	Total	$100	Total	$80	Total	$80		

Step 4: Eternal Savings lends money to Herman's Hardware. Deposits, loans, and M all increase by $64.

University Bank				Eternal Savings				Banking System	
Assets		Liabilities		Assets		Liabilities		Change in Transaction Deposits	Change in M
Required reserves	$ 20	Your account	$100	Required reserves	$28.80	Atlas Antenna account	$ 80	+$64	+$64
Excess reserves	0	Campus Radio account	0	Excess reserves	51.20	Herman's Hardware account	64		
Loan	80			Loans	64				
Total	$100	Total	$100		$ 144		$144		
⋮		⋮		⋮		⋮		⋮	⋮

***n*th step:** Some bank lends $1.00		+1	+1

Cumulative Change in Banking System

Bank Reserves	Transactions Deposits	Money Supply
+$100	+$500	+$400

TABLE 13.3
Deposit Creation

Excess reserves (step 1) are the basis of bank loans. When a bank uses its excess reserves to make a loan, it creates a deposit (step 2). When the loan is spent, a deposit will be made somewhere else (step 3). This new deposit creates additional excess reserves (step 3) that can be used for further loans (step 4, etc.). The process of deposit creation continues until the money supply has increased by a multiple of the initial deposit.

Table 13.3 also shows the use of balance sheets. Notice how the balance of University Bank now looks immediately after it receives your initial deposit (step 1, Table 13.3). Your deposit of coins is entered on both sides of University's balance sheet. On the left side, your deposit is regarded as an asset, because your piggy bank's coins have an immediate market value and can be used to pay off the bank's liabilities. The coins now appear as *reserves*. The reserves these coins represent are further divided into required reserves ($20, or 20 percent of your deposit) and excess reserves ($80).

On the right side of the balance sheet, the bank reminds itself that it has an obligation (liability) to return your deposit when you so demand. Thus, the bank's accounts balance, with assets and liabilities being equal. In fact, *a bank's books must always balance because all the bank's assets must belong to someone (its depositors or its owners).*

University Bank wants to do more than balance its books, however; it wants to earn profits. To do so, it will have to make loans—that is, put its excess reserves to work. Suppose that it lends $80 to Campus Radio.[2] As step 2 in Table 13.3 illustrates, this loan alters both sides of University Bank's balance sheet. On the right-hand side, the bank creates a new transactions deposit for (credits the account of) Campus Radio; this item represents an additional liability (promise to pay). On the left-hand side of the balance sheet, two things happen. First, the bank notes that Campus Radio owes it $80 ("loans"). Second, the bank recognizes that it's now required to hold $36 in *required* reserves, in accordance with its higher level of transactions deposits ($180). (Recall we're assuming that required reserves are 20 percent of total transactions deposits.) Since its total reserves are still $100, $64 is left as *excess* reserves. Note again that *excess reserves are reserves a bank isn't required to hold.*

Changes in the Money Supply. Before examining further changes in the balance sheet of University Bank, consider again what's happened to the economy's money supply during these first two steps. In the first step, you deposited $100 of cash in your checking account. This initial transaction didn't change the value of the money supply. Only the composition of the money supply (M1 or M2) was affected ($100 less cash held by the public, $100 more in transactions accounts).

Not until step 2—when the bank makes a loan—does all the excitement begin. In making a loan, the bank automatically increases the total money supply by $80. Why? Because someone (Campus Radio) now has more money (a transactions deposit) than it did before, *and no one else has any less.* And Campus Radio can use its money to buy goods and services, just like anybody else.

This second step is the heart of money creation. Money effectively appears out of thin air when a bank makes a loan. To understand how this works, you have to keep reminding yourself that money is more than the coins and currency we carry around. Transactions deposits are money too. Hence, *the creation of transactions deposits via new loans is the same thing as creating money.*

More Deposit Creation. Suppose again that Campus Radio actually uses its $80 loan to buy an antenna. The rest of Table 13.3 illustrates how this additional transaction leads to further changes in balance sheets and the money supply.

In step 3, we see that when Campus Radio buys the $80 antenna, the balance in its checking account at University Bank drops to zero because it has spent all its money. As University Bank's liabilities fall (from $180 to $100), so does the level of its required reserves (from $36 to $20). (Note that required reserves are still 20 percent of its remaining transactions deposits.) But University Bank's excess reserves have disappeared completely! This disappearance reflects the fact that Atlas Antenna keeps *its* transactions account at another bank (Eternal Savings). When Atlas deposits

---

[2]Because of the Fed's assumed minimum reserve requirement (20 percent), University Bank can now lend only $80 rather than $100, as before.

the check it received from Campus Radio, Eternal Savings does two things: First it credits Atlas's account by $80. Second, it goes to University Bank to get the reserves that support the deposit.[3] The reserves later appear on the balance sheet of Eternal Savings as both required ($16) and excess ($64) reserves.

Observe that the money supply hasn't changed during step 3. The increase in the value of Atlas Antenna's transactions account balance exactly offsets the drop in the value of Campus Radio's transactions account. Ownership of the money supply is the only thing that has changed.

In step 4, Eternal Savings takes advantage of its newly acquired excess reserves by making a loan to Herman's Hardware. As before, the loan itself has two primary effects. First, it creates a transactions deposit of $64 for Herman's Hardware and thereby increases the money supply by the same amount. Second, it increases the required level of reserves at Eternal Savings. (To how much? Why?)

THE MONEY MULTIPLIER

By now it's perhaps obvious that the process of deposit creation won't come to an end quickly. On the contrary, it can continue indefinitely, just like the income multiplier process in Chapter 10. Indeed, people often refer to deposit creation as the money multiplier process, with the **money multiplier** expressed as the reciprocal of the required reserve ratio.[4] That is,

$$\frac{\text{Money}}{\text{multiplier}} = \frac{1}{\text{required reserve ratio}}$$

money multiplier: The number of deposit (loan) dollars that the banking system can create from $1 of excess reserves; equal to 1 ÷ required reserve ratio.

Figure 13.2 illustrates the money multiplier process. When a new deposit enters the banking system, it creates both excess and required reserves. The required reserves represent leakage from the flow of money since they can't be used to create new loans. Excess reserves, on the other hand, can be used for new loans. Once those loans are made, they typically become transactions deposits elsewhere in the banking system. Then some additional leakage into required reserves occurs, and further loans are made. The process continues until all excess reserves have leaked into required reserves. Once excess reserves have completely disappeared, the total value of new loans will equal initial excess reserves multiplied by the money multiplier.

The potential of the money multiplier to create loans is summarized by the equation

$$\frac{\text{Excess}}{\text{reserves}} \times \frac{\text{money}}{\text{multiplier}} = \frac{\text{potential}}{\text{deposit creation}}$$
$$\text{of banking system}$$

Notice how the money multiplier worked in our previous example. The value of the money multiplier was equal to 5, since we assumed that the required reserve ratio was 0.20. Moreover, the initial level of excess reserves was $80, as a consequence of your original deposit (step 1). According to the money multiplier, then, the deposit-creation potential of the banking system was

$$\frac{\text{Excess reserves}}{(\$80)} \times \frac{\text{money multiplier}}{(5)} = \frac{\text{potential deposit creation (\$400)}}{}$$

---

[3]In actuality, banks rarely "go" anywhere; such interbank reserve movements are handled by bank clearing houses and regional Federal Reserve banks. The effect is the same, however. The nature and use of bank reserves are discussed more fully in Chapter 14.

[4]The money multiplier $(1/r)$ is the sum of the infinite geometric progression

$1 + (1 - r) + (1 - r)^2 + (1 - r)^3 + \cdots + (1 - r)^\infty$.

FIGURE 13.2
The Money Multiplier Process
Part of every new bank deposit leaks into required reserves. The rest—excess reserves—can be used to make loans. These loans, in turn, become deposits elsewhere. The process of money creation continues until all available reserves become required reserves.

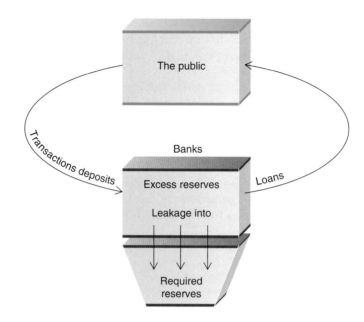

When all the banks fully utilized their excess reserves at each step of the money multiplier process, the ultimate increase in the money supply was in fact $400 (see the last row in Table 13.3).

Excess Reserves as Lending Power

While you're struggling through Table 13.3, notice the critical role that excess reserves play in the process of deposit creation. A bank can make additional loans only if it has excess reserves. Without excess reserves, all of a bank's reserves are required, and no further liabilities (transactions deposits) can be created with new loans. On the other hand, a bank with excess reserves can make additional loans. In fact,

- *Each bank may lend an amount equal to its excess reserves and no more.*

As such loans enter the circular flow and become deposits elsewhere, they create new excess reserves and further lending capacity. As a consequence,

- *The entire banking system can increase the volume of loans by the amount of excess reserves multiplied by the money multiplier.*

By keeping track of excess reserves, then, we can gauge the lending capacity of any bank or, with the aid of the money multiplier, the entire banking system.

Table 13.4 summarizes the entire money multiplier process. In this case, we assume that all banks are initially "loaned up"—that is, without any excess reserves. The money multiplier process begins when someone deposits $100 in cash into a transactions account at Bank A. If the required reserve ratio is 20 percent, this initial deposit creates $80 of excess reserves at Bank A while adding $100 to total transactions deposits.

If Bank A uses its newly acquired excess reserves to make a loan that ultimately ends up in Bank B, two things happen: Bank B acquires $64 in excess reserves (0.80 × $80), and total transactions deposits increase by another $80.

The money multiplier process continues with a series of loans and deposits. When the twenty-sixth loan is made (by bank Z), total loans grow by only $0.30 and transactions deposits by an equal amount. Should the process continue further, the *cumulative* change in loans will ultimately equal $400, that is, the money multiplier times initial excess reserves. The money supply will increase by the same amount.

Required reserves = 0.20	Change in Transactions Deposits	Change in Total Reserves	Change in Required Reserves	Change in Excess Reserves	Change in Lending Capacity
If $100 in cash is deposited in Bank A, Bank A acquires	$100.00	$100.00	$ 20.00	$80.00	$ 80.00
If loan made and deposited elsewhere, Bank B acquires	80.00	80.00	16.00	64.00	64.00
If loan made and deposited elsewhere, Bank C acquires	64.00	64.00	12.80	51.20	51.20
If loan made and deposited elsewhere, Bank D acquires	51.20	51.20	10.24	40.96	40.96
If loan made and deposited elsewhere, Bank E acquires	40.96	40.96	8.19	32.77	32.77
If loan made and deposited elsewhere, Bank F acquires	32.77	32.77	6.55	26.27	26.22
If loan made and deposited elsewhere, Bank G acquires	26.22	26.22	5.24	20.98	20.98
. . .					
If loan made and deposited elsewhere, Bank Z acquires	0.38	0.38	0.08	0.30	0.30
Cumulative, through Bank Z	$498.80	$100.00	$ 99.76	$ 0.24	$398.80
. . .					
And if the process continues indefinitely	$500.00	$100.00	$100.00	$ 0.00	$400.00

Note: A $100 cash deposit creates $400 of new lending capacity when the required reserve ratio is 0.20. Initial excess reserves are $80 (= $100 deposit − $20 required reserves). The money multiplier is 5 (= 1 ÷ 0.20). New lending potential equals $400 (= $80 excess reserves × 5).

TABLE 13.4
The Money Multiplier at Work

The process of deposit creation continues as money passes through different banks in the form of multiple deposits and loans. At each step, excess reserves and new loans are created. The lending capacity of this system equals the money multiplier times excess reserves. In this case, initial excess reserves of $80 create the possibility of $400 of new loans when the reserve ratio is 0.20 (20 percent).

BANKS AND THE CIRCULAR FLOW

The bookkeeping details of bank deposits and loans are rarely exciting and often confusing. But they do demonstrate convincingly that banks can create money. In that capacity, *banks perform two essential functions for the macro economy:*

- *Banks transfer money from savers to spenders by lending funds (reserves) held on deposit.*
- *The banking system creates additional money by making loans in excess of total reserves.*

In performing these two functions, banks change the size of the money supply—that is, the amount of purchasing power available for buying goods and services. Market participants may respond to these changes in the money supply by altering their spending behavior and shifting the aggregate demand curve.

Figure 13.3 on the next page is a simplified perspective on the role of banks in the circular flow. As before, income flows from product markets through business firms to factor markets and returns to consumers in the form of disposable income. Consumers spend most of their income but also save (don't spend) some of it.

FIGURE 13.3
Banks in the Circular Flow

Banks help transfer income from savers to spenders by using their deposits to make loans to business firms and consumers who want to spend more money than they have. By lending money, banks help maintain any desired rate of aggregate demand.

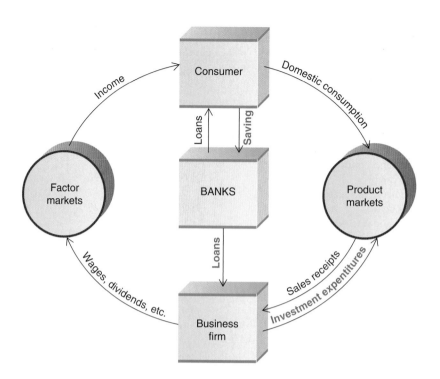

Financing Injections

The leakage represented by consumer saving is a potential source of stabilization problems, particularly unemployment. If additional spending by business firms, foreigners, or governments doesn't compensate for consumer saving at full employment, a recessionary GDP gap will emerge, creating unemployment (see Chapters 9 and 10). Our interest here is in the role the banking system can play in encouraging such additional spending.

Suppose for the moment that *all* consumer saving was deposited in piggy banks rather than depository institutions (banks) and that no one used checks. Under these circumstances, banks couldn't transfer money from savers to spenders by holding deposits and making loans.

In reality, a substantial portion of consumer saving *is* deposited in banks. These and other bank deposits can be used as the basis of loans, thereby returning purchasing power to the circular flow. In fact, the primary economic function of banks isn't to store money but to transfer purchasing power from savers to spenders. They do so by lending money to businesses for new plant and equipment, to consumers for new homes or cars, and to government entities that desire greater purchasing power. Moreover, because the banking system can make *multiple* loans from available reserves, banks don't have to receive all consumer saving in order to carry out their function. On the contrary, *the banking system can create any desired level of money supply if allowed to expand or reduce loan activity at will.*

Constraints on Deposit Creation

There are three major constraints on the deposit creation of the banking system.

Deposits. The first constraint is the willingness of consumers and businesses to continue using and accepting checks rather than cash in the marketplace. If people preferred to hold cash rather than checkbooks, banks wouldn't be able to acquire or maintain the reserves that are the foundation of bank lending activity.

Borrowers. The second constraint on deposit creation is the willingness of consumers, businesses, and governments to borrow the money that banks make available. The chain of events we've observed in deposit creation depends on the willingness of Campus Radio to borrow $80, of Herman's Hardware to borrow $64, and so on. If no one wanted to borrow any money, deposit creation would never begin. By the same reasoning, if all excess reserves aren't borrowed (lent), deposit creation won't live up to its theoretical potential.

Regulation. The third major constraint on deposit creation is the Federal Reserve System. As we've observed, the Fed may limit deposit creation by imposing reserve requirements. These and other tools of monetary policy are discussed in Chapter 14.

THE ECONOMY TOMORROW

The power of banks to create money originates in the *fractional reserve* system. As we've observed, a bank holds reserves that are a small fraction of its liabilities, implying that no bank could pay off its customers if they all sought to withdraw their deposits at one time.

When Banks Fail

Bank Panics

In earlier times, banks did experience occasional "runs" when depositors would rush to withdraw their funds. Such depositor runs usually began when word spread that a particular bank was running low on cash and might close. Depositor runs became self-fulfilling confirmation of a bank's insolvency. The resulting bank closing wiped out customer deposits, curtailed bank lending, and often pushed the economy into recession.

During the Great Depression there was widespread fear that the banking system would collapse. Borrowers weren't able to repay their loans and depositors were withdrawing more cash. As their reserves dwindled, banks' ability to create money evaporated. Suddenly, a chunk of money (bank deposits and loans) just disappeared. With little cash coming in and a lot of cash flowing out, banks quickly ran out of cash reserves and had to shut their doors. Between 1930 and 1933, over 9,000 banks failed. To prevent total collapse of the banking system, newly elected president Franklin Roosevelt declared a "bank holiday" that closed all the nation's banks for one week.

Deposit Insurance

Congress used that opportunity to create a deposit insurance that would protect customer deposits. The Federal Deposit Insurance Corporation (FDIC) and the Federal Savings and Loan Insurance Corporation (FSLIC) were created in 1933 and 1934 to ensure depositors that they'd get their money back even it their bank failed. The guarantee of insured deposits eliminated the motivation for deposit runs. If a bank closed, the federal government would step in and repay deposits.

The S&L Crisis

Federal deposit insurance provided a foundation for public confidence in the banking system. It didn't, however, ward off bank failures. In some respects, deposit insurance even contributed to bank failures. By insuring deposits, the federal government eliminated a major risk for bank customers. Depositors no longer had to concern themselves with the soundness of a bank's lending practices; their deposits were insured. This created the opportunity for bank owners to engage in riskier loans that had greater profit potential.

During the 1970s, accelerating inflation pushed interest rates up. To attract deposits, banks had to offer higher rates of interest on customer deposits. Many of their loans, however, were already set at lower interest rates. This was particularly true for savings and loan associations (S&Ls), which traditionally lent most of their funds in long-term home mortgages. Suddenly, they were stuck earning low interest rates on long-term mortgages while paying high interest rates on short-term deposits. This was a recipe for failure.

The woes of the S&Ls were exacerbated by increased competition from new financial institutions (like money market mutual funds) that enticed deposits away from S&Ls. Sharp downturns in oil prices and real estate also weakened borrowers' ability to repay their loans. These and other forces caused more than half the S&Ls that existed in 1970 to disappear by 1990. In 1988, more banks failed (200) than in any year since the Great Depression. The 1990–91 recession pushed still more banks into insolvency.

IN THE NEWS

Bank Reopens to Customers' Questions

Worried customers streamed into a Superior Bank branch here Monday to find out if their money was safe three days after federal regulators seized the failed thrift.

Among the concerned customers was John Piotrowski, a Downers Grove management consultant, who had money stashed at the bank for his daughter's October wedding. "My wife almost fainted," when they heard about the bank's closure, he said.

The Office of Thrift Supervision closed Superior on Friday after federal regulators said the bank, based in suburban Oak Brook Terrace, was insolvent. The Federal Deposit Insurance Corp. was appointed the bank's receiver and reopened it Monday under the new name Superior Federal. Most customers who came to the Downers Grove branch on Monday got the good news that their money was safe because the FDIC insures accounts up to $100,000. However, accounts of more than $100,000 can be set up so they are FDIC insured, said David Barr, an FDIC spokesman.

—Deanna Bellandi

Source: Associated Press, July 31, 2001. Reprinted with permission. www.ap.org

Analysis: When a bank fails, the FDIC (or SAIF for savings banks) steps in to guarantee that deposited funds will be returned to depositors. The government then tries to sell the bank or its remaining assets (loans).

Bank Bailouts

The FSLIC and FDIC averted bank panics by paying off depositors in failed banks. So many S&Ls failed, however, that the FSLIC itself ran out of funds. Congress had to appropriate ever larger sums of money to bail out the banks. In 1992 alone, over $60 billion was spent on bank bailouts.

When the federal government steps in to pay insured deposits, it also assumes control of a failing bank (see News). The government then tries to arrange a merger or acquisition with a stronger bank. In the process, the federal government acquires some or all of the outstanding loans of the failed bank. The Resolution Trust Corporation (RTC) was created in 1989 to manage these loans. The RTC tried to collect outstanding loans or sell the properties (such as office buildings, shopping centers, homes) that were financed with those loans. Part of the huge outlays for bank bailouts in the early 1990s were offset by the proceeds from these RTC property sales.

Banks will continue to compete for deposits and loans in the economy tomorrow. They'll have the advantage of deposit insurance—provided by the FDIC and the renamed Savings Association Insurance Fund (SAIF)—in attracting new funds. Congress, however, has set more stringent requirements on the types of loans and investments banks can make. It has also forced bank owners to put more of their own funds at risk. The intent of these changes is to improve the financial stability of banks while assuring the public that their deposits are safe—even in banks with only fractional reserves.

SUMMARY

- In a market economy, money serves a critical function in facilitating exchanges and specialization, thus permitting increased output. *Money* refers to any medium that's generally accepted in exchange.

- Because people use bank account balances to buy goods and services, such balances are also regarded as money. The money supply M1 includes cash plus transactions account (checkable) deposits. M2 adds savings account balances and other deposits to form a broader measure of the money supply.

- Banks have the power to create money by making loans. In making loans, banks create new transactions deposits, which become part of the money supply.

- Banks' ability to make loans—create money—depends on their reserves. Only if a bank has excess reserves—reserves greater than those required by federal regulation—can it make new loans.
- As loans are spent, they create deposits elsewhere, making it possible for other banks to make additional loans. The money multiplier (1 ÷ required reserve ratio) indicates the total value of deposits that can be created by the banking system from excess reserves.
- The role of banks in creating money includes the transfer of money from savers to spenders as well as deposit creation

in excess of deposit balances. Taken together, these two functions give banks direct control over the amount of purchasing power available in the marketplace.
- The deposit-creation potential of the banking system is limited by government regulation. It's also limited by the willingness of market participants to hold deposits or borrow money.
- When banks fail, the federal government (FDIC or SAIF) guarantees to pay deposits. To reduce bank failures, bank owners are now required to put more of their own assets at risk.

Key Terms

barter
money
money supply (M1, M2)
transactions account

aggregate demand
deposit creation
bank reserves
reserve ratio

required reserves
excess reserves
money multiplier

Questions for Discussion

1. Why are checking account balances, but not credit cards, regarded as "money"?
2. How are an economy's production possibilities affected when workers are paid in bras and coffins rather than cash? (See World View, page 267, about bartering in Russia.)
3. What percentage of your monthly bills do you pay with (a) cash, (b) check, (c) credit card, and (d) automatic transfers. How do you pay off the credit card balance? How does your use of cash compare with the composition of the money supply (Figure 13.1)?
4. If you can purchase airline tickets with online computer services, should your electronic account be counted in the money supply? Explain.
5. Does the fact that your bank keeps only a fraction of your account balance in reserve make you uncomfortable?

Why don't people rush to the bank and retrieve their money? What would happen if they did?
6. If people never withdrew cash from banks, how much money could the banking system potentially create? Could this really happen? What might limit deposit creation in this case?
7. If all banks heeded Shakespeare's admonition "Neither a borrower nor a lender be," what would happen to the circular flow?
8. How does federal deposit insurance encourage greater risk-taking by banks? Could the banking system function without government deposit insurance? How?
9. If Internet e-cash systems could make loans, how would the money supply be affected?

ALERT!

PROBLEMS The Student Problem Set at the back of this book contains numerical and graphing problems for this chapter.

WEB ACTIVITIES to accompany this chapter can be found on the Online Learning Center: **http://www.mhhe.com/economics/schiller10**

The Federal Reserve System

W e've seen how money is created. We've also gotten a few clues about how the government limits money creation and thus influences aggregate demand. This chapter examines the mechanics of government control more closely. The basic issues addressed are

- **How does the government control the amount of money in the economy?**
- **Which government agency is responsible for exercising this control?**
- **How are banks and bond markets affected by the government's policies?**

Most people have a ready answer for the first question. The popular view is that the government controls the amount of money in the economy by printing more or fewer dollar bills. But we've already observed that the concept of "money" isn't so simple. In Chapter 13 we demonstrated that banks, not the printing presses, create most of our money. In making loans, banks create transactions deposits that are counted as part of the money supply.

Because bank lending activities are the primary source of money, the ***government must regulate bank lending if it wants to control the amount of money in the economy.*** That's exactly what the Federal Reserve System does. The Federal Reserve System—the "Fed"—not only limits the volume of loans that the banking system can make from available reserves; it can also alter the amount of reserves banks hold.

The Federal Reserve System's control over the supply of money is the key mechanism of **monetary policy.** The potential of this policy lever to alter macro outcomes (unemployment, inflation, etc.) is examined in Chapter 15. For the time being, however, we focus on the *tools* of monetary policy.

monetary policy: The use of money and credit controls to influence macroeconomic outcomes.

STRUCTURE OF THE FED

In the absence of any government regulation, the supply of money would be determined by individual banks. Moreover, individual depositors would bear all the risks of bank failures. In fact, this is the way the banking system operated until 1914. The money supply was subject to abrupt changes, and consumers frequently lost their savings in recurrent bank failures.

A series of bank failures resulted in a severe financial panic in 1907. Millions of depositors lost their savings, and the economy was thrown into a tailspin. In the wake of this panic, a National Monetary Commission was established to examine ways of restructuring the banking system. The mandate of the commission was to find ways to avert recurrent financial crises. After five years of study, the commission recommended the creation of a Federal Reserve System. Congress accepted the commission's recommendations, and President Wilson signed the Federal Reserve Act in December 1913.

The core of the Federal Reserve System consists of 12 Federal Reserve banks. Each bank acts as a central banker for the private banks in its region. In this role, the regional Fed banks perform the following services:

Federal Reserve Banks

- *Clearing checks between private banks.* Suppose the Bank of America in San Francisco receives a deposit from one of its customers in the form of a share draft written on the New York State Employees Credit Union. The Bank of America doesn't have to go to New York to collect the cash or other reserves that support that draft. Instead, the Bank of America can deposit the draft (check) at its account with the Federal Reserve Bank of San Francisco. The Fed then collects from the credit union. This vital clearinghouse service saves the Bank of America and other private banks a great deal of time and expense in processing the 40 *billion* checks that are written every year. (The Fed employs 5,000 people for this processing activity.)

- *Holding bank reserves.* Notice that the Fed's clearinghouse service was facilitated by the fact that the Bank of America and the New York Employees Credit Union had their own accounts at the Fed. As we noted in Chapter 13, banks are *required* to hold some minimum fraction of their deposits in reserve. Only a small amount of reserves is held as cash in a bank's vaults. The rest is held in reserve accounts at the regional Federal Reserve banks. These accounts not only provide greater security and convenience for bank reserves but also enable the Fed to monitor the actual level of bank reserves.

- *Providing currency.* Before every major holiday there's a great demand for cash. People want some pocket money during holidays and know that it's difficult to cash checks on weekends or holidays, especially if they're going out of town. So they load up on cash at their bank or ATMs. After the holiday is over, most of this cash is returned to the banks, typically by the stores, gas stations, and restaurants that benefited from holiday spending. Because banks hold very little cash in their vaults, they turn to the Fed to meet these sporadic cash demands. A private bank can simply call the regional Federal Reserve bank and order a supply of cash, to be delivered (by armored truck) before a weekend or holiday. The cash will be deducted from the bank's own account at the Fed. When all the cash comes back in after the holiday, the bank can reverse the process, sending the unneeded cash back to the Fed.

- *Providing loans.* The Federal Reserve banks may also loan reserves to private banks. This practice, called "discounting," is examined more closely in a moment.

At the top of the Federal Reserve System's organization chart (Figure 14.1) is the Board of Governors, which is responsible for setting monetary policy. The Board,

The Board of Governors

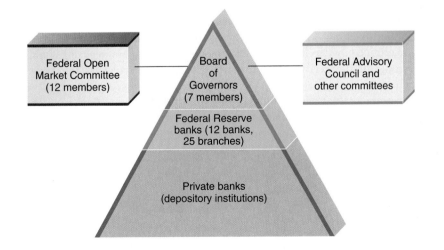

FIGURE 14.1

Structure of the Federal Reserve System

The Fed's broad policies are determined by the seven-member Board of Governors. The 12 Federal Reserve banks provide central banking services to individual banks in their respective regions. The Federal Open Market Committee directs Federal Reserve transactions in the money market. Various committees offer formal and informal advice to the Board of Governors.

located in Washington, D.C., consists of seven members (governors), appointed by the president of the United States and confirmed by the U.S. Senate. Board members are appointed for 14-year terms and can't be reappointed. Their exceptionally long appointments give the Fed governors a measure of political independence. They're not beholden to any elected official and will hold office longer than any president.

The intent of the Fed's independence is to keep control of the nation's money supply beyond the immediate reach of politicians (especially members of Congress, elected for two-year terms). The designers of the Fed system feared that political control of monetary policy would cause wild swings in the money supply and macro instability. Critics argue, however, that the Fed's independence makes it unresponsive to the majority will.

The president selects one of the governors to serve as chairman of the Board for four years. Alan Greenspan was first appointed as chairman by President Reagan, then reappointed for a four-year term by President George H. Bush in 1991, twice reappointed by President Clinton (in 1996 and 2000) and reappointed for a final term by President George W. Bush in June 2004.[1] Chairman Greenspan is the primary spokesperson for Fed policy and reports to Congress every six months on the conduct of monetary policy.

WEBNOTE

Who runs the Fed? Read profiles of the governors at www.federalreserve.gov/bios.

The Federal Open Market Committee (FOMC)

A key arm of the Board is the Federal Open Market Committee (FOMC), which is responsible for the Fed's daily activity in financial markets. The FOMC plays a critical role in setting short-term interest rates and the level of reserves held by private banks. The membership of the FOMC includes all seven governors and 5 of the 12 regional Reserve bank presidents. The FOMC meets in Washington, D.C., every four or five weeks throughout the year to review the economy's performance. It decides whether the economy is growing fast enough (or too fast) and then adjusts monetary policy as needed.

MONETARY TOOLS

money supply (M1): Currency held by the public, plus balances in transactions accounts.

Our immediate interest isn't in the structure of the Federal Reserve but the way the Fed is able to alter the **money supply.** The Fed's control of the money supply is exercised by use of three policy instruments:

M2 money supply: M1 plus balances in most savings accounts and money market mutual funds.

- Reserve requirements
- Discount rates
- Open market operations

Reserve Requirements

required reserves: The minimum amount of reserves a bank is required to hold; equal to required reserve ratio times transactions deposits.

The Fed's first policy tool focuses on reserve requirements. As noted in Chapter 13, the Fed requires private banks to keep some stated fraction of their deposits "in reserve." These **required reserves** are held either in the form of actual vault cash or, more commonly, as credits (deposits) in the bank's "reserve account" at a regional Federal Reserve bank. ***By changing the reserve requirements, the Fed can directly alter the lending capacity of the banking system.***

Recall that the banking system's ability to make additional loans—create deposits—is determined by two factors: (1) the amount of excess reserves banks hold and (2) the money multiplier. Both factors are directly influenced by the Fed's required reserve ratio.

Suppose, for example, that banks hold $100 billion of deposits and total reserves of $30 billion. Assume too that the minimum reserve requirement is 20 percent. Under these circumstances, banks are holding more reserves than they have to. Recall that

$$\text{Required reserves} = \text{required reserves ratio} \times \text{total deposits}$$

[1]Greenspan's 14-year term as a Governor ends on February 1, 2006, but he could continue to serve as chairman until a successor is confirmed by the U.S. Senate.

so, in this case

$$\text{Required reserves} = 0.20 \times \$100 \text{ billion}$$

$$= \$20 \text{ billion}$$

Banks are *required* to hold $20 billion in reserve to meet Federal Reserve regulations. They're actually holding $30 billion, however. The $10 billion difference between actual and required reserves is **excess reserves**—that is,

$$\text{Excess reserves} = \text{total reserves} - \text{required reserves}$$

excess reserves: Bank reserves in excess of required reserves.

The existence of excess reserves implies that banks aren't fully utilizing their lending powers. With $10 billion of excess reserves and the help of the **money multiplier** the banks *could* lend an additional $50 billion.

The potential for additional loans is calculated as

$$\text{Available lending capacity of banking system} = \text{excess reserves} \times \text{money multiplier}$$

money multiplier: The number of deposit (loan) dollars that the banking system can create from $1 of excess reserves; equal to 1 ÷ required reserve ratio.

or, in this case,

$$\$10 \text{ billion} \times \frac{1}{0.20} = \$50 \text{ billion of unused lending capacity}$$

That is, the banking system could create another $50 billion of money (transactions account balances) without any additional reserves.

A simple way to confirm this—and thereby check your arithmetic—is to note what would happen to total deposits if the banks actually made further loans. Total deposits would increase to $150 billion in this case (the initial $100 billion plus the new $50 billion), an amount that could be supported with $30 billion in reserves (20 percent of $150 billion).

But what if the Fed doesn't want the money supply to increase this much? Maybe prices are rising and the Fed wants to restrain rather than stimulate total spending in the economy. Under such circumstances, the Fed would want to restrict the availability of credit (loans). Does it have the power to do so? Can the Fed reduce the lending capacity of the banking system?

The answer to both questions is clearly yes. ***By raising the required reserve ratio, the Fed can immediately reduce the lending capacity of the banking system.***

Table 14.1 summarizes the impact of an increase in the required reserve ratio. In this case, the required reserve ratio is increased from 20 to 25 percent. Notice that this change in the reserve requirement has no effect on the amount of deposits in the banking system (row 1, Table 14.1) or the amount of total reserves (row 2). They remain at $100 billion and $30 billion, respectively. What the increased reserve requirement does affect is the way those reserves can be used. Before the increase, only $20 billion in

	Required Reserve Ratio	
	20 Percent	**25 Percent**
1. Total deposits	$100 billion	$100 billion
2. Total reserves	30 billion	30 billion
3. Required reserves	20 billion	25 billion
4. Excess reserves	10 billion	5 billion
5. Money multiplier	5	4
6. Unused lending capacity	$ 50 billion	$ 20 billion

TABLE 14.1
The Impact of an Increased Reserve Requirement

An increase in the required reserve ratio reduces both excess reserves (row 4) and the money multiplier (row 5). As a consequence, changes in the reserve requirement have a substantial impact on the lending capacity of the banking system (row 6).

Analysis: A reduction in the reserve requirement transforms some of the banking system's required reserves into excess reserves, thus increasing potential lending activity and profits. It also increases the size of the money multiplier.

reserves were *required,* leaving $10 billion of *excess* reserves. Now, however, banks are required to hold $25 billion (0.25 × $100 billion) in reserves, leaving them with only $5 billion in excess reserves. Thus an increase in the reserve requirement immediately reduces excess reserves, as illustrated in row 4, Table 14.1.

There's also a second effect. Notice what happens to the money multiplier (1 ÷ reserve ratio). Previously it was 5(= 1 ÷ 0.20); now it's only 4(= 1 ÷ 0.25). Consequently, a higher reserve requirement not only reduces excess reserves but diminishes their lending power as well.

A change in the reserve requirement, therefore, hits banks with a triple whammy. ***A change in the reserve requirement causes a change in***

- *Excess reserves.*
- *The money multiplier.*
- *The lending capacity of the banking system.*

These changes lead to a sharp reduction in bank lending power. Whereas the banking system initially had the power to increase the volume of loans by $50 billion ($10 billion of excess reserves × 5), it now has only $20 billion ($5 million × 4) of unused lending capacity, as noted in the last row in Table 14.1.

Changes in reserve requirements are a powerful weapon for altering the lending capacity of the banking system. The Fed uses this power sparingly, so as not to cause abrupt changes in the money supply and severe disruptions of banking activity. From 1970 to 1980, for example, reserve requirements were changed only twice, and then by only half a percentage point each time (for example, from 12.0 to 12.5 percent). The Fed last cut the reserve requirement from 12 to 10 percent in 1992 to increase bank profits and encourage more lending (see News). Smaller banks have a lower reserve requirement (3 percent), which gives them a competitive advantage.

The Discount Rate

Banks have a tremendous incentive to maintain their reserves at or close to the minimum established by the Fed. Bank reserves held at the Fed earn no interest, but loans and bonds do. Hence, a profit-maximizing bank seeks to keep its excess reserves as low as possible, preferring to put its reserves to work. In fact, banks have demonstrated an uncanny ability to keep their reserves close to the minimum federal requirement. As Figure 14.2 illustrates, the only time banks held huge excess reserves was in the Great Depression of the 1930s. The banks didn't want to make any more loans and were fearful of panicky customers withdrawing their deposits.

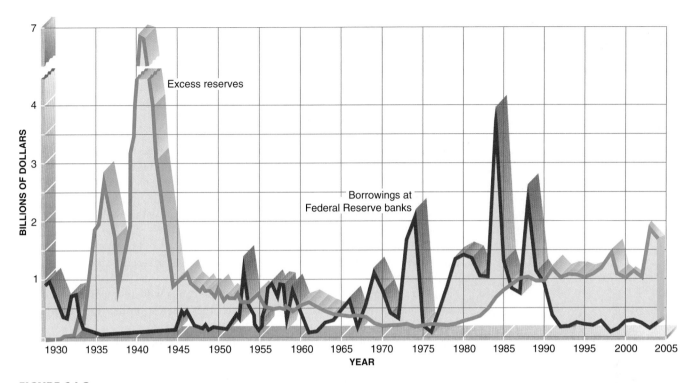

FIGURE 14.2
Excess Reserves and Borrowings

Excess reserves represent unused lending capacity. Hence, banks strive to keep excess reserves at a minimum. One exception to this practice occurred in the Great Depression, when banks were hesitant to make any loans. In trying to minimize excess reserves, banks occasionally fall short of required reserves. At such times they may borrow from other banks (the federal funds market), or they may borrow reserves from the Fed. Borrowing from the Fed is called "discounting."

Because banks continually seek to keep excess reserves at a minimum, they run the risk of falling below reserve requirements. A large borrower may be a little slow in repaying a loan, or the rate of deposit withdrawals and transfers may exceed expectations. At such times, a bank may find that it doesn't have enough reserves to satisfy Fed requirements.

Banks could ensure continual compliance with reserve requirements by maintaining large amounts of excess reserves. But that's an unprofitable procedure, and a profit-maximizing bank will seek other alternatives.

The Federal Funds Market. A bank that finds itself short of reserves can turn to other banks for help. If a reserve-poor bank can borrow some reserves from a reserve-rich bank, it may be able to bridge its temporary deficit and satisfy the Fed. *Reserves borrowed by one bank from another are referred to as "federal funds" and are lent for short periods, usually overnight.* Although trips to the federal funds market—via telephone and computer—will usually satisfy Federal Reserve requirements, such trips aren't free. The lending bank will charge interest (the **federal funds rate**) on its interbank loan.[2] The use of the federal funds market to satisfy Federal Reserve requirements also depends on other banks having excess reserves to lend.

The St. Louis Fed bank tracks bank reserves and borrowings; to update Figure 14.2, go to http://research.stlouisfed.org/fred2/categories/122.

federal funds rate: The interest rate for interbank reserve loans.

---

[2]An overnight loan of $1 million at 6 percent interest (per year) costs $165 in interest charges plus any service fees that might be added. Banks make multimillion-dollar loans in the federal funds market.

Sale of Securities. Another option available to reserve-poor banks is the sale of securities. Banks use some of their excess reserves to buy government bonds, which pay interest. If a bank needs more reserves to satisfy federal regulations, it may sell these securities and deposit the proceeds at a regional Federal Reserve bank. Its reserve position is thereby increased. This option also involves distinct costs, however, both in forgone interest-earning opportunities and in the possibility of capital losses when the bond is offered for quick sale.

Discounting. A third option for avoiding a reserve shortage lies in the structure of the Federal Reserve System itself. The Fed not only establishes certain rules of behavior for banks but also functions as a central bank, or banker's bank. Banks maintain accounts with the regional Federal Reserve banks, much the way you and I maintain accounts with a local bank. Individual banks deposit and withdraw "reserve credits" from these accounts, just as we deposit and withdraw dollars. Should a bank find itself short of reserves, it can go to the Fed's "discount window" and borrow some reserves. This process is called **discounting.** Discounting means the Fed is lending reserves directly to private banks.[3]

discounting: Federal Reserve lending of reserves to private banks.

The Fed's discounting operation provides private banks with an important source of reserves, but not without cost. The Fed too charges interest on the reserves it lends to banks, a rate of interest referred to as the **discount rate.**

discount rate: The rate of interest the Federal Reserve charges for lending reserves to private banks.

The discount window is a mechanism for directly influencing the size of bank reserves. ***By raising or lowering the discount rate, the Fed changes the cost of money for banks and therewith the incentive to borrow reserves.*** At high discount rates, borrowing from the Fed is expensive. High discount rates also signal the Fed's desire to restrain the money supply and an accompanying reluctance to lend reserves. Low discount rates, on the other hand, make it profitable to acquire additional reserves and exploit one's lending capacity to the fullest. Low discount rates also indicate the Fed's willingness to support credit expansion. The accompanying News tells how the Fed reduced both the federal funds rate and the discount rate in August 2001 to encourage more borrowing and spending. After the September 11 attacks on the World Trade Center and Pentagon, the Fed reduced both rates again, and quite sharply.

Open Market Operations

Reserve requirements and discount window operations are important tools of monetary policy. But they don't come close to open market operations in day-to-day impact on the money supply. ***Open market operations are the principal mechanism for directly altering the reserves of the banking system.*** Since reserves are the lifeblood of the banking system, open market operations are of immediate and critical interest to private banks and the larger economy.

Portfolio Decisions. To appreciate the impact of open market operations, you have to think about the alternative uses for idle funds. Just about all of us have some idle funds, even if they amount to just a few dollars in our pocket or a minimal balance in our checking account. Other consumers and corporations have great amounts of idle funds, even millions of dollars at any time. Here we're concerned with what people decide to do with such funds.

People (and corporations) don't hold all their idle funds in transactions accounts or cash. Idle funds are also used to purchase stocks, build up savings account balances, and purchase bonds. These alternative uses of idle funds are attractive because they promise some additional income in the form of interest, dividends, or capital appreciation, such as higher stock prices. Deciding where to place idle funds is referred to as the **portfolio decision.**

portfolio decision: The choice of how (where) to hold idle funds.

---

[3]In the past banks had to present loan notes to the Fed in order to borrow reserves. The Fed "discounted" the notes by lending an amount equal to only a fraction of their face value. Although banks no longer have to present loans as collateral, the term "discounting" endures.

IN THE NEWS

Fed Again Reduces Key Rate

Federal Reserve officials, concerned about the uncertain outlook for the U.S. economy amid a global slowdown in growth, lowered their target for short-term interest rates yesterday for a seventh time this year and left the door open for more cuts if needed.

In announcing its decision, the Fed's top policymaking group, the Federal Open Market Committee, noted that U.S. consumer spending has held up recently "but business profits and capital spending continue to weaken and growth abroad is slowing, weighing on the U.S. economy."

The committee lowered the central bank's target for the federal funds rate, the interest rate financial institutions charge one another on overnight loans, by another quarter of a percentage point, to 3.5 percent. The key rate, which influences many other interest rates, including banks' prime lending rate, is now 3 percentage points lower than it was Jan. 1. . . .

In a separate but related action, the Federal Reserve Board reduced the central bank's largely symbolic discount rate, the interest rate financial institutions pay when they borrow money from one of the 12 regional Federal Reserve banks, to 3 percent from 3.25 percent.

—John M. Berry

Source: *Washington Post*, August 22, 2001. © 2001 The Washington Post. Reprinted with permission. www.thewashingtonpost.com

Analysis: By reducing the federal funds and discount rates, the Fed encourages banks to borrow reserves and make more loans. Lower interest rates also encourage businesses and consumers to borrow and spend more.

Hold Money or Bonds? The Fed's open market operations focus on one of the portfolio choices people make: whether to deposit idle funds in bank accounts or purchase government bonds. The Fed attempts to influence this choice by making bonds more or less attractive, as circumstances warrant. The Fed's goal is to encourage people to move funds from banks to bond markets or vice versa. In the process, reserves either enter or leave the banking system, thereby altering the lending capacity of banks.

Figure 14.3 depicts the general nature of the Fed's open market operations. As we first observed in Chapter 13 (Figure 13.2), the process of deposit creation begins when people deposit money in the banking system. But people may also hold their assets in the form of bonds. The Fed's objective is to alter this portfolio decision by buying or selling bonds. ***When the Fed buys bonds from the public, it increases the flow of deposits (reserves) to the banking system. Bond sales by the Fed reduce the inflow.***

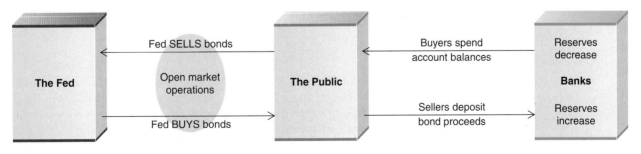

FIGURE 14.3
Open Market Operations

People may hold assets in the form of bank deposits (money) or bonds. When the Fed buys bonds from the public, it increases the flow of deposits (and reserves) to the banks. When the Fed sells bonds, it diminishes the flow of deposits and therewith the banks' capacity to lend (create money).

The Bond Market. To understand how open market operations work, let's look closer at the bond market. Not all of us buy and sell bonds, but a lot of consumers and corporations do: Daily volume in bond markets exceeds $500 billion. What's being exchanged in this market, and what factors influence decisions to buy or sell?

In our discussion thus far, we've portrayed banks as intermediaries between savers and spenders. Banks aren't the only mechanism available for transferring purchasing power from nonspenders to spenders. Funds are lent and borrowed in bond markets as well. In this case, a corporation may borrow money directly from consumers or other institutions. When it does so, it issues a bond as proof of its promise to repay the loan. A **bond** is simply a piece of paper certifying that someone has borrowed money and promises to pay it back at some future date. In other words, a bond is nothing more than an IOU. In the case of bond markets, however, the IOU is typically signed by a giant corporation or a government agency rather than a friend. It's therefore more widely accepted by lenders.

> **bond:** A certificate acknowledging a debt and the amount of interest to be paid each year until repayment; an IOU.

Because most corporations and government agencies that borrow money in the bond market are well known and able to repay their debts, their bonds are actively traded. If I lend $1,000 to General Motors on a 10-year bond, for example, I don't have to wait 10 years to get my money back; I can resell the bond to someone else at any time. If I do, that person will collect the face value of the bond (plus interest) from GM when it's due. The actual purchase and sale of bonds take place in the bond market. Although a good deal of the action occurs on Wall Street in New York, the bond market has no unique location. Like other markets we've discussed, the bond market exists whenever and however bond buyers and sellers get together.

Bond Yields. People buy bonds because bonds pay interest. If you buy a General Motors bond, GM is obliged to pay you interest during the period of the loan. For example, an 8 percent 2015 GM bond in the amount of $1,000 states that GM will pay the bondholder $80 interest annually (8 percent of $1,000) until 2015. At that point GM will repay the initial $1,000 loan (the "principal").

> **yield:** The rate of return on a bond; the annual interest payment divided by the bond's price.

The current **yield** paid on a bond depends on the promised interest rate (8 percent in this case) and the actual purchase price of the bond. Specifically,

$$\text{Yield} = \frac{\text{annual interest payment}}{\text{price paid for bond}}$$

If you pay $1,000 for the bond, then the current yield is

$$\text{Yield} = \frac{\$80}{\$1,000} = 0.08, \text{ or } 8\%$$

which is the same as the interest rate printed on the face of the bond. But what if you pay only $900 for the bond? In this case, the interest rate paid by GM remains at 8 percent, but the *yield* jumps to

$$\text{Yield} = \frac{\$80}{\$900} = 0.089, \text{ or } 8.9\%$$

Buying a $1,000 bond for only $900 might seem like too good a bargain to be true. But bonds are often bought and sold at prices other than their face value (see News on the next page). In fact, *a principal objective of Federal Reserve open market activity is to alter the price of bonds, and therewith their yields.* By doing so, the Fed makes bonds a more or less attractive alternative to holding money.

Open Market Activity. The basic premise of open market activity is that participants in the bond market will respond to changes in bond prices and yields. As we've observed, *the less you pay for a bond, the higher its yield.* Accordingly, the Fed can induce people to *buy* bonds by offering to sell them at a lower price (e.g., a $1,000,

Zero-Coupon Bonds

Conventional bonds make interest payments each year, often quarterly. However, some bonds pay no current interest. Because so-called zero-coupon bonds make no interest payments, they have a *current* yield of zero. In effect, a zero-coupon bond accumulates interest payments, paying them all at once when the bond comes due. The *yield* to *maturity* on such bonds is implied by the difference between the purchase price and the face value of the bond. A $1,000 "zero" due in 10 years, for example, might cost only $400 today. You lend $400 now and get back $1,000 in 10 years. The implied yield to maturity is approximately 9 percent.

Analysis: The yield (return) on a bond depends not only on annual interest payments but also on the difference between the price paid for the bond and its face (payoff) value.

8 percent bond for only $900). Similarly, the Fed can induce people to *sell* bonds by offering to buy them at higher prices. In either case, the Fed hopes to move reserves into or out of the banking system. In other words, **open market operations** entail the purchase and sale of government securities (bonds) for the purpose of altering the flow of reserves into and out of the banking system.

open market operations: Federal Reserve purchases and sales of government bonds for the purpose of altering bank reserves.

Open Market Purchases. Suppose the Fed wants to increase the money supply and therefore desires to provide the banking system with additional reserves. To do so, it must persuade people to deposit a larger share of their financial assets in banks and hold less in other forms, particularly government bonds. *If the Fed offers to pay a higher price for bonds ("bids up bonds"), it will effectively lower bond yields and market interest rates.* The higher prices and lower yields will reduce the attractiveness of holding bonds. If the price offered by the Fed is high enough, people will sell some of their bonds to the Fed and deposit some or all of the proceeds of the sale in their bank accounts. This influx of money into bank accounts will directly increase bank reserves.

Figure 14.4 illustrates the dynamics of open market operations in more detail. When the Fed buys a bond from the public, it pays with a check written on itself (Step 1 in Figure 14.4). What will the bond seller do with the check? There really aren't any options. If the seller wants to use the proceeds of the bond sale, he or she will have

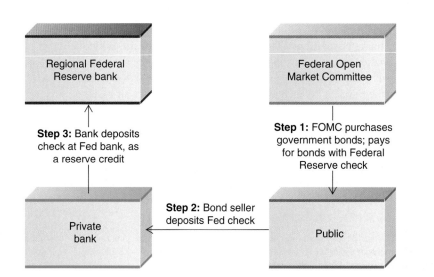

FIGURE 14.4
An Open Market Purchase

The Fed can increase bank reserves by buying bonds from the public. The Fed check used to buy bonds (step 1) gets deposited in a private bank (step 2). The bank returns the check to the Fed (step 3), thereby obtaining additional reserves. To decrease bank reserves, the Fed would sell bonds, thus reversing the flow of reserves.

to deposit the Fed check at a bank (Step 2 in the figure). The bank, in turn, deposits the check at a regional Federal Reserve bank, in exchange for a reserve credit (Step 3). The bank's reserves are directly increased by the amount of the check. Thus, *by buying bonds, the Fed increases bank reserves.* These reserves can be used to expand the money supply still further, as banks put their newly acquired reserves to work making loans.

Open Market Sales. Should the Fed desire to slow the growth in the money supply, it can reverse the whole process. Instead of offering to *buy* bonds, the Fed in this case will try to *sell* bonds. If the Fed "bids bonds down" (offers to sell them at low prices), bond yields will rise. In response, individuals, corporations, and government agencies will convert some of their transactions deposits into bonds. When they do so, they write a check, paying the Fed for the bonds.[4] The Fed then returns the check to the depositor's bank, taking payment through a reduction in the bank's reserve account. The reserves of the banking system are thereby diminished, as is the capacity to make loans. Thus, *by selling bonds, the Fed reduces bank reserves.*

The Fed Funds Rate. A market signal of these changing reserve flows is provided by the federal funds rate. Recall that "fed funds" are excess reserves traded among banks. If the Fed pumps more reserves into the banking system (by buying bonds), the interest rate charged for overnight reserve loans—the federal funds rate—will decline. Conversely, if the Fed is reducing bank reserves (by selling bonds), the federal funds rate will increase. Hence, the federal funds rate is a highly visible signal of Federal Reserve open market operations. When Alan Greenspan reduced the federal funds rate *11 times* in 2001, the Fed was underscoring the urgency of monetary stimulus to combat the recession and the after-effects of the September 11 terrorist attacks.

Volume of Activity. To appreciate the significance of open market operations, you need a sense of the magnitudes involved. The volume of trading in U.S. government securities exceeds $100 billion per day. The Fed alone owned over $500 billion worth of government securities at the beginning of 2005 and bought or sold enormous sums daily. Thus, open market operations involve tremendous amounts of money and, by implication, potential bank reserves. Each $1 of reserves represents something like $10 of potential lending capacity (via the money multiplier). Thus, open market operations can have a profound impact on the money supply.

INCREASING THE MONEY SUPPLY

The three major instruments of monetary policy are reserve requirements, discount rates, and open market operations. The Fed can use these levers individually or in combination to change the money supply. This section illustrates the use of each tool to attain a specific policy goal.

Suppose the policy goal is to increase the money supply from an assumed level of $340 billion to $400 billion. In surveying the nation's banks, the Fed discovers the facts shown in Table 14.2. On the basis of the facts presented in Table 14.2, it's evident that

- The banking system is "loaned up." Because excess reserves are zero (see row 5 in Table 14.2), there's no additional lending capacity.
- The required reserve ratio must be equal to 25 percent, because this is the current ratio of required reserves ($60 billion) to total deposits ($240 billion).

---

[4]In actuality, the Fed deals directly with only 36 "primary" bond dealers. These intermediaries then trade with each other, "secondary" dealers, financial institutions, and individuals. These additional steps don't significantly alter the flow of funds depicted here.

WEBNOTE

How has the federal funds rate changed in the past eight weeks? What does it signal about Federal Reserve activity? For data on the fed funds rate visit the Fed's Web site at www.federalreserve.gov.

Item	Amount
1. Cash held by public	$100 billion
2. Transactions deposits	240 billion
3. Total money supply (M1)	$340 billion
4. Required reserves	$ 60 billion
5. Excess reserves	0
6. Total reserves of banks	$ 60 billion
7. U.S. bonds held by public	$460 billion
8. Discount rate	7%

TABLE 14.2
How to Increase the Money Supply

The accompanying data depict a banking system that has $340 billion of money (M1) and no further lending capacity (excess reserves = 0). To enlarge M1 to $400 billion, the Fed can (1) lower the required reserve ratio, (2) reduce the discount rate, or (3) buy bonds held by the public.

Accordingly, if the Fed wants to increase the money supply, it will have to pump additional reserves into the banking system or lower the reserve requirement. *To increase the money supply the Fed can*

- *Lower reserve requirements.*
- *Reduce the discount rate.*
- *Buy bonds.*

Lowering Reserve Requirements

Lowering the reserve requirements is an expedient way of increasing the lending capacity of the banking system. But by how much should the reserve requirement be reduced?

Recall that the Fed's policy objective is to increase the money supply from $340 billion to $400 billion, an increase of $60 billion. If the public isn't willing to hold any additional cash, this entire increase in money supply will have to take the form of added transactions deposits. In other words, total deposits will have to increase from $240 billion to $300 billion. These additional deposits will have to be *created* by the banks, in the form of new loans to consumers or business firms.

If the banking system is going to support $300 billion in transactions deposits with its *existing* reserves, the reserve requirement will have to be reduced from 25 percent; thus,

$$\frac{\text{Total reserves}}{\text{Desired level of deposits}} = \frac{\$60 \text{ billion}}{\$300 \text{ billion}} = 0.20$$

At the moment the Fed lowers the minimum reserve ratio to 0.20, *total* reserves won't change. The bank's potential lending power will change, however. Required reserves will drop to $48 billion (0.20 × $240 billion), and excess reserves will jump from zero to $12 billion. These new excess reserves imply an additional lending capacity:

$$\underset{(\$12 \text{ billion})}{\text{Excess reserves}} \times \underset{(5)}{\text{money multiplier}} = \underset{(\$60 \text{ billion})}{\text{unused lending capacity}}$$

If the banks succeed in putting all this new lending power to work—actually make $60 billion in new loans—the Fed's objective of increasing the money supply will be attained.

Lowering the Discount Rate

The second monetary tool available to the Fed is the discount rate. We assumed it was 7 percent initially (see row 8 in Table 14.2). If the Fed lowers this rate, it will become cheaper for banks to borrow reserves from the Fed. The banks will be more willing to borrow (cheaper) reserves so long as they can make additional loans to their own customers at higher interest rates. The profitability of discounting depends on the *difference* between the discount rate and the interest rate the bank charges its loan customers. The Fed increases this difference when it lowers the discount rate.

There's no way to calculate the appropriate discount rate without more detailed knowledge of the banking system's willingness to borrow reserves from the Fed.

Nevertheless, we can determine how much reserves the banks *must* borrow if the Fed's money supply target is to be attained. The Fed's objective is to increase transactions deposits by $60 billion. If these deposits are to be created by the banks—and the reserve requirement is unchanged at 0.25—the banks will have to borrow an additional $15 billion of reserves ($60 billion divided by 4, the money multiplier).

Buying Bonds

The Fed can also get additional reserves into the banking system by buying U.S. bonds in the open market. As row 7 in Table 14.2 indicates, the public holds $460 billion in U.S. bonds, none of which are counted as part of the money supply. If the Fed can persuade people to sell some of these bonds, bank reserves will surely rise.

To achieve its money supply target, the Fed will offer to buy $15 billion of U.S. bonds. It will pay for these bonds with checks written on its own account at the Fed. The people who sold the bonds will deposit these checks in their own transactions accounts. As they do so, they'll directly increase bank deposits and reserves by $15 billion.

Is $15 billion of open market purchases enough? Yes. The $15 billion is a direct addition to transactions deposits, and therefore to the money supply. The additional deposits bring in $15 billion of reserves, only $3.75 billion of which is required (0.25 × $15 billion). Hence, the new deposits bring in $11.25 billion of excess reserves, which themselves create an additional lending capacity:

$$\begin{matrix} \text{Excess reserves} \\ (\$11.25 \text{ billion}) \end{matrix} \times \begin{matrix} \text{money multiplier} \\ (4) \end{matrix} = \begin{matrix} \text{unused lending capacity} \\ (\$45 \text{ billion}) \end{matrix}$$

Thus, the $15 billion of open market purchases will eventually lead to a $60 billion increase in M1 as a consequence of both direct deposits ($15 billion) and subsequent loan activity ($45 billion).

Federal Funds Rate. When the Fed starts bidding up bonds, bond yields and market interest rates will start falling. So will the federal funds rate. This will give individual banks an incentive to borrow any excess reserves available, thereby accelerating deposit (loan) creation.

WEBNOTE

For an inside view of how the Fed uses its policy tools, visit www.federalreserveeducation.org.

WORLD VIEW

China Pulls Reins on Its Economy
Moves Meant to Slow Industrial Growth

China acted to brake its speeding economy Wednesday. . . .

Chinese regulators issued new landuse guidelines to rein in booming industrial growth, the latest in a series of measures to cool an overheating economy. Earlier this week, Beijing:

- Raised reserve requirements for banks—for the third time in seven months—to slow lending.
- Capped the percentage of debt companies can use to fund cement, steel, aluminum and real estate projects.
- Signaled tighter credit policies are coming. Several Chinese commercial banks confirmed they have halted new loans in anticipation of rewritten rules.

Chinese leaders are concerned the country could face a banking collapse, surging unemployment and falling prices if the economy zooms ahead unchecked.

In an interview Wednesday with Reuters, Chinese Premier Wen Jiabao vowed "very forceful measures" to bring the economy under control. Chinese officials say their 2004 growth target is between 7% and 8%, a slowdown from the 9.7% annual rate China posted in the first quarter.

—James Cox

Source: *USA Today*, April 29, 2004. USA TODAY. Copyright 2004. Reprinted with permission.

Analysis: Central banks raise interest rates and slow money-supply growth when they sense inflationary pressures.

DECREASING THE MONEY SUPPLY

All the tools used to increase the money supply can also be used to decrease it. *To reduce the money supply, the Fed can*

- *Raise reserve requirements.*
- *Increase the discount rate.*
- *Sell bonds.*

On a week-to-week basis the Fed does occasionally seek to reduce the total amount of cash and transactions deposits held by the public. These are minor adjustments, however, to broader policies. A growing economy needs a steadily increasing supply of money to finance market exchanges. Hence, the Fed rarely seeks an outright reduction in the size of the money supply. What it does do is regulate the *rate of growth* in the money supply. When the Fed wants to slow the rate of consumer and investor spending, it restrains the *growth* of money and credit. Although many people talk about "reducing" the money supply, they're really talking about slowing its rate of growth. More immediately, they expect to see *rising* interest rates. To slow economic growth (and potential price inflation) China pursued this sort of monetary restraint in 2004 (see World View on the previous page).

THE ECONOMY TOMORROW

The policy tools at the Fed's disposal imply tight control of the nation's money supply. By altering reserve requirements, discount rates, or open market purchases, the Fed apparently has the ability to increase or decrease the money supply at will. But the Fed's control is far from complete. The nature of "money," as well as our notion of what a "bank" is, keeps changing. As a result, the Fed has to run pretty fast just to stay in place.

Is the Fed Losing Control?

Before 1980, the Fed's control of the money supply wasn't only incomplete but actually weakening. The Fed didn't have authority over all banks. Only one-third of all commercial banks were members of the Federal Reserve System and subject to its regulations. All savings and loan associations and other savings banks remained outside the Federal Reserve System. These banks were subject to regulations of state banking commissions and other federal agencies but not to Federal Reserve requirements. As a consequence, a substantial quantity of money and near-money lay beyond the control of the Fed.

Monetary Control Act

To increase the Fed's control of the money supply, Congress passed the Depository Institutions Deregulation and Monetary Control Act of 1980. Commonly referred to simply as the Monetary Control Act, that legislation subjected *all* commercial banks, S&Ls, savings banks, and most credit unions to Fed regulation. All depository institutions now have to satisfy Fed reserve requirements. All depository institutions also enjoy access to the Fed's discount window. These reforms (phased in over a period of seven years) obliterated the distinction between member and nonmember banks and greatly strengthened the Fed's control of the banking system.

Ironically, **as the Fed's control of the banks was increasing, the banks themselves were declining in importance.** Banks are part of a larger financial services industry that provides deposit, credit, and payment services. Many of these services are provided by financial institutions other than banks. These nonbank financial institutions have grown in importance while traditional banks have declined in number and importance.

Decline of Traditional Banks

Accepting and holding deposits is a core bank function. Consumers can also place idle funds in money market mutual funds (MMMF), however. MMMFs typically pay higher interest rates than traditional bank accounts and also permit limited check writing privileges. They thus serve as a potential substitute for traditional banks. Many brokerage houses also offer to hold idle cash in interest-earning accounts for their stock and bond customers.

Nonbanks are also competing against banks for loan business; 30 percent of all consumer loans are now made through credit cards. Banks themselves were once the primary source of credit cards. Now corporate giants like AT&T, GM, Sears, and American Airlines offer nonbank credit cards. Large corporations also offer loans to consumers who want to buy their products and even extend loans to unaffiliated businesses.

Insurance companies and pension funds also use their vast financial resources to make loans. The Teachers Insurance and Annuity Association (TIAA)—the pension fund for college professors—has lent over $10 billion directly to corporations. Many insurance companies provide long-term loans for commercial real estate.

Foreign banks, corporations, and pension funds may also extend credit to American businesses. They may also hold deposits of U.S. dollars abroad (for example, Eurodollars). As the accompanying World View illustrates, money—even terrorists' money—travels easily across national borders.

All this credit and deposit activity by global and nonbank institutions competes with traditional banks. And the nonbanks are winning the competition. In the past 20 years, the share of all financial institution assets held by banks has dropped from 37 percent to 27 percent, which means that banks are less important than they once were. This has made control of the money supply increasingly difficult.

WORLD VIEW

Fighting Terror/Targeting Funds; Laws May Not Stop Flow of Terror Funds

Congress is expected to approve legislation as early as today aimed at crippling the ability of terrorists to send money around the world. But law enforcement officials say that the increased globalization of electronic money transfer systems has made it easier than ever to move cash and avoid detection. . . .

The question, money laundering specialists say, is whether any unilateral action Congress takes can do much to stop the flow of dirty money across the world's borders. "The technology is changing all the time that makes it easier to transfer funds anonymously and to send money through five or six countries in one day," said William Schroeder, former director of the FBI's legal forfeiture division. "That makes it extremely difficult to connect people with money, to locate a money trail and follow it from person to person . . ."

Security cameras in Portland, Maine, captured pictures of suspected terrorists Muhammad Atta and Abdulaziz Alomari visiting two different ATMs on Sept. 10. Bank cash machines hardly qualify as cutting edge, but ATMs help criminals, according to the Treasury Department's Financial Crimes Enforcement Network, by allowing them "to wire funds into accounts in the United States from other nations and almost instantaneously and virtually anonymously to withdraw those funds."

Last year, federal prosecutors revealed that a husband-and-wife team with little more than a laptop computer and a license for what turned out to be a shell bank in Russia laundered more than $7 billion between 1996 and 1998. Using wire transfer software from the Bank of New York, the couple allegedly worked with the Russian mafia to send money from Moscow to New York to a series of offshore banks without tipping off regulators.

"If you know what you're doing, you can send money from the US to Spain to Cyprus to the Cayman Islands to Peru in a matter of minutes," said Schroeder.

—Scott Bernard Nelson

Source: *Boston Globe*, October 24, 2001. Copyright 2001 by Globe Newspaper Co. (MA). Reprinted with permission.

Analysis: Nearly two-thirds of all U.S. currency circulates outside the United States, and over $1.5 trillion is transmitted by bank wire every day. This globalization of money makes it hard not only to track terrorists' money but also to control the domestic money supply.

Because of the difficulties in managing an increasingly globalized and electronic flow of funds, the Fed has shifted away from money-supply targets to interest rate targets. Although changes in the money supply and in interest rates are intrinsically related, interest rates are easier and faster to track. The Fed also has the financial power to change short-term interest rates through its massive open market operations. If it chooses, the Fed can also offset abrupt changes in the flow of funds across national borders that might otherwise disrupt domestic interest rates. Last, but not least, the Fed recognizes that interest rates, not more obscure data on the money-supply or bank reserves, are the immediate concern in investment and "big-ticket" consumption decisions. As a result, the Fed will continue to use the federal funds rate as its primary barometer of monetary policy in the economy tomorrow.

Focus on Fed Funds Rate, not Money Supply

SUMMARY

- The Federal Reserve System controls the nation's money supply by regulating the loan activity (deposit creation) of private banks (depository institutions).
- The core of the Federal Reserve System is the 12 regional Federal Reserve banks, which provide check-clearance, reserve deposit, and loan ("discounting") services to individual banks. Private banks are required to maintain minimum reserves on deposit at one of the regional Federal Reserve banks.
- The general policies of the Fed are set by its Board of Governors. The Board's chair is selected by the U.S. president and confirmed by the Senate. The chair serves as the chief spokesperson for monetary policy. The general policies of the Fed are carried out by the Federal Open Market Committee (FOMC), which directs open market sales and purchase of U.S. bonds.
- The Fed has three basic tools for changing the money supply. By altering the reserve requirement, the Fed can immediately change both the quantity of excess reserves in the banking system and the money multiplier, which limits banks' lending capacity. By altering discount rates (the rate of interest charged by the Fed for reserve borrowing), the Fed can also influence the amount of reserves maintained by banks. Finally, and most important, the Fed can increase or decrease the reserves of the banking system by buying or selling government bonds, that is, by engaging in open market operations.
- When the Fed buys bonds, it causes an increase in bank reserves (and lending capacity). When the Fed sells bonds, it induces a reduction in reserves (and lending capacity).
- The federal funds (interest) rate is a market signal of Fed open market activity and intentions.
- In the 1980s, the Fed gained greater control of the banking system. Global and nonbank institutions such as pension funds, insurance companies, and nonbank credit services have grown in importance, however, making control of the money supply more difficult.

Key Terms

monetary policy	money multiplier	portfolio decision
money supply (M1, M2)	federal funds rate	bond
required reserves	discounting	yield
excess reserves	discount rate	open market operations

Questions for Discussion

1. Why do banks want to maintain as little excess reserves as possible? Under what circumstances might banks want to hold excess reserves? (*Hint:* see Figure 14.2.)
2. Why do people hold bonds rather than larger savings account or checking account balances? Under what circumstances might they change their portfolios, moving their funds out of bonds into bank accounts?
3. What is the current price and yield of 30-year U.S. Treasury bonds? Of General Motors bonds? (Check the financial section of your daily newspaper.) What accounts for the difference?
4. Why did China raise reserve requirements in 2004? How did they expect consumers and businesses to respond? (See World View, page 296.)

5. Why might the Fed want to decrease the money supply?
6. Why would a zero-coupon bond (see News page 293) have a lower price than a bond paying annual interest?
7. In 2000–2001, bond yields in Japan fell to less than 1.5 percent as the Bank of Japan bid up bond prices. Yet, relatively few people moved their assets out of bonds into banks. How might this failure of open market operations be explained?

8. In 2001, the Fed reduced both the discount and federal fund rates dramatically. But bank loan volume didn't increase. What considerations might have constrained the market's response to Fed policy?
9. If bondholders expect the Fed to raise interest rates, what action might they take? How would this affect the Fed's goal?

ALERT!

PROBLEMS — The Student Problem Set at the back of this book contains numerical and graphing problems for this chapter.

WEB ACTIVITIES — to accompany this chapter can be found on the Online Learning Center: **http://www.mhhe.com/economics/schiller10**

Monetary Policy

So what if the Federal Reserve System controls the nation's money supply? Why is this significant? Does it matter how much money is available?

Vladimir Lenin thought so. The first communist leader of the Soviet Union once remarked that the best way to destroy a society is to destroy its money. If a society's money became valueless, it would no longer be accepted in exchange for goods and services in product markets. People would have to resort to barter, and the economy's efficiency would be severely impaired. Adolf Hitler tried unsuccessfully to use this weapon against Great Britain during World War II. His plan was to counterfeit British currency, then drop it from planes flying over England. He believed that the sudden increase in the quantity of money, together with its suspect origins, would render the British pound valueless.

Even in peacetime, the quantity of money in circulation influences its value in the marketplace. Moreover, interest rates and access to credit (bank loans) are basic determinants of spending behavior. Consequently, control over the money supply implies an ability to influence macroeconomic outcomes.

But how much influence does the money supply have on macro performance? Specifically,

- **What's the relationship between the money supply, interest rates, and aggregate demand?**
- **How can the Fed use its control of the money supply or interest rates to alter macro outcomes?**
- **How effective is monetary policy, compared to fiscal policy?**

Economists offer very different answers to these questions. Some argue that changes in the money supply directly affect macro outcomes; others argue that the effects of such changes are indirect and less certain.

Paralleling these arguments about *how* **monetary policy** works are debates over the relative effectiveness of monetary and fiscal policy. Some economists argue that monetary policy is more effective than fiscal policy; others contend the reverse is true. This chapter examines these different views of money and assesses their implications for macro policy.

THE MONEY MARKET

The best place to learn how monetary policy works is the money *market*. You must abandon any mystical notions you may harbor about money and view it like any other commodity that's traded in the marketplace. Like other goods, there's a supply of money and a demand for money. Together they determine the "price" of money, or the **interest rate.**

At first glance, it may appear strange to call interest rates the price of money. But when you borrow money, the "price" you pay is measured by the interest rate

monetary policy: The use of money and credit controls to influence macroeconomic outcomes.

interest rate: The price paid for the use of money.

you're charged. When interest rates are high, money is "expensive." When interest rates are low, money is "cheap."

Money Balances

money supply (M1): Currency held by the public, plus balances in transactions accounts.

money supply (M2): M1 plus balances in most savings accounts and money market mutual funds.

Even people who don't borrow must contend with the price of money. Money, as we've seen, comes in many different forms. A common characteristic of all money is that it can be held as a store of value. People hold cash and maintain positive bank balances for this purpose. Most of the money in our common measures of **money supply (M1, M2)** is in the form of bank balances. There's an opportunity cost associated with such money balances, however. Money held in transactions accounts earns little or no interest. Money held in savings accounts and money market mutual funds does earn interest but usually at relatively low rates. By contrast, money used to buy bonds or stocks or to make loans is likely to earn a higher interest rate of return.

The Price of Money. The nature of the "price" of money should be apparent: People who hold *cash* are forgoing an opportunity to earn interest. So are people who hold money in checking accounts that pay no interest. In either case, *forgone interest is the opportunity cost (price) of money people choose to hold.* How high is that price? It's equal to the market rate of interest.

Money held in interest-paying bank accounts does earn some interest. In this case, the opportunity cost of holding money is the *difference* between the prevailing rate of interest and the rate paid on deposit balances. As is the case with cash and regular checking accounts, opportunity cost is measured by the forgone interest.

The Demand for Money

demand for money: The quantities of money people are willing and able to hold at alternative interest rates, *ceteris paribus.*

Once we recognize that money does have a price, we can easily formulate a demand for money. As is the case with all goods, the **demand for money** is a schedule (or curve) showing the quantity of money demanded at alternative prices (interest rates).

The decision to hold (demand) money balances is the kind of **portfolio decision** we examined in Chapter 14. While at first glance it might seem irrational to hold money balances that pay little or no interest, there are many good reasons for doing so.

portfolio decision: The choice of how (where) to hold idle funds.

Transactions Demand. Even people who've mastered the principles of economics hold money. They do so because they want to buy goods and services. In order to transact business in product or factor markets, we need money in the form of either cash or a positive bank account balance. Debit cards and ATM cards don't work unless there's money in the bank. Payment by e-cash also requires a supporting bank balance. Even when we use credit cards, we're only postponing the date of payment by a few weeks or so. Accordingly, we recognize the existence of a basic **transactions demand for money.**

transactions demand for money: Money held for the purpose of making everyday market purchases.

Precautionary Demand. Another reason people hold money is their fear of the proverbial rainy day. A sudden emergency may require money purchases over and above normal transactions needs. Moreover, such needs may arise when the banks are closed or in a community where one's checks aren't accepted. Also, future income is uncertain and may diminish unexpectedly. Therefore, people hold a bit more money (cash or bank account balances) than they anticipate spending. This **precautionary demand for money** is the extra money being held as a safeguard against the unexpected.

precautionary demand for money: Money held for unexpected market transactions or for emergencies.

Speculative Demand. People also hold money for speculative purposes. Suppose you were interested in buying stocks or bonds but hadn't yet picked the right ones or regarded their present prices as too high. In such circumstances, you might want to hold some money so that you could later buy a "hot" stock or bond at a price you think attractive. Thus, you'd be holding money in the hope that a better financial opportunity would later appear. In this sense, you'd be *speculating* with your money, forgoing present opportunities to earn interest in the hope of hitting a real jackpot later. These money balances represent a **speculative demand for money.**

speculative demand for money: Money held for speculative purposes, for later financial opportunities.

The Market Demand Curve. These three motivations for holding money combine to create a *market demand* for money. The question is, what shape does this demand

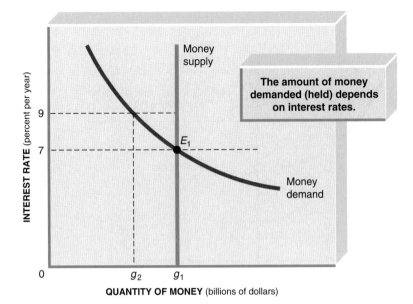

Money supply

The amount of money demanded (held) depends on interest rates.

E_1

Money demand

INTEREST RATE (percent per year)

9

7

0   g_2 g_1

QUANTITY OF MONEY (billions of dollars)

FIGURE 15.1
Money Market Equilibrium

All points on the market demand curve represent the quantity of money people are willing to hold at a specific interest rate. The equilibrium interest rate occurs at the intersection (E_1) of the money supply and money demand curves. At that rate of interest, people are willing to hold as much money as is available. At any other interest rate (for example, 9 percent), the quantity of money people are *willing* to hold won't equal the quantity available, and people will adjust their portfolios.

curve take? Does the quantity of money demanded decrease sharply as the rate of interest rises? Or do people tend to hold the same amount of money, regardless of its price?

People do cut down on their money balances when interest rates rise. At such times, the opportunity cost of holding money is simply too high. This explains why so many people move their money out of transactions deposits (M1) and into money market mutual funds (M2) when interest rates are extraordinarily high (for example, in 1980–82). Corporations are even more careful about managing their money when interest rates rise. Better money management requires watching checking account balances more closely and even making more frequent trips to the bank, but the opportunity costs are worth it.

Figure 15.1 illustrates the total market demand for money. Like nearly all demand curves, the market demand curve for money slopes downward. The downward slope indicates that *the quantity of money people are willing and able to hold (demand) increases as interest rates fall* (ceteris paribus).

Once a money demand curve and a money supply curve are available, the action in money markets is easy to follow. Figure 15.1 summarizes this action. The money demand curve in Figure 15.1 reflects existing demands for holding money. The money supply curve is drawn at an arbitrary level of g_1. In practice, its position depends on Federal Reserve policy (Chapter 14), the lending behavior of private banks, and the willingness of consumers and investors to borrow money.

The intersection of the money demand and money supply curves (E_1) establishes an **equilibrium rate of interest.** Only at this interest rate is the quantity of money supplied equal to the quantity demanded. In this case, we observe that an interest rate of 7 percent equates the desires of suppliers and demanders.

At any rate of interest other than 7 percent, the quantity of money demanded wouldn't equal the quantity supplied. Look at the imbalance that exists, for example, when the interest rate is 9 percent. At that rate, the quantity of money supplied (g_1 in Figure 15.1) exceeds the quantity demanded (g_2). All the money (g_1) must be held by someone, of course. But the demand curve indicates that people aren't *willing* to hold so much money at that interest rate (9 percent). People will adjust their portfolios by moving money out of cash and bank accounts into bonds or other assets that offer higher returns. This will tend to lower interest rates (recall that buying bonds tends to lower their yields). As interest rates drop, people are willing to hold more money. Ultimately we get to E_1, where the quantity of money demanded equals the quantity supplied. At that equilibrium, people are content with their portfolio choices.

Equilibrium

equilibrium rate of interest: The interest rate at which the quantity of money demanded in a given time period equals the quantity of money supplied.

FIGURE 15.2
Changing the Rate of Interest

FIGURE 15.2
Changing the Rate of Interest

Changes in the money supply alter the equilibrium rate of interest. In this case, an increase in the money supply (from g_1 to g_3) lowers the equilibrium rate of interest (from 7 percent to 6 percent).

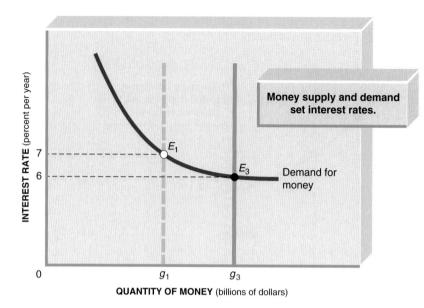

Money supply and demand set interest rates.

QUANTITY OF MONEY (billions of dollars)

Changing Interest Rates

The equilibrium rate of interest is subject to change. As we saw in Chapter 14, the Federal Reserve System can alter the money supply through changes in reserve requirements, changes in the discount rate, or open market operations. By implication, then, *the Fed can alter the equilibrium rate of interest.*

Figure 15.2 illustrates the potential impact of monetary policy on the equilibrium rate of interest. Assume that the money supply is initially at g_1 and the equilibrium interest rate is 7 percent. The Fed then increases the money supply to g_3 by lowering the reserve requirement, reducing the discount rate, or, most likely, purchasing additional bonds in the open market. This expansionary monetary policy brings about a new equilibrium, at E_3. At this intersection, the market rate of interest is only 6 percent. Hence, by increasing the money supply, the Fed tends to lower the equilibrium rate of interest. To put the matter differently, people are *willing* to hold larger money balances only at lower interest rates.

Were the Fed to reverse its policy and reduce the money supply, interest rates would rise. You can see this result in Figure 15.2 by observing the change in the rate of interest that occurs when the money supply *shrinks* from g_3 to g_1.

Federal Funds Rate. As we noted in Chapter 14, the most visible market signal of the Fed's activity is the **federal funds rate.** When the Fed injects or withdraws reserves from the banking system (via open market operations), the interest rate on interbank loans is most directly affected. Any change in the federal funds rate, moreover, is likely to affect a whole hierarchy of interest rates (see Table 15.1).

federal funds rate: The interest rate for interbank reserve loans.

TABLE 15.1
The Hierarchy of Interest Rates

Interest rates reflect the risks and duration of loans. Because risks and loan terms vary greatly, dozens of different interest rates are available. Here are a few of the more common rates as of July 2004.

Interest Rate	Type of Loan	Rate
Federal funds rate	Interbank reserves, overnight	1.25%
Discount rate	Reserves lent to banks by Fed	2.25
Prime rate	Bank loans to blue chip corporations	4.25
Mortgage rate	Loans for house purchases; up to 30 years	5.86
Auto loan	Financing of auto purchase	3.32
Consumer installment credit	Loans for general purposes	11.80
Credit cards	Financing of unpaid credit card purchases	12.93
Source: Federal Reserve.		

The federal funds rate reflects the cost of funds for banks. When that cost decreases, banks respond by lowering the interest rates *they* charge to businesses (the prime rate), home buyers (the mortgage rate), and consumers (e.g., auto loans, installment credit, credit cards).

INTEREST RATES AND SPENDING

A change in the interest rate isn't the end of this story. The ultimate objective of monetary policy is to alter macroeconomic outcomes: prices, output, employment. This requires a change in aggregate demand. Hence, the next question is how changes in interest rates affect consumer, investor, government, and net export spending.

Consider first a policy of monetary stimulus. The goal of monetary stimulus is to increase **aggregate demand.** A mechanism for doing so is lower interest rates.

Investment. Will lower interest rates encourage spending? In Chapter 9 we observed that investment decisions are sensitive to the rate of interest. Specifically, we demonstrated that lower rates of interest reduce the cost of buying plant and equipment, making capital investment more profitable. Lower interest rates also reduce the opportunity cost of holding inventories. Accordingly, a lower rate of interest should result in a higher rate of desired investment spending, as shown by the movement down the investment-demand curve in Step 2 of Figure 15.3.

Aggregate Demand. The increased investment brought about by lower interest rates represents an injection of new spending into the circular flow. That jump in spending will kick off multiplier effects and result in an even larger increase in aggregate demand. Step 3 in Figure 15.3 illustrates this increase by the rightward *shift* of the aggregate demand curve. Market participants, encouraged by lower interest rates, are now willing to buy more output at the prevailing price level.

Consumers too may change their behavior when interest rates fall. As interest rates fall, mortgage payments decline. Monthly payments on home equity and credit card balances may also decline. These lower interest changes can free up billions of consumer dollars. This increased net cash flow and lower interest rates may encourage consumers

Monetary Stimulus

aggregate demand: The total quantity of output demanded at alternative price levels in a given time period, *ceteris paribus.*

Compare the interest rates in Table 15.1 with today's rates at www.stls.frb.org.

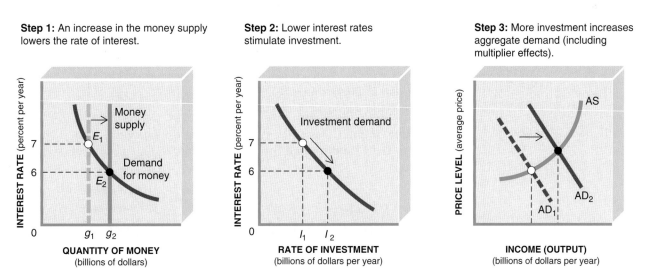

Step 1: An increase in the money supply lowers the rate of interest.

Step 2: Lower interest rates stimulate investment.

Step 3: More investment increases aggregate demand (including multiplier effects).

FIGURE 15.3
Monetary Stimulus

An increase in the money supply may reduce interest rates and encourage more investment. The increase in investment will trigger multiplier effects that increase aggregate demand by an even larger amount.

IN THE NEWS

More People Refinance to Wring Cash Out of Their Homes

McLEAN, Va.—Jay and Sharon Sebastian refinanced the mortgage on their 30-year-old home this month for the second time in less than a year. And, like millions of others, they took out some cold, hard cash that soon will be spent.

Not only did they reduce their 30-year fixed interest rate from 6⅝% to 6%, they upped the mortgage on their four-bedroom, three-bath home in this Washington, D.C., suburb to $300,000 from the previous $275,000 balance. The bank cut them a check for $25,000, which they're using to remodel their outdated kitchen with granite countertops, hardwood floors and stainless steel appliances.

"The check is going in the mail today for the (remodeling) deposit, so it's going right back into the economy," says Jay, a 40-year-old software development manager.

Luckily for the economy, many homeowners are doing the same thing.

Most Take Extra Cash

As mortgage rates hover near record lows, nearly two-thirds of the millions of Americans who are refinancing their homes are doing "cash-outs"—when homeowners increase their mortgage amounts based on the appreciation of their homes and pocket the difference. . . .

The extra cash, along with lower monthly mortgage payments from a raft of refinancings, is acting as a key source of spending as the U.S. economy struggles to stay on its feet, many economists say. . . .

An estimated $140 billion was cashed out last year. That helped boost consumer spending in a year that saw a recession, a falling stock market and the Sept. 11 attacks—all blows that were expected to lead consumers into hibernation. Instead, consumer spending rose 2.5% last year to an inflation-adjusted $6.4 trillion, accounting for more than two-thirds of all U.S. economic activity. . . .

The benefit to the economy doesn't stop at the first sale. If the Sebastians' contractor decides to use his cut to take his family on a trip to Disney World, which then hires a new person to play a dwarf and that person buys a new stereo, the economy has benefited three more times.

—Barbara Hagenbaugh

Source: *USA Today,* October 28, 2002. USA TODAY. Copyright 2002. Reprinted with permission.

Analysis: Lower interest rates encourage market participants to borrow and spend more money. This shifts the AD curve rightward.

---

to buy new cars, appliances, or other "big-ticket" items (see News). State and local governments may also conclude that lower interest rates increase the desirability of bond-financed public works. All such responses would add to aggregate demand.

From this perspective, *the Fed's objective of stimulating the economy is achieved in three distinct steps:*

- *An increase in the money supply.*
- *A reduction in interest rates.*
- *An increase in aggregate demand.*

Quantitative Impact. Just how much stimulus can monetary policy create? According to Fed Chairman Alan Greenspan, the impact of monetary policy can be impressive:

$$\text{Greenspan's policy guide:} \quad \frac{\text{1/10 point reduction in}}{\text{long-term interest rate}} = \frac{\text{\$10 billion}}{\text{fiscal stimulus}}$$

By this rule of thumb, a full-point reduction in long-term interest rates would increase aggregate demand just as much as a $100 billion injection of new government spending. This kind of stimulus was evident in 2002–3: low interest rates prompted a consumer-driven spending spree (see News). This injection of new spending shifted the AD curve rightward, propelling the economy out of recession.

Monetary Restraint

Like fiscal policy, monetary policy is a two-edged sword, at times seeking to increase aggregate demand and at other times trying to restrain it. When inflation threatens, the objective of monetary policy is to reduce the rate of total spending, which puts the Fed in the position of "leaning against the wind." If successful, the resulting reduction in spending will keep aggregate demand from increasing inflationary pressures.

Higher Interest Rates. The mechanics of monetary policy designed to combat inflation are similar to those used to fight unemployment; only the direction is reversed. In this case, we seek to discourage spending by increasing the rate of interest. The Fed can push interest rates up by selling bonds, increasing the discount rate, or increasing the reserve requirement. All these actions reduce the money supply and help establish a new and higher equilibrium rate of interest.

The ultimate objective of a restrictive monetary policy is to reduce aggregate demand. For monetary restraint to succeed, spending behavior must be responsive to interest rates.

Reduced Aggregate Demand. Figure 15.3 showed the impact of interest rates on investment and aggregate demand. If the interest rate rises from 6 to 7 percent, investment declines from I_2 to I_1 and aggregate demand shifts *leftward*. At higher rates of interest, many marginal investments will no longer be profitable. Likewise, many consumers will decide that they can't afford the higher monthly payments associated with increased interest rates; purchases of homes, cars, and household appliances will be postponed. State and local governments may also decide to cancel or postpone bond-financed projects. Thus, ***monetary restraint is achieved with***

- *A decrease in the money supply.*
- *An increase in interest rates.*
- *A decrease in aggregate demand.*

The resulting leftward shift of the aggregate demand curve lessens inflationary pressures.

Ironically, the monetary stimulus of 2001–2 was so effective, that the Fed started worrying about inflation in mid-2004 (see News). In June 2004, monetary policy switched to restraint, not stimulus.

WEBNOTE

For an official explanation of monetary policy, with links to relevant data, visit the Minneapolis Fed at woodrow.mpls.frb.fed.us/info/policy.

IN THE NEWS

Fed Shifts Focus From Job Growth To Rising Prices

WASHINGTON—An unexpected quickening in the pace of price increases in the past two months is challenging the Federal Reserve's plan to raise short-term interest rates only slowly from today's 46-year lows.

The recent shift in prices is at odds with Fed officials' forecast that the combination of unemployment, unused industrial capacity and rapid growth in productivity would keep inflation very low for another year or two.

Fed officials, though not ready to abandon the forecast, acknowledge that their primary concern has shifted in the past few months from sluggish job growth to rising prices. If inflation moves higher in coming months, they are likely to re-examine

their public assessment, made earlier this month, that rates will rise "at a pace that is likely to be measured."

"The flareup in inflation in the first quarter is a matter for concern," Fed Governor Ben Bernanke said yesterday in a speech in Seattle. "The inflation data bear close watching." . . .

The Fed is almost certain to raise its target for the federal-funds rate, charged on overnight loans between banks, from 1% at its late June meeting. Markets are assuming the rate will then rise rapidly to about 2% by the end of the year. . . .

—Greg Ip

Analysis: When inflationary pressures build up, monetary restraint is appropriate. Higher interest rates may slow spending and restrain aggregate demand.

POLICY CONSTRAINTS

The mechanics of monetary policy are simple enough. They won't always work as well as we might hope, however. Several constraints can limit the Fed's ability to alter the money supply, interest rates, or aggregate demand.

Constraints on Monetary Stimulus

Short- vs. Long-Term Rates. One of the most visible constraints on monetary policy is the distinction between short-term interest rates and long-term interest rates. Greenspan's policy guide (previous page) focuses on changes in *long-term* rates like mortgages and installment loans. Yet, the Fed's open market operations have the most direct effect on *short-term* rates (e.g., the overnight federal funds rate). As a consequence, ***the success of Fed intervention depends in part on how well changes in long-term interest rates mirror changes in short-term interest rates.***

In 2001, the Fed reduced the federal funds rate by three full percentage points between January and September, the biggest reduction in short-term rates since 1994. Long-term rates fell much less, however. The interest rate on 30-year mortgages, for example, fell less than half a percentage point in the first few months of monetary stimulus.

Reluctant Lenders. There are several reasons why long-term rates might not closely mirror changes in short-term rates. The first potential constraint is the willingness of private banks to increase lending activity. The Fed can reduce the cost of funds to the banking system; the Fed can even reduce reserve requirements. But the money supply won't increase as much as expected unless banks lend more money.

If the banks instead choose to accumulate excess reserves, the money supply won't increase as much as intended. This happened in 2001, when the Fed was trying to stimulate the economy but banks were reluctant to increase their loan activity (see News). Banks were trying to shore up their own equity and were wary of making any

IN THE NEWS

Uneasy Banks May Tighten Loans, Stunt Recovery

Institutions Seeing More Write-Offs, Delinquencies

A rising tide of bad commercial loans could make banks more reluctant to lend and blunt the impact of the Federal Reserve's latest interest rate cut.

Banks earned a record $19.9 billion in the first quarter, but the proportion of commercial loans 90 days or more past due increased to 1.8 percent—a seven year high, according to a report released Wednesday by the Federal Deposit Insurance Corp.

In the same period, banks wrote off $7 billion in bad loans, up 38 percent from a year earlier.

The combination of higher write-offs and delinquent loans is worrisome, experts say. . . .

Banks will have to set aside more money as a reserve against loan losses, which will hurt their earnings.

More worrisome: Banks tend to reduce lending when write-offs rise. Even though the Fed's rate cuts could spur loan demand from corporate borrowers, companies could find loans harder to get, which could slow an economic recovery.

Last week, Fed Chief Alan Greenspan noted in a speech the increase in problem loans and urged banks not to choke off credit to healthy borrowers.

But about half of all banks have tightened their commercial loan standards this year, according to a survey released Wednesday by the Comptroller of the Currency, which regulates national banks. The most frequently cited reason was the economic outlook.

—Christine Dugas

Source: *USA Today,* June 23, 2001. USA TODAY. Copyright 2001. Reprinted with permission.

Analysis: If banks are reluctant to make new loans in an depressed economy, new bank reserves created by the Fed won't bolster more spending.

(a) A liquidity trap can stop interest rates from falling.

(b) Inelastic investment demand can also impede monetary policy.

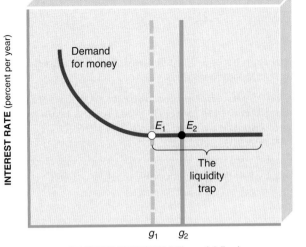

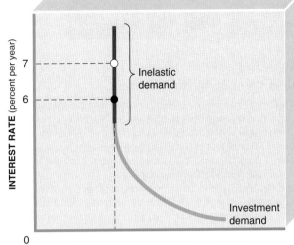

FIGURE 15.4
Constraints on Monetary Stimulus

(a) Liquidity Trap   If people are willing to hold unlimited amounts of money at the prevailing interest rate, increases in the money supply won't push interest rates lower. A liquidity trap— the horizontal segment of the money demand curve—prevents interest rates from falling.

(b) Inelastic Demand   A lower interest rate won't always stimulate investment. If investors have unfavorable expectations for future sales, small reductions in interest rates may not alter their investment decisions. Here the rate of investment remains constant when the interest rate drops from 7 to 6 percent. This kind of situation blocks the second step in the Keynesian approach to monetary policy (see Figure 15.3b).

new loans that might not get repaid in a weak economy. During the Great Depression banks also held onto their excess reserves instead of using them for new loans (recall Figure 14.2). In such cases, long-term rates stay relatively high even when short-term rates are falling.

Liquidity Trap. There are circumstances in which even *short-term* rates may not fall when the Fed wants them to. The possibility that interest rates may not respond to changes in the money supply is illustrated by the liquidity trap. When interest rates are low, the opportunity cost of holding money is cheap. At such times people may decide to hold all the money they can get, waiting for income-earning opportunities to improve. Bond prices, for example, may be high and their yields low. Buying bonds at such times entails the risk of capital losses (when bond prices fall) and little reward (since yields are low). Accordingly, market participants may decide just to hold any additional money the Fed supplies. At this juncture—a phenomenon Keynes called the **liquidity trap**—further expansion of the money supply has no effect on the rate of interest. The horizontal section of the money demand curve in Figure 15.4a portrays this situation.

What happens to interest rates when the initial equilibrium falls into this trap? Nothing at all. Notice that the equilibrium rate of interest doesn't fall when the money supply is increased from g_1 to g_2 (Figure 15.4a). People are willing to hold all that additional money without a reduction in the rate of interest. This is the behavior that neutralized Japan's monetary stimulus in 1999–2001 (see World View on next page).

Low Expectations. Even if both short- and long-term interest rates do fall, we've no assurance that desired *spending* will increase as expected. Keynes put great emphasis

liquidity trap: The portion of the money demand curve that is horizontal; people are willing to hold unlimited amounts of money at some (low) interest rate.

Why Japan Is Stuck
Free Money Can't Budge the Economy

Decades from now, people may still be arguing over one of the most intriguing economic mysteries of the 1990s: How did a country as rich and sophisticated as Japan fall into a liquidity trap, a bizarre state of affairs in which even near-zero interest rates fail to get banks lending, businesses investing, consumers spending, and the real economy moving?

By any measure, Japan's economic crisis this decade has been a nightmare. A vortex of falling asset prices, banking crises, declining corporate profits, and rising government debt has sucked the economy down. . . .

Until recently it was barely credible that an advanced economy could face Japan's dilemma. True, academics once thought a lot about liquidity traps, which Depression-era economist John Maynard Keynes raised as a possibility in the 1930s. But interest in the issue waned in the inflationary post-war decades. And periodic recessions responded to the usual measures.

Blunt Tools. Then came the great Japanese recession. Today, the BOJ is virtually giving money away, and nobody wants it. Japan has vast savings but no credit creation. Japan may have waited far too long to apply classic remedies. Fiscal and monetary tools become blunted once a depression psychology, such as Japan now suffers, sets in.

Japan has cut its official discount rate to 0.5 percent and short-term rates to nearly zero. Yet the economy isn't growing. Here's why:

Banks

Burdened by bad debts and short of capital, they aren't lending; instead, they are putting excess reserves in the bond market.

Companies

They have little incentive to borrow to finance new investment because industrial Japan is already saddled with excess capacity.

Consumers

They are so anxious that they are saving, not spending, even though bank deposits yield less than 1 percent.

Source: *BusinessWeek*, April 12, 1999. Reprinted by permission. Copyright 1999 by The McGraw-Hill Companies.

Analysis: When consumers and businesses are very pessimistic, they are likely to hold more money rather than spend it. Such a liquidity trap blunts monetary stimulus.

---

on *expectations.* Recall that investment decisions are motivated not only by interest rates but by expectations as well. During a recession—when unemployment is high and the rate of spending low—corporations have little incentive to expand production capacity. With little expectation of future profit, investors are likely to be unimpressed by "cheap money" (low interest rates) and may decline to use the lending capacity that banks make available.

Investment demand that's slow to respond to the stimulus of cheap money is said to be *inelastic* because it won't expand. Consumers too are reluctant to borrow when current and future income prospects are uncertain or distinctly unfavorable. Accordingly, even if the Fed is successful in lowering interest rates, there's no assurance that lower interest rates will stimulate borrowing and spending. Such a reluctance to spend was evident early in 2001, even before the September 11 terrorist attacks. Although the Fed managed to push interest rates down to 20-year lows, investors and consumers preferred to pay off old debts rather than incur new ones (see News on page 312). The September 11 attacks made people even more reluctant to borrow and spend.

Monetary stimulus was even less effective in Japan in 1999–2001. When the Japanese central bank cut the discount rate from an extraordinary low ½ percent to an unheard of ¼ percent, no one responded. In the lengthening recession Japanese

Lag Time Is a Variable to Watch in Fed Rate Cut

NEW YORK—Here is a New Economy paradox: Thanks to the increasingly free flow of information, it takes less time than ever for companies and individuals to adjust to changes in the economy. Yet shifts in monetary policy, while perhaps having a faster impact than in the past, can still take between six and 12 months to make their presence really felt.

"We're not going to see growth any stronger tomorrow than it was yesterday," says Bruce Steinberg, chief economist at Merrill Lynch & Co. In fact, he says, "It is going to be the second half of the year at the soonest," before the economy feels the full impact of the half percentage-point decline in interest rates that the Federal Reserve pushed through on Wednesday.

Why such a long lag? Economists say that makets and information may be traveling at supercharged speeds, but simple decisions about how to invest in stocks, whether to buy a new home and when's the right time to upgrade business equipment, travel at very human speeds—and can take months to play out.

—Jon E. Hilsenrath

Source: *The Wall Street Journal*, January 5, 2000. Reprinted by permission of The Wall Street Journal, © 2000 Dow Jones & Company. All rights reserved worldwide.

Analysis: It takes time for consumers and businesses to develop and implement new loan and expenditure decisions. This creates a time lag for monetary-policy effects.

consumers were trying to save more of their money and producer expectations were glum. So even *really* cheap loans didn't budge the aggregate demand curve.

The vertical portion of the investment demand curve in Figure 15.4*b* illustrates the possibility that investment spending may not respond to changes in the rate of interest. Notice that a reduction in the rate of interest from 7 percent to 6 percent doesn't increase investment spending. In this case, businesses are simply unwilling to invest any more funds. As a consequence, aggregate spending doesn't rise. The Fed's policy objective remains unfulfilled, even though the Fed has successfully lowered the rate of interest. Recall that the investment demand curve may also *shift* if expectations change. If expectations worsened, the investment demand curve would shift to the left and might result in even *less* investment at 6 percent interest (see Figure 15.4*b*).

Time Lags. Even when expectations are good, businesses won't respond *instantly* to changes in interest rates. Lower interest rates make investments more profitable. But it still takes time to develop and implement new investments. Hence, **there is always a time lag between interest-rate changes and investment responses.**

The same is true for consumers. Consumers don't rush out the door to refinance their homes or buy new ones the day to Fed reduces interest rates. They might start *thinking* about new financing, but aren't likely to *do* anything for a while. As the accompanying News suggests, it may take 6–12 months before market behavior responds to monetary policy. It took at least that long before investors and consumers responded to the monetary stimulus of 2001–2002.

Expectations. Time lags and expectations could also limit the effectiveness of monetary restraint. In pursuit of "tight" money, the Fed could drain bank reserves and force interest rates higher. Yet market participants might continue to borrow and spend if high expectations for rising sales and profits overwhelm high interest rates in investment decisions. Consumers too might believe that future incomes will be sufficient to cover larger debts and higher interest charges. Both groups

Limits on Monetary Restraint

IN THE NEWS

Vicious Cycle

Despite Rate Cuts, Mood in Boardrooms Is Darkening Further

WASHINGTON—Despite Wall Street's widespread hopes for an economic recovery in the second half of 2001, America's business leaders have adopted a decidedly gloomier view.

At companies across the nation, sales and earnings continue to fall below already-lowered expectations. Federal Reserve officials attempted to drive away that storm cloud yesterday by cutting interest rates by a quarter percentage point, their sixth rate cut in as many months. . . .

Fed officials, citing the risks of "economic weakness in the foreseeable future," sent a clear signal that they were poised to keep easing credit conditions through the summer.

The nation's businesses, meanwhile, have dealt with those same uncertainties by cutting spending, closing facilities and laying off workers—actions that, in turn, further dim the prospects for an imminent turnaround and complicate the Fed's job of keeping the economy out of the ditch. . . .

—Greg Ip

Source: *The Wall Street Journal*, June 28, 2001. Reprinted by permission of The Wall Street Journal, © 2001 Dow Jones & Company. All rights reserved.

Analysis: Interest rate cuts are supposed to stimulate investment and consumption. But gloomy expectations may deter people from borrowing and spending.

might foresee accelerating inflation that would make even high interest rates look cheap in the future. This was apparently the case in Britain in 2004, as the World View below documents.

Global Money. Market participants might also tap global sources of money. If money gets too tight in domestic markets, business may borrow funds from foreign banks or institutions. GM, Disney, ExxonMobil, and other multinational corporations can borrow funds from foreign subsidiaries, banks, and even bond markets. As we saw in Chapter 14, market participants can also secure funds from nonbank sources in the United States. These nonbank and global lenders make it harder for the Fed to restrain aggregate demand.

WORLD VIEW

Rising Rates Haven't Thwarted Consumers

THE BANK OF ENGLAND continued its tightening of monetary policy on June 10. And with the British economy still expanding at a decent clip, more hikes are on the way.

As expected by most economists, the BOE raised its lending rate by a quarter-point, to 4.5%. It was the fourth bump up since November, 2003. In explaining the move, the BOE's statement pointed to above-trend output growth, strong household, business, and public spending, as well as a labor market that "has tightened further." . . .

The BOE is the first of the world's major central banks to raise rates, but the moves have done little to curb borrowing, especially by consumers. Home buying remains robust. . . .

The easy access to credit and the strong labor markets are boosting consumer spending.

Source: *BusinessWeek*, June 28, 2004. Reprinted by permission. Copyright 2004 by The McGraw-Hill Companies.

Analysis: Strong expectations and rising incomes may fuel continued spending even when interest rates are rising.

Analysis: Sometimes monetary stimulus doesn't get a stalled economy moving again.

How Effective? In view of all these constraints on monetary policies, some observers have concluded that monetary policy is an undependable policy lever. Keynes, for example, emphasized that monetary policy wouldn't be very effective in ending a deep recession. He believed that the combination of reluctant bankers, the liquidity trap, and low expectations would render monetary stimulus ineffective. Using monetary policy to stimulate the economy in such circumstances would be akin to "pushing on a string." Alan Greenspan came to much the same conclusion in September 1992 when he said that further Fed stimulus would be ineffective in accelerating a recovery from the 1990–1991 recession. He believed, however, that earlier cuts in interest rates would help stimulate spending once banks, investors, and consumers gained confidence in the economic outlook. The same kind of problem existed in 2001: The Fed's actions to reduce interest rates (11 times in as many months!) weren't enough to propel the economy forward in 2001–2002 (see cartoon). Market participants had to recover their confidence in the future before they would start spending "cheap" money. When that happened, the market response was strong (see News, p. 306).

The limitations on monetary restraint aren't considered as serious. The Fed has the power to reduce the money supply. If the money supply shrinks far enough, the rate of spending will have to slow down.

THE MONETARIST PERSPECTIVE

The Keynesian view of money emphasizes the role of interest rates in fulfilling the goals of monetary policy. *In the Keynesian model, changes in the money supply affect macro outcomes primarily through changes in interest rates.* The three-step sequence of (1) money supply change, (2) interest rate movement, and (3) aggregate demand shift makes monetary policy subject to several potential uncertainties. As we've seen, the economy doesn't always respond as expected to Fed policy.

An alternative view of monetary policy seizes on those occasional failures to offer another explanation of how the money supply affects macro outcomes. The so-called monetarist school dismisses changes in short-term interest rates (e.g., the federal funds rate) as unpredictable and ineffective. They don't think real output levels are affected by monetary stimulus. As they see it, only the price level is affected by Fed policy, and then only by changes in the money supply. Monetarists conclude that monetary policy isn't an effective tool for fighting short-run business cycles, but it is a powerful tool for managing inflation.

The Equation of Exchange

Monetarists assert that the potential of monetary policy can be expressed in a simple equation called the **equation of exchange,** written as

$$MV = PQ$$

equation of exchange: Money supply (*M*) times velocity of circulation (*V*) equals level of aggregate spending (*P* × *Q*).

where M refers to the quantity of money in circulation and V to its **velocity** of circulation. Total spending in the economy is equal to the average price (P) of goods times the quantity (Q) of goods sold in a period. This spending is financed by the supply of money (M) times the velocity of its circulation (V).

income velocity of money (*V*): The number of times per year, on average, a dollar is used to purchase final goods and services; *PQ* ÷ *M*.

Suppose, for example, that only two participants are in the market and that the money supply consists of one crisp $20 bill. What's the limit to total spending in this case? If you answer "$20," you haven't yet grasped the nature of the circular flow. Suppose I begin the circular flow by spending $20 on eggs, bacon, and a gallon of milk. The money I spend ends up in Farmer Brown's pocket because he is the only other market participant. Once in possession of the money, Farmer Brown may decide to satisfy his long-smoldering desire to learn something about economics and buy one of my books. If he acts on that decision, the $20 will return to me. At that point, both Farmer Brown and I have sold $20 worth of goods. Hence, $40 of total spending has been financed with one $20 bill.

As long as we keep using this $20 bill to buy goods and services from each other, we can continue to do business. Moreover, the faster we pass the money from hand to hand during any period of time, the greater the value of sales each of us can register. If the money is passed from hand to hand eight times, then I'll be able to sell $80 worth of textbooks and Farmer Brown will be able to sell $80 worth of produce during that period, for a total nominal output of $160. *The quantity of money in circulation and the velocity with which it travels (changes hands) in product markets will always be equal to the value of total spending and income (nominal GDP).* The relationship is summarized as

$$M \times V = P \times Q$$

In this case, the *equation of exchange* confirms that

$$\$20 \times 8 = \$160$$

The value of total sales for the year is $160.

Monetarists use the equation of exchange to simplify the explanation of how monetary policy works. There's no need, they argue, to follow the effects of changes in M through the money markets to interest rates and further to changes in total spending. The basic consequences of monetary policy are evident in the equation of exchange. The two sides of the equation of exchange must always be in balance. Hence, we can be absolutely certain that *if* **M** *increases, prices* **(P)** *or output* **(Q)** *must rise, or* **V** *must fall.*

The equation of exchange is an incontestable statement of how the money supply is related to macro outcomes. The equation itself, however, says nothing about *which* variables will respond to a change in the money supply. The *goal* of monetary policy is to change the macro outcomes on the right side of the equation. It's *possible,* however, that a change in M might be offset with a reverse change in V, leaving P and Q unaffected. Or it could happen that the *wrong* macro outcome is affected. Prices (P) might rise, for example, when we're trying to increase real output (Q).

Stable Velocity

Monetarists add some important assumptions to transform the equation of exchange from a simple identity to a behavioral *model* of macro performance. The first assumption is that the velocity of money (V) is stable. How fast people use their money balances depends on the institutional structure of money markets and people's habits. Neither the structure of money markets nor people's habits are likely to change when

IN THE NEWS

Monetarists Reject Focus on Lowering Rates

A group of monetarist economists urged the . . . administration and the Federal Reserve yesterday to stop trying to encourage faster economic growth by insisting on lower interest rates.

The group, known as the Shadow Open Market Committee, said that the gross national product, adjusted for inflation, has grown during the past two years at a 2½ percent annual rate, only slightly less than its average for the last 100 years.

"Efforts to force interest rates lower, to depreciate the dollar and to stimulate the economy to head off protectionist (trade) legislation are based on the mistaken belief that we have

learned how to stimulate now and prevent inflation later," the committee said in a statement issued after one of its semiannual meetings in New York. . . .

The Shadow Committee, headed by economists Allan H. Meltzer of Carnegie-Mellon University and Karl Brunner of the University of Rochester, was formed more than a decade ago to provide economic analysis and policy recommendations from a monetarist point of view.

—John M. Berry

Source: *The Washington Post*, September 23, 1986. © 1986 The Washington Post. Reprinted with permission. www.washingtonpost.com

Analysis: Monetarists reject the notion that lower interest rates will necessarily stimulate aggregate demand. What matters is the supply of money, not the rate of interest.

M is altered. Accordingly, an increase in M won't be offset by a reduction in V. Instead, the impact of an increased money supply will be transmitted to the right-hand side of the equation of exchange, which means that ***total spending must rise if the money supply* (M) *grows and* V *is stable*.**

Money Supply Focus

From a monetarist perspective, there's no need to trace the impacts of monetary policy through interest rate movements. The focus on interest rates is a uniquely Keynesian perspective. Monetarists claim that interest rate movements are secondary to the major thrust of monetary policy. *As monetarists see it, changes in the money supply must alter total spending, regardless of how interest rates move.*

A monetarist perspective leads to a whole different strategy for the Fed. Because interest rates aren't part of the monetarist explanation of how monetary policy works, the Fed shouldn't try to manipulate interest rates (see News); instead, it should focus on the money supply itself. Monetarists also argue that the Fed can't really control interest rates well since they depend on both the supply of and the demand for money. What the Fed *can* control is the supply of money, and the equation of exchange clearly shows that money matters.

"Natural" Unemployment

Some monetarists add yet another perspective to the equation of exchange. They assert that not only V but Q as well is stable. If this is true, then changes in the money supply (M) would affect only prices (P).

What does it mean for Q to be stable? The argument here is that the quantity of goods produced is primarily dependent on production capacity, labor market efficiency, and other "structural" forces. These structural forces establish a **"natural" rate of unemployment** that's fairly immune to short-run policy intervention. This is the *long-run* aggregate supply curve we first encountered in Chapter 8. From this perspective, there's no reason for producers to depart from this "natural" rate of output when the money supply increases. Producers are smart enough to know that both prices and costs will rise when spending increases. Hence, rising prices won't create any new profit incentives for increasing output. Firms will just continue producing at the "natural" rate with higher (nominal) prices and costs. As a result, increases in aggregate spending—whether financed by more M or faster V—aren't likely to alter real output levels. Q will stay constant.

natural rate of unemployment: long-term rate of unemployment determined by structural forces in labor and product markets.

The Dropouts—Used by permission of Howard Post.

Analysis: If the money supply shrinks (or its growth rate slows), price levels will rise less quickly.

If the quantity of real output is in fact stable, then P is the only thing that can change. Thus, *the most extreme monetarist perspective concludes that changes in the money supply affect prices only.* As the "simple economics" in the accompanying cartoon suggests, a decrease in M should directly reduce the price level. When M *increases,* total spending rises, but the higher nominal value of spending is completely absorbed by higher prices. In this view, monetary policy affects only the rate of inflation. This is the kind of money-driven inflation that bedeviled George Washington's army (see News).

Figure 15.5 illustrates the extreme monetarist argument in the context of aggregate supply and demand. The assertion that real output is fixed at the natural rate of unemployment is reflected in the vertical aggregate supply curve. With real output stuck at Q^*, any increase in aggregate demand directly raises the price level.

Monetarist Policies

At first glance, the monetarist argument looks pretty slick. Keynesians worry about how the money supply affects interest rates, how interest rates affect spending, and

IN THE NEWS

"Not Worth a Continental": The U.S. Experience with Hyperinflation

The government of the United States had no means to pay for the Revolutionary War. Specifically, the federal government had no power to levy taxes that might transfer resources from the private sector to the public sector. Instead, it could only request the states to levy taxes of their own and contribute them to the war effort. The states were not very responsive, however: state contributions accounted for only 6 percent of federal revenues during the war years.

To pay for needed weapons and soldiers, the federal government had only two other options, either (1) borrow money or (2) create new money. When loans proved to be inadequate, the Continental Congress started issuing new paper money—the "Continental" dollar—in 1775. By the end of 1779, Congress had authorized issuance of over $250 million in Continental dollars.

At first the paper money enabled George Washington's troops to acquire needed supplies, ammunition, and volunteers. But soon the flood of paper money inundated product markets. Wholesale prices of key commodities skyrocketed. Commodity prices *doubled* in 1776, in 1777, and again in 1778. Then prices increased *tenfold* in the next two years.

Many farmers and storekeepers refused to sell goods to the army in exchange for Continental dollars. Rapid inflation had taught them that the paper money George Washington's troops offered was nearly worthless. The expression "not worth a Continental" became a popular reference to things of little value.

The states tried price controls and even empowered themselves to seize needed war supplies. But nothing could stop the inflation fueled by the explosive increase in the money supply. Fortunately, the war ended before the economy collapsed. After the war, the U.S. Congress established a new form of money, and in 1787 it empowered the federal government to levy taxes and mint gold and silver coins.

—Sidney Ratner, James H. Soltow, and Richard Sylla

Source: *The Evolution of the American Economy,* 2nd ed. (1993). © 1979 Sidney Ratner Estate. Reprinted by permission of the authors.

Analysis: Rapid expansion of the money supply will push the price level up. As inflation accelerates, money becomes less valuable.

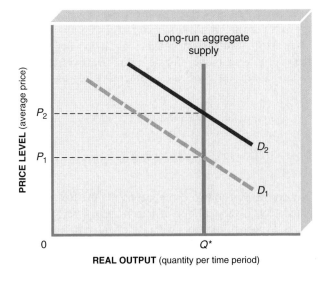

FIGURE 15.5
The Monetarist View

Monetarists argue that the rate of real output is set by structural factors. Furthermore, firms aren't likely to be fooled into producing more just because prices are rising if costs are rising just as much. Hence, long-run aggregate supply remains at the "natural" level Q^*. Any increases in aggregate demand, therefore, raise the price level (inflation) but not output.

how spending affects output. By contrast, monetarists point to a simple equation ($MV = PQ$) that produces straightforward responses to monetary policy.

There are fundamental differences between the two schools here, not only about how the economy works but also about how successful macro policy might be. To appreciate those differences, consider monetarist responses to inflationary and recessionary gaps.

Fighting Inflation. Consider again the options for fighting inflation. The objective of policy is to reduce aggregate spending. From a Keynesian perspective, the way to achieve this reduction is to shrink the money supply and drive up interest rates. But monetarists argue that nominal interest rates are already likely to be high. Furthermore, if an effective anti-inflation policy is adopted, interest rates will come *down,* not go up.

Real vs. Nominal Interest. To understand this monetarist conclusion, we have to distinguish between *nominal* interest rates and *real* ones. Nominal interest rates are the ones we actually see and pay. When a bank pays 5½ percent interest on your bank account, it's quoting (and paying) a nominal rate.

Real interest rates are never actually seen and rarely quoted. These are "inflation-adjusted" rates. Specifically, the **real interest rate** equals the nominal rate *minus* the anticipated rate of inflation; that is,

$$\begin{array}{ccc} \text{Real} & \text{nominal} & \text{anticipated} \\ \text{interest} = \text{interest} - \text{inflation} \\ \text{rate} & \text{rate} & \text{rate} \end{array}$$

real interest rate: The nominal rate of interest minus anticipated inflation rate.

Recall what inflation does to the purchasing power of the dollar: As inflation continues, each dollar purchases fewer goods and services. As a consequence, dollars borrowed today are of less real value when they're paid back later. The real rate of interest reflects this inflation adjustment.

Suppose you lend someone $100 at the beginning of the year, at 8 percent interest. You expect to get more back at the end of the year than you start with. That "more" you expect refers to *real* goods and services, not just dollar bills. Specifically, you anticipate that when the loan is repaid with interest at the end of the year, you'll be able to buy more goods and services than you could at the beginning. This expectation of a *real* gain is at least part of the reason for making a loan.

Your expected gain won't materialize, however, if all prices rise by 8 percent during the year. If the inflation rate is 8 percent, you'll discover that $108 buys you no more at the end of the year than $100 would have bought you at the beginning. Hence, you'd have given up the use of your money for an entire year without any real compensation. In such circumstances, the *real* rate of interest turns out to be zero; that is,

$$\begin{array}{c} \text{Real} \\ \text{interest} \\ \text{rate} \end{array} = \begin{array}{c} 8\% \text{ nominal} \\ \text{interest} \\ \text{rate} \end{array} - \begin{array}{c} 8\% \text{ inflation} \\ \text{rate} \end{array}$$

$$= 0\%$$

The nominal rate of interest, then, really has two components: (1) the real rate of interest, and (2) an inflation adjustment. If the real rate of interest was 4 percent and an inflation rate of 9 percent was expected, the nominal rate of interest would be 13 percent. If inflationary expectations *improved,* the *nominal* interest rate would *fall.* This is evident in the rearranged formula:

$$\begin{array}{c} \text{Nominal} \\ \text{interest rate} \end{array} = \begin{array}{c} \text{real} \\ \text{interest rate} \end{array} + \begin{array}{c} \text{anticipated rate} \\ \text{of inflation} \end{array}$$

If the real interest rate is 4 percent and anticipated inflation falls from 9 to 6 percent, the nominal interest rate would decline from 13 to 10 percent.

A central assumption of the monetarist perspective is that the real rate of interest is fairly stable. This is a critical point. ***If the real rate of interest is stable, then changes in the nominal interest rate reflect only changes in anticipated inflation.*** From this perspective, high nominal rates of interest are a symptom of inflation, not a cure. Indeed, high nominal rates may even look cheap if inflationary expectations are worsening faster than interest rates are rising (see News below).

Consider the implications of all this for monetary policy. Suppose we want to close an inflationary GDP gap. Monetarists and Keynesians alike agree that a reduced money supply (*M*) will deflate total spending. But Keynesians rely on a "quick fix" of *higher* interest rates to slow consumption and investment spending. Monetarists,

IN THE NEWS

Money Is Free!

"Money's not tight, it's cheap. It's free!"

So says one of our most articulate friends along Wall Street. The point is that short-term interest rates, horrendous as they are, are below the short-term inflation rate, horrendous as it is. The August numbers showed a six-month inflation rate of 9.4 percent, for example, while six months earlier the prime interest rate was 8.0 percent. If you borrowed and paid back in cheaper dollars, you got your money for free.

We relate the quote because we have the impression a lot of folks in Washington don't realize how those of us out here in the real world look at these matters. In particular, the observation ought to be of interest to the Federal Reserve's Open Market Committee, which meets today to set money growth targets for both the next two months and the next year.

Out here in the real world, folks know free money when they see it. That is why interest rates will not go down, nor the dollar recover meaningfully, until inflation is reduced. And the longer the Fed delays in starting to curb money growth, the higher price the nation will have to pay before inflation is ultimately brought under control.

Analysis: Monetarists argue that changes in nominal interest rates have little effect on investment. In their view, *real* (inflation-adjusted) interest rates determine investment behavior.

by contrast, assert that nominal interest rates will *fall* if the Fed tightens the money supply. Once market participants are convinced that the Fed is going to reduce money supply growth, inflationary expectations diminish. When inflationary expectations diminish, nominal interest rates will begin to fall.

To get a global view of how interest rates and inflation move together, visit Australia (their central bank) at www.rba.gov.au.

Short- vs. Long-Term Rates (again). The monetarist argument is supported by the different movements of short-term and long-term interest rates. As we observed earlier, short-run rates (like the federal funds rate) are very responsive to Fed intervention. But long-term rates are much slower to respond. This suggests that banks and borrowers look beyond current economic conditions in making long-term financial commitments.

If the Fed is reducing money-supply growth, short-term rates may rise quickly. But long-term rates won't increase unless market participants expect inflation to worsen. Given the pivotal role of long-term rates in investment decisions, the Fed may have to stall GDP growth—even spark a recession—to restrain aggregate demand enough to stop prices from rising. Rather than take such risks, ***monetarists advocate steady and predictable changes in the money supply.*** Such a policy, they believe, would reduce uncertainties and thus stabilize both long-term interest rates and GDP growth.

Fighting Unemployment. The link between anticipated inflation and nominal interest rates also constrains expansionary monetary policy. The Keynesian cure for a recession is to expand M and lower interest rates. But monetarists fear that an increase in M will lead—via the equation of exchange—to higher P. If everyone believed this would happen, then an unexpectedly large increase in M would immediately raise people's inflationary expectations. Even if short-term interest rates fell, long-term interest rates might actually rise. This would defeat the purpose of monetary stimulus.

From a monetarist perspective, expansionary monetary policies aren't likely to lead us out of a recession (look again at the cartoon on p. 313). On the contrary, such policies might double our burden by heaping inflation on top of our unemployment woes. The rate of real output and employment is more dependent on structural characteristics of the economy than on changes in the money supply. All monetary policy should do is ensure a stable and predictable rate of growth in the money supply. Then people could concentrate on real production decisions without worrying so much about fluctuating prices.

THE CONCERN FOR CONTENT

Monetary policy, like fiscal policy, can affect more than just the *level* of total spending. We must give some consideration to the impact of Federal Reserve actions on the *content* of the GDP if we're going to be responsive to the "second crisis" of economic theory.[1]

Both Keynesians and monetarists agree that monetary policy will affect nominal interest rates. When interest rates change, not all spending decisions will be affected equally. Investment decisions that are highly sensitive to interest rates are more susceptible to monetary policy than others. The construction industry, especially the residential housing market, stands out in this respect. The sensitivity of housing costs to interest rate changes forces the construction industry to bear a disproportionate burden of restrictive monetary policy. Accordingly, when the Fed pursues a policy of tight money—high interest rates and limited lending capacity—it not only restrains total spending but reduces the share of housing in that spending. Utility industries,

The Mix of Output

[1]See the quotation from Joan Robinson in Chapter 11, calling attention to the exclusive focus of economists on the *level* of economic activity (the "first crisis"), to the neglect of content (the "second crisis").

public works projects, and state and local finances are also disproportionately affected by monetary policy.

In addition to altering the content of demand and output, monetary policy affects the competitive structure of the market. When money is tight, banks must ration available credit among loan applicants. Large and powerful corporations aren't likely to run out of credit because banks will be hesitant to incur their displeasure and lose their business. Thus, General Motors and IBM stand a much better chance of obtaining tight money than does the corner grocery store. Moreover, if bank lending capacity becomes too small, GM and IBM can always resort to the bond market and borrow money directly from the public. Small businesses seldom have such an alternative.

Income Redistribution

Monetary policy also affects the distribution of income. When interest rates fall, borrowers pay smaller interest charges. On the other hand, lenders get smaller interest payments. Hence, a lower interest rate redistributes income from lenders to borrowers. When interest rates declined sharply in 2001, homeowners refinanced their mortgages and saved billions of dollars in interest payments (News, p. 306). The decline in interest rates, however, *reduced* the income of retired persons, who depend heavily on interest payments from certificates of deposit, bonds, and other assets.

THE ECONOMY TOMORROW

Which Lever to Pull?

Our success in managing the macro economy of tomorrow depends on pulling the right policy levers at the right time. But which levers should be pulled? Keynesians and monetarists offer very different prescriptions for treating an ailing economy. Can we distill some usable policy guidelines from this discussion for policy decisions in the economy tomorrow?

The Policy Levers

The equation of exchange is a convenient summary of the differences between Keynesian and monetarist perspectives. There's no disagreement about the equation itself: aggregate spending ($M \times V$) *must* equal the value of total sales ($P \times Q$). *What Keynesians and monetarists argue about is which of the policy levers—M or V—is likely to be effective in altering aggregate spending.*

- *Monetarists* point to changes in the money supply (M) as the principal lever of macroeconomic policy. They assume V is reasonably stable.
- *Keynesian* fiscal policy *must* rely on changes in the velocity of money (V) because tax and expenditure policies have no direct impact on the money supply.

Crowding Out

The extreme monetarist position that *only* money matters is based on the assumption that the velocity of money (V) is constant. *If V is constant, changes in total spending can come about only through changes in the money supply.* There are no other policy levers on the left side of the equation of exchange.

Think about an increase in government spending designed to stimulate the economy. How does the government pay for this fiscal policy initiative? Monetarists argue that there are only two ways to pay for this increased expenditure (G): The government must either raise additional taxes or borrow more money. If the government raises taxes, the disposable income of consumers will be reduced, and private spending will fall. On the other hand, if the government borrows more money to pay for its expenditures, there will be less money available for loans to private consumers and investors. In either case, more government spending (G) implies less private spending (C or I). Thus, *increased G* effectively **"crowds out"** some C or I, leaving total

crowding out: A reduction in private-sector borrowing (and spending) caused by increased government borrowing.

spending unchanged. From this viewpoint, fiscal policy is ineffective; it can't even shift the aggregate demand curve. At best, fiscal policy can change the composition of demand and thus the mix of output. Only changes in M (monetary policy) can shift the aggregate demand curve.

Milton Friedman, formerly of the University of Chicago, champions the monetarist view with this argument:

> I believe that the state of the government budget matters; matters a great deal—for some things. The state of the government budget determines what fraction of the nation's income is spent through the government and what fraction is spent by individuals privately. The state of the government budget determines what the level of our taxes is, how much of our income we turn over to the government. The state of the government budget has a considerable effect on interest rates. If the federal government runs a large deficit, that means the government has to borrow in the market, which raises the demand for loanable funds and so tends to raise interest rates.
>
> If the government budget shifts to a surplus, that adds to the supply of loanable funds, which tends to lower interest rates. It was no surprise to those of us who stress money that enactment of the surtax was followed by a decline in interest rates. That's precisely what we had predicted and what our analysis leads us to predict. But—and I come to the main point— in my opinion, the state of the budget by itself has no significant effect on the course of nominal income, on inflation, on deflation, or on cyclical fluctuations.[2]

Keynesians reply that the alleged constant velocity of money is a monetarist's pipe dream. Some even argue that the velocity of money is so volatile that changes in V can completely offset changes in M, leaving us with the proposition that money doesn't matter.

The liquidity trap illustrates the potential for V to change. Keynes argued that people tend to accumulate money balances—slow their rate of spending—during recessions. A slowdown in spending implies a reduction in the velocity of money. Indeed, in the extreme case of the liquidity trap, the velocity of money falls toward zero. Under these circumstances, changes in M (monetary policy) won't influence total spending. The velocity of money falls as rapidly as M increases. On the other hand, increased government spending (fiscal policy) can stimulate aggregate spending by putting idle money balances to work (thereby increasing V). Changes in fiscal policy will also influence consumer and investor expectations, and thereby further alter the rate of aggregate spending.

Tables 15.2 and 15.3 summarize these different perspectives on fiscal and monetary policy. The first table evaluates fiscal policy from both Keynesian and monetarist viewpoints. The central issue is whether and how a change in government spending (G) or taxes (T) will alter macroeconomic outcomes. Keynesians assert that aggregate demand will be affected as the velocity of money (V) changes. Monetarists say no, because they anticipate an unchanged V.

How Fiscal Policy Works: Two Views

If aggregate demand isn't affected by a change in G or T, then fiscal policy won't affect prices (P) or real output (Q). Thus, monetarists conclude that fiscal policy isn't a viable tool for combating either inflation or unemployment. By contrast, Keynesians believe V will change and that output and prices will respond accordingly.

Insofar as interest rates are concerned, monetarists recognize that nominal interest rates will be affected (read Friedman's quote again) but *real* rates won't be because real interest rates depend on real output and growth, both of which are seen as immune to fiscal policy. Keynesians see less impact on nominal interest rates and more on real interest rates.

[2]Milton Friedman and Walter W. Heller, *Monetary vs. Fiscal Policy* (New York: Norton, 1969), pp. 50–51.

TABLE 15.2
How Fiscal Policy Matters: Monetarist vs. Keynesian Views

Monetarists and Keynesians have very different views on the impact of fiscal policy. Monetarists assert that changes in government spending (G) and taxes (T) don't alter the velocity of money (V). As a result, fiscal policy alone can't alter total spending. Keynesians reject this view, arguing that V is changeable. They claim that tax cuts and increased government spending increase the velocity of money and so alter total spending.

Do Changes in G or T Affect:	Monetarist View	Keynesian View
1. Aggregate demand?	No (stable V causes crowding out)	Yes (V changes)
2. Prices?	No (aggregate demand not affected)	Maybe (if at capacity)
3. Real output?	No (aggregate demand not affected)	Yes (output responds to demand)
4. Nominal interest rates?	Yes (crowding out)	Maybe (may alter demand for money)
5. Real interest rates?	No (determined by real growth)	Yes (real growth and expectations may vary)

What all this boils down to is this: Fiscal policy, by itself, will be effective only if it can alter the velocity of money. ***How well fiscal policy works depends on how much the velocity of money can be changed by government tax and spending decisions.***

How Monetary Policy Works: Two Views

Table 15.3 is a similar summary of monetary policy. This time the positions of monetarists and Keynesians are reversed, or nearly so. Monetarists say a change in M must alter total spending ($P \times Q$) because V is stable. Keynesians assert that V may vary, so they aren't convinced that monetary policy will always work. The heart of the controversy is again the velocity of money. Monetary policy works as long as V is stable, or at least predictable. ***How well monetary policy works depends on how stable or predictable V is.***

Once the central role of velocity is understood, everything else falls into place. Monetarists assert that prices but not output will be directly affected by a change in

TABLE 15.3
How Money Matters: Monetarist vs. Keynesian Views

Because monetarists believe that V is stable, they assert that changes in the money supply (M) must alter total spending. But all the monetary impact is reflected in prices and nominal interest rates; *real* output and interest rates are unaffected.

Keynesians think that V is variable and thus that changes in M might *not* alter total spending. If monetary policy does alter aggregate spending, however, Keynesians expect all outcomes to be affected.

Do Changes in M Affect:	Monetarist View	Keynesian View
1. Aggregate demand?	Yes (V stable)	Maybe (V may change)
2. Prices?	Yes (V and Q stable)	Maybe (V and Q may change)
3. Real output?	No (rate of unemployment determined by structural forces)	Maybe (output responds to demand)
4. Nominal interest rates?	Yes (but direction unknown)	Maybe (liquidity trap)
5. Real interest rates?	No (depends on real growth)	Maybe (real growth may vary)

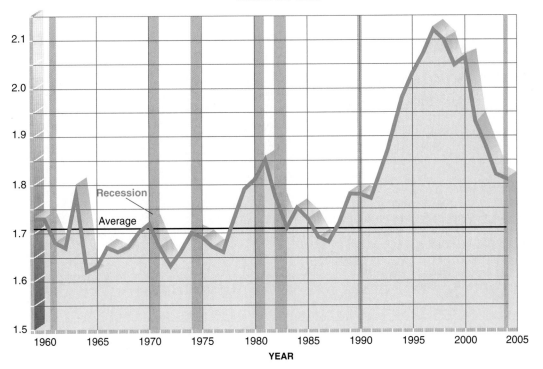

Ratio of GDP to M2

FIGURE 15.6
The Velocity of M2

The velocity of money (the ratio of GDP to M2) averages about 1.64. However, *V* appears to decline in recessions. Keynes urged the use of fiscal stimulus to boost *V*. Monetarists caution that short-run changes in *V* are too unpredictable.

Source: Federal Reserve.

M because the right-hand side of the equation of exchange contains only two variables (*P* and *Q*), and one of them (*Q*) is assumed unaffected by monetary policy. Keynesians, by contrast, aren't so sure prices will be affected by *M* or that real output won't be. It all depends on *V* and the responsiveness of *P* and *Q* to changes in aggregate spending.

Finally, monetarists predict that nominal interest rates will respond to changes in *M*, although they're not sure in what direction. It depends on how inflationary expectations adapt to changes in the money supply. Keynesian economists aren't so sure nominal interest rates will change but are sure about the direction if they do.

Tables 15.2 and 15.3 highlight the velocity of money as a critical determinant of policy impact. The critical question appears to be whether *V* is stable or not. Why hasn't someone answered this simple question and resolved the debate over fiscal versus monetary policy?

Is Velocity Stable?

Long-Run Stability. The velocity of money (*V*) turns out, in fact, to be quite stable over long periods of time. Over the past 30 years the velocity of money (M2) has averaged about 1.64, as Figure 15.6 illustrates. Moreover, the range of velocity has been fairly narrow, extending from a low of 1.56 in 1987 to a high of 2.05 in 1997. Monetarists conclude that the historical pattern justifies the assumption of a stable *V*.

Deflation Still Haunts the Bank of Japan

Critics Say Pledge to Raise a Money-Supply Target Hasn't Produced Results

TOKYO—The Japanese central bank, which had raised hopes it would try to reflate the nation's weak economy, again faces mounting criticism that it is failing to fight the demon of deflation.

The Bank of Japan said in March it would start aiming for a higher money supply, departing from the ordinary practice of targeting a key interest rate, to ease the price declines hammering Japanese companies. But since the March 19 announcement, economists note that Japan's key money-supply indicator has risen modestly, while prices are falling faster. . . .

Deflation is getting worse. The central bank said domestic wholesale prices fell 0.8 percent from a year earlier, dropping for the 10th month in a row.

The data put fresh pressure on central bank governor Masaru Hayami to do more to boost Japan's weakening economy. The bank's policy board meets Monday; most analysts expect it to ease credit in the next few months, but not right away.

In March, the bank unveiled a policy dubbed "quantitative easing," saying it would begin targeting increases in a part of the money supply—the reserve funds that private-sector banks keep at the Bank of Japan—starting with a boost to five trillion yen ($40.48 billion) from four trillion yen. The bank also said it would increase its outright purchases of long-term Japanese government bonds if necessary to top up the money supply.

—Michael Williams

Analysis: When low (near zero) interest rates failed to spark an economy recovery, the Bank of Japan focused on increases in the money supply. Their goal was to keep the price level (P) from falling.

Short-Run Instability. Keynesians reply that monetarists are farsighted and so fail to see significant short-run variations in V. The difference between a velocity of 1.56 and velocity of 2.05 translates into hundreds of billions of dollars in aggregate demand. Moreover, there's a pattern to short-run variations in V: Velocity tends to decline in recessions (see Figure 15.6). These are precisely the situations in which fiscal stimulus (increasing V) would be appropriate.

Money Supply Targets

The differing views of Keynesians and monetarists clearly lead to different conclusions about which policy lever to pull.

Monetarist Advice. The monetarists' policy advice to the Fed is straightforward. *Monetarists favor fixed money supply targets.* They believe that V is stable in the long run and unpredictable in the short run. Hence, the safest course of action is to focus on M. All the Fed has to do is announce its intention to increase the money supply by some fixed amount (such as 3 percent per year), then use its central banking powers to hit that money growth target. After rock-bottom interest rates failed to ignite the Japanese economy, the Bank of Japan decided to adopt the monetarist approach in 2001 (see World View).

Keynesian Advice. *Keynesians reject fixed money supply targets,* favoring more flexibility in control of the money supply. In their view, a fixed money supply target would render monetary policy useless in combating cyclical swings of the economy. Keynesians prefer the risks of occasional policy errors to the straitjacket of a fixed money supply target. *Keynesians advocate targeting interest rates, not the money supply.* Keynesians also advocate liberal use of the fiscal policy lever.

The Fed's Eclecticism. For a brief period (1979–82) the Fed adopted the monetarists' policy of fixed money supply targets. On October 6, 1979, the chairman of the Fed (Paul Volcker) announced that the Fed would begin focusing on the money supply exclusively, without worrying about interest rates. The Fed's primary goal was to reduce inflation, which was then running at close to 14 percent a year. To slow the inflationary spiral, the Fed decided to limit sharply growth of the money supply.

The Fed succeeded in reducing money supply growth and the inflationary spiral. But its tight-money policies sent interest rates soaring and pushed the economy into a deep recession (1981–82). Exactly three years after adopting the monetarist approach, the Fed abandoned it.

In place of a strict monetarist approach,[3] the Fed adopted an eclectic mixture of monetarist and Keynesian policies. For many years the Fed announced targets for money supply growth. But the targets were very broad and not very stable. At the beginning of 1986, for example, the Fed set a target of 3 to 8 percent growth for M1. That wide target gave it plenty of room to adjust to changing interest rates and cyclical changes. But the Fed actually missed the target by a mile—M1 increased by 15 percent in 1986. In explaining this mile-wide miss to Congress, Chairman Volcker emphasized pragmatism. "Success," he asserted, "will not be measured by whether or not we meet some preordained, arbitrary target: but by our macroeconomic performance." Since the economy was growing steadily in 1987, and inflation wasn't increasing, he concluded that monetary policy had been a success. He concluded his testimony by telling Congress that the Fed would no longer set targets for M1 but would instead keep an eye on broader money supply measures (M2 and M3; see Table 13.1) and interest rates. Nobel Laureate Paul Samuelson provided a glib explanation of this approach by noting that "God gave us two eyes so we can keep one on the money supply and the other on interest rates."

Fed watchers say that Alan Greenspan not only uses both eyes but also some personal radar to track the economy and formulate monetary policy. In early 1990, he refused to set a target for growth of the narrowly defined money supply (M1) and set very wide targets (3 to 7 percent) for broader measures of the money supply (M2). For 1993, the Fed set a very broad target range for M2 growth (2 to 6 percent). By midyear it was evident the Fed couldn't even hit that target. Rather than establish yet another target, however, the Fed chairman told Congress that M2 growth was an unreliable policy guide. A more eclectic mix of indicators—including several measures of both the money supply and interest rates—was more appropriate, Greenspan told Congress.

Focus on Federal Funds Rate. Since then, money-supply targets have all but been abandoned. For the last 8–10 years, the focus of Fed policy has been the federal funds rate. The Fed governors assess the state of the economy, then adjust the federal funds rate (via open market operations) as they deem necessary. How do they decide how much of an adjustment is needed? As Alan Greenspan himself explained, "The Federal Reserve specializes in precision guesswork."

Precision guesswork seemed OK when the economy was booming. But many critics blamed the 1990–91 and 2000–2001 recessions on excessive monetary restraint. The pattern of a rapidly rising federal funds rate in 2000 followed by an abrupt reversal in 2001 (see Figure 15.7) caused a lot of second-guessing about Fed policy. When people peer into the economy tomorrow, they wonder how much we should continue to rely on the Fed's "precision guesswork."

---

[3]The Fed's policy of 1979–82 was not strict monetarism. Although the Fed emphasized money supply targets, it allowed the money supply to fluctuate much more than strict monetarists prescribed.

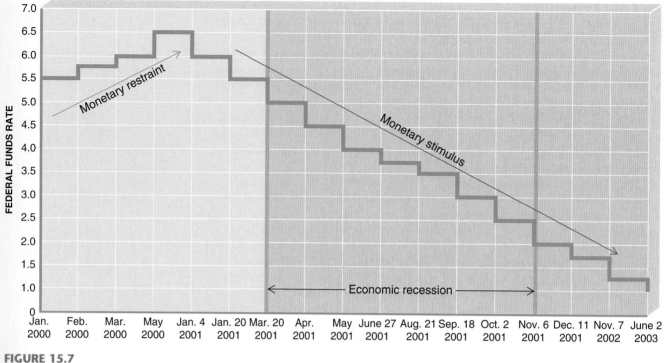

FIGURE 15.7
Policy Reversals

The Fed raised the federal funds rate sharply in 2000, hoping to engineer a "soft landing." The Fed then reversed course abruptly in 2001 when the economy slowed too much. It pursued mone- tary stimulus for 2½ years with 13 interest-rate cuts. The Fed reversed direction again in 2004. (News, p. 307).

SUMMARY

- The essence of monetary policy lies in the Federal Reserve's control over the money supply. By altering the money supply, the Fed can determine the amount of pur- chasing power available.
- There are sharp disagreements about how monetary pol- icy works. Keynesians argue that monetary policy works indirectly, through its effects on interest rates and spend- ing. Monetarists assert that monetary policy has more di- rect and more certain impacts, particularly on price levels.
- In the Keynesian view, the demand for money is impor- tant. This demand reflects desires to hold money (in cash or bank balances) for transactions, precautionary, and speculative purposes. The interaction of money supply and money demand determines the equilibrium rate of interest.
- From a Keynesian perspective, the impact of monetary policy on the economy occurs in three distinct steps: (1) changes in the money supply alter interest rates; (2) changes in interest rates alter the rate of expendi- ture; and (3) the change in desired expenditure alters (shifts) aggregate demand.
- For Keynesian monetary policy to be fully effective, interest rates must be responsive to changes in the money supply, and spending must be responsive to

changes in interest rates. Neither condition is assured. In a liquidity trap, people are willing to hold unlimited amounts of money at some low rate of interest. The interest rate won't fall below this level as the money sup- ply increases. Also, investor expectations of sales and profits may override interest rate considerations in the investment decision.
- Fed policy has the most direct impact on short-term interest rates, particularly the overnight federal funds rate. Long- term rates are less responsive to open market operations.
- The monetarist school emphasizes long-term linkages. Using the equation of exchange ($MV = PQ$) as a base, monetarists assert that the velocity of money (V) is stable, so that changes in M must influence ($P \times Q$). Monetarists focus on the money supply; Keynesians, on interest rates.
- Some monetarists also argue that the level of real output (Q) is set by structural forces, as illustrated by the verti- cal, long-run aggregate supply curve. Q is therefore in- sensitive to changes in aggregate spending. If both V and Q are constant, changes in M directly affect P.
- Monetary policy attempts to influence total expenditure by changing M and will be fully effective only if V is constant. Fiscal policy attempts to influence total expenditure by

changing V and will be fully effective only if M doesn't change in the opposite direction. The controversy over the effectiveness of fiscal versus monetary policy depends on whether the velocity of money (V) is stable or instead is subject to policy influence.

- The velocity of money is more stable over long periods of time than over short periods. Keynesians conclude that

this makes fiscal policy more powerful in the short run. Monetarists conclude that the unpredictability of short-run velocity makes *any* short-run policy risky.

- Fed policy has evolved from an emphasis on money-supply targets, to dual targeting of the money supply and interest rates, to a focus on short-term interest rates.

Key Terms

monetary policy
interest rate
money supply (M1, M2)
demand for money
portfolio decision
transactions demand for money

precautionary demand for money
speculative demand for money
equilibrium rate of interest
federal funds rate
aggregate demand
liquidity trap

equation of exchange
income velocity of money (V)
natural rate of unemployment
real interest rate
crowding out

Questions for Discussion

1. What proportions of your money balance are held for transactions, precautionary, and speculative purposes? Can you think of any other purposes for holding money?
2. Why do high interest rates so adversely affect the demand for housing and yet have so little influence on the demand for pizzas?
3. If the Federal Reserve banks mailed everyone a brand-new $100 bill, what would happen to prices, output, and income? Illustrate your answer by using the equation of exchange.
4. Can there be any inflation without an increase in the money supply? How?
5. How might the existence of multiplier effects increase the risk of inflation when interest rates are cut?
6. When prices started doubling (see News, page 316), why didn't the Continental Congress print even *more* money

so Washington's army could continue to buy supplies? What brings an end to such "inflation financing"?
7. How can money be truly "free" if you have to pay interest on loans? (See News, page 318.)
8. Could long-term interest rates rise when short-term rates are falling? What would cause such a pattern?
9. In the News on p. 306, what starts the multiplier process? When will it stop?
10. Why were banks reluctant to use their lending capacity in 2001? (See News, page 308.) What did they do with their increased reserves?
11. How did the Bank of Japan hope to increase the money supply in 2001? (See World View, page 324.) If M did increase, would the economy necessarily recover?
12. Why don't businesses and consumers respond more quickly to interest-rate changes? (News, p. 311). Which responses are particularly slow?

PROBLEMS   The Student Problem Set at the back of this book contains numerical and graphing problems for this chapter.

WEB ACTIVITIES   to accompany this chapter can be found on the Online Learning Center: **http://www.mhhe.com/economics/schiller10**

PART 6

Supply-Side Options

Fiscal and monetary levers attempt to alter macro outcomes by managing aggregate demand. Supply-side policies focus on possibilities for shifting the aggregate *supply* curve instead. In the short run, any increase in aggregate supply promotes more output and less inflation. Supply-siders also emphasize how shifts of aggregate supply are critical to long-run economic growth. Chapter 16 focuses on short-run supply-side options; Chapter 17 takes the long-run view.

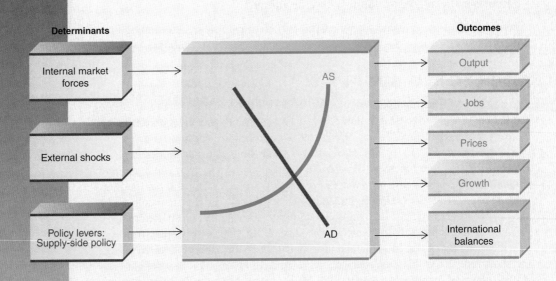

CHAPTER 10

Supply-Side Policy: Short-Run Options

Fiscal and monetary policies focus on the *demand* side of the macro economy. The basic premise of both approaches is that macro goals can be achieved by shifting the aggregate demand curve. The aggregate demand curve isn't the only game in town, however; there's an aggregate supply curve as well. Why not focus instead on possibilities for shifting the aggregate *supply* curve?

Any policies that alter the willingness or ability to supply goods at various price levels will shift the aggregate supply curve. This chapter identifies some of those policy options and examines how they affect macro outcomes. The focus is on two questions:

- **How does the aggregate supply curve affect macro outcomes?**
- **How can the aggregate supply curve be shifted?**

As we'll see, the aggregate supply curve plays a critical role in determining how difficult it is to achieve the goals of full employment and price stability.

AGGREGATE SUPPLY

The impetus for examining the supply side of the macro economy sprang up in the stagflation of the 1970s. **Stagflation** occurs when both unemployment *and* inflation increase at the same time. From 1973 to 1974, for example, consumer price inflation surged from 8.7 to 12.3 percent. At the same time, the unemployment rate jumped from 4.9 to 5.6 percent. How could this happen? *No shift of the aggregate demand curve can increase inflation and unemployment at the same time.* If aggregate demand increases (shifts right), the price level may rise but unemployment should decline with increased output. If aggregate demand decreases (shifts left), inflation should subside but unemployment increase. In other words, most demand-side theories predict that inflation and unemployment move in *opposite* directions in the short run. When this didn't happen, an alternative explanation was sought. The explanation was found on the supply side of the macro economy. Two critical clues were (1) the shape of the **aggregate supply** curve and (2) potential AS shifts.

stagflation: The simultaneous occurrence of substantial unemployment and inflation.

SHAPE OF THE AS CURVE

As we've seen, the basic short-run objective of fiscal and monetary policy is to attain full employment and price stability. The strategy is to shift the aggregate demand curve to a more favorable position. Now the question turns to the *response* of producers to an aggregate demand shift. Will they increase real output? Raise prices? Or some combination of both?

The answer depends on the shape of the aggregate supply curve: *The response of producers to an AD shift is expressed in the slope and position of the aggregate supply curve.* Until now we've used a generally upward-sloping curve

aggregate supply: The total quantity of output producers are willing and able to supply at alternative price levels in a given time period, *ceteris paribus*.

to depict aggregate supply, but we have to recognize that other supply responses are possible.

Figure 16.1 illustrates three very different supply behaviors.

Keynesian AS. Part (*a*) depicts what we've called the "naive" Keynesian view. Recall that Keynes was primarily concerned with the problem of unemployment. He didn't think there was much risk of inflation in the depths of a recession. He expected producers to increase output, not prices, when aggregate demand expanded. This expectation is illustrated by a *horizontal* AS curve. When fiscal or monetary stimulus shifts the AD curve rightward, output (*Q*) rises but not the price level (*P*). Only when capacity (*Q**) is reached do prices start rising abruptly.

Monetarist AS. The monetarist view of supply behavior is very different. In the most extreme monetarist view, real output remains at its "natural" rate, regardless of fiscal or monetary interventions. Rising prices don't entice producers to increase output because costs are likely to rise just as fast. They instead make output decisions based on more fundamental factors like technology and market size. The AS curve is *vertical* because output doesn't respond to changing price levels. (This is the long-run AS curve we first encountered in Chapter 8.) With a vertical AS curve, only prices can respond to a shift in aggregate demand. In Figure 16.1*b*, the AS curve is anchored at the natural rate of unemployment Q_N. When aggregate demand increases from AD_4 to AD_5, the price level (*P*) rises, but output (*Q*) is unchanged.

Hybrid AS. Figure 16.1*c* blends these Keynesian and monetarist perspectives into a hybrid AS curve. At low rates of output, the curve is nearly horizontal; at high rates of output, the AS curve becomes nearly vertical. In the broad middle of the AS curve, the curve slopes gently upward. In this area, shifts of aggregate demand affect *both* prices and output. The message of this hybrid AS curve is that the outcomes of fiscal and monetary policy depend on how close the economy is to full employment. *The closer we are to capacity, the greater the risk that fiscal or monetary stimulus will spill over into price inflation.*

Until now we've used the upward-sloping AS curve depicted in Figure 16.1*c* to characterize producer behavior. Because it allows for varying output/price responses at different levels of economic activity, the AS curve in Figure 16.1*c* is generally regarded as the most realistic for short-run outcomes. However, the upward-sloping section of the AS curve in Figure 16.1*c* has some disturbing implications. Because both prices and output respond to demand-side shifts, the economy can't attain both full employment and price stability at the same time—at least not with fiscal and monetary policies. Consider the simple geometry of policy stimulus and restraint.

Demand Stimulus. Monetary and fiscal stimulus shift the aggregate demand curve rightward. This demand-side effect is evident in all three graphs in Figure 16.1. However, *all rightward shifts of the aggregate demand curve increase both prices and output if the aggregate supply curve is upward-sloping.* This implies that fiscal and monetary efforts to reduce unemployment will also cause some inflation.

Demand Restraint. Monetary and fiscal restraint shift the aggregate demand curve leftward. *If the aggregate supply curve is upward-sloping, leftward shifts of the aggregate demand curve cause both prices and output to fall.* Therefore, fiscal and monetary efforts to reduce inflation will also increase unemployment.

FIGURE 16.1

Contrasting Views of Aggregate Supply

(a) Keynesian AS In the simple Keynesian model, the rate of output responds fully and automatically to increases in demand until full employment (Q^*) is reached. If demand increases from AD_1 to AD_2, equilibrium GDP will expand from Q_1 to Q^*, without any inflation. Inflation becomes a problem only if demand increases beyond capacity—to AD_3, for example.

(b) Monetarist AS Monetarists assert that changes in the money supply affect prices but not output. They regard aggregate supply as a fixed quantum, at the long-run, natural rate of unemployment (here noted as Q_N). Accordingly, a shift of demand (from AD_4 to AD_5) can affect only the price level (from P_4 to P_5).

(c) Hybrid AS The consensus view incorporates Keynesian and monetarist perspectives but emphasizes the upward slope that dominates the middle of the AS curve. When demand increases, both price levels and the rate of output increase. Hence, the slope and position of the AS curve limit the effectiveness of fiscal and monetary policies.

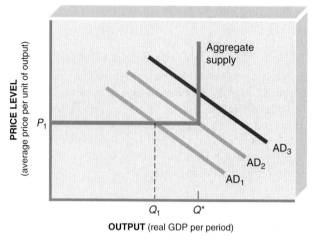

(a) The Keynesian view

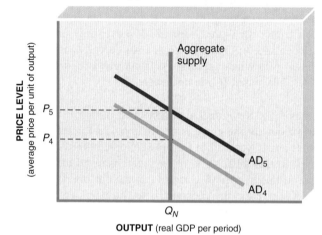

(b) The monetarist view

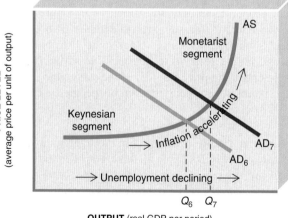

(c) The consensus view

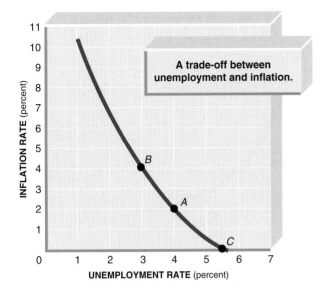

FIGURE 16.2
The Phillips Curve

The Phillips curve illustrates a trade-off between full employment and price stability. In the 1960s it appeared that efforts to reduce unemployment rates below 5.5 percent (point C) led to increasing rates of inflation (points A and B). Inflation threatened to reach unacceptable heights long before everyone was employed.

The Phillips Curve. The message of the upward-sloping aggregate supply curve is clear: *Demand-side policies alone can never succeed completely; they'll always cause some unwanted inflation or unemployment.*

Our macro track record provides ample evidence of this dilemma. Consider, for example, our experience with unemployment and inflation during the 1960s, as shown in Figure 16.2. This figure shows a **Phillips curve,** indicating that prices (P) generally started rising before the objective of expanded output (Q) had been completely attained. Inflation struck before full employment was reached.

The Phillips curve was developed by a New Zealand economist, Alban W. Phillips, to summarize the relationship between unemployment and inflation in England for the years 1826–1957.[1] The Phillips curve was raised from the status of an obscure graph to that of a policy issue by the discovery that the same kind of relationship apparently existed in other countries and at other times. Paul Samuelson and Robert Solow of the Massachusetts Institute of Technology were among the first to observe that the Phillips curve was a reasonable description of U.S. economic performance for the years 1900–1960. For the post–World War II years in particular, Samuelson and Solow noted that an unemployment rate of 4 percent was likely to be accompanied by an inflation rate of approximately 2 percent. This relationship is expressed by point A in Figure 16.2. By contrast, lower rates of unemployment were associated with higher rates of inflation, as at point B. Alternatively, complete price stability appeared attainable only at the cost of an unemployment rate of 5.5 percent (point C). A seesaw kind of relationship existed between inflation and unemployment: When one went up, the other fell.

The trade-off between unemployment and inflation originates in the upward-sloping AS curve. Figure 16.3a illustrates this point. Suppose the economy is initially at equilibrium A, with fairly stable prices but low output. When aggregate demand expands to AD_2, prices rise along with output, so we end up with higher inflation but less unemployment. This is also shown in Figure 16.3b by the move from point a to point b on the Phillips curve. The move from point a to point b indicates a decline in unemployment (more output) but an increase in inflation (higher price level). If demand is increased further, to AD_3, a still lower unemployment rate is achieved but at the cost of higher inflation (point c).

Phillips curve: A historical (inverse) relationship between the rate of unemployment and the rate of inflation; commonly expresses a trade-off between the two.

---

[1]A. W. Phillips. "The Relationship Between Unemployment and the Rate of Change of Money Wage Rates in the United Kingdom, 1826–1957," *Economica* (November 1958). Phillips's paper studied the relationship between unemployment and *wage* changes rather than *price* changes; most later formulations (and public policy) focus on prices.

(a) Increases in aggregate demand cause...

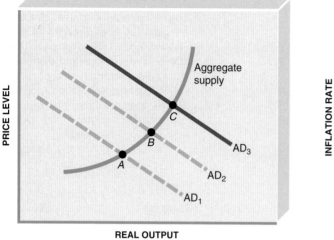

(b) A trade-off between unemployment and inflation.

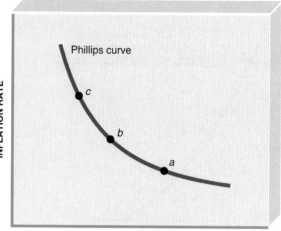

FIGURE 16.3
The Phillips Curve Trade-Off

If the aggregate supply curve slopes upward, increases in aggregate demand always cause both prices and output to rise. Thus, higher inflation becomes a cost of achieving lower unemployment. In (a), increased demand moves the economy from point A to point B. At B, unemployment is lower, but prices are higher. This trade-off is illustrated on the Phillips curve in (b). Each point on the Phillips curve represents a different AS/AD equilibrium from the graph on the left.

SHIFTS OF THE AS CURVE

The unemployment inflation trade-off implied by the upward-sloping AS curve is not etched in stone. Many economists argue that the economy can attain lower levels of unemployment *without* higher inflation. This certainly appeared to be the case in the 1990s: Unemployment rates fell sharply from 1992 to 2000 without any increase in inflation. How could this have happened? There's no AD shift in any of part of Figure 16.1 that would reduce both unemployment *and* inflation.

Rightward AS Shifts: All Good News

Only a rightward shift of the AS curve can reduce unemployment and inflation at the same time. When aggregate supply increases from AS_1 to AS_2 in Figure 16.4, macro equilibrium moves from E_1 to E_2. At E_2 real output is higher, so the unemployment rate

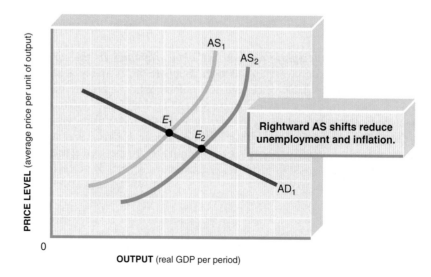

Rightward AS shifts reduce unemployment and inflation.

FIGURE 16.4
Shifts of Aggregate Supply

A rightward AS shift (AS_1 to AS_2) reduces both unemployment and inflation. A leftward shift has the opposite effect, creating stagflation.

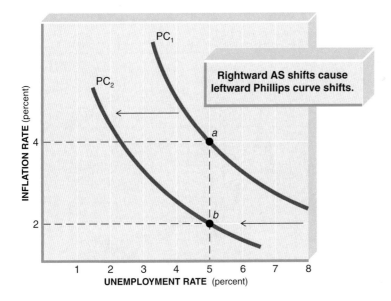

FIGURE 16.5
A Phillips Curve Shift

If the Phillips curve shifts leftward, the short-run unemployment inflation trade-off eases. With PC$_1$, 5 percent unemployment ignites 4 percent inflation (point *a*). With PC$_2$, 5 percent unemployment causes only 2 percent inflation (point *b*).

must be lower. At E_2 the price level is also lower, indicating reduced inflation. Hence, a rightward shift of the AS curve offers the best of two worlds—something aggregate *demand* shifts (Figure 16.1) can't do.

Phillips Curve Shift. As we saw in Figure 16.3, the Phillips curve is a direct by-product of the AS curve. Accordingly, ***When the AS curve shifts, the Phillips curve shifts as well.*** As Figure 16.5 illustrates, the Phillips curve shifts to the left, the opposite of the AS shift in Figure 16.4. No new information is conveyed here. The Phillips curve simply focuses more directly on the implied change in the unemployment-inflation trade-off. ***When the Phillips curve shifts to the left, the unemployment-inflation trade-off eases.***

The Misery Index. To keep track of simultaneous changes in unemployment and inflation, Arthur Okun developed the "misery index"—a simple sum of the inflation and unemployment rates. As the News feature on the next page illustrates, macro misery diminished substantially during the first Reagan administration (1981–84). President Clinton also benefited from a leftward shift of the Phillips curve through 1998, but saw the misery index climb in 1999–2000. President George W. Bush experienced a sharp increase in the misery index during the recession of 2001. The misery index didn't recede until 2004, when strong output growth reduced the unemployment rate.

Whereas rightward AS shifts appear to be a dream come true, leftward AS shifts are a real nightmare. Imagine in Figure 16.4 that the AS shift is reversed, that is, from AS$_2$ to AS$_1$. What would happen? Output would decrease and prices would rise, exactly the kind of dilemma depicted in the accompanying cartoon. In other words, nothing would go in the right direction. This would be rampant stagflation.

A natural disaster can trigger a leftward shift of the AS curve, especially in smaller nations. In 2003, an earthquake struck Iran with a vengeance, killing upward of 40,000 people. In addition, the earthquake leveled homes and office buildings, tore up roads and water systems, and shut down communications networks (see World View on next page). This supply-side shock diminished the capacity for future production.

In a large economy like that of the United States, leftward shifts of aggregate supply are less dramatic. When the Organization of Petroleum Exporting Countries (OPEC) abruptly raises oil prices, many industries experience higher production costs that reduce the ability and willingness to supply output at given price levels. The end result is an increase in both inflation and unemployment. Oil shocks also divert consumer spending from domestic goods and services to imported oil (a form of

The Great Divide

Analysis: Leftward shifts of the aggregate supply curve push price levels up and output down. The remedy for such stagflation is a rightward shift of aggregate supply.

Leftward AS Shifts: All Bad News

To update the misery index, retrieve data on unemployment and inflation from the U.S. Bureau of Labor Statistics at www.bls.gov.

IN THE NEWS

The Misery Index

Unemployment is a problem and so is inflation. Being burdened with both problems at the same time is real misery.

The late Arthur Okun proposed measuring the extent of misery by adding together the inflation and unemployment rates. He called the sum of the two rates the "discomfort index". Political pundits quickly renamed it the "misery index".

In essence, the misery index is a measure of stagflation—the simultaneous occurrence of inflation and unemployment. In 1980, the misery index peaked at 19.6 percent as a result of high inflation (12.5 percent) as well as high unemployment (7.1 percent). Stagflation—and the misery it causes—has since receded markedly.

Source: *Economic Report of the President, 2004.*

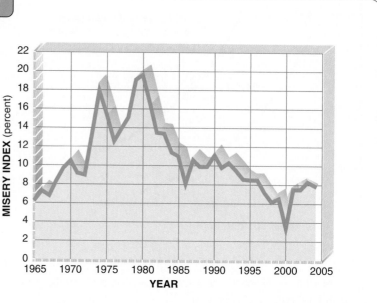

Analysis: Stagflation refers to the simultaneous occurrence of inflation and unemployment. The "misery index" combines both problems into a single measure of macro performance.

circular flow leakage). This kind of external shock contributed to the big increase in macro misery during the years 1975–89 (see above News) and hurt the economy again in 2004 (News on next page).

The September 11, 2001, terrorist attacks on the World Trade Center and Pentagon were another form of external shock. The attacks directly destroyed some production capacity (office space, telecommunications links, transportation links). But they took

WORLD VIEW

Quake Victims Snatch Up Aid As Death Toll Reaches 28,000

BAM, Iran—Survivors of Iran's earthquake scavenged the rubble for their battered belongings and desperately jostled for aid handouts Tuesday as some officials speculated the death toll could reach 50,000.

While the chief U.N. official in Bam, Ted Peran, put the death toll at 28,000, Iranian President Mohammad Khatami said it was expected to climb above 30,000—roughly a third of the city's population. Other government officials said they feared more than 50,000 had been killed. At least 12,000 people were injured in the earthquake, which had a magnitude of 6.6. . . .

Along the ruined streets of Bam, crowds of people surrounded aid trucks. Women in black chadors, some carrying infants, scrambled for old clothes tossed from the back of a truck. Some young men tried to clamber onto the truck to help themselves, but they were pushed back.

Others scavenged in the rubble in search of their belongings. One man extracted a pair of trousers and a bottle of water from a pile of rocks where his house used to be.

—Matthew Pennington,
The Associated Press

Source: *Associated Press,* December 29, 2003. Reprinted with permission of the Associated Press.

Analysis: A natural disaster that destroys both human and physical capital shifts the aggregate supply curve to the left, reducing output and raising price levels.

'Oil Shock' Has Some Economists Worried

Crude oil prices soared yesterday to nearly $49 a barrel, heightening concerns that sustained high energy costs could drag the slowing U.S. and world economies into a more serious downturn.

With growth slowing in China, Europe and Japan, some economists worry that rapidly escalating oil prices will trigger a self-reinforcing spiral of falling demand in the U.S. economy and among its trading partners. . . .

If the price of oil hits $50 a barrel, U.S. households will see their weekly costs rise by an average $14.80 per family, according to a recent study by the National Energy Assistance Directors' Association.

Higher diesel fuel prices raise truckers' costs to haul automobile parts, milk, furniture and other goods from one place to another. Trucking companies increasingly are passing those costs on to other companies. . . .

United Parcel Service Inc., the delivery company that operates a fleet of 88,000 vehicles and 270 aircraft, is paying more for both diesel and jet fuel.

The company adds a surcharge for express packages delivered by air, and it has been raising the surcharge steadily, said Susan Rosenberg, a company spokeswoman. It plans to lift it to 8.5 percent next month.

—Nell Henderson and Justin Blum

Source: *The Washington Post*, August 20, 2004. © 2004 The Washington Post. Reprinted with permission.

Analysis: Higher oil prices increase the costs of production and transportation, shifting the short-run AS curve leftward.

an even greater toll on the *willingness* to supply goods and services. In the aftermath of the attacks businesses, perceiving new risks to investment and production, held back from making new commitments. Increased security measures also made transporting goods more expensive. All of these responses shifted the AS curve leftward and the Phillips curve rightward, adding to macro misery.

From the supply side of macro markets, the appropriate response to negative external shocks is clear: shift the AS curve rightward. As the forgoing graphs have demonstrated, ***rightward shifts of the aggregate supply curve always generate desirable macro outcomes.*** The next question, of course, is how to shift the aggregate supply curve in the desired (rightward) direction. Supply-side economists look for clues among the forces that influence the supply-side response to changes in demand. Among those forces, the following policy options have been emphasized:

Policy Levers

- Tax incentives for saving, investment, and work.
- Human capital investment.
- Deregulation.
- Trade liberalization.
- Infrastructure development.

All these policies have the potential to change supply decisions *independently* of any changes in aggregate demand. If they're effective, they'll result in a rightward shift of the aggregate supply curve and an *improved* trade-off between unemployment and inflation.

TAX INCENTIVES

The most renowned supply-side policy option for improving the unemployment-inflation trade-off was the "supply-side" tax cuts of the early 1980s. Tax cuts are of course a staple of Keynesian economics. But tax cuts take on a whole new role on the supply side of the economy. ***In Keynesian economics, tax cuts are used to increase aggregate demand.***

FIGURE 16.6

Two Theories for Getting the Economy Moving

Keynesians and supply-siders both advocate cutting taxes to reduce unemployment. But they have very different views on the kind of tax cuts required and the impact of any cuts enacted.

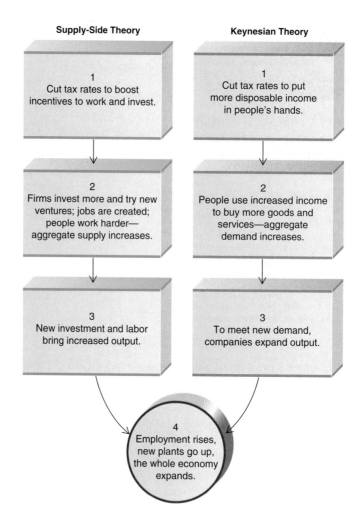

Supply-Side Theory

1 Cut tax rates to boost incentives to work and invest.

2 Firms invest more and try new ventures; jobs are created; people work harder— aggregate supply increases.

3 New investment and labor bring increased output.

Keynesian Theory

1 Cut tax rates to put more disposable income in people's hands.

2 People use increased income to buy more goods and services—aggregate demand increases.

3 To meet new demand, companies expand output.

4 Employment rises, new plants go up, the whole economy expands.

By putting more disposable income in the hands of consumers, Keynesian economists seek to increase expenditure on goods and services. Output is expected to increase in response. From a Keynesian perspective, the form of the tax cut is not very important, as long as disposable income increases.

The supply side of the economy encourages a different view of taxes. Taxes not only alter disposable income but also affect the incentives to work and produce. High tax rates destroy the incentives to work and produce, so they end up reducing total output. Low tax rates, by contrast, allow people to keep more of what they earn and so stimulate greater output. ***The direct effects of taxes on the supply of goods are the concern of supply-side economists.*** Figure 16.6 shows the difference between demand-side and supply-side perspectives on tax policy.

Marginal Tax Rates

marginal tax rate: The tax rate imposed on the last (marginal) dollar of income.

Supply-side theory places special emphasis on *marginal* tax rates. The **marginal tax rate** is the tax rate imposed on the last (marginal) dollar of income received. In our progressive income tax system, marginal tax rates increase as more income is received. Uncle Sam takes a larger share out of each additional dollar earned. In 2005, the highest marginal tax rate on personal income was 35 percent. That top tax rate was far below the 91 percent rate that existed in 1944, but it was also a lot higher than the 12 percent tax rate imposed in 1914 (see Figure 16.7).

In view of the wild history of tax rates, one might wonder whether the rate selected matters. Specifically, does the marginal tax rate affect supply decisions? Will people work and invest as much when the marginal tax rate is 91 percent as when it is only 12 percent? Doesn't seem likely, does it.

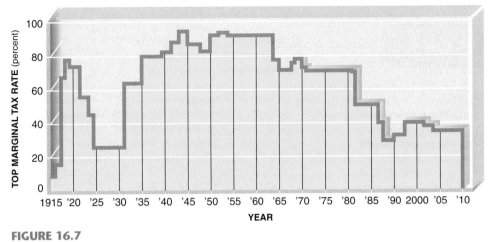

FIGURE 16.7

Changes in Marginal Tax Rates Since 1915

The top marginal tax rate on income has varied from a low of 12 percent in 1914 to a high of 91 percent in 1944. Supply-side theory emphasizes how these varying tax rates affect work, investment, and production decisions, that is, aggregate supply.

Labor Supply. The marginal tax rate directly changes the financial incentive to *increase* one's work. *If the marginal tax rate is high, there's less incentive to work more*—Uncle Sam will get most of the added income. Confronted with high marginal tax rates, workers may choose to stay home rather than work an extra shift. Families may decide that it doesn't pay to send both parents into the labor market. When marginal tax rates are low, by contrast, those extra work activities generate bigger increases in disposable income.

Entrepreneurship. Marginal tax rates affect not only labor-supply decisions but also decisions on whether to start or expand a business. Most small businesses are organized as sole proprietorships or partnerships and subject to *personal,* not *corporate,* tax rates. Hence, a decline in personal tax rates will affect the risk/reward balance for potential entrepreneurs. Columbia Business School professors William Gentry and Glenn Huber have demonstrated that progressive marginal tax rates discourage entry into self-employment. Syracuse professor Douglas Holtz-Eakin and Princeton economist Harvey Rosen have shown that the growth rate, investment, and employment of small businesses are also affected by marginal tax rates. As Holtz-Eakin concluded, "taxes matter."

Investment. Taxes matter for corporations too. Corporate entities account for nearly 90 percent of business output and 84 percent of business assets. Like small proprietorships, corporations, too, are motivated by *after*-tax profits. Hence, corporate **investment** decisions will be affected by corporate tax rates. If Uncle Sam imposes a high tax rate on corporate profits, the payoff to investors will be diminished. Potential investors may decide to consume their income or to purchase tax-free bonds rather than to invest in plant and equipment. If that happens, total investment will decline and output will suffer. Accordingly, *if high tax rates discourage investment, aggregate supply will be constrained.*

If tax rates affect supply decisions, then *changes* in tax rates will shift aggregate supply. Specifically, supply-siders conclude that *a reduction in marginal tax rates will shift the aggregate supply curve to the right.* The increased supply will come from three sources: more work effort, more entrepreneurship, and more investment. This increased willingness to produce will reduce the rate of unemployment. The additional output will also help reduce inflationary pressures. Thus we end up with less unemployment *and* less inflation.

> **investment:** Expenditures on (production of) new plant, equipment, and structures (capital) in a given time period, plus changes in business inventories.

Tax-Induced Supply Shifts

IN THE NEWS

Congress Passes Tax Cut Package

The House and Senate gave final approval to a far-reaching package of tax breaks yesterday, handing President Bush a major victory on his top legislative priority at the close of a tumultuous week in which he and the Republicans lost control of the Senate.

The tax cut, the largest approved by Congress in two decades, provides for millions of refund checks of up to $600 apiece to be mailed to Americans this summer, and grants reductions in most tax rates, tax relief for married couples and parents of young children, and a repeal of the estate tax, though not until 2010.

All of these were priorities set out by the president, who welcomed the tax bill's passage after returning to the White House from Camp David. The plan "cuts income taxes for everyone who pays them. Nothing could be more profound, and nothing could be more fair," Bush said. . . .

The concept of issuing checks to provide immediate tax relief—and help stimulate the economy—was not in Bush's original plan and had not been included in either the House or Senate versions of the legislation; the House and Senate proposals had instead called for adjusting taxpayers' withholding tables.

But the administration, confronting claims from economists that adjusting the withholding tables would not provide a big enough economic boost and charges from Democrats that the tax cut was geared for the wealthy, pressed for including the refund checks in the final tax deal. . . .

The tax bill reduces the top rate from 39.6 percent to 35 percent by 2006, while the president had sought a 33 percent rate.

—Glenn Kessler and Juliet Eilperin

Source: *The Washington Post,* May 27, 2001. © 2001 The Washington Post. Reprinted with permission. www.washingtonpost.com

Analysis: Tax cuts can focus on demand-side or supply-side incentives. The 2001 tax-cut package included both: tax rebates to stimulate demand and reductions in marginal tax rates to stimulate supply.

tax rebate: A lump-sum refund of taxes paid.

From a supply-side perspective, the form of the tax cut is critical. For example, **tax rebates** are a one-time windfall to consumers and have no effect on marginal tax rates. As a consequence, disposable income rises, but not the incentives for work or production. Rebates directly affect only the demand side of the economy.

To stimulate aggregate *supply,* tax *rates* must be reduced, particularly at the margin. These cuts can take the form of reductions in personal income tax rates or reductions in the marginal tax rates imposed on businesses. In either case, the lower tax rates will give people a greater incentive to work, invest, and produce. This was the motivation for the Reagan tax cuts of 1981–84. Shifting the aggregate supply curve rightward was also the goal of President George W. Bush's 2001 proposal to cut the top marginal tax rate from 39.6 percent to 33 percent. Congress ultimately adopted a package of supply-side and demand-side incentives (see News above). On the supply side it phased in a cut in the top marginal tax rate to 35 percent. To shift aggregate demand, Congress also authorized $38 billion of tax rebates in 2001.

Table 16.1 illustrates the distinction between Keynesian and supply-side tax cuts. Under both tax systems (A and B), a person earning $200 pays $80 in taxes before the tax cut and $60 after the tax cut. But under system A, the marginal tax rate is always 50 percent, which means that Uncle Sam is getting half of every dollar earned above $100. By contrast, system B imposes a marginal tax rate of only 30 percent—$0.30 of every dollar above $100 goes to the government. Under system B, people have a greater incentive to earn more than $100. Although both systems raise the same amount of taxes, system B offers greater incentives to work extra hours and produce more output.

Tax Elasticity of Supply

Virtually all economists agree that tax rates influence people's decisions to work, invest, and produce. But the policy-relevant question is, *how much* influence do taxes have? Do reductions in the marginal tax rate shift the aggregate supply curve far to the right? Or are the resultant shifts quite small?

TABLE 16.1
Average vs. Marginal Tax Rates

The same amount of taxes can be raised via two very different systems. Here a person earning $200 pays $80 in taxes under either system (A or B). Thus, the *average* tax rate (total tax ÷ total income) is the same in both cases ($80 ÷ $200 = 40%) but the *marginal* tax rates are very different. System A has a high marginal rate (50%), whereas system B has a low marginal tax rate (30%). System B provides a greater incentive for people to earn over $100.

Initial Alternatives					
Tax System	Initial Tax Schedule	Tax on Income of $200	Average	Marginal	Disposable Income
A	$30 + 50% of income over $100	$80	40%	50%	$120
B	$50 + 30% of income over $100	$80	40%	30%	$120

The average tax rate could be cut to 30 percent under either system. Under both systems, the revised tax would be $60 and disposable income would be increased to $140. Keynesians would be happy with either form of tax cut. But supply-siders would favor system B because the lower marginal tax rate gives people more incentive to earn higher incomes.

Alternative Forms of Tax Cut					
Tax System	Initial Tax Schedule	Tax on Income of $200	Average	Marginal	Disposable Income
A	$10 + 50% of income over $100	$60	30%	50%	$140
B	$30 + 30% of income over $100	$60	30%	30%	$140

The response of labor and capital to a change in tax rates is summarized by the **tax elasticity of supply.** Like other elasticities, this one measures the proportional response of supplies to a change in price (in this case, a tax *rate*). Specifically, the tax elasticity of supply is the percentage change in quantity supplied divided by the percentage in tax rates, that is,

> **tax elasticity of supply:** The percentage change in quantity supplied divided by the percentage change in tax rates.

$$\text{Tax elasticity of supply} = \frac{\%\ \text{change in quantity supplied}}{\%\ \text{change in tax rate}}$$

Normally we expect quantity supplied to go up when tax rates go down. Elasticity (E) is therefore negative, although it's usually expressed in absolute terms (without the minus sign). The (absolute) value of E must be greater than zero, since we expect *some* response to a tax cut. The policy issue boils down to the question of how large E actually is.

If the tax elasticity of supply were large enough, a tax cut might actually *increase* tax revenues. Suppose the tax elasticity were equal to 1.5. In that case a tax cut of 10 percent would cause output supplied to increase by 15 percent (= 1.5 × 10%). Such a large increase in the tax base (income) would result in *more* taxes being paid even though the tax *rate* was reduced. One of President Reagan's economic advisers, Arthur Laffer, actually thought such an outcome was possible. He predicted that tax revenues would increase after the Reagan supply-side tax cuts were made. In reality, the tax elasticity of supply turned out to be much smaller (around 0.15) and tax revenues fell substantially. The aggregate supply curve *did* shift to the right, but not very far, when marginal tax rates were cut.

The evidently low tax elasticity of supply helped President Clinton convince Congress to *increase* marginal tax rates in 1993. Although opponents objected that higher tax rates would reduce work and investment, the Clinton administration pointed out that any leftward shift of aggregate supply was likely to be small. President George W. Bush reversed that shift with the 2001–04 marginal tax-rate cuts.

Savings Incentives

Supply side economists emphasize the importance of *long-run* responses to changed tax incentives. On the demand side, an increase in income translates very quickly into increased spending. On the supply side, things don't happen so fast. It takes time to construct new plants and equipment. People are also slow to respond to new work and investment incentives. Hence, the full benefits of supply-side tax cuts—or the damage done by tax hikes—won't be immediately visible.

Of particular concern to supply-side economists is the rate of saving in the economy. Demand-side economists emphasize spending and tend to treat **saving** as a leakage problem. Supply-siders, by contrast, emphasize the importance of saving for financing investment and economic growth. At full employment, a greater volume of investment is possible only if the rate of consumption is cut back. In other words, additional investment requires additional saving. Hence, *supply-side economists favor tax incentives that encourage saving as well as greater tax incentives for investment.* This kind of perspective contrasts sharply with the Keynesian emphasis on stimulating consumption, as the accompanying cartoon emphasizes.

saving: That part of disposable income not spent on current consumption; disposable income less consumption.

Investment Incentives

An alternative lever for shifting aggregate supply is to offer tax incentives for investment. The 1981 tax cuts focused on *personal* income tax rates. By contrast, President George H. Bush advocated cutting capital gains taxes. These are taxes levied on the increase in the value of property, such as land, buildings, and corporate stock, when it's sold. Lower capital gains taxes, Bush argued, would encourage people to start businesses or invest in them.

President Clinton also emphasized the need for investment incentives. His very first proposal for stimulating the economy was a temporary investment tax credit. People who invested in new plant and equipment would receive a tax credit equal to 10 percent

Don Wright, *The Palm Beach Post.* Reprinted with permission.

Analysis: In the short run, consumer saving may reduce aggregate demand. However, saving also finances increased investment, which is essential to long-run growth.

of their investment. In effect, Uncle Sam would pay for part of any new investment by collecting less taxes. Because the credit is available only to those who make new investments, it's a particularly efficient lever for shifting the aggregate supply curve. President Clinton withdrew the investment-credit proposal, however, when he decided that deficit reduction was a higher priority.

President George W. Bush pulled this supply-side lever more firmly. After securing the huge *personal* tax cuts in 2001, Bush sought *business* tax cuts. In 2002 Congress approved larger capital expensing, which reduced the after-tax cost of new investments. In 2003, tax rates on dividends and capital gains were reduced.

Find out *ways* to save taxes at www.irs.gov. Click on "Information for Individuals."

HUMAN CAPITAL INVESTMENT

A nation's ability to supply goods and services depends on its *human* capital as well as its *physical* capital. If the size of the labor force increased, more output could be produced in any given price level. Similarly, if the *quality* of the workforce were to increase, more output could be supplied at any given price level. In other words, increases in **human capital**—the skills and knowledge of the workforce—add to the nation's potential output.

human capital: The knowledge and skills possessed by the workforce.

Structural Unemployment

A mismatch between the skills of the workforce and the requirements of new jobs is a major cause of the unemployment-inflation trade-off. When aggregate demand increases, employers want to hire more workers. But the available (unemployed) workers may not have the skills employers require. This is the essence of **structural unemployment.** The consequence is that employers can't increase output as fast as they'd like to. Prices, rather than output, increase.

structural unemployment: Unemployment caused by a mismatch between the skills (or location) of job seekers and the requirements (or location) of available jobs.

The larger the skills gap between unemployed workers and the requirements of emerging jobs, the worse will be the Phillips curve trade-off. To improve the trade-off, the skills gap must be reduced. This is another supply-side imperative. *Investments in human capital reduce structural unemployment and shift the aggregate supply curve rightward.*

Worker Training

The tax code is a policy tool for increasing human capital investment as well as physical capital investment. In this case tax credits are made available to employers who offer more worker training. Such credits reduce the employer's after-tax cost of training.

President Clinton proposed even stronger incentives for employer-based training. He wanted to *require* employers to spend at least 1.5 percent of their total payroll costs on training activities. Those employers who didn't provide training activities directly would have to pay an equivalent sum into a public training fund. This "play-or-pay" approach would force employers to invest in the human capital of their employees.

Although the "play-or-pay" concept is intriguing, it might actually shift the aggregate supply curve the *wrong* way. The *costs* of employing workers would rise in the short run as employers shelled out more money for training or taxes. Hence, the aggregate supply curve would shift *leftward* in the short run, worsening the unemployment-inflation trade-off. Only later might AS shift rightward, and then only to the extent that training actually improved **labor productivity.**

labor productivity: Amount of output produced by a worker in a given period of time; output per hour.

Education Spending

Another way to increase human capital is to expand and improve the efficacy of the education system. President George H. Bush encouraged local school systems to become more competitive. He suggested they experiment with vouchers that would allow students to attend the school of their choice. Schools would then have to offer services that attracted voucher-carrying students. Those schools that didn't compete successfully wouldn't have enough funds (vouchers) to continue.

President Clinton advocated a more conventional approach. He urged Congress to allocate more funds to the school system, particularly programs for preschoolers, like Head Start, and for disadvantaged youth. He acknowledged the potential value of vouchers in increasing school quality but wanted to limit their use to public schools. If successful, these efforts will shift the aggregate supply curve rightward. They're more likely to develop human capital gradually, however, than to spur short-term economic growth.

President George W. Bush characterized himself as the "education President." He increased federal spending on education and improved tax incentives for college-savings accounts and tuition payments. Here again, however, any improvements in labor productivity are likely to emerge many years later. There is little potential for short-run AS shifts.

Affirmative Action

Lack of skills and experience aren't the only reasons it's sometimes hard to find the "right" workers. The mismatch between employed workers and jobs is often less a matter of skills than of race, gender, or age. In other words, discrimination can create an artificial barrier between job seekers and available job openings.

If discrimination tends to shift the aggregate supply curve leftward, then reducing discriminatory barriers should shift it to the right. Equal opportunity programs are thus a natural extension of a supply-side approach to macro policy. However, critics are also quick to point out the risks inherent in government regulation of hiring decisions. From a supply-side perspective, laws that forbid discrimination are welcome and should be enforced. But aggressive affirmative action programs that require employers to hire specific numbers of women or minority workers limit productive capabilities and can lead to excessive costs.

Transfer Payments

transfer payments: Payments to individuals for which no current goods or services are exchanged, like Social Security, welfare, unemployment benefits.

Welfare programs also discourage workers from taking available jobs. Unemployment and welfare benefits provide a source of income when a person isn't working. Although these **transfer payments** are motivated by humanitarian goals, they also inhibit labor supply. Transfer recipients must give up some or all of their welfare payments when they take a job, which makes working less attractive and therefore reduces the number of available workers. The net result is a leftward shift of the aggregate supply curve.

In 1996, Congress reformed the nation's core welfare program. The supply-side emphasis of that reform was manifest in the very title of the reform legislation: the Personal Responsibility and Work Opportunity Act. Congress set time limits on how long people can draw welfare benefits. The act also required recipients to engage in job-related activities like job search and training while still receiving benefits.

The 1996 reforms had a dramatic effect on recipient behavior. Nationally, over 5 million adults left welfare between 1996 and 2001. Over half of these ex-welfare recipients entered the labor force, thereby shifting the AS curve rightward.

Recognizing that income transfers reduce aggregate supply doesn't force us to eliminate all welfare programs. Welfare programs are also intended to serve important social needs. The AS/AD framework reminds us, however, that the structure of such programs will affect aggregate supply. With over 60 million Americans receiving income transfers, the effect on aggregate supply can be significant.

DEREGULATION

Government intervention affects the shape and position of the aggregate supply curve in other ways. The government intervenes directly in supply decisions by *regulating* employment and output behavior. In general, such regulations limit the flexibility of producers to respond to changes in demand. Government regulation also tends to raise production costs. The higher costs result not only from required changes in the production process but also from the expense of monitoring government regulations and filling out endless government forms. Thomas Hopkins, a Rochester Institute of Technology economist, estimates that the total costs of regulation exceed $700 billion a year. These added costs of production shift the aggregate supply curve to the left.

Government intervention in factor markets increases the cost of supplying goods and services in many ways.

Factor Markets

Minimum Wages. Minimum wage laws are one of the most familiar forms of factor-market regulation. The Fair Labor Standards Act of 1938 required employers to pay workers a minimum of 25 cents per hour. Over time, Congress has increased the coverage of that act and the minimum wage itself repeatedly (to $5.15 in 2004).

The goal of the minimum wage law is to ensure workers a decent standard of living. But the law has other effects as well. By prohibiting employers from using lower-paid workers, it limits the ability of employers to hire additional workers. Teenagers, for example, may not have enough skills or experience to merit the federal minimum wage. Employers may have to rely on more expensive workers rather than hire unemployed teenagers. In the absence of a minimum wage, employers would hire and train more teenagers and other low-skill workers. With minimum wage requirements, the costs of production increase.

Here again the issue is not whether minimum wage laws serve any social purposes but how they affect macro outcomes. By shifting the aggregate supply curve leftward, minimum wage laws make it more difficult to achieve full employment with stable prices.

Mandatory Benefits. Government-directed fringe benefits have the same kind of effect on aggregate supply. One of the first bills President Clinton signed into law was the Family and Medical Leave Act, which requires all businesses with 50 or more employees to grant leaves of absence for up to 12 weeks. The employer must continue to pay health benefits during such absences and must also incur the costs of recruiting and training temporary replacements. The General Accounting Office estimated this would add nearly $700 million per year to payroll costs. These added payroll costs add to the costs of production, making producers less willing to supply output at any given price level.

Occupational Health and Safety. Government regulation of factor markets extends beyond wages and benefits. The government also sets standards for workplace safety and health. The Occupational Safety and Health Administration (OSHA), for example, issued new rules in November 2000 to reduce ergonomic injuries at work. The rules would have required employers to redesign workplaces (assembly lines, computer workstations) to accommodate individual workers. The rules would have also required employers to pay higher health care costs and grant more injury-related leave. OSHA itself estimated that the new regulations would cost employers $4.5 billion a year. Employers said the ergonomics regulations would cost *far* more that—up to $125 billion a year. Concern over the implied upward shift of aggregate supply prompted Congress to rescind the new ergonomics rules in early 2001, before they took effect (see News on next page).

The government's regulation of factor markets tends to raise production costs and inhibit supply. The same is true of regulations imposed directly on product markets, as the following examples illustrate.

Product Markets

Transportation Costs. At the federal level, various agencies regulate the output and prices of transportation services. Until 1984, the Civil Aeronautics Board (CAB) determined which routes airlines could fly and how much they could charge. The Interstate Commerce Commission (ICC) has had the same kind of power over trucking, interstate bus lines, and railroads. The routes, services, and prices for ships (in U.S. coastal waters and foreign commerce) have been established by the Federal Maritime Commission. In all these cases, the regulations constrained the ability of producers to respond to increases in demand. Existing producers couldn't increase output at will, and new producers were excluded from the market. Hence, the rate of output was kept too low and prices too high.

Bush Signs Repeal of Ergonomics Rules

President Bush signed his first bill carrying national impact yesterday, repealing workplace safety regulations that he called "unduly burdensome and overly broad," and sending his administration to work on a business-friendlier substitute that is months or years away.

Republicans see the repeal, which was whisked through Congress, as a major step in diminishing the regulatory legacy of former president Bill Clinton. Speaking to female business leaders in the East Room, Bush praised Congress for beginning "a culture of accomplishment in Washington." . . .

The ergonomics regulations, which were 10 years in the making, would have taken effect in October. Labor Department officials said they have begun working on an alternative, which could include replacement regulations or voluntary guidelines. A third possibility is a new regulation written at the direction of Congress.

In the meantime, the Occupational Safety and Health Administration will continue to investigate complaints. "OSHA is still charged with ensuring a safe workplace," labor spokesman Stuart D. Roy said.

—Mike Allen

Source: *Washington Post*, March 21, 2001. © 2001 The Washington Post. Reprinted with permission. www.washingtonpost.com

Analysis: Workplace-safety regulations increase production costs and so shift the AS curve leftward. In this case, the implied shift was regarded as excessive.

The Cato Institute, a conservative Washington, D.C., think tank, publishes lots of studies on regulatory costs; visit www.cato.org/research/reglt-st.html.

For the EPA's assessment of how its own regulations affect the U.S. economy, go to www.epa.gov. Click on "Browse EPA Topics," then choose "Economics."

Similar problems continue to inflate intrastate trucking costs. All but eight states limit the routes, the loads, and the prices of intrastate trucking companies. These regulations promote inefficient transportation and protect producer profits. The net cost to the economy is at least $8 billion, or about $128 a year for a family of four.

Many cities and counties also limit the number of taxicabs and regulate their prices. The net effect of such regulation is to limit competition and drive up the cost of transportation.

Food and Drug Standards. The Food and Drug Administration (FDA) has a broad mandate to protect consumers from dangerous products. In fulfilling this responsibility, the FDA sets health standards for the content of specific foods. A hot dog, for example, can be labeled as such only if it contains specific mixtures of skeletal meat, pig lips, snouts, and ears. By the same token, a milk chocolate bar is a milk chocolate bar, according to the FDA, only if it

contains not less than 3.66 percent by weight of milk fat, not less than 12 percent by weight of milk solids, and not less than 10 percent by weight of chocolate liquor as calculated by subtracting from the weight of chocolate liquor used the weight of cacao fat therein and the weights therein of alkali and seasoning ingredients, if any, multiplying the remainder by 2.2, dividing the result by the weight of the finished milk chocolate, and multiplying the quotient by 100.

The FDA also sets standards for the testing of new drugs and evaluates the test results. In all three cases, the goal of regulation is to minimize health risks to consumers.

Like all regulation, however, the FDA standards entail real costs. The tests required for new drugs are expensive and time-consuming. Getting a new drug approved for sale can take years of effort and require a huge investment. The net results are that (1) fewer new drugs are brought to market and (2) those that do reach the market are more expensive than they would have been in the absence of regulation. In other words, the aggregate supply of goods is shifted to the left.

Other examples of government regulation are commonplace. The Environmental Protection Agency (EPA) regulates auto emissions, the discharge of industrial wastes, and water pollution. The U.S. Congress restricts foreign imports and raises their prices.

The Federal Trade Commission (FTC) limits firms' freedom to increase their output or advertise their products.

Many—perhaps most—of these regulatory activities are beneficial. In fact, all were originally designed to serve specific public purposes. As a result of such regulation, we get safer drugs, cleaner air, and less deceptive advertising. We must also consider the costs involved, however. All regulatory activities impose direct and indirect costs. These costs must be compared to the benefits received. ***The basic contention of supply-side economists is that regulatory costs are now too high.*** To improve our economic performance, they assert, we must *deregulate* the production process, thereby shifting the aggregate supply curve to the right again. According to a recent World Bank study, this supply-side insight has global validity (see World View).

Reducing Costs

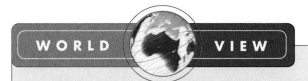

WORLD   VIEW

World Bank Faults Tight Regulation

Study to Argue Fewest Rules Foster Strongest Economies; Goal Is to Promote Changes

WASHINGTON—The World Bank, hoping to spur officials in developing countries to consider changes, plans to release a new survey finding that the least amount of business regulation fosters the strongest economies.

The bank, in cooperation with academics, management-consulting firms and law firms, measured the costs of five basic business-development functions in 130 nations. Titled "Doing Business," the report analyzes how regulation and legal systems affect companies' ability to register with the government, obtain credit, hire and fire workers, enforce contracts and work through bankruptcy courts.

The least regulated and most efficient economies are concentrated among countries with well-established common-law traditions, including Australia, Canada, New Zealand, the United Kingdom and the U.S. On par with the best performers are Singapore and Hong Kong. . . .

The countries with the most inefficient across-the-board regulations and laws are Bolivia, Burkina Faso, Chad, Costa Rica, Guatemala, Mali, Mozambique, Paraguay, the Philippines and Venezuela . . .

"In much of Africa, Latin America and the former Soviet Union, excess regulation stifles productive activity," the authors said.

The report uses its comparisons to advance the thesis that heavier regulation is usually associated with more inefficiency in public institutions, causing longer delays and higher cost. The consequence often is more unemployment and corruption, and less productivity and investment.

— Michael Schroeder and Terence Roth

Let's Make a Deal

Number of days to enforce a commercial business contract:

Fastest Countries	Days	Slowest Countries	Days
Tunisia	7	Guatemala	1,460
Netherlands	39	Serbia and Montenegro	1,028
New Zealand	50	Slovenia	1,003
Singapore	50	Poland	1,000
Botswana	56	Ethiopia	895

Top 10 countries whose regulation systems make it easiest for companies to register, obtain credit, hire and fire workers, enforce contracts and work through the bankruptcy courts.

• Australia	• Denmark	• New Zealand	• Singapore	• U.K.
• Canada	• Netherlands	• Norway	• Sweden	• U.S.

Source: *The Wall Street Journal*, October 7, 2003. Reprinted by permission of The Wall Street Journal, © 2003 Dow Jones & Company. All rights reserved worldwide.

Analysis: More government regulation raises business costs and constrains productivity. Countries with less obtrusive regulation grow faster.

EASING TRADE BARRIERS

Government regulation of international trade also influences the shape and position of aggregate supply. Trade flows affect both factor and product markets.

Factor Markets   In factor markets, U.S. producers buy raw materials, equipment parts, and components from foreign suppliers. Tariffs (taxes on imported goods) make such inputs more expensive, thereby increasing the cost of U.S. production. Regulations or quotas that make foreign inputs less accessible or more expensive similarly constrain the U.S. aggregate supply curve. The quota on imported sugar, for example, increases the cost of U.S.-produced soda, cookies, and candy. Just that one trade barrier has cost U.S. consumers over $2 billion in higher prices.

Product Markets   The same kind of trade barriers affect product markets directly. With completely unrestricted ("free") trade, foreign producers would be readily available to supply products to U.S. consumers. If U.S. producers were approaching capacity or incurring escalating cost pressures, foreign suppliers would act as a safety valve. By increasing the quantity of output available at any given price level, foreign suppliers help flatten out the aggregate supply curve.

Despite the success of the North American Free Trade Agreement (NAFTA) and the World Trade Organization (WTO) in reducing trade barriers, half of all U.S. imports are still subject to tariffs. Nontariff barriers (regulation, quotas, and so forth) also still constrain aggregate supply. This was evident in the multiyear battle over Mexican trucking. Although NAFTA authorized Mexican trucking companies to compete freely in the United States by 2000, U.S. labor unions (Teamsters) and trucking companies vigorously protested their entry, delaying the implied reduction in transportation costs for four years.

Immigration   Another global supply-side policy lever is immigration policy. Skill shortages in U.S. labor markets can be overcome with education and training. But even faster relief is available in the vast pool of foreign workers. In 2000, Congress increased the quota for software engineers and other high-tech workers by 70 percent, to 195,000 workers. The intent was to relieve the skill shortage in high-tech industries and with it, the cost pressures that were increasing the slope of the aggregate supply curve. Temporary visas for farm workers also help avert cost-push inflation in the farm sector. By regulating the flow of immigrant workers, Congress has the potential to alter the shape and position of the short-run AS curve.

INFRASTRUCTURE DEVELOPMENT

infrastructure: The transportation, communications, education, judicial, and other institutional systems that facilitate market exchanges.

Another way to reduce the costs of supplying goods and services is to improve the nation's **infrastructure,** that is, the transportation, communications, judicial, and other systems that bind the pieces of the economy into a coherent whole. The interstate highway system, for example, enlarged the market for producers looking for new sales opportunities. Improved air traffic controls and larger airports have also made international markets and factors of production readily accessible. Without interstate highways and international airports, the process of supplying goods and services would be more localized and much more expensive.

It's easy to take infrastructure for granted until you have to make do without it. In recent years, U.S. producers have rushed into China, Russia, and Eastern Europe looking for new profit opportunities. What they discovered is that even simple communication is difficult where telephones are scarce and unreliable. In China, there are only nine telephones for every 100 people; Russia has 21. By contrast, the United States has 66 phones for every 100 people. Cars and taxicabs are almost as hard to locate in Russia or China, and conference facilities are primitive. There are few established clearinghouses for marketing information, and labor markets are fragmented and localized. Getting started sometimes requires doing everything from scratch.

"I blame government, labor, business, and my ex-wife."

Analysis: Because many constraints on aggregate supply contribute to stagflation, it's hard to single out any one cause (or cure).

Although the United States has a highly developed infrastructure, it too could be improved. There are roads and bridges to repair, more airports to be built, faster rail systems to construct, and space-age telecommunications networks to install. Spending on this kind of infrastructure will not only increase aggregate demand (fiscal stimulus) but also shift aggregate supply.

EXPECTATIONS

Last, but not least, we must again take expectations into account. Expectations play a crucial role not only in consumer expenditure decisions but in production and investment decisions as well. Hence, expectations will influence the shape of the short-run aggregate supply curve—the *willingness* and ability to supply output at various prices. If producers expect more "business-friendly" government policies (see News, page 346), they will be more willing to invest in new plant, equipment, and software. By contrast, the prospect of increasing government regulation or higher taxes deters investors from expanding production capacity. ***Because investment is always a bet on future economic conditions, expectations directly affect the shape of the AS curve.*** Hence, an improvement in expectations will shift the AS curve rightward. In the aftermath of the September 11, 2001, terrorist attacks rebuilding consumer and investor confidence was the most important task for both supply-side and demand-side policy.

THE ECONOMY TOMORROW

Rebuilding America

The output of the U.S. economy depends not only on *private* investment but on *public* investment as well. The infrastructure of transportation, communications, and environmental systems all affect the nation's production possibilities. As we look to the future, we have to wonder whether that infrastructure will satisfy the needs of the economy tomorrow. If it doesn't, it will become increasingly difficult and costly to increase output. Inadequate infrastructure would not only worsen short-term macro outcomes but also impair our ability to compete in world markets.

Declining Infrastructure Investment

The United States has over $2 trillion worth of public, nonmilitary infrastructure, including highways, bridges, sewage systems, buildings, hospitals, and schools. Like private capital (business plant, equipment, and structures), this *public* capital contributes to our production possibilities.

Investment in public infrastructure slowed down in the 1970s and 1980s. As Figure 16.8 shows, the rate of infrastructure investment peaked at around 3.5 percent

FIGURE 16.8
Declining Infrastructure Investment

Relative investments in civilian infrastructure dropped sharply in the 1970s and early 1980s. The investment ratio peaked at about 3.5 percent of GDP in the mid-1960s and plummeted to only 0.5 percent in 1981–82.

Source: David Alan Aschauer, "Infrastructure: America's Third Deficit," *Challenge* (March–April 1991). Reprinted with permission of publisher, M. E. Sharpe, Inc.

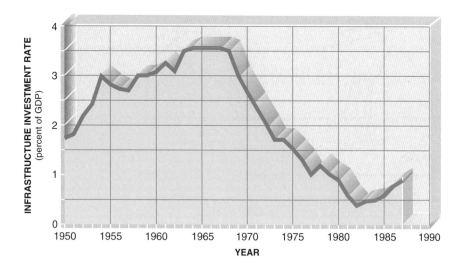

of GDP in the mid-1960s. It then declined steadily to a low of about 0.5 percent of GDP in the early 1980s. As a result of this decline in spending, the United States has barely been able to *maintain* existing infrastructure much less *expand* it. Studies by Alan Aschauer and others suggest that ***declining infrastructure investment has reduced actual and potential output.*** In other words, crumbling infrastructure has shifted the aggregate supply curve leftward.

Not everyone agrees that the nation's infrastructure is actually crumbling. Accident rates on the roads, rails, and in the air have been declining. Moreover, the quality of interstate roads—including the 155,000-mile National Highway system—has improved significantly since 1980. But everyone agrees that ***the transportation system isn't keeping up with a growing economy.*** Highway traffic is increasing at 2.5 percent a year, while airline passenger traffic is rising at closer to 4 percent a year. To accommodate this growth, we need more and better transportation systems.

The Cost of Delay

The failure to expand the infrastructure could prove costly. The U.S. Department of Transportation estimates that people now spend nearly 800 *million* hours a year in traffic delays. If the nation's highways don't improve, those delays will skyrocket to 3.9 *billion* hours a year a decade from now. That's a lot of labor resources to leave idle. Moreover, cars stuck on congested highways waste a lot of gasoline: nearly 3 billion gallons a year.

Delays in air travel impose similar costs. The Federal Aviation Administration says air travel delays increase airline operating costs by over $2 billion a year and idle over $3 billion worth of passenger time. That time imposes a high opportunity cost in forgone business transactions and shortened vacations. Ultimately, all these costs are reflected in lower productivity, reduced output, and higher prices.

The Rebuilding Process

To alleviate these constraints on aggregate supply, Congress voted to accelerate infrastructure spending. The Transportation Equity Act of 2000 raised federal spending to over $60 billion a year. Among the public investments:

- *Highways:* Highway construction and rehabilitation.
- *Air traffic control:* Modernization of the air traffic control system.
- *Weather service:* Modernization of the weather service (new satellites, a supercomputer).
- *Maglev trains:* Research on magnetically levitated ("maglev") trains that can travel at 300 miles per hour and are environmentally clean.
- *Smart cars and highways:* Research and testing of cars and highways outfitted with radar, monitors, and computers to reduce congestion and accidents.

Other legislation authorized more spending on sewage systems, access to space (for example, the space shuttle), modernization of the postal service, and construction of more hospitals, prisons, and other buildings. These infrastructure improvements increase aggregate supply, improving both short- and long-run economic outcomes. To keep track of such activity, the GDP accounts now distinguish government *investment* spending from government *consumption* spending.

SUMMARY

- Fiscal and monetary policies seek to attain full employment and price stability by altering the level of aggregate demand. Their success depends on microeconomic responses, as reflected in the price and output decisions of market participants.
- The market's response to shifts in aggregate demand is reflected in the shape and position of the aggregate supply curve. If the curve slopes upward, a trade-off between unemployment and inflation exists. The Phillips curve illustrates the trade-off.
- If the aggregate supply curve shifts to the left, the trade-off between unemployment and inflation worsens. Stagflation—a combination of substantial inflation and unemployment—results. This is illustrated by rightward shifts of the Phillips curve.
- Supply-side policies attempt to alter price and output decisions directly. If successful, they'll shift the aggregate supply curve to the right. A rightward AS shift implies less inflation *and* less unemployment.
- Marginal tax rates are a major concern of supply-side economists. High tax rates discourage extra work, investment, and saving. A reduction in marginal tax rates should shift aggregate supply to the right.
- The tax elasticity of supply measures the response of quantity supplied to changes in tax rates. Empirical evidence suggests that tax elasticity is low and that short-run shifts of the aggregate supply curve are therefore small.
- Investments in human capital increase productivity and therefore shift aggregate supply also. Workers' training and education enhancement are policy levers.
- Government regulation often raises the cost of production and limits output. Deregulation is intended to reduce costly restrictions on price and output behavior, thereby shifting aggregate supply to the right.
- Public infrastructure is part of the economy's capital resources. Investments in infrastructure (such as transportation systems) facilitate market exchanges and expand production possibilities.
- Trade barriers shift the AS curve leftward by raising the cost of imported imports and the price of imported products. Lowering trade barriers increases aggregate supply.

Key Terms

stagflation
aggregate supply
Phillips curve
marginal tax rate
investment

tax rebate
tax elasticity of supply
saving
human capital
structural unemployment

labor productivity
transfer payments
infrastructure

Questions for Discussion

1. Why might prices rise when aggregate demand increases? What factors might influence the extent of price inflation?
2. What were the unemployment and inflation rates last year? Where would they lie on Figure 16.5? Can you explain the implied shift from curve PC$_2$?
3. Why would a business prefer to locate in Tunisia rather than Guatemala, according to the World View on p. 347?
4. Which of the following groups are likely to have the highest tax elasticity of labor supply? (*a*) college students, (*b*) single parents, (*c*) primary earners in two-parent families, (*d*) secondary earners in two-parent families. Why are there differences?
5. How is the aggregate supply curve affected by (*a*) minimum wage laws, (*b*) Social Security payroll taxes and retirement benefits?

6. OSHA predicted that its proposed ergonomics rules (News, page 346) would have cut repetitive-stress injuries by 50 percent. Was Congress correct in repealing those rules?

7. If all workplace-safety regulations both (*a*) improve workers well-being and (*b*) raise production costs, how should the line between "good" regulations and "bad" regulations be drawn?

8. How do each of the following infrastructure items affect aggregate supply? (*a*) highways, (*b*) schools, (*c*) sewage systems, (*d*) courts and prisons.

9. How would the volume and timing of capital investments be affected by (*a*) a permanent cut in the capital-gains tax, (*b*) a temporary 10-percent tax credit?

10. Why would Democrats oppose a capital-gains tax cut that might invigorate a stalled economy?

11. In the cartoon on page 342, which "expert" is the supply-sider?

ALERT!

PROBLEMS   The Student Problem Set at the back of this book contains numerical and graphing problems for this chapter.

WEB ACTIVITIES   to accompany this chapter can be found on the Online Learning Center:
http://www.mhhe.com/economics/schiller10

Growth and Productivity: Long-Run Possibilities

> Economic growth is the fundamental determinant of the long-run success of
> any nation, the basic source of rising living standards, and the key to meeting
> the needs and desires of the American people.
>
> —*Economic Report of the President, 1992*

Imagine a world with no fax machines, no cellular phones, no satellite TV, and no digital sound. Such a world actually existed—and only 30 years ago! At the time, personal computers were still on the drawing board, and laptops weren't even envisioned. Web sites were a place where spiders gathered, not locations in the Internet. Home video hadn't been seen, and no one had yet popped any microwave popcorn. Biotechnology hadn't yet produced any blockbuster drugs, and people wore the same pair of athletic shoes for a wide variety of sports.

New products are evidence of economic progress. Over time, we produce not only *more* goods and services but also *new* and *better* goods and services. In the process, we get richer: Our material living standards rise.

Rising living standards aren't inevitable, however. According to World Bank estimates, almost 3 *billion* people—nearly half the world's population—continue to live in abject poverty (with incomes of less than $2 per day). Worse still, living standards in many of the poorest countries have *fallen* in the last decade. Living standards also fell in Eastern Europe when communism collapsed and a painful transition to market economies began. Those living in the former Soviet bloc countries are counting on the power of free markets to jump-start their economies and raise living standards.

This chapter takes a longer-term view of economic performance. Chapters 8 to 16 were concerned with the business cycle—that is, *short-run* variations in output and prices. This chapter looks at the prospects for *long-run* growth and considers three questions:

- **How important is economic growth?**
- **How does an economy grow?**
- **Is continued economic growth possible? Is it desirable?**

We develop answers to these questions by first examining the nature of economic growth and then examining its sources and potential limits.

THE NATURE OF GROWTH

Economic growth refers to increases in the output of goods and services. But there are two distinct ways in which output increases, and they have very different implications for our economic welfare.

FIGURE 17.1

Two Types of Growth

Increases in output may result from increased use of existing capacity or from increases in that capacity itself. In part *a* the mix of output at point *A* doesn't make full use of production possibilities. Hence, we can get more output by employing more of our available resources or using them more efficiently. This is illustrated by point *B* (or any other point on the curve).

Once we're on the production possibilities curve, we can get more output only by *increasing* our productive capacity. This is illustrated by the outward *shift* of the production possibilities curve in part *b*.

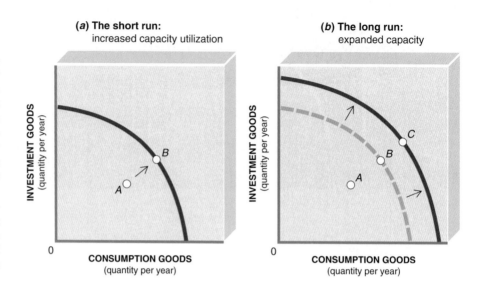

(a) The short run: increased capacity utilization

(b) The long run: expanded capacity

Short-Run Changes in Capacity Utilization

production possibilities: The alternative combinations of final goods and services that could be produced in a given time period with all available resources and technology.

Long-Run Changes in Capacity

economic growth: An increase in output (real GDP); an expansion of production possibilities.

Nominal vs. Real GDP

The easiest kind of growth comes from increased use of our productive capabilities. In any given year there's a limit to an economy's potential output. This limit is determined by the quantity of resources available and our technological know-how. We've illustrated these short-run limits with a **production possibilities** curve, as in Figure 17.1*a*. By using all our available resources and our best expertise, we can produce any combination of goods and services on the production possibilities curve.

We don't always take full advantage of our productive capacity. The economy often produces a mix of output that lies *inside* our production possibilities, like point *A* in Figure 17.1*a*. When this happens, a major *short-run* goal of macro policy is to achieve full employment—to move us from point *A* to some point on the production possibilities curve (such as point *B*). In the process, we produce more output.

Once we're fully utilizing our productive capacity, further increases in output are attainable only if we *expand* that capacity. To do so we have to *shift* the production possibilities curve outward as in Figure 17.1*b*. Such shifts imply an increase in *potential* GDP—that is, our productive capacity.

Over time, increases in capacity are critical. Short-run increases in the utilization of existing capacity can generate only modest increases in output. Even high unemployment rates, such as 7 percent, leave little room for increased output. *To achieve large and lasting increases in output we must push our production possibilities outward.* For this reason, economists often define **economic growth** in terms of changes in *potential* GDP.

The unique character of economic growth can also be illustrated with aggregate supply and demand curves. Figure 17.2 depicts both a sloped, *short-run* AS curve and a vertical, *long-run* AS curve. In the short run, macro stabilization policies try to shift the AD curve to a more desirable price-output equilibrium. Such demand-side policies are unlikely to change the country's long-run capacity to produce, however. At best they move the macro equilibrium to a more desirable point on the *short-run* AS curve (for example, from E_1 to E_2 in Figure 17.2).

Our productive capacity may increase nevertheless. If it does, the "natural" long-run AS curve will also shift. In this framework, *economic growth implies a rightward shift of the long-run aggregate supply curve.* Should that occur, the economy will be able to produce still more output with less inflationary pressure (e.g., as at E_3 in Figure 17.2).

Notice we refer to *real* GDP, not *nominal* GDP, in our concept of economic growth. Nominal GDP can rise even when the quantity of goods and services falls, as was the

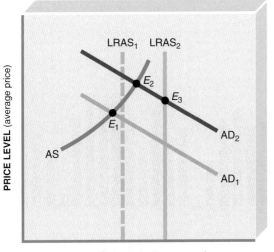

PRICE LEVEL (average price)

REAL OUTPUT (dollars per year)

FIGURE 17.2
Shifts of Long-Run Supply

Macro stabilization policies try to shift the aggregate demand curve (e.g., from AD_1 to AD_2) to achieve greater output and employment. The vertical long-run AS curve implies that these efforts will have no lasting impact on the natural rate of output, however. To achieve economic growth, the long-run aggregate supply curve must be shifted to the right (e.g., from $LRAS_1$ to $LRAS_2$).

case in 1991. The total quantity of goods and services produced in 1991 was less than the quantity produced in 1990. Nevertheless, prices rose enough in 1991 to keep nominal GDP growing.

Real GDP refers to the actual quantity of goods and services produced. Real GDP avoids the distortions of inflation by adjusting for changing prices. By using 1992 prices as a **base period,** we observe that real GDP fell from $6139 billion in 1990 to only $6079 billion in 1991. Since then real GDP has increased nearly 60 percent—an impressive growth achievement.

real GDP: The value of final output produced in a given period, adjusted for changing prices.

base period: The time period used for comparative analysis; the basis for indexing, e.g., of price changes.

MEASURES OF GROWTH

Typically, changes in real GDP are expressed in percentage terms, as a growth *rate*. The **growth rate** is simply the change in real output between two periods divided by total output in the base period. The percentage decline in real output during 1991 was thus $60 billion ÷ $6139 billion, or 1 percent. By contrast, real output grew in 1992 by 2.7 percent.

Figure 17.3 illustrates the recent growth experience of the U.S. economy. In the 1960s, real GDP grew by an average of 4.1 percent per year. Economic growth slowed to only 2.8 percent in the 1970s, however, with actual output declines in three years. The steep recession of 1982, as seen in Figure 17.3, reduced GDP growth in the 1980s to an even lower rate: 2.5 percent per year. The 1990s started out even worse, with negligible growth in 1990 and a recession in 1991. The economy performed significantly better after that, however. From 1997 to 2000, real GDP grew by more than 4 percent a year. That acceleration of the growth rate was so impressive that observers began to talk about a "New Economy," in which faster growth would be the norm (see News on next page).

The notion of a fast-growth New Economy was badly shaken in 2001. In the first quarter of 2001, GDP fell by 0.2 percent and then by 0.6 percent in the second quarter. In the third quarter (which included the Sept. 11 terrorist attacks), real GDP again declined by 1.3 percent. Analysts fretted over whether the economy would ever get back on the "fast track" of 3.5–4.0 percent growth or would instead be saddled with years of more sluggish growth (2.0–2.5 percent)—or worse.

The Growth Rate

growth rate: Percentage change in real output from one period to another.

The U.S. Bureau of Economic Analysis (BEA) maintains quarterly data on real GDP growth in their "overview of the U.S. economy" at www.bea.doc.gov.

The Exponential Process. At first blush, all the anxiety about growth rates seems a bit overblown. Indeed, the whole subject of economic growth looks rather dull when you discover that "big" gains in economic growth are measured in fractions of a percent.

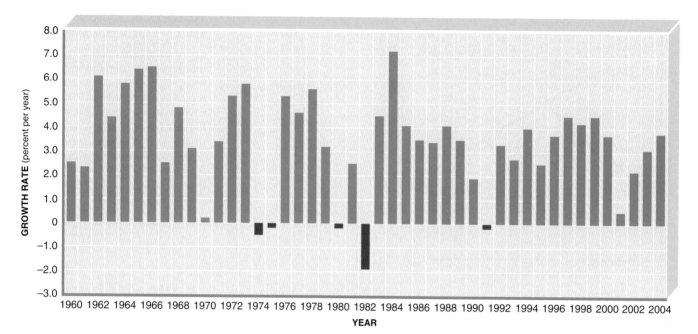

FIGURE 17.3
Recent U.S. Growth Rates

Total output typically increases from one year to another. The focus of policy is on the growth *rate*, that is, how fast real GDP increases from one year to the next. Annual growth rates since 1960 have ranged from a high of 7.2 percent (1984) to a low of *minus* 1.9 percent (1982).

Source: *Economic Report of the President, 2004.*

However, this initial impression isn't fair. First, even one year's "low" growth implies lost output. If we had just *maintained* output in 1991 at its 1990 level—that is, "achieved" a *zero* growth rate rather than a 1 percent decline—we would have had $60 billion more worth of goods and services, which works out to over $200 worth of goods and services per person. Lots of people would have liked that extra output. In today's $11 trillion economy, each 1 percent of economic growth is even more significant.

IN THE NEWS

The New Economy

The U.S. economy today displays several exceptional features. The first is its strong rate of productivity growth. . . . A second is its unusually low levels of both inflation and unemployment. . . . A third is the disappearance of Federal budget deficits. . . . A fourth is the strength of the U.S. economy's performance relative to other industrial economies. . . . These developments reveal profound changes in economic trends that justify the term "New Economy."

Three interrelated factors lie behind these extraordinary economic gains: technological innovation, organizational changes in business, and public policy. . . . The interactions among these three factors have created a virtuous cycle in which developments in one area reinforce and stimulate developments in another. The result is an economic system in which the whole is greater than the sum of the parts. . . .

This Report defines the New Economy by the extraordinary gains in performance—including rapid productivity growth, rising incomes, low unemployment, and moderate inflation—that have resulted from this combination of virtually reinforcing advances in technologies, business practices, and economic policies.

Source: *Economic Report of the President, 2001*, pp. 22–23.

Analysis: The successes of the late 1990s spawned the hope of continuing rapid gains in productivity and GDP growth—a "new" economy. The recession of 2001, coupled with widespread "dot.com" failures, shed doubt on this concept.

Second, economic growth is a *continuing* process. Gains made in one year accumulate in future years. It's like interest you earn at the bank: If you leave your money in the bank for several years, you begin to earn interest on your interest. Eventually you accumulate a nice little bankroll.

The process of economic growth works the same way. Each little shift of the production possibilities curve broadens the base for future GDP. As shifts accumulate over many years, the economy's productive capacity is greatly expanded. Ultimately we discover that those "little" differences in annual growth rates generate tremendous gains in GDP.

This cumulative process, whereby interest or growth is compounded from one year to the next, is called an "exponential process." At growth rates of 2.5 percent, GDP doubles in 28 years. With 3.5 percent growth, GDP doubles in only 20 years. In a single generation the *difference* between 2.5 percent growth and 3.5 percent growth amounts to more than $5 trillion of output a year. That *difference* is about half of this year's total output. From this longer-term perspective, the difference between 2.5 percent and 3.5 percent growth begins to look very meaningful.

The exponential process looks even more meaningful when we translate it into *per capita* terms. We can do so by looking at GDP *per capita* rather than total GDP. **GDP per capita** is simply total output divided by total population. In 2003, the total output of the U.S. economy was $11 trillion. Since there were 290 million of us to share that output, GDP per capita was

$$\text{GDP per capita} \atop (2003) = \frac{\$11 \text{ trillion of output}}{290 \text{ million people}} = \$37,931$$

This does not mean that every man, woman, and child in the United States received $37,931 worth of goods and services in 2003; it simply indicates how much output was potentially available to the "average" person. GDP per capita is often used as a basic measure of our standard of living.

Growth in GDP per capita is attained only when the growth of output exceeds population growth. In the United States, this condition is usually achieved. Even when *total* GDP growth slowed in the 1970s and 1980s, *per capita* GDP kept rising because the U.S. population was growing by only 1 percent a year. Hence, even relatively slow economic growth of 2.5 percent a year was enough to keep raising living standards.

The developing nations of the Third World aren't so fortunate. Many of these countries bear both slower *economic* growth and faster *population* growth. They have a difficult time *maintaining* living standards, much less increasing them. Ethiopia, for example, is one of the poorest countries in the world, with GDP per capita of roughly $720 (see World View in Chapter 2, page 29). Yet its population continues to grow rapidly (2.6 percent per year), putting constant pressure on living standards. The population of Nigeria grew by an average of 2.8 percent per year in the 1990s, while GDP grew at a slower rate of only 2.4 percent (see Table 2.1). As a consequence, GDP per capita *declined* nearly 0.4 percent per year.

By comparison with these countries, the United States has been most fortunate. Our GDP per capita has more than doubled since 1980s, despite several recessions. This means that the average person today has twice as many goods and services as the average person had a generation ago.

What about the future? Will we continue to enjoy substantial gains in living standards? Many Americans harbor great doubts. A 2003 poll revealed that 40 percent of adults believe their children's living standards will be no higher than today's. That would happen only if population growth outstrips or equals GDP growth. That seems most unlikely. Table 17.1 displays more optimistic scenarios in which GDP continues to grow faster than the population. If GDP *per capita* continues to grow at 2 percent per year—as it did in the 1990s—it will take 35 years to double our standard of living. If GDP per capita grows just half a percent faster, say, by 2.5 percent per year, our standard of living will double in only 30 years.

WEBNOTE

Find growth rates of various countries from the World Bank at www.worldbank.org/data. Click on "Data by Topic," then choose "Macroeconomics and Growth." Under "Economic Growth and Structure," click on "Growth of Output."

GDP per Capita: A Measure of Living Standards

GDP per capita: Total GDP divided by total population; average GDP.

TABLE 17.1
The Rule of 72

Small differences in annual growth rates cumulate into large differences in GDP. Shown here are the number of years it would take to double GDP per capita at various net growth rates. *"Net" growth* refers to the GDP growth rate minus the population growth rate.

Doubling times can be approximated by the "rule of 72." Seventy-two divided by the growth rate equals the number of years it takes to double.

Net Growth Rate (%)	Doubling Time (years)
0.0%	Never
0.5	140
1.0	70
1.5	47
2.0	35
2.5	30
3.0	24
3.5	20
4.0	18

GDP per Worker: A Measure of Productivity

labor force: All persons over age 16 who are either working for pay or actively seeking paid employment.

employment rate: The percentage of the adult population that is employed.

The potential increases in living standards depicted in Table 17.1 won't occur automatically. Someone is going to have to produce more output if we want GDP per capita to rise. One reason our living standard rose in the 1980s is that the labor force grew faster than the population. Those in the World War II baby boom had reached maturity and were entering the **labor force** in droves. At the same time, more women took jobs outside the home, a trend that continued into the 1990s. As a consequence, the **employment rate** increased significantly, as Figure 17.4 shows. With the number of workers growing faster than the population, GDP per capita was sure to rise.

The employment rate can't increase forever. At the limit, everyone would be in the labor market, and no further workers could be found. Further increases in GDP per capita could only come from increases in output *per worker*.

FIGURE 17.4
A Rising Employment Rate

The entry of Baby Boomers (born 1946–60) into the labor force and increased labor-force attachment of women caused the ratio of workers to total population (the employment rate) to rise. This boosted per capita GDP.

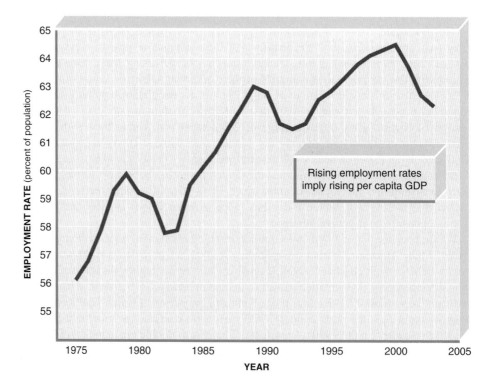

The most common measure of **productivity** is output per labor-hour, which is simply the ratio of total output to the number of hours worked. As noted earlier, total GDP in 2003 was $11 trillion. In that same year the labor force was employed for a total of 242 billion hours. Hence, the average worker's productivity was

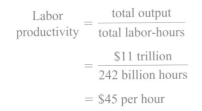

The increase in our GDP per capita in recent decades is directly related to the higher productivity of the average U.S. worker. The average worker today produces twice as many goods and services as the average worker did in 1970.

The Productivity Turnaround. For economic growth to continue, the productivity of the average U.S. worker must rise still further. Will it? As Figure 17.5 reveals, productivity grew at an average pace of 1.4 percent from 1973 to 1995. Along the way, however, there were many years (e.g., 1978–84) in which productivity advances slowed to a snail's pace. This productivity slowdown constrained GDP growth.

After 1995, productivity advances accelerated sharply, as seen in Figure 17.5. This productivity jump was so impressive that it raised hopes for a "New Economy" (see News, page 356), in which technological breakthroughs, better management, and enlightened public policy would keep both productivity and GDP growing at faster rates.

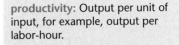

productivity: Output per unit of input, for example, output per labor-hour.

The U.S. Bureau of Labor Statistics (BLS) maintains quarterly data on labor productivity at www.bls.gov/data.

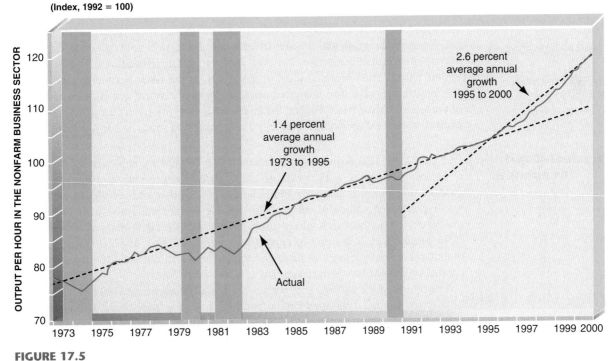

FIGURE 17.5
Productivity Gains

Increasing productivity (output per worker) is the critical factor in raising per capita GDP over time. Productivity advances slowed in 1978–84 but accelerated sharply in 1995–2000.

Note: Shaded areas indicate recessions.

Source: *U.S. Department of Commerce.*

SOURCES OF GROWTH

The arithmetic of economic growth is simple. Future output growth depends on two factors:

$$\begin{array}{c} \text{Growth rate of} \\ \text{total output} \end{array} = \begin{array}{c} \text{growth rate of} \\ \text{labor force} \end{array} + \begin{array}{c} \text{growth rate of} \\ \text{productivity} \end{array}$$

Accordingly, how fast GDP increases in the future depends on how fast the labor force grows and how fast productivity advances. Since the long-run growth of the labor force has stabilized at around 1.1 percent, the real uncertainty about future economic growth originates in the unpredictability of productivity advances. Will output per worker increase at the snail's pace of only 1 percent a year or at much faster rates of 2, 3, or even 4 percent per year?

To assess the potential for U.S. productivity gains, we need to examine the sources of productivity improvement. *The sources of productivity gains include*

*   *Higher skills*—an increase in labor skills.
*   *More capital*—an increase in the ratio of capital to labor.
*   *Technological advance*—the development and use of better capital equipment and products.
*   *Improved management*—better use of available resources in the production process.

Human-Capital Investment

Continuing advances in education and skills training have greatly increased the quality of U.S. labor. In 1950, less than 8 percent of all U.S. workers had completed college. Today, nearly 30 percent of the workforce has completed four years of college. There has also been a substantial increase in vocational training, both in the public sector and by private firms.

In the 1970s, these improvements in the quality of individual workers were offset by a change in the composition of the labor force. As we observed in Chapters 6 and 16, the proportion of teenagers and women in the labor force grew tremendously in the 1960s and 1970s. These Baby Boomers and their mothers contributed to higher output. Because teenagers and women (re)entering the labor market generally have less job experience than adult men, however, *average* productivity fell.

human capital: The knowledge and skills possessed by the workforce.

This phenomenon reversed itself in the 1990s, as the Baby Boomers reached their prime working years. The increased productivity of the workforce is not a reflection of the aging process itself. Rather, the gains in productivity reflect the greater **human-capital** investment associated with more schooling and more on-the-job learning.

Physical-Capital Investment

The knowledge and skills a worker brings to the job don't completely determine his or her productivity. A worker with no tools, no computers, and no machinery won't produce much even if she has a Ph.D. Similarly, a worker with outmoded equipment won't produce as much as an equally capable worker equipped with the newest machines and the best technology. From this perspective, *a primary determinant of labor productivity is the rate of capital investment.* In other words, improvements in output per *worker* depend in large part on increases in the quantity and quality of *capital* equipment (see World View).

The efforts of the average U.S. worker are presently augmented with over $100,000 of invested capital. This huge capital endowment is a prime source of high productivity. To *increase* productivity, however, the quality and quantity of capital available to the average worker must continue to increase. That requires capital spending to increase faster than the labor force. With the labor force growing at 1.1 percent a year, that's not a hard standard to beat. How *much* faster capital investment grows is nevertheless a decisive factor in productivity gains. In the 1980s, investment growth was slow and erratic. In the 1990s, however, capital investment accelerated markedly. In 1996, 1997, 1998, 1999, and again in 2000, capital investment growth exceeded

WORLD VIEW

Comparative Investment and Growth

Investment in new plant and equipment is essential for economic growth. In general, countries that allocate a larger share of output to investment will grow more rapidly. In the 1990s, China had the highest growth rate and one of the highest investment rates.

Country	Investment as Percentage of GDP (average, 1990–1999)	Growth Rate of GDP (average, 1990–1999)
China	39	10.7
Thailand	36	4.7
Singapore	35	8.0
India	23	6.0
United States	18	3.3
Great Britain	17	2.5
South Africa	15	1.9

Source: World Bank.

Analysis: Investment increases production possibilities. Countries that devote a larger share of output to investment tend to grow faster.

10 percent a year. Investment in information technology (computers, software, and telecommunications equipment) was exceedingly robust, reaching growth rates as high as 25 percent. In the process, workers got "smarter," communications improved, and productivity jumped. The Council of Economic Advisers credited this boom in information-technology investment with nearly one-third of *all* the 1995–99 GDP growth.

Saving and Investment Rates. The dependence of productivity gains on capital investment puts a new perspective on consumption and saving. In the short run, the primary concern of macroeconomic policy is to balance aggregate demand and aggregate supply. In this context, savings are a form of leakage that requires offsetting injections of investment or government spending. From the longer-run perspective of economic growth, saving and investment take on added importance. *Savings aren't just a form of leakage but a basic source of investment financing.* If we use all our resources to produce consumer, export, and public-sector goods, there won't be any investment. In that case, we might not face a short-run stabilization problem—our productive capacity might be fully utilized—but we'd confront a long-run *growth* problem. Indeed, if we consumed our entire output, our productive capacity would actually shrink since we wouldn't even be replacing worn-out plant and equipment. We must have at least enough savings to finance **net investment**.

net investment: Gross investment less depreciation.

Household and Business Saving. Household saving rates in the United States have been notoriously low and falling since the early 1980s. In 2000, U.S. households actually *dis*saved—spending more on consumption than their disposable incomes. Despite the meager flow of household saving, investment growth actually accelerated in the late 1990s. Virtually all of that investment was financed with *business saving* and *foreign investment*. The retained earnings and depreciation allowances that create business savings generated a huge cash flow for investment in the 1990s.

Foreign Investment. In addition to this business-saving flow, foreign investors poured money into U.S. plant, equipment, software, and financial assets. These two income flows more than compensated for the virtual absence of household saving. Many people worry, though, that foreign investments may get diverted elsewhere and that business saving will drop when profits diminish. Then continued investment growth will be more dependent on a flow of funds from household saving.

Management Training

The accumulation of more and better capital equipment does not itself guarantee higher productivity or faster GDP growth. The human factor is still critical: How well resources are organized and managed will affect the rate of growth. Hence, entrepreneurship and the quality of continuing management are also major determinants of economic growth.

It's difficult to characterize differences in management techniques or to measure their effectiveness. However, much attention has been focused in recent years on the alleged shortsightedness of U.S. managers. The rumor is that U.S. firms focus too narrowly on short-term profits, neglecting long-term gains in productivity. They also emphasize quantity over quality of output. And they fail to include workers in key decisions, thus depriving themselves of important insights and goodwill. By contrast, firms in Japan and elsewhere concentrate on longer-term gains, quality control, and strong bonds between labor and management. As a consequence, Japanese firms enjoy remarkably good labor and customer relations, intense worker loyalty, and faster productivity gains.

If all these accusations about U.S. corporate management were true, the U.S. economy would surely be in a sorry state. At best, these contrasts between management practices serve as precautionary tales. The time horizons used for developing investment and production plans can affect long-run growth prospects. Management-labor relations can also materially affect productivity. Furthermore, management familiarity with *global* markets will affect a firm's ability to grow and prosper in both foreign and domestic markets. Corporations in the United States spend billions of dollars on management training to help keep company executives up to speed on these and other determinants of long-run productivity. Such investments in managerial talent are an important source of economic growth.

Research and Development

The National Science Foundation tracks R&D spending. Visit www.nsf.gov. and click on "Science Statistics."

A fourth and vital source of productivity advance is research and development (R&D), a broad concept that includes scientific research, product development, innovations in production techniques, and the development of management improvements. R&D activity may be a specific, identifiable activity such as in a research lab, or it may be part of the process of learning by doing. In either case, the insights developed from R&D generally lead to new products and cheaper ways of producing them. Over time, R&D is credited with the greatest contributions to economic growth. In his study of U.S. growth during the period 1929–82, Edward Denison concluded that 26 percent of *total* growth was due to "advances in knowledge."

New Growth Theory. The evident contribution of "advances in knowledge" to economic growth has spawned a new perspective called "new growth theory." "Old growth theory," it is said, emphasized the importance of bricks and mortar, that is, saving and investing in new plant and equipment. By contrast, "new" growth theory emphasizes the importance of investing in ideas. Paul Romer, a Stanford economist, asserts that new ideas and the spread of knowledge are the primary engines of growth. Unfortunately, neither Romer nor anyone else is exactly sure how one spawns new ideas or best disseminates knowledge. The only evident policy lever appears to be the support of research and development, a staple of "old" growth theory.

There's an important link between R&D and capital investment. As noted earlier, part of each year's gross investment compensates for the depreciation of existing plant and equipment. However, new machines are rarely identical to the ones they replace. When you get a new computer, you're not just *replacing* an old one; you're *upgrading* your computing capabilities with more memory, faster speed, and a lot of new features. Indeed, the availability of *better* technology is often the motive for such capital investment. The same kind of motivation spurs businesses to upgrade machines and structures. Hence, advances in technology and capital investment typically go hand in hand.

POLICY LEVERS

Once the sources of growth are known, policies for accelerating long-run economic growth can be developed. Although the pace of economic growth is primarily set by market forces, government policy may be able to affect that pace. Most of the policy options are distinctly *micro* in nature, although *macro* policy decisions are also important.

Governments at all levels already play a tremendous role in human-capital development by building, operating, and subsidizing schools. The quantity and quality of continuing investments in America's schools will have a major effect on future productivity. Government policy also plays an *indirect* role in schooling decisions by offering subsidized college loans.

Immigration policy is also a determinant of the nation's stock of human capital. At least 1 million immigrants enter the United States every year. As we noted in Chapter 16, Congress in 2000 increased the immigration quota for software engineers and other high-tech workers to 195,000 workers per year. This increased labor inflow not only relieved *short-run* wage and cost pressures but also enhanced the foundation for *long-run* growth. By regulating the number and skills of immigrants, the federal government can affect the size and quality of the U.S. labor force (see World View). Canada's immigration policy is designed explicitly to raise the skill level of its labor force, by awarding points for education, job skills, work experience and other productivity attributes.

Increasing Human-Capital Investment

The U.S. Immigration and Naturalization Service (INS) maintains a profile of immigrants, including their occupational skills. Visit http://uscis.gov/graphics/shared/aboutus/statistics/index.htm.

WORLD VIEW

Work Visas Are Allowing Washington to Sidestep Immigration Reform

The inscription on the Statue of Liberty is quietly being rewritten: "Give me your tired, your poor, your huddled masses yearning to breathe free; I'll also take your skilled employees under the temporary visa program, H-1B."

The H-1B visa was established in 1990 to permit foreigners with a college degree or higher to work in the United States for a renewable three-year term for employers who petition on their behalf. In 1998, the program was expanded to allow 115,000 workers, up from 65,000, to enter the United States in fiscal years 1999 and 2000. Demand for H-1B visas by employers is high, particularly among high-technology companies.

Workers admitted under the H-1B program are not immigrants, but experts in the field expect that most of them will end up staying permanently in the United States.

In addition to workers with H-1B visas, hundreds of thousands of other foreigners are admitted to work temporarily in the United States under visa categories covering intracompany transfers, individuals with extraordinary ability, registered nurses and workers in nonprofit religious organizations. A fast-growing category is the Nafta TN visa, which offers an unlimited number of temporary visas for professional workers from Canada and soon Mexico.

In a new book, "Heaven's Door," George Borjas, a Harvard economist, proposes that the United States adopt a Canadian-style point system, in which applicants for visas are assigned points on the basis of characteristics like their ability to speak English, work-force skills, family ties, refugee status and ethnic diversity. Those whose total points exceed a certain threshold would be admitted.

—Alan B. Krueger

The New York Times

Source: *The New York Times*, May 25, 2000. © 2000 The New York Times Company. Reprinted with permission. www.nytimes.com

Analysis: Immigrant flows affect a nation's stock of human capital. Can or should immigrants be selected on the basis of human-capital traits?

Increasing Physical-Capital Investment

As in the case of human capital, the possibilities for increasing physical-capital investment are also many and diverse.

Investment Incentives. The tax code is a mechanism for stimulating investment. Faster depreciation schedules, tax credits for new investments, and lower business tax rates all encourage increased investment in physical capital. The 2002 and 2003 tax cuts were designed for this very purpose.

Savings Incentives. In principle, the government can also deepen the savings pool that finances investment. Here again, the tax code offers some policy levers. Tax preferences for Individual Retirement Accounts and other pension savings may increase the marginal propensity to save or at least redirect savings flows to longer-term investments. The Bush 2001 tax package (Chapter 11) included not only a *short-run* fiscal stimulus (e.g., tax rebates) but also enhanced incentives for *long-term* savings (retirement and college savings accounts).

Infrastructure Development. The government also directly affects the level of physical capital through its public works spending. As we observed in Chapter 16, the $2 trillion already invested in bridges, highways, airports, sewer systems, and other infrastructure is an important part of America's capital stock. In 2004, Congress passed a new Highway bill that authorizes nearly $300 billion in infrastructure spending. Investments of that sort reduce transportation and commuting costs, making more resources available for production.

Fiscal Responsibility. In addition to these many supply-side interventions, the government's *macro* policies also affect the rate of investment and growth. Of particular interest in this regard is the federal government's budget balance. As we've seen, budget deficits may be a useful mechanism for attaining short-run macro stability. Those same deficits, however, may have negative long-run effects. If Uncle Sam borrows more funds from the national savings pool, other borrowers may end up with less. As we saw in Chapter 12, there's no guarantee that federal deficits will result in the **crowding out** of private investment. Let's recognize the risk of such an outcome, however. Hence, *fiscal and monetary policies must be evaluated in terms of their impact not only on (short-run) aggregate demand but also on long-run aggregate supply.*

> **crowding out:** A reduction in private-sector borrowing (and spending) caused by increased government borrowing.

> **crowding in:** An increase in private-sector borrowing (and spending) caused by decreased government borrowing.

In this regard, the transformation of federal budget deficits to budget surpluses after 1997 facilitated the **crowding in** of private investment. After 1997, more funds were available to private investors and at lower interest rates. This surely contributed to the accelerated growth of capital investment in 1996–2000. Since then, budget balances have swung sharply into the red (see Figure 12.1).

Maintaining Stable Expectations

The position of the long-run AS curve also depends on a broader assessment of the economic outlook. Expectations are a critical factor in both consumption and investment behavior. People who expect to lose their job next year are unlikely to buy a new car or house this year. Likewise, if investors expect interest rates to jump next year, they may be less willing to initiate long-run capital projects.

A sense of political and economic stability is critical to any long-run current trend. Within that context, however, specific perceptions of government policy may also alter investment plans. Investors may look to the Fed for a sense of monetary stability. They may be looking for a greater commitment to long-run price stability than to short-run adjustments of aggregate demand. In the fiscal policy area the same kind of commitment to long-run fiscal discipline rather than to short-run stimulus may be sought. Such possibilities imply that macro policy must be sensitive to long-run expectations. It also implies that short-run goals may at times conflict with longer-run growth and investment objectives.

Institutional Context

Last, but not least, the prospects for economic growth depend on the institutional context of a nation's economy. We first encountered this proposition in Chapter 1. In the

World View on page 15, nations were ranked on the basis of an Index of Freedom. Studies have shown how greater economic freedom—secure property rights, open trade, lower taxes, less regulation—typically fosters faster growth. In less regulated economies there's more scope for entrepreneurship and more opportunity to invest (see World View, p. 347). Recognizing this, nations around the world, from India to China, to Russia, to Latin America, have deregulated industries, privatized state enterprises, and promoted more open trade and investment.

THE ECONOMY TOMORROW

Limitless Growth?

Suppose we pulled all the right policy levers and were able to keep the economy on a fast-paced growth track. Could the economy keep growing forever? Wouldn't we use up all available resources and ruin the environment in the process? How much long-term growth is really possible—or even desirable?

The Malthusian Formula for Destruction

The prospect of an eventual limit to economic growth originated in the eighteenth-century warnings of the Reverend Thomas Malthus. Malthus argued that continued economic growth was impossible because food production couldn't keep pace with population growth. His dire projections earned the economics profession its characterization as the "dismal science."

When Malthus first issued his warnings, in 1798, the population of England (including Wales) was about 9 million. Annual production of barley, oats, and related grains was approximately 162 million bushels, and wheat production was around 50 million bushels, just about enough to feed the English population (a little had to be imported from other countries). Although the relationship between food and population was satisfactory in 1798, Malthus reasoned that starvation was not far off. First of all, he observed that "population, when unchecked, goes on doubling itself every 25 years, or increases in a geometrical ratio."[1] Thus, he foresaw the English population increasing to 36 million people by 1850, 144 million by 1900, and more than 1 billion by 1975, unless some social or natural restraints were imposed on population growth.

Limits to Food Production

One natural population check that Malthus foresaw was a scarcity of food. England had only a limited amount of land available for cultivation and was already farming the most fertile tracts. Before long, all available land would be in use and only improvements in agricultural productivity (output per acre) could increase food supplies. Some productivity increases were possible, Malthus concluded, but "the means of subsistence, under circumstances the most favorable to human industry, could not possibly be made to increase faster than in an arithmetical ratio."[2]

With population increasing at a *geometric* rate and food supplies at an *arithmetic* rate, the eventual outcome is evident. Figure 17.6 illustrates how the difference between a **geometric growth** path and an **arithmetic growth** path ultimately leads to starvation. As Malthus calculated it, per capita wheat output would decline from 5.5 bushels in 1800 to only 1.7 bushels in 1900 (Figure 17.5*b*). This wasn't enough food to feed the English people. According to Malthus's projections, either England died off about 100 years ago or it has been maintained at the brink of starvation for more than a century only by recurrent plagues, wars, or the kind of "moral restraint" that's commonly associated with Victorian preachments.

geometric growth: An increase in quantity by a constant proportion each year.

arithmetic growth: An increase in quantity by a constant amount each year.

[1]Thomas Malthus, *An Essay on the Principle of Population* (1798; reprint ed., Homewood, IL: Richard D. Irwin, 1963), p. 4.
[2]Ibid., p. 5.

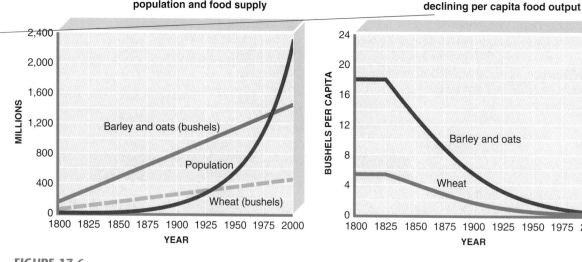

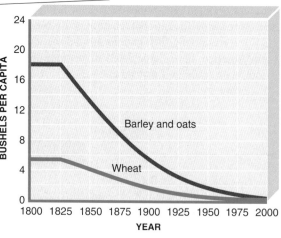

(a) Malthus's projections of population and food supply

(b) Malthus's projections of declining per capita food output

FIGURE 17.6

The Malthusian Doomsday

By projecting the growth rates of population and food output into the future, Malthus foresaw England's doomsday. At that time, the amount of available food per capita would be too small to sustain human life. Fortunately, Malthus overestimated population growth and underestimated productivity growth.

Source: Mathus' arithmetic applied to actual data for 1800 (see text).

Malthus's logic was impeccable. As long as population increased at a geometric rate while output increased at an arithmetic rate, England's doomsday was as certain as two plus two equals four. Malthus's error was not in his logic but in his empirical assumptions. He didn't know how fast output would increase over time, any more than we know whether people will be wearing electronic wings in the year 2203. He had to make an educated guess about future productivity trends. He based his estimates on his own experiences at the very beginning of the Industrial Revolution. As it turned out (fortunately), he had no knowledge of the innovations that would change the world, and he grossly underestimated the rate at which productivity would increase. ***Output, including agricultural products, has increased at a geometric rate, not at the much slower arithmetic rate foreseen by Malthus.*** As we observed earlier, U.S. output has grown at a long-term rate of roughly 3 percent a year. This *geometric* growth has doubled output every 25 years or so. That rate of economic growth is more than enough to raise living standards for a population growing by only 1 percent a year.

Resource Constraints

As Yale historian Paul Kennedy has suggested, maybe Malthus's doomsday predictions were just premature, not wrong. Maybe growth will come to a screeching halt when we run out of arable land, water, oil, or some other vital resource.

Malthus focused on arable land as the ultimate resource constraint. Other doomsday prophets have focused on the supply of whale oil, coal, oil, potatoes, and other "essential" resources. All such predictions ignore the role of markets in both promoting more efficient uses of scarce resources and finding substitutes for them. If, for example, the world were really running out of oil, what would happen to oil prices? Oil prices would rise substantially, prompting consumers to use oil more efficiently and prompting producers to develop alternative fuel sources. If productivity and the availability of substitutes increase fast enough, the price of "scarce" resources might actually fall rather than rise. This possibility prompted a famous "Doomsday bet" between University of Maryland business professor Julian Simon and Stanford ecologist Paul Ehrlich. In 1980, Paul Ehrlich identified five metals that he predicted would become so scarce as to slow economic growth. Simon wagered that the price of those metals would actually *decline* over the ensuing decade as productivity and available substitutes increased. In 1990, their prices had fallen, and Ehrlich paid Simon for the bet.

The market's ability to circumvent resource constraints would seem to augur well for our future. Doomsayers warn, though, that other limits to growth will emerge, even in a world of "unlimited" resources and unending productivity advance. The villain this time is pollution. Over 20 years ago, Paul Ehrlich warned about this second problem:

Environmental Destruction

> Attempts to increase food production further will tend to accelerate the deterioration of our environment, which in turn will eventually *reduce* the capacity of the Earth to produce food. It is not clear whether environmental decay has now gone so far as to be essentially irreversible; it is possible that the capacity of the planet to support human life has been permanently impaired. Such technological "successes" as automobiles, pesticides, and inorganic nitrogen fertilizers are major contributors to environmental deterioration.[3]

The "inevitability" of environmental destruction led G. Evelyn Hutchinson to conclude in 1970 that the limits of habitable existence on Earth would be measured "in decades."[4]

It's not difficult for anyone with the basic five senses to comprehend the pollution problem. Pollution is as close these days as the air we breathe. Moreover, we can't fail to observe a distinct tendency for pollution levels to rise along with GDP and population expansion. If one projects such pollution trends into the future, things are bound to look pretty ugly.

Although pollution is universally acknowledged to be an important and annoying problem, we can't assume that the *rate* of pollution will continue unabated. On the contrary, the growing awareness of the pollution problem has already led to significant abatement-policy efforts. The Environmental Protection Agency (EPA), for example, is unquestionably a force working for cleaner air and water. Indeed, active policies to curb pollution are as familiar as auto-exhaust controls and DDT bans. A computer programmed 10 or 20 years ago to project present pollution levels wouldn't have foreseen these abatement efforts and would thus have overestimated current pollution levels.

This isn't to say that we have in any final way "solved" the pollution problem or that we're even doing the best job we possibly can. It simply says that geometric increases in pollution aren't inevitable. There's simply no compelling reason why we have to continue polluting the environment; if we stop, another doomsday can be averted. Julian Simon was so confident of our ability to do so that he offered another doomsday wager in 1996. He offered a $100,000 bet that by any measure human well-being will improve in the next decade.

Julian Simon may have been right that there are no limits to growth, at least none emanating from resource constraints or pollution thresholds. As Robert Solow summed up the issue:

The Possibility of Growth

> My real complaint about the Doomsday school [is that] it diverts attention from the really important things that can actually be done, step by step, to make things better. The end of the world *is* at hand—the earth, if you take the long view, will fall into the sun in a few billion years anyway, unless some other disaster happens first. In the meantime, I think we'd be better off passing a strong sulfur-emissions tax, or getting some Highway Trust Fund money allocated to mass transit, or building a humane and decent floor under family incomes, or overriding President Nixon's veto of a strong Water Quality Act, or reforming the tax system, or fending off starvation in Bengal—instead of worrying about the generalized "predicament of mankind."[5]

Karl Marx expressed these same thoughts nearly a century earlier. Marx chastised "the contemptible Malthus" for turning the attention of the working class away from what he regarded as the immediate problem of capitalist exploitation to some distant and ill-founded anxiety about "natural" disaster.[6]

---

[3]Paul R. Ehrlich and Anne H. Ehrlich, *Population, Resources, Environment: Issues in Human Ecology,* 2nd ed. (San Francisco: W. H. Freeman, 1972), p. 442.

[4]Evelyn Hutchinson, "The Biosphere," *Scientific American,* September 1970, p. 53: Dennis L. Meadows et al., *The Limits to Growth* (New York: Universe Books, 1972), Chapter 4.

[5]Robert M. Solow. "Is the End of the World at Hand?" *Challenge,* March 1973, p. 50.

[6]Cited by John Maddox in *The Doomsday Syndrome* (New York: McGraw-Hill, 1972), pp. 40 and 45.

"And so, extrapolating from the best figures available, we see that current trends, unless dramatically reversed, will inevitably lead to a situation in which the sky will fall."

Analysis: Most doomsday predictions fail to recognize the possibilities for behavioral change—or the role of market incentives in encouraging it.

The Desirability of Growth

Let's concede, then, that continued, perhaps even "limitless" growth is *possible*. Can we also agree that it's *desirable?* Those of us who commute on congested highways, worry about global warming, breathe foul air, and can't find a secluded camping site may raise a loud chorus of nos. But before reaching a conclusion let's at least determine what it is people don't like about the prospect of continued growth. Is it really economic growth per se that people object to, or instead the specific ways GDP has grown in the past? To state the question this way may provoke a few second thoughts.

First of all, let's distinguish very clearly between economic growth and population growth. Congested neighborhoods, dining halls, and highways are the consequence of too many people, not of too many goods and services. Indeed, if we had *more* goods and services—if we had more houses and transit systems—much of the population congestion we now experience might be relieved. Maybe if we had enough resources to meet our existing demands *and* to build a solar-generated "new town" in the middle of Montana, people might move out of the crowded neighborhoods of Chicago and St. Louis. Well, probably not, but at least one thing is certain; with fewer goods and services, more people will have to share any given quantity of output.

Which brings us back to the really essential measure of growth, GDP per capita. Are there any serious grounds for desiring *less* GDP per capita, a reduced standard of living? And don't say yes just because you think we already have too many cars on our roads or calories in our bellies. That argument refers to the *mix* of output again and doesn't answer the question of whether we want *any* more goods or services per person. Increasing GDP per capita can take a million forms, including the educational services you're now consuming. The rejection of economic growth per se implies that none of those forms is desirable.

SUMMARY

- Economic growth refers to increases in real GDP. Short-run growth may result from increases in capacity utilization (like less unemployment). In the long run, however, growth requires increases in capacity itself—rightward shifts on the long-run aggregate supply curve.
- GDP per capita is a basic measure of living standards. GDP per worker is a basic measure of productivity.

- The rate of economic growth is set by the growth rate of the labor force *plus* the growth rate of output per worker (productivity). Over time, increases in productivity have been the primary cause of rising living standards.
- Productivity gains comes from many sources, including better labor quality, increased capital investment, research and development, improved management, and supportive government policies.
- Supply-side policies increase both the short- and long-run capacity to produce. Monetary and fiscal policies may also affect capital investment and thus the rate of economic growth.
- Productivity growth accelerated in 1995–2000 due to fast investment growth, especially in information technology. Sustaining rapid productivity gains is the critical challenge for long-run GDP growth.

- Recent U.S. investment growth has been financed with business saving and foreign investment. U.S. households save very little.
- The argument that there are identifiable and imminent limits to growth—perhaps even a cataclysmic doomsday—are founded on one of two concerns: (1) the depletion of resources and (2) pollution of the ecosystem.
- The general weakness of doomsday arguments is that they regard existing patterns of resource use or pollution as unalterable. As a consequence, they consistently underestimate the possibilities for technological advance or adaptation. Even optimistic projections of technological possibilities turn out to be pessimistic.
- Continued economic growth is desirable as long as it brings a higher standard of living for people and an increased ability to produce and consume socially desirable goods and services.

Key Terms

production possibilities	GDP per capita	net investment
economic growth	labor force	crowding out
real GDP	employment rate	crowding in
base period	productivity	geometric growth
growth rate	human capital	arithmetic growth

Questions for Discussion

1. In what specific ways (if any) does a college education increase a worker's productivity?
2. Why do productivity gains slow down in recessions? (See Figure 17.5.)
3. Why don't we consume all our current output instead of sacrificing some present consumption for investment?
4. Should we grant immigration rights based on potential contributions to economic growth as Canada does? (See World View, page 363.)
5. How would a growing federal budget surplus affect the prospects for long-run economic growth? Why might a growing surplus *not* be desirable?
6. Should fiscal policy encourage more consumption or more saving? Does it matter?
7. In 1866, Stanley Jevons predicted that economic growth would come to a halt when England ran out of coal, a doomsday that he reckoned would occur in the mid-1970s. How did we avert that projection?
8. Fertility rates in the United States have dropped so low that we're approaching zero population growth, a condition that France has maintained for decades. How will this affect our economic growth? Our standard of living?
9. Is limitless growth really possible? What forces do you think will be most important in slowing or halting economic growth?
10. Would you accept Julian Simon's second (1996) doomsday wager (page 367)? What dimensions of human well-being might worsen in 10 years?

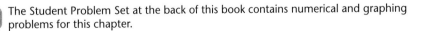

ALERT!

PROBLEMS — The Student Problem Set at the back of this book contains numerical and graphing problems for this chapter.

WEB ACTIVITIES — to accompany this chapter can be found on the Online Learning Center: **http://www.mhhe.com/economics/schiller10**

PART 7

Policy Constraints

Macro theories often provide conflicting advice about whether and how the government ought to intervene. To make matters worse, the information needed to make a decision is typically incomplete. Politics muddies the waters too by changing priorities and restricting the use of policy levers. Finally, there's the inescapable reality that everything changes at once—there's no *ceteris paribus* in the real world. Chapters 18 and 19 consider these constraints on policy development and implementation.

CHAPTER

18

Global Macro

In this global economy there is no such thing as a purely domestic policy.
—President Bill Clinton
American University, February 26, 1993

Two years after making that statement, President Clinton got a crash course in global macroeconomics. The Mexican economy took a nosedive in 1995: Unemployment rose, prices skyrocketed, and the value of the Mexican peso plunged. President Clinton and his economic advisers quickly realized that this turn of events wasn't simply a Mexican problem. Mexico is one of America's largest export markets. If the Mexican economy sinks into a recession, Mexican consumers and businesses won't be able to buy so many U.S.-made goods. The U.S. economy would suffer export losses and related job losses.

The financial markets of Mexico and the United States are also linked. When the peso collapsed, many Mexicans rushed to convert their currency into U.S. dollars. As they moved assets into American banks, U.S. bank reserves increased. This capital inflow made the Fed's job of controlling the money supply that much more difficult.

There was no way the United States could seal off its economy from the Mexican crisis. So long as resources, goods, and money can move across national borders, countries are economically interdependent. Ironically, the 1993 North American Free Trade Agreement (NAFTA) had increased the interdependence between Mexico and the United States. Therefore, helping Mexico was also a way of helping the United States avert economic damage. This realization helped convince President Clinton to "bail out" Mexico with a multibillion-dollar loan. The U.S. Federal Reserve also helped control disruptions in currency flows and values.

The global economy got an even greater jolt when terrorists destroyed the World Trade Center in September 2001. The economic shock disrupted not only U.S. markets but global ones as well. As the accompanying World View relates, nations around the world worried that the economic shock to the U.S. economy would destabilize their economies too. If U.S. consumers and businesses curtailed their spending, export sales of other nations would decline. A *global* crisis, not just an *American* crisis, would ensue. Mindful of that possibility, the world's leaders quickly worked out a coordinated policy response.

This chapter explores this global interdependence. Of particular concern are the following questions:

- **How does the U.S. economy interact with the rest of the world?**
- **How does the rest of the world affect U.S. macro outcomes?**
- **How does global interdependence limit macro policy options?**

As we'll see, international transactions significantly affect U.S. economic performance and policy.

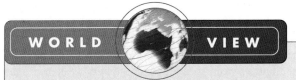

Tragedy Dashes Hopes for Europe's Economy

The economic fallout doesn't stop at the U.S. border.

In the aftermath of last week's terror strikes, European companies say the uncertainty over what happens next will weigh on an already weak European economy for weeks, even months.

Economies around the world—including Japan, which has been struggling for years—had all been hoping to avoid recession this year, based on the prospect of the U.S. economy recovering. Those hopes are now gone.

Unease spells trouble for any economy: Businesses delay big orders; potential merger partners put their deal talks on ice; companies hold off on expansion plans; and consumers save rather than buy. "People won't be ordering big machines for a couple of million marks right now," said Diether Klingelnberg, whose company in Hueckeswagen,

Germany, makes machine parts for the airline industry, among other sectors. "People want to wait and see what will happen.". . .

Baudouin Velge, chief economist of the Belgian Federation of Employers, a trade group representing 30,000 Belgian companies, figures, "The American economy will be hit by this for another six months," which delays the main boost Europe was counting on for its own recovery. The U.S. buys 22 percent of Europe's exports. Economists estimate a percentage-point drop in U.S. economic growth translates into a half-percentage point decline in European growth.

—Christopher Rhoads and G. Thomas Sims

Analysis: The flow of goods, labor, and money across national borders makes countries economically interdependent. A shock to the U.S. economy disrupts foreign economies as well, and vice versa.

INTERNATIONAL TRADE

Japanese cars are the most visible reminders of America's global interdependence. American consumers purchase over 1 million cars from Japan each year and buy another million or so Toyotas, Nissans, Hondas, Mazdas, and Subarus produced in the United States. On the other side of the Pacific Ocean, Japanese autoworkers are apt to wear Levis, sip Coca-Cola, and grab a quick meal at McDonald's.

The motivations for international trade are explained at length in Chapter 35. Also discussed in Chapter 35 are the *microeconomic* demands for greater protection from "unfair" imports. What concerns us here is how such trade affects our domestic *macro* performance. Does trade help or hinder our efforts to attain full employment, price stability, and economic growth?

We first noticed in Chapter 9 that **imports** are a source of **leakage** in the circular flow. The income that U.S. consumers spend on Japanese cars *could* be spent in America. When that income instead leaks out of the circular flow, it limits domestic spending and related **multiplier** effects.

The basic macro model can be expanded easily to include this additional leakage. In a closed (no-trade) economy, total income and domestic spending are always equal—that is,

$$\text{Closed economy: } C + I + G = Y$$

When some goods are sold as exports and others can be purchased from abroad, however, this equality no longer holds. In an open economy, we have to take account of imports and exports: that is,

$$\text{Open economy: } C + I + G + X = Y + M$$

where X refers to exports and M to imports. ***In an open economy, the combined spending of consumers, investors, and the government may not equal domestic output.*** Total

Imports as Leakage

imports: Goods and services purchased from international sources.

leakage: Income not spent directly on domestic output but instead diverted from the circular flow, such as saving, imports, taxes.

multiplier: The multiple by which an initial change in aggregate spending will alter total expenditure after an infinite number of spending cycles.

spending is augmented by the demand for exports, and the supply of goods is increased by imports.

Although imported goods may be desired, their availability complicates macro policy. Increases in aggregate spending are supposed to boost domestic output and employment. With imports, however, the link between spending and output is weakened. *Part of any increase in income will be spent on imports.* This fraction is called the **marginal propensity to import (MPM).** Like its cousin, the **marginal propensity to save (MPS),** the marginal propensity to import

- Reduces the initial impact on domestic demand of any income change.
- Reduces the size of the multiplier.

Reduced Multiplier Effects. Table 18.1 illustrates the impact of imports on the Keynesian multiplier process. The process starts with an increase of $10 billion in new government spending. This injection directly adds $10 billion to consumer income (assuming an economy with no income taxes).

The successive panels of Table 18.1 illustrate the sequence of events that follows. In the closed economy, consumers have only two uses for their income: to spend it on domestic consumption (B1) or to save it (B2). We assume here the marginal propensity to save is 0.10. Hence consumers save $1 billion and spend the remaining $9 billion on domestic consumption.

In an open economy, consumers have an additional choice. They may spend their income on domestic goods (B1), save it (B2), *or* spend it on imported goods (B3). In Table 18.1 we assume that the marginal propensity to import is 0.10. Hence, consumers use their additional $10 billion of income the following way:

$8 billion spent on domestic consumption.
$1 billion saved.
$1 billion spent on imports.

In the open economy, only $8 billion rather than $9 billion is initially spent on domestic consumption. Thus, *imports reduce the initial spending impact of added income.*

marginal propensity to import (MPM): The fraction of each additional (marginal) dollar of disposable income spent on imports.

marginal propensity to save (MPS): The fraction of each additional (marginal) dollar of disposable income not spent on consumption; 1 − MPC.

TABLE 18.1
Imports as Leakage

Import leakage reduces the initial spending impact of autonomous changes in consumer income. Continuing import leakage reduces the size of the multiplier as well. In this case, the ultimate impact of added government spending is cut in half by import leakage: Aggregate demand increases by $50 billion rather than $100 billion in response to a $10 billion increase in government spending.

Action	Cumulative Change in Aggregate Demand	
	Closed Economy	Open Economy
A. Government spends additional $10 billion	+$10 billion	+$10 billion
B. Consumers use added $10 billion of income for:		
1. Domestic consumption	+$9 billion	+$8 billion
2. Saving (MPS = 0.1)	($1 billion)	($1 billion)
3. Imports (MPM = 0.1)	0	($1 billion)
C. Multiplier	$\frac{1}{MPS} = 10$	$\frac{1}{MPS + MPM} = 5$
D. Additional multiplier-induced consumption = C × B1	+$90 billion	+$40 billion
E. Cumulative change = A + D	+$100 billion	+$50 billion

Import leakage continues through every round of the circular flow. As a consequence, *imports also reduce the value of the multiplier.* In this case, the multiplier is reduced from 10 to 5.

To see how this change in the multiplier comes about, note that *the value of the multiplier depends on the extent of leakage.* The most general form of the multiplier is

$$\text{Generalized multiplier} = \frac{1}{\text{leakage fraction}}$$

In a closed (no trade) and private (no taxes) economy, the multiplier takes the familiar Keynesian form:

$$\genfrac{}{}{0pt}{}{\text{Closed economy}}{\genfrac{}{}{0pt}{}{\text{multiplier}}{\text{(without taxes)}}} = \frac{1}{\text{MPS}}$$

In this case, consumer saving is the only form of leakage. Therefore, the marginal propensity to save (MPS) is the entire leakage fraction. In Table 18.1 the closed-economy multiplier is equal to 10 (see panel C).

Once we open the economy to trade, we have to contend with additional leakage. In an open economy, leakage results from the MPS *and* the MPM. Thus, the generalized multiplier becomes:

$$\genfrac{}{}{0pt}{}{\text{Open economy}}{\genfrac{}{}{0pt}{}{\text{multiplier}}{\text{(without taxes)}}} = \frac{1}{\text{MPS} + \text{MPM}}$$

Imports act just like saving leakage, decreasing the multiplier bang of each autonomous buck. In Table 18.1 (panel C),

$$\text{Open economy multiplier} = \frac{1}{\text{MPS} + \text{MPM}} = \frac{1}{0.1 + 0.1} = \frac{1}{0.2} = 5$$

The consequences of these different multipliers are striking. Panel D shows that additional consumption of $90 billion is induced in the closed economy. By comparison, the open economy generates only $40 billion of additional consumption.

The last panel of Table 18.1 summarizes the consequences for aggregate demand. The cumulative increase in aggregate demand is

$$\genfrac{}{}{0pt}{}{\text{Cumulative change}}{\text{in aggregate demand}} = \genfrac{}{}{0pt}{}{\text{initial change}}{\text{in spending}} \times \genfrac{}{}{0pt}{}{\text{income}}{\text{multiplier}}$$

In this example, the initial injection of spending is the $10 billion spent by the government. In the closed economy, this injection leads to a $100 billion increase in aggregate demand (panel E). In the open economy, the same injection increases aggregate demand—only $50 billion!

This end result is also illustrated in Figure 18.1, which shows how imports limit the shift of aggregate demand. The smaller shift that occurs in the open economy results in a smaller increase in equilibrium real GDP. In this sense *imports, by increasing leakage, reduce the impact of fiscal stimulus.* Notice in Figure 18.1 the much larger induced consumption in the closed economy. The fiscal stimulus shifts aggregate demand to AD_4 in the closed economy but only to AD_3 in the open economy. The end result is less of an increase in domestic output (and less inflationary pressure as well).

Global Stabilizer. The import leakage that reduces the effectiveness of fiscal stimulus can also act as an automatic stabilizer. This was particularly evident in early 2001. The slowdown in U.S. aggregate demand was heavily concentrated in high-tech sectors

FIGURE 18.1
Imports Reduce Multiplier Effects

The amount of additional demand created by a fiscal stimulus depends on the marginal propensity to import. In a closed economy (MPM = 0) aggregate demand increases from AD_1 to AD_4. In an open economy (MPM > 0) imports limit spending on domestic goods, shifting aggregate demand only to AD_3.

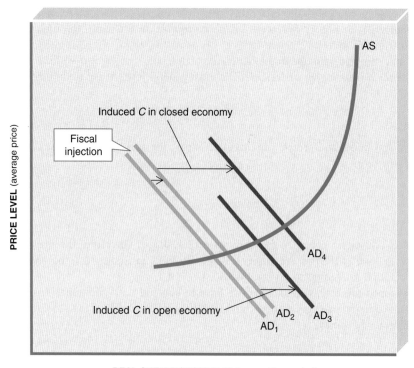

REAL OUTPUT (INCOME) (dollars per time period)

that are highly dependent on imported equipment and components, that is, industries with a very high marginal propensity to import. Hence, foreign producers absorbed a large share of the pain caused by the U.S. slowdown (see World View). In the absence of that safety valve, the U.S. economy would have suffered larger multiplier effects and a more severe slowdown.

WORLD VIEW

U.S. Growth Slows—and Foreign Economies Feel the Pain

But the Falloff in American Imports Is Limiting U.S. Weakness

If you want a vivid illustration of America's role in the global slowdown, consider that the U.S. buys up nearly one-fourth of the rest of the world's exports. And the growth rate of the volume of goods coming into the U.S. has swung from a 17 percent annual pace last autumn to a −5 per-cent pace currently. No wonder many economies abroad are struggling.

To an important extent, though, the rest of the world's pain is America's gain. True, the growing weakness in exports has been a considerable drag on the ailing manufacturing sector. But the dropoff in imports is acting like a shock absorber, because much of the fallout from weaker demand is being felt by foreign producers, not the U.S. economy. . . .

In this particular slowdown, the stabilizing influence of falling imports is especially large. That's because the slump is concentrated in business-sector cuts in capital spending and inventories, mainly for tech-equipment. About 36 percent of U.S. dollar outlays for capital goods goes to imports. For tech gear alone, imports account for about 16 percent. That means foreign companies—and countries—are absorbing a large share of the burden of dealing with U.S. corporate cutbacks. One case in point: Singapore is in recession mostly because its shipments to the U.S. of semiconductors and other tech components have plunged dramatically.

—James C. Cooper and Kathleen Madigan

Source: *BusinessWeek,* August 6, 2001. © 2001 The McGraw-Hill Companies, Inc. Reprinted with permission. www.businessweek.com

Analysis: Imports act as an automatic stabilizer by (1) absorbing some of lost sales in an economic downturn and (2) adding to aggregate supply as domestic capacity is approached.

International trade is a two-way street. Whereas we import goods and services from the rest of the world, other countries buy our **exports.** Thus, *export sales inject spending into our circular flow at the same time that imports cause leakage from it.*

Any changes in exports are regarded as autonomous, since export sales depend primarily on the income and spending behavior of foreigners. Hence, *a change in export demand causes a shift of the aggregate demand curve.* Like any other injection, an increase in export demand would set off a chain of multiplier effects. In other words, small changes in exports generate larger (multiplied) shifts of aggregate demand. This was a distinct risk for the U.S. economy in the 1997–98 Asian crisis: a reduction in American exports to Asia could have snowballed into very large job losses. When Japan fell into another recession in early 2001, U.S. exporters again lost sales and laid off workers.

TRADE IMBALANCES

With exports adding to aggregate spending, and imports subtracting from the circular flow, the net impact of international trade on the domestic economy comes down to a question of balance. *What counts is the difference between exports (injections) and imports (leakages).* If exports and imports were exactly equal, there would be no net stimulus or leakage from the rest of the world.

A convenient way of emphasizing the offsetting effects of exports and imports is to rearrange the income identity to

$$C + I + G + (X - M) = Y$$

where $(X - M)$ equals **net exports.**

If exports and imports were always equal, the term $(X - M)$ would disappear and we could focus on domestic spending behavior. But why would we expect imports and exports to be equal? We now know that even *domestic* injections such as investment aren't likely to equal domestic leakages like saving. Indeed, the short-run macro stability problem arises because investment and saving decisions are made by different people and for very different reasons. There's no *a priori* reason to expect those outcomes to be identical.

The same problem affects international trade. Foreign decisions about how much to spend on American exports are made outside U.S. borders. Decisions in the United States about how much to spend on imports are made by American consumers, investors, and government agencies. Because these sets of shoppers are so isolated from one another, it seems unlikely that exports will ever equal imports. Instead, we have to expect a trade imbalance.

There are specific terms for characterizing trade imbalances. A U.S. **trade surplus** exists when America is exporting more goods and services than it's importing—that is, when net exports $(X - M)$ are positive. When U.S. net exports are negative, imports exceed exports and the United States has a **trade deficit.** In 2003 the United States had a trade deficit of $490 billion. That deficit implies that U.S. consumers, investors, and government agencies were buying $490 billion more output in 2003 than American factories and offices were producing.

A trade deficit isn't all bad. After all, when imports exceed exports, we end up consuming more than we're producing. In effect, *a trade deficit permits domestic living standards to exceed domestic output.* It's almost like getting something for nothing—the proverbial free lunch. A trade deficit can also be an important safety valve for rising inflation pressures. In 2004, the U.S. economy was growing very fast and signs of demand-pull inflation were emerging (in June 2004 the Fed began raising interest rates). The ready availability of imported inputs and products helped keep inflation in check.

Trade deficits aren't always so beneficial. A trade deficit represents net leakage. That leakage may frustrate attempts to attain full employment. As we observed (Figure 18.1),

exports: Goods and services sold to foreign buyers.

net exports: The value of exports minus the value of imports: $(X - M)$.

trade surplus: The amount by which the value of exports exceeds the value of imports in a given time period (positive net exports).

trade deficit: The amount by which the value of imports exceeds the value of exports in a given time period (negative net exports).

Macro Effects

To track changes in the U.S. trade balance, see the import and export data in "Balance of Payments" at the Bureau of Economic Analysis: www.bea.doc.gov.

crowding out: A reduction in private-sector borrowing (and spending) caused by increased government borrowing.

import leakage necessitates a larger fiscal injection to reach any particular spending goal. Larger injections may not be possible, especially if *budget* deficit concerns limit fiscal-policy initiatives.

Crowding Out Net Exports. One reason people worry about budget deficits is that increased government spending may supplant private investment and consumption. This is the **crowding out** problem we first encountered in Chapter 12. It takes on a new dimension in an open economy. In an open economy, increased government purchases need not reduce private-sector spending—even at full employment! Increased imports can satisfy the increase in aggregate demand. Thus, in an open economy *an increase in imports can reduce domestic crowding out.*

The elbow room provided by imports relieves some of the worries about federal *budget* deficits. New concerns arise, however, about *trade* deficits. As imports increase, our net export position deteriorates. Hence, *in an open economy fiscal stimulus tends to crowd out net exports by boosting imports.* Indeed, any fiscal stimulus intended to boost domestic output will *worsen* the trade deficit. Consumers will spend some fraction of their additional income—the marginal propensity to import (MPM)—on imports. These added imports will widen the trade gap. Thus, *the objective of reducing the trade deficit may conflict with the goal of attaining full employment.*

A trade surplus can create similar problems. The additional spending implied by positive net exports may fuel inflationary pressures. If the economy is overheating, the policy objective is to restrain aggregate spending. But fiscal and monetary restraints don't directly affect the incomes, expectations, or tastes of foreign consumers. Foreign spending on U.S. goods may continue unabated, even as domestic monetary and fiscal restraint squeezes domestic consumers and investors. Indeed, domestic monetary and fiscal restraint will have to be harder, just to offset continuing export demand.

Worse yet, the trade surplus may grow in response to restrictive macro policies. Domestic consumers, squeezed by monetary and fiscal restraint, will reduce purchases of imported goods. On the other hand, if fiscal and monetary restraint reduces domestic inflation, foreigners may increase their export purchases. Here again, *trade goals and domestic macro goals may conflict.*

Foreign Perspectives

Who cares if our trade balance worsens? Why don't we just focus on our domestic macro equilibrium and ignore any trade imbalances that result? If we ignored trade imbalances, we wouldn't have a goal conflict and could achieve our domestic policy goals.

Unfortunately, our trading partners have their own policy objectives and may not be content to ignore our trade imbalances. *If the United States has a trade deficit, other countries must have a trade surplus.* This is simple arithmetic. Its implications are potentially worrisome, however. The rest of the world might not be happy about shipping us more output than they're getting in return. In real economic terms, they'd be picking up the tab for our "free lunch." Their exports would be financing a higher standard of living for us than our output alone permitted. At the same time, their living standards would be less than their own output made possible. These disparities could cause tension. In addition, foreign nations might also be concerned about inflationary pressures of their own and so resist additional demand for their exports (our imports).

The whole notion of macro equilibrium gets much more complicated when we adopt these global views. From a global perspective, *we can't focus exclusively on domestic macro goals and ignore international repercussions.* If our trade balance upsets other economies, foreign nations may respond with their own macro and trade initiatives. These responses, in turn, would affect America's trade flows and so alter domestic outcomes. A *global* macro equilibrium would be attained only when no trading partner had reason to change macro or trade policy.

A Policy Constraint

From a macro perspective, our basic objective in both an open and a closed economy remains the same: to find the optimal balance of aggregate demand and aggregate supply. Trade flows may help or hinder this effort, depending on the timing, size, and

Oil Shocks

In 1973, in 1979, in 2000, and again in 2004, the Organization of Petroleum Exporting Countries (OPEC) sharply increased crude oil prices. The price of oil quadrupled in 1973 and doubled again in 1979. In 2004, the price of oil again doubled, to nearly $50 per barrel. The resulting "shock" to macro equilibrium caused both higher unemployment and more inflation in oil-importing nations.

Inflationary Impact

An increase in the price of oil sets the stage for cost-push inflation. Industries using oil to fuel their machines or heat their furnaces are hit with an increase in production costs. These higher costs shift the aggregate *supply* curve to the left, as in the accompanying figure (AS_1 to AS_2).

Recessionary Impact

The leftward shift of the aggregate supply curve not only pushes the average price level up (to P_2) but also reduces output (to Q_2). In the United States, the 1973 reduction in total domestic output was aggravated by price controls on domestic oil and gas. As a consequence, many manufacturers were forced to shut down because they couldn't get the oil they were willing and able to purchase. Others shut down because higher fuel costs made continued production unprofitable.

Decreased Consumption

Although the most visible effects of oil shocks are inflation and shortages, the greatest threat often lies on the demand side of

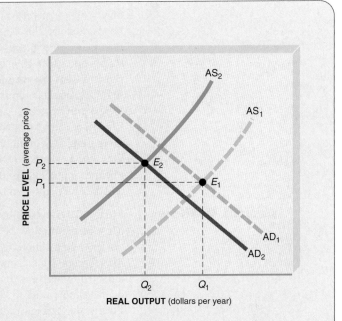

product and factor markets. OPEC price boosts force consumers to spend more of their income on foreign oil imports. In 2004, the jump in oil prices raised fuel costs for U.S. household by over $700 per year (see News, p. 337). This sudden increase in import leakage left consumers with less income to spend on domestic output. Thus, the aggregate *demand* curve shifted to the left, as from AD_1 to AD_2.

Analysis: Abrupt changes in the price or availability of imported goods will alter domestic output and spending. Such external shocks can worsen domestic inflation and unemployment.

source of the trade imbalance. Sudden *changes* in trade flows can create an external shock that upsets macro policy goals (see World View). All we know for certain is

- Imports and exports alter the levels of aggregate demand and aggregate supply.
- Trade flows may help or impede domestic macro policy attain its objectives.
- Macro policy decisions need to take account of international trade repercussions.

Thus, international trade adds an important new wrinkle to macro policy decision making.

INTERNATIONAL FINANCE

Our global interactions with the rest of the world are further complicated by international money flows. Money flows across international borders as easily as goods and services. In fact, money *must* move across borders to pay for imports and exports. In addition, people move money across borders to get bigger profits, higher interest rates, or more security. Like trade in goods and services, these international money flows alter macro outcomes and complicate macro decision making.

Capital Inflows

In 2003, over $1 trillion of foreign capital flowed into the United States. A lot of this capital inflow was used to purchase U.S. bonds. The Treasury bonds were attractive to international investors for two reasons. First, real interest rates in the U.S. economy were relatively high, making them a more attractive investment than foreign bonds. Second, the U.S. economy looked more prosperous and more politically stable than many other places, making Treasury bonds appear more secure. Corporate bonds, stocks and other U.S. investments also looked attractive in early 2003, for much the same reasons. So people and institutions around the world moved some of their funds into U.S. markets, creating a tremendous capital inflow.

The profits of U.S. corporations operating abroad added to that capital inflow. When U.S. firms build plants abroad, they anticipate earning profits they can bring home. Over time, U.S. multinational firms have accumulated a sizable share of world markets, giving them a regular inflow of international profits. McDonald's, for example, operates more than 30,000 restaurants in 119 countries. Profits from its foreign outlets add to America's capital inflow.

Capital Outflows

Money flows out of the United States to the rest of the world for the same purposes. Most of the outflow is used to pay for U.S. imports (including foreign travel by U.S. citizens). In addition, U.S. investors may seek to invest in foreign countries and need to buy foreign land, labor, and capital. And U.S. households and institutions may be attracted to overseas *financial* investments, for example, foreign bonds or stocks. Some people simply want to keep their money in Swiss banks to avoid scrutiny or evade taxes. Finally, the U.S. government spends money in foreign countries to maintain American defenses, operate embassies, encourage economic development, and provide emergency relief. The war in Iraq required the U.S. government to spend tens of billions of dollars on foreign goods and services. All these activities cause a dollar outflow.

Part of the dollar outflow is also prompted by foreign investors and institutions. We already noted that a motivation for capital *inflows* is the desire for U.S.-based investments and profits. As interest and profits accumulate, foreign investors may want to retrieve some of their assets. Those repatriated interest and profit payments are part of the capital *outflows*. If the relative attractiveness of investments in the United States diminishes, even more foreign capital will flow out. When the U.S. stock market crashed in 2000–2001, many foreign investors took their money and ran.

CAPITAL IMBALANCES

Like trade flows, capital flows won't always be balanced. At times, the outflow of dollars will exceed the inflow, and the United States will experience a **capital deficit.** At other times, the balance may be reversed, leaving the United States with a **capital surplus.** In 2003, the United States had a capital surplus of nearly $400 billion.

The huge capital surplus of 2003 is directly related to the huge trade deficit in that same year. When we import more than we export, we're effectively buying foreign goods and services on credit. The bulk of that credit is derived from the net inflow of foreign capital. The net inflow of money prompted by foreign investors creates a pool of funds that can be used to purchase foreign goods and services. If the capital inflow were smaller, our ability to purchase imports would be less, too. The reverse of this is true as well. If Americans weren't buying so many imports, foreigners wouldn't have as many dollars to invest in U.S. banks, corporations, and property. Thus, *capital imbalances are directly related to trade imbalances.*

Macro Effects

Capital imbalances are a problem for monetary policy. The essence of monetary policy is control of the money supply. When money is able to move across international borders at will, control of the money supply becomes more difficult.

Suppose inflationary forces are building and the Fed wants to reduce money supply growth. To do so, it might engage in open market operations, with the objective of net selling. By selling bonds, the Fed would seek to draw reserves out of the banking

capital deficit: The amount by which the capital outflow exceeds the capital inflow in a given time period.

capital surplus: The amount by which the capital inflow exceeds the capital outflow in a given time period.

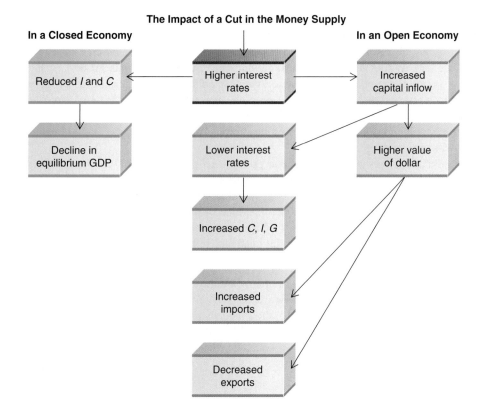

The Impact of a Cut in the Money Supply

In a Closed Economy

In an Open Economy

Higher interest rates

Reduced *I* and *C*

Increased capital inflow

Decline in equilibrium GDP

Lower interest rates

Higher value of dollar

Increased *C, I, G*

Increased imports

Decreased exports

FIGURE 18.2
International Constraints on Monetary Policy

A reduction in the money supply is intended to reduce consumption and investment spending and thereby relieve inflationary pressures. If the money supply reduction increases domestic interest rates, however, it may trigger additional capital inflow. That increased capital inflow will frustrate monetary policy by increasing the money supply and holding down interest rates. The capital inflow will also tend to increase the value of the U.S. dollar and so widen the trade deficit.

system and thereby slow money supply growth. The bond sales will also tend to raise interest rates and thus dampen both consumer and investor spending. This now-familiar sequence of events is illustrated on the left side of Figure 18.2.

The figure also illustrates how an open economy complicates monetary policy. The higher interest rates caused by the Fed's bond sales attract foreign investors. As the return on U.S. bonds increases, the inflow of foreign capital will accelerate. This will frustrate the Fed's goal of reducing money supply growth and tend to put downward pressure on domestic interest rates. The Fed will have to work harder (e.g., sell more bonds) to achieve any desired money supply target.

An important feature of Figure 18.2 is the box marked "higher value of dollar." When we purchase goods and services from foreign countries, we must exchange our dollars for foreign currency. The Japanese workers who make Toyotas, for example, are paid in yen. Their willingness to supply cars is based on how many yen, not dollars, they'll receive. Thus, we must first exchange dollars for yen before we can import Toyotas. When you travel abroad, you do these exchanges yourself, typically at banks, hotels, or foreign-exchange offices. When you stay at home and buy imported goods, someone else handles the exchange for you.

Whether you or some middleperson does the exchange is irrelevant. What matters is how many yen you get for your dollars. The more yen you get, the more Toyotas and other Japanese goods you're able to buy. In other words, *if the dollar's value in the world markets is high, imports are cheap.*

The dollar's value in international trade is reflected in the **exchange rate.** The exchange rate is simply the price (value) of one currency, measured in terms of another. The exchange rate prevailing at any time reflects the interplay of trade and capital flows and all their determinants. (Foreign exchange markets are examined in Chapter 36.) What matters here is that exchange rates *change,* often in response to monetary and fiscal policy.

Exchange Rates

exchange rate: The price of one country's currency expressed in terms of another's; the domestic price of a foreign currency.

In Figure 18.2. restrictive monetary policy causes domestic interest rates to rise. These higher interest rates make U.S. bonds more attractive and so increase capital inflow from the rest of the world. To buy Treasury bonds, however, foreign investors need dollars. As they clamor to exchange their yen, euros, and pounds for dollars, the value (price) of the dollar will increase. A higher dollar means that you can get more yen for every dollar. Imports thus become cheaper, and so Americans buy more of them. On the other hand, a stronger (more expensive) dollar makes U.S. exports costlier for foreign consumers, and so they buy fewer American products. The end result is a widening trade gap.

Similar global obstacles can impede policies of monetary stimulus. Suppose the Fed cut interest rates to stimulate aggregate demand. Those lower interest rates might start a capital outflow, as global investors sought higher returns elsewhere. This accelerated outflow would reduce the value of the dollar, making imports more expensive. The implied upward shift of aggregate supply would frustrate efforts to accelerate real GDP growth. The capital outflow would also make it harder to reduce interest rates.

Capital Flows—Another Policy Constraint

International capital flows add yet another complication to macro policy. The very existence of international capital flows weakens the Fed's ability to control the money supply. As the accompanying World View suggests, these global linkages were a significant policy constraint in 2001: the weakening U.S. dollar kept the Fed from offering more monetary stimulus. We conclude, then, that global money links create

WORLD VIEW

Another Chink in the Economy's Armor
But If the Dollar's Down, Is the Bottom Near?

The dollar is too strong. That's what American steelmakers and other manufacturers who depend on selling their products overseas have complained all summer.

Not anymore. Since early July, the dollar is down 8 percent against the euro, its chief competitor. While that dip may be welcome among old-line exporters, it raises more serious questions about the health of the economy. That is because one key reason for the dollar's dip is that currency traders are beginning to concede that a rebound in the U.S. economy may be further off than expected. So they're selling greenbacks—literally taking their cash and betting that it will do better overseas.

Dollar drop
The dollar is declining against the euro.

1.18
1.16
1.14
1.12 **Euros per**
1.10 **dollar**
1.08

| June | July | Aug. |

The dollar's sudden weakness isn't all bad news. U.S. manufacturers such as General Motors and International Paper have pushed Treasury Secretary Paul O'Neill to talk down the dollar, figuring that a weaker currency will pump up the value of profit from overseas sales. That would shore up their earnings statements and, conceivably, their stock prices.

Weakling. The evidence on past efforts to boost the economy with a weak dollar is mixed at best. A policy launched in 1985 cut the currency's value by 40 percent, boosting exports, but was later cited by some economists as a cause of the October 1987 stock market crash. Some economists argue that a weak dollar assures one thing and one thing only: inflation. That's because a weaker dollar could prompt importers to boost prices to maintain profit margins, allowing domestic manufacturers to simply do the same, rather than focus on gaining market share.

The fear of inflation may have figured into the Fed's decision to hold off on a more dramatic move last week, some economists say.

—Noam Neusner

Source: *U.S. News & World Report*, September 3, 2001. Copyright 2001 U.S. News & World Report, L.P. Reprinted with permission. www.usnews.com

Analysis: The Fed may be reluctant to pursue a monetary stimulus if lower interest rates might spark a capital outflow, a weaker dollar, and higher import prices (inflation).

another policy headache: In addition to all our other macro worries, we now have to be concerned about

- The flow of capital into and out of the country.
- The effect of capital imbalances on domestic macro performance.
- How macro policy will affect international capital flows, exchange rates, and trade balances.

PRODUCTIVITY AND COMPETITIVENESS

The global dimensions of the economy add a whole new layer of complexity to macro policy. One might reasonably wonder whether international trade and finance is really worth all the trouble. Couldn't we get along just as well without the rest of the world?

Perhaps. But we wouldn't be able to drink much coffee. Or spend summer vacations in Europe. Or buy Japanese cars and Mexican beer.

Specialization

To decide whether international trade and finance is worth all the trouble, we have to consider how international exchanges affect our standard of living. One obvious advantage of trade is that it gives us access to goods and services we don't or can't produce at home, such as coffee, vacations abroad, bananas, and Italian shoes. These *imported goods and services broaden our consumption possibilities.*

Most of the goods and services we import *could* be produced at home. Cars and shoes are made in America as well as abroad, as is a small quantity of coffee and bananas (in Hawaii). Even more coffee and bananas *could* be produced in the United States if we invested enough in greenhouses that duplicated tropical conditions. Homegrown coffee and bananas would turn out to be terribly expensive, however, so we're better off importing them. This leaves domestic resources available for the production of other goods that we can more easily grow (corn), manufacture (airplanes), or build (houses). In other words, we're better off *specializing* in the production of things we do relatively well and *trading* with other nations for the rest of the goods and services we desire. This is the principle of **comparative advantage** we first encountered in Chapter 2. In essence, it recommends that we produce what we do best and trade with other nations for goods they produce best. *Specialization among countries increases world efficiency and output, making all nations richer.*

comparative advantage: The ability of a country to produce a specific good at a lower opportunity cost than its trading partners.

Chapter 35 demonstrates the benefits of international specialization (the theory of comparative advantage). At this juncture we may note that the same principles that motivate *individuals* to specialize and then exchange their goods and services also motivate *nations* to specialize and then exchange their goods and services in international trade. In both cases, **productivity** and total output increase.

productivity: Output per unit of input, for example, output per labor-hour.

Competitiveness

The increased output and productivity that specialization makes possible aren't the only benefits of international trade. *Trade stimulates improvements in productivity.* The presence of foreign producers keeps domestic producers on their toes. To compete in international markets, domestic producers must reduce costs and increase efficiency.

In recent years, America's huge trade deficits have provoked questions about the competitiveness of U.S. producers. The excess of imports over exports suggests to many people that America isn't producing goods of the quality and value that consumers demand. Productivity may have lagged in some U.S. industries. And other nations inevitably become more efficient in producing certain goods and services. But the trade gap isn't a general indictment of U.S. competitiveness.

The U.S. Bureau of Labor Statistics (BLS) assembles international comparisons of manufacturing productivity (also published in the *Monthly Labor Review*); visit www.bls.gov/fls.

As we've observed, international trade and capital flows are interrelated, and both are directly influenced by exchange rates. In the early 1980s, the relative attractiveness of America's capital markets led to a surge of capital inflows and a higher exchange rate for the U.S. dollar. Between 1981 and 1985, the world value of the

U.S. dollar rose by 50 percent, which made all American goods more expensive in international markets. To *maintain* their prices in international markets, U.S. producers would have had to cut costs enough to offset that increase in the dollar's value. Although American productivity increased faster than foreign productivity in those years, few U.S. producers could stay ahead of the rising dollar. The resulting increase in the trade deficit was a product of the rising dollar, not of a decline in U.S. productivity. The same thing happened again during the period 1996–99, when the value of the dollar and the trade deficit both jumped. The same sequence was repeated in 2001.

Although a trade gap isn't necessarily evidence of declining competitiveness, it does draw policy attention to productivity issues. Productivity improvements are essential to economic growth and rising living standards. If a trade gap stimulates fiscal, monetary, and supply-side policies that foster productivity advances, then the economy may be better off as a result. By the same token, trade gaps remind us that policies that restrain productivity improvements (research, innovation, and investment) also have international consequences.

GLOBAL COORDINATION

As all countries begin to acknowledge the international dimensions of their economies, the desire for coordination grows. The coordination is pursued both through formal institutions and informal "understandings" among the major industrialized nations.

IMF

The most visible institution for global coordination is the International Monetary Fund (IMF). The IMF is sort of a bankers' United Nations. All nations contribute funds to the IMF, which then uses those funds to assist nations whose currency is in trouble. When Thailand devalued its currency (the baht) in July 1997, for example, the currencies of other Asian nations also plunged. This Asian crisis threatened U.S. exports as well as those of other nations. There was a distinct threat that the "Asian flu" would become a global contagion. To keep the Asian flu from spreading, the IMF lent more than $100 billion to Thailand, Korea, Indonesia, and other Asian nations. The IMF also loaned Brazil over $40 billion in 1998–99 and Argentina $22 billion in 2001 to avoid a "Latin flu" from spreading to other South American nations and the global economy.

Although the IMF often provides global "first aid," IMF assistance typically comes with strings attached. The IMF often insists that a debtor nation alter its domestic monetary fiscal or trade policies as a condition of an IMF bailout. Such intrusions into domestic macro policy are often resented, especially when they entail high political costs in the debtor nation (as in Argentina in 2001–2).

WEBNOTE

For a summary of IMF activities and recent bailouts, visit www.imf.org.

Group of Eight

The eight largest industrial countries (the United States, Japan, Canada, Germany, France, Italy, Great Britain, and Russia) attain a less formal mode of global coordination. The finance economic ministers of these nations meet periodically to assess the global outlook and coordinate macro policy. Although the Group of Eight (the G-8) has no formal apparatus for joint actions, any informal agreements it reaches can have a substantial effect on global trade and capital flow. Reaching agreement isn't always easy, however. In mid-2001, the Federal Reserve's attempts to stimulate the U.S. economy were frustrated by higher interest rates in Europe. Despite Fed pleas for greater monetary stimulus (see World View), the European Central Bank kept interest rates relatively high. In 2004, U.S. trading partners worried that Fed rate hikes would strengthen the U.S. dollar and add to their inflationary pressures.

Global interests will never fully displace national policy priorities. However, even limited global coordination helps smooth out some of the rough spots of macro performance in an increasingly interdependent world.

WORLD VIEW

U.S. Wants Europe, Japan to Ease Rates
Moves Could Help Fortify Economies Overseas, Lift Dollar in Short Term

WASHINGTON—The Bush administration, hoping to see stronger economic growth overseas, wants Europe and Japan to follow the U.S. Federal Reserve's lead in easing monetary policy more aggressively.

U.S. officials hope the moves eventually will invigorate slack overseas markets for American companies. But they recognize that the more immediate effect is likely to be a stronger dollar that will make it tougher for American manufacturers to compete against foreign producers. Already, many companies complain that the strong dollar is hurting their exports at the same time that the weak euro is crimping profits from their European operations.

Unfazed by such concerns, a senior Bush administration official yesterday said the European Central Bank still "needs to ease up quite a bit," while Japan's financial authorities should combine expansion of that country's money supply with tough-minded economic reforms. . . .

On July 7, Mr. O'Neill will meet in Rome with his finance ministry counterparts from the other Group of Seven major industrialized nations. Treasury officials say that, while the secretary may push for enhanced growth, he won't press directly for rate cuts. "It's none of our business how they stimulate growth." Mr. O'Neill said yesterday. "It's entirely up to them."

But the U.S. is likely to find others around the table who think the ECB should do more to stimulate the economy.

The Italian and German governments—whose economies are among the worst-performing in the 12-nation euro area—are growing increasingly disgruntled with the central bank. The ECB has hardly budged on rates since the global slowdown began, cutting its key rate just a quarter point to 4.5 percent on May 10.

—Michael M. Phillips and Rebecca Quick

Analysis: Global coordination of economic policies is limited by the different priorities of individual nations. In the absence of coordination, policy success is more difficult.

THE ECONOMY TOMORROW

A Global Currency?

On January 1, 1999, 11 European nations adopted a simple currency, the *euro*. That wasn't an easy or quick policy decision. As the World View on the next page notes, the quest for a common European currency began in the Middle Ages. The latest push for the euro began over 40 years ago. In view of this history, one has to wonder why a single European currency has been sought and why it has taken so long to attain.

The New Euro

The allure of a common currency is that it facilitates trade and capital flows across national borders. A common currency eliminates the uncertainties and added costs of diverse currencies. European businesses spent nearly $13 billion a year just on currency conversions. Exchange rate fluctuation also impeded cross-border business transactions, which is why the U.S. Congress created a national currency to replace the hundreds of state and private bank currencies that existed prior to 1863.

Macro Coordination

There's a huge difference, however, between creating a common *national* currency (the U.S. dollar) and a common *cross-national* currency like the euro. The 50 states that make up the United States share a common set of laws, monetary institutions, and government. The nations of the European Union (EU) don't even share a common language, much less governmental authority. Accordingly, in creating a common currency, they agreed to submerge some national interests to broader European goals.

WORLD VIEW

The Long History of Europe's Single Currency

- **Middle Ages:** Feudal rulers frequently try to unify coins with trading partners.
- **1865–1927:** "Latin coin union" (France, Belgium, Italy, Switzerland, and Greece) undermined by policy rows.
- **1872–1924:** "Scandinavian coin union" (Sweden, Norway, and Denmark) works smoothly for a time but eroded by World War I.
- **1957:** European Community's founding Treaty of Rome provides for coordination of economic and monetary policies.
- **1970:** "Werner Plan" seeks to achieve monetary union by 1980, but is derailed by international oil crisis.
- **1972:** European nations link currencies in "snake" that limits fluctuations.
- **1979:** Founding of European Monetary System tying exchange rates.
- **1987:** Single European Act fixed objective of monetary union in a treaty for first time.
- **1989:** Delores Report outlines three-stage plan for monetary union.

- **1991:** EC heads of state agree in Maastricht, the Netherlands, to create a monetary union in 1997 or 1999.
- **1993:** After currency turmoil ejects Britain and Italy from exchange-rate mechanism, fluctuation bands are widened.
- **1994:** Founding of European Monetary Institute, forerunner of a European central bank.
- **1995:** EU governments agree they won't be able to meet the 1997 deadline.
- **1998:** Using 1997 data, EU rules which nations can participate in monetary union.
- **1999:** Parities of currencies are irrevocably fixed, European central bank takes over monetary policy.
- **2002:** Notes and coins in new currency issued to public; national currencies eliminated.

Source: *Deutsche Bank Research.* From *The Wall Street Journal.* December 13, 1995. Reprinted by permission of The Wall Street Journal. © 1995 Dow Jones & Company, Inc. All rights reserved worldwide. www.wsj.com. Updated by author 2002.

Analysis: The adoption of a common currency requires nations to give up control of monetary policy. Few countries are willing to do so.

WEBNOTE

Information on the euro and economic conditions in Euroland is posted at europa.eu.int/index_en.htm.

To maintain a common currency, nations must maintain common macro policies. Germany, for example, has been particularly vigilant about inflation, while Italy has given higher priority to reducing unemployment. As a result, German monetary policy tended to be tighter (more restrictive) than Italian monetary policy. When they adopted a common currency, Germany, Italy and the other nine original EU members had to find a middle ground for monetary policy. If unemployment or growth rates vary significantly across the EU nations, such a middle ground may be politically difficult to maintain.

Recognizing these obstacles, the EU nations initially hedged on their commitment to a common currency. Although the euro became the official currency of the original 11 nations in 1999, each country maintained its own currency for three additional years. Euros did not circulate publicly until January 2002. And although the EU nations established a new European central bank, the central banks of the member nations still functioned for several years. Now the "trial marriage" is over, and the euro is the common currency of Europe, or at least most of Europe: Great Britain, Sweden, Denmark, and Switzerland opted to keep their national currencies. Submerging national priorities to the common interests of "Euroland" was viewed as too great a price to pay for greater cross-border efficiency. Other nations, however, concluded that the benefits of global integration justify the loss of policy independence and have eagerly joined the EU.

SUMMARY

- The United States exports about 11 percent of total output and imports an even larger percentage. This international trade ties our macro performance to that of the rest of the world.
- Imports represent leakage from the circular flow and so tend to reduce equilibrium GDP. The marginal propensity to import also diminishes the multiplier impact of fiscal and monetary policies.
- Exports represent added spending on domestic output and so tend to increase equilibrium GDP. This added demand may conflict with restrictive macro policy objectives.
- Trade imbalances occur when exports and imports are unequal. Trade deficits imply that we're consuming more output than we're producing. Trade surpluses indicate the opposite.
- Fiscal stimulus increases imports and crowds out net exports. The resulting increase in the trade deficit may constrain policy options.

- Capital imbalances occur when capital inflows don't equal capital outflows. Capital surpluses help finance trade deficits but may also conflict with macro policy goals at home or abroad.
- International trade and capital flows place additional constraints on macro policy. Macro policy must both anticipate and respond to changes in trade and capital flows.
- The benefits of international trade and capital markets are the broadening of consumption possibilities and the enhanced productivity they promote. Productivity advances arise from specialization in production and from the competitive pressure of foreign producers and markets.
- In adopting a common currency, EU nations have broadened markets and accelerated productivity and growth. To maintain that currency, they have had to submerge some national priorities.

Key Terms

imports	exports	capital deficit
leakage	net exports	capital surplus
multiplier	trade surplus	exchange rate
marginal propensity to import (MPM)	trade deficit	comparative advantage
marginal propensity to save (MPS)	crowding out	productivity

Questions for Discussion

1. How is the U.S. economy affected by (*a*) a recession in Mexico, (*b*) simulative monetary policies in Mexico, (*c*) a drop in the value of the peso?
2. Suppose investors in other countries increased their purchases of U.S. corporate stock. How would this influx of capital affect the U.S. economy?
3. Why is it unrealistic to expect trade flows to be balanced?
4. Farmers in the United States export about one-third of their major crops. What would happen to U.S. farmers if foreign consumers stopped buying American food? What would happen to our macro equilibrium?
5. Japan imports most of the raw materials it uses in the production of finished goods. If the international prices of

raw materials rose sharply, how would Japan's economy be affected? Would Japanese exports be affected?
6. How would a tax cut in the United States affect international capital and trade flows?
7. Why would the European Central Bank (ECB) need to be prodded into reducing interest rates (see World View, page 385)? What might have held the ECB back?
8. Who gains and who loses when the global value of the U.S. dollar rises?
9. Would a higher marginal propensity to import help or hinder domestic macro policy?

PROBLEMS   The Student Problem Set at the back of this book contains numerical and graphing problems for this chapter.

WEB ACTIVITIES   to accompany this chapter can be found on the Online Learning Center:
http://www.mhhe.com/economics/schiller10

Theory and Reality

There is no one solution. It isn't just a question of the budget. It isn't just the question of inflationary labor rates. It isn't just the question of sticky prices. It isn't just the question of what the Government does to keep prices up or to make regulations that tend to be inflationary. It isn't just the weather or just the drought.

It is all these things. The interaction of these various factors is what is so terribly difficult for us to understand and, of course, what is so terribly difficult for us to deal with.

—Former Secretary of the Treasury W. Michael Blumenthal

Macroeconomic theory is supposed to explain the business cycle and show policymakers how to control it. But something is obviously wrong. Despite our relative prosperity, we haven't consistently achieved the goals of full employment, price stability, and vigorous economic growth. All too often, either unemployment or inflation surges or economic growth slows down. No matter how hard we try to eliminate it, the business cycle seems to persist.

What accounts for this gap between the promises of economic theory and the reality of economic performance? Are the theories inadequate? Or is sound economic advice being ignored?

Many people blame the economists. They point to the conflicting advice of Keynesians, monetarists, and supply-siders and wonder what theory is supposed to be followed. If economists themselves can't agree, it is asked, why should anyone else listen to them?

Not surprisingly, economists see things a bit differently. First, they point out, the **business cycle** isn't as bad as it used to be. Since World War II, the economy has had many ups and downs, but none as severe as the Great Depression or earlier catastrophes. Second, economists complain that "politics" often takes precedence over good economic advice. Politicians are reluctant, for example, to raise taxes, cut spending, or slow money growth in order to control inflation. Their concern is winning the next election, not solving the country's economic problems.

When President Jimmy Carter was in office, he anguished over another problem: the complexity of economic decision making. In the real world, neither theory nor politics can keep up with all our economic goals. As President Carter observed: "We cannot concentrate just on inflation or just on unemployment or just on deficits in the federal budget or our international payments. Nor can we act in isolation from other countries. We must deal with all of these problems simultaneously and on a worldwide basis."

No president learned this lesson faster or more forcefully than George W. Bush. Just as he was putting the final touches on a bipartisan consensus on taxes, spending, and debt reduction, terrorists destroyed the World Trade Center and damaged the Pentagon. In response to those attacks, all major economic policy decisions had to be revised.

business cycle: Alternating periods of economic growth and contraction.

As if the burdens of a continuously changing world weren't enough, the president must also contend with sharply differing economic theories and advice, a slow and frequently hostile Congress, a massive and often unresponsive bureaucracy, and a complete lack of knowledge about the future.

This chapter confronts these and other frustrations of the real world head on. In so doing, we provide answers to the following questions:

- **What's the ideal "package" of macro policies?**
- **How well does our macro performance live up to the promises of that package?**
- **What kinds of obstacles prevent us from doing better?**

The answers to these questions may shed some light on a broader concern that has long troubled students and policymakers alike, namely, "If economists are so smart, why is the economy always in such a mess?"

POLICY LEVERS

Table 19.1 summarizes the macroeconomic tools available to policymakers. Although this list is brief, we hardly need a reminder at this point of how powerful each instrument can be. Every one of these major policy instruments can significantly change our answers to the basic economic questions of WHAT, HOW, and FOR WHOM to produce.

The basic tools of **fiscal policy** are contained in the federal budget. Tax cuts are supposed to increase aggregate demand by putting more income in the hands of consumers and businesses. Tax increases are intended to curtail spending and reduce inflationary pressures. Table 19.2 summarizes some of the major tax changes of recent years.

The expenditure side of the federal budget is another fiscal policy tool. From a Keynesian perspective, increases in government spending raise aggregate demand and so encourage more production. A slowdown in government spending is supposed to restrain aggregate demand and lessen inflationary pressures.

Who Makes Fiscal Policy? As we first observed in Chapter 11, changes in taxes and government spending originate both in economic events and explicit policy decisions. When the economy slows, tax revenues decline, and government spending increases automatically. Conversely, when real GDP grows, tax revenues automatically rise, and government transfer payments decline. These **automatic stabilizers** are a basic countercyclical feature of the federal budget. They don't represent active fiscal policy. On the contrary, *fiscal policy refers to deliberate changes in tax or spending legislation.* These changes can be made only by the U.S. Congress. Every year the president proposes specific budget and tax changes, negotiates with Congress, then accepts or vetoes specific acts that Congress has passed. The resulting policy decisions represent

WEBNOTE

The Library of Congress maintains a summary of recent congressional tax legislation at thomas.loc.gov. Go to "Bill Summary and Status." Enter "taxes."

Fiscal Policy

fiscal policy: The use of government taxes and spending to alter macroeconomic outcomes.

automatic stabilizer: Federal expenditure or revenue item that automatically responds counter-cyclically to changes in national income—such as unemployment benefits, income taxes.

Type of Policy	Policy Instruments
Fiscal	Tax cuts and increases
	Changes in government spending
Monetary	Open market operations
	Reserve requirements
	Discount rates
Supply-side	Tax incentives for investment and saving
	Deregulation
	Human-capital investment
	Infrastructure development
	Free trade
	Immigration

TABLE 19.1
The Policy Levers

Economic policymakers have access to a variety of policy instruments. The challenge is to choose the right tools at the right time. The mix of tools required may vary from problem to problem.

TABLE 19.2
Fiscal Policy Milestones

1986	Tax Reform Act	Major reduction in tax rates coupled with broadening of tax base
1990	Budget Enforcement Act	Limits set on discretionary spending; pay-as-you-go financing required
1993	Clinton "New Direction"	Tax increases and spending cuts to achieve $300 billion deficit reduction
1994	Contract with America	Republican-led Congress cuts spending, sets seven-year target for balanced budget
1997	Balanced Budget Act, Taxpayer Relief Act	Package of tax cuts and spending cuts to balance budget by 2002
2001	Economic Growth and Tax Relief Act	Eight year, $1.35 trillion in personal tax cuts
2002	Job Creation and Worker Assistance Act	Business investment tax cuts
2003	Jobs and Growth Tax Relief Act	Cuts in dividend and capital-gains taxes
2004	Working Families Tax Relief Act	Extends 2001–03 tax cuts until 2008–10

structural deficit: Federal revenues at full employment minus expenditures at full employment under prevailing fiscal policy.

fiscal stimulus: Tax cuts or spending hikes intended to increase (shift) aggregate demand.

fiscal restraint: Tax hikes or spending cuts intended to reduce (shift) aggregate demand.

"discretionary" fiscal policy. Those policy decisions expand or shrink the **structural deficit** and thus give the economy a shot of **fiscal stimulus** or **fiscal restraint.**

Monetary Policy

monetary policy: The use of money and credit controls to influence macroeconomic outcomes.

The policy arsenal in Table 19.1 also contains monetary tools. Tools of **monetary policy** include open market operations, discount rate changes, and reserve requirements.

As we saw in Chapter 15, there are disagreements over how these monetary tools should be used. Keynesians believe that interest rates are the critical policy lever. In their view, the money supply should be expanded or curtailed in order to achieve whatever interest rate is needed to shift aggregate demand. Monetarists, on the other hand, contend that the money supply itself is the critical policy lever and that it should be expanded at a steady and predictable rate. This policy, they believe, will ensure price stability and a **natural rate of unemployment.**

natural rate of unemployment: Long-term rate of unemployment determined by structural forces in labor and product markets.

Who Makes Monetary Policy? Actual monetary policy decisions are made by the Federal Reserve's Board of Governors. Twice a year the Fed provides Congress with a broad overview of the economic outlook and monetary objectives. The Fed's assessment of the economy is updated each month at meetings of the Federal Open Market Committee (FOMC). The FOMC decides which monetary policy levers to pull.

Table 19.3 depicts milestones in recent monetary policy. Of particular interest is the October 1979 decision to adopt a pure monetarist approach. This involved an exclusive focus on the money supply, without regard for interest rates. After interest rates soared and the economy appeared on the brink of a depression, the Fed abandoned the monetarist approach and again began keeping an eye on both interest rates (the Keynesian focus) and the money supply.

Monetarists contend that the Fed never fully embraced their policy. The money supply grew at a very uneven pace in 1980, they argue, not at the steady, predictable rate that they demanded. Nevertheless, the policy shifts of 1979 and 1982 were distinctive and had dramatic effects.

A quick review of Table 19.3 reveals that such monetary policy reversals have been quite frequent. There were U-turns in monetary policy between 1982 and 1983, 1989 and 1991, 1998 and 1999, 2000 and 2001, and again between 2003 and 2004.

Supply-Side Policy

Supply-side theory offers the third major set of policy tools. The focus of **supply-side policy** is to provide incentives to work, invest, and produce. Of particular concern are high tax rates and regulations that reduce supply incentives. Supply-siders argue that marginal tax rates and government regulation must be reduced in order to get more output without added inflation.

TABLE 19.3
Monetary Policy Milestones

October 1979	Fed adopts monetarist approach, focusing exclusively on money supply; interest rates soar
July 1982	Deep into recession, Fed votes to ease monetary restraint
October 1982	Fed abandons pure monetarist approach and expands money supply rapidly
May 1983	Fed reverses policy and begins slowing money supply growth
1985	Fed increases money supply with discount-rate cuts and open market purchases
1987	Fed abandons money supply targets as policy guides; money supply growth decreases; discount rate increased
1989	Greenspan announces goal of "zero inflation," exercises more monetary restraint
1991	Deep in recession, the Fed begins to ease monetary restraint
1994	Fed slows M2 growth to 1 percent; raises federal funds rate by 3 percentage points as economy nears full employment
1995	Greenspan trumpets "soft landing" and eases monetary restraint
1998	Fed cuts interest rates to cushion U.S. economy from Asian crisis
1999–2000	Fed raises interest rates six times
2001–2003	Fed cuts interest rates 13 times
2004	Fed begins raising interest rates

In the 1980s tax rates were reduced dramatically. The maximum marginal tax rate on individuals was cut from 70 to 50 percent in 1981, and then still further, to 28 percent, in 1987. The 1980s also witnessed major milestones in the deregulation of airlines, trucking, telephone service, and other industries (see Table 19.4).

Some of the momentum toward less regulation was reversed during the 1990s. New regulatory costs on business were created by the Americans with Disabilities Act, the 1990 amendments to the Clean Air Act, and the Family Leave Act of 1993. All three laws provide important benefits to workers or the environment. At the same time, however, they also make supplying goods and services more expensive.

The Clinton administration broadened supply-side efforts to include infrastructure development and increased investment in human capital (through education and skill training programs). These activities increase the capacity to produce and so shift the aggregate supply curve rightward. The Clinton administration also toughened environmental regulation, however, and sought legislation that would require employers to provide more training and fringe benefits (like health insurance), initiatives that shift the aggregate supply curve leftward. George W. Bush sought to reduce such regulations.

Who Makes Supply-Side Policy? Because tax rates are a basic tool of supply-side policy, fiscal and supply-side policies are often intertwined. When Congress changes the tax laws, it almost always alters marginal tax rates and thus changes production incentives. Notice, for example, that tax legislation appears in Table 19.4 as well as in Table 19.2. The Taxpayer Relief Act of 1997 not only changed total tax revenues (fiscal policy) but also restructured production and investment incentives (supply-side policy). The 2001–3 tax cuts also had both demand-side and supply-side provisions.

Supply-side and fiscal policies also interact on the outlay side of the budget. The Transportation Equity Act of 2000, for example, authorized accelerated public works spending (fiscal stimulus) on infrastructure development (increase in supply capacity). President Clinton's Rebuild America program also affected both aggregate demand and aggregate supply. *Deciding **whether** to increase spending is a fiscal policy decision; deciding **how** to spend available funds may entail supply-side policy.*

Regulatory policy is also fashioned by Congress. The president and executive agencies play a critical role in this supply-side area in the day-to-day decisions on how to interpret and enforce regulatory policies.

supply-side policy: The use of tax incentives, (de)regulation, and other mechanisms to increase the ability and willingness to produce goods and services.

TABLE 19.4
Supply-Side Milestones

1990	Social Security Act amendments	Increased payroll tax to 7.65 percent
1990	Americans with Disabilities Act	Required employers to provide greater access for disabled individuals
1990	Immigration Act	Increased immigration, especially for high-skill workers
1990	Clean Air Act amendments	Increased pollution controls
1993	Rebuild America Program	Increased spending on infrastructure and human-capital investment
	Family Leave Act	Required employers to provide unpaid leaves of absence for workers
	NAFTA	Lowered North American trade barriers
1994	GATT renewed	Lowered World trade barriers
1996	Telecommunications Act	Permitted greater competition in cable and telephone industries
1996–1997	Minimum Wage Hike	Raised minimum wage from $4.25 to $5.15 per hour
1996	Personal Responsibility and Work Opportunity Act	Required more welfare recipients to work
1997	Taxpayer Relief Act	Created tuition tax credits, cut capital gains tax
1998	Workforce Investment Act	Increased funds for skills training
2000	Transportation Equity Act	Provided new funding for highways, rails
2001	Economic Growth and Tax Relief Act	Increased savings incentives; reduced marginal tax rates
2002	Job Creation and Worker Assistance Act	Provided more tax incentives for investment
2003	Jobs and Growth Tax Relief Act	Reduced taxes on capital gains and dividends

IDEALIZED USES

These fiscal, monetary, and supply-side tools are potentially powerful levers for controlling the economy. In principle, they can cure the excesses of the business cycle and promote faster economic growth. To see how, let's review their use in three distinct macroeconomic settings.

Case 1: Recession

When output and employment levels fall far short of the economy's full-employment potential, the mandate for public policy is clear. Aggregate demand must be increased so that producers can sell more goods, hire more workers, and move the economy toward its productive capacity. At such times the most urgent need is to get people back to work and close the **recessionary GDP gap.**

recessionary GDP gap: The amount by which equilibrium GDP falls short of full-employment GDP.

How can the government end a recession? Keynesians emphasize the need to increase aggregate demand by cutting taxes or boosting government spending. The resulting stimulus will set off a **multiplier** reaction. If the initial stimulus and multiplier are large enough, the recessionary GDP gap can be closed, propelling the economy to full employment.

multiplier: The multiple by which an initial change in aggregate spending will alter total expenditure after an infinite number of spending cycles; $1/(1 - MPC)$.

Modern Keynesians acknowledge that monetary policy might also help. Specifically, increases in the money supply may lower interest rates and thus give investment spending a further boost. To give the economy a really powerful stimulus, we might want to pull all these policy levers at the same time. That's what the government did in early 2001—using tax cuts, lower interest rates, and increased spending to jump start the economy (see cartoon and News).

Analysis: When the economy is flat on its back, it may need both monetary and fiscal stimulus.

Finding a Fix for the Declining Economy

Government's Options Include Spending, Cutting Rates and Taxes

WASHINGTON—With unemployment rising and the stock market slumping, politicians are nearing a panic, howling for the government to do *something* to stop the economic decline.

Of course, it isn't like policymakers have been sitting idly by. The Federal Reserve has cut interest rates seven times this year, while President Bush and Congress approved an emergency tax rebate. Those measures may well turn out to be sufficient to prevent a recession.

But with each passing day of scary data, patience inside the Beltway is wearing thin, especially for those folks running for re-election next year. Fed Chairman Alan Greenspan and his central-bank colleagues have a clear course: They will likely keep cutting interest rates. Here is a look at the more complex set of options facing the White House and Capitol Hill:

Q: Politics aside, does it really make economic sense to do anything?

A: Until recently, conventional wisdom told us no. The experts concluded that the wheels of government—outside the Fed—worked too slowly to give any short-term assistance, and by the time federal action kicked in, the economy would be recovering anyway, risking overstimulation. "I don't think the government really has the power to prevent recessions," says Murray Weidenbaum, who was chairman of President Reagan's Council of Economic Advisers.

Yet most economists—liberal and conservative alike—grudgingly admit that the answer may indeed be "yes," saying this year's tax rebate was well-timed, thus reviving interest in short-term measures.

Q: So what are the choices?

A: The most likely to succeed is fiscal stimulus—either spending increases or further tax cuts. That is, the federal government pumps more money into the economy. . . .

Q: If the government does end up accepting some fiscal stimulus, which is better, spending increases or tax cuts?

A: The case can be made that increasing spending makes more sense. The government can tweak outlays in a way to make sure every dollar gets spent. Tax cuts are less certain; recipients may stash some away. Indeed, some analysts think consumers are saving a good chunk of their rebates.

Yet spending has its own disadvantages. There can be long lags between congressional approval of a program and the time the money gets spent. And government spending, insulated from market forces, can be highly inefficient, diminishing its positive benefits. A decade of failed public-works-spending programs in Japan has done much to discredit the idea.

Q: What is the best kind of tax cut?

A: One that is likely to be spent quickly.

—Jacob M. Schlesinger

Analysis: The federal government has many policy levers at its disposal; they aren't certain to work as intended or on time, however.

velocity of money (*V*): The number of times per year, on average, that a dollar is used to purchase final goods and services; $PQ \div M$.

Monetarists would proceed differently. First, they see no point in toying with the federal budget. In the pure monetarist model, changes in taxes or government spending may alter the mix of output but not its level. So long as the **velocity of money (*V*)** is constant, fiscal policy doesn't matter. In this view, the appropriate policy response to a recession is patience. As sales and output slow, interest rates decline, and new investment will be stimulated.

Supply-siders emphasize the need to improve production incentives. They urge cuts in marginal tax rates on investment and labor. They also look for ways to reduce government regulation. Finally, they urge that any increase in government spending (fiscal stimulus) focus on long-run capacity expansion such as infrastructure development.

Case 2: Inflation

inflationary GDP gap: The amount by which equilibrium GDP exceeds full-employment GDP.

An overheated economy provides as clear a policy mandate as does a sluggish one. In this case, the immediate goal is to restrain aggregate demand until the rate of total expenditure is compatible with the productive capacity of the economy. This entails shifting the aggregate demand curve to the left in order to close the **inflationary GDP gap.** Keynesians would do this by raising taxes and cutting government spending. Keynesians would also see the desirability of increasing interest rates to curb investment spending.

Monetarists would simply cut the money supply. In their view, the short-run aggregate supply curve is unknown and unstable. The only predictable response is reflected in the vertical, long-run aggregate supply curve. According to this view, changes in the money supply alter prices, not output. Inflation is seen simply as "too much money chasing too few goods." Monetarists would turn off the money spigot. The Fed's job in this situation isn't only to reduce money supply growth but to convince market participants that a more cautious monetary policy will be continued. This was the intent of Chairman Greenspan's 1989 public commitment to zero inflation.

Supply-siders would point out that inflation implies both "too much money" and "not enough goods." They'd look at the supply side of the market for ways to expand productive capacity. In a highly inflationary setting, they'd propose more incentives to save. The additional savings would automatically reduce consumption while creating a larger pool of investable funds. Supply-siders would also cut taxes and regulations that raise production costs and lower import barriers that keep out cheaper foreign goods.

Case 3: Stagflation

stagflation: The simultaneous occurrence of substantial unemployment and inflation.

Although serious inflations and recessions provide clear mandates for economic policy, there's a vast gray area between these extremes. Occasionally, the economy suffers from both inflation and unemployment at the same time, a condition called **stagflation.** In 1980, for example, the unemployment rate (7.1 percent) and the inflation rate (12.5 percent) were both too high. With an upward-sloping aggregate supply curve, the easy policy options were foreclosed. If aggregate demand were stimulated to reduce unemployment, the resultant pressure on prices might fuel the existing inflation. And if fiscal and monetary restraints were used to reduce inflationary pressures, unemployment might worsen. In such a situation, there are no simple solutions.

Knowing the causes of stagflation will help achieve the desired balance. If prices are rising before full employment is reached, some degree of structural unemployment is likely. An appropriate policy response might include more vocational training in skill-shortage areas as well as a redirection of aggregate demand toward labor-surplus sectors.

High tax rates or costly regulations might also contribute to stagflation. If either constraint exists, high prices (inflation) may not be a sufficient incentive for increased output. In this case, reductions in tax rates and regulation might help reduce both unemployment and inflation, which is the basic goal of supply-side policies.

Stagflation may also arise from a temporary contraction of aggregate supply that both reduces output and drives up prices. In this case, neither structural unemployment nor excessive demand is the culprit. Rather, an "external shock" (such as a natural disaster or a terrorist attack) or an abrupt change in world trade (such as an oil embargo) is likely to be the cause of the policy dilemma. Accordingly, none of our familiar policy tools is likely to provide a complete "cure." In most cases, the economy simply has to adjust to a temporary setback.

The apparently inexhaustible potential of public policy to alter the economy's performance has often generated optimistic expectations about the efficacy of fiscal, monetary, and supply-side tools. In the early 1960s, such optimism pervaded even the highest levels of government. Those were the days when prices were relatively stable, unemployment rates were falling, the economy was growing rapidly, and preparations were being made for the first trip into space. The potential of economic policy looked great indeed. It was also during the 1960s that a lot of people (mostly economists) spoke of the potential for **fine-tuning,** or altering economic outcomes to fit very exacting specifications. Flexible responses to changing market conditions, it was argued, could ensure fulfillment of our economic goals. The prescription was simple: When unemployment is the problem, simply give the economy a jolt of fiscal or monetary stimulus; when inflation is worrisome, simply tap on the fiscal or monetary brakes. To fulfill our goals for content and distribution, simply pick the right target for stimulus or restraint. With a little attention and experience, the right speed could be found and the economy guided successfully down the road to prosperity. As the economic expansion of the 1990s stretched into the record books, the same kind of economic mastery was claimed. More that a few prominent economists claimed the business cycle was dead.

THE ECONOMIC RECORD

The economy's track record doesn't live up to these high expectations. To be sure, the economy has continued to grow and we've attained an impressive standard of living. We can't lose sight of the fact that our per capita income greatly exceeds the realities and even the expectations in most other countries of the world. Nevertheless, we must also recognize that our economic history is punctuated by periods of recession, high unemployment, inflation, and recurring concern for the distribution of income and mix of output.

The graphs in Figure 19.1 provide a quick summary of the gap between the theory and reality of economic policy. The Employment Act of 1946 committed the federal government to macro stability. It's evident that we haven't kept that commitment. In the 1970s we rarely came close. Although we approached all three goals in the mid-1980s, our achievements were short-lived. Economic growth ground to a halt in 1989, and the economy slipped into yet another recession in 1990. Although inflation stayed low, unemployment rates jumped.

The economy performed very well again from 1992 until early 2000. After that, however, growth came to an abrupt halt again. With the economy teetering on recession, the unemployment rate started rising in mid-2000. Some of the people who had proclaimed the business cycle to be dead were out of work. Then the economy was hit by the external shock of a terrorist attack that suspended economic activity and shook investor and consumer confidence.

Looking back over the entire postwar period, the record includes nine years of outright recession (actual declines in output) and another 20 years of **growth recession** (growth of less than 3 percent). Moreover, the distribution of income in 2004 looked virtually identical to that of 1946, and more than 30 million people were still officially counted as poor in the later year.

Fine-Tuning

fine-tuning: Adjustments in economic policy designed to counteract small changes in economic outcomes; continuous responses to changing economic conditions.

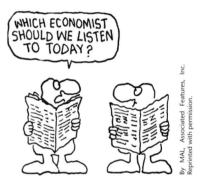

WHICH ECONOMIST SHOULD WE LISTEN TO TODAY?

By MAL, Associated Features, Inc. Reprinted with permission.

Analysis: There are different theories about when and how the government should "fix" the economy. Policymakers must decide which advice to follow in specific situations.

growth recession: A period during which real GDP grows, but at a rate below the long-term trend of 3 percent.

FIGURE 19.1

The Economic Record

The Full Employment and Balanced Growth Act of 1978 established specific goals for unemployment (4 percent), inflation (3 percent), and economic growth (4 percent). We've rarely attained those goals, however, as these graphs illustrate. Measurement, design, and policy implementation problems help explain these shortcomings.

Source: *Economic Report of the President, 2004.*

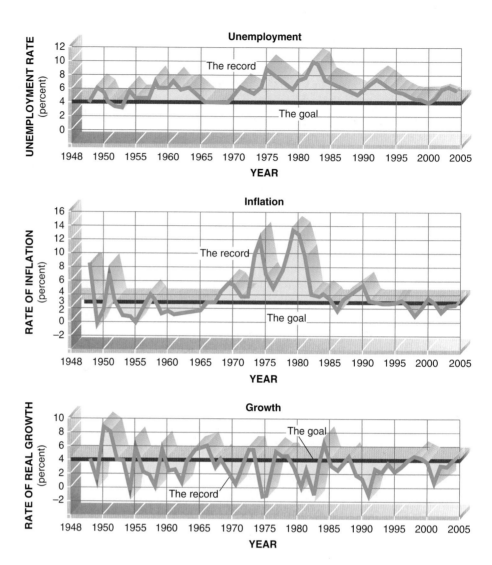

The economic performance of the United States was better than that of other Western nations in the 1990s. The economies of most countries didn't grow as fast as the U.S. economy in the 1990s. But, as the accompanying World View shows, some countries did a better job of restraining prices.

When one looks at the specific policy initiatives of various administrations, the gap between theory and practice is even larger. The Fed's decision to reduce the money supply on repeated occasions during the Great Depression was colossally perverse. Only slightly less so was the Fed's decision to expand the money supply rapidly in 1978, despite evidence that inflationary pressures were already building up. During 1980–81 and again in 1989–90, the Fed slowed money supply growth much more and far longer than was justified. As a consequence, the economy suffered two consecutive recessions in the early 1980s and another one in the early 1990s. Pretty much the same sequence occured in 1999–2001.

On the fiscal side of the ledger, we must recall President Roosevelt's timid efforts to expand aggregate demand during the Great Depression. Also worth remembering is President Johnson's refusal to pay for the Vietnam War by either raising taxes or cutting nonmilitary expenditures. The resulting strain on the economy's capacity kindled inflationary pressures that lasted for years. For his part, President Carter increased labor costs (higher payroll taxes and minimum wages), farm prices, and government

Macro Performance in the 1990s

The performance of the U.S. economy in the 1990s was better than most developed economies. Japan had the greatest success in restraining inflation (1.2 percent) but suffered from sluggish growth (1.5 percent per year). The United States grew faster and also experienced less unemployment than most European countries.

Performance (annual average percentage)	U.S.	Japan	Germany	United Kingdom	France	Italy	Canada
Real growth	2.4	1.5	2.4	1.6	1.8	1.4	1.8
Inflation	3.0	1.2	2.5	3.9	2.0	4.1	2.2
Unemployment	5.8	3.0	9.0	7.3	11.2	11.4	9.7

Source: International Monetary Fund. www.imf.org

Analysis: Macroeconomic performance varies a lot, both over time and across countries. In the 1990s, U.S. economic performance was above average on most measures.

spending at a time when inflation was a foremost policy concern. President Reagan made his share of mistakes too, including the pursuit of deep budget cuts in the early stages of a recession. President George H. Bush ignored the recession for an entire year, believing that "self-adjustment" would ensure recovery. That mistake cost him his job.

President Clinton pushed through a tax increase in 1993 that helped subdue the recovery from the 1990–91 recession. He also caused the aggregate supply curve to shift upward by forcing employers to pay higher labor costs. President George W. Bush cut taxes and regulation to shift both aggregate supply and aggregate demand in the right direction. But his insistence on cutting the growth of federal spending in the midst of the 2001 recession was ill-timed (and ultimately reversed).

WHY THINGS DON'T ALWAYS WORK

There's plenty of blame to go around for all the blemishes on our economic record. Some people blame the Fed, others blame Congress, still others blame China or Mexico. Some forces, however, constrain economic policy even when no one is specifically to blame. In this regard, we can distinguish *four obstacles to policy success:*

- *Goal conflicts*
- *Measurement problems*
- *Design problems*
- *Implementation problems*

Goal Conflicts

The first factor to take note of is potential conflicts in policy priorities. President Clinton had to confront this problem his first day in office. He had pledged to create new jobs by increasing public infrastructure spending and offering a middle-class tax cut. He had also promised to reduce the deficit, however. This created a clear goal conflict. In the end, President Clinton had to settle for a smaller increase in infrastructure spending and a tax *increase.* President George W. Bush confronted similar problems. In the 2000 presidential campaign he had promised a big increase in federal spending on education. By the time he took office, however, the federal budget surplus was rapidly shrinking, and

IN THE NEWS

Deficit-Cutting Wilts in Heat from Voters

Entitlements Remain Mostly Off-Limits

In April, Sen. Pete V. Domenici (R-N.M.) suggested a plan for digging out of the massive federal deficit. His idea seemed modest on its face but was revolutionary by Washington standards.

Domenici proposed capping cost-of-living increases in entitlement programs, the automatic spending engines such as Medicaid, Medicare and federal retirement that are exempt from annual congressional review. . . .

Even before his proposal took shape, more than 3,000 New Mexico constituents sent him identical postcards opposing any effort to cap entitlement programs.

The National Council of Senior Citizens dubbed the plan "the most outrageous attack on the elderly we have seen in years." The Veterans of Foreign Wars expressed "shock and outrage." Milk producers accused Domenici of trying to balance the budget "on the back of farmers."

That was enough for the Senate, which voted 69 to 28 to reject the proposal.

—Eric Pianin

Source: *The Washington Post,* August 4, 1992. © 1992 The Washington Post. Reprinted with permission. www.washingtonpost.com

Analysis: Changes in economic policy inevitably alter incomes and stir political opposition. Cuts in spending are particularly difficult to enact.

---

the goal of preserving the non–Social Security ("off budget") surplus took precedence. The conflict between spending priorities and budget balancing became much more intense when President Bush decided to attack Iraq.

These and other goal conflicts have their roots in the short-run trade-off between unemployment and inflation. Should we try to cure inflation, unemployment, or just a bit of both? Answers are likely to vary. Unemployed people put the highest priority on attaining full employment. Labor unions press for faster economic growth. Bankers, creditors, and people on fixed incomes demand an end to inflation.

This goal conflict is often institutionalized in the decision-making process. The Fed is traditionally viewed as the guardian of price stability. The president and Congress worry more about people's jobs and government programs, so they are less willing to raise taxes or cut spending.

Distributional goals may also conflict with macro objectives. Anti-inflationary policies may require cutbacks in programs for the poor, the elderly, or needy students. These cutbacks may be politically impossible (see News). Likewise, tight-money policies may be viewed as too great a burden for small businesses.

Although the policy levers in Table 19.1 are powerful, they can't grant all our wishes. Since we still live in a world of scarce resources, ***all policy decisions entail opportunity costs,*** which means that we'll always be confronted with trade-offs. The best we can hope for is a set of compromises that yields *optimal* outcomes, not ideal ones.

Measurement Problems

One reason firefighters are pretty successful in putting out fires before entire cities burn down is that fires are highly visible phenomena. But such visibility isn't characteristic of economic problems. An increase in the unemployment rate from 5 to 6 percent, for example, isn't the kind of thing you notice while crossing the street. Unless you work in the unemployment insurance office or lose your own job, the increase in unemployment isn't likely to attract your attention. The same is true of prices; small increases in product prices aren't likely to ring many alarms. Hence, both inflation and unemployment may worsen considerably before anyone takes serious notice. Were we as slow and ill-equipped to notice fires, whole neighborhoods would burn before someone rang the alarm.

Analysis: In the absence of timely information, today's policy decisions are inevitably based on yesterday's perceptions.

Measurement problems are a very basic policy constraint. To formulate appropriate economic policy, we must first determine the nature of our problems. To do so, we must measure employment changes, output changes, price changes, and other macro outcomes. The old adage that governments are willing and able to solve only those problems they can measure is relevant here. Indeed, before the Great Depression, a fundamental constraint on public policy was the lack of statistics on what was happening in the economy. One lasting benefit of that experience is that we now try to keep informed on changing economic conditions. The information at hand, however, is always dated and incomplete. *At best, we know what was happening in the economy last month or last week.* The processes of data collection, assembly, and presentation take time, even in this age of high-speed computers. The average recession lasts about 11 months, but official data generally don't even confirm the existence of a recession until 8 months after a downturn starts! As the accompanying News reveals, the 2001 recession ended nearly two years before researchers confirmed its demise!

Forecasts. In an ideal world, policymakers wouldn't just *respond* to economic problems but would also *anticipate* their occurrence. If an inflationary GDP gap is emerging, for example, we want to take immediate action to keep aggregate spending from increasing. That is, the successful firefighter not only responds to a fire but also looks for hazards that might start one.

Unfortunately, economic policymakers are again at a disadvantage. Their knowledge of future problems is even worse than their knowledge of current problems. *In designing policy, policymakers must depend on economic forecasts,* that is, informed guesses about what the economy will look like in future periods.

Macro Models. Those guesses are often based on complex computer models of how the economy works. These models—referred to as *econometric macro models*—are mathematical summaries of the economy's performance. The models try to identify the key determinants of macro performance and then show what happens to macro outcomes when they change. As the News on the next page suggests, the apparent precision of such computer models may disguise "a black art."

An economist "feeds" the computer two essential inputs. One is a quantitative model of how the economy allegedly works. A Keynesian model, for example, includes equations that show multiplier spending responses to tax cuts. A monetarist model shows that tax cuts raise interest rates, not total spending ("crowding out"),

Tough Calls in Economic Forecasting

Seers Often Peer into Cracked Crystal Balls

In presenting his annual economic outlook last Thursday, the chairman of President Clinton's Council of Economic Advisers was having nothing to do with all the recession talk going around.

"Let me be clear," Martin Baily said, "we don't think that we're going into recession."

The same message was delivered the next day by Clinton in a Rose Garden economic valedictory. Citing the predictions of 50 private forecasters known as the Blue Chip Consensus— "the experts who make a living doing this," as he put it— Clinton assured Americans that the economy would continue to grow this year at an annual rate of 2 percent to 3 percent.

What the president and his adviser failed to mention was that "the experts" have not predicted any of the nine recessions since the end of World War II. . . .

Allen Sinai of Decision Economics, a respected private forecaster, agreed. "Its probably only fair for forecasters to admit at times like this that we're simply not well equipped to predict turning points," he said. "A recession, by its nature, is a speculative call."

On first blush, such humility may seem at odds with the aura surrounding the modern day forecaster. Using high-speed computers and sophisticated models of the U.S. economy, they constantly revise their two-year predictions for everything from unemployment to business investment to long-term interest rates, expressed numerically to the first decimal point.

But according to the forecasters themselves, what may appear to be a precise science is a black art, one that is constantly confounded by the changing structure of the economy and the refusal of investors, consumers and business executives to behave as rationally and predictably in real life as they do in the economic models.

The reason we have trouble calling recessions is that all recessions are anomalies," said Joel Prakken, president of Macroeconomic Advisers of St. Louis, one of the nation's leading forecasting firms.

—Steven Peablstein

Source: *The Washington Post,* January 15, 2001. © 2001 The Washington Post. Reprinted with permission. www.washingtonpost.com

Analysis: Even the most sophisticated computer models rely on basic assumptions about consumer and investor behavior. If the assumptions are wrong, the forecasts will likely be wrong as well (as they were in early 2001).

WEBNOTE

For an overview of the forecasting model the Congressional Budget Office uses, visit www.cbo.gov and search for the 2001 report, "Description of Economic Models."

and a supply-side model stipulates labor-supply and production responses. The computer can't tell which theory is right; it just predicts what it's programmed to see. In other words, the computer sees the world through the eyes of its economic master.

The second essential input in a computer forecast is the assumed values for critical variables. A Keynesian model, for example, must specify how large a multiplier to expect. All the computer does is carry out the required mathematical routines, once it's told that the multiplier is relevant and what its value is. It can't discern the true multiplier any better than it can pick the right theory.

Given the dependence of computers on the theories and perceptions of their economic masters, it's not surprising that computer forecasts often differ greatly. It's also not surprising that they're often wrong. Even policymakers who are familiar with both economic theory and computer models can make some pretty bad calls. In January 1990, Fed chairman Alan Greenspan assured Congress that the risk of a recession was as low as 20 percent. Although he said he "wouldn't bet the ranch" on such a low probability, he was confident that the odds of a recession were below 50 percent; five months after his testimony, the 1990–91 recession began.

Leading Indicators. Given the complexity of macro models, many people prefer to use simpler tools for divining the future. One of the most popular is the Index of Leading Economic Indicators. As noted in Chapter 9 (see Table 9.2), the Leading Indicators are things we can observe today that are logically linked to future production (e.g., orders for new equipment). Unfortunately, the logical sequence of events doesn't always unfold as anticipated. All too often, the links in the chain of Leading Indicators are broken by changing expectations and unanticipated events.

Crystal Balls. In view of the fragile foundations and spotty record of computer and index-based forecasts, many people shun them altogether, preferring to use their own "crystal balls." The Foundation for the Study of Cycles has identified 4,000 different crystal balls that people use to gauge the health of the economy, including the ratio of used-car to new-car sales (it rises in recession); the number of divorce petitions (it rises in bad times); animal population cycles (they peak just before economic downturns); and even the optimism/pessimism content of popular music (a reflection of consumer confidence). Corporate executives claim that such crystal balls are as valuable as professional economic forecasts. In a Gallup survey of CEOs, most respondents said economists' forecasts had little or no influence on company plans or policies. The head of one large company said, "I go out of my way to ignore them." The general public apparently shares this view, giving higher marks to the forecasts of sportswriters and weather forecasters than to those of economists.

Economic forecasters defend themselves in two ways. First, they note that economic policy decisions are inevitably based on anticipated changes in the economy's performance. The decision to stimulate or restrain the economy can't be made by a flip of a coin; *someone* must try to foresee the future course of the economy. Second, forecasters claim that their quantitative approach is the only honest one. Because forecasting models require specific behavioral assumptions and estimates, they force people to spell out their versions of the future. Less rigorous ("gut feeling") approaches are too ambiguous and often inconsistent.

These are valid arguments. Still, one must be careful to distinguish the precision of computers from the inevitable uncertainties of their spoon-fed models. The basic law of the computer is GIGO: garbage in, garbage out. If the underlying models and assumptions are no good, the computer's forecasts won't be any better.

Policy and Forecasts. The task of forecasting the economic future is made still more complex by the interdependency of forecasts, policy decisions, and economic outcomes (see Figure 19.2). First, a forecast is made, based on current economic conditions, likely disturbances to the economy, and anticipated economic policy. These forecasts are then used to project likely budget deficits and other policy variables. Congress and the president react to these projections by revising fiscal, monetary, or supply-side policies. These changes, in turn, alter the basis for the initial forecasts.

WEBNOTE

The Dismal Sciences company assembles economic forecasts and a broad array of economic statistics, along with user-friendly commentary. You can visit the company at www.dismal.com.

WEBNOTE

To review the latest forecasts of 50 noted economists, see the Blue Chip average at www.bluechippubs.com.

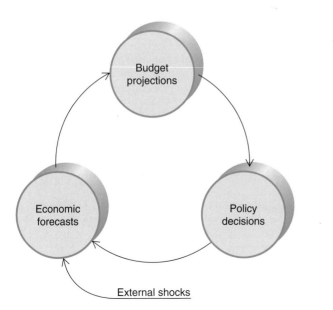

FIGURE 19.2
The Mutual Dependence of Forecasts and Policy

Because tax revenues and government spending are sensitive to economic conditions, budget projections must rely on economic forecasts. The budget projections may alter policy decisions, however, and so change the basis for the initial forecasts. This interdependence among macro forecasts, budget projections, and policy decisions is virtually inevitable.

This interdependence among forecasts, budget projections, and policy decisions was superbly illustrated in the early months of the George W. Bush presidency. At the beginning of 2001, both the White House and the Congress were forecasting enormous budget surpluses. The central policy debate focused on what to do with those surpluses. The Democrats wanted to spend the surplus; the Republicans wanted to give it back to households with larger tax cuts. As the debate dragged on, however, the weakening economy shrunk the surplus. In August 2001, the Congressional Budget Office (CBO) announced that the "on-budget" (non–Social Security) surplus it had forecast just seven months earlier had vanished. This forced both political parties to change their policy proposals. Protecting the vanishing surplus became the political priority. Spending proposals were scaled back, as were hopes of debt repayment.

External Shocks. The CBO's forecasts of budget surpluses were already far wrong *before* the September 11, 2001, terrorist attack on the World Trade Center. That attack created an external shock that caused everyone to revise their economic forecasts. In the immediate aftermath of the attack, financial markets closed, air travel was suspended, sports events and concerts were canceled, businesses closed, and consumers stayed away from shopping malls. As a result, GDP declined, raising new fears of a global recession (see World View).

The very nature of external *shocks* is that they are *unanticipated*. Hence, even if we knew enough about the economy to forecast "shockless" outcomes perfectly, an external shock could always disrupt the economy and ruin our forecasts. In reality, forecasting methods aren't even good enough to predict the behavior of a "shockless" economy with precision.

WORLD VIEW

Worldwide, Hope for Recovery Dims
Economic Shock in the U.S. May Trigger a Global Recession

The National Association for Business Economics was holding its annual meeting in the Marriott Hotel at the World Trade Center when disaster struck. "The chandeliers shook, we heard a concussive sound, and as we were herding out, we could see that one tower was burning," says Carl Tannenbaum, the chief economist of LaSalle Bank in Chicago, who was attending the meeting.

Just the day before, a panel of NABE economists had predicted slow growth, but no recession. That forecast was obsolete, however, the moment the first plane hit. In addition to destroying thousands of lives and billions of dollars in property, the terrorist attacks forced the shutdown of the financial markets, the temporary closure of U.S. businesses, and the grounding of air passenger and cargo traffic. Around the country, customers vanished from stores. With the U.S. already near zero growth, these impacts themselves are almost certain to tip the country into negative growth. "People are going to pause. And that pause is going to have a real impact on the third quarter and probably the fourth quarter," says Fred Poses, chairman and CEO of American Standard Companies.

A U.S. downturn will have repercussions all around the world. With Japan imploding economically, Asia in trouble, and Europe struggling, a recession in the U.S. would remove the last remaining source of demand from the global economy. "It's like throwing cold water on any prospects for a recovery," says Chang Il Hyung, senior vice-president of South Korea's Samsung Electronics Co., the world's largest memory chipmaker. With people around the globe watching the carnage in New York, consumer confidence and business investment could be hit everywhere. "Since the global economy is interwoven through trade and investment, all of us will be worse off," says Sung Won Sohn, chief economist at Wells Fargo & Co.

Source: *BusinessWeek*, September 24, 2001. © 2001 The McGraw-Hill Companies, Inc. Reprinted with permission. www.businessweek.com

Analysis: An external shock is by its very nature unanticipated. When it occurs, forecasts and policy decisions have to be revised.

IN THE NEWS

CBO's Flawed Forecasts

Every year the Congressional Budget Office (CBO) forecasts the federal budget balance for the next five years. Those forecasts are rarely accurate. The typical CBO forecasting error for the *current* fiscal year amounts to 0.5 percent of GDP, or about $60 billion. Moreover, the errors widen for future years: For the *fifth* year out, CBO's forecasts typically miss the actual budget balance by a startling 3 percent of GDP. This implies that CBO's January 2004 forecast of the 2009

budget balance (a $268 billion deficit) will be off the mark by $438 billion!

Since 1981, CBO has both over- and underestimated federal budget balances. There has been a slightly pessimistic bias, however, especially in the boom years of 1992–2000. Forecasts from the president's Office of Management and Budget (OMB) haven't been any better.

Source: Congressional Budget Office, *The Budget and Economic Outlook, Fiscal Years 2005–2014,* January 2004.

Analysis: The economic and budget forecasts that guide policy decisions are often flawed. This reduces the chances of policy success.

As the accompanying News reveals, the CBO's forecasting errors in 2001 were not an exception; they were the norm. When policymakers rely on such forecasts, they are likely to fail all too often.

Design Problems

Assume for the moment that we somehow are able to get a reliable forecast of where the economy is headed. The outlook, let's suppose, is bad. Now we're in the driver's seat to steer the economy past looming dangers. We need to chart our course—to design an economic plan. What action should we take? Which theory of macro behavior should guide us? How will the marketplace respond to any specific action we take?

Suppose, for example, that we adopt a Keynesian approach to ending a recession. Specifically, we cut income taxes to stimulate consumer spending. How do we know that consumers will respond as anticipated? In 1998, Japanese households used their tax cut to increase *savings* rather than consumption. In 2001, U.S. households were also slow to spend their tax rebates. When consumers don't respond as anticipated, the intended fiscal stimulus doesn't materialize. Such behavioral responses frustrate even the best-intentioned policy. The successful policymaker needs a very good crystal ball, one that will also foretell how market participants are going to respond to any specific actions taken.

WEBNOTE

For the latest CBO and Office of Management and Budget (OMB) macro forecasts, visit www.cbo.gov. Click on "Current Economic Projections."

Measurement and design problems can break the spirit of even the best policymaker (or the policymaker's economic advisers). Yet measurement and design problems are only part of the story. A good idea is of little value unless someone puts it to use. Accordingly, to understand fully why things go wrong, we must also consider the difficulties of *implementing* a well-designed policy.

Implementation Problems

Congressional Deliberations. Suppose that the president and his Council of Economic Advisers (perhaps in conjunction with the National Economic Council, the secretary of the Treasury, and the director of the Office of Management and Budget) decide that aggregate demand is slowing. A tax cut, they believe, is necessary to stimulate demand for goods and services. Can they simply go ahead and cut tax rates? No, because only the Congress can legislate tax changes. Once the president decides on the appropriate policy, he must ask Congress for authority to take the required action, which means a delay in implementing policy or possibly no policy at all.

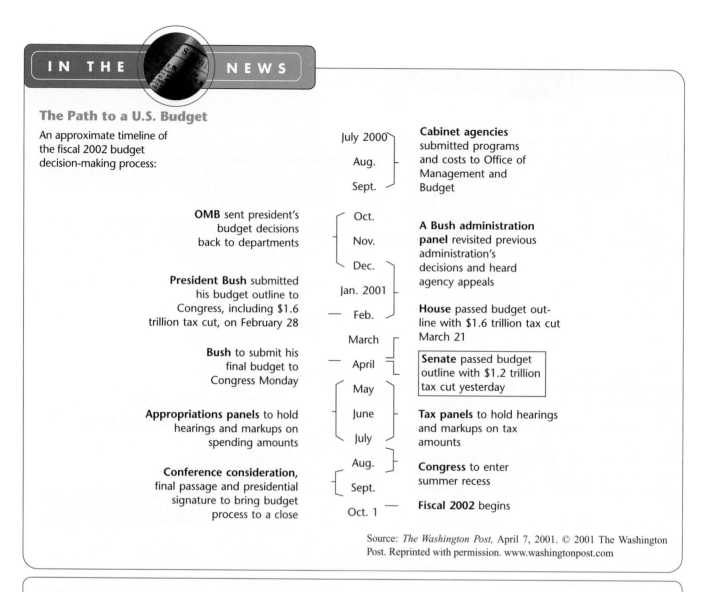

IN THE NEWS

The Path to a U.S. Budget

An approximate timeline of the fiscal 2002 budget decision-making process:

	July 2000 — **Cabinet agencies** submitted programs and costs to Office of Management and Budget
	Aug.
	Sept.
OMB sent president's budget decisions back to departments	Oct.
	Nov. — **A Bush administration panel** revisited previous administration's decisions and heard agency appeals
	Dec.
President Bush submitted his budget outline to Congress, including $1.6 trillion tax cut, on February 28	Jan. 2001
	Feb. — **House** passed budget outline with $1.6 trillion tax cut March 21
	March
Bush to submit his final budget to Congress Monday	April — Senate passed budget outline with $1.2 trillion tax cut yesterday
	May
Appropriations panels to hold hearings and markups on spending amounts	June — **Tax panels** to hold hearings and markups on tax amounts
	July
	Aug. — **Congress** to enter summer recess
Conference consideration, final passage and presidential signature to bring budget process to a close	Sept.
	Oct. 1 — **Fiscal 2002** begins

Source: *The Washington Post*, April 7, 2001. © 2001 The Washington Post. Reprinted with permission. www.washingtonpost.com

Analysis: Fiscal policy decisions must be processed through lengthy administrative and congressional processes. This delays fiscal-policy responses to economic problems.

At the very least, the president must convince Congress of the wisdom of his proposed policy. The tax proposal must work its way through separate committees of both the House of Representatives and the Senate, get on the congressional calendar, and be approved in each chamber. If there are important differences in Senate and House versions of the tax-cut legislation, they must be compromised in a joint conference. The modified proposal must then be returned to each chamber for approval (see News).

The same kind of process applies to the outlay side of the budget. Once the president has submitted his budget proposals (in January), Congress reviews them, then sets its own spending goals. After that, the budget is broken down into 13 different categories, and a separate appropriations bill is written for each one. These bills spell out in detail how much can be spent and for what purposes. Once Congress passes them, they go to the president for acceptance or veto.

Budget legislation requires Congress to finish these deliberations by October 1 (the beginning of the federal fiscal year), but Congress rarely meets this deadline. In most years, the budget debate continues well into the fiscal year. In some years, the budget

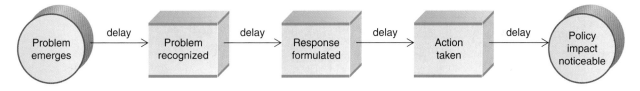

FIGURE 19.3
Policy Response: A Series of Time Lags

Even the best-intentioned economic policy can be frustrated by time lags. It takes time for a problem to be recognized, time to formulate a policy response, and still more time to implement

that policy. By the time the policy begins to affect the economy, the underlying problem may have changed.

debate isn't resolved until the fiscal year is nearly over! The final budget legislation is typically more than 1,000 pages long and so complex that few people understand all its dimensions.

Time Lags. This description of congressional activity isn't an outline for a civics course; rather, it's an important explanation of why economic policy isn't fully effective. ***Even if the right policy is formulated to solve an emerging economic problem, there's no assurance that it will be implemented. And if it's implemented, there's no assurance that it will take effect at the right time.*** One of the most frightening prospects for economic policy is that a policy design intended to serve a specific problem will be implemented much later, when economic conditions have changed. This isn't a remote danger. According to Christina Romer and Paul Romer, the Fed doesn't pull the monetary-stimulus lever until a recession is underway, and Congress is even slower in responding to an economic downturn. Indeed, a U.S. Treasury Department study concluded that almost every postwar fiscal stimulus package was enacted well after the end of the recession it was intended to cure!

Figure 19.3 is a schematic view of why macro policies don't always work as intended. There are always delays between the time a problem emerges and the time it's recognized. There are additional delays between recognition and response design, between design and implementation, and finally between implementation and impact. Not only may mistakes be made at each juncture, but even correct decisions may be overcome by changing economic conditions.

We can illustrate the processes in Figure 19.3 by considering how the income surtax of 1968 came about. The expansion of the Vietnam War in July 1965 added something like $15 billion to aggregate demand at a time when the economy was already fully employed.[1] To offset resulting inflationary pressures, the president and Congress initiated some fiscal restraint, including the restoration of excise taxes on cars and telephones. Much stronger action was necessary, however. But President Lyndon Johnson insisted that the escalation of the war was temporary. From his perspective, the imposition of stronger fiscal restraints was tantamount to an admission that the war wouldn't be won quickly. Only after another 18 months of war did the administration propose further action. In January 1967, President Johnson called for a 6 percent surtax to correct the "imbalances created by the special pressures of Vietnam procurement." The problem that emerged in July 1965 wasn't recognized until 1966, and a response wasn't formulated until January 1967. Compounding these delays was the reluctance of Congress to help finance an undeclared war. Congress didn't take the requested action until June 1968. Thus, there was a three-year lag between the time the problem emerged and the policy response. In the interim, inflationary pressures worsened.

---

[1]This figure includes multiplier effects through the first quarter of 1966.

SHOE JEFF MacNELLY

Analysis: Budget cuts are not popular with voters—even when economic conditions warrant fiscal restraint.

Senator John McCain maintains a list of political "pork" spending at http://mccain.senate.gov/index.cfm?fuseaction=NewsCenter.Pork.

Politics vs. Economics. The delayed fiscal response to accelerated Vietnam expenditures also illustrates the very first barrier to policy implementation: *goal conflicts.* Just as the design of policy is compromised by conflicting interests, so too is the implementation of those designs. Especially noteworthy in this regard is the potential conflict of economic policy with political objectives. The conflict that existed between President Johnson's war objectives and his economic objectives is obvious. So was the conflict between George W. Bush's goal of reducing the deficit and the cost of the war in Iraq. Wars aside, observers have noted that the president and Congress are reluctant to impose fiscal restraints (tax increases or budget cutbacks) in election years, regardless of economic circumstances. As the accompanying cartoon emphasizes, fiscal restraint is never popular.

The tendency of Congress to hold fiscal policy hostage to electoral concerns has created a pattern of short-run stops and starts—a kind of policy-induced business cycle. Indeed, some argue that the business cycle has been replaced with the political cycle: The economy is stimulated in the year of an election and then restrained in the postelection year. The conflict between the urgent need to get reelected and the necessity to manage the economy results in a seesaw kind of instability.

Even when the need for fiscal *stimulus* seems urgent—like after the September 11 terrorist attacks—politics can slow and distort the policy response. Two months after the attacks Republican and Democrat lawmakers were still far apart on how much fiscal stimulus to provide and what form the stimulus should take (see News). Critics feared that by the time Congress acted, the stimulus would be too late and possibly excessive.

In theory, the political independence of the Fed's Board of Governors provides some protection from ill-advised but politically advantageous policy initiatives. In practice, however, the Fed's relative obscurity and independence may backfire. The president and the Congress know that if they don't take effective action against inflation—by raising taxes or cutting government spending—the Fed can and will take stronger action to restrain aggregate demand. This is a classic case of having one's cake and eating it too. Elected officials win votes for not raising taxes or cutting some constituent's favorite spending program. They then take credit for any reduction in the rate of inflation brought about by Federal Reserve policies. To top it off, Congress and the president can also blame the Fed for driving up interest rates or starting a recession if monetary policy becomes too restrictive!

Finally, we must recognize that policy design is obstructed by a certain attention deficit (see cartoon). Neither people on the street nor elected public officials focus constantly on economic goals and activities. Even students enrolled in economics courses have a hard time keeping their minds on the economy and its problems. The

IN THE NEWS

Stimulus Package Stalled over Tax Breaks, Spending

WASHINGTON—A multibilliondollar economic stimulus package aimed at energizing the faltering economy, helping the unemployed and giving low-income workers a tax rebate faces a stalemate in a deeply divided Senate this week.

Democrats and Republicans said Tuesday that bipartisan negotiations are needed if Congress is to find agreement on a bill that President Bush wants passed by the end of the month. But the two parties remain so far apart that they are only talking about talking, not actually working out a solution.

Democrats lack the votes to pass their $66.4 billion tax package and an additional $20 billion in domestic security spending that they want to attach. Republicans don't have enough votes for their alternative, either.

The problem for both sides: Passing anything in the Senate, controlled 50-49 by Democrats with one independent, requires consensus. Either side can invoke Senate rules that set a 60-vote hurdle, rather than a simple majority, for passage.

How does either side get there? "That's a good question," Sen. Daschle said. "Neither side has 60 votes at this point. So we know we've got to work together. . . ".

Adding to the disarray is a dispute over the Democrats' proposal to spend $20 billion more on homeland security, which Bush vowed to veto last week. Republicans say Democrats have simply dusted off old wish lists for public works and pork-barrel projects. And they say Democrats have even more spending cloaked in their tax bill, including $6 billion in farm aid that provides subsidies to bison ranchers.

"I thought this was going to be a stimulus package instead of a pork package," Lott said.

—William M. Welch

Source: *USA Today,* November 14, 2001. © 2001 USA TODAY. Reprinted with permission. www.usatoday.com

Analysis: Political disputes over the size and content of budget initiatives can slow and distort economic policy responses.

Analysis: Economic problems often don't arouse public or policy interest until they become severe.

executive and legislative branches of government, for their part, are likely to focus on economic concerns only when economic problems become serious or voters demand action. Otherwise, policymakers are apt to be complacent about economic policy as long as economic performance is within a tolerable range of desired outcomes.

THE ECONOMY TOMORROW

Hands On or Hands Off?

In view of the goal conflicts and the measurement, design, and implementation problems that policymakers confront, it's less surprising that things sometimes go wrong than that things so often work out right. The maze of obstacles through which theory must pass before it becomes policy explains many economic disappointments. On this basis alone, we may conclude that *consistent fine-tuning of the economy isn't compatible with either our design capabilities or our decision-making procedures.* We have exhibited a strong capability to avoid major economic disruptions in the last four decades. We haven't, however, been able to make all the minor adjustments necessary to fulfill our goals completely. As Arthur Burns, former chairman of the Fed's Board of Governors, said:

> There has been much loose talk of "fine tuning" when the state of knowledge permits us to predict only within a fairly broad level the course of economic development and the results of policy actions.[2]

Hands Off   Some critics of economic policy take this argument a few steps further. If fine-tuning isn't really possible, they say, we should abandon discretionary policies altogether and follow fixed rules for fiscal and monetary intervention.

As we saw in Chapter 15, pure monetarism would require the Fed to increase the money supply at a constant rate. Critics of fiscal policy would require the government to maintain balanced budgets, or at least to offset deficits in sluggish years with surpluses in years of high growth. Such rules would prevent policymakers from over- or understimulating the economy. Such rules would also add a dose of certainty to the economic outlook.

Milton Friedman has been one of the most persistent advocates of fixed policy rules. With discretionary authority, Friedman argues.

> the wrong decision is likely to be made in a large fraction of cases because the decision-makers are examining only a limited area and not taking into account the cumulative consequences of the policy as a whole. On the other hand, if a general rule is adopted for a group of cases as a bundle, the existence of that rule has favorable effects on people's attitudes and beliefs and expectations that would not follow even from the discretionary adoption of precisely the same policy on a series of separate occasions.[3]

The case for a hands-off policy stance is based on practical, not theoretical, arguments. *Everyone agrees that flexible, discretionary policies* could *result in better economic performance. But Friedman and others argue that the practical requirements of monetary and fiscal management are too demanding and thus prone to failure.* Moreover, required policies may be compromised by political pressures.

New Classical Economics. Monetarist critiques of discretionary policy are echoed by a new perspective referred to as new classical economics (NCE). Classical economists saw no need for discretionary macro policy. In their view, the private sector is inherently stable and government intervention serves no purpose. New classical economics reaches the same conclusion. As Robert Barro, a proponent of NCE, put it: "It is best for the government to provide a stable environment, and then mainly stay out of the way."[4] Barro

---

[2]*Newsweek,* August 27, 1973, p. 4.
[3]Milton Friedman, *Capitalism and Freedom* (Chicago: University of Chicago Press, 1962), p. 53.
[4]Robert Barro, "Don't Fool with Money, Cut Taxes," *The Wall Street Journal,* November 21, 1991, p. A14.

and other NCE economists based this laissez-faire conclusion on the intriguing notion of **rational expectations.** This notion contends that people make decisions on the basis of all available information, including the *future* effects of *current* government policy.

Suppose, for example, that the Fed decided to increase the money supply in order to boost output. If people had rational expectations, they'd anticipate that this money supply growth will fuel inflation. To protect themselves, they'd immediately demand higher prices and wages. As a result, the stimulative monetary policy would fail to boost real output. (Monetarists reach the same conclusion but for different reasons; for monetarists, the countervailing forces are technological and institutional rather than rational expectations.)

Discretionary fiscal policy could be equally ineffective. Suppose Congress accelerated government spending in an effort to boost aggregate demand. Monetarists contend that the accompanying increase in the deficit would push interest rates up and crowd out private investment and consumption. New classical economists again reach the same conclusion via a different route. They contend that people with rational expectations would anticipate that a larger deficit now will necessitate tax increases in later years. To prepare for later tax bills, consumers will reduce spending now, thereby saving more. This "rational" reduction in consumption will offset the increased government expenditure, thus rendering fiscal policy ineffective.

If the new classical economists are right, then the only policy that works is one that surprises people—one that consumers and investors don't anticipate. But a policy based on surprises isn't very practical. Accordingly, new classical economists conclude that minimal policy intervention is best. This conclusion provides yet another guideline for policy decisions (see Table 19.5 for a roster of competing theories).

rational expectations: Hypothesis that people's spending decisions are based on all available information, including the anticipated effects of government intervention.

Keynesians	Keynesians believe that the private sector is inherently unstable and prone to stagnate at low levels of output and employment. They want the government to manage aggregate demand with changes in taxes and government's spending.
Modern ("neo") Keynesians	Post–World War II followers of Keynes worry about inflation as well as recession. They urge budgetary restraint to cool an overheated economy. They also use monetary policy to change interest rates.
Monetarists	The money supply is their only heavy hitter. By changing the money supply, they can raise or lower the price level. Pure monetarists shun active policy, believing that it destabilizes the otherwise stable private sector. Output and employment gravitate to their natural levels.
Supply-siders	Incentives to work, invest, and produce are the key to their plays. Cuts in marginal tax rates and government regulation are used to expand production capacity, thereby increasing output and reducing inflationary pressures.
New classical economists	They say fine-tuning won't work because once the private sector realizes what the government is doing, it will act to offset it. They also question the credibility of quick-fix promises. They favor steady, predictable policies.
Marxists	Marxists contend that the failures of the economy are inherent in its capitalist structure. The owners of capital won't strive for full employment or a more equitable income distribution. Workers, without any capital, have little incentive to excel. This team proposes starting a new game, with entirely different rules.

**TABLE 19.5
Who's on First? Labeling Economists**

It sometimes hard to tell who's on what side in economic debates. Although some economists are proud to wear the colors of monetarists, Keynesians, or other teams, many economists shun such allegiances. Indeed, economists are often accused of playing on one team one day and on another team the next, making it hard to tell which team is at bat. To simplify matters, this guide may be used for quick identification of the players. Closer observation is advised, however, before choosing up teams.

Hands On

Proponents of a hands-on policy strategy acknowledge the possibility of occasional blunders. They emphasize, however, the greater risks of doing nothing when the economy is faltering. Some proponents of the quick fix even turn the new classical economics argument on its head. Even the wrong policy, they argue, might be better than doing nothing if enough market participants believed that *change* implied *progress*. They cite the jump in consumer confidence that followed the election of Bill Clinton, who had emphasized the need for a *change* in policy but hadn't spelled out the details of that change. The surge in confidence itself stimulated consumer purchases, even before President Clinton took office. The same kind of response occurred after the September 11, 2001, terrorist attacks. Consumers were dazed and insecure. There was a serious risk that they would curtail spending if the government didn't *do something.* Details aside, they just wanted reassurance that someone was taking charge of events. Quick responses by the Fed (increasing the money supply), the Congress (authorizing more spending), and President Bush (mobilizing security and military forces) kept consumer confidence from plunging.

Just doing *something* isn't the purpose of a hands-on policy, of course. Policy activists believe that we have enough knowledge about how the economy works to pull the right policy levers most of the time. They also point to the historical record. Our economic track record may not be perfect, but the historical record of prices, employment, and growth has improved since active fiscal and monetary policies were adopted. Without flexibility in the money supply and the budget, they argue, the economy would be less stable and our economic goals would remain unfulfilled.

The historical evidence for discretionary policy is ambiguous. Victor Zarnowitz showed that the U.S. economy has been much more stable since 1946 than it was in earlier periods (1875–1918 and 1919–1945).[5] Recessions have gotten shorter and economic expansions longer. But a variety of factors—including a shift from manufacturing to services, a larger government sector, and automatic stabilizers—has contributed to this improved macro performance. The contribution of discretionary macro policy is less clear. It's easy to observe what actually happened but almost impossible to determine what would have occurred in other circumstances.

Finally, one must contend with the difficulties inherent in adhering to any fixed rules. How is the Fed, for example, supposed to maintain a steady rate of growth in the money supply? As we observed in Chapter 13, people move their funds back and forth between different kinds of "money." Also, the demand for money is subject to unpredictable shifts. To maintain a steady rate of growth in M2 or any other measure of money would require superhuman foresight and responses. As former Fed chairman Paul Volcker told Congress, it would be "exceedingly dangerous and in fact practically impossible to eliminate substantial elements of discretion in the conduct of Federal Reserve policy."

The same is true of fiscal policy. Government spending and taxes are directly influenced by changes in unemployment, inflation, interest rates, and growth. These automatic stabilizers make it virtually impossible to maintain any fixed rule for budget balancing. Moreover, if we eliminated the automatic stabilizers, we'd risk greater instability.

Modest Expectations

The clamor for fixed policy rules is more a rebuke of past policy than a viable policy alternative. We really have no choice but to pursue discretionary policies. Recognition of measurement, design, and implementation problems is important for an understanding of the way the economy functions. Even though it's impossible to reach all our goals, we can't abandon conscientious attempts to get as close as possible to

---

[5]Victor Zarnowitz, *Facts and Factors in the Recent Evolution of the Business Cycle in the United States* (Cambridge, MA: National Bureau of Economic Research, 1989).

goal fulfillment. If public policy can create a few more jobs, a better mix of output, a little more growth and price stability, or an improved distribution of income, those initiatives are worthwhile.

SUMMARY

- The government possesses an array of macro policy levers, each of which can significantly alter economic outcomes. To end a recession, we can cut taxes, expand the money supply, or increase government spending. To curb inflation, we can reverse each of these policy levers. To overcome stagflation, we can combine fiscal and monetary levers with improved supply-side incentives.
- Although the potential of economic theory seems impressive, the economic record doesn't look as good. Persistent unemployment, recurring economic slowdowns, and nagging inflation suggest that the realities of policy making are more difficult than theory implies.
- To some extent, the failures of economic policy are a reflection of scarce resources and competing goals. Even when consensus exists, however, serious obstacles to effective economic policy remain. These obstacles include

(a) Measurement problems. Our knowledge of economic performance is always dated and incomplete.
(b) Design problems. We don't know exactly how the economy will respond to specific policies.
(c) Implementation problems. It takes time for Congress and the president to agree on an appropriate plan of action. Moreover, political needs may take precedence over economic needs.

For all these reasons, discretionary policy rarely lives up to its theoretical potential.

- Monetarists and new classical economists favor rules rather than discretionary macro policies. They argue that discretionary policies are unlikely to work and risk being wrong. Critics respond that discretionary policies are needed to cope with ever-changing economic circumstances.

Key Terms

business cycle
fiscal policy
automatic stabilizer
structural deficit
fiscal stimulus
fiscal restraint

monetary policy
natural rate of unemployment
supply-side policy
recessionary GDP gap
multiplier
velocity of money (V)

inflationary GDP gap
stagflation
fine-tuning
growth recession
rational expectations

Questions for Discussion

1. What policies would Keynesian, monetarists, and supply-siders advocate for (a) restraining inflation, (b) reducing unemployment?
2. Why do policymakers respond so slowly to economic problems?
3. If policymakers have instant data on the economy's performance, should they respond immediately? Why or why not?
4. Suppose it's an election year and aggregate demand is growing so fast that it threatens to set off an inflationary movement. Why might Congress and the president

hesitate to cut back on government spending or raise taxes, as economic theory suggests is appropriate?
5. In his fiscal 2002 budget, President Bush proposed increases in defense spending while arguing for cutbacks in total spending. Should military spending be subject to macroeconomic constraints? What programs should be expanded or contracted to bring about needed changes in the budget? Is this feasible?
6. Prior to assuming office, President-elect Clinton pledged to propose a tax credit for new investment during the first months of his administration. How

might such an announcement affect the timing of investment decisions?

7. Suppose the government proposes to cut taxes while maintaining the current level of government expenditures. To finance this deficit, it may either (*a*) sell bonds to the public or (*b*) print new money (via Federal Reserve cooperation). What are the likely effects of each of these alternatives on each of the following? Would Keynesians, monetarists, and supply-siders give the same answers?
   (*a*) Interest rates
   (*b*) Consumer spending
   (*c*) Business investment
   (*d*) Aggregate demand

8. Suppose the economy is slumping into recession and needs a fiscal policy boost. Voters, however, are opposed to larger federal deficits. What should policymakers do?

9. How were each of the following affected by the 2001 terrorist attack on the World Trade Center? (See World View, page 402.)
   (*a*) Federal tax revenues
   (*b*) Federal spending
   (*c*) U.S. imports
   (*d*) Short-run GDP growth
   (*e*) Long-run GDP growth

10. According to the News on page 393, why did Murray Weidenbaum conclude that the government can't prevent recessions? Is he right?

ALERT!

PROBLEMS — The Student Problem Set at the back of this book contains numerical and graphing problems for this chapter.

WEB ACTIVITIES — to accompany this chapter can be found on the Online Learning Center: http://www.mhhe.com/economics/schiller10

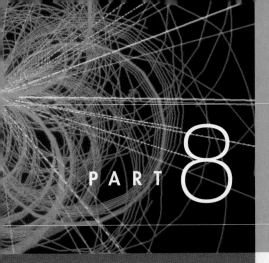

PART 8

International Economics

Our interactions with the rest of the world have a profound impact on the mix of output (WHAT), the methods of production (HOW), and the distribution of income (FOR WHOM). Trade and global money flows can also affect the stability of the macro economy. Chapters 20 and 21 explore the motives, the nature, and the effects of international trade and finance.

International Trade

The 2004 World Series between the Boston Red Sox and the St. Louis Cardinals was played with Japanese gloves, baseballs made in Costa Rica, and Mexican bats. Most of the players were wearing shoes made in Korea or China. And during the regular season, many of the games throughout the league were played on artificial grass made in Taiwan. Baseball, it seems, has become something less than the "all-American" game.

Imported goods have made inroads into other activities as well. All DVDs, VCRs, and video-game machines are imported, as are most televisions, fax machines, personal computers, and cell phones. Most of these imported goods could have been produced in the United States. Why did we purchase them from other countries? For that matter, why does the rest of the world buy computers, tractors, chemicals, airplanes, and wheat from us rather than produce such products for themselves? Wouldn't we all be better off relying on ourselves for the goods we consume (and the jobs we need) rather than buying and selling products in international markets? Or is there some advantage to be gained from international trade?

This chapter begins with a survey of international trade patterns—what goods and services we trade, and with whom. Then we address basic issues related to such trade:

- **What benefit, if any, do we get from international trade?**
- **How much harm do imports cause, and to whom?**
- **Should we protect ourselves from "unfair" trade by limiting imports?**

After examining the arguments for and against international trade, we draw some general conclusions about trade policy. As we'll see, international trade tends to increase *average* incomes, although it may diminish the job and income opportunities for specific industries and workers.

U.S. TRADE PATTERNS

The United States is by far the largest player in global product and resource markets. In 2003, we purchased 20 percent of the world's exports and sold 15 percent of the same total.

In dollar terms, our imports in 2003 exceeded $1.5 trillion. These **imports** included the consumer items mentioned earlier as well as capital equipment, raw materials, and food. Table 20.1 is a sampler of the goods and services we purchase from foreign suppliers.

Although imports represent only 14 percent of total GDP, they account for larger shares of specific product markets. Coffee is a familiar example. Since virtually all coffee is imported (except for a tiny amount produced in Hawaii), Americans would have a harder time staying awake without imports. Likewise, there'd be no aluminum if we didn't import bauxite, no chrome bumpers if we didn't import chromium, no tin cans without imported tin, and a lot fewer computers without

Imports

imports: Goods and services purchased from international sources.

Country	Imports from	Exports to
Australia	Beef Alumina Autos	Airplanes Computers Auto parts
Belgium	Jewelry Cars Optical glass	Cigarettes Airplanes Diamonds
Canada	Cars Trucks Paper	Auto parts Cars Computers
China	Toys Shoes Clothes	Fertilizer Airplanes Cotton
Germany	Cars Engines Auto parts	Airplanes Computers Cars
Japan	Cars Computers Telephones	Airplanes Computers Timber
Russia	Oil Platinum Artworks	Corn Wheat Oil seeds
South Korea	Shoes Cars Computers	Airplanes Leather Iron ingots and oxides

Source: U.S. Department of Commerce.

TABLE 20.1
A U.S. Trade Sampler

The United States imports and exports a staggering array of goods and services. Shown here are the top exports and imports with various countries. Notice that we export many of the same goods we import (such as cars and computers). What's the purpose of trading goods we produce ourselves?

imported components. We couldn't even play the all-American game of baseball without imports, since baseballs are no longer made in the United States.

We import *services* as well as *goods.* If you fly to Europe on Virgin Airways you're importing transportation services. If you stay in a London hotel, you're importing lodging services. When you go to Barclay's Bank to cash traveler's checks, you're importing foreign financial services. These and other services now account for one-sixth of U.S. imports.

While we're buying goods (merchandise) and services from the rest of the world, global consumers are buying our **exports.** In 2003, we exported $726 billion of *goods,* including farm products (wheat, corn, soybeans), tobacco, machinery (computers), aircraft, automobiles and auto parts, raw materials (lumber, iron ore), and chemicals (see Table 20.1 for a sample of U.S. merchandise exports). We also exported $320 billion of services (movies, software licenses, tourism, engineering, financial services, etc.).

Although the United States is the world's largest exporter of goods and services, exports represent a relatively modest fraction of our total output. As the World View illustrates, other nations export much larger proportions of their GDP. Ireland is one of the most export-oriented countries, with tourist services pushing its export ratio to an incredible 98 percent. By contrast, Myanmar (Burma) is basically a closed economy, with few exports (other than opium and other drugs traded in the black market).

The low U.S. export ratio disguises our heavy dependence on exports in specific industries. We export 25 to 50 percent of our rice, corn, and wheat production each year, and still more of our soybeans. Clearly, a decision by international consumers to stop

Exports

exports: Goods and services sold to foreign buyers.

Find the most recent trends in trade statistics at www.whitehouse.gov/fsbr/international.html.

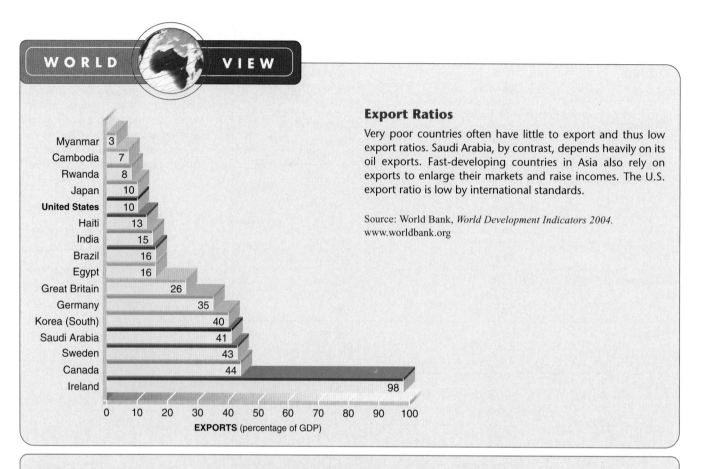

Export Ratios

Very poor countries often have little to export and thus low export ratios. Saudi Arabia, by contrast, depends heavily on its oil exports. Fast-developing countries in Asia also rely on exports to enlarge their markets and raise incomes. The U.S. export ratio is low by international standards.

Source: World Bank, *World Development Indicators 2004*.
www.worldbank.org

Country	Exports (percentage of GDP)
Myanmar	3
Cambodia	7
Rwanda	8
Japan	10
United States	10
Haiti	13
India	15
Brazil	16
Egypt	16
Great Britain	26
Germany	35
Korea (South)	40
Saudi Arabia	41
Sweden	43
Canada	44
Ireland	98

EXPORTS (percentage of GDP)

Analysis: The relatively low U.S. export ratio reflects the vast size of our domestic market and our relative self-sufficiency in food and resources. European nations are smaller and highly interdependent.

eating U.S. agricultural products could devastate a lot of American farmers. Such companies as Boeing (planes), Caterpillar Tractor (construction and farm machinery), Weyerhaeuser (logs, lumber), Eastman Kodak (film), Dow (chemicals), and Sun Microsystems (computer workstations) sell over one-fourth of their output in foreign markets. McDonald's sells hamburgers to 47 million people a day in 121 countries around the world; to do so, the company exports management and marketing services (as well as frozen food) from the United States. The Walt Disney Company produces the most popular TV shows in Russia and Germany, publishes Italy's best-selling weekly magazine, and has the most popular tourist attraction in Japan (Tokyo Disneyland). The 500,000 foreign students attending U.S. universities are purchasing $5 billion of American educational services. All these activities are part of America's service exports.

Trade Balances

Although we export a lot of products, we often have an imbalance in our trade flows. The trade balance is the difference between the value of exports and imports; that is,

$$\text{Trade balance} = \text{exports} - \text{imports}$$

During 2003, we imported much more than we exported and so had a negative trade balance. A negative trade balance is called a **trade deficit.**

Although the overall trade balance includes both goods and services, these flows are usually reported separately, with the *merchandise* trade balance distinguished from the *services* trade balance. As Table 20.2 shows, the United States had a merchandise (goods) trade deficit of $556 billion in 2003 and a *services* trade *surplus* of $58 billion, leaving the overall trade balance in the red.

trade deficit: The amount by which the value of imports exceeds the value of exports in a given time period.

Product Category	Exports ($ billions)	Imports ($ billions)	Surplus (Deficit) ($ billions)
Merchandise	$ 726	$1,282	$(556)
Services	320	262	58
Total trade	$1,046	$1,544	$(498)

Source: U.S. Department of Commerce.

TABLE 20.2
Trade Balances

Both merchandise (goods) and services are traded between countries. The United States typically has a merchandise deficit and a services surplus. When combined, an overall trade deficit remained in 2003.

When the United States has a trade deficit with the rest of the world, other countries must have an offsetting **trade surplus.** On a global scale, imports must equal exports, since every good exported by one country must be imported by another. Hence, *any imbalance in America's trade must be offset by reverse imbalances elsewhere.*

Whatever the overall balance in our trade accounts, bilateral balances vary greatly. Table 20.3 shows, for example, that our 2003 aggregate trade deficit ($498 billion) incorporated huge bilateral trade deficits with Japan and China. In the same year, however, we had trade surpluses with the Netherlands, Belgium, Australia, Hong Kong, and the United Arab Emirates.

trade surplus: The amount by which the value of exports exceeds the value of imports in a given time period.

WEBNOTE

For more data on bilateral trade, visit the U.S. Census Bureau at www.census.gov/foreign-trade.

MOTIVATION TO TRADE

Many people wonder why we trade so much, particularly since (1) we import many of the things we also export (like computers, airplanes, clothes), (2) we *could* produce many of the other things we import, and (3) we worry so much about trade imbalances. Why not just import those few things that we can't produce ourselves, and export just enough to balance that trade?

Although it might seem strange to be importing goods we could produce ourselves, such trade is entirely rational. Our decision to trade with other countries arises from the same considerations that motivate individuals to specialize in production: satisfying their remaining needs in the marketplace. Why don't you become self-sufficient, growing all your own food, building your own shelter, recording your own songs? Presumably because you've found that you can enjoy a much higher standard of living (and better music) by working at just one job then buying other goods in the

Specialization

Country	Exports to ($ billions)	Imports from ($ billions)	Trade Balance ($ billions)
Top Deficit Countries			
China	$ 28	$152	−$124
Japan	52	118	−66
Canada	168	222	−54
Mexico	97	138	−41
Germany	68	107	−39
Top Surplus Countries			
Netherlands	21	11	+10
Australia	13	6	+7
Belgium	15	10	+5
Hong Kong	14	9	+5
United Arab Emirates	3	1	+2

Source: U.S. Census Bureau, Foreign Trade Division.

TABLE 20.3
Bilateral Trade Balances

The U.S. trade deficit is the net result of bilateral deficits and surpluses. We had huge trade deficits with Japan and China in 2003, for example, but small trade surpluses with the Netherlands, Belgium, Australia, and Hong Kong. International trade is multinational, with surpluses in some countries being offset by trade deficits elsewhere.

marketplace. When you do so, you're no longer self-sufficient. Instead, you are *specializing* in production, relying on others to produce the array of goods and services you want. When countries trade goods and services, they are doing the same thing—*specializing* in production, then *trading* for other desired goods. Why do they do this? Because **specialization increases total output.**

To see how nations benefit from trade, we'll examine the production possibilities of two countries. We want to demonstrate that two countries that trade can together produce more output than they could in the absence of trade. If they can, ***the gain from trade is increased world output and a higher standard of living in all trading countries.*** This is the essential message of the *theory of comparative advantage.*

Production and Consumption without Trade

Consider the production and consumption possibilities of just two countries—say, the United States and France. For the sake of illustration, assume that both countries produce only two goods: bread and wine. Let's also set aside worries about the law of diminishing returns and the substitutability of resources, thus transforming the familiar **production possibilities** curve into a straight line, as in Figure 20.1.

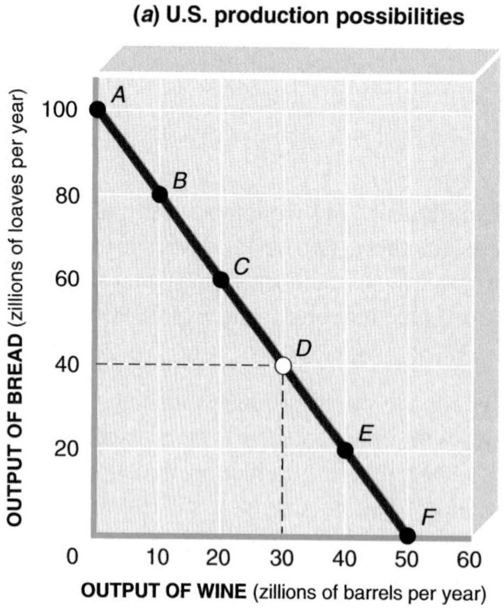

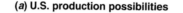

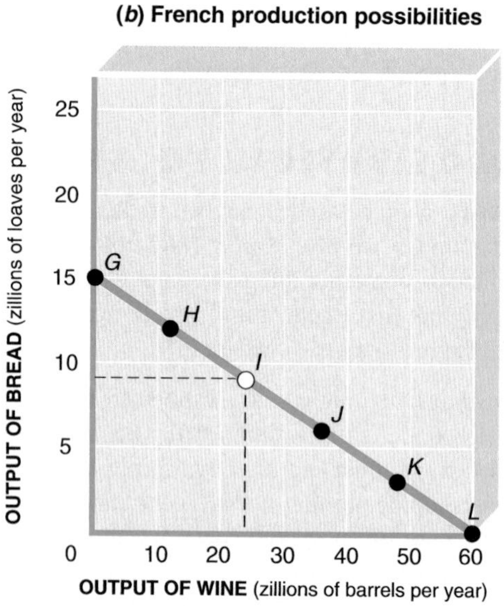

(a) U.S. production possibilities

(b) French production possibilities

U.S. Production Possibilities		
	Bread (zillions of loaves) +	Wine (zillions of barrels)
A	100 +	0
B	80 +	10
C	60 +	20
D	40 +	30
E	20 +	40
F	0 +	50

French Production Possibilities		
	Bread (zillions of loaves) +	Wine (zillions of barrels)
G	15 +	0
H	12 +	12
I	9 +	24
J	6 +	36
K	3 +	48
L	0 +	60

FIGURE 20.1

Consumption Possibilities without Trade

In the absence of trade, a country's consumption possibilities are identical to its production possibilities. The assumed production possibilities of the United States and France are illustrated in the graphs and the corresponding schedules. Before entering into trade, the United States chose to produce and consume at point *D*, with 40 zillion loaves of bread and 30 zillion barrels of wine. France chose point *I* on its own production possibilities curve. By trading, each country hopes to increase its consumption beyond these levels.

The "curves" in Figure 20.1 suggest that the United States is capable of producing much more bread than France. With our greater abundance of labor, land, and other resources, we assume that the United States is capable of producing up to 100 zillion loaves of bread per year. To do so, we'd have to devote all our resources to that purpose. This capability is indicated by point A in Figure 20.1a and in row A of the accompanying production possibilities schedule. France (Figure 20.1b), on the other hand, confronts a *maximum* bread production of only 15 zillion loaves per year (point G) because it has little available land, less fuel, and fewer potential workers.

The capacities of the two countries for wine production are 50 zillion barrels for us (point F) and 60 zillion for France (point L), largely reflecting France's greater experience in tending vines. Both countries are also capable of producing alternative *combinations* of bread and wine, as evidenced by their respective production possibilities curves (points A–F for the United States and G–L for France).

In the absence of contact with the outside world, the production possibilities curve for each country would also define its **consumption possibilities.** Without imports, a country cannot consume more than it produces. Thus, the only immediate issue in a closed economy is which mix of output to choose—*what* to produce and consume—out of the domestic choices available.

Assume that Americans choose point D on their production possibilities curve, producing and consuming 40 zillion loaves of bread and 30 zillion barrels of wine. The French, on the other hand, prefer the mix of output represented by point I on their production possibilities curve. At that point they produce and consume 9 zillion loaves of bread and 24 zillion barrels of wine.

To assess the potential gain from trade, we must focus the *combined* output of the United States and France. In this case, total world output (points D and I) comes to 49 zillion loaves of bread and 54 zillion barrels of wine. What we want to know is whether world output would increase if France and the United States abandoned their isolation and started trading. Could either country, or both, consume more output by engaging in a little trade?

Because both countries are saddled with limited production possibilities, trying to eke out a little extra wine and bread from this situation might not appear very promising. Such a conclusion is unwarranted, however. Take another look at the production possibilities confronting the United States, as reproduced in Figure 20.2. Suppose the

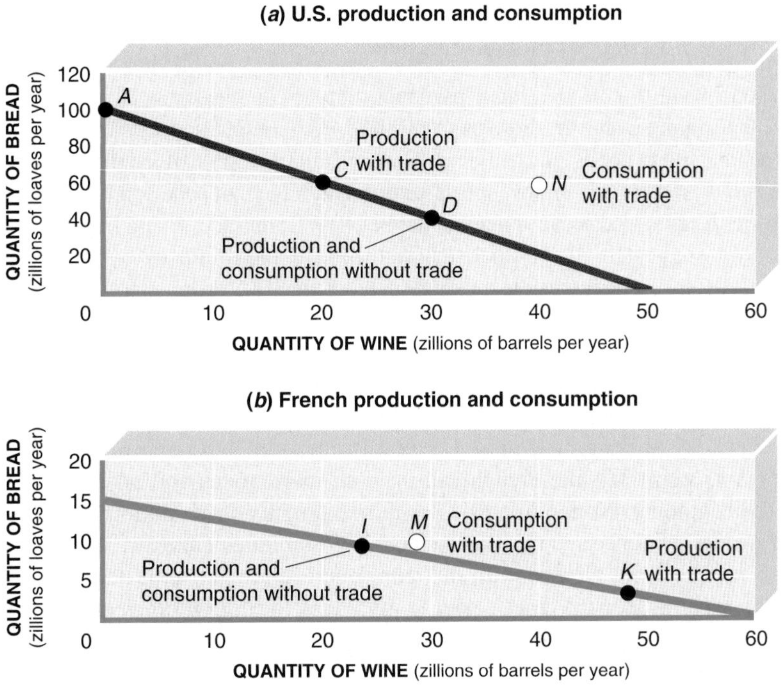

production possibilities: The alternative combinations of final goods and services that could be produced in a given time period with all available resources and technology.

consumption possibilities: The alternative combinations of goods and services that a country could consume in a given time period.

Production and Consumption with Trade

(a) U.S. production and consumption

(b) French production and consumption

FIGURE 20.2
Consumption Possibilities with Trade

A country can increase its consumption possibilities through international trade. Each country alters its mix of domestic output to produce more of the good it produces best. As it does so, total world output increases, and each country enjoys more consumption. In this case, trade allows U.S. consumption to move from point D to point N. France moves from point I to point M.

United States were to produce at point *C* rather than point *D*. At point *C* we could produce 60 zillion loaves of bread and 20 zillion barrels of wine. That combination is clearly possible, since it lies on the production possibilities curve. We didn't choose that point earlier because we assumed the mix of output at point *D* was preferable. The mix of output at point *C* could be produced, however.

We could also change the mix of output in France. Assume that France moved from point *I* to point *K*, producing 48 zillion barrels of wine and only 3 zillion loaves of bread.

Two observations are now called for. The first is simply that output mixes have changed in each country. The second, and more interesting, is that total world output has increased. When the United States and France were at points *D* and *I*, their *combined* output consisted of

	Bread (zillions of loaves)	Wine (zillions of barrels)
United States (at point *D*)	40	30
France (at point *I*)	9	24
Total pretrade output	49	54

After moving along their respective production possibilities curves to points *C* and *K*, the combined world output becomes

	Bread (zillions of loaves)	Wine (zillions of barrels)
United States (at point *C*)	60	20
France (at point *K*)	3	48
Total output with trade	63	68

Total world output has increased by 14 zillion loaves of bread and 14 zillion barrels of wine. *Just by changing the mix of output in each country, we've increased total world output.* This additional output creates the potential for making both countries better off than they were in the absence of trade.

The United States and France weren't producing at points *C* and *K* before because they simply didn't want to *consume* those particular output combinations. Nevertheless, our discovery that points *C* and *K* allow us to produce *more* output suggests that everybody can consume more goods and services if we change the mix of output in each country. This is our first clue as to how specialization and trade can benefit an economy.

Suppose we're the first to discover the potential benefits from trade. Using Figure 20.2 as our guide, we suggest to the French that they move their mix of output from point *I* to point *K*. As an incentive for making such a move, we promise to give them 6 zillion loaves of bread in exchange for 20 zillion barrels of wine. This would leave them at point *M*, with as much bread to consume as they used to have, plus an extra 4 zillion barrels of wine. At point *I* they had 9 zillion loaves of bread and 24 zillion barrels of wine. At point *M* they can have 9 zillion loaves of bread and 28 zillion barrels of wine. Thus, by altering their mix of output (from point *I* to point *K*) and then trading (point *K* to point *M*), the French end up with more goods and services than they had in the beginning. Notice in particular that this new consumption possibility (point *M*) lies *outside* France's domestic production possibilities curve.

The French will be quite pleased with the extra output they get from trading. But where does this leave us? Does France's gain imply a loss for us? Or do we gain from trade as well?

TABLE 20.4
Gains from Trade

When nations specialize in production, they can export one good and import another and end up with more goods to consume than they had without trade. In this case, the United States specializes in bread production.

| | Production and Consumption with Trade | | | | | | Production and Consumption with No Trade |
	Production	+	Imports	−	Exports	=	Consumption	
United States at . . .	Point C						Point N	Point D
Bread	60	+	0	−	6	=	54	40
Wine	20	+	20	−	0	=	40	30
France at . . .	Point K						Point M	Point I
Bread	3	+	6	−	0	=	9	9
Wine	48	+	0	−	20	=	28	24

Mutual Gains

As it turns out, *both* the United States and France gain by trading. The United States, too, ends up consuming a mix of output that lies outside our production possibilities curve.

Note that at point C we produce 60 zillion loaves of bread per year and 20 zillion barrels of wine. We then export 6 zillion loaves to France. This leaves us with 54 zillion loaves of bread to consume. In return for our exported bread, the French give us 20 zillion barrels of wine. These imports, plus our domestic production, permit us to *consume* 40 zillion barrels of wine. Hence, we end up consuming at point N, enjoying 54 zillion loaves of bread and 40 zillion barrels of wine. Thus, by first changing our mix of output (from point D to point C), then trading (point C to point N), we end up with 14 zillion more loaves of bread and 10 zillion more barrels of wine than we started with. International trade has made us better off, too.

Table 20.4 recaps the gains from trade for both countries. Notice that U.S. imports match French exports and vice versa. Also notice how the trade-facilitated consumption in each country exceeds no-trade levels.

There's no sleight of hand going on here; the gains from trade are due to specialization in production. When each country goes it alone, it's a prisoner of its own production possibilities curve; it must make production decisions on the basis of its own consumption desires. When international trade is permitted, however, each country can concentrate on the exploitation of its production capabilities. ***Each country produces those goods it makes best and then trades with other countries to acquire the goods it desires to consume.***

The resultant specialization increases total world output. In the process, each country is able to escape the confines of its own production possibilities curve, to reach beyond it for a larger basket of consumption goods. ***When a country engages in international trade, its consumption possibilities always exceed its production possibilities.*** These enhanced consumption possibilities are emphasized by the positions of points N and M outside the production possibilities curves (Figure 20.2). If it weren't possible for countries to increase their consumption by trading, there'd be no incentive for trading, and thus no trade.

PURSUIT OF COMPARATIVE ADVANTAGE

Although international trade can make everyone better off, it's not so obvious which goods should be traded, or on what terms. In our previous illustration, the United States ended up trading bread for wine in terms that were decidedly favorable to us. Why did we export bread rather than wine, and how did we end up getting such a good deal?

Opportunity Costs

comparative advantage: The ability of a country to produce a specific good at a lower opportunity cost than its trading partners.

opportunity cost: The most desired goods or services that are forgone in order to obtain something else.

The decision to export bread is based on **comparative advantage,** that is, the *relative* cost of producing different goods. Recall that we can produce a maximum of 100 zillion loaves of bread per year or 50 zillion barrels of wine. Thus, the domestic **opportunity cost** of producing 100 zillion loaves of bread is the 50 zillion barrels of wine we forsake in order to devote our resources to bread production. In fact, at every point on the U.S. production possibilities curve (Figure 20.2*a*), the opportunity cost of a loaf of bread is $\frac{1}{2}$ barrel of wine. We're effectively paying half a barrel of wine to get a loaf of bread.

Although the cost of bread production in the United States might appear outrageous, even higher opportunity costs prevail in France. According to Figure 20.2*b*, the opportunity cost of producing a loaf of bread in France is a staggering 4 barrels of wine. To produce a loaf of bread, the French must use factors of production that could otherwise be used to produce 4 barrels of wine.

Comparative Advantage. A comparison of the opportunity costs prevailing in each country exposes the nature of comparative advantage. The United States has a comparative advantage in bread production because less wine has to be given up to produce bread in the United States than in France. In other words, the opportunity costs of bread production are lower in the United States than in France. *Comparative advantage refers to the relative (opportunity) costs of producing particular goods.*

A country should specialize in what it's *relatively* efficient at producing, that is, goods for which it has the lowest opportunity costs. In this case, the United States should produce bread because its opportunity cost ($\frac{1}{2}$ barrel of wine) is less than France's (4 barrels of wine). Were you the production manager for the whole world, you'd certainly want each country to exploit its relative abilities, thus maximizing world output. Each country can arrive at that same decision itself by comparing its own opportunity costs to those prevailing elsewhere. *World output, and thus the potential gains from trade, will be maximized when each country pursues its comparative advantage.* Each country does so by exporting goods that entail relatively low domestic opportunity costs and importing goods that involve relatively high domestic opportunity costs. That's the kind of situation depicted in Table 20.4.

Absolute Costs Don't Count

absolute advantage: The ability of a country to produce a specific good with fewer resources (per unit of output) than other countries.

In assessing the nature of comparative advantage, notice that we needn't know anything about the actual costs involved in production. Have you seen any data suggesting how much labor, land, or capital is required to produce a loaf of bread in either France or the United States? For all you and I know, the French may be able to produce both a loaf of bread and a barrel of wine with fewer resources than we're using. Such an **absolute advantage** in production might exist because of their much longer experience in cultivating both grapes and wheat or simply because they have more talent.

We can envy such productivity, and even try to emulate it, but it shouldn't alter our production or trade decisions. All we really care about are *opportunity costs*—what *we* have to give up in order to get more of a desired good. If we can get a barrel of wine for less bread in trade than in production, we have a comparative advantage in producing bread. As long as we have a *comparative* advantage in bread production we should exploit it. It doesn't matter to us whether France could produce either good with fewer resources. For that matter, even if France had an absolute advantage in *both* goods, we'd still have a *comparative* advantage in bread production, as we've already confirmed. The absolute costs of production were omitted from the previous illustration because they were irrelevant.

To clarify the distinction between absolute advantage and comparative advantage, consider this example. When Charlie Osgood joined the Willamette Warriors football team, he was the fastest runner ever to play football in Willamette. He could also throw the ball farther than most people could see. In other words, he had an *absolute advantage* in both throwing and running. Charlie would have made the greatest quarterback or the greatest end ever to play football. *Would have.* The problem was that he could play only one position at a time. Thus, the Willamette coach had to play Charlie either as a quarterback or as an end. He reasoned that Charlie could throw only a bit farther than some of the other top quarterbacks but could far outdistance all the other ends. In other words, Charlie had a *comparative advantage* in running and was assigned to play as an end.

TERMS OF TRADE

It definitely pays to pursue one's comparative advantage by specializing in production. It may not yet be clear, however, how we got such a good deal with France. We're clever traders, but beyond that, is there any way to determine the **terms of trade,** the quantity of good A that must be given up in exchange for good B? In our previous illustration, the terms of trade were very favorable to us; we exchanged only 6 zillion loaves of bread for 20 zillion barrels of wine (Table 20.4). The terms of trade were thus 6 loaves = 20 barrels.

The terms of trade with France were determined by our offer and France's ready acceptance. But why did France accept those terms? France was willing to accept our offer because the terms of trade permitted France to increase its wine consumption without giving up any bread consumption. Our offer of 6 loaves for 20 barrels was an improvement over France's domestic opportunity costs. France's domestic possibilities required it to give up 24 barrels of wine in order to produce 6 loaves of bread (see Figure 20.2*b*). Getting bread via trade was simply cheaper for France than producing bread at home. France ended up with an extra 4 zillion barrels of wine (Table 20.4).

Our first clue to the terms of trade, then, lies in each country's domestic opportunity costs. ***A country won't trade unless the terms of trade are superior to domestic opportunities.*** In our example, the opportunity cost of 1 barrel of wine in the United States is 2 loaves of bread. Accordingly, we won't export bread unless we get at least 1 barrel of wine in exchange for every 2 loaves of bread we ship overseas.

All countries want to gain from trade. Hence, we can predict that ***the terms of trade between any two countries will lie somewhere between their respective opportunity costs in production.*** That is, a loaf of bread in international trade will be worth at least $\frac{1}{2}$ barrel of wine (the U.S. opportunity cost) but no more than 4 barrels (the French opportunity cost). In our example, the terms of trade ended up at 1 loaf = 3.33 barrels (that is, at 6 loaves = 20 barrels). This represented a very large gain for the United States and a small gain for France. Figure 20.3 illustrates this outcome and several other possibilities.

Limits to the Terms of Trade

The Role of Markets and Prices

Relatively little trade is subject to such direct negotiations between countries. More often than not, the decision to import or export a particular good is left up to the market decisions of individual consumers and producers.

Individual consumers and producers aren't much impressed by such abstractions as comparative advantage. Market participants tend to focus on prices, always trying to allocate their resources in order to maximize profits or personal satisfaction. Consumers tend to buy the products that deliver the most utility per dollar of expenditure, while producers try to get the most output per dollar of cost. Everybody's looking for a bargain.

So what does this have to do with international trade? Well, suppose that Henri, an enterprising Frenchman, visited the United States before the advent of international trade. He observed that bread was relatively cheap while wine was relatively expensive—the opposite of the price relationship prevailing in France. These price comparisons brought to his mind the opportunity for making a fast franc. All he had to do was bring over some French wine and trade it in the United States for a large quantity of bread. Then he could return to France and exchange the bread for a greater quantity of wine. *Alors!* Were he to do this a few times, he'd amass substantial profits.

FIGURE 20.3

Searching for the Terms of Trade

Assume the United States can produce 100 zillion loaves of bread per year (point *A*). If we reduce output to only 85 zillion loaves, we could move to point *X*. At point *X* we have 7.5 zillion barrels of wine and 85 zillion loaves of bread.

Trade increases consumption possibilities. If we continued to produce 100 zillion loaves of bread, we could trade 15 zillion loaves to France in exchange for as much as 60 zillion barrels of wine. This would leave us *producing* at point *A* but *consuming* at point *Y*. At point *Y* we have more wine and no less bread than we had at point *X*.

A country will end up on its consumption possibilities curve only if it gets *all* the gains from trade. It will remain on its production possibilities curve only if it gets *none* of the gains from trade. The terms of trade determine how the gains from trade are distributed, and thus at what point in the shaded area each country ends up.

Note: The kink in the consumption possibilities curve at point *Y* occurs because France is unable to produce more than 60 zillion barrels of wine.

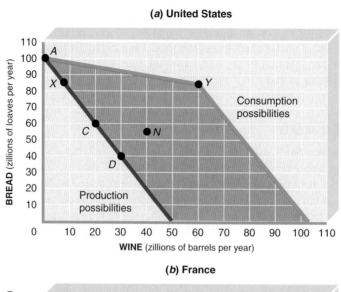

(a) United States

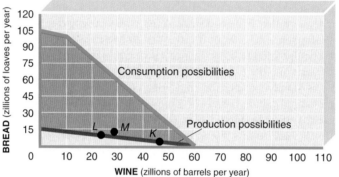

(b) France

WEBNOTE

Find out more about trade patterns and policy from the International Trade Commission at dataweb.usitc.gov.

Henri's entrepreneurial exploits will not only enrich him but will also move each country toward its comparative advantage. The United States ends up exporting bread to France, and France ends up exporting wine to the United States, exactly as the theory of comparative advantage suggests. The activating agent isn't the Ministry of Trade and its 620 trained economists but simply one enterprising French trader. He's aided and encouraged, of course, by consumers and producers in each country. American consumers are happy to trade their bread for his wines. They thereby end up paying less for wine (in terms of bread) than they'd otherwise have to. In other words, the terms of trade Henri offers are more attractive than the prevailing (domestic) relative prices. On the other side of the Atlantic, Henri's welcome is equally warm. French consumers are able to get a better deal by trading their wine for his imported bread than by trading with the local bakers.

Even some producers are happy. The wheat farmers and bakers in the United States are eager to deal with Henri. He's willing to buy a lot of bread and even to pay a premium price for it. Indeed, bread production has become so profitable in the United States that a lot of people who used to grow and mash grapes are now growing wheat and kneading dough. This alters the mix of U.S. output in the direction of more bread, exactly as suggested in Figure 20.2*a*.

In France, the opposite kind of production shift is taking place. French wheat farmers are planting more grape vines so they can take advantage of Henri's generous purchases. Thus, Henri is able to lead each country in the direction of its comparative advantage while raking in a substantial profit for himself along the way.

Where the terms of trade and the volume of exports and imports end up depends partly on how good a trader Henri is. It will also depend on the behavior of the thousands of individual consumers and producers who participate in the market exchanges. In other words, trade flows depend on both the supply and the demand for bread and wine in each country. ***The terms of trade, like the price of any good, depend on the willingness of market participants to buy or sell at various prices.*** All we know for sure is that the terms of trade will end up somewhere between the limits set by each country's opportunity costs.

PROTECTIONIST PRESSURES

Although the potential gains from world trade are impressive, not everyone will smile at the Franco-American trade celebration. On the contrary, some people will be upset about the trade routes that Henri has established. They'll not only boycott the celebration but actively seek to discourage us from continuing to trade with France.

Consider, for example, the winegrowers in western New York. Do you think they're going to be happy about Henri's entrepreneurship? Americans can now buy wine more cheaply from France than they can from New York. Before long we may hear talk about unfair foreign competition or about the greater nutritional value of American grapes (see News). The New York winegrowers may also emphasize the importance of maintaining an adequate grape supply and a strong wine industry at home, just in case of terrorist attacks.

Microeconomic Pressures

Import-Competing Industries. Joining with the growers will be the farm workers and the other producers and merchants whose livelihood depends on the New York wine industry. If they're clever enough, the growers will also get the governor of the state to join their demonstration. After all, the governor must recognize the needs of his people, and his people definitely don't include the wheat farmers in Kansas who are making a bundle from international trade. New York consumers are of course benefiting from lower wine prices, but they're unlikely to demonstrate over a few cents a bottle. On the other hand, those few extra pennies translate into millions of dollars for domestic wine producers.

The wheat farmers in France are no happier about international trade than are the winegrowers in the United States. They'd dearly love to sink all those boats bringing wheat from America, thereby protecting their own market position.

IN THE NEWS

Whining over Wine

A new type of wine bar has sprung up on Capitol Hill, and it's not likely to tickle the palate of a dedicated oenophile. California wine makers are hawking a bill that could slap higher tariffs on imported wine, and Congress shows some sign of becoming intoxicated with what the wine makers have to offer. First introduced last summer, the Wine Equity Act, as the measure is called, is already sponsored by 345 Congressmen and 60 Senators.

The wine makers aren't putting all their grapes into one bottle. Behind the scenes they have been making common cause with the American Grape Growers Alliance for Fair Trade, a group that represents many of the farmer cooperatives that supply domestic wineries. In a suit they filed with the Commerce Department and International Trade Commission in January, the growers complained that the Europeans, and particularly the Italians, are unfairly subsidizing the wine producers. If their suit is upheld, the ITC could impose stiff duties on the imports. The importers say there is no good evidence of substantial government subsidies.

Source: *Fortune*, February 20, 1984. From FORTUNE. © 1984 Time Inc. All rights reserved. www.fortune.com

Analysis: Although trade increases consumption possibilities, imports typically compete with a domestic industry. The affected industries will try to restrict imports in order to preserve their own jobs and incomes.

If we're to make sense of trade policies, then, we must recognize one central fact of life: Some producers have a vested interest in restricting international trade. In particular, *workers and producers who compete with imported products—who work in import-competing industries—have an economic interest in restricting trade.* This helps explain why GM, Ford, and Chrysler are unhappy about auto imports and why workers in Massachusetts want to end the importation of Italian shoes. It also explains why textile producers in South Carolina think China is behaving irresponsibly when it sells cotton shirts and dresses in the United States.

Export Industries. Although imports typically mean fewer jobs and less income for some domestic industries, exports represent increased jobs and income for other industries. Producers and workers in export industries gain from trade. Thus, on a microeconomic level there are identifiable gainers and losers from international trade. *Trade not only alters the mix of output but also redistributes income from import-competing industries to export industries.* This potential redistribution is the source of political and economic friction.

Net Gain. We must be careful to note, however, that the microeconomic gains from trade are greater than the microeconomic losses. It's not simply a question of robbing Peter to enrich Paul. We must remind ourselves that consumers in general enjoy a higher standard of living as a result of international trade. As we saw earlier, trade increases world efficiency and total output. Accordingly, we end up slicing up a larger pie rather than just reslicing the same old smaller pie.

The gains from trade will mean nothing to workers who end up with a smaller slice of the (larger) pie. It's important to remember, however, that the gains from trade are large enough to make everybody better off. Whether we actually choose to distribute the gains from trade in this way is a separate question, to which we shall return shortly. Note here, however, that *trade restrictions designed to protect specific microeconomic interests reduce the total gains from trade.* Trade restrictions leave us with a smaller pie to split up.

Additional Pressures

Import-competing industries are the principal obstacle to expanded international trade. Selfish micro interests aren't the only source of trade restrictions, however. Other arguments are also used to restrict trade.

National Security. The national security argument for trade restrictions is twofold. We can't depend on foreign suppliers to provide us with essential defense-related goods, it is said, because that would leave us vulnerable in time of war. The machine tool industry used this argument to protect itself from imports. In 1991, the Pentagon again sided with the toolmakers, citing the need for the United States to "gear up military production quickly in case of war," a contingency that couldn't be assured if weapons manufacturers relied on imported lathes, milling machines, and other tools. After the September 11, 2001, terrorist attacks on the World Trade Center and Pentagon, U.S. farmers convinced Congress to safeguard the nation's food supply with additional subsidies (see Chapter 29). The steel industry emphasized the importance of not depending on foreign suppliers.

dumping: The sale of goods in export markets at prices below domestic prices.

Dumping. Another argument against free trade arises from the practice of **dumping.** Foreign producers "dump" their goods when they sell them in the United States at prices lower than those prevailing in their own country, perhaps even below the costs of production.

Dumping may be unfair to import-competing producers, but it isn't necessarily unwelcome to the rest of us. As long as foreign producers continue dumping, we're getting foreign products at low prices. How bad can that be? There's a legitimate worry, however. Foreign producers might hold prices down only until domestic producers are

China Accuses Corning of 'Dumping'

Corning Inc., the big U.S. fiber-optic and glass maker, said the Chinese government has charged it with selling optical-fiber products in China at an unfairly low price that damaged Chinese producers, a practice known as dumping.

Corning denied the charge, which followed a nearly year-long investigation by China's Ministry of Commerce after two Chinese companies alleged that optical-fiber imports were priced below what market conditions justified. . . .

Since it joined the WTO, China has brought about 25 dumping cases against foreign companies, according to a King & Spalding estimate. In that same period, U.S. companies have brought 24 dumping cases against China, according to the International Trade Commission. . . .

Recent U.S. trade actions against China, most notably an antidumping case launched in October against $1 billion worth of Chinese wood and bedroom furniture imports, have likely played a role, too, according to trade experts.

The high-profile U.S. furniture case against China and China's charge against fiber makers such as Corning also exemplify the chief economic concerns in each economy: The U.S. is preoccupied with protecting workers in its hard-hit manufacturing sector, while China is interested in nurturing its technology industry. . . .

With the filing of the Chinese charges, Corning customers in China will have to pay a 16% deposit on the purchase price of the company's products, starting immediately. That money will be held in an escrow account until the matter is resolved.

Source: The Wall Street Journal, June 17, 2004. Reprinted by permission of The Wall Street Journal, © 2004 Dow Jones & Company. All rights reserved worldwide.

Analysis: *Dumping* means that a foreign producer is selling exports at prices below cost or below prices in the home market, putting import-competing industries at a competitive disadvantage. *Accusations* of dumping are an effective trade barrier.

driven out of business. Then we might be compelled to pay the foreign producers higher prices for their products. In that case, dumping could consolidate market power and lead to monopoly-type pricing. The fear of dumping, then, is analogous to the fear of predatory pricing.

The potential costs of dumping are serious. It's not always easy to determine when dumping occurs, however. Those who compete with imports have an uncanny ability to associate any and all low prices with predatory dumping. The United States has used dumping *charges* to restrict imports of Chinese shrimp, furniture, lingerie, and other products in which China has an evident comparative advantage. The Chinese have retaliated with dozens of their own dumping investigations, including the 2004 accusation for fiber-optic cable (in which the United States has a comparative advantage), as the accompanying World View explains.

Infant Industries. Actual dumping threatens to damage already established domestic industries. Even normal import prices, however, may make it difficult or impossible for a new domestic industry to develop. Infant industries are often burdened with abnormally high startup costs. These high costs may arise from the need to train a whole workforce and the expenses of establishing new marketing channels. With time to grow, however, an infant industry might experience substantial cost reductions and establish a comparative advantage. When this is the case, trade restrictions might help nurture an industry in its infancy. Trade restrictions are justified, however, only if there's tangible evidence that the industry can develop a comparative advantage reasonably quickly.

Improving the Terms of Trade. A final argument for restricting trade rests on how the gains from trade are distributed. As we observed, the distribution of the gains from trade depends on the terms of trade. If we were to buy fewer imports, foreign producers might lower their prices. If that happened, the terms of trade would move in our favor, and we'd end up with a larger share of the gains from trade.

One way to bring about this sequence of events is to put restrictions on imports, making it more difficult or expensive for Americans to buy foreign products. Such restrictions will reduce the volume of imports, thereby inducing foreign producers to lower their prices. Unfortunately, this strategy can easily backfire: Retaliatory restrictions on imports, each designed to improve the terms of trade, will ultimately eliminate all trade and therewith all the gains people were competing for in the first place.

BARRIERS TO TRADE

The microeconomic losses associated with imports give rise to a constant clamor for trade restrictions. People whose jobs and incomes are threatened by international trade tend to organize quickly and air their grievances. The News depicts the efforts of farmers in Montana and North Dakota to limit imports of Canadian wheat and livestock. They hope to convince Congress to impose restrictions on imports. More often than not, Congress grants the wishes of these well-organized and well-financed special interests.

Embargoes

embargo: A prohibition on exports or imports.

The surefire way to restrict trade is simply to eliminate it. To do so, a country need only impose an embargo on exports or imports, or both. An **embargo** is nothing more than a prohibition against trading particular goods.

In 1951, Senator Joseph McCarthy convinced the U.S. Senate to impose an embargo on Soviet mink, fox, and five other furs. He argued that such imports helped finance world communism. Senator McCarthy also represented the state of Wisconsin, where most U.S. minks are raised. The Reagan administration tried to end the fur embargo in 1987 but met with stiff congressional opposition. By then, U.S. mink ranchers had developed a $120 million per year industry.

The United States has also maintained an embargo on Cuban goods since 1959, when Fidel Castro took power there. This embargo severely damaged Cuba's sugar industry and deprived American smokers of the famed Havana cigars. It also fostered the development of U.S. sugar beet and tobacco farmers, who now have a vested interest in maintaining the embargo.

Tariffs

A more frequent trade restriction is a **tariff,** a special tax imposed on imported goods. Tariffs, also called *customs duties,* were once the principal source of revenue for

IN THE NEWS

Farmers Stage Protests over Import of Products

Farmers claiming that imports of Canadian grain and other agricultural products are depressing U.S. prices threatened on Tuesday more blockades at border crossings unless the U.S. government acts to slow the flow of goods.

Farmers also want Canadian wheat and livestock tested for diseases and additives that are banned here.

Blockades and other protests have appeared at various border crossings in North Dakota and Montana for several days. In Montana, 20 long-haul truckers were ticketed Monday, the first day of a state crackdown on border inspections. And farmers in North Dakota dumped grain on U.S. Highway 281, stopping truck traffic for eight hours.

"We've got an oversupply of wheat, hogs and cattle already," said Curt Trulson, a farmer in Ross, N.D. "We don't need any more foreign commodities."

Source: *USA Today,* September 23, 1998. USA TODAY. © 1998, USA Today. Reprinted with permission. www.usatoday.com

Analysis: Import-competing industries cite lots of reasons for restricting trade. Their primary concern, however, is to protect their own jobs and profits.

governments. In the eighteenth century, tariffs on tea, glass, wine, lead, and paper were imposed on the American colonies to provide extra revenue for the British government. The tariff on tea led to the Boston Tea Party in 1773 and gave added momentum to the American independence movement. In modern times, tariffs have been used primarily as a means to protect specific industries from import competition. The current U.S. tariff code specifies tariffs on over 9,000 different products—nearly 50 percent of all U.S. imports. Although the average tariff is only 5 percent, individual tariffs vary widely. The tariff on cars, for example, is only 2.5 percent, while cotton sweaters confront a 17.8 percent tariff.

> **tariff:** A tax (duty) imposed on imported goods.

The attraction of tariffs to import-competing industries should be obvious. *A tariff on imported goods makes them more expensive to domestic consumers and thus less competitive with domestically produced goods.* Among familiar tariffs in effect in 2004 were $0.50 per gallon on Scotch whiskey and 76 cents per gallon on imported champagne. These tariffs made American-produced spirits look relatively cheap and thus contributed to higher sales and profits for domestic distillers and grape growers. In the same manner, imported baby food is taxed at 34.6 percent, maple sugar at 9.4 percent, golf shoes at 8.5 percent, and imported sailboats at 1.5 percent. In each case, domestic producers in import-competing industries gain. The losers are domestic consumers, who end up paying higher prices. The tariff on orange juice, for example, raises the price of drinking orange juice by $525 million a year. Tariffs also hurt foreign producers, who lose business, and world efficiency, as trade is reduced.

The harmonized tariff schedule for imported products is available online from the U.S. International Trade Commission. Go to www.usitc.gov, and click on "Publications" then "Harmonized Tariff Schedule."

"Beggar Thy Neighbor." Microeconomic interests aren't the only source of pressure for tariff protection. Imports represent leakage from the domestic circular flow and a potential loss of jobs at home. From this perspective, the curtailment of imports looks like an easy solution to the problem of domestic unemployment. Just get people to "buy American" instead of buying imported products, so the argument goes, and domestic output and employment will surely expand. Congressman Willis Hawley used this argument in 1930. He assured his colleagues that higher tariffs would "bring about the growth and development in this country that has followed every other tariff bill, bringing as it does a new prosperity in which all people, in all sections, will increase their comforts, their enjoyment, and their happiness."[1] Congress responded by passing the Smoot-Hawley Tariff Act of 1930, which raised tariffs to an average of nearly 60 percent, effectively cutting off most imports.

Tariffs designed to expand domestic employment are more likely to fail than to succeed. If a tariff wall does stem the flow of imports, it effectively transfers the unemployment problem to other countries, a phenomenon often referred to as "beggar thy neighbor." The resultant loss of business in other countries leaves them less able to purchase our exports. The imported unemployment also creates intense political pressures for retaliatory action. That's exactly what happened in the 1930s. Other countries erected trade barriers to compensate for the effects of the Smoot-Hawley tariff. World trade subsequently fell from $60 billion in 1928 to a mere $25 billion in 1938. This trade contraction increased the severity of the Great Depression (see World View).

Quotas

Tariffs reduce the flow of imports by raising import prices. The same outcome can be attained more directly by imposing import **quotas,** numerical restrictions on the quantity of a particular good that may be imported. The United States limits the quantity of ice cream imported from Jamaica to 950 gallons a year. Only 1.4 million kilograms of Australian cheddar cheese and no more than 7,730 tons of Haitian sugar can be imported. Textile quotas are imposed on every country that wants to ship textiles to the U.S. market. According to the U.S. Department of State, approximately 12 percent of our imports are subject to import quotas.

> **quota:** A limit on the quantity of a good that may be imported in a given time period.

---

[1] *The New York Times,* June 15, 1930, p. 25.

"Beggar-Thy-Neighbor" Policies in the 1930s

President Herbert Hoover, ignoring the pleas of 1,028 economists to veto it, signed the Smoot-Hawley Tariff Act on June 17, 1930. It was a hollow celebration. The day before, anticipating the signing, the stock market suffered its worst collapse since November 1929, and the law quickly helped push the Great Depression deeper.

The new tariffs, which by 1932 rose to an all-time high of 59 percent of the average value of imports (today it's 5 percent), were designed to save American jobs by restricting foreign competition. Economists warned that angry nations would retaliate, and they did.

- Spain passed the Wais tariff in July in reaction to U.S. tariffs on grapes, oranges, cork, and onions.
- Switzerland, objecting to new U.S. tariffs on watches, embroideries, and shoes, boycotted American exports.
- Italy retaliated against tariffs on hats and olive oil with high tariffs on U.S. and French automobiles in June 1930.
- Canada reacted to high duties on many food products, logs, and timber by raising tariffs threefold in August 1932.

- Australia, Cuba, France, Mexico, and New Zealand also joined in the tariff wars.

From 1930 to 1931 U.S. imports dropped 29 percent, but U.S. exports fell even more, 33 percent, and continued their collapse to a modern-day low of $2.4 billion in 1933. World trade contracted by similar proportions, spreading unemployment around the globe.

In 1934 the U.S. Congress passed the Reciprocal Trade Agreements Act to empower the president to reduce tariffs by half the 1930 rates in return for like cuts in foreign duties on U.S. goods. The "beggar-thy-neighbor" policy was dead. Since then, the nations of the world have been reducing tariffs and other trade barriers.

Source: World Bank, *World Development Report 1987;* and *The Wall Street Journal,* April 28, 1989, Reprinted by permission of The Wall Street Journal, © 1989 Dow Jones & Company. All rights reserved. www.worldbank.org; www.wsj.com

Analysis: Tariffs inflict harm on foreign producers. If foreign countries retaliate with tariffs of their own, world trade will shrink and unemployment will increase in all countries.

Comparative Effects

Quotas, like all barriers to trade, reduce world efficiency and invite retaliatory action. Moreover, their impact can be even more damaging than tariffs. To see this, we may compare market outcomes in four different contexts: no trade, free trade, tariff-restricted trade, and quota-restricted trade.

No-Trade Equilibrium. Figure 20.4*a* depicts the supply-and-demand relationships that would prevail in an economy that imposed a trade *embargo* on foreign textiles. In this situation, the **equilibrium price** of textiles is completely determined by domestic demand and supply curves. The no-trade equilibrium price is p_1, and the quantity of textiles consumed is q_1.

> **equilibrium price:** The price at which the quantity of a good demanded in a given time period equals the quantity supplied.

Free-Trade Equilibrium. Suppose now that the embargo is lifted. The immediate effect of this decision will be a rightward shift of the market supply curve, as foreign supplies are added to domestic supplies (Figure 20.4*b*). If an unlimited quantity of textiles can be bought in world markets at a price of p_2, the new supply curve will look like S_2 (infinitely elastic at p_2). The new supply curve (S_2) intersects the old demand curve (D_1) at a new equilibrium price of p_2 and an expanded consumption of q_2. At this new equilibrium, domestic producers are supplying the quantity q_d while foreign producers are supplying the rest ($q_2 - q_d$). Comparing the new equilibrium to the old one, we see that ***free trade results in reduced prices and increased consumption.***

Domestic textile producers are unhappy, of course, with their foreign competition. In the absence of trade, the domestic producers would sell more output (q_1) and get higher prices (p_1). Once trade is opened up, the willingness of foreign producers to sell unlimited quantities of textiles at the price p_2 puts a lid on domestic prices.

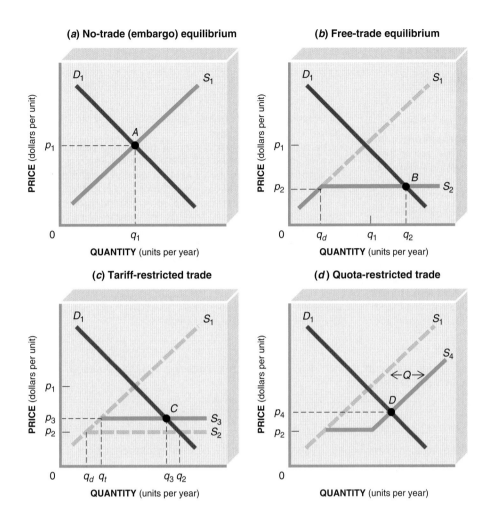

(a) No-trade (embargo) equilibrium

(b) Free-trade equilibrium

(c) Tariff-restricted trade

(d) Quota-restricted trade

FIGURE 20.4
The Impact of Trade Restrictions

In the *absence of trade,* the domestic price and sales of a good will be determined by domestic supply and demand curves (point A in part *a*). Once trade is permitted, the market supply curve will be altered by the availability of imports. With *free trade* and unlimited availability of imports at price p_2, a new market equilibrium will be established at world prices (point B).

Tariffs raise domestic prices and reduce the quantity sold (point C). *Quotas* put an absolute limit on imported sales and thus give domestic producers a great opportunity to raise the market price (point D).

Tariff-Restricted Trade. Figure 20.4*c* illustrates what would happen to prices and sales if the United Textile Producers were successful in persuading the government to impose a tariff. Assume that the tariff raises imported textile prices from p_2 to p_3, making it more difficult for foreign producers to undersell domestic producers. Domestic production expands from q_d to q_1, imports are reduced from $q_2 - q_d$ to $q_3 - q_t$, and the market price of textiles rises. Domestic textile producers are clearly better off, whereas consumers and foreign producers are worse off. In addition, the U.S. Treasury will collect increased tariff revenues.

Quota-Restricted Trade. Now consider the impact of a textile *quota.* Suppose we eliminate tariffs but decree that imports can't exceed the quantity Q. Because the quantity of imports can never exceed Q, the supply curve is effectively shifted to the right by that amount. The new curve S_4 (Figure 20.4*d*) indicates that no imports will occur below the world price p_2 and above that price the quantity Q will be imported. Thus, the *domestic* demand curve determines subsequent prices. Foreign producers are precluded from selling greater quantities as prices rise further. This outcome is in marked contrast to that of tariff-restricted trade (Figure 20.4*c*), which at least permits foreign producers to respond to rising prices. Accordingly, ***quotas are a greater threat to competition than tariffs, because quotas preclude additional imports at any price.*** The actual quotas on textile imports raise the prices of shirts, towels, and other textile products by 58 percent. As a result, a $10 shirt ends up costing consumers $15.80. All told, U.S. consumers end up paying an extra $25 billion a year for textile products.

Differing views on the cost of sugar quotas are offered by The Foundation for American Communications at www.facsnet.org and by the Sugar Alliance at www.sugaralliance.org and at www.opensecrets.org.

Some See Bush Sheltering Sugar for Votes

The Bush administration is shielding the sugar industry from competition in a new trade pact with Australia, rather than damage the president's re-election hopes in swing states such as Florida and Michigan, industry groups say. . . .

"It all boils down to electoral politics. It's very raw," says Sarah Thorn, a lobbyist at the Grocery Manufacturers of America. . . .

President Bush edged Al Gore four years ago after the Supreme Court ruled on the vote in Florida, the biggest sugar-producing state. Michigan and Minnesota, home to thousands of sugar beet growers, are considered up for grabs this fall.

The industry is among the largest contributors to both parties. Growers and processors, along with makers of corn-based sweetener, made $25.5 million in political action committee contributions and soft money gifts between 1997 and June 2003, Common Cause says.

The sugar industry is protected by quotas that restrict imports to about 15% of the U.S. market. The government also has a price-support program and offers loans to sugar processors, who can repay in sugar rather than cash if prices fall. . . .

Critics of the program say U.S. growers and processors aren't globally competitive. They say the program hurts sugar users such as candymakers and forces consumers to pay inflated prices. U.S. sugar prices last year were 21.4 cents a pound, nearly three times the world price of 7.5 cents a pound.

—James Cox

Source: *USA Today,* February 11, 2004. USA TODAY. Copyright 2004. Reprinted with permission. www.usatoday.com

Analysis: Import quotas preclude increased foreign competition when domestic prices rise. Protected domestic producers enjoy higher prices and profits while consumers pay higher prices.

The sugar industry is one of the greatest beneficiaries of quota restrictions. By limiting imports to 15 percent of domestic consumption, sugar quotas keep U.S. prices artificially high (see News). This costs consumers nearly $2 billion a year in higher prices. Candy and soda producers lose sales and profits. Foreign sugar producers (mainly in poor nations) lose sales and income. Who gains? Domestic sugar producers—who, coincidentally, are highly concentrated in key electoral states.

Voluntary Restraint Agreements

voluntary restraint agreement (VRA): An agreement to reduce the volume of trade in a specific good; a voluntary quota.

A slight variant of quotas has been used in recent years. Rather than impose quotas on imports, the U.S. government asks foreign producers to "voluntarily" limit their exports. These so-called **voluntary restraint agreements** have been negotiated with producers in Japan, South Korea, Taiwan, China, the European Union, and other countries. Korea, for example, agreed to reduce its annual shoe exports to the United States from 44 million pairs to 33 million pairs. Taiwan reduced its shoe exports from 156 million pairs to 122 million pairs per year. In 1989, China agreed to slow its exports of clothing, limiting its sales growth to 3 percent a year. For their part, the Japanese agreed to reduce sales of color TV sets in the United States from 2.8 million to 1.75 million per year. In 1989, President George H. Bush extended voluntary restraint agreements on foreign steel exports, limiting imported steel to 18.4 percent of total U.S. sales. In 1996, President Clinton forced Canada to limit its exports of lumber to the United States, and in 1999, Russia reluctantly agreed to limit steel exports.

All these voluntary export restraints, as they're often called, represent an informal type of quota. The only difference is that they're negotiated rather than imposed. But these differences are lost on consumers, who end up paying higher prices for these goods. The voluntary limit on Japanese auto exports to the United States alone cost consumers $15.7 billion in only four years.

Nontariff Barriers

Tariffs and quotas are the most visible barriers to trade, but they're only the tip of the iceberg. Indeed, the variety of protectionist measures that have been devised is testimony to the ingenuity of the human mind. At the turn of the century, the Germans were committed to a most-favored-nation policy, a policy of extending equal treatment

WORLD · VIEW

High Court Opens U.S. Roads to Mexican Trucks

The Supreme Court ruled yesterday that the Bush administration can open U.S. roads to Mexican trucks as soon as it wants, overruling a lower court judgment that the government must first study the environmental effects.

Under NAFTA, which went into effect in 1994, the United States was supposed to phase out restrictions on Mexican trucks crossing the border by 2000, provided those trucks meet U.S. safety standards. But under pressure from members of Congress and the Teamsters union, which feared losing jobs to low-wage Mexican drivers, the Clinton administration maintained the existing barriers, citing safety concerns. As a result, Mexican trucks have been confined to a 20-mile zone along the border, where they transfer their loads to U.S. carriers in cities such as San Diego and Laredo, Tex.

The Bush administration vowed to open the border in 2001 after a NAFTA panel held that Washington was violating the agreement.

—Paul Blustein

Source: *The Washington Post*, June 8, 2004. © 2004 The Washington Post. Reprinted with permission.

Analysis: Nontariff barriers like extraordinary safety requirements on Mexican trucks limit import competition.

to all trading partners. The Germans, however, wanted to lower the tariff on cattle imports from Denmark without extending the same break to Switzerland. Such a preferential tariff would have violated the most-favored-nation policy. Accordingly, the Germans created a new and higher tariff on "brown and dappled cows reared at a level of at least 300 meters above sea level and passing at least one month in every summer at an altitude of at least 800 meters." The new tariff was, of course, applied equally to all countries. But Danish cows never climb that high, so they weren't burdened with the new tariff.

With the decline in tariffs over the last 20 years, nontariff barriers have increased. The United States uses product standards, licensing restrictions, restrictive procurement practices, and other nontariff barriers to restrict roughly 15 percent of imports. In 1999–2000, the European Union banned imports of U.S. beef, arguing that the use of hormones on U.S. ranches created a health hazard for European consumers. Although both the U.S. government and the World Trade Organization disputed that claim, the ban was a highly effective nontariff trade barrier. The United States responded by slapping 100 percent tariffs on dozens of European products. In 2001, the U.S. Congress blocked Mexican trucks from open access to U.S. highways. Although the safety of Mexican trucks was spotlighted, the underlying motive was to limit competition in the multibillion-dollar U.S. transport services market. It took a U.S. Supreme Court ruling to open the roads to foreign competition (see World View).

"TELL ME AGAIN HOW THE QUOTAS ON JAPANESE CARS HAVE PROTECTED US"

—from *Herblock at Large* (Pantheon Books, 1987).

Analysis: Trade restrictions that protect import-competing industries also raise consumer prices.

THE ECONOMY TOMORROW

An Increasingly Global Market

Proponents of free trade and representatives of special interests that profit from trade protection are in constant conflict. But most of the time the trade-policy deck seems stacked in favor of the special interests. Because the interests of import-competing firms and workers are highly concentrated, they're quick to mobilize politically. By contrast, the benefits of freer trade are less direct and spread over millions of consumers. As a consequence, the beneficiaries of freer trade are less likely to monitor trade policy—much less lobby actively to change it. Hence, the political odds favor the spread of trade barriers.

Multilateral Trade Pacts

Despite these odds, the long-term trend is toward *lowering* trade barriers, thereby increasing global competition. Two forces encourage this trend. The principal barrier to protectionist policies is worldwide recognition of the gains from freer trade. Since world nations now understand that trade barriers are ultimately self-defeating, they're more willing to rise above the din of protectionist cries and dismantle trade barriers. They diffuse political opposition by creating across-the-board trade pacts that seem to spread the pain (and gain) from freer trade across a broad swath of industries. Such pacts also incorporate multiyear timetables that give affected industries time to adjust.

The opposition of import-competing industries to these multilateral, multiyear trade pacts is countered by a second force: the interests of *export*-oriented industries and other multilateral firms. Barriers to auto imports from Japan may keep out cars produced by General Motors in that country. Tariffs on imported steel raise product costs for U.S.-based auto producers. Foreign retaliation to our trade barriers may hurt our own exports. Increasing awareness of such damage has created a political climate for freer trade.

Global Pacts: GATT and WTO

The granddaddy of the multilateral, multiyear free-trade pacts was the 1947 *General Agreement on Tariffs and Trade (GATT)*. Twenty-three nations pledged to reduce trade barriers and give all GATT nations equal access to their domestic markets.

Since the first GATT pact, seven more "rounds" of negotiations have expanded the scope of GATT: 117 nations signed the 1994 pact. As a result of these GATT pacts, average tariff rates in developed countries have fallen from 40 percent in 1948 to less than 4 percent today.

WTO. The 1994 GATT pact also created the *World Trade Organization (WTO)* to enforce free-trade rules. If a nation feels its exports are being unfairly excluded from another country's market, it can file a complaint with the WTO. This is exactly what the United States did when the European Union (EU) banned U.S. beef imports. The WTO ruled in favor of the United States. When the EU failed to lift its import ban, the WTO authorized the United States to impose retaliatory tariffs on European exports.

The EU turned the tables on the United States in 2003. They complained to the WTO that U.S. tariffs on steel violated trade rules. The WTO agreed and gave the EU permission to impose retaliatory tariffs on $2.2 billion of U.S. exports. That prompted the Bush administration to scale back the tariffs in December 2003.

In effect, the WTO is now the world's trade police force. It is empowered to cite nations that violate trade agreements and even to impose remedial action when violations persist. Why do sovereign nations give the WTO such power? Because they are all convinced that free trade is the surest route to GDP growth.

WTO Protests. Although freer trade clearly boosts economic growth, some people say that it does more harm than good. Environmentalists question the very desirability of continued economic growth. They worry about the depletion of resources, congestion and pollution, and the social friction that growth often promotes. Labor organizations worry that global competition will depress wages and working conditions. And many Third World nations are concerned about playing by trade rules that always seem to benefit rich nations (e.g., copyright protection, import protection, farm subsidies).

Despite some tumultuous street protests (e.g., Seattle in 1999), WTO members continue the difficult process of dismantling trade barriers. The latest round of negotiations began in Daha, Qatar, in 2001. The key issue in the "Daha Round" has been

NAFTA Reallocates Labor: Comparative Advantage at Work

More Jobs in These Industries		but . . .	Few Jobs in These Industries	
Agriculture	+10,600		Construction	−12,800
Metal products	+6,100		Medicine	−6,000
Electrical appliances	+5,200		Apparel	−5,900
Business services	+5,000		Lumber	−1,200
Motor vehicles	+5,000		Furniture	−400

Source: Congressional Budget Office.

The lowering of trade barriers between Mexico and the United States is changing the mix of output in both countries. New export opportunities create jobs in some industries while increased imports eliminate jobs in other industries. (Estimated gains and losses are during the first five years of NAFTA.)

Analysis: The specialization encouraged by free trade creates new jobs in export but reduces employment in import-competing industries. In the process, total world output increases.

---

farm subsidies in rich nations. Poor nations protest that farm subsidies in the United States and Europe not only limit their exports but also lower global farm prices (hurting farmers in developing nations). By the end of 2004, the WTO had secured pledges to reduce those farm subsidies.

Because worldwide trade pacts are so complex, many nations have also pursued *regional* free-trade agreements. In December 1992, the United States, Canada, and Mexico signed the *North American Free Trade Agreement (NAFTA),* a 1,000-page document covering more than 9,000 products. The ultimate goal of NAFTA is to eliminate all trade barriers between these three countries. At the time of signing, intraregional tariffs averaged 11 percent in Mexico, 5 percent in Canada, and 4 percent in the United States. NAFTA requires that all tariffs between the three countries be eliminated by 2007. The pact also requires the elimination of specific nontariff barriers.

The NAFTA-initiated reduction in trade barriers substantially increased trade flows between Mexico, Canada, and the United States. It also prompted a wave of foreign investment in Mexico, where both cheap labor and NAFTA access were available. Overall, NAFTA accelerated economic growth and reduced inflationary pressures in all three nations. Some industries (like construction and apparel) suffered from the freer trade, but others (like trucking, farming, and finance) reaped huge gains (see News).

The *European Union* is another regional pact, but one that virtually eliminates national boundaries among 25 countries. The EU not only eliminates trade barriers but also enhances full intercountry mobility of workers and capital. In 1999, the EU nations also created a new currency (the euro) that has replaced the German mark, the French franc, and other national currencies. In effect, Europe has become one large, unified market. As trade barriers continue to fall around the world, the global marketplace is likely to become more like an open bazaar as well. The resulting increase in competition should spur efficiency and growth in the economy tomorrow.

*Regional Pacts:
NAFTA and EU*

To see how detailed a trade pact can be, access the NAFTA pact at www.nafta-sec-alena.org.

SUMMARY

- International trade permits each country to specialize in areas of relative efficiency, increasing world output. For each country, the gains from trade are reflected in consumption possibilities that exceed production possibilities.
- One way to determine where comparative advantage lies is to compare the quantity of good A that must be given up in order to get a given quantity of good B from domestic production. If the same quantity of B can be obtained for less A by engaging in world trade, we have a comparative advantage in the production of good A. Comparative advantage rests on a comparison of relative opportunity costs.
- The terms of trade—the rate at which goods are exchanged—are subject to the forces of international supply and demand. The terms of trade will lie somewhere between the opportunity costs of the trading partners. The terms of trade determine how the gains from trade are shared.

- Resistance to trade emanates from workers and firms that must compete with imports. Even though the country as a whole stands to benefit from trade, these individuals and companies may lose jobs and incomes in the process.
- Trade barriers take many forms. Embargoes are outright prohibitions against import or export of particular goods. Quotas limit the quantity of a good imported or exported. Tariffs discourage imports by making them more expensive. Other nontariff barriers make trade too costly or time-consuming.
- The World Trade Organization (WTO) seeks to reduce worldwide trade barriers and enforce trade rules. Regional accords such as the European Union (EU) and North American Free Trade Agreement (NAFTA) pursue similar objectives among fewer countries.

Key Terms

imports	comparative advantage	tariff
exports	opportunity cost	quota
trade deficit	absolute advantage	equilibrium price
trade surplus	terms of trade	voluntary restraint agreement (VRA)
production possibilities	dumping	
consumption possibilities	embargo	

Questions for Discussion

1. Suppose a lawyer can type faster than any secretary. Should the lawyer do her own typing? Can you demonstrate the validity of your answer?
2. What would be the effects of a law requiring bilateral trade balances?
3. If a nation exported much of its output but imported little, would it be better or worse off? How about the reverse, that is, exporting little but importing a lot?
4. How does international trade restrain the price behavior of domestic firms?
5. Suppose we refused to sell goods to any country that reduced or halted its exports to us. Who would benefit and who would lose from such retaliation? Can you suggest alternative ways to ensure import supplies?
6. Domestic producers often base their claim for import protection on the fact that workers in country X are paid substandard wages. Is this a valid argument for protection?
7. Based on the News on page 435, how do U.S. furniture manufacturers feel about NAFTA? How about farmers?
8. Who would gain or lose from the proposed Wine Equity Act? (See the News, page 425.)
9. Who pays for sugar quotas? (See News, page 432.) How could the quotas be eliminated?
10. Who gains and who loses from restrictions on the access of Mexican trucks to U.S. markets? (See World View, page 433.)

ALERT!

PROBLEMS — The Student Problem Set at the back of this book contains numerical and graphing problems for this chapter.

WEB ACTIVITIES — to accompany this chapter can be found on the Online Learning Center: **http://www.mhhe.com/economics/schiller10**

21

International Finance

U.S. textile, furniture, and shrimp producers want China to increase the value of the yuan. They say China's undervalued currency makes Chinese exports too cheap, undercutting American firms. On the other hand, Wal-Mart thinks a cheap yuan is a good thing, as it keeps prices low for the $12 *billion* of toys, tools, linens, and other goods it buys from China each year. Those low import prices help Wal-Mart keep its prices low and sales volume high.

This chapter examines how currency values affect trade patterns and ultimately the core questions of WHAT, HOW, and FOR WHOM to produce. We focus on the following questions:

- **What determines the value of one country's money as compared to the value of another's?**
- **What causes the international value of currencies to change?**
- **Should governments intervene to limit currency fluctuations?**

EXCHANGE RATES: THE GLOBAL LINK

As we saw in Chapter 20, the United States exports and imports a staggering volume of goods and services. Although we trade with nearly 200 nations around the world, we seldom give much thought to where imports come from and much less to how we acquire them. Most of the time, all we want to know is which products are available and at what price.

Suppose you want to buy a Magnavox DVD player. You don't have to know that Magnavox players are produced by the Dutch company Philips Electronics. And you certainly don't have to fly to the Netherlands to pick it up. All you have to do is drive to the nearest electronics store; or you can just "click and buy" at the Internet's virtual mall.

But you may wonder how the purchase of an imported product was so simple. Dutch companies sell their products in euros, the currency of Europe. But you purchase the DVD player in dollars. How is such an exchange possible?

There's a chain of distribution between your dollar purchase in the United States and the euro-denominated sale in the Netherlands. Somewhere along that chain someone has to convert your dollars into euros. The critical question for everybody concerned is how many euros we can get for our dollars—that is, what the **exchange rate** is. If we can get two euros for every dollar, the exchange rate is 2 euros = 1 dollar. Alternatively, we could note that the price of a euro is 50 U.S. cents when the exchange rate is 2 to 1. Thus, *an exchange rate is the price of one currency in terms of another.*

exchange rate: The price of one country's currency expressed in terms of another's; the domestic price of a foreign currency.

FOREIGN-EXCHANGE MARKETS

Most exchange rates are determined in foreign-exchange markets. Stop thinking of money as some sort of magical substance, and instead view it as a useful commodity that facilitates market exchanges. From that perspective, an exchange rate—the price of money—is subject to the same influences that determine all market prices: demand and supply.

The Demand for Dollars

When Daimler-Benz bought Chrysler in 1998, it paid $36 billion. When the Sony Corporation bought Columbia Pictures, it also needed dollars—over 3 billion of them! In both cases, the objective of the foreign investor was to acquire an American business. To attain their objectives, however, the buyers first had to buy *dollars*. The German and Japanese buyers had to exchange their own currency for American dollars.

Canadian tourists also need American dollars. Few American restaurants or hotels accept Canadian currency as payment for goods and services; they want to be paid in U.S. dollars. Accordingly, Canadian tourists must buy American dollars if they want to see the United States.

Europeans love iPods. The Apple Corporation, however, wants to be paid in U.S. dollars. Hence, European consumers must exchange their currencies for U.S. dollars if they want an iPod. Individual consumers can spend euros at their local electronics store. When they do so, however, they're initiating a series of market transactions that will end when Apple Corporation gets paid in U.S. dollars. In this case, some intermediary exchanges the European currency for American dollars.

Some foreign investors also buy U.S. dollars for speculative purposes. When the ruble collapsed, Russians feared that the value of the ruble would drop further and preferred to hold U.S. dollars. Barclay's Bank also speculates in dollars on occasions when it fears that the value of the British pound will drop.

All these motivations give rise to a demand for U.S. dollars. Specifically, ***the market demand for U.S. dollars originates in***

- *Foreign demand for American exports* (including tourism).
- *Foreign demand for American investments.*
- *Speculation.*

Governments may also create a demand for dollars through currency *swaps* and other activities.

The Supply of Dollars

The *supply* of dollars arises from similar sources. On the supply side, however, it's Americans who initiate most of the exchanges. Suppose you take a trip to Mexico. You'll need to buy Mexican pesos at some point. When you do, you'll be offering to *buy* pesos by offering to *sell* dollars. In other words, **the demand *for foreign currency* represents a supply *of U.S. dollars*.**

When Americans buy BMW cars, they also supply U.S. dollars. American consumers pay for their BMWs in dollars. Somewhere down the road, however, those dollars will be exchanged for European euros. At that exchange, dollars are being *supplied* and euros *demanded.*

American corporations demand foreign exchange too. General Motors builds cars in Germany, Coca-Cola produces Coke in China, Exxon produces and refines oil all over the world. In nearly every such case, the U.S. firm must first build or buy some plant and equipment, using another country's factors of production. This activity requires foreign currency and thus becomes another component of our demand for foreign currency.

We may summarize these market activities by noting that ***the supply of dollars originates in***

- *American demand for imports* (including tourism).
- *American investments in foreign countries.*
- *Speculation.*

As on the demand side, government intervention can also contribute to the supply of dollars.

Whether American consumers will choose to buy a BMW depends partly on what the car costs. The price tag isn't always apparent in international transactions. Remember that the BMW producer and workers want to be paid in their own currency. Hence, the *dollar* price of a BMW depends on two factors: (1) the German price of a BMW and (2) the *exchange rate* between U.S. dollars and euros. Specifically, the U.S. price of a BMW is

$$\frac{\text{Dollar price}}{\text{of BMW}} = \frac{\text{euro price}}{\text{of BMW}} \times \frac{\text{dollar price}}{\text{of euro}}$$

Suppose the BMW company is prepared to sell a BMW for 100,000 euros and that the current exchange rate is 2 euros = \$1. At these rates, a BMW will cost you

$$\frac{\text{Dollar price}}{\text{of BMW}} = 100{,}000 \text{ euros} \times \frac{\$1}{2 \text{ euros}}$$

$$= \$50{,}000$$

If you're willing to pay this much for a shiny new BMW, you may do so at current exchange rates.

Now suppose the exchange rate changes from 2 euros = \$1 to 1 euro = \$1. *A higher dollar price for euros will raise the dollar costs of European goods.* In this case, the dollar price of a euro increases from \$0.50 to \$1. At this new exchange rate, the BMW plant in Germany is still willing to sell BMWs at 100,000 euros apiece. And German consumers continue to buy BMWs at that price. But this constant euro price now translates into a higher *dollar* price. Thus a BMW now costs you \$100,000.

As the dollar price of a BMW rises, the number of BMWs sold in the United States will decline. As BMW sales decline, the quantity of euros demanded may decline as well. Thus, the quantity of foreign currency demanded declines when the exchange rate rises because foreign goods become more expensive and imports decline.[1] When the dollar price of European currencies actually increased in 1992, BMW decided to start producing cars in South Carolina. A year later Mercedes-Benz decided to produce cars in the United States as well. Sales of American-made BMWs and Mercedes no longer depend on the exchange rate of the U.S. dollars.

The Supply Curve. These market responses suggest that the supply of dollars is upward-sloping. If the value of the dollar rises, Americans will be able to buy more euros. As a result, the dollar price of imported BMWs will decline. American consumers will respond by demanding more imports, thereby supplying a larger quantity of dollars. The supply curve in Figure 21.1 shows how the quantity of dollars supplied rises as the value of the dollar increases.

The Demand Curve. The demand for dollars can be explained in similar terms. Remember that the demand for dollars arises from the foreign demand for U.S. exports and investments. If the exchange rate moves from 2 euros = \$1 to 1 euro = \$1, the euro price of dollars falls. As dollars become cheaper for Germans, all American exports effectively fall in price. Germans will buy more American products (including trips to Disney World) and therefore demand a greater quantity of dollars. In addition, foreign investors will perceive in a cheaper dollar the opportunity to buy U.S. stocks, businesses, and property at fire-sale prices. Accordingly, they join foreign consumers in demanding more dollars. Not all these behavioral responses will occur overnight, but they're reasonably predictable over a brief period of time.

The Value of the Dollar

What's a euro? Read more about the European currency at www.europe-euro.com.

---

[1] The extent to which imports decline as the cost of foreign currency rises depends on the *price elasticity of demand.*

FIGURE 21.1

The Foreign-Exchange Market

The foreign-exchange market operates like other markets. In this case, the "good" bought and sold is dollars (foreign exchange). The price and quantity of dollars actually exchanged are determined by the intersection of market supply and demand.

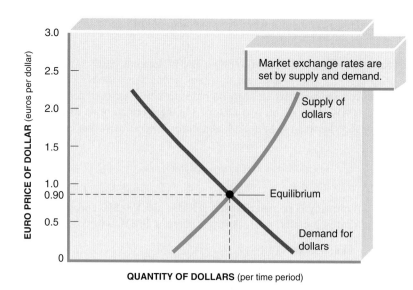

Equilibrium

equilibrium price: The price at which the quantity of a good demanded in a given time period equals the quantity supplied.

Given market demand and supply curves, we can predict the **equilibrium price** of any commodity, that is, the price at which the quantity demanded will equal the quantity supplied. This occurs in Figure 21.1 where the two curves cross. At that equilibrium, the value of the dollar (the exchange rate) is established. In this case, the euro price of the dollar turns out to be 0.90.

The value of the dollar can also be expressed in terms of other currencies. The World View below displays a sampling of dollar exchange rates in August 2004.

WORLD VIEW

Foreign-Exchange Rates

The foreign exchange mid-range rates below apply to trading among banks in amounts of $1 million and more, as quoted at 4 P.M. Eastern time by Reuters and other sources. Retail transactions provide fewer units of foreign currency per dollar.

Country	U.S. Dollar per Unit (dollar price of foreign currency)	Currency per U.S. Dollar (foreign price of U.S. dollar)
Brazil (real)	0.3292	3.0377
Britain (pound)	1.8211	0.5491
Canada (dollar)	0.7523	1.3293
China (renminbi)	0.1208	8.2781
Indonesia (rupiah)	0.0001	9,141.00
Japan (yen)	0.0090	111.20
Mexico (peso)	0.0876	11.4155
Russia (ruble)	0.0344	29.104
Euroland (euro)	1.2024	0.8317

Source: *The Wall Street Journal,* August 2, 2004. Reprinted by permission of *The Wall Street Journal,* © 2004 Dow Jones & Company, Inc. All rights reserved worldwide. www.wsj.com

Analysis: The exchange rates between currencies are determined by supply and demand in foreign-exchange markets. The rates reported here represent the equilibrium exchange rates on a particular day.

(Notice how many Indonesian rupiah you could buy for $1.) The *average* value of the dollar is a weighted mean of the exchange rates between the U.S. dollar and all these currencies. The value of the dollar is "high" when its foreign-exchange price is above recent levels, "low" when it is below recent averages.

The equilibrium depicted in Figure 21.1 determines not only the *price* of the dollar but also a specific *quantity* of international transactions. Those transactions include the exports, imports, international investments, and other sources of dollar supply and demand. A summary of all those international money flows is contained in the **balance of payments**—an accounting statement of all international money flows in a given period of time.

Trade Balance. Table 21.1 depicts the U.S. balance of payments for 2003. Notice first how the millions of separate transactions are classified into a few summary measures. The trade balance is the difference between exports and imports of goods (merchandise) and services. In 2003, the United States imported over $1.5 trillion of goods and services but exported only $1 trillion. This created a **trade deficit** of $498 billion. That trade deficit represents a net outflow of dollars to the rest of the world.

$$\text{Trade balance} = \text{exports} - \text{imports}$$

The excess supply of dollars created by the trade gap widened further by other net outflows. U.S. government grants to foreign nations (line 7 in Table 21.1) contributed $94 billion to the net *supply* of dollars.

Current-Account Balance. The current-account balance is a subtotal in Table 21.1. It includes the merchandise, services, and investment balances as well as government grants and private transfers such as wages sent home by foreign citizens working in the United States.

$$\frac{\text{Current-account}}{\text{balance}} = \frac{\text{trade}}{\text{balance}} + \frac{\text{unilateral}}{\text{transfers}}$$

The current-account balance is the most comprehensive summary of our trade relations. As indicated in Table 21.1, the United States had a current-account deficit of $530 billion in 2003.

The Balance of Payments

balance of payments: A summary record of a country's international economic transactions in a given period of time.

trade deficit: The amount by which the value of imports exceeds the value of exports in a given time period.

Item	Amount ($ billions)
1. Merchandise exports	$713
2. Merchandise imports	(1,261)
3. Service exports	307
4. Service imports	(256)
Trade balance (items 1–4)	−497
5. Income from U.S. overseas investments	188
6. Income outflow for foreign-owned U.S. investments	(69)
7. Net U.S. government grants	(94)
8. Net private transfers and pensions	(57)
Current-account balance (items 1–8)	−530
9. U.S. capital inflow	581
10. U.S. capital outflow	(285)
11. Increase in U.S. official reserves	(2)
12. Increase in foreign official assets in U.S.	249
Capital-account balance (items 9–12)	547
13. Statistical discrepancy	−13
Net balance (items 1–13)	0

Source: U.S. Department of Commerce (2003 data).

TABLE 21.1
The U.S. Balance of Payments

The balance of payments is a summary statement of a country's international transactions. The major components of that activity are the trade balance (merchandise exports minus merchandise imports), the current-account balance (trade, services, and transfers), and the capital-account balance. The net total of these balances must equal zero, since the quantity of dollars paid must equal the quantity received.

The latest statistics on the balance of payments are available from the Bureau of Economic Analysis at www.bea.doc.gov.

Capital-Account Balance. The current-account deficit is offset by the capital-account surplus. The capital-account balance takes into consideration assets bought and sold across international borders; that is,

$$\text{Capital-account balance} = \text{foreign purchases of U.S. assets} - \text{U.S. purchases of foreign assets}$$

As Table 21.1 shows, foreign consumers demanded $581 billion worth of dollars in 2003 to buy farms and factories as well as U.S. bonds, stocks, and other investments (item 9). This exceeded the flow of U.S. dollars going overseas to purchase foreign assets (item 10). In addition, the United States and foreign governments bought and sold dollars, creating an additional outflow of dollars (items 11 and 12).

The net capital inflows were essential in financing the U.S. trade deficit (negative trade balance). As in any market, the number of dollars demanded must equal the number of dollars supplied. Thus, ***the capital-account surplus must equal the current-account deficit.*** In other words, there can't be any dollars left lying around unaccounted for. Item 13 in Table 21.1 reminds us that our accounting system isn't perfect—that we can't identify every transaction. Nevertheless, all the accounts must eventually "balance out":

$$\text{Net balance of payments} = \text{current-account balance} + \text{capital-account balance} = 0$$

That's the character of a market *equilibrium:* The quantity of dollars demanded equals the quantity of dollars supplied.

MARKET DYNAMICS

The interesting thing about markets isn't their character in equilibrium but the fact that prices and quantities are always changing in response to shifts in demand and supply. The U.S. demand for BMWs shifted overnight when Japan introduced a new line of sleek, competitively priced cars (e.g., Lexus). The reduced demand for BMWs shifted the supply of dollars leftward. That supply shift raised the value of the dollar vis-á-vis the euro, as illustrated in Figure 21.2. (It also increased the demand for Japanese yen, causing the yen value of the dollar to *fall.*)

Depreciation and Appreciation

depreciation (currency): A fall in the price of one currency relative to another.

appreciation: A rise in the price of one currency relative to another.

Exchange-rate changes have their own terminology. **Depreciation** of a currency occurs when one currency becomes cheaper in terms of another currency. In our earlier discussion of exchange rates, for example, we assumed that the exchange rate between euros and dollars changed from 2 euros = $1 to 1 euro = $1, making the euro price of a dollar cheaper. In this case, the dollar *depreciated* with respect to the euro.

The other side of depreciation is **appreciation,** an increase in value of one currency as expressed in another country's currency. ***Whenever one currency depreciates, another currency must appreciate.*** When the exchange rate changed from 2 euros = $1 to 1 euro = $1, not only did the euro price of a dollar fall, but also the dollar price of a euro rose. Hence, the euro appreciated as the dollar depreciated.

Figure 21.3 illustrates actual changes in the exchange rate of the U.S. dollar since 1980. The trade-adjusted value of the U.S. dollar is the (weighted) average of all exchange rates for the dollar. Between 1980 and 1985, the U.S. dollar appreciated over 80 percent. This appreciation greatly reduced the price of imports and thus increased their quantity. At the same time, the dollar appreciation raised the foreign price of U.S. exports and so reduced their volume. U.S. farmers, aircraft manufacturers, and tourist services suffered huge sales losses. The trade deficit ballooned.

The value of the dollar reversed course after 1985. This brief dollar depreciation set in motion forces that reduced the trade deficit in the late 1980s. Then the dollar

How much are 100 Japanese yen worth in U.S. dollars? Find out at the currency converter at www.oanda.com/site/cc_index.shtml.

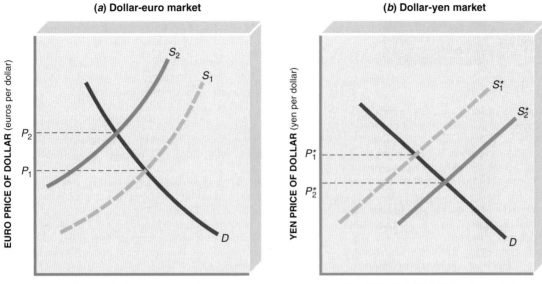

(a) Dollar-euro market   (b) Dollar-yen market

QUANTITY OF DOLLARS (per time period)   QUANTITY OF DOLLARS (per time period)

FIGURE 21.2
Shifts in Foreign-Exchange Markets

When the Japanese introduced luxury autos into the United States, the American demand for German cars fell. As a consequence, the supply of dollars in the dollar-euro market (part *a*) shifted to the left and the euro value of the dollar rose. At the same time, the increased American demand for Japanese cars shifted the dollar supply curve in the yen market (part *b*) to the right, reducing the yen price of the dollar.

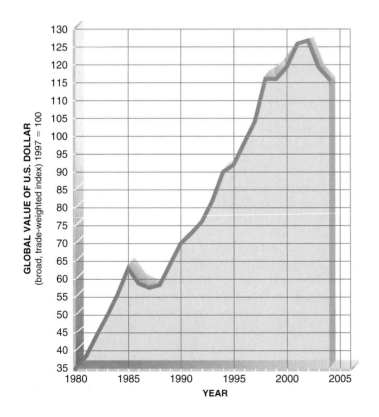

YEAR

FIGURE 21.3
Changing Values of U.S. Dollar

Since 1973, exchange rates have been flexible. As a result, the value of the U.S. dollar has fluctuated with international differences in inflation, interest rates, and economic growth. U.S. economic stability has given the U.S. dollar increasing value over time.

Weak Dollar Helps U.S. Firms

The dollar's precipitous decline against European currencies has brought overseas customers to Al Lubrano's small Rhode Island manufacturing firm that he hasn't heard from in five years.

Gerry Letendre's manufacturing plant in New Hampshire just hired five employees to keep up with growing European demand, two and a half years after Letendre laid off a quarter of his work force.

The dollar's slide has made U.S. goods far cheaper for European consumers, and European exports considerably more expensive here. Letendre's Diamond Casting and Machine Co. in Hollis, N.H., has already boosted shipments of its circuit board printing equipment and industrial valves to Europe by 30 percent. Lubrano, president of Technical Materials Inc., in Lincoln, R.I., said his export business should jump as much as 25 percent this year.

"On balance, the weak dollar has been tremendous for us," Lubrano said.

—Jonathan Weisman

Source: *The Washington Post,* January 26, 2004. © 2004 The Washington Post. Reprinted with permission.

Dollar's Fall Puts Big Crimp in European Tourism

ROME—As the euro continues to strengthen against the battered U.S. dollar, tourists, businesses and Americans living abroad complain that Europe is pricing itself out of the market.

"It has become so expensive it almost makes me ill," says Nancy Oliveira, 55, an American living in Rome on what she says was once a "comfortable fixed income." . . .

The Italian National Tourist office reports a 15% decline in the number of Americans visiting from 2000 to 2002. . . .

Companies that rely on tourists and visitors estimate business is down 20% to 30%. . . .

Sales at Florence Moon, a leather store in Rome that caters primarily to Americans, are down 50%, says Farshad Shahabadi, whose family owns the store. "If it's bad for us, then it must be bad for everyone else, too," Shahabadi says.

—Ellen Hale

Source: *USA Today,* February 20, 2004. USA TODAY. Copyright 2004. Reprinted with permission. www.usatoday.com.

Analysis: Depreciation of a nation's currency is good for that nation's exporters but bad for that nation's importers (including its tourists).

---

started appreciating again, slowing export growth and increasing imports throughout the 1990s. After a long steep appreciation, the dollar started losing value in 2003. This was good for U.S. exporters, but bad for U.S. tourists (see World View).

Market Forces

Exchange rates change for the same reasons that any market price changes: The underlying supply or demand (or both) has shifted. Among the more important sources of such shifts are

- *Relative income changes.* If incomes are increasing faster in country A than in country B, consumers in A will tend to spend more, thus increasing the demand for B's exports and currency. B's currency will appreciate.
- *Relative price changes.* If domestic prices are rising rapidly in country A, consumers will seek out lower-priced imports. The demand for B's exports and currency will increase. B's currency will appreciate.
- *Changes in product availability.* If country A experiences a disastrous wheat crop failure, it will have to increase its food imports. B's currency will appreciate.
- *Relative interest rate changes.* If interest rates rise in country A, people in country B will want to move their deposits to A. Demand for A's currency will rise and it will appreciate.
- *Speculation.* If speculators anticipate an increase in the price of A's currency, for the preceding reasons or any other, they'll begin buying it, thus pushing its price up. A's currency will appreciate.

foreign-exchange markets: Places where foreign currencies are bought and sold.

All these various changes are taking place every minute of every day, thus keeping **foreign-exchange markets** active. On an average day, over *$1 trillion* of foreign

Money Crisis Pulling Asian Students Home

The financial tsunami that swamped Asian economies in the last few months is sloshing back across the Pacific toward American colleges and universities, where thousands of Asian students are suddenly short of dollars.

Since last July, the Indonesian currency, the rupiah, has lost 80 percent of its value as measured against the U.S. dollar. A half-dozen Asian currencies have lost about half their value against the dollar.

That means, for example, that what would have been $20,000 in Korean money (the won) a year ago is now worth only $10,000. Consequently, Korean and Indonesian students—

plus Malaysians, Thais, Singaporeans and Japanese—are struggling to pay their tuition bills. Some can't—so they're going home.

There are about 458,000 foreign students in the USA—about 3 percent of total higher education enrollment, according to the Institute of International Education, a non-profit cultural exchange organization that conducts an annual census of foreign students. About 57 percent of the students are Asians.

Source: *USA Today*, February 18, 1998. USA TODAY. Copyright 1998. Reprinted with permission. www.usatoday.com

Analysis: When the foreign price of the U.S. dollar rises (dollar appreciation), American exports (including educational services) become more expensive, which causes a decline in enrollments (quantity demanded).

---

exchange is bought and sold in the market. Significant changes occur in currency values, however, only when several of these forces move in the same direction at the same time. This is what caused the Asian crisis of 1997–98.

In July 1997, the Thai government decided the baht was overvalued and let market forces find a new equilibrium. Within days, the dollar prices of the baht plunged 25 percent. This sharp decline in the value of the Thai baht simultaneously increased the Thai price of the U.S. dollar. As a consequence, Thais could no longer afford to buy as many American products.

The devaluation of the baht had a domino effect on other Asian currencies. The plunge in the baht shook confidence in the Malaysian ringget, the Indonesian rupiah, and even the Korean won. People wanted to hold "hard" currencies like the U.S. dollar. As people rushed to buy U.S. dollars with their local currencies, the value of those currencies plunged. At one point the Indonesian rupiah had lost 80 percent of its dollar value, making U.S. exports five times more expensive for Indonesians. As a result, Indonesians could no longer afford to buy imported rice, machinery, cars, or pork. Indonesian students attending U.S. colleges could no longer afford to pay tuition (see World View). The sudden surge in prices and scarcity of goods led to street demonstrations and a change in government. Similar problems erupted throughout Southeast Asia.

The "Asian contagion" unfortunately wasn't confined to that area of the world. Hog farmers in the United States saw foreign demand for their pork evaporate. Koreans stopped taking vacations in Hawaii. Thai Airways canceled orders for Boeing jets. And Japanese consumers bought fewer Washington state apples and California oranges. This loss of export markets slowed economic growth in the United States, Europe, Japan, and other nations.

The Asian Crisis of 1997–98

Check out the latest exchange rates for the euro and the baht at www.x-rates.com.

RESISTANCE TO EXCHANGE-RATE CHANGES

Given the scope and depth of the Asian crisis of 1997–98, it's easy to understand why people crave *stable* exchange rates. The resistance to exchange-rate fluctuations originates in various micro- and macroeconomic interests.

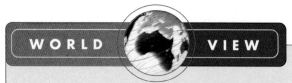

Nobel Prize Was Nobler in October

STOCKHOLM—Winners of the four Nobel science awards said yesterday that the honor is more important than the money, so it does not matter much that each award has lost $242,000 in value since October.

"If we had been more intelligent, we would have done some hedging," said Gary S. Becker, 61, a University of Chicago professor and a Nobel economics laureate. Sweden's decision last month to let the krona float caused the prizes' value to drop from $1.2 million each when announced in October to $958,000 when King Carl XVI Gustaf presents them Thursday.

The recipients are Becker; American Rudolph A. Marcus, the chemistry laureate; Frenchman Georges Charpak, the physics laureate; and medicine prize winners Edmond Fischer and Edwin Krebs of the University of Washington in Seattle.

—Associated Press

Source: *Boston Globe,* December 8, 1992. Reprinted with permission of The Associated Press. www.ap.org.

Analysis: Currency depreciation reduces the external value of domestic income and assets. The dollar value of the Nobel Prize fell when the Swedish krona depreciated.

Micro Interests

The microeconomic resistance to changes in the value of the dollar arises from two concerns. First, people who trade or invest in world markets want a solid basis for forecasting future costs, prices, and profits. Forecasts are always uncertain, but they're even less dependable when the value of money is subject to change. An American firm that invests $2 million in a ski factory in Sweden expects not only to make a profit on the production there but also to return that profit to the United States. If the Swedish krona depreciates sharply in the interim, however, the profits amassed in Sweden may dwindle to a mere trickle, or even a loss, when the kronor are exchanged back into dollars. Even the Nobel Prize loses a bit of its luster when the krona depreciates (see World View). From this view, the uncertainty associated with fluctuating exchange rates is an unwanted burden.

Even when the direction of an exchange rate move is certain, those who stand to lose from the change are prone to resist. ***A change in the price of a country's money automatically alters the price of all its exports and imports.*** When the Russian ruble and Japanese yen depreciated in 2000–2001, for example, the dollar price of Russian and Japanese steel declined as well. This prompted U.S. steelmakers to accuse Russia and Japan of "dumping" steel. Steel companies and unions appealed to Washington to protect their sales and jobs.

Even in the country whose currency becomes cheaper, there'll be opposition to exchange-rate movements. When the U.S. dollar appreciates, Americans buy more foreign products. This increased U.S. demand for imports may drive up prices in other countries. In addition, foreign firms may take advantage of the reduced American competition by raising their prices. In either case, some inflation will result. The consumer's insistence that the government "do something" about rising prices may turn into a political force for "correcting" foreign-exchange rates.

Macro Interests

Any microeconomic problem that becomes widespread enough can turn into a macroeconomic problem. The huge U.S. trade deficits of the 1980s effectively exported jobs to foreign nations. Although the U.S. economy expanded rapidly in 1983–85, the unemployment rate stayed high, partly because American consumers were spending more of their income on imports. Yet fear of renewed inflation precluded more stimulative fiscal and monetary policies.

The U.S. trade deficits of the 1980s were offset by huge capital-account surpluses. Foreign investors sought to participate in the U.S. economic expansion by buying land, plant, and equipment and by lending money in U.S. financial markets. These capital inflows complicated monetary policy, however, and greatly increased U.S. foreign debt and interest costs.

U.S. a Net Debtor

The inflow of foreign investment also raised anxieties about "selling off" America. As Japanese and other foreign investors increased their purchases of farmland, factories, and real estate (e.g., Rockefeller Center), many Americans worried that foreign investors were taking control of the U.S. economy.

Fueling these fears was the dramatic change in America's international financial position. From 1914 to 1984, the United States had been a net creditor in the world economy. We owned more assets abroad than foreign investors owned in the United States. Our financial position changed in 1985. Continuing trade deficits and offsetting capital inflows transformed the United States into a net debtor in that year. Since then, foreigners have owned more U.S. assets than Americans own of foreign assets.

America's new debtor status can complicate domestic policy. A sudden flight from U.S. assets could severely weaken the dollar and disrupt the domestic economy. To prevent that from occurring, policymakers must consider the impact of their decisions on foreign investors. This may necessitate difficult policy choices.

There's a silver lining to this cloud, however. The inflow of foreign investment is a reflection of confidence in the U.S. economy. Foreign investors want to share in our growth and profitability. In the process, their investments (like BMW's auto plant) expand America's production possibilities and stimulate still more economic growth.

Foreign investors actually assume substantial risk when they invest in the United States. If the dollar falls, the foreign value of their U.S. investments will decline. Hence, foreigners who've already invested in the United States have no incentive to start a flight from the dollar. On the contrary, a strong dollar protects the value of their U.S. holdings.

EXCHANGE-RATE INTERVENTION

Given the potential opposition to exchange-rate movements, governments often feel compelled to intervene in foreign-exchange markets. The intervention is usually intended to achieve greater exchange-rate stability. But such stability may itself give rise to undesirable micro- and macroeconomic effects.

Fixed Exchange Rates

One way to eliminate fluctuations in exchange rates is to fix the rate's value. To fix exchange rates, each country may simply proclaim that its currency is worth so much in relation to that of other countries. The easiest way to do this is for each country to define the worth of its currency in terms of some common standard. Under a **gold standard,** each country determines that its currency is worth so much gold. In so doing, it implicitly defines the worth of its currency in terms of all other currencies, which also have a fixed gold value. In 1944, the major trading nations met at Bretton Woods, New Hampshire, and agreed that each currency was worth so much gold. The value of the U.S. dollar was defined as being equal to 0.0294 ounce of gold, while the British pound was defined as being worth 0.0823 ounce of gold. Thus, the exchange rate between British pounds and U.S. dollars was effectively fixed at $1 = 0.357 pound, or 1 pound = $2.80 (or $2.80/0.0823 = $1/0.0294).

gold standard: An agreement by countries to fix the price of their currencies in terms of gold; a mechanism for fixing exchange rates.

Balance-of-Payments Problems. It's one thing to proclaim the worth of a country's currency; it's quite another to *maintain* the fixed rate of exchange. As we've observed, foreign-exchange rates are subject to continual and often unpredictable

FIGURE 21.4
Fixed Rates and Market Imbalance

If exchange rates are fixed, they can't adjust to changes in market supply and demand. Suppose the exchange rate is initially fixed at e_1. When the demand for British pounds increases (shifts to the right), an excess demand for pounds emerges. More pounds are demanded (q_D) at the rate e_1 than are supplied (q_S). This causes a balance-of-payments deficit for the United States.

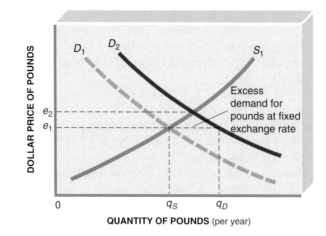

QUANTITY OF POUNDS (per year)

changes in supply and demand. Hence, two countries that seek to stabilize their exchange rate at some fixed value are going to find it necessary to compensate for such foreign-exchange market pressures.

Suppose the exchange rate officially established by the United States and Great Britain is equal to e_1, as illustrated in Figure 21.4. As is apparent, that particular exchange rate is consistent with the then-prevailing demand and supply conditions in the foreign-exchange market (as indicated by curves D_1 and S_1).

Now suppose that Americans suddenly acquire a greater taste for British cars and start spending more income on Jaguars and the like. Although Ford Motor owns Jaguar, the cars are still produced in Great Britain. Hence, as U.S. purchases of British goods increase, the demand for British currency will *shift* from D_1 to D_2 in Figure 21.4. Were exchange rates allowed to respond to market influences, the dollar price of a British pound would rise, in this case to the rate e_2. But we've assumed that government intervention has fixed the exchange rate at e_1. Unfortunately, at e_1, American consumers want to buy more pounds (q_D) than the British are willing to supply (q_s). The difference between the quantity demanded and the quantity supplied in the market at the rate e_1 represents a **market shortage** of British pounds.

The excess demand for pounds implies a **balance-of-payments deficit** for the United States: More dollars are flowing out of the country than into it. The same disequilibrium represents a **balance-of-payments surplus** for Britain, because its outward flow of pounds is less than its incoming flow.

Basically, there are only two solutions to balance-of-payments problems brought about by the attempt to fix exchange rates:

- Allow exchange rates to rise to e_2 (Figure 21.4), thereby eliminating the excess demand for pounds.
- Alter market supply or demand so that they intersect at the fixed rate e_1.

Since fixed exchange rates were the initial objective of policy, only the second alternative is of immediate interest.

The Need for Reserves. One way to alter market conditions would be for someone simply to supply British pounds to American consumers. The U.S. Treasury could have accumulated a reserve of foreign exchange in earlier periods. By selling some of those **foreign-exchange reserves** now, the Treasury could help to stabilize market conditions at the officially established exchange rate. The rightward shift of the pound supply curve in Figure 21.5 illustrates the sale of accumulated British pounds—and related purchase of U.S. dollars—by the U.S. Treasury. (In 2003, the U.S. Treasury increased foreign-exchange reserves by $2 billion; see item 12 in Table 21.1.)

market shortage: The amount by which the quantity demanded exceeds the quantity supplied at a given price; excess demand.

balance-of-payments deficit: An excess demand for foreign currency at current exchange rates.

balance-of-payments surplus: An excess demand for domestic currency at current exchange rates.

foreign-exchange reserves: Holdings of foreign exchange by official government agencies, usually the central bank or treasury.

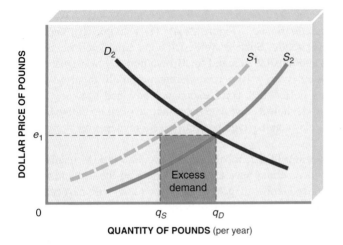

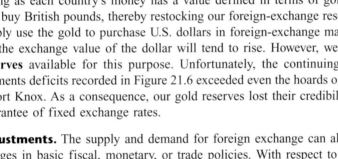

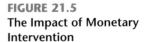
FIGURE 21.5
The Impact of Monetary Intervention

If the U.S. Treasury holds reserves of British pounds, it can use them to buy U.S. dollars in foreign-exchange markets. As it does so, the supply of pounds will shift to the right, to S_2, thereby maintaining the desired exchange rate, e_1. The Bank of England could bring about the same result by offering to buy U.S. dollars with pounds.

Although foreign-exchange reserves can be used to fix exchange rates, such reserves may not be adequate. Indeed, Figure 21.6 should be testimony enough to the fact that today's deficit isn't always offset by tomorrow's surplus. A principal reason that fixed exchange rates didn't live up to their expectations is that the United States had balance-of-payments deficits for 22 consecutive years. This long-term deficit overwhelmed our stock of foreign-exchange reserves.

The Role of Gold. Gold reserves are a potential substitute for foreign-exchange reserves. As long as each country's money has a value defined in terms of gold, we can use gold to buy British pounds, thereby restocking our foreign-exchange reserves. Or we can simply use the gold to purchase U.S. dollars in foreign-exchange markets. In either case, the exchange value of the dollar will tend to rise. However, we must have **gold reserves** available for this purpose. Unfortunately, the continuing U.S. balance-of-payments deficits recorded in Figure 21.6 exceeded even the hoards of gold buried under Fort Knox. As a consequence, our gold reserves lost their credibility as a potential guarantee of fixed exchange rates.

Domestic Adjustments. The supply and demand for foreign exchange can also be shifted by changes in basic fiscal, monetary, or trade policies. With respect to trade

gold reserves: Stocks of gold held by a government to purchase foreign exchange.

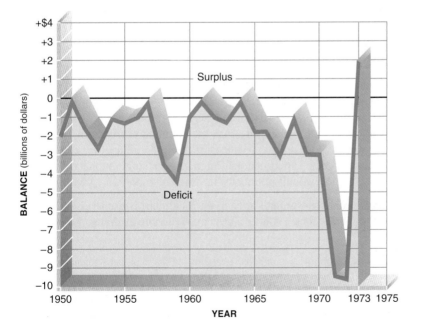

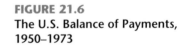
FIGURE 21.6
The U.S. Balance of Payments, 1950–1973

The United States had a balance-of-payments deficit for 22 consecutive years. During this period, the foreign-exchange reserves of the U.S. Treasury were sharply reduced. Fixed exchange rates were maintained by the willingness of foreign countries to accumulate large reserves of U.S. dollars. However, neither the Treasury's reserves nor the willingness of foreigners to accumulate dollars was unlimited. In 1973, fixed exchange rates were abandoned.

policy, *trade protection can be used to prop up fixed exchange rates.* We could eliminate the excess demand for pounds (Figure 21.4), for example, by imposing quotas and tariffs on British goods. Such trade restrictions would reduce British imports to the United States and thus the demand for British pounds. In August 1971, President Nixon imposed an emergency 10 percent surcharge on all imported goods to help reduce the payments deficit that fixed exchange rates had spawned. Such restrictions on international trade, however, violate the principle of comparative advantage and thus reduce total world output. Trade protection also invites retaliatory trade restrictions.

Fiscal policy is another way out of the imbalance. An increase in U.S. income tax rates will reduce disposable income and have a negative effect on the demand for all goods, including imports. A reduction in government spending will have similar effects. In general, *deflationary (or restrictive) policies help correct a balance-of-payments deficit by lowering domestic incomes and thus the demand for imports.*

Monetary policies in a deficit country could follow the same restrictive course. A reduction in the money supply will tend to raise interest rates. The balance of payments will benefit in two ways. The resultant slowdown in spending will reduce import demand. In addition, higher interest rates may induce international investors to move some of their funds into the deficit country. Such moves will provide immediate relief to the payments imbalance.[2] Russia tried this strategy in 1998, tripling key interest rates (to as much as 150 percent). But even that wasn't enough to restore confidence in the ruble, which kept depreciating. Within three months of the monetary policy tightening, the ruble lost half its value.

A surplus country could help solve the balance-of-payments problem. By pursuing expansionary—even inflationary—fiscal and monetary policies, a surplus country could stimulate the demand for imports. Moreover, any inflation at home will reduce the competitiveness of exports, thereby helping to restrain the inflow of foreign demand. Taken together, such efforts would help reverse an international payments imbalance.

Even under the best of circumstances, domestic economic adjustments entail significant costs. In effect, *domestic adjustments to payments imbalances require a deficit country to forsake full employment and a surplus country to forsake price stability.* China has had to grapple with these domestic consequences of fixing the value of its currency. The artificially low value of the yuan has promoted Chinese exports and accelerated China's GDP growth. It has also caused prices in China to rise faster than the government desires, however. To maintain the yuan's fixed exchange rate, the Chinese government began introducing restrictive monetary and fiscal policies in 2003–4. There's no easy way out of this impasse. Market imbalances caused by fixed exchange rates can be corrected only with abundant supplies of foreign-exchange reserves or deliberate changes in fiscal, monetary, or trade policies.

The Euro Fix. As noted earlier in the chapter, the original 12 nations of the European Monetary Union (EMU) did fix their exchange rates in 1999. They went far beyond the kind of exchange-rate fix we're discussing here. Members of the EMU *eliminated* their national currencies, making the euro the common currency of Euroland. They don't have to worry about reserve balances or domestic adjustments. However, they do have to reconcile their varied national interests to a single monetary authority, which may prove to be difficult politically in times of economic stress.

Flexible Exchange Rates

Balance-of-payments problems wouldn't arise in the first place if exchange rates were allowed to respond to market forces. Under a system of **flexible exchange rates** (often

---

[2]Before 1930, not only were foreign-exchange rates fixed, but domestic monetary supplies were tied to gold stocks as well. Countries experiencing a balance-of-payments deficit were thus forced to contract their money supply, and countries experiencing a payments surplus were forced to expand their money supply by a set amount. Monetary authorities were powerless to control domestic money supplies except by erecting barriers to trade. The system was abandoned when the world economy collapsed into the Great Depression.

called floating exchange rates), the exchange rate moves up or down to choke off any excess supply of or demand for foreign exchange. Notice again in Figure 21.4 that the exchange-rate move from e_1 to e_2 prevents any excess demand from emerging. ***With flexible exchange rates, the quantity of foreign exchange demanded always equals the quantity supplied,*** and there's no imbalance. For the same reason, there's no need for foreign-exchange reserves.

flexible exchange rates: A system in which exchange rates are permitted to vary with market supply-and-demand conditions; floating exchange rates.

Although flexible exchange rates eliminate balance-of-payments and foreign-exchange reserves problems, they don't solve all of a country's international trade problems. ***Exchange-rate movements associated with flexible rates alter relative prices and may disrupt import and export flows.*** As noted before, depreciation of the dollar raises the price of all imported goods. The price increases may contribute to domestic cost-push inflation. Also, domestic businesses that sell imported goods or use them as production inputs may suffer sales losses. On the other hand, appreciation of the dollar raises the foreign price of U.S. goods and reduces the sales of American exporters. Hence, ***someone is always hurt, and others are helped, by exchange-rate movements.*** The resistance to flexible exchange rates originates in these potential losses. Such resistance creates pressure for official intervention in foreign-exchange markets or increased trade barriers.

The United States and its major trading partners abandoned fixed exchange rates in 1973. Although exchange rates are now able to fluctuate freely, it shouldn't be assumed that they necessarily undergo wild gyrations. On the contrary, experience with flexible rates since 1973 suggests that some semblance of stability is possible even when exchange rates are free to change in response to market forces.

Speculation. One force that often helps maintain stability in a flexible exchange-rate system is speculation. Speculators often counteract short-term changes in foreign-exchange supply and demand. If an exchange rate temporarily rises above its long-term equilibrium, speculators will move in to sell foreign exchange. By selling at high prices and later buying at lower prices, speculators hope to make a profit. In the process, they also help stabilize foreign-exchange rates.

Speculation isn't always stabilizing, however. Speculators may not correctly gauge the long-term equilibrium. Instead, they may move "with the market" and help push exchange rates far out of kilter. This kind of destabilizing speculation sharply lowered the international value of the U.S. dollar in 1987, forcing the Reagan administration to intervene in foreign-exchange markets, borrowing foreign currencies to buy U.S. dollars. In 1997, the Clinton administration intervened for the opposite purpose: stemming the rise in the

"Damn it! How can I relax, knowing that out there, somewhere, somehow, someone's attacking the dollar?"

Analysis: A "weak" dollar reduces the buying power of American tourists.

U.S. dollar. the Bush administration has been more willing to stay on the sidelines, letting global markets set the exchange rates for the U.S. dollar.

Managed Exchange Rates. Governments can intervene in foreign-exchange markets without completely fixing exchange rates. That is, they may buy and sell foreign exchange for the purpose of *narrowing* rather than *eliminating* exchange-rate movements. Such limited intervention in foreign-exchange markets is often referred to as **managed exchange rates,** or, popularly, "dirty floats."

> **managed exchange rates:** A system in which governments intervene in foreign-exchange markets to limit but not eliminate exchange-rate fluctuations; "dirty floats."

The basic objective of exchange-rate management is to provide a stabilizing force. The U.S. Treasury, for example, may use its foreign-exchange reserves to buy dollars when they're depreciating too much. Or it will buy foreign exchange if the dollar is rising too fast. From this perspective, exchange-rate management appears as a fail-safe system for the private market. Unfortunately, the motivation for official intervention is sometimes suspect. Private speculators buy and sell foreign exchange for the sole purpose of making a profit. But government sales and purchases may be motivated by other considerations. A falling exchange rate increases the competitive advantage of a country's exports. A rising exchange rate makes international investment less expensive. Hence, a country's efforts to manage exchange-rate movements may arouse suspicion and outright hostility in its trading partners.

Although managed exchange rates would seem to be an ideal compromise between fixed rates and flexible rates, they can work only when some acceptable "rules of the game" and mutual trust have been established. As Sherman Maisel, a former governor of the Federal Reserve Board, put it, "Monetary systems are based on credit and faith: If these are lacking, a . . . crisis occurs."[3]

THE ECONOMY TOMORROW

Currency Bailouts

The world has witnessed a string of currency crises, including the one in Asia during 1997–98, the Brazilian crisis of 1999, the Argentine crisis of 2001–2, recurrent ruble crises in Russia, and periodic panics in Mexico and South America. In every instance, the country in trouble pleads for external help. In most cases, a currency "bailout" is arranged, whereby global monetary authorities lend the troubled nation enough reserves (such as U.S. dollars) to defend its currency. Typically, the International Monetary Fund (IMF) heads the rescue party, joined by the central banks of the strongest economies.

The Case for Bailouts

> **devaluation:** An abrupt depreciation of a currency whose value was fixed or managed by the government.

The argument for currency bailouts typically rests on the domino theory. Weakness in one currency can undermine another. This seemed to be the case during the 1997–98 Asian crisis. After the **devaluation** of the Thai baht, global investors began worrying about currency values in other Asian nations. Choosing to be safe rather than sorry, they moved funds out of Korea, Malaysia, and the Philippines and invested in U.S. and European markets (notice in Figure 21.3 the 1997–98 appreciation of the U.S. dollar).

The initial baht devaluation also weakened the competitive trade position of these same economies. Thai exports became cheaper, diverting export demand from other Asian nations. To prevent loss of export markets, Thailand's neighbors felt they had to devalue as well. Speculators who foresaw these effects accelerated the domino effect by selling the region's currencies.

When Brazil devalued its currency (the *real*) in January 1999, global investors worried that a "samba effect" might sweep across Latin American (see World View). The domino effect could reach across the ocean and damage U.S. and European exports as well. Hence, the industrial countries often offer a currency bailout as a form of self-defense.

[3]Sherman Maisel, *Managing the Dollar* (New York: W. W. Norton, 1973), p. 196.

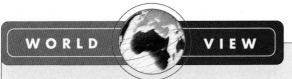
WORLD VIEW

Brazil's Ills Distress Continent
Money Crisis Shakes Investors' Confidence

BUENOS AIRES—Fallout from the continuing currency crisis in Brazil has sparked the most serious financial turmoil in Latin America since the Mexican peso crisis of four years ago, scaring away foreign investors and undermining growth after years of rapid gains.

In the days since Brazil, Latin America's largest nation, devalued its currency on January 12, a number of leading economists have scaled back their forecasts for Latin American growth, predicting it will be flat or negative for the first half of 1999.

The "samba effect," as Brazil's impact on its neighbors is called, is exacerbating regional unemployment rates and sending already high interest rates climbing. Even more significantly, perhaps, it is eroding foreign investment and confidence in the region amid fears that Brazil may default on its foreign debt despite government promises to the contrary.

To encourage investors to keep their money in Brazil, the central bank raised interest rates to stratospheric levels, with dire consequences for Brazilian borrowers. Economists predict that the world's eighth-largest economy will contract by 6 percent this year.

With the Brazilian real's value having fallen sharply, Brazil's neighbors, especially Argentina, are now discovering that one of their biggest markets has been closed off—essentially because of the weaker real, which has raised the price of imported goods in the nation of 165 million people.

—Anthony Faiola

Source: *The Washington Post*, February 1, 1999. © 1999 *The Washington Post*. Reprinted with permission. www.washingtonpost.com

Analysis: When a nation devalues its currency, its imports become more expensive and its exports cheaper. These price changes disrupt trade flows of other nations. Devaluations also shake the confidence of global investors.

Critics of bailouts argue that such interventions are ultimately self-defeating. They say that once a country knows for sure that currency bailouts are in the wings, it doesn't have to pursue the domestic policy adjustments that might stabilize its currency. A nation can avoid politically unpopular options such as high interest rates, tax hikes, or cutbacks in government spending. It can also turn a blind eye to trade barriers, monopoly power, lax lending policies, and other constraints on productive growth. Hence, the expectation of readily available bailouts may foster the very conditions that cause currency crises.

The Case against Bailouts

The decision to bail out a depreciating currency isn't as simple as it appears. To minimize the ill effects of bailouts, the IMF and other institutions typically require the crisis nation to pledge more prudent monetary, fiscal, and trade policies. Usually there's a lot of debate about what kinds of adjustments will be made—and how soon. As long as the crisis nation is confident of an eventual bailout, however, it has a lot of bargaining power to resist policy changes. Only after the IMF finally said no to further bailouts in 2001 did Argentina devalue its currency and pursue more domestic reforms.

Future Bailouts?

SUMMARY

- Money serves the same purposes in international trade as it does in the domestic economy, namely, to facilitate productive specialization and market exchanges. The basic challenge of international finance is to create acceptable standards of value from the various currencies maintained by separate countries.

- Exchange rates are the basic mechanism for translating the value of one national currency into the equivalent value of another. An exchange rate of $1 = 2$ euros means that one dollar is worth two euros in foreign-exchange markets.

- Foreign currencies have value because they can be used to acquire goods and resources from other countries. Accordingly, the supply of and demand for foreign currency reflect the demands for imports and exports, for international investment, and for overseas activities of governments.

- The balance of payments summarizes a country's international transactions. Its components are the trade balance, the current-account balance, and the capital-account balance. The current and capital accounts must offset each other.
- The equilibrium exchange rate is subject to any and all shifts of supply and demand for foreign exchange. If relative incomes, prices, or interest rates change, the demand for foreign exchange will be affected. A depreciation is a change in market exchange rates that makes one country's currency cheaper in terms of another currency. An appreciation is the opposite kind of change.
- Changes in exchange rates are often resisted. Producers of export goods don't want their currencies to rise in value (appreciate); importers and people who travel dislike it when their currencies fall in value (depreciate).
- Under a system of fixed exchange rates, changes in the supply and demand for foreign exchange can't be expressed in exchange-rate movements. Instead, such shifts will be reflected in excess demand for or excess supply of foreign exchange. Such market imbalances are referred to as balance-of-payments deficits or surpluses.
- To maintain fixed exchange rates, monetary authorities must enter the market to buy and sell foreign exchange. In order to do so, deficit countries must have foreign-exchange reserves. In the absence of sufficient reserves, a country can maintain fixed exchange rates only if it's willing to alter basic fiscal, monetary, or trade policies.
- Flexible exchange rates eliminate balance-of-payments problems and the crises that accompany them. But complete flexibility can lead to excessive changes. To avoid this contingency, many countries prefer to adopt managed exchange rates, that is, rates determined by the market but subject to government intervention.

Key Terms

exchange rate	foreign-exchange markets	foreign-exchange reserves
equilibrium price	gold standard	gold reserves
balance of payments	market shortage	flexible exchange rates
trade deficit	balance-of-payments deficit	managed exchange rates
depreciation (currency)	balance-of-payments surplus	devaluation
appreciation		

Questions for Discussion

1. Why would a decline in the value of the dollar prompt foreign manufacturers such as BMW to build production plants in the United States?
2. How do changes in the foreign value of the U.S. dollar affect foreign enrollments at U.S. colleges? (See World View, page 445.)
3. How would rapid inflation in Canada alter our demand for travel to Canada and for Canadian imports? Does it make any difference whether the exchange rate between Canadian and U.S. dollars is fixed or flexible?
4. Under what conditions would a country welcome a balance-of-payments deficit? When would it *not* want a deficit?
5. In what sense do fixed exchange rates permit a country to "export its inflation"?
6. In the World View on p. 444, who is Farshad Shahabadi referring to as "everyone else"?
7. If a nation's currency depreciates, are the reduced export prices that result "unfair"?
8. How would each of these events affect the supply or demand for Japanese yen?
   (a) Stronger U.S. economic growth.
   (b) A decline in Japanese interest rates.
   (c) Higher inflation in the USA.
9. Is a stronger dollar good or bad for America? Explain.
10. Who will gain and who will lose if China depreciates the yuan?

ALERT!

PROBLEMS   The Student Problem Set at the back of this book contains numerical and graphing problems for this chapter.

WEB ACTIVITIES   to accompany this chapter can be found on the Online Learning Center:
http://www.mhhe.com/economics/schiller10

GLOSSARY

Note: Numbers in parentheses indicate the chapters in which the definitions appear.

absolute advantage: The ability of a country to produce a specific good with fewer resources (per unit of output) than other countries. (20)

AD excess: The amount by which aggregate demand must be reduced to achieve full-employment equilibrium after allowing for price-level changes. (11)

AD shortfall: The amount of additional aggregate demand needed to achieve full employment after allowing for price-level changes. (11)

adjustable-rate mortgage (ARM): A mortgage (home loan) that adjusts the nominal interest rate to changing rates of inflation. (7)

aggregate demand (AD): The total quantity of output (real GDP) demanded at alternative price levels in a given time period, *ceteris paribus.* (8)(9)(10)(11)(13)(15)

aggregate expenditure: The rate of total expenditure desired at alternative levels of income, *ceteris paribus.* (9)

aggregate supply (AS): The total quantity of output (real GDP) producers are willing and able to supply at alternative price levels in a given time period, *ceteris paribus.* (8)(9)(10)(11)(16)

antitrust: Government intervention to alter market structure or prevent abuse of market power. (4)

appreciation: A rise in the price of one currency relative to another. (21)

arithmetic growth: An increase in quantity by a constant amount each year. (17)

asset: Anything having exchange value in the marketplace; wealth. (12)

automatic stabilizer: Federal expenditure or revenue item that automatically responds countercyclically to changes in national income, like unemployment benefits, income taxes. (12)(19)

average propensity to consume (APC): Total consumption in a given period divided by total disposable income. (9)

balance of payments: A summary record of a country's international economic transactions in a given period of time. (21)

balance-of-payments deficit: An excess demand for foreign currency at current exchange rates. (21)

balance-of-payments surplus: An excess demand for domestic currency at current exchange rates. (21)

bank reserves: Assets held by a bank to fulfill its deposit obligations. (13)

barter: The direct exchange of one good for another, without the use of money. (13)

base period: The time period used for comparative analysis; the basis for indexing, e.g., of price changes. (5)(7)(17)

bond: A certificate acknowledging a debt and the amount of interest to be paid each year until repayment; an IOU. (14)

bracket creep: The movement of taxpayers into higher tax brackets (rates) as nominal incomes grow. (7)

budget deficit: Amount by which government spending exceeds government revenue in a given time period. (12)

budget surplus: An excess of government revenues over government expenditures in a given time period. (12)

business cycle: Alternating periods of economic growth and contraction. (8)(9)(19)

capital: Final goods produced for use in the production of other goods, e.g., equipment, structures. (1)

capital deficit: The amount by which the capital outflow exceeds the capital inflow in a given time period. (18)

capital-intensive: Production processes that use a high ratio of capital to labor inputs. (2)

capital surplus: The amount by which the capital inflow exceeds the capital outflow in a given time period. (18)

categorical grants: Federal grants to state and local governments for specific expenditure purposes. (4)

ceteris paribus: The assumption of nothing else changing. (1)(3)

comparative advantage: The ability of a country to produce a specific good at a lower opportunity cost than its trading partners. (2)(18)(20)

complementary goods: Goods frequently consumed in combination; when the price of good *x* rises, the demand for good *y* falls, *ceteris paribus.* (3)

Consumer Price Index (CPI): A measure (index) of changes in the average price of consumer goods and services. (7)

consumption: Expenditure by consumers on final goods and services. (9)

consumption function: A mathematical relationship indicating the rate of desired consumer spending at various income levels. (9)

consumption possibilities: The alternative combinations of goods and services that a country could consume in a given time period. (20)

cost-of-living adjustment (COLA): Automatic adjustments of nominal income to the rate of inflation. (7)

crowding in: An increase in private-sector borrowing (and spending) caused by decreased government borrowing. (12)(17)

crowding out: A reduction in private-sector borrowing (and spending) caused by increased government borrowing. (11)(12)(15)(17)(18)

cyclical deficit: That portion of the budget deficit attributable to unemployment or inflation. (12)

cyclical unemployment: Unemployment attributable to a lack of job vacancies, that is, to inadequate aggregate demand. (6)(9)(10)

debt ceiling: An explicit, legislated limit on the amount of outstanding national debt. (12)

debt service: The interest required to be paid each year on outstanding debt. (12)

deficit ceiling: An explicit, legislated limitation on the size of the budget deficit. (12)

deficit spending: The use of borrowed funds to finance government expenditures that exceed tax revenues. (12)

deflation: A decrease in the average level of prices of goods and services. (7)

demand: The willingness and ability to buy specific quantities of a good at alternative prices in a given time period, *ceteris paribus.* (3)

demand curve: A curve describing the quantities of a good a consumer is willing and able to buy at alternative prices in a given time period, *ceteris paribus.* (3)

demand for money: The quantities of money people are willing and able to hold at alternative interest rates, *ceteris paribus.* (15)

demand-pull inflation: An increase in the price level initiated by excessive aggregate demand. (9)(10)

demand schedule: A table showing the quantities of a good a consumer is willing and able to buy at alternative prices in a given time period, *ceteris paribus.* (3)

deposit creation: The creation of transactions deposits by bank lending. (13)

depreciation: The consumption of capital in the production process; the wearing out of plant and equipment. (5)

depreciation (currency): A fall in the price of one currency relative to another. (21)

devaluation: An abrupt depreciation of a currency whose value was fixed or managed by the government. (21)

discount rate: The rate of interest the Federal Reserve charges for lending reserves to private banks. (14)

discounting: Federal Reserve lending of reserves to private banks. (14)

discouraged worker: An individual who isn't actively seeking employment but would look for or accept a job if one were available. (6)

discretionary fiscal spending: Those elements of the federal budget not determined by past legislative or executive commitments. (12)

disposable income (DI): After-tax income of households; personal income less personal taxes. (5)(9)(11)

dissaving: Consumption expenditure in excess of disposable income; a negative saving flow. (9)

dumping: The sale of goods in export markets at prices below domestic prices. (20)

economic growth: An increase in output (real GDP); an expansion of production possibilities. (1)(2)(6)(17)

economics: The study of how best to allocate scarce resources among competing uses. (1)

efficiency: Maximum output of a good from the resources used in production. (1)

embargo: A prohibition on exports or imports. (20)

employment rate: The percentage of the adult population that is employed. (17)

entrepreneurship: The assembling of resources to produce new or improved products and technologies. (1)

equation of exchange: Money supply (M) times velocity of circulation (V) equals level of aggregate spending ($P \times Q$). (15)(16)

equilibrium (macro): The combination of price level and real output that is compatible with both aggregate demand and aggregate supply. (8)(9)(11)

equilibrium GDP: The value of total output at (real GDP) produced at macro equilibrium (AS-AD). (9)(10)

equilibrium price: The price at which the quantity of a good demanded in a given time period equals the quantity supplied. (3)(20)(21)

equilibrium rate of interest: The interest rate at which the quantity of money demanded in a given time period equals the quantity of money supplied. (15)

excess reserves: Bank reserves in excess of required reserves. (13)(14)

exchange rate: The price of one country's currency expressed in terms of another's; the domestic price of a foreign currency. (18)(21)

expenditure equilibrium: The rate of output at which desired spending equals the value of output. (9)

exports: Goods and services sold to foreign buyers. (2)(5)(18)(20)

external debt: U.S. government debt (Treasury bonds) held by foreign households and institutions. (12)

externalities: Costs (or benefits) of a market activity borne by a third party; the difference between the social and private costs (benefits) of a market activity. (2)(4)

factor market: Any place where factors of production (e.g., land, labor, capital) are bought and sold. (3)

factors of production: Resource inputs used to produce goods and services, e.g., land, labor, capital, entrepreneurship. (1)(2)

federal funds rate: The interest rate for interbank reserve loans. (14)(15)

fine-tuning: Adjustments in economic policy designed to counteract small changes in economic outcomes; continuous responses to changing economic conditions. (19)

fiscal policy: The use of government taxes and spending to alter macroeconomic outcomes. (8)(11)(12)(19)

fiscal restraint: Tax hikes or spending cuts intended to reduce (shift) aggregate demand. (11)(12)(19)

fiscal stimulus: Tax cuts or spending hikes intended to increase (shift) aggregate demand. (11)(12)(19)

fiscal year (FY): The 12-month period used for accounting purposes; begins October 1 for the federal government. (12)

flexible exchange rates: A system in which exchange rates are permitted to vary with market supply-and-demand conditions; floating exchange rates. (21)

foreign-exchange markets: Places where foreign currencies are bought and sold. (21)

foreign-exchange reserves: Holdings of foreign exchange by official government agencies, usually the central bank or treasury. (21)

free rider: An individual who reaps direct benefits from someone else's purchase (consumption) of a public good. (4)

frictional unemployment: Brief periods of unemployment experienced by people moving between jobs or into the labor market. (6)

full employment: The lowest rate of unemployment compatible with price stability; variously estimated at between 4 and 6 percent unemployment. (6)(10)

full-employment GDP: The value of total market output (real GDP) produced at full employment. (8)(9)(10)

GDP deflator: A price index that refers to all goods and services included in GDP. (7)

GDP gap (real): The difference between full-employment GDP and equilibrium GDP. (10)(11)(19)

GDP per capita: Total GDP divided by total population; average GDP. (5)(17)

geometric growth: An increase in quantity by a constant proportion each year. (17)

gold reserves: Stocks of gold held by a government to purchase foreign exchange. (21)

gold standard: An agreement by countries to fix the price of their currencies in terms of gold; a mechanism for fixing exchange rates. (21)

government failure: Government intervention that fails to improve economic outcomes. (1)(4)

gross business saving: Depreciation allowances and retained earnings. (10)

gross domestic product (GDP): The total market value of all final goods and services produced within a nation's borders in a given time period. (2)(5)

gross investment: Total investment expenditure in a given time period. (5)

growth rate: Percentage change in real output from one period to another. (17)

growth recession: A period during which real GDP grows but at a rate below the long-term trend of 3 percent. (8)(19)

human capital: The knowledge and skills possessed by the workforce. (2)(16)(17)

hyperinflation: Inflation rate in excess of 200 percent, lasting at least one year. (7)

imports: Goods and services purchased from international sources. (2)(5)(18)(20)

income quintile: One-fifth of the population, rank-ordered by income (e.g., top fifth). (2)

income transfers: Payments to individuals for which no current goods or services are exchanged, e.g., Social Security, welfare, unemployment benefits. (2)(11)(12)

income velocity of money (V): The number of times per year, on average, a dollar is used to purchase final goods and services; $PQ \div M$. (15)

inflation: An increase in the average level of prices of goods and services. (4)(5)(7)(8)

inflation rate: The annual percentage rate of increase in the average price level. (7)

inflationary GDP gap: The amount by which equilibrium GDP exceeds full employment GDP. (9)(10)(11)(19)

infrastructure: The transportation, communications, education, judicial, and other institutional systems that facilitate market exchanges. (16)

injection: An addition of spending to the circular flow of income. (10)

interest rate: The price paid for the use of money. (15)

intermediate goods: Goods or services purchased for use as input in the production of final goods or in services. (5)

internal debt: U.S. government debt (Treasury bonds) held by U.S. households and institutions. (12)

investment: Expenditures on (production of) new plant, equipment, and structures (capital) in a given time period, plus changes in business inventories. (2)(5)(9)(16)

item weight: The percentage of total expenditure spent on a specific product; used to compute inflation indexes. (7)

labor force: All persons over age 16 who are either working for pay or actively seeking paid employment. (6)(17)

labor-force participation rate: The percentage of the working-age population working or seeking employment. (6)

labor productivity: Amount of output produced by a worker in a given period of time; output per hour (or day, etc.). (16)

laissez faire: The doctrine of "leave it alone," of nonintervention by government in the market mechanism. (1)(8)

law of demand: The quantity of a good demanded in a given time period increases as its price falls, *ceteris paribus*. (3)(8)

law of supply: The quantity of a good supplied in a given time period increases as its price increases, *ceteris paribus*. (3)

leakage: Income not spent directly on domestic output but instead diverted from the circular flow, e.g., saving, imports, taxes. (10)(18)

liability: An obligation to make future payment; debt. (12)

liquidity trap: The portion of the money demand curve that is horizontal; people are willing to hold unlimited amounts of money at some (low) interest rate. (15)

macroeconomics: The study of aggregate economic behavior, of the economy as a whole. (1)(8)

managed exchange rates: A system in which governments intervene in foreign-exchange markets to limit but not eliminate exchange-rate fluctuations; "dirty floats." (21)

marginal propensity to consume (MPC): The fraction of each additional (marginal) dollar of disposable income spent on consumption; the change in consumption divided by the change in disposable income. (9)(10)(11)

marginal propensity to import (MPM): The fraction of each additional (marginal) dollar of disposable income spent on imports. (18)

marginal propensity to save (MPS): The fraction of each additional (marginal) dollar of disposable income not spent on consumption; $1 - MPC$. (9)(18)

marginal tax rate: The tax rate imposed on the last (marginal) dollar of income. (16)

market demand: The total quantities of a good or service people are willing and able to buy at alternative prices in a given time period; the sum of individual demands. (3)

market failure: An imperfection in the market mechanism that prevents optimal outcomes. (1)(4)

market mechanism: The use of market prices and sales to signal desired outputs (or resource allocations). (1)(3)(4)

market power: The ability to alter the market price of a good or service. (4)

market shortage: The amount by which the quantity demanded exceeds the quantity supplied at a given price; excess demand. (3)(21)

market supply: The total quantities of a good that sellers are willing and able to sell at alternative prices in a given time period, *ceteris paribus*. (3)

market surplus: The amount by which the quantity supplied exceeds the quantity demanded at a given price; excess supply. (3)

merit good: A good or service society deems everyone is entitled to some minimal quantity of. (4)

microeconomics: The study of individual behavior in the economy, of the components of the larger economy. (1)

mixed economy: An economy that uses both market signals and government directives to allocate goods and resources. (1)

monetary policy: The use of money and credit controls to influence macroeconomic outcomes. (8)(14)(15)(19)

money: Anything generally accepted as a medium of exchange. (13)

money illusion: The use of nominal dollars rather than real dollars to gauge changes in one's income or wealth. (7)

money multiplier: The number of deposit (loan) dollars that the banking system can create from $1 of excess reserves; equal to $1 \div$ required reserve ratio. (13)(14)

money supply (M1): Currency held by the public, plus balances in transactions accounts. (13)(14)(15)

money supply (M2): M1 plus balances in most savings accounts and money market funds. (13)(14)(15)

monopoly: A firm that produces the entire market supply of a particular good or service. (2)(4)

multiplier: The multiple by which an initial change in aggregate spending will alter total expenditure after an infinite number of spending cycles; $1/(1 - MPC)$. (10)(11)(18)(19)

national debt: Accumulated debt of the federal government. (12)

national income (NI): Total income earned by current factors of production: NDP less depreciation and indirect business taxes; plus net foreign factor income. (5)

national-income accounting: The measurement of aggregate economic activity, particularly national income and its components. (5)

natural monopoly: An industry in which one firm can achieve economies of scale over the entire range of market supply. (4)

natural rate of unemployment: Long-term rate of unemployment determined by structural forces in labor and product markets. (6)(15)(19)

net domestic product (NDP): GDP less depreciation. (5)

net exports: The value of exports minus the value of imports: $(X - M)$. (2)(5)(18)

net investment: Gross investment less depreciation. (5)(17)

nominal GDP: The value of final output produced in a given period, measured in the prices of that period (current prices). (5)(7)

nominal income: The amount of money income received in a given time period, measured in current dollars. (7)

Okun's Law: 1 percent more unemployment is estimated to equal 2 percent less output. (6)

open market operations: Federal Reserve purchases and sales of government bonds for the purpose of altering bank reserves. (14)

opportunity cost: The most desired goods or services that are forgone in order to obtain something else. (1)(3)(4)(12)(20)

optimal mix of output: The most desirable combination of output attainable with existing resources, technology, and social values. (4)(12)

outsourcing: The relocation of production to foreign countries. (6)

per capita GDP: The dollar value of GDP divided by total population; average GDP. (2)(17)

personal income (PI): Income received by households before payment of personal taxes. (5)

Phillips curve: An historical (inverse) relationship between the rate of unemployment and the rate of inflation; commonly expresses a trade-off between the two. (16)

portfolio decision: The choice of how (where) to hold idle funds. (14)(15)

precautionary demand for money: Money held for unexpected market transactions or for emergencies. (15)

price ceiling: Upper limit imposed on the price of a good. (3)

price floor: Lower limit set for the price of a good. (3)

price stability: The absence of significant changes in the average price level; officially defined as a rate of inflation of less than 3 percent. (7)

private good: A good or service whose consumption by one person excludes consumption by others. (4)

product market: Any place where finished goods and services (products) are bought and sold. (3)

production possibilities: The alternative combinations of final goods and services that could be produced in a given time period with all available resources and technology. (1)(5)(6)(17)(20)

productivity: Output per unit of input, e.g., output per labor-hour. (2)(17)(18)

progressive tax: A tax system in which tax rates rise as incomes rise. (4)

proportional tax: A tax that levies the same rate on every dollar of income. (4)

public choice: Theory of public-sector behavior emphasizing rational self-interest of decision makers and voters. (4)

public good: A good or service whose consumption by one person does not exclude consumption by others. (4)

quota: A limit on the quantity of a good that may be imported in a given time period. (20)

rational expectations: Hypothesis that people's spending decisions are based on all available information, including the anticipated effects of government intervention. (19)

real GDP: The value of final output produced in a given period, adjusted for changing prices. (5)(7)(8)(17)

real income: Income in constant dollars; nominal income adjusted for inflation. (7)

real interest rate: The nominal interest rate minus the anticipated inflation rate. (7)(15)

recession: A decline in total output (real GDP) for two or more consecutive quarters. (8)

recessionary GDP gap: The amount by which equilibrium GDP falls short of full-employment GDP. (9)(10)(11)(19)

refinancing: The issuance of new debt in payment of debt issued earlier. (12)

regressive tax: A tax system in which tax rates fall as incomes rise. (4)

relative price: The price of one good in comparison with the price of other goods. (7)

required reserves: The minimum amount of reserves a bank is required to hold; equal to required reserve ratio times transactions deposits. (13)(14)

reserve ratio: The ratio of a bank's reserves to its total transactions deposits. (13)

saving: That part of disposable income not spent on current consumption; disposable income less consumption. (5)(9)(16)

Say's Law: Supply creates its own demand. (8)

scarcity: Lack of enough resources to satisfy all desired uses of those resources. (1)

seasonal unemployment: Unemployment due to seasonal changes in employment or labor supply. (6)

shift in demand: A change in the quantity demanded at any (every) given price. (3)

speculative demand for money: Money held for speculative purposes, for later financial opportunities. (15)

stagflation: The simultaneous occurrence of substantial unemployment and inflation. (16)(19)

structural deficit: Federal revenues at full employment minus expenditures at full employment under prevailing fiscal policy. (12)(19)

structural unemployment: Unemployment caused by a mismatch between the skills (or location) of job seekers and the requirements (or location) of available jobs. (6)(16)

substitute goods: Goods that substitute for each other; when the price of good x rises, the demand for good y increases, *ceteris paribus*. (3)

supply: The ability and willingness to sell (produce) specific quantities of a good at alternative prices in a given time period, *ceteris paribus*. (3)

supply-side policy: The use of tax incentives, (de)regulation, and other mechanisms to increase the ability and willingness to produce goods and services. (8)(19)

tariff: A tax (duty) imposed on imported goods. (20)

tax elasticity of supply: The percentage change in quantity supplied divided by the percentage change in tax rates. (16)

tax rebate: A lump-sum refund of taxes paid. (16)

terms of trade: The rate at which goods are exchanged; the amount of good A given up for good B in trade. (20)

trade deficit: The amount by which the value of imports exceeds the value of exports in a given time period (negative net exports). (18)(20)(21)

trade surplus: The amount by which the value of exports exceeds the value of imports in a given time period (positive net exports). (18)(20)

transactions account: A bank account that permits direct payment to a third party, for example, with a check. (13)

transactions demand for money: Money held for the purpose of making everyday market purchases. (15)

transfer payments: Payments to individuals for which no current goods or services are exchanged, like Social Security, welfare, unemployment benefits. (4)(16)

Treasury bonds: Promissory notes (IOUs) issued by the U.S. Treasury. (12)

underemployment: People seeking full-time paid employment who work only part-time or are employed at jobs below their capability. (6)

unemployment: The inability of labor-force participants to find jobs. (4)(6)

unemployment rate: The proportion of the labor force that is unemployed. (6)

user charge: Fee paid for the use of a public-sector good or service. (4)

value added: The increase in the market value of a product that takes place at each stage of the production process. (5)

velocity of money (V): The number of times per year, on average, that a dollar is used to purchase final goods and services; $PQ \div M$. (19)

voluntary restraint agreement (VRA): An agreement to reduce the volume of trade in a specific good; a "voluntary" quota. (20)

wealth effect: A change in consumer spending caused by a change in the value of owned assets. (9)

yield: The rate of return on a bond; the annual interest payment divided by the bond's price. (14)

REAL GROSS DOMESTIC PRODUCT IN CHAIN-WEIGHTED DOLLARS, 1929–2003 (2000 = 100)

Year	GDP	Personal Consumption Expenditures Total	Gross Private Domestic Investment Total	Net Exports			Government Purchases					Percent Change from Prior Year GDP
								Federal				
				Net	Exports	Imports	Total	Total	National Defense	Non-Defense	State and Local	
1929	865	661	91		35	44	121	25	—	—	104	—
1930	791	626	61	−10	29	39	133	28	—	—	111	−8.9
1931	740	607	38	−10	24	34	139	28	—	—	115	−7.7
1932	644	553	12	−9	19	28	134	27	—	—	108	−13.3
1933	636	541	17	−10	19	29	129	35	—	—	101	−2.1
1934	704	579	31	−9	21	30	146	45	—	—	94	7.7
1935	767	615	57	−17	22	39	156	46	—	—	113	7.7
1936	867	677	73	−15	23	38	175	72	—	—	109	14.2
1937	911	702	91	−14	29	43	167	67	—	—	112	4.3
1938	880	670	60	−15	29	34	180	71	—	—	114	−4.0
1939	951	729	77	−4	31	35	196	97	17	56	124	7.9
1940	1,034	767	108	−1	35	36	202	87	45	54	119	7.8
1941	1,211	822	132	−9	36	45	335	215	169	40	114	18.2
1942	1,435	803	70	−16	24	40	789	564	484	28	107	20.0
1943	1,671	826	41	−31	20	51	1,173	895	781	17	99	19.9
1944	1,807	850	51	−32	21	53	1,321	1,014	882	21	96	8.4
1945	1,786	903	67	−27	30	57	1,153	852	748	12	99	−4.0
1946	1,589	1,013	172	18	65	47	397	201	166	29	109	−20.8
1947	1,575	1,032	165	29	74	45	337	127	97	33	124	−1.5
1948	1,643	1,054	211	6	58	52	362	144	94	50	131	3.8
1949	1,635	1,083	161	8	58	50	405	160	105	54	147	.4
1950	1,777	1,153	228	−9	50	59	405	167	125	41	159	8.7
1951	1,915	1,171	228	0	62	62	554	294	257	36	161	8.8
1952	1,988	1,208	267	−8	59	67	666	372	326	45	164	4.3
1953	2,080	1,266	216	−18	55	73	714	389	329	60	172	3.7
1954	2,065	1,291	206	−12	58	70	665	335	288	47	174	−.7
1955	2,213	1,386	257	−14	64	78	641	307	267	40	198	5.6
1956	2,256	1,425	253	−11	74	85	641	303	266	37	205	2.0
1957	2,301	1,461	242	−7	81	88	670	316	279	37	217	1.8
1958	2,279	1,472	222	−12	70	92	691	312	265	46	234	−.5
1959	2,441	1,554	266	−34	77	101	714	395	325	65	260	7.1
1960	2,501	1,597	266	−21	90	103	715	380	322	58	275	2.5
1961	2,560	1,630	264	−19	91	102	751	395	332	63	298	2.3
1962	2,715	1,711	298	−26	95	114	797	423	345	78	306	6.1
1963	2,834	1,781	318	−22	102	117	818	425	338	82	322	4.4
1964	2,998	1,888	344	−15	114	123	836	418	323	95	344	5.8
1965	3,191	2,007	393	−26	117	136	861	424	321	98	367	6.4
1966	3,399	2,121	427	−40	126	157	937	466	362	99	391	6.5
1967	3,484	2,185	408	−49	128	168	1,008	504	404	100	418	2.5
1968	3,652	2,310	431	−78	139	193	1,040	514	415	95	442	4.8
1969	3,765	2,396	457	−70	145	204	1,038	493	391	98	459	3.1
1970	3,771	2,451	427	−64	161	213	1,012	456	354	98	471	.2
1971	3,898	2,545	475	−75	164	224	990	426	324	102	484	3.4
1972	4,105	2,701	532	−88	176	250	983	423	315	108	487	5.3
1973	4,341	2,833	594	−62	209	261	980	402	294	104	506	5.8
1974	4,319	2,812	550	−36	226	255	1,004	396	284	109	528	−.5
1975	4,311	2,876	453	−7	224	227	1,027	397	279	115	545	−.2
1976	4,540	3,035	544	−41	234	271	1,031	393	277	115	548	5.3
1977	4,750	3,164	627	−66	240	301	1,043	404	280	122	548	4.6
1978	5,015	3,303	702	−67	265	327	1,074	412	285	127	568	5.6
1979	5,173	3,383	725	−45	292	333	1,094	420	291	129	579	3.2
1980	5,161	3,374	645	+10	323	310	1,115	439	303	134	581	−.2
1981	5,291	3,422	704	+5	327	319	1,125	459	322	137	570	2.5
1982	5,189	3,470	606	−15	302	315	1,145	477	349	128	567	−1.9
1983	5,423	3,668	662	−64	294	354	1,187	506	371	135	575	4.5
1984	5,813	3,863	857	−129	318	441	1,227	525	395	129	593	7.2
1985	6,053	4,064	849	−149	328	469	1,312	560	423	137	629	4.1
1986	6,263	4,228	843	−165	353	510	1,392	586	445	141	669	3.5
1987	6,475	4,369	870	−156	391	540	1,426	597	450	146	695	3.4
1988	6,742	4,546	890	−112	454	561	1,445	586	446	138	721	4.1
1989	6,981	4,675	926	−79	506	586	1,482	594	443	150	749	3.5
1990	7,112	4,770	895	−54	552	607	1,530	659	479	178	868	1.9
1991	7,100	4,778	822	−14	589	603	1,547	658	474	182	886	−.2
1992	7,336	4,934	889	−15	629	645	1,555	646	450	195	906	3.3
1993	7,532	5,099	968	−52	650	702	1,541	619	425	194	919	2.7
1994	7,835	5,290	1,099	−79	706	785	1,541	596	404	191	943	4.0
1995	8,031	5,433	1,134	−71	778	849	1,549	580	389	191	968	2.5
1996	8,328	5,619	1,234	−79	843	923	1,564	573	383	189	990	3.7
1997	8,703	5,831	1,387	−104	943	1,048	1,594	567	373	194	1,025	4.5
1998	9,066	6,125	1,524	−203	966	1,170	1,624	561	365	195	1,063	4.2
1999	9,470	6,438	1,642	−296	1,008	1,304	1,686	573	372	201	1,113	4.5
2000	9,817	6,739	1,735	−379	1,096	1,475	1,721	578	370	208	1,142	3.7
2001	9,866	6,904	1,590	−398	1,039	1,437	1,768	600	384	215	1,168	.5
2002	10,083	7,140	1,572	−470	1,014	1,484	1,836	648	418	229	1,189	2.2
2003	10,381	7,356	1,629	−519	1,032	1,550	1,909	690	452	238	1,220	3.0

Source: U.S. Department of Commerce.

Note: Subtotals within Government Purchases based on 1992 prices for years 1929–1989

CONSUMER PRICE INDEX, 1925–2003 (1982–84 = 100)

Year	Index (all items)	Percent Change
1925	17.5	3.5
1926	17.7	−1.1
1927	17.4	−2.3
1928	17.1	−1.2
1929	17.1	0.6
1930	16.7	−6.4
1931	15.2	−9.3
1932	13.7	−10.3
1933	13.0	0.8
1934	13.4	1.5
1935	13.7	3.0
1936	13.9	1.4
1937	14.4	2.9
1938	14.1	−2.8
1939	13.9	0.0
1940	14.0	0.7
1941	14.7	9.9
1942	16.3	9.0
1943	17.3	3.0
1944	17.6	2.3
1945	18.0	2.2
1946	19.5	18.1
1947	22.3	8.8
1948	24.1	3.0
1949	23.8	−2.1
1950	24.1	5.9
1951	26.0	6.0
1952	26.5	0.8
1953	26.7	0.7
1954	26.9	−0.7
1955	26.8	0.4
1956	27.2	3.0
1957	28.1	2.9
1958	28.9	1.8
1959	29.1	1.7
1960	29.6	1.4
1961	29.9	0.7
1962	30.2	1.3
1963	30.6	1.6
1964	31.0	1.0
1965	31.5	1.9
1966	32.4	3.5
1967	33.4	3.0
1968	34.8	4.7
1969	36.7	6.2
1970	38.8	5.6
1971	40.5	3.3
1972	41.8	3.4
1973	44.4	8.7
1974	49.3	12.3
1975	53.8	6.9
1976	56.9	4.9
1977	60.6	6.7
1978	65.2	9.0
1979	72.6	13.3
1980	82.4	12.5
1981	90.9	8.9
1982	96.5	3.8
1983	99.6	3.8
1984	103.9	3.9
1985	107.6	3.8
1986	109.6	1.1
1987	113.6	4.4
1988	118.3	4.6
1989	124.0	4.6
1990	130.7	6.1
1991	136.2	3.1
1992	140.3	2.9
1993	144.5	2.7

Note: Data beginning 1978 are for all urban consumers: earlier data are for urban wage earners and clerical workers.

Source: U.S. Department of Labor. Bureau of Statistics.

T-2

CONSUMER PRICE INDEX, 1925–2003 (continued)

Year	Index (all items)	Percent Change
1994	148.2	2.7
1995	152.4	2.5
1996	156.9	3.3
1997	160.5	1.7
1998	163.0	1.6
1999	166.6	2.7
2000	172.2	3.4
2001	177.1	2.8
2002	179.7	1.6
2003	184.0	2.3

CHAIN-WEIGHTED PRICE DEFLATORS FOR GROSS DOMESTIC PRODUCT, 1959–2003 (2000 = 100)

Year	Index (all items)	Percent Change
1959	20.7	1.2
1960	21.0	1.4
1961	21.2	1.1
1962	21.5	1.4
1963	21.8	1.1
1964	22.1	1.5
1965	22.5	1.8
1966	23.1	2.8
1967	23.8	3.1
1968	24.9	4.3
1969	26.1	5.0
1970	27.5	5.3
1971	28.9	5.0
1972	30.1	4.3
1973	31.8	5.6
1974	34.7	9.0
1975	38.0	9.5
1976	40.2	5.8
1977	42.7	6.4
1978	45.7	7.0
1979	49.5	8.3
1980	54.0	9.1
1981	59.1	9.4
1982	62.7	6.1
1983	65.2	3.9
1984	67.6	3.8
1985	69.7	3.0
1986	71.2	2.2
1987	73.2	2.7
1988	75.7	3.4
1989	78.5	3.8
1990	81.6	3.9
1991	84.4	3.5
1992	86.4	2.3
1993	88.3	2.3
1994	90.2	2.1
1995	92.1	2.0
1996	93.8	1.9
1997	95.4	1.7
1998	96.4	1.1
1999	97.8	1.4
2000	100.0	2.2
2001	102.3	2.4
2002	104.1	1.7
2003	106.0	1.8

Source: U.S. Department of Commerce, Bureau of Economic Analysis.

INTEREST RATES, 1929–2003 (percent per annum)

Year	Prime Rate Charged by Banks	Discount Rate, Federal Reserve Bank of New York
1929	5.50–6.00	5.16
1933	1.50–4.00	2.56
1939	1.50	1.00
1940	1.50	1.00
1941	1.50	1.00
1942	1.50	1.00
1943	1.50	1.00
1944	1.50	1.00
1945	1.50	1.00
1946	1.50	1.00
1947	1.50–1.75	1.00
1948	1.75–2.00	1.34
1949	2.00	1.50
1950	2.07	1.59
1951	2.56	1.75
1952	3.00	1.75
1953	3.17	1.99
1954	3.05	1.60
1955	3.16	1.89
1956	3.77	2.77
1957	4.20	3.12
1958	3.83	2.15
1959	4.48	3.36
1960	4.82	3.53
1961	4.50	3.00
1962	4.50	3.00
1963	4.50	3.23
1964	4.50	3.55
1965	4.54	4.04
1966	5.63	4.50
1967	5.61	4.19
1968	6.30	5.16
1969	7.96	5.87
1970	7.91	5.95
1971	5.72	4.88
1972	5.25	4.50
1973	8.03	6.44
1974	10.81	7.83
1975	7.86	6.25
1976	6.84	5.50
1977	6.83	5.46
1978	9.06	7.46
1979	12.67	10.28
1980	15.27	11.77
1981	18.87	13.42
1982	14.86	11.02
1983	10.79	8.50
1984	12.04	8.80
1985	9.93	7.69
1986	8.83	6.33
1987	8.21	5.66
1988	9.32	6.20
1989	10.87	6.93
1990	10.01	6.98
1991	8.46	5.45
1992	6.25	3.25
1993	6.00	3.00
1994	7.15	3.60
1995	8.83	5.21
1996	8.27	5.02
1997	8.44	5.00
1998	8.35	4.92
1999	8.00	4.62
2000	9.23	5.73
2001	6.91	3.40
2002	4.67	1.17
2003	4.12	1.15

Source: Board of Governors of the Federal Reserve System.

Problems for Chapter 1

Name: _____

1. According to Table 1.1 (or Figure 1.1), what is the opportunity cost of the

    (a) Fourth truck? _____

    (b) Fifth truck? _____

2. (a) According to Figure 1.2, what is the opportunity cost of North Korea's military force at point N? _____

    (b) How much of a peace dividend would North Korea get if it cut the military establishment from OD to OH? _____

3. How much of a peace dividend is generated in a $11 trillion economy when defense spending is cut from 3.5 percent to 3.0 percent of total output? $_____

4. What is the opportunity cost (in dollars) to attend an hour-long econ lecture for

    (a) A minimum-wage teenager $_____

    (b) A $100,000 per year corporate executive $_____

5. Suppose either computers or televisions can be assembled with the following labor inputs:

Units produced	1	2	3	4	5	6	7	8	9	10
Total labor used	3	7	12	18	25	33	42	54	70	90

    (a) Draw the production possibilities curve for an economy with 54 units of labor. Label it P54.

    (b) What is the opportunity cost of the eighth computer? _____

    (c) Suppose immigration brings in 36 more workers. Redraw the production possibilities curve to reflect this added labor. Label the new curve P90.

    (d) Suppose advancing technology (e.g., the miniaturization of electronic circuits) increases the productivity of the 90-laborer workforce by 20 percent. Draw a third production possibilities curve (PT) to illustrate this change.

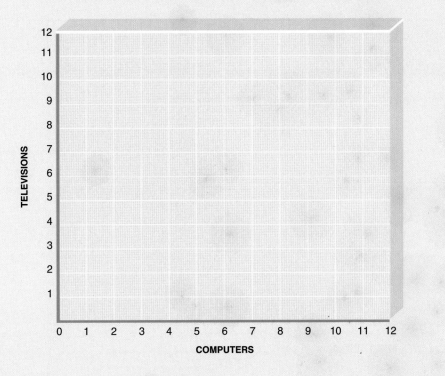

6. Suppose there's a relationship of the following sort between study time and grades:

	(a)	(b)	(c)	(d)	(e)
Study time (hours per week)	0	2	6	12	20
Grade-point average	0	1.0	2.0	3.0	4.0

If you have only 20 hours per week to use for either study time or fun time,
(a) Draw the (linear) production possibilities curve on the graph below that represents the alternative uses of your time.
(b) What is the cost, in lost fun time, of raising your grade-point average from 2.0 to 3.0? Illustrate this effort on the graph (point *C* to point *D*).   _____
(c) What is the opportunity cost of increasing your grades from 3.0 to 4.0? Illustrate as point *D* to point *E*.   _____
(d) Why does the opportunity cost change? _____

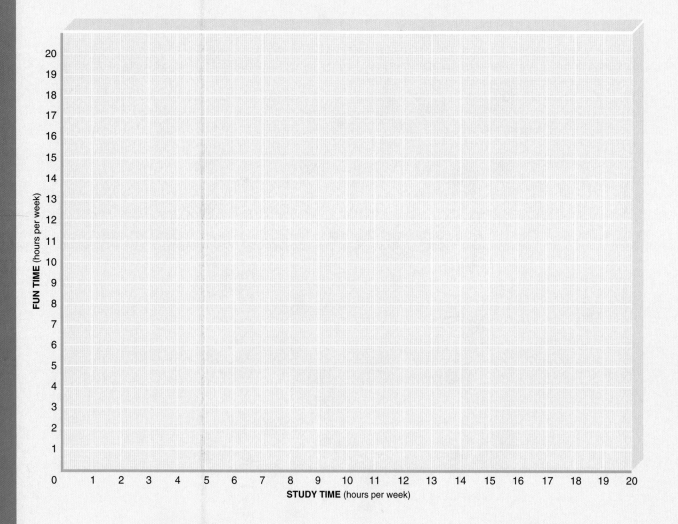

Problems for Chapter 2

Name: _____

1. In 2002, the worlds' total output (real GDP) was roughly $46 trillion. What percent of this total was produced by the three largest economies (World View, p. 28)?   _____%

2. According to the World View on p. 29, what percentage of America's GDP per capita is available to the average citizen of

    (*a*) Mexico   _____%
    (*b*) China   _____%
    (*c*) Ethiopia   _____%

3. If Haiti's per capita GDP of roughly $1,280 increases by an exceptionally fast 5 percent a year, what will its per capita GDP be in

    (*a*) 10 years? $_____
    (*b*) 20 years? $_____
    (*c*) In 20 years, what percent of America's 2002 per capita income would it attain at that rate?   _____%

4. According to Table 2.1, how fast does total output have to grow in order to raise per capita GDP in

    (*a*) France?   _____
    (*b*) Nigeria?   _____

5. U.S. real gross domestic product increased from $3.8 trillion in 1980 to $4.8 trillion in 1990. During that same decade the share of durable goods (e.g., cars, appliances) fell from 18.5 percent to 17.0 percent. What was the value of durable-goods output

    (*a*) In 1980? $_____
    (*b*) In 1990? $_____
    (*c*) By how much did durable output change?   _____%

6. Using the data in Figure 2.6,
    (*a*) Compute the average income of U.S. households. $_____
    (*b*) If all incomes were equalized by government taxes and transfer payments, how much would the average household in each income quintile gain (via transfers) or lose (via taxes)?

        (*i*) Highest fifth $_____
        (*ii*) Second fifth $_____
        (*iii*) Third fifth $_____
        (*iv*) Fourth fifth $_____
        (*v*) Lowest fifth $_____

    (*c*) What is the implied tax rate on the highest quintile?   _____%

7. What percent of U.S. exports go to

    (*a*) China?   _____%
    (*b*) Canada?   _____%

What percent of U.S. imports come from

    (*a*) China?   _____%
    (*b*) Canada?   _____%

8. How much more output (income) per year will have to be produced in the world
    (*a*) Just to reduce the "extreme poverty" (less than $2 per day) of 3 billion people by $1 per day? $_____
    (*b*) To raise the incomes of the world's "extremely poor" population to the official threshold of U.S. poverty (roughly $5,000 per year)? $_____

9. **(Macro course only)** Using the data from the endpapers of this book, complete the following table.

| | Share of Total Output | |
Sector	1950	2000
Consumption	_____	_____
Investment	_____	_____
Government purchases	_____	_____
Exports	_____	_____
Imports	_____	_____

(*a*) Which sector share has increased the most?   _____

(*b*) Which sector share has decreased the most?   _____

10. **(Macro course only)** Using data from the endpapers, illustrate on the graph below
   (*a*) The federal government's share of the total output.
   (*b*) The state/local government's share of total output.

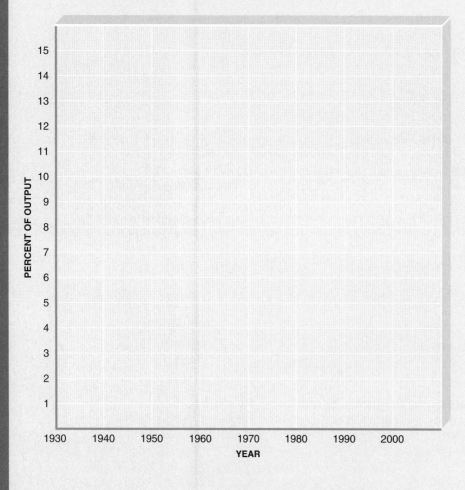

1. According to Figure 3.3, at what price would Tom buy 15 hours of web tutoring?

           (*a*) Without a lottery win.   _____

           (*b*) With a lottery win.   _____

2. According to Figures 3.5 and 3.6, what would the new equilibrium price of tutoring services be if Ann decided to stop tutoring?   _____

3. Given the following data, identify the amount of shortage or surplus that would exist at a price of

           (*a*) $5.00   _____

           (*b*) $3.00   _____

           (*c*) $1.00   _____

A. Price	$5.00	$4.00	$3.00	$2.00	$1.00			$5.00	$4.00	$3.00	$2.00	$1.00
B. Quantity demanded						C. Quantity supplied						
Al	1	2	3	4	5		Alice	3	3	3	3	3
Betsy	0	1	1	1	2		Butch	7	5	4	4	2
Casey	2	2	3	3	4		Connie	6	4	3	3	1
Daisy	1	3	4	4	6		Dutch	6	5	4	3	0
Eddie	1	2	2	3	5		Ellen	4	2	2	2	1
Market total	__	__	__	__	__		Market total	__	__	__	__	__

4. Graph the official and equilibrium prices for the U2 rock concert (see News, page 61).

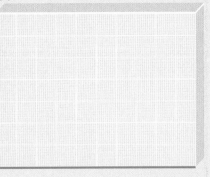

PRICE (dollars per ticket)

QUANTITY (tickets per show)

5. In the World View on page 64, menu prices are continuously adjusted. Graph the initial and final (adjusted) prices for the following situations. Be sure to label axes and graph completely.

(*a*) **Customers are ordering too little haddock.**

(*b*) **The kitchen is running out of beef ribs.**

6. What factors caused the supply and demand shifts in the California electricity market (see "Economy Tomorrow" p. 65–67)?

Demand Shift Factors _____

Supply Shift Factors _____

_____   _____

_____   _____

_____   _____

Problems for Chapter 3 (cont'd)

Name: _____

7. In Figure 3.8, when a price ceiling is imposed on the "new" market by how much does
   (a) The quantity of electricity demanded increase? _____
   (b) The quantity of electricity supplied decrease? _____
   (c) How large is the resulting shortage? _____

8. In the California electricity market (Figure 3.8),
   (a) What is the "new" equilibrium price? _____
   (b) How large is the market shortage at that price? _____

9. What is the relationship of Idaho power to California power? (circle one)
   (a) Complementary good   (b) Substitute good
   Illustrate on the graphs below the impacts of a California price ceiling (at P_c) on the California and Idaho electricity markets.
   (c) Which determinant of demand for Idaho electricity changes in this case? _____

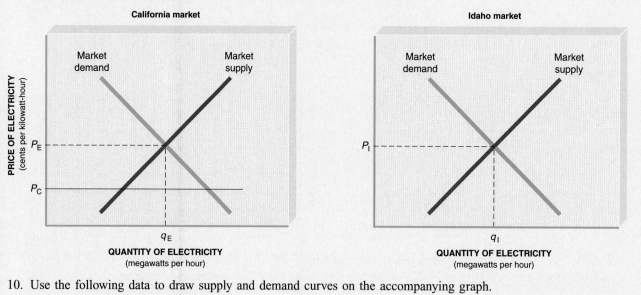

10. Use the following data to draw supply and demand curves on the accompanying graph.

Price	$ 8	7	6	5	4	3	2	1
Quantity demanded	2	3	4	5	6	7	8	9
Quantity supplied	10	9	8	7	6	5	4	3

   (a) What is the equilibrium price? _____
   (b) If a *minimum* price (price floor) of $6 is set, what disequilibrium results? _____
   (c) If a *maximum* price (price ceiling) of $3 is set, what disequilibrium results? _____

   Illustrate these answers.

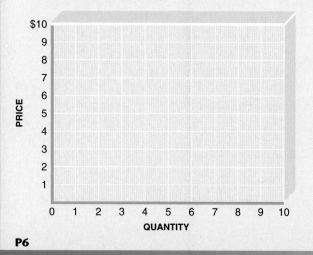

Problems for Chapter 4

Name: _____

1. In Figure 4.2, by how much is the market
   (a) Overproducing private goods? _____
   (b) Underproducing public goods? _____

2. Use Figure 4.3 to illustrate on the accompanying production possibilities curve
   (a) The market mix of output (M).
   (b) The optimal mix of output (X).

3. Assume that the product depicted below generates external costs in consumption of $5 per unit.
   (a) Draw the social demand curve.

   (b) What is the socially optimal output? _____
   (c) By how much does the market overproduce this good? _____

4. In the previous problem's market equilibrium, what is
   (a) The market value of the good? _____
   (b) The social value of the good? _____

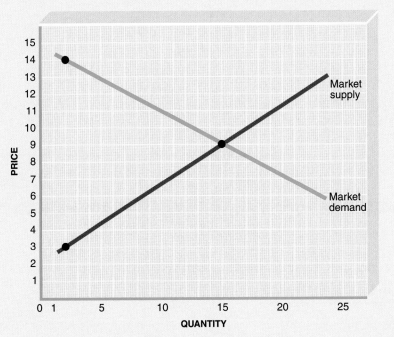

5. (a) Assuming a 10 percent sales tax is levied on all consumption, complete the following table:

Income	Consumption	Sales Tax	Percent of Income Paid in Taxes
$10,000	$10,000	_____	_____
20,000	19,000	_____	_____
40,000	36,000	_____	_____
80,000	68,000	_____	_____

   (b) Is the sales tax progressive or regressive? _____

Problems for Chapter 4 (cont'd)

Name: _____

6. If a new home can be constructed for $120,000, what is the opportunity cost of federal defense spending, measured in terms of private housing? (Assume a defense budget of $400 billion.) _____

7. Suppose the following data represent the market demand for college education:

Tuition (per year)	$1,000	2,000	3,000	4,000	5,000	6,000	7,000	8,000
Enrollment demanded (in millions per year)	8	7	6	5	4	3	2	1

(a) If tuition is set at $5,000, how many students will enroll? _____

Now suppose that society gets an external benefit of $1,000 for every enrolled student.

(b) Draw the social and market demand curves for this situation on the graph below (left).
(c) What is the socially optimal level of enrollments at the same tuition price of $5,000? _____
(d) How can this optimal enrollment level be achieved? _____

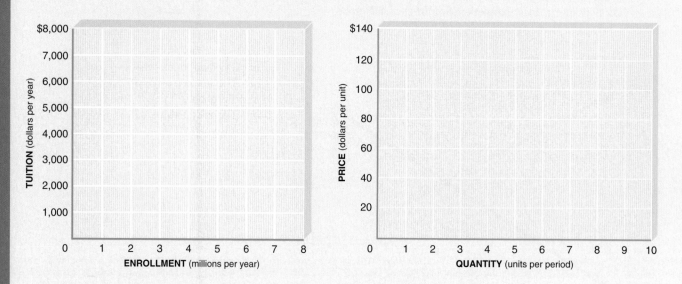

8. Suppose the following data represent the prices that each of three consumers is willing to pay:

Quantity	Consumer A	Consumer B	Consumer C
1	$50	$40	$30
2	30	20	20
3	20	15	10

(a) Construct the market demand curve for this good on the graph above (right).
(b) If this good were priced in the market at $40, how many units would be demanded? _____
(c) Now suppose that this is a public good, in the sense that all consumers receive satisfaction from the good even if only one person buys it. Under these conditions, what is the social value of the
  (i) First unit? _____
  (ii) Second unit? _____

9. According to the News on p. 84, what percent of income is spent on lottery tickets by
(a) A poor family with income of $18,000 per year? _____
(b) An affluent family with income of $80,000 per year? _____

Problems for Chapter 5

Name: _____

1. Suppose that furniture production encompasses the following stages:

Stage 1: Trees sold to lumber company	$1,000
Stage 2: Lumber sold to furniture company	$1,700
Stage 3: Furniture company sells furniture to retail store	$3,200
Stage 4: Furniture store sells furniture to consumer	$5,995

   (a) What is the value added at each stage?

                     Stage 1: _____

                     Stage 2: _____

                     Stage 3: _____

                     Stage 4: _____

   (b) How much does this output contribute to GDP? _____

   (c) How would answer b change if the lumber were imported from Canada? _____

2. If real GDP increases by 5 percent next year and the price level goes up by 3 percent, what will happen to nominal GDP? _____

3. What was real per capita GDP in 1933 measured in 2003 prices? (Use the data in Table 5.4 to compute your answer.) _____

4. (a) Calculate national income from the following figures:

Consumption	$200 billion
Depreciation	20
Retained earnings	12
Gross investment	30
Imports	40
Social Security taxes	25
Exports	50
Indirect business taxes	15
Government purchases	60
Personal income taxes	40

                     NI: _____

   (b) If there were 80 million people in this country, what would the GDP per capita be? _____

   (c) If all prices were to double overnight, what would happen to the values of real and nominal GDP per capita?

                     Change in real GDP: _____

                     Change in nominal GDP: _____

5. What is the value of net investment in Problem 4? _____

6. What share of total income consists of
   (a) Wages and salaries _____
   (b) Corporate profits _____
   (*Note:* See Table 5.5 for data)

7. (a) Compute real GDP for 1995 using average prices of 1985 as the base year. (On the inside covers of this book you'll find data for GDP and the GDP "price deflator" used to measure inflation.)
   (b) By how much did real GDP increase between 1985 and 1995? _____
   (c) By how much did nominal GDP increase between 1985 and 1995? _____

8. Suppose all the dollar values in Problem 4 were in 1990 dollars. Use the Consumer Price Index shown on the end cover of this book to convert the numbers to 2003 dollars. What is the value of national income in 2003 dollars? (You'll be converting the figures from their nominal to their real values, with 2003 as the base year.) _____

Name: _____

9. On the accompanying graph, illustrate (*A*) nominal per capita GDP and (*B*) real per capita GDP
   for each year. (The necessary data appear on the endpapers of this book.)
   (*a*) By what percent did nominal per capita GDP increase in the 1990s? _____
   (*b*) By what percent did real per capita GDP increase in the 1990s? _____
   (*c*) In how many years did nominal per capita GDP decline? _____
   (*d*) In how many years did real per capita GDP decline? _____
   (*e*) What explains the divergence between nominal and real growth rates? _____
   _____

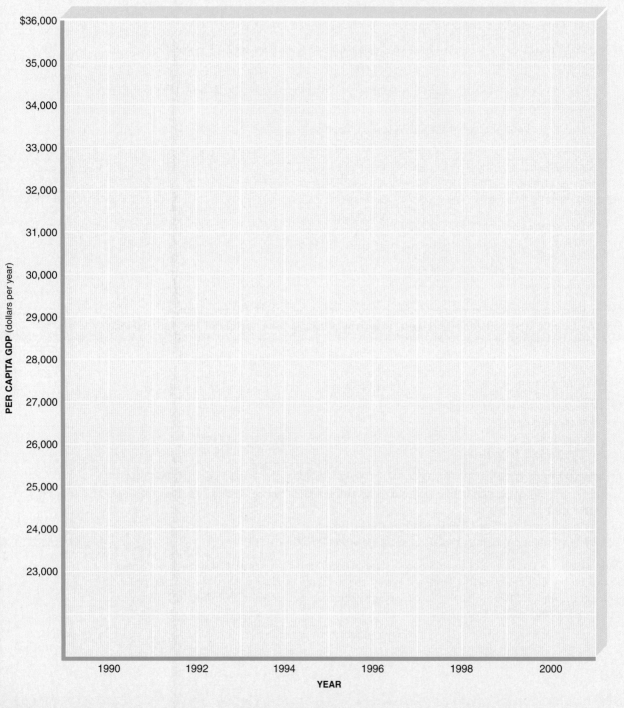

Problems for Chapter 6

Name: _____

1. According to Figure 6.1, what percent of the civilian labor force was
   (a) Employed? _____%
   (b) Unemployed? _____%
   (c) What percent of the *population* was employed in civilian jobs? _____%

2. Between 1997 and 2000, by how much did
   (a) The labor force increase? _____%
   (b) Total output (real GDP) increase? _____%
   (c) The national unemployment rate change? _____
   (*Note:* Data on inside covers of the text.)

3. If the labor force is growing by 1.5 percent per year, how many new jobs have to be created each *month* to keep unemployment from increasing? _____
   Web query: By how much did U.S. employment actually increase last month (www.bls.gov) _____

4. Between 1980 and 2004, by how much did the labor-force participation rate (Figure 6.2) of
   (a) Men fall? _____
   (b) Women rise? _____

5. According to Okun's Law (updated), how much output (real GDP) was lost in 2002 when the nation's unemployment rate increased from 4.7 percent to 5.8 percent? _____

6. Suppose the following data describe a nation's population:

	Year 1	Year 2
Population	200 million	203 million
Labor force	120 million	125 million
Unemployment rate	6 percent	6 percent

   (a) How many people are unemployed in each year? Year 1: _____ Year 2: _____
   (b) How many people are employed in each year? Year 1: _____ Year 2: _____
   (c) Compute the employment rate (i.e., number employed ÷ population) in each year. Year 1: _____ Year 2: _____
   (d) How can the employment rate rise when the *un*employment rate is constant?

7. Based on the data in the previous problem, what happens to each of the following numbers in Year 2 when 1 million jobseekers become "discouraged workers"?
   (a) number of unemployed persons _____
   (b) unemployment rate _____
   (c) employment rate _____

8. According to the News on p. 127, how many additional people became *under*employed in October 2001? _____

9. On the accompanying graph, illustrate both the unemployment rate and the percentage change in real
   GDP (output) for each year. (The data required for this exercise are on the inside cover of this book.)
   (*a*) In how many years was "full employment" achieved? (Use current benchmark.)   _____
   (*b*) Unemployment and growth rates tend to move in opposite directions. Which appears to
         change direction first?   _____
   (*c*) Does the unemployment rate ever increase even when output is expanding?   _____

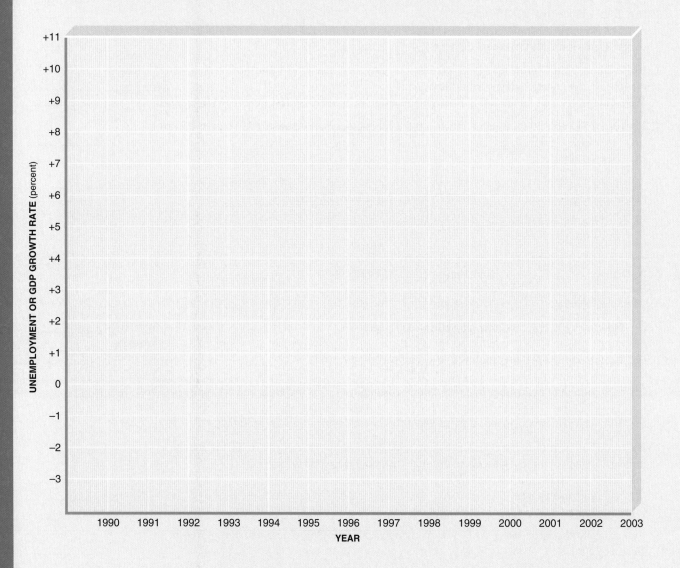

Problems for Chapter 7

Name: _____

1. If tuition keeps increasing at the same rate as in 2003 (see News, page 134), what will it cost to attend a community college five years from now? _____

2. Suppose you'll have an annual nominal income of $40,000 for each of the next three years, and the inflation rate is 5 percent per year.

   (a) Find the real value of your $40,000 salary for each of the next three years.

   Year 1: _____

   Year 2: _____

   Year 3: _____

   (b) If you have a COLA in your contract, and the inflation rate is 5 percent, what is the real value of your salary for each year?

   Year 1: _____

   Year 2: _____

   Year 3: _____

3. In the World View on page 148, what was the real rate of interest in Zimbabwe in 2004? _____

4. Suppose you borrow $1,000 of principal that must be repaid at the end of two years, along with interest of 5 percent a year. If the annual inflation rate turns out to be 10 percent,

   (a) What is the real value of the principal repayment? _____

   (b) What is the real rate of interest on the loan? _____

   (c) Whose real wealth is diminished in this case? _____

5. Assuming that the following table describes a typical consumer's complete budget, compute the item weights for each product.

Item	Quantity	Unit Price	Item Weight:
Coffee	20 pounds	$ 3	_____
Tuition	1 year	4,000	_____
Pizza	100 pizzas	8	_____
VCR rental	75 days	15	_____
Vacation	2 weeks	300	_____
		Total:	_____

6. Suppose the prices listed in the table for Problem 5 changed from one year to the next, as shown below. Use the rest of the table to compute the average inflation rate.

Item	Unit Price Last Year	Unit Price This Year	Percent Change in Price	×	Item Weight	=	Inflation Impact
Coffee	$ 3	$ 4	_____		_____		_____
Tuition	4,000	7,000	_____		_____		_____
Pizza	8	10	_____		_____		_____
VCR rental	15	10	_____		_____		_____
Vacation	300	500	_____		_____		_____
					Average inflation:		_____

7. Use the item weights in Figure 7.2 to determine the percentage change in the CPI that would result from a

   (a) 10 percent increase in entertainment prices. _____

   (b) 6 percent decrease in transportation costs. _____

   (c) Doubling of clothing prices. _____

   (*Note:* Review Table 7.4 for assistance.)

8. Use the GDP deflator data on the inside cover of this book to compute real GDP in 1970 at 2000 prices. _____

9. According to Table 7.3, what happened during the period shown to the
   (*a*) Nominal price of gold?   _____
   (*b*) Real price of gold?   _____

10. On the accompanying graph, illustrate for each year (*A*) the nominal interest rate (use the prime
    rate of interest), (*B*) the CPI inflation rate, and (*C*) the real interest rate (adjusted for same-year
    CPI inflation). The required data appear in the inside cover of the book.
    (*a*) In what year was the official goal of price stability met?   _____
    (*b*) In that year, what was the
       (*i*) Nominal interest rate?   _____
       (*ii*) Real interest rate?   _____
    (*c*) What was the range of rates during this period for
       (*i*) Nominal interest rates?   _____
       (*ii*) Real interest rates?   _____
    (*d*) On a year-to-year basis which varies more, nominal or real interest rates?_____

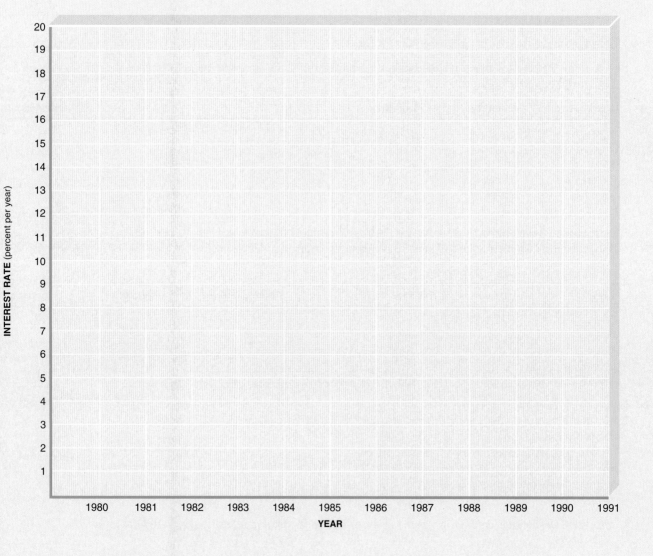

Problems for Chapter 8

Name: _____

1. (*a*) How much output is unsold at the price level P_l in Figure 8.7? _____
   (*b*) At what price level is all output produced sold? _____

2. Suppose you have $500 in savings when the price level index is at 100.
   (*a*) If inflation pushes the price level up by 20 percent, what will be the real value of your savings? _____
   (*b*) What happens to the real value of your savings if the price level *declines* by 10 percent? _____

3. Use the following information to draw aggregate demand and aggregate supply curves on the graph below. Both curves are assumed to be straight lines.

Average Price	Real Output Demanded (per year)	Real Output Supplied (per year)
$1,000	0	$1,000
100	$900	100

   (*a*) At what price level does equilibrium occur? _____
   (*b*) What curve would have shifted if a new equilibrium were to occur at an output level of 700 and a price level of 700? _____
   (*c*) What curve would have shifted if a new equilibrium were to occur at an output level of 700 and a price level of 500? _____
   (*d*) What curve would have shifted if a new equilibrium were to occur at an output level of 700 and a price level of 300? _____
   (*e*) Compared to the initial equilibrium (*a*), how have price levels or output changed in
       (*b*) Output: _____ Price level: _____
       (*c*) Output: _____ Price level: _____
       (*d*) Output: _____ Price level: _____

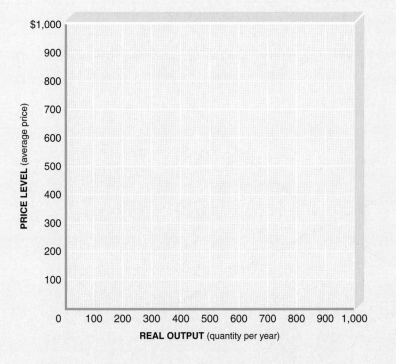

4. According to the World View on page 171, which direction did aggregate demand shift in
       (*a*) The United States? _____
       (*b*) Japan? _____
       (*c*) China? _____

Problems for Chapter 8 (cont'd)

Name: _____

5. Illustrate these events with AS or AD shifts:

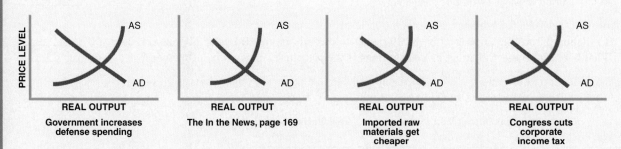

| Government increases defense spending | The In the News, page 169 | Imported raw materials get cheaper | Congress cuts corporate income tax |

6. Assume that the accompanying graph depicts aggregate supply and demand conditions in an economy. Full employment occurs when $6 trillion of real output is produced.
   - (a) What is the equilibrium rate of output? _____
   - (b) How far short of full employment is the equilibrium rate of output? _____
   - (c) Illustrate a shift of aggregate demand that would change the equilibrium rate of output to $6 trillion. Label the new curve AD$_2$.
   - (d) What is the price level at the new equilibrium? _____
   - (e) Illustrate a shift of aggregate supply (AS$_2$) that would, when combined with AD$_1$, move equilibrium output to $6 trillion.
   - (f) What is the price level at this new equilibrium? _____

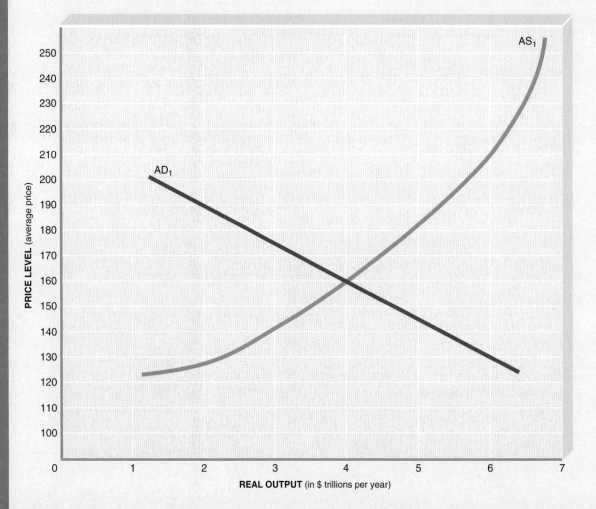

Problems for Chapter 9

Name: _____

1. (a) What is the implied MPC in the News on p. 187? _____
   (b) What is the implied APC? _____

2. On the accompanying graph, draw the consumption function $C = \$150 + 0.8Y_D$.
   (a) At what level of income do households begin to save? _____
       Designate that point on the graph with the letter *A*.
   (b) By how much does consumption increase when income rises \$200 beyond point *A*?
       Designate this new level of consumption with point *B*. _____
   (c) Illustrate the impact on consumption of the change in consumer confidence described in the
       News on page 187.

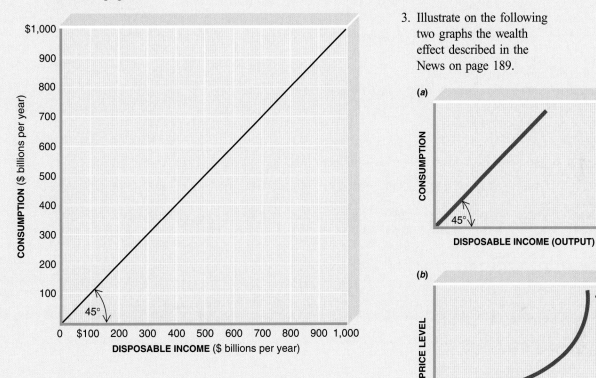

3. Illustrate on the following two graphs the wealth effect described in the News on page 189.

4. Illustrate on the following graph what was happening to aggregate demand in Canada according to the World View on page 193.

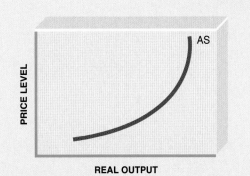

5. What was the range, in percentage points, of the variation in quarterly growth rates between 1999 and 2003 of
   (a) Consumer spending _____
   (b) Investment spending _____
   (*Note:* See Figure 9.8 for data)

6. Complete the following table:

Price Level	Real Output Demanded (in $ billions) by:							Aggregate Demand	Aggregate Supply
	Consumers	+	Investors	+	Government	+	Net Exports	=	
120	80		15		20		10	___	170
110	92		16		20		12	___	160
100	104		17		20		14	___	150
90	116		18		20		16	___	140
80	128		19		20		18	___	120
70	140		20		20		20	___	95
60	154		21		20		22	___	65

(a) What is the level of equilibrium GDP?   _____

(b) What is the equilibrium price level?   _____

(c) If full employment occurs at real GDP = $165 billion, what kind of
    GDP gap exists?   _____

(d) How large is that gap?   _____

(e) Which macro problem exists here?   _____

7. On the graph below, draw the AD and AS curves with these data:

Price level	140	130	120	110	100	90	80	70	60	50
Real output										
Demanded	600	700	800	900	1,000	1,100	1,200	1,300	1,400	1,500
Supplied	1,200	1,150	1,100	1,050	1,000	950	900	800	600	400

(a) What is the equilibrium
    (i) Real output level?   _____
    (ii) Price level?   _____

Suppose net exports decline by $150 at all price levels, but all other components of aggregate
demand remain constant.

(b) Draw the new AD curve.

(c) What is the new equilibrium
    (i) Output level?   _____
    (ii) Price level?   _____

(d) What macro problem has arisen in this economy? _____

Problems for Chapter 10

Name: _____

1. From 1929 to 2003, in how many years did
   (*a*) real consumption decline? _____
   (*b*) real investment decline? _____
   (*c*) real government spending increase at least $100 billion? (Data on end covers of text.) _____

2. If the consumption function is $C = \$200 + 0.9Y$,
   (*a*) What does the saving function look like? _____
   (*b*) What is the rate of desired saving when disposable income equals
        (*i*) $500? _____
        (*ii*) $1,000? _____
        (*iii*) $2,000? _____

3. What is the value of the multiplier when the marginal propensity to consume is
        (*a*)   0.10 _____
        (*b*)   0.25 _____

4. Suppose that autonomous investment increases by $100 billion in a closed and private economy (no government or foreign trade). Assume further that households have a marginal propensity to consume of 90 percent.
   (*a*) Compute four rounds of multiplier effects:

	Changes in This Cycle's Spending	Cumulative Change in Spending
First cycle	_____	_____
Second cycle	_____	_____
Third cycle	_____	_____
Fourth cycle	_____	_____

   (*b*) What will be the final cumulative impact on spending? _____
   (*c*) Compare your results with those in Table 10.1. With a higher marginal propensity to consume, does the cumulative change in expenditure become larger or smaller? _____

5. Illustrate in the graph on the left below the impact of a sudden decline in consumer confidence that reduces autonomous consumption by $50 billion at the price level P_F. Assume MPC = 0.8.
   (*a*) What is the new equilibrium level of real output? (Don't forget the multiplier.) _____
   (*b*) How large is the real GDP gap? _____
   (*c*) What has happened to average prices? _____

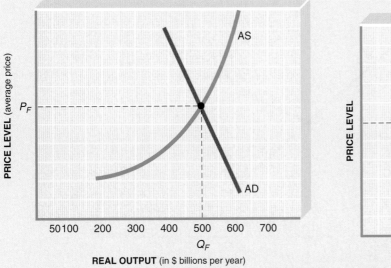

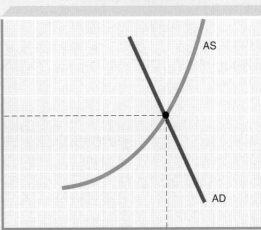

Asia's economy (Problem 6)

6. (*a*) Show on the previous graph (right) the effects of the U.S. slump on Asia's economy
    (World View, p. 214).
   (*b*) If Asian net exports to the U.S. declined by $40 billion per year, by how much would *total*
    Asian spending decline if Asian consumers have an MPC of 0.90?   _____

7. How large is the inflationary GDP gap in Figure 10.9?   _____

8. The accompanying graph depicts a macro equilibrium. Answer the questions based on the
   information in the graph.
   (*a*) What is the equilibrium rate of GDP?   _____
   (*b*) If full-employment real GDP is $1,200, what problem does this economy have?   _____
   (*c*) How large is the real GDP gap?   _____
   (*d*) If the multiplier were equal to 4, how much additional investment would be needed to
    increase aggregate demand by the amount of the initial GDP gap?   _____
   (*e*) Illustrate the changes in autonomous investment and induced consumption that occur in *d*.
   (*f*) What happens to prices when aggregate demand increases by the amount of
    the initial GDP gap?   _____
   (*g*) Is full employment restored by the AD shift?   _____

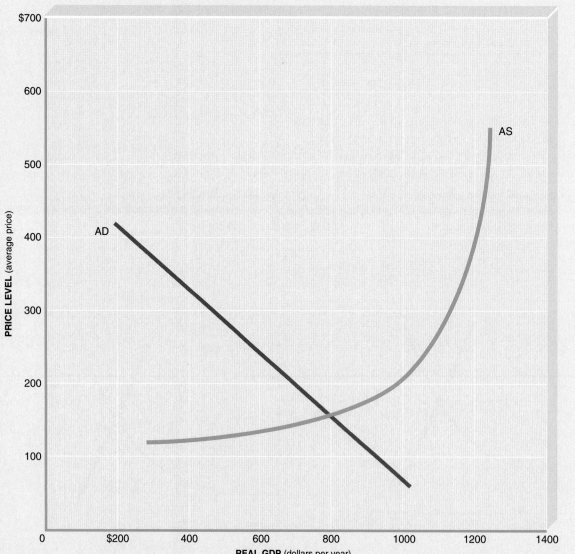

1. In the tax-cut example on pp. 230–231,
   (a) By how much does consumer saving increase initially?   _____
   (b) What is the marginal propensity to save?   _____

2. Suppose the consumption function is

$$C = \$400 \text{ billion} + 0.8Y$$

   and the government wants to stimulate the economy. By how much will aggregate demand at current prices shift initially (before multiplier effects) with
   (a) A $50 billion increase in government purchases?   _____
   (b) A $50 billion tax cut?   _____
   (c) A $50 billion increase in income transfers?   _____

   What will the cumulative AD shift be for
   (d) The increased G?   _____
   (e) The tax cut?   _____
   (f) The increased transfers?   _____

3. Suppose the government decides to increase taxes by $20 billion in order to increase Social Security benefits by the same amount. How will this combined tax-transfer policy affect aggregate demand at current prices?   _____

4. On the accompanying graph, identify and label
   (a) Macro equilibrium.
   (b) The real GDP gap.
   (c) The AD excess or shortfall.
   (d) The new equilibrium that would occur with appropriate fiscal policy.

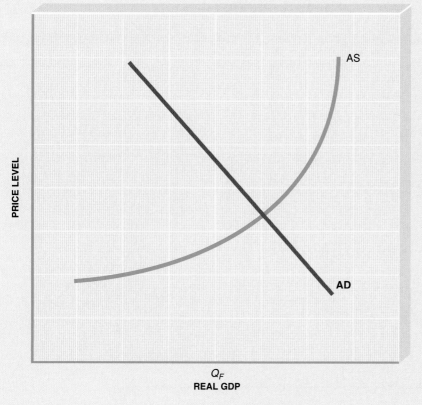

5. According to the World View on page 230,
   (a) By how much did South Korea's government *increase* public-works spending?   _____
   (b) By how much might this fiscal stimulus have increased aggregate demand if the marginal propensity to consume was 0.9?   _____

6. (a) According to the News on page 233, by how much were tax cuts expected to boost consumer spending in 2001?   _____
   (b) By how much would total spending have changed as a result of such an initial consumption surge?   _____

7. Suppose that an increase in income transfers rather than government spending was the preferred policy for stimulating the economy depicted in Figure 11.4. By how much would transfers have to increase to attain the desired shift of AD?   _____

8. If the marginal propensity to consume was 0.9, how large would each of the following need to be in order to restore a full-employment equilibrium in Figure 11.6?
   (a) A tax increase.   _____
   (b) A government spending cut.   _____
   (c) A cut in income transfers.   _____

9. Use the following data to complete the graph and to answer the following questions:

Price level	10	20	30	40	50	60	70	80	90	100
Real GDP supplied	$500	600	680	750	820	880	910	940	960	970
Real GDP demanded	$960	920	880	840	800	760	720	680	640	600

   (a) If full employment occurs at a real output rate of $880, how large is the real GDP gap?   _____
   (b) How large is the AD shortfall?   _____
   (c) What will happen to prices if AD increases enough to restore full employment?   _____
   (d) Assuming MPC = 0.75, how will macro equilibrium change if the government purchases increase by $20? Illustrate your answer on the graph.   _____

Problems for Chapter 12

Name: _____

1. From 2002 to 2003 how did each of the following change?
   (*a*) Tax revenue _____
   (*b*) Government spending _____
   (*c*) Budget deficit _____
   (*Note:* See Table 12.1)

2. Since 1970, in how many years has the federal budget had a surplus? _____

3. What country had the largest budget deficit (as percent of GDP) in 2003? _____

4. What would happen to the budget deficit if the
   (*a*) GDP growth rate jumped from 1 percent to 3 percent? _____
   (*b*) Inflation rate increased by 2 percentage points? _____
   (*Note:* See Table 12.2 for clues.)

5. Use Table 12.3 to determine how much fiscal stimulus or restraint occured between
   (*a*) 1999 and 2000 _____
   (*b*) 2001 and 2002 _____

6. Suppose a government has no debt and a balanced budget. Suddenly it decides to spend $10 billion while raising only $8 billion worth of taxes.
   (*a*) What will be the government's deficit? _____
   (*b*) If the government finances the deficit by issuing bonds, what amount of bonds will it issue? _____
   (*c*) At a 10 percent rate of interest, how much interest will the government pay each year? _____
   (*d*) Add the interest payment to the government's $10 billion expenditures for the next year, and assume that taxes remain at $8 billion. In the second year, compute the
     (*i*) Deficit. _____
     (*ii*) Amount of new debt (bonds) issued. _____
     (*iii*) Debt-service requirement. _____
   (*e*) Repeat these calculations for the third, fourth, and fifth years, assuming that the government taxes at a rate of $8 billion each year and has noninterest expenditures of $10 billion annually.

	Year 3	Year 4	Year 5
Deficit	_____	_____	_____
New debt	_____	_____	_____
Debt service	_____	_____	_____

   (*f*) What is the ratio of interest payments, relative to the deficit, with each passing year?

Year 2	Year 3	Year 4	Year 5
_____	_____	_____	_____

   (*g*) What will happen to the ratio of government debt to government expenditure with each passing year? _____

7. (*a*) According to the News on page 250, how much fiscal restraint occurred between 1931 and 1933? _____
   (*b*) By how much did this policy reduce aggregate demand if the MPC was 0.8? _____

8. In Figure 12.5, what is the opportunity cost of increasing government spending from g_1 to g_2 if
   (*a*) No external financing is available?   _____
   (*b*) Complete external financing is available?   _____

9. Use the accompanying graph to illustrate *changes* in the structural and total deficits for the years
   1997–2003 (data in Table 12.3). Why do the two measures move in different directions?

   _____

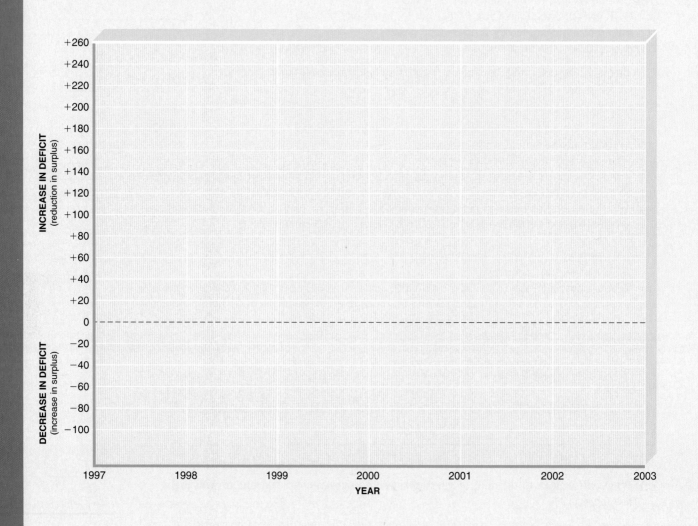

Problems for Chapter 13

Name: _____

1. If you cash a $20 traveler's check at a bank, by how much does

    (a) M1 change? _____

    (b) M2 change? _____

    (c) bank reserves change? _____

  If you deposit the traveler's check in your bank account, by how much does

    (d) M1 change? _____

    (e) M2 change? _____

    (f) bank reserves change? _____

2. Suppose a bank's balance sheet looks as follows:

Assets		Liabilities	
Reserves	$500	Deposits	$3,600

  and banks are required to hold reserves equal to 10 percent of deposits.

  (a) How much excess reserves does the bank hold? _____

  (b) How much more can this bank lend? _____

3. Suppose a bank's balance sheet looks like this:

Assets		Liabilities	
Reserves		Deposits	$500
Excess	$ 60		
Required	40		
Loans	400		
Total	$500	Total	$500

  What is the required reserve ratio? _____

4. What is the value of the money multiplier when the required reserve ratio is

    (a) 20 percent? _____

    (b) 4 percent? _____

5. In December 1994, a man in Ohio decided to deposit all of the 8 *million* pennies he'd been saving for nearly 65 years. (His deposit weighed over 48,000 pounds!) With a reserve requirement of 5 percent, what will be the cumulative change for the banking system in

    (a) Transactions deposits? _____

    (b) Total reserves? _____

    (c) Lending capacity? _____

6. (a) When the reserve requirement changes, which of the following will change for the bank that receives the initial deposit (Bank *A*)? (Check those items that will change.)

    Transactions deposits _____

    Total reserves _____

    Required reserves _____

    Excess reserves _____

    Lending capacity _____

  (b) When the reserve requirement changes, which of the following will experience a cumulative change in the total banking system? (Check all that apply.)

    Transactions deposits _____

    Total reserves _____

    Required reserves _____

    Excess reserves _____

    Lending capacity _____

7. In Table 13.3, how much unused lending capacity does Eternal Savings have at step 4? _____

8. Suppose that a lottery winner deposits $10 million in cash into her transactions account at the Bank of America (B of A). Assume a reserve requirement of 25 percent and no excess reserves in the banking system prior to this deposit.

(a) Use step 1 in the T-accounts below to show how her deposit affects the balance sheet at B of A.

(b) Has the money supply been changed by her deposit?   _____

(c) Use step 2 below to show the changes at B of A after B of A fully uses its new lending capacity.

(d) Has the money supply been changed in step 2?   _____

(e) In step 3 the new borrower(s) writes a check for the amount of the loan. That check is deposited at another bank, and B of A pays the other bank when the check clears. What does the B of A balance sheet look like now?

(f) After the entire banking system uses the lending capacity of the initial ($10 million) deposit, by how much will the following have changed?

Total reserves	_____
Total deposits	_____
Total loans	_____
Cash held by public	_____
The money supply	_____

Step 1: Winnings Deposited
Bank of America

Assets (in millions)		Liabilities (in millions)	
Reserves:		Deposits	_____
Required	_____		
Excess	_____		
Subtotal	_____		
Loans	_____		
Total assets	_____	Total liabilities	_____

Step 2: Loans Made
Bank of America

Assets (in millions)		Liabilities (in millions)	
Reserves:		Deposits	_____
Required	_____		
Excess	_____		
Subtotal	_____		
Loans	_____		
Total assets	_____	Total liabilities	_____

Step 3: Check Clears
Bank of America

Assets (in millions)		Liabilities (in millions)	
Reserves:		Deposits	_____
Required	_____		
Excess	_____		
Subtotal	_____		
Loans	_____		
Total assets	_____	Total liabilities	_____

Problems for Chapter 14

Name: _____

1. What is the money multiplier when the reserve requirement is:

     (a) 0.100   _____

     (b) 0.125   _____

2. In Table 14.1, what would the following values be if the required reserve ratio fell to 0.15?

     (a) Total deposits   _____

     (b) Total reserves   _____

     (c) Required reserves   _____

     (d) Excess reserves   _____

     (e) Money multiplier   _____

     (f) Unused lending capacity   _____

3. Assume that the following data describe the condition of the banking system:

Total reserves	$200 billion
Transactions deposits	$800 billion
Cash held by public	$100 billion
Reserve requirement	0.20

     (a) How large is the money supply (MI)?   _____

     (b) How large are *required* reserves?   _____

     (c) How large are *excess* reserves?   _____

     (d) By how much could the banks increase their lending activity?   _____

4. In Problem 3, suppose the Fed wanted to stop further lending activity. To do this, what reserve requirement should the Fed impose?   _____

5. According to the News on page 288, what is

     (a) The required reserve rate?   _____

     (b) The money multiplier?   _____

6. Assume the banking system contains

Total reserves	$60 billion
Transactions deposits	$600 billion
Cash held by public	$100 billion
Reserve requirement	0.10

     (a) Are the banks fully utilizing their lending capacity?   _____

     (b) What would happen to the money supply *initially* if the public deposited another $50 billion of cash in transactions accounts?   _____

     (c) What would the lending capacity of the banking system be after such a portfolio switch?   _____

     (d) How large would the money supply be if the banks fully utilized their lending capacity?   _____

     (e) What three steps could the Fed take to offset that potential growth in M1?   _____

           _____

           _____

7. Assume that a $1,000 bond issued in 2005 pays $100 in interest each year. What is the current yield on the bond if it can be purchased for

     (a) $1,200?   _____

     (b) $1,000?   _____

     (c) $800?   _____

     (d) $600?   _____

8. Suppose a $1,000 bond pays $50 per year in interest.

     (a) What is the contractual interest rate on the bond?   _____

     (b) If market interest rates rise to 10 percent, what price will the bond sell for?   _____

Problems for Chapter 14 (cont'd)

Name: _____

9. Suppose a banking system with the following balance sheet has no excess reserves. Assume that banks will make loans in the full amount of any excess reserves that they acquire and will immediately be able to eliminate loans from their portfolio to cover inadequate reserves.

Assets (in billions)		Liabilities (in billions)	
Total reserves	$ 30	Transactions accounts	$300
Securities	90		
Loans	180		
Total	$300	Total	$300

(a) What is the reserve requirement? _____

(b) Suppose the reserve requirement is changed to 5 percent. Reconstruct the balance sheet of the total banking system after all banks have fully utilized their lending capacity.

Assets (in billions)		Liabilities (in billions)	
Total reserves	_____	Transactions accounts	_____
Securities	_____		
Loans	_____		
Total	_____	Total	_____

(c) By how much has the money supply changed as a result of the lower reserve requirement (step b)? _____

(d) Suppose the Fed now buys $10 billion of securities directly from the banks. What will the banks' books look like after this purchase?

Assets (in billions)		Liabilities (in billions)	
Total reserves	_____	Transactions accounts	_____
Securities	_____		
Loans	_____		
Total	_____	Total	_____

(e) How much excess reserves do the banks have now? _____

(f) By how much can the money supply now increase? _____

1. Suppose homeowners owe $800 billion in mortgage loans.
   (a) If the mortgage interest rate is 9 percent, approximately how much are homeowners paying in
       annual mortgage interest?   _____
   (b) If the interest rate drops to 8 percent, by how much will annual interest payments drop?   _____
   (c) What are homeowners likely to do with their interest rate "savings"?   _____

2. If all of the "cash out" described in the News on p. 306 was spent on consumption, by how much
   did AD shift
                                                              (a) initially?   _____
                                                              (b) cumulatively?   _____

3. Illustrate the effects on investment of
   (a) an interest-rate hike (point A)
   (b) an interest-rate hike accompanied by increased sales expectations
       (point B)

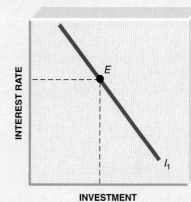

4. Suppose that an economy is characterized by

$$M = \$4{,}000 \text{ billion}$$

$$V = 2$$

$$P = 100$$

   (a) What is the real value of output (Q)?   _____
   Now assume that the Fed increases the money supply by 10 percent and velocity remains unchanged.
   (b) If the price level remains constant, what will happen to real output?   _____
   (c) If, instead, real output is fixed at the natural level of unemployment, what will happen when
       M increases?   _____
   (d) By how much would V have to fall to offset the increase in M?   _____

5. If the nominal rate of interest is 8 percent and the real rate of interest is 3 percent, what rate of
   inflation is anticipated?   _____

6. Suppose the Fed decided to purchase $10 billion worth of government securities in the open
   market. What impact would this action have on the economy? Specifically, answer the following
   questions:
   (a) How will M1 be affected initially?   _____
   (b) How will the banking system's lending capacity be affected if the reserve requirement is
       25 percent?   _____
   (c) How will banks induce investors to utilize this expanded lending capacity? _____
   (d) How will aggregate demand be affected if investors borrow and spend all the newly available
       credit?   _____
   (e) Under what circumstances would the Fed be pursuing such an open market policy? _____
   (f) How could those same objectives be achieved through changes in the discount rate or reserve
       requirement?

   _____

   _____

7. According to Greenspan's rule of thumb, how much fiscal restraint would be equivalent to a
   2-point hike in long-term interest rates?   _____

8. The following data describe market conditions:

Money supply (in billions)	$100	$200	$300	$400	$ 500	$ 600	$ 700
Interest rate	8.0	7.5	7.0	6.5	6.0	5.5	5.5
Rate of investment (in billions)	$ 12	$ 12	$ 15	$ 16	$16.5	$16.5	$16.5

   (*a*) At what rate of interest does the liquidity trap emerge?   _____
   (*b*) At what rate of interest does investment demand become totally inelastic?   _____

9. Use the accompanying graphs to show what happens in the economy when *M* increases from $300
   billion to $400 billion.
   (*a*) By how much does *PQ* change if *V* is constant?   _____
   (*b*) If aggregate supply were fixed (vertical) at the initial output level, what would happen to the
          price level?   _____
   (*c*) What is the value of *V*?   _____

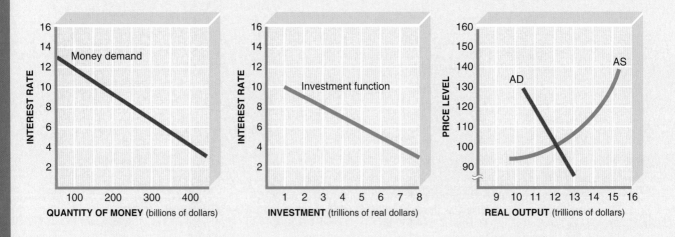

Problems for Chapter 16

Name: _____

1. On the graph below, draw the (*A*) Keynesian, (*B*) Monetarist, and (*C*) hybrid AS curves, all intersecting AD at point *E*. If AD shifts rightward, which AS curve generates

    (*a*) The biggest increase in output? _____

    (*b*) The biggest increase in prices? _____

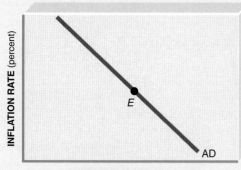

2. The Economy Tomorrow section provides estimates of time spent in traffic delays. If the average worker produces $35 of output per hour, what is the opportunity cost of

    (*a*) Current traffic delays? $_____

    (*b*) Estimated delays in 10 years? $_____

3. Suppose taxpayers are required to pay a base tax of $50 plus 30 percent on any income over $100, as in the initial tax system *B* in Table 16.1. Suppose further that the taxing authority wishes to raise by $20 the taxes of people with incomes of $200.

    (*a*) If marginal tax rates are to remain unchanged, what will the new base tax have to be? $_____

    (*b*) If the base tax of $50 is to remain unchanged, what will the marginal tax rate have to be?   _____%

4. Suppose households supply 230 billion hours of labor per year and have a tax elasticity of supply of 0.20. If the tax rate is increased by 10 percent, by how many hours will the supply of labor decline?   _____

5. By how much did the disposable income of rich people increase as a result of the 2001–4 reduction in the top marginal tax rate from 39.6 to 35 percent? Assume they have $2 trillion of income in the highest bracket.   _____

6. According to Figure 16.5, what inflation rate would occur if the unemployment rate fell to 4 percent, with

    (*a*) PC_1?   _____

    (*b*) PC_2?   _____

7. On the following graph, plot the unemployment and inflation rates for the years 1992–2003. Is there any evidence of a Phillips curve trade-off?   _____

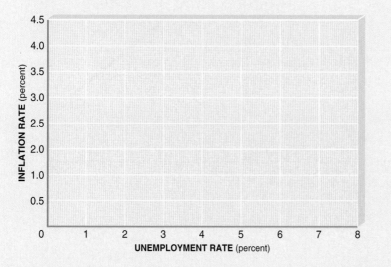

8. According to the "oil shock" News on page 337,
   (a) How much more will the average family spend on oil products *per year* as a result of the
       price spike? $_____
   (b) Where will the money come from? _____

9. If the tax elasticity of supply is 0.15, by how much do taxes have to be reduced to increase the
   labor supply by 3 percent?   _____

10. Suppose an economy is characterized by the AS/AD curves in the accompanying graph. A
    decision is then made to increase infrastructure spending by $20 billion a year.
    (a) Illustrate the direct impact of the increased spending on aggregate demand on the graph
        (ignore multiplier effects).
    (b) If AS is unaffected, what is the new equilibrium rate of outout?   _____
    (c) What is the new equilibrium price level?   _____
    (d) Now assume that the infrastructure investments increase aggregate supply by $30 billion
        a year (from the initial equilibrium). Illustrate this effect on the graph.
    (e) After both demand and supply adjustments occur, what is the final equilibrium
        (i) Rate of output?   _____
        (ii) Price level?   _____

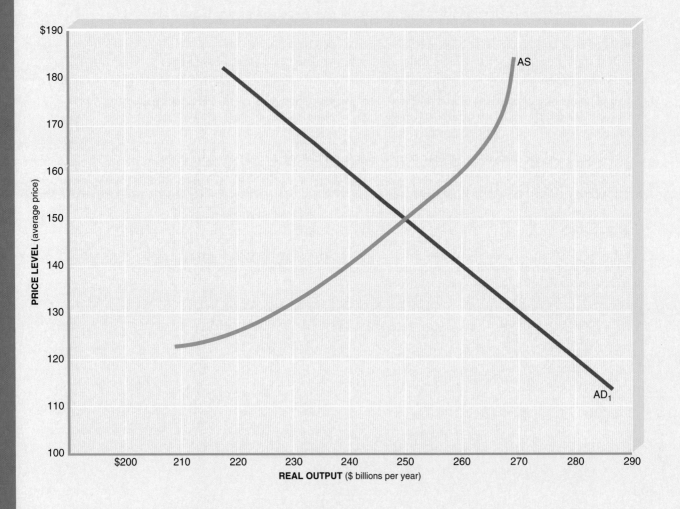

Problems for Chapter 17

Name: _____

1. According to the rule of 72 (Table 17.1), how many years will it take for GDP to double if the economy is growing at:
   (*a*) 3 percent a year? _____
   (*b*) 4.5 percent a year? _____

2. According to the Rule of 72 (Table 17.1), how long will it be before GDP doubles in
   (*a*) The United States? _____
   (*b*) China? _____
   (*c*) Venezuela? _____
   (*Note:* See Table 2.1 for GDP growth rates.)

3. If real GDP is growing at 3 percent a year, how long will it take for
   (*a*) Real GDP to double? _____
   (*b*) Real GDP per capita to double if the population is increasing each year by

                                            (*i*) 0 percent? _____
                                            (*ii*) 1 percent? _____
                                            (*iii*) 2 percent? _____

4. Suppose that every additional 5 percentage points in the investment rate ($I \div$ GDP) boost economic growth by 1 percentage point. Assume also that all investment must be financed with consumer saving. The economy is now assumed to be fully employed at

GDP	$6 trillion
Consumption	5 trillion
Saving	1 trillion
Investment	1 trillion

   If the goal is to raise the growth rate by 1 percent,
   (*a*) By how much must investment increase? _____
   (*b*) By how much must consumption decline for this to occur? _____

5. If the labor force increases by 1 percent each year and productivity increases by 2 percent, how fast will output grow? _____

6. According to the World View on page 361, by how much did GDP increase in the 1990s (the entire decade, not the annual average) in
                                            (*a*) China? _____
                                            (*b*) The United States? _____
                                            (*c*) Great Britain? _____

7. In 2003, approximately 62 percent of the adult population (221 million) was employed. If the employment rate increased to 65 percent.
   (*a*) How many more people would be working? _____
   (*b*) By how much would output increase if per worker GDP is $80,000? _____

8. If output per worker is now $80,000 per year, how much will the average worker produce 10 years from now if productivity improves by
   (*a*) 1.0 percent per year? _____
   (*b*) 2.0 percent per year? _____

Name: _____

9. On the accompanying graph, illustrate the investment rate for each year and plot the annual growth rate of GDP, using data from the inside endcover of the text. Then answer the following questions.

   (*a*) What was the range for the annual investment rate?   Highest _____

                                                                       Lowest _____

   (*b*) What was the range of annual growth rates?   Highest _____

                                                                        Lowest _____

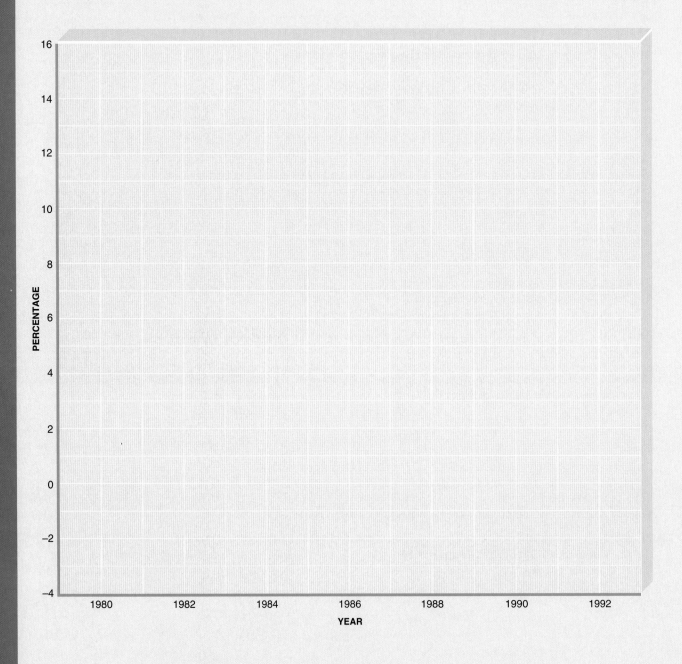

1. Using the data from the inside front cover and the first page of this book, compute the
   (*a*) Import/GDP ratio in 2003.   _____
   (*b*) Export/GDP ratio in 2003.   _____

2. (*a*) If the marginal propensity to save in a closed (no-trade) economy is 0.05, what is the value
         of the multiplier?   _____
   (*b*) If this same economy opens up to trade and exhibits a marginal propensity to import of
         0.10, what does the value of the multiplier become?   _____

3. According to the World View on page 373,
   (*a*) What percent of European exports go to the United States?   _____
   (*b*) By how much does European GDP growth slow if U.S. GDP growth slows by 2 percentage
         points?   _____

4. According to the World View on page 376, what is the marginal propensity to import for capital
   investment?   _____

5. Use data from the inside cover to compute the marginal propensity to import between 1997 and
   2000.   _____

6. Suppose that the expenditure patterns of a country are as follows:

$$C = \$60 \text{ million per year} + 0.8Y$$

$$I = \$100 \text{ billion per year}$$

$$G = 0 \quad \text{(no taxes either)}$$

$$\text{Exports} = \text{imports} = \$10 \text{ billion per year}$$

   (*a*) What is the value of equilibrium GDP?   _____
   (*b*) As a result of higher oil prices, this country must now spend an additional $10 billion per
         year on imported oil. Assuming that prices of other goods do not change, what impact will
         the higher oil prices have on equilibrium GDP? _____

7. Recompute the answer to Problem 6 by assuming that the marginal propensity to import equals
   0.1 (and thus that the MPC for domestic goods is 0.7). _____

8. Using the data from the inside front cover and the first page of this text, compute the
   1990–2000 percentage growth for the following:
                                                    (*a*) Consumption   _____
                                                    (*b*) Investment   _____
                                                    (*c*) Government spending   _____
                                                    (*d*) Exports   _____

   What was the fastest-growing component of aggregate demand?   _____
   How did this component affect U.S. job growth? _____
   _____

Name: _____

9. On the graph plot (*a*) U.S. exports, (*b*) U.S. imports, and (*c*) nominal GDP growth for each year. Which trade flow is more related to GDP growth? _____

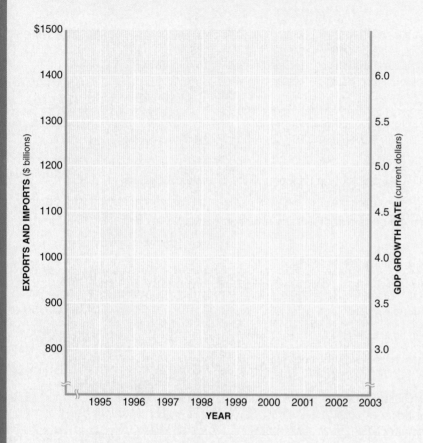

10. Illustrate on the graphs below the impact of monetary stimulus in

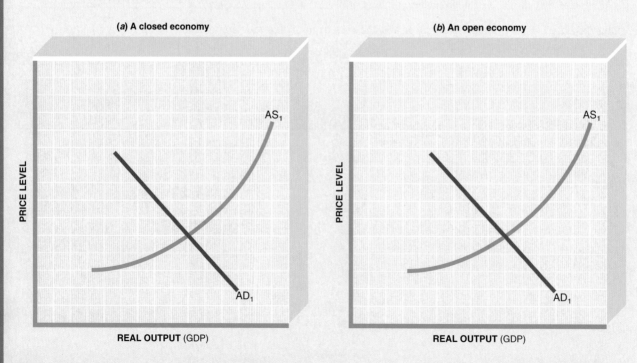

Problems for Chapter 19

Name: _____

1. If the Congressional Budget Office makes its average error this year, by how much will it underestimate next year's budget deficit? (See News on page 403.)

     _____

2. If the unemployment rate stays 2 percentage points above full employment for an entire year,
   (a) How many jobs will be lost?
   (b) If the average worker produces $80,000 of output, how much output will be lost?

     _____
     _____

3. According to the World View on page 397,
   (a) Which country had the greatest macro misery in the 1990s? (Compute the "misery in the index" from Chapter 16.)
   (b) Who had the fastest growth?

     _____
     _____

4. Complete the following chart by summarizing the policy prescriptions of various economic theories:

	Policy Prescription for	
Policy Approach	Recession	Inflation
Fiscal	_____	_____
Classical	_____	_____
Keynesian	_____	_____
Monetarist	_____	_____
Monetary	_____	_____
Keynesian	_____	_____
Monetarist	_____	_____
Supply-Side	_____	_____

Name: _____

5. The following table displays Congressional Budget Office forecasts of federal budget balances for the following year. Graph these forecasts on the graph below, along with *actual* surplus and deficits for those same years (see Table 12.3 for data).

Year:	1995	1996	1997	1998	1999	2000	2001	2002
Budget balance forecast (in billions of dollars)	−162	−189	−165	−120	−2	+131	+281	+313

(a) In how many years was CBO too optimistic (underestimating the deficit or overestimating the surplus)? _____

(b) In how many years was CBO too pessimistic? _____

(c) Why was the forecast so wrong in 2002?

_____

_____

Problems for Chapter 20

Name: _____

1. Which countries are the two largest export markets for the United States? (See Table 20.3.)   1. _____
                                                                                                    2. _____

2. Suppose a country can produce a maximum of 1,000 jumbo airliners or 800 aircraft carriers.
   (*a*) What is the opportunity cost of an aircraft carrier?   _____
   (*b*) If another country offers to trade six planes for four aircraft carriers, should the offer be
         accepted?   _____
   (*c*) What are the implied terms of trade?   _____

3. If it takes 64 farm workers to harvest one ton of strawberries and 16 farm workers to harvest one
   ton of wheat, what is the opportunity cost of five tons of strawberries?   _____

4. Alpha and Beta, two tiny islands off the east coast of Tricoli, produce pearls and pineapples. The
   following production possibilities schedules describe their potential output in tons per year.

Alpha		Beta	
Pearls	Pineapples	Pearls	Pineapples
0	30	0	20
2	25	10	16
4	20	20	12
6	15	30	8
8	10	40	4
10	5	45	2
12	0	50	0

   (*a*) Graph the production possibilities confronting each island.
   (*b*) What is the opportunity cost of pineapples on each island (before trade)?   Alpha: _____
                                                                                                Beta: _____

   (*c*) Which island has a comparative advantage in pearl production?   _____
   (*d*) Graph the consumption possibilities of each island with free trade.

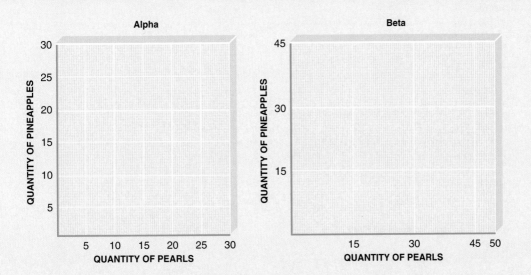

5. (*a*) How much more are U.S. consumers paying for the 20 billion pounds of sugar they consume
         each year as a result of the quotas on sugar imports? (See News, p. 432.)   _____
   (*b*) How much sales revenue are foreign sugar producers losing as a result of those same quotas? _____

6. Suppose the two islands in Problem 4 agree that the terms of trade will be one for one and exchange 10 pearls for 10 pineapples.
   (a) If Alpha produced 6 pearls and 15 pineapples while Beta produced 30 pearls and 8 pineapples before they decided to trade, how much would each be producing after trade? Assume that the two countries specialize just enough to maintain their consumption of the item they export, and make sure each island follows its comparative advantage.
   (b) How much would each island be consuming after specializing and trading?   Alpha: _____
   (c) How much would the combined production of pineapples increase for the two islands due to   Beta: _____
       trade? _____
   (d) How much would the combined production of pearls increase? _____
   (e) How could both countries produce and consume even more? _____
       _____

   (f) Assume the two islands are able to trade as much as they want with the rest of the world, with the terms of trade at one pineapple for one pearl. Draw the ultimate consumption possibilities curve for each island.

7. Suppose the following table reflects the domestic supply and demand for compact disks (CDs):

Price ($)	16	14	12	10	8	6	4	2
Quantity supplied	8	7	6	5	4	3	2	1
Quantity demanded	2	4	6	8	10	12	14	16

   (a) Graph these market conditions and identify the equilibrium price and sales.   Price/sales: _____
   (b) Now suppose that foreigners enter the market, offering to sell an unlimited supply of CDs for $6 apiece. Illustrate and identify
       (i) The market price   _____
       (ii) Domestic consumption   _____
       (iii) Domestic production   _____
   (c) If a tariff of $2 per CD is imposed, what will happen to
       (i) The market price?   _____
       (ii) Domestic consumption?   _____
       (iii) Domestic production?   _____
   Graph your answers.

Problems for Chapter 21

Name: _____

1. If a euro is worth $1.25, what is the euro price of a dollar? _____

2. If a pound of U.S. pork cost 40 rupiah in Indonesia before the Asian crisis, how much did it cost during the crisis? See World View on page 445 for clues. _____

3. If a PlayStation 2 costs 20,000 yen in Japan, how much will it cost in U.S. dollars if the exchange rate is

                                          (*a*) 120 yen = $1? _____
                                          (*b*) 1 yen = $0.00833? _____
                                          (*c*) 100 yen = $1? _____

4. Between 1980 and 2000,
    (*a*) By how much did the dollar appreciate (Figure 21.3)? _____%
    (*b*) How did that appreciation affect the relative price of U.S. exports? _____

5. If inflation raises U.S. prices by 3 percent and the U.S. dollar appreciates by 2 percent, by how much does the foreign price of U.S. exports change? _____%

6. According to the World View on p. 440, what was the peso price of a euro in August 2004? _____

7. For each of the following possible events, indicate whether the demand or supply curve for dollars would shift, the direction of the shift, the determinant of the change, the inflow or outflow effect on the balance of payments (and the specific account that would be affected), and the resulting movement of the equilibrium exchange rate for the value of the dollar.

    (*a*) American cars become suddenly more popular abroad. _____

    (*b*) Inflation rates in the United States accelerate. _____

    (*c*) The United States falls into a depression. _____

    (*d*) Interest rates in the United States drop. _____

    (*e*) The United States suddenly experiences rapid increases in productivity. _____

    (*f*) Anticipating a return to the gold standard, Americans suddenly rush to buy gold from the two big producers, South Africa and the Soviet Union. _____

    (*g*) War is declared in the Middle East. _____

    (*h*) The stock markets in the United States suddenly collapse. _____

8. The following schedules summarize the supply and demand for trifflings, the national currency of Tricoli:

Triffling price (U.S. dollars per triffling)	0	$4	$8	$12	$16	$20	$24
Quantity demanded (per year)	40	38	36	34	32	30	28
Quantity supplied (per year)	1	11	21	31	41	51	61

Use the above schedules for the following:

(*a*) Graph the supply and demand curves.

(*b*) Determine the equilibrium exchange rate.   _____

(*c*) Determine the size of the excess supply or excess demand that would exist if the Tricolian government fixed the exchange rate $22 = 1 triffling.   _____

(*d*) How might this imbalance be remedied?

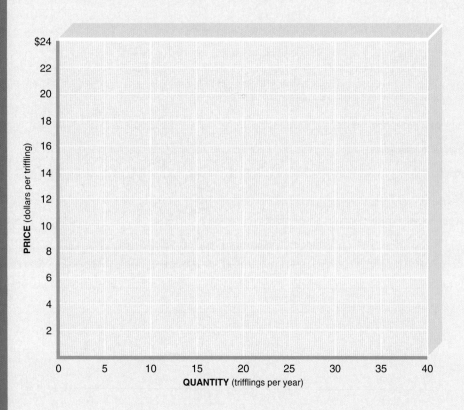